TERRORISM

Commentary on Security Documents

VOLUME 108

TERRORISM

Commentary on Security Documents

VOLUME 108

EXTRAORDINARY RENDITION

Kristen E. Boon, Professor
Seton Hall School of Law

Aziz Huq, Assistant Professor
University of Chicago School of Law

Douglas C. Lovelace, Jr., Esquire
Senior National Securities Strategist

OXFORD
UNIVERSITY PRESS

OXFORD
UNIVERSITY PRESS

Oxford University Press, Inc., publishes works that further Oxford University's objective of excellence in research, scholarship, and education.

Published by Oxford University Press, Inc.
198 Madison Avenue, New York, New York 10016

Cataloging-in-Publication information is available from the Library of Congress.

ISSN 1062-4007
Terrorism: Commentary on Security Documents

ISBN 978-0-19-539813-7 (v. 108)

Note to Readers:

This publication is designed to provide accurate and authoritative information in regard to the subject matter covered. It is based upon sources believed to be accurate and reliable and is intended to be current as of the time it was written. It is sold with the understanding that the publisher is not engaged in rendering legal, accounting, or other professional services. If legal advice or other expert assistance is required, the services of a competent professional person should be sought. Also, to confirm that the information has not been affected or changed by recent developments, traditional legal research techniques should be used, including checking primary sources where appropriate.

(Based on the Declaration of Principles jointly adopted by a Committee of the American Bar Association and a Committee of Publishers and Associations.)

TABLE OF CONTENTS

VOLUME 108

EXTRAORDINARY RENDITION

DOCUMENTS

B. REPORTS FROM NATIONAL JURISDICTIONS

INTRODUCTION

Overview: The American Policy of "Extraordinary Rendition"

This volume addresses the phenomenon of "extraordinary rendition." This is defined here as the transfer between national jurisdictions of a person, outside the channels of the normal judicial process of extradition, deportation, etc., to which there attends a substantial likelihood that the person transferred will be tortured in the receiving country. The policy of extraordinary rendition is national—American—in its origins, but international in its scope. Countries from Africa to North America and from Asia to Europe have been implicated in the policy's workings. As a consequence, several countries and intergovernmental organizations have conducted extensive investigations into the law and facts of extraordinary rendition. Foremost amongst these have been European and Canadian governments, echoing a geographic pattern familiar from other human rights contexts. Either the entirety or parts of these reports are collected and reproduced in this volume. The collected materials paint a partial, but nonetheless revealing image of the trajectory of extraordinary rendition. A full picture, however, awaits historians in the future who have access to state documentation about a practice that to date remains half submerged in the shadows.

From Rendition to Extraordinary Rendition

Extraordinary rendition is an American innovation of the modern era. While this volume deals with non-American and international documents, it is thus appropriate, and not at all parochial, to begin with a discussion of the etiology of the policy from an American perspective. The United States have grappled with the problem of transferring criminal suspects between nations since its inception with varying degrees of successes. The issue has also previously been politically contentious. Two of the America's first international treaties, a 1788 Consular Convention with France and the 1794 Jay Treaty, for example, provided for extradition, the formal legal process allowing for challenge in a federal court that ends in an individual's transfer to another jurisdiction. But one of America's earliest foreign policy debates concerned an English request under the Jay Treaty for the extradition of an American citizen, a naturally delicate subject for the newly independent Republic. President John Adams's resulting 1799 extradition order came under heavy fire, with his Democratic-Republican opponents in Congress submitting a resolution censuring Adams for "a dangerous interference of the executive with judicial decisions."[1] The legal and procedural framework for transfer between jurisdictions—and in particular the sufficiency of ex ante legal review in the sending country—were thus salient points of contention in the early American republic.

But rendition as it was long practice raised more concerns about strict legality than about the risk of more grave human rights violations. Generally a transfer ended in the process of a criminal trial in which a suspect was entitled to contest his innocence. Prior to the September 2001 attacks, "rendition"—or the extraterritorial transfer of criminal suspect to trial in another country outside the channel of the extradition system—was thus used to further the ends of justice by bringing a suspect back to the United States for a criminal trial. Domestic courts saw little ground for concern in consequence. In 1886, for example, the U.S. Supreme Court ruled that a criminal suspect who had fled to war-torn Peru and was seized there by the Pinkerton Detective Agency could be tried in the United States.[2] The Court reiterated that same position in later cases. In 1992, the Supreme Court similarly allowed the trial of a kidnapped Mexican physician for the torture and murder of a federal drug enforcement agent. And in 1989, the U.S. Department of Justice also took the position that the President had "inherent constitutional authority" to deploy FBI agents beyond United States' borders to arrest individuals for trial in the United States. Even though the rendition itself was extra-legal, the suspect at the end of the day had access to a judicial process, which provided a forum for challenges to wrongful detention or abusive treatment.[3]

Extraordinary Rendition and Terrorism

The first important shift in the modality of rendition came in the mid-1980s. At this time, as America faced a growing international terrorism threat rendition became a national security tool rather than a law enforcement implement. But even received as a national security tactic, rendition still meant bringing suspects back to the United States. In 1987, the FBI and CIA collaborated in "Operation Goldenrod." American agents kidnapped Jordanian terrorism suspect Fawaz Yunis, wanted in connection with the hijacking of a Jordanian airliner. Yunis was lured into international waters

---

[1] Convention with the Purpose of Defining and Establishing the Functions and Privileges of Respective Consuls and Vice-Consuls, Nov. 14, 1788, U.S.-Fr., 8 Stat. 106, T.S. 84; Treaty of Amity, Commerce and Navigation, Nov. 19, 1794, U.S.-U.K., 8 Stat. 116, T.S. No. 106.

[2] See Charles Fairman, Editorial Comment, "*Ker v. Illinois* Revisited," *American Journal of International Law*, 47 (1953), 678.

[3] *United States v. Alvarez-Machain*, 504 U.S. 655 (1992).

off the Cypriot coast. He arrested there for transfer to and trial in the U.S. Prosecutors secured convictions for air piracy and hostage taking against him. The U.S. government expanded rendition efforts in the mid-1990s to deal with the emerging threat of Islamist terrorism in the wake of the Afghanistan war. In 1995, for example, Pakistani intelligence arrested Ramzi Yousef, instigator of the 1993 World Trade Center bombing and handed him over to members of an FBI Joint Terrorism Task Force for transport and trial in the federal court. That is, rendition targeted al Qaeda and its affiliates before the September 2001 attacks, but did so in a way that at least arguably furthered the rule of law.

Nevertheless, at this time, the CIA grew increasingly worried that a U.S. court might make embarrassing inquiries about the circumstances of a terrorist suspect's capture and transfer back to the United States. The Agency thus began to explore other models of rendition. It began using rendition to transfer suspects *to* a foreign government, not just *back* to the United States. Egypt became the first destination of choice.[4] The decision to begin sending suspects to other countries, especially countries such as Egypt, breached an significant legal threshold. Once the CIA began sending suspects to other countries, even with the promise of a criminal trial at the other end, there was a risk that a trial might not be fair. Indeed, it is unclear whether sending suspects for trial and imprisonment in countries such as Egypt or Syria is that different from sending them to those same countries without *any* promise of legal process. In countries with a weak rule of law, where courts would often be weak or under a government thumb, that is, rendition inevitably created a risk of ill-treatment. It is the weakness of the rule of law—and not the specific form of the transfer, that creates the concern for human rights.

The seeds of extraordinary rendition were planted before 9/11. But its full flowering had to await the 9/11 attacks. The Reagan and Clinton administration had used secret "presidential findings" (the analog to an executive order directing the President's subordinates to pursue a particular policy) to authorize renditions. On September 17, 2001, President George W. Bush signed a new presidential "finding", giving the CIA broad new authorization to kill, capture, or detain members of Al Qaeda anywhere in the world. This finding is the *fons et origo* of the new policy of "extraordinary rendition." It is with regret that this volume must be published without a copy of that finding because to this day it remains classified and undisclosed.

[4] On the development of 1990s rendition, see Jane Mayer, "Outsourcing Torture," *The New Yorker* (February 14, 2005), 106; Michael Scheuer, "A Fine Rendition," *New York Times*, March 11, 2005, A23. For confirmation of 1990s rendition efforts, see Testimony of Christopher Kojm, 9/11 Commission Deputy, Transcript of 9/11 Commission Hearings, Wednesday, 24 March, 2004; *The 9/11 Commission Report: Final Report of the National Commission on Terrorist Attacks Upon the United States* (W.W. Norton: New York, 2004), 127.

The finding did not require the CIA, when detaining and transferring suspects, to seek case-by-case approval from the White House, the State Department, or the Justice Department. The same finding released the "vast" new funds to coax foreign intelligence services into new cooperation with the CIA. There is no reason to believe that finding has been rescinded at the time of this writing (in late 2009). After the Sept 17, 2001 finding, the number of renditions escalated, to at least 150 in the first five years after 9/11. Egypt's prime minister reported his country alone received "60 to 70" detainees between September 2001 and May 2005 via the American rendition system.[5] With this change in volume also came a critical shift in the *purpose* of renditions. Before 9/11, renditions had a nexus with a criminal justice process, either in the United States or another country. By contrast, individuals "rendered" after 9/11 are rarely formally charged with a criminal offense or tried in a court of law.[6]

The post-9/11 practice of extraordinary rendition is interwoven with the legal question of what forms of interrogation are permitted under domestic law and international human rights treaties. Senior intelligence officials have explained collaboration with Egyptian or Jordanian intelligence services as a way to circumvent U.S. rules against torture. As CIA Director George Tenet explained to Congress, "it might be better sometimes for . . . suspects to remain in the hands of foreign authorities, who might be able to use more aggressive interrogation techniques." Speaking off the record to the *Washington Post*, another official confirmed that Tenet's statement accurately described the Administration's purpose in expanding the use of extraordinary renditions: "Someone"—i.e., another country's intelligence agency—"might be able to get information we can't from detainees."[7] The use of extraordinary rendition expands the United States' repertoire of possible interrogation tactics at the same time as it minimizes the legal exposure of the United States to responsibility under international law. It also limits the exposure of U.S. agents to possible criminal prosecutions, whether under U.S. law, under the domestic law of another country, or through the exercise of universal jurisdiction. Evaluations of extraordinary rendition thus tend to be inextricable from responses to the Bush Administration's use of interrogation techniques that violated norms under the December 1984 Convention against Torture and Other Cruel, Inhuman or Degrading Treatment or Punishment.

---

[5] Jane Mayer, "Outsourcing Torture," *The New Yorker* (February 14, 2005), 106; Shaun Waterman, "Terror Detainees sent to Egypt, U.S. deny torture is condoned," *Washington Times*, May 16, 2004.

[6] The Agiza and al-Zari cases discussed below are an exception.

[7] John Barry, Michael Hirsch, and Michael Isikoff, "The Roots of Torture," Newsweek, May 24, 2004, 16; DeNeen L. Brown and Dana Priest, "Deported Terror Suspects Details Torture in Syria; Canada's Case Called Typical of CIA," *Washington Post*, November 5, 2003, A1.

The policy of transfers outside the normal channels of either criminal justice (i.e., extradition) or immigration enforcement (i.e., "removal" as it is known in U.S. law) is linked to a second practice. Beginning in March 2002, the CIA operated a series of secret detention facilities outside the United States at which it held terrorism suspects. These have become known as "black sites." The use of black sites appears to have been coterminous with and linked to the use of rendition. That is, individuals would be "rendered" and then either brought to and kept in black sites, or else channeled through black sites to third countries or publically known U.S. facilities such as the one at Guantanamo Bay. The use of black site was apparently first prompted by the arrest of Abu Zubaybah on March 28 2002 by Pakistani intelligence services. The CIA first kept Abu Zubaybah in a small, disused warehouse on an active airbase in Thailand. In June 2003, media reports of the Thai facility surfaced, and Thailand's government insisted that the site be closed, souring relations with the CIA. Abu Zubaybah was transferred to another site. According to a *Washington Post* article from November 2005, only one-third of the hundred or so suspects rendered until then were "considered major terrorism suspects."[8] It is likely that this ration would have dropped thereafter given that most high-value suspects were picked up soon after 9/11 rather than later.

Extraordinary rendition and the global network of black sites made up an interconnected global detention system. That system stretched from the United States—where decisions were made and information gathered—to Europe to Asia and Africa. These practices not only challenged conventional norms of legality and humane treatment under U.S. law, they also raised questions about legal and institutional globalizations. As some of the documents gathered in this volume make clear, extraordinary rendition was only made possible because of a preexisting network of legal arrangements to enable military cooperation. These were often embodied in the form of "status of forces agreements," or SOFAs. Arrangements designed to foster collective security became tools for the circumvention of domestic norms against torture. Further, the documents collected in this volume suggest that debates on globalizations have not adequately grappled with the complex possibilities that globalized flows of security-related information, money, and cooperation create. Just as the al Qaeda network itself is in some measure a response to globalization—to wit, the support received by Saudi and other Middle Eastern regimes from the United States—so the globalized response to terrorism engenders new questions about how shared values such as the rule of law are to be protected.

[8] Dana Priest, "CIA Holds Terror Suspects in Secret Prisons: Debate is Growing within Agency about Legality and Morality of Overseas System Set Up After 9/11," *Washington Post*, November 2, 2005, A1; Dana Priest, "CIA Holds Terror Suspects in Secret Prisons: Debate is Growing over Legality and Morality of Overseas System Set Up After 9/11," *Washington Post*, November 2, 2005.

International institutions charged with concern for human rights and domestic investigators tasked with eliminating gross violations of legality have inevitably grappled with these legal and policy questions in the course of dealing with extraordinary rendition. The documents in this volume detail that effort to come to terms (both moral and legal) with this new face of globalization. The network of black sites, secret prisons, and clandestine flights that was set in motion between 2001 and 2008 drew in countries across the globe, and responses have been geographically varied.[9] The volume is divided into two main sections. In both, the perspective is from outside the United States. This volume hence looks not at how extraordinary rendition was justified by Tenet, Condoleezza Rice, and others in the American Administration. Rather it considers how the remainder of the world saw, and reacted to, this innovation in American security policy.

The volume's first section contains documents from international agencies and entities describing extraordinary rendition, principally United Nations agencies and constituent parts of the Council of Europe. The second section turns to documentation from national sources—either executive or legislative branches—concerning specific instances of extraordinary rendition. Documents from British, Swedish, Irish, Canadian, and Italian investigations are included. An afterward to the volume considers briefly the future of extraordinary rendition.

[9] As discussed further below, the absence of Asian and African voices in this volume is a matter of regret, even if it fairly reflects the absence of institutional resources and capital when it comes to intergovernmental initiatives to promote legality and human rights in those parts of the world.

A. REPORTS FROM INTERNATIONAL BODIES

COMMENTARY

COMMENTARY ON REPORTS FROM INTERNATIONAL BODIES

The first selection of documents concerning extraordinary rendition emerge from international organizations, in particular bodies within the United Nations and bodies within the European system. Absent are documents from African, Eurasian, or Asian international organizations or rights bodies. Regional organizations with human rights mandates in those parts of the world have not generated the kind of legal, policy, and factual analysis that has emerged from the European and the United Nations systems. This is best understood as a symptom of their weakness rather than as an indication that no legal and policy issues concern those countries. To the contrary, the work of the rapporteur for the Council of Europe's Parliamentary Assembly's Committee on Legal Affairs and Human Rights Dick Marty suggests that many Asian and African countries were heavily involved in extraordinary rendition. Geographic asymmetry of reporting and analytic attention to extraordinary rendition has policy consequences. Given the asymmetry, the regional attention documented below may not have the effect of eliminating renditions. Investment in networks for rendition will instead flow to other less well-regulated parts of the world. Hence, the net effect of international attention is by no means clear.

This section first addresses two documents that emerge from bodies within the United Nations system. It then turns to a series of European documents from the Council of Europe and then from the European Union that address different factual, legal, and policy considerations.

[*Commentary for Documents 1 and 2*] The United Nations "CAT Committee": al-Zari and Agiza Communication and the U.S. Report

Within the United Nations structure, the Convention against Torture and Other Cruel, Inhuman or Degrading Treatment or Punishment ("CAT" or "Convention against Torture") creates a committee to monitor compliance with that treaty—commonly known as "the CAT Committee."[1] The CAT Committee comprises "ten experts of high moral standing and recognized competence in the field of human rights, who shall serve in their personal capacity" who sit for two years. Under Article 19 of CAT, state parties are required to submit reports concerning their compliance with CAT's various requirements every four years. Under Article 21, states can also agree to allow the CAT Committee to hear complaints from individual. Two documents relevant to extraordinary rendition have emerged from that committee.

On May 20, 2005, issued a communication finding that Sweden had violated provisions of the Convention against Torture in December 2001 when it cooperated with the United States in what in effect was an extraordinary rendition from Swedish soil. The CAT Communication is reproduced in its entirety here.

That communication arose from the expulsion of two Egyptian asylum seekers from Sweden on December 18, 2001. The Swedish government had previously acknowledged in immigration proceedings that Mohammed al-Zari and Ahmed Agiza had a well-founded fear of being persecuted if they were returned to Egypt (which suffices as a matter of law to establish refugee status). Nevertheless, with the logistical support and apparent encouragement of the United States, the Swedish government nonetheless decided to expel both al-Zari and Agiza even though it knew or should have known that Egypt resorted to consistent and widespread use of torture against detainees held for political or security reasons. The Swedish government relied in so doing on "diplomatic assurances" from Egypt. In essence, these are unenforceable statements generated in the course of country-to-country diplomacy that are generally not even subject to public airing, scrutiny, and criticism.

The evening of the Foreign Ministry's decision, the two men were taken to a Swedish airport and handed over to non-Swedish personnel (who were either American officials or in the employ of the United States[2]) who restrained then, placed them on an airplane, and few them to Egypt. The men's lawyers, as a consequence, did not have a chance to contest the expulsion decision. While members of the Swedish Security Police were present during the handover, they permitted American officials to do the restraining and to handle the physical transfer. As discussed below, this aspect of the case generated an inquiry by Sweden's parliamentary ombudsman. After their arrival in Egypt, both Agiza and al-Zari were tortured and

[1] See Convention against Torture and Other Cruel, Inhuman or Degrading Treatment or Punishment, art. 17, S. Treaty Doc. No. 100-20, p. 20, 1465 U.N.T.S. 85.

[2] The Swedish government subsequently confirmed American involvement in the transfer. See Craig Whitlock, A Secret Deportation of Terror Suspects, *Washington Post*, July 25, 2004, at A1.

ill-treated according to independent inquiries by Human Rights Watch and by Swedish human rights groups.

The CAT Committee's inquiry was limited to the legal questions raised by the Agiza and al-Zari cases. It concluded that Sweden had in their case violated Article 3 of the Convention against Torture, which provides that "[n]o State Party shall expel, return ("refouler") or extradite a person to another State where there are substantial grounds for believing that he would be in danger of being subjected to torture." The CAT Committee concluded that the substantiality of the risk to Agiza and al-Zari was indeed confirmed by their harsh treatment on Swedish soil at American hands. Further, the Committee stated that "[t]he procurement of diplomatic assurances . . . [that] provided no mechanism for their enforcement, did not suffice to protect against this manifest risk."

The legal analysis of the CAT Committee is significant for two reasons. First, the Committee looked past Sweden's formal compliance with the international law of asylum to discern the practical realities of its actions. Hence, although the expulsion of Agiza and al-Zari complied (almost and in a superficial fashion) with the substantive and procedural law of asylum and refugee status, the Committee viewed it as another example of an extraordinary rendition. The abbreviated timeframe of the expulsion, the evasion of procedures, the de facto side-lining of legal counsel, and the illegal coercion used at both the pick-up and in the Egyptian detention align the case of Agiza and al-Zari with the practice of extraordinary rendition. The CAT Committee communication thus confirms that superficial compliance with procedural regularities does not constitute fulfillment of international law obligations barring torture.

Second, the CAT Committee's rejection of Sweden's reliance on Egypt's "diplomatic assurances" is important because it eliminates a safe harbor for countries wishing to cooperate with extraordinary rendition while maintaining a minimal veneer of legality. Diplomatic assurances are only ever sought from countries that engage routinely in torture. No country that has relied on them has explained why it is plausible to rely on non-enforceable promissory language generated in the course of diplomatic negotiations by a country pursuing a self-interested goal when the promise in question is facially inconsistent with the known violations by the country of its own law, international treaties, and "jus cogens" rules of customary international law.

The second document to emerge from the CAT Committee concerning extraordinary rendition is the Committee s response to the mandated report from the United States delivered in May 2006. This document is a useful analysis of the gap between the international law of torture on the one hand and the domestic law and practice within the United States.

For example, the CAT Committee noted the gap between the CAT's requirement that all forms of torture be criminalized and prosecuted, federal law in the United States leaves gaps in territorial coverage. Further, the committee noted the absence of prosecutions. Turning to extraordinary rendition, the Committee expressed its concern about the evidence of "black sites" and renditions to torture. Of special note, the Committee not only stressed the need to fill any gaps in the law, it also provided practical guidance on how to satisfy the CAT's anti-torture regime. For example, the CAT Committee emphasized the role of International Committee of the Red Cross in monitoring the conditions and treatment of detainees. And echoing the Agiza and al-Zari communication, the Committee's response to the American submission cautions against reliance on "diplomatic assurances." According to the Committee, the latter should be relied upon only "in regard to States which do not systematically violate the Convention's provisions, and after a thorough examination of the merits of each individual case." Given the distribution of diplomatic assurances' usage, this would seem to be a recipe for eliminating reliance on such assurances altogether.

[*Commentary for Documents 3 and 4*] **Reports of the Committee on Legal Affairs and Human Rights, Parliamentary Assembly of the Council of Europe**

Founded in 1947, the Council of Europe is a pan-European organization comprising 47 member states and more than 800 million inhabitants. Its mandate reaches the fostering of shared legal standards, development, and human rights. Among its most important constituent institutions is the European Court of Human Rights, which enforces the European Convention on Human Rights. The court, however, is not the only body within the Council that has an interest in human rights. In addition, the Parliamentary Assembly, which is made up of legislators from each of the constituent country's legislatures, also takes an interest in human rights questions. That attention has extended to extraordinary renditions and takes the form of two documents excerpted here. These documents in turn have triggered other legal and policy inquiries by distinct European bodies.

Council of Europe attention to the issue of extraordinary rendition was catalyzed by news reports in November 2005 that the Central Intelligence Agency had maintained secret detention facilities in Poland and Romania, both Council members. The Council later concluded that other Council members had been implicated in the policy. According to a fax from the Egyptian Ministry of European Affairs to the Egyptian Embassy in London that was intercepted by Swiss intelligence, Bulgaria, Macedonia, Kosovo, and the Ukraine had also housed such centers at one time or another after September 2001.

On November 3, 2005, the Council's Commissioner for Human Rights, Alvaro Gil-Robles called for an investigation. The same day, the President of the Parliamentary Assembly René van der Linden directed the Assembly's Committee on Legal Affairs and Human Rights to commence an investigation. In December 2005, the European Parliament—which is the directly-elected parliamentary institution within the European Union–also created a temporary committee to investigate the alleged illegal transfer of detainees and the suspected existence of secret CIA detention facilities. The Committee on Legal Affairs and Human Rights appointed Dick Marty, a Swiss former state prosecutor from the canton of Ticino and politician affiliated with the Free Democratic Party.

The Marty inquiry yielded two reports, a preliminary one published in January 2006 and an ampler document issued in June 2006. Marty and his team conduct investigations aimed at uncovering direct evidence of the practice and extent of extraordinary rendition in Council of Europe member countries. Rather, Marty and his investigators interviewed state officials, human rights groups, subjects of renditions, and others with both first- and second-hand knowledge of extraordinary rendition. The net result does not directly contribute to the historical record about rendition. The value of Marty's work is instead synthetic. It distills and describes the information available in some public form or another concerning extraordinary rendition. By placing the imprimatur of an intergovernmental organization on such material, Marty apparently aimed to change debate about rendition. What previously were a set of accusations leveled by non-governmental actors became an officially endorsed portrayal of a wide-spread and systemic policy that, in Marty's view, violated both European and international human rights law.

The first Marty report summarizes ongoing investigations (or campaigns for investigations) in Italy, Germany, Poland, Romania, the United Kingdom, Germany, Armenia, Bosnia-Herzegovina, Denmark, Finland, France, and the Republic of Eire. The summary testifies to the diversity of institutional forms that investigations can take from criminal investigations in Germany to mere requests for information directed to U.S. authorities from the Danish and the Finnish governments. It is striking that few of these inquiries have generated meaningful new information concerning extraordinary rendition or yielded legal outcomes; the Arar Commission and the Italian prosecution of 23 CIA agents are rare exceptions to this trend.

The second Marty report, issued on June 12, 2006, is a more substantial portrayal of the "'spider's web' spun across the globe" linking rendition, black sites, and various forms of proxy detention in the hands of American allies. While accepting that "hard evidence" was still lacking, the second report concluded with greater certainty that secret detention sites had existed in Council of Europe member states. The report then goes on to paint in more detail than any other intergovernmental document the functioning and extent of the extraordinary rendition system. This report first adduces the circumstantial and direct evidence of extraordinary rendition and its linkages to the use of torture. Marty and his investigators relied on photographic evidence, documentation of flights gleaned from public logs, and eye-witness accounts to build a comprehensive portrayal of the rendition system and its collateral components. The report then profiles nine case studies of persons who were either seized in Council of Europe states or who passed through such states in the course of a rendition. Finally, the report discusses the then-ongoing criminal and parliamentary investigations in various nations. Because this data has been superseded in part in each case, it is the part of the Marty report that is of the least continuing use.

The second Marty report concludes with a set of recommendations organized around the aim of bolstering the anti-torture norm of international law. One of the most interesting of these recognizes and responds to the use of American military bases on European soil. These bases are the result of the military alliance NATO, and depend on either multilateral or bilateral treaties with the United States. One of the important legal contributions of the Marty report is to emphasize the salience of these legal arrangements, and to promote the inclusion of "human rights protection clauses" in such treaties.

[*Commentary for Document 5*] **Legal Opinion of the Venice Commission**

Created in 1990, the Venice Commission is the Council of Europe's advisory body on matters of constitutional law. In December 2005, Dick Marty, then chairing the Committee on Legal Affairs and Human Rights of the Parliamentary Assembly of the Council of Europe requested a legal opinion from the Venice Commission on the legal obligations under European laws of Council of Europe members concerning extraordinary rendition and the operation of secret detention sites on European soil. Where the Marty report deal with the facts and policy consequences of extraordinary rendition, the Venice Commission was concerned with its legal aspects. The ensuing opinion, issued on March 17, 2006, is included in this volume.

The legal opinion is a useful guide to the international law of prisoner transfers. According to the Venice Commission, such transfers are lawful when part of a deportation, an extradition, the transit of a sentenced prisoner to a third country or the transfer of sentenced prisoner to serve a sentence in their nation of origin. Even "transits," where the state has only fleeting contact with the prisoner, must be accomplished under European law "with due respect for human rights and fundamental freedoms."

The legal opinion then explores the content of European human rights law, in particular Article 5 of the European Convention on Human Rights, which protects "the right to liberty and security of the person." Of interest to American lawyers, the Venice Commission emphasized Article 5's requirement of "proceedings by which the lawfulness of . . . detention shall be decided speedily by a court" parallels the constitutional entitlement of habeas corpus under Article I of the U.S. Constitution.

The Venice Commission also underlined the significance of the 1944 Chicago Convention on International Civil Aviation, which regulates international aviation. The Commission emphasized that under international law aircraft controlled by states do not have a right to overfly other states without express authorization. It is unclear whether this analysis, however, has bearing on the actual practice of rendition to the extent that the latter appeared to rely on private chartered flights. Like the second Marty report, the Venice Commission also examines the significance of bilateral and multilateral treaties governing military cooperation, called "status of forces" agreements, or SOFAs. A SOFA defines the rights and powers of foreign troops stationed on another sovereign's soil. Significantly, the Commission emphasized that host nations maintain an ongoing right of access to a military base. Such access, however, is of course relevant only to the extent a host nation is willing to expend political capital on investigations.

[*Commentary for Documents 6 and 7*] **The European Parliament**

Other European bodies have also explored the consequences and legality of rendition. This volume includes two documents from the European parliament. The first is a May 2006 opinion from the European Union Network of Independent Experts on Fundamental Rights that concerned the human rights responsibilities of member states with respect to rendition programs. Like the Venice Commission it emphasizes the interaction of human rights law with the international law of military cooperation embodied in multiple SOFAs. The report goes on to detail the legal tools available for effective investigations into possible renditions to torture.

The European Parliament also issued in January 2007 a report of allegations of European countries' collaboration with the CIA on the transportation and illegal detention of prisoners. The report draws on other sources, including the Marty reports. One contribution it makes is a country-by-country break down of the various levels of involvement by European countries in the extraordinary rendition program. In so doing, it identifies some variance in European nations' willingness to respond to the rendition of their own nationals and also allegations of wrongdoing on their soil. The parliamentary report thus praises the criminal investigation of one rendition from Milan, Italy to Cairo, Egypt (which is explored at greater length in the following section of the volume). It praises Germany for its willingness to push for the release of its citizens, in contrast to Austria, which has demonstrated indifference to the detention in Jordan of an Austrian resident. The variance is illustrative of differences in levels of commitment to human-rights norms in a continent generally viewed as strong on such liberties.

DOCUMENT NO. 1

CONSIDERATION OF REPORTS SUBMITTED BY STATES PARTIES UNDER ARTICLE 19 OF THE CONVENTION

UN Committee Against Torture

July 25, 2006

Conclusions and Recommendations of the Committee Against Torture

United States of America

1. The Committee against Torture considered the second report of the United States of America (CAT/C/48/Add.3/Rev.1) at its 702nd and 705th meetings (CAT/C/SR.702 and 705), held on 5 and 8 May 2006, and adopted, at its 720th and 721st meetings, on 17 and 18 May 2006 (CAT/C/SR.720 and 721), the following conclusions and recommendations.

A. Introduction

2. The second periodic report of the United States of America was due on 19 November 2001, as requested by the Committee at its twenty-fourth session in May 2000 (A/55/44, para. 180 (f)) and was received on 6 May 2005. The Committee notes that the report includes a point-by-point reply to the Committee's previous recommendations.

3. The Committee commends the State party for its exhaustive written responses to the Committee's list of issues, as well as the detailed responses provided both in writing and orally to the questions posed by the members during the examination of the report. The Committee expresses its appreciation for the large and high-level delegation, comprising representatives from relevant departments of the State party, which facilitated a constructive oral exchange during the consideration of the report.

4. The Committee notes that the State party has a federal structure, but recalls that the United States of America is a single State under international law and has the obligation to implement the Convention against

Torture and Other Cruel, Inhuman or Degrading Treatment or Punishment ("the Convention") in full at the domestic level.

5. Recalling its statement adopted on 22 November 2001 condemning utterly the terrorist attacks of 11 September 2001, the terrible threat to international peace and security posed by acts of international terrorism and the need to combat by all means, in accordance with the Charter of the United Nations, the threats caused by terrorist acts, the Committee recognizes that these attacks caused profound suffering to many residents of the State party. The Committee acknowledges that the State party is engaged in protecting its security and the security and freedom of its citizens in a complex legal and political context.

B. Positive Aspects

6. The Committee welcomes the State party's statement that all United States officials, from all government agencies, including its contractors, are prohibited from engaging in torture at all times and in all places, and that all United States officials from all government agencies, including its contractors, wherever they may be, are prohibited from engaging in cruel, inhuman or degrading treatment or punishment, in accordance with the obligations under the Convention.

7. The Committee notes with satisfaction the State party's statement that the United States does not transfer persons to countries where it believes it is "more likely than not" that they will be tortured, and that this also applies, as a matter of policy, to the transfer of any individual, in the State party's custody, or control, regardless of where they are detained.

8. The Committee welcomes the State party's clarification that the statement of the United States President on signing the Detainee Treatment Act on 30 December 2005 is not to be interpreted as a derogation by the President from the absolute prohibition of torture.

9. The Committee also notes with satisfaction the enactment of:

(a) The Prison Rape Elimination Act of 2003, which addresses sexual assault of persons in the custody of correctional agencies, with the purpose, inter alia, of establishing a "zero-tolerance standard" for rape in detention facilities in the State party; and

(b) That part of the Detainee Treatment Act of 2005 which prohibits cruel, inhuman, or degrading treatment and punishment of any person, regardless of nationality or physical location, in the custody or under the physical control of the State party.

10. The Committee welcomes the adoption of National Detention Standards in 2000, which set minimum standards for detention facilities holding Department of Homeland Security detainees, including asylum-seekers.

11. The Committee also notes with satisfaction the sustained and substantial contributions of the State party to the United Nations Voluntary Fund for the Victims of Torture.

12. The Committee notes the State party's intention to adopt a new Army Field Manual for intelligence interrogation, applicable to all its personnel, which, according to the State party, will ensure that interrogation techniques fully comply with the Convention.

C. Subjects of Concern and Recommendations

13. Notwithstanding the statement by the State party that "every act of torture within the meaning of the Convention is illegal under existing federal and/or state law", the Committee reiterates the concern expressed in its previous conclusions and recommendations with regard to the absence of a federal crime of torture, consistent with article 1 of the Convention, given that sections 2340 and 2340 A of the United States Code limit federal criminal jurisdiction over acts of torture to extraterritorial cases. The Committee also regrets that, despite the occurrence of cases of extraterritorial torture of detainees, no prosecutions have been initiated under the extraterritorial criminal torture statute (arts. 1, 2, 4 and 5).

The Committee reiterates its previous recommendation that the State party should enact a federal crime of torture consistent with article 1 of the Convention, which should include appropriate penalties, in order to fulfil its obligations under the Convention to prevent and eliminate acts of torture causing severe pain or suffering, whether physical or mental, in all its forms.

The State party should ensure that acts of psychological torture, prohibited by the Convention, are not limited to "prolonged mental harm" as set out in the State party's understandings lodged at the time of ratification of the Convention, but constitute a wider category of acts, which cause severe mental suffering, irrespective of their prolongation or its duration.

The State party should investigate, prosecute and punish perpetrators under the federal extraterritorial criminal torture statute.

14. The Committee regrets the State party's opinion that the Convention is not applicable in times and in the context of armed conflict, on the basis of the argument that the "law of armed conflict" is the exclusive *lex specialis* applicable, and that the Convention's application "would result in an overlap of the different treaties which would undermine the objective of eradicating torture" (arts. 1 and 16).

The State party should recognize and ensure that the Convention applies at all times, whether in peace, war or armed conflict, in any territory under its jurisdiction and that the application of the Convention's provisions

are without prejudice to the provisions of any other international instrument, pursuant to paragraph 2 of its articles 1 and 16.

15. The Committee notes that a number of the Convention's provisions are expressed as applying to "territory under [the State party's] jurisdiction" (arts. 2, 5, 13, 16). The Committee reiterates its previously expressed view that this includes all areas under the de facto effective control of the State party, by whichever military or civil authorities such control is exercised. The Committee considers that the State party's view that those provisions are geographically limited to its own de jure territory to be regrettable.

The State party should recognize and ensure that the provisions of the Convention expressed as applicable to "territory under the State party's jurisdiction" apply to, and are fully enjoyed, by all persons under the effective control of its authorities, of whichever type, wherever located in the world.

16. The Committee notes with concern that the State party does not always register persons detained in territories under its jurisdiction outside the United States, depriving them of an effective safeguard against acts of torture (art. 2).

The State party should register all persons it detains in any territory under its jurisdiction, as one measure to prevent acts of torture. Registration should contain the identity of the detainee, the date, time and place of the detention, the identity of the authority that detained the person, the ground for the detention, the date and time of admission to the detention facility and the state of health of the detainee upon admission and any changes thereto, the time and place of interrogations, with the names of all interrogators present, as well as the date and time of release or transfer to another detention facility.

17. The Committee is concerned by allegations that the State party has established secret detention facilities, which are not accessible to the International Committee of the Red Cross. Detainees are allegedly deprived of fundamental legal safeguards, including an oversight mechanism in regard to their treatment and review procedures with respect to their detention. The Committee is also concerned by allegations that those detained in such facilities could be held for prolonged periods and face torture or cruel, inhuman or degrading treatment. The Committee considers the "no comment" policy of the State party regarding the existence of such secret detention facilities, as well as on its intelligence activities, to be regrettable (arts. 2 and 16).

The State party should ensure that no one is detained in any secret detention facility under its de facto effective control. Detaining persons in such conditions constitutes, per se, a violation of the Convention. The State party should investigate and disclose the existence of any such facilities and the authority under which they have been established and the manner

in which detainees are treated. The State party should publicly condemn any policy of secret detention.

The Committee recalls that intelligence activities, notwithstanding their author, nature or location, are acts of the State party, fully engaging its international responsibility.

18. The Committee is concerned by reports of the involvement of the State party in enforced disappearances. The Committee considers the State party's view that such acts do not constitute a form of torture to be regrettable (arts. 2 and 16).

The State party should adopt all necessary measures to prohibit and prevent enforced disappearance in any territory under its jurisdiction, and prosecute and punish perpetrators, as this practice constitutes, per se, a violation of the Convention.

19. Notwithstanding the State party's statement that "[u]nder U.S. law, there is no derogation from the express statutory prohibition of torture" and that "[n]o circumstances whatsoever . . . may be invoked as a justification or defense to committing torture", the Committee remains concerned at the absence of clear legal provisions ensuring that the Convention's prohibition against torture is not derogated from under any circumstances, in particular since 11 September 2001 (arts. 2, 11 and 12).

The State party should adopt clear legal provisions to implement the principle of absolute prohibition of torture in its domestic law without any possible derogation. Derogation from this principle is incompatible with paragraph 2 of article 2 of the Convention, and cannot limit criminal responsibility. The State party should also ensure that perpetrators of acts of torture are prosecuted and punished appropriately.

The State party should also ensure that any interrogation rules, instructions or methods do not derogate from the principle of absolute prohibition of torture and that no doctrine under domestic law impedes the full criminal responsibility of perpetrators of acts of torture.

The State party should promptly, thoroughly, and impartially investigate any responsibility of senior military and civilian officials authorizing, acquiescing or consenting, in any way, to acts of torture committed by their subordinates.

20. The Committee is concerned that the State party considers that the non-refoulement obligation, under article 3 of the Convention, does not extend to a person detained outside its territory. The Committee is also concerned by the State party's rendition of suspects, without any judicial procedure, to States where they face a real risk of torture (art. 3).

The State party should apply the *non-refoulement* guarantee to all detainees in its custody, cease the rendition of suspects, in particular by its intelligence agencies, to States where they face a real risk of torture, in order

to comply with its obligations under article 3 of the Convention. The State party should always ensure that suspects have the possibility to challenge decisions of *refoulement*.

21. The Committee is concerned by the State party's use of "diplomatic assurances", or other kinds of guarantees, assuring that a person will not be tortured if expelled, returned, transferred or extradited to another State. The Committee is also concerned by the secrecy of such procedures including the absence of judicial scrutiny and the lack of monitoring mechanisms put in place to assess if the assurances have been honoured (art. 3).

When determining the applicability of its *non-refoulement* obligations under article 3 of the Convention, the State party should only rely on "diplomatic assurances" in regard to States which do not systematically violate the Convention's provisions, and after a thorough examination of the merits of each individual case. The State party should establish and implement clear procedures for obtaining such assurances, with adequate judicial mechanisms for review, and effective post-return monitoring arrangements. The State party should also provide detailed information to the Committee on all cases since 11 September 2001 where assurances have been provided.

22. The Committee, noting that detaining persons indefinitely without charge constitutes per se a violation of the Convention, is concerned that detainees are held for protracted periods at Guantánamo Bay, without sufficient legal safeguards and without judicial assessment of the justification for their detention (arts. 2, 3 and 16).

The State party should cease to detain any person at Guantánamo Bay and close this detention facility, permit access by the detainees to judicial process or release them as soon as possible, ensuring that they are not returned to any State where they could face a real risk of being tortured, in order to comply with its obligations under the Convention.

23. The Committee is concerned that information, education and training provided to the State party's law-enforcement or military personnel are not adequate and do not focus on all provisions of the Convention, in particular on the non-derogable nature of the prohibition of torture and the prevention of cruel, inhuman and degrading treatment or punishment (arts. 10 and 11).

The State party should ensure that education and training of all law-enforcement or military personnel, are conducted on a regular basis, in particular for personnel involved in the interrogation of suspects. This should include training on interrogation rules, instructions and methods, and specific training on how to identify signs of torture and cruel, inhuman or degrading treatment. Such personnel should also be instructed to report such incidents.

The State party should also regularly evaluate the training and education provided to its law-enforcement and military personnel as well as ensure regular and independent monitoring of their conduct.

24. The Committee is concerned that in 2002 the State party authorized the use of certain interrogation techniques that have resulted in the death of some detainees during interrogation. The Committee also regrets that "confusing interrogation rules" and techniques defined in vague and general terms, such as "stress positions", have led to serious abuses of detainees (arts. 11, 1,2 and 16).

The State party should rescind any interrogation technique, including methods involving sexual humiliation, "waterboarding", "short shackling" and using dogs to induce fear, that constitutes torture or cruel, inhuman or degrading treatment or punishment, in all places of detention under its de facto effective control, in order to comply with its obligations under the Convention.

25. The Committee is concerned at allegations of impunity of some of the State party's law-enforcement personnel in respect of acts of torture or cruel, inhuman or degrading treatment or punishment. The Committee notes the limited investigation and lack of prosecution in respect of the allegations of torture perpetrated in areas 2 and 3 of the Chicago Police Department (art. 12).

The State party should promptly, thoroughly and impartially investigate all allegations of acts of torture or cruel, inhuman or degrading treatment or punishment by law-enforcement personnel and bring perpetrators to justice, in order to fulfil its obligations under article 12 of the Convention. The State party should also provide the Committee with information on the ongoing investigations and prosecution relating to the above-mentioned case.

26. The Committee is concerned by reliable reports of acts of torture or cruel, inhuman and degrading treatment or punishment committed by certain members of the State party's military or civilian personnel in Afghanistan and Iraq. It is also concerned that the investigation and prosecution of many of these cases, including some resulting in the death of detainees, have led to lenient sentences, including of an administrative nature or less than one year's imprisonment (art. 12).

The State party should take immediate measures to eradicate all forms of torture and ill-treatment of detainees by its military or civilian personnel, in any territory under its jurisdiction, and should promptly and thoroughly investigate such acts, prosecute all those responsible for such acts, and ensure they are appropriately punished, in accordance with the seriousness of the crime.

27. The Committee is concerned that the Detainee Treatment Act of 2005 aims to withdraw the jurisdiction of the State party's federal courts with respect to habeas corpus petitions, or other claims by or on behalf of Guantánamo Bay detainees, except under limited circumstances. The Committee is also concerned that detainees in Afghanistan and Iraq, under the control of the Department of Defense, have their status determined and reviewed by an administrative process of that department (art. 13).

The State party should ensure that independent, prompt and thorough procedures to review the circumstances of detention and the status of detainees are available to all detainees, as required by article 13 of the Convention.

28. The Committee is concerned at the difficulties certain victims of abuses have faced in obtaining redress and adequate compensation, and that only a limited number of detainees have filed claims for compensation for alleged abuse and maltreatment, in particular under the Foreign Claims Act (art. 14).

The State party should ensure, in accordance with the Convention, that mechanisms to obtain full redress, compensation and rehabilitation are accessible to all victims of acts of torture or abuse, including sexual violence, perpetrated by its officials.

29. The Committee is concerned at section 1997 e (e) of the 1995 Prison Litigation Reform Act which provides "that no federal civil action may be brought by a prisoner for mental or emotional injury suffered while in custody without a prior showing of physical injury" (art. 14).

The State party should not limit the right of victims to bring civil actions and amend the Prison Litigation Reform Act accordingly.

30. The Committee, while taking note of the State party's instruction number 10 of 24 March 2006, which provides that military commissions shall not admit statements established to be made as a result of torture in evidence, is concerned about the implementation of the instruction in the context of such commissions and the limitations on detainees' effective right to complain. The Committee is also concerned about the Combatant Status Review Tribunals and the Administrative Review Boards (arts. 13 and 15).

The State party should ensure that its obligations under articles 13 and 15 are fulfilled in all circumstances, including in the context of military commissions and should consider establishing an independent mechanism to guarantee the rights of all detainees in its custody.

31. The Committee is concerned at the fact that substantiated information indicates that executions in the State party can be accompanied by severe pain and suffering (arts. 16, 1 and 2).

The State party should carefully review its execution methods, in particular lethal injection, in order to prevent severe pain and suffering.

32. The Committee is concerned at reliable reports of sexual assault of sentenced detainees, as well as persons in pretrial or immigration detention, in places of detention in the State party. The Committee is concerned that there are numerous reports of sexual violence perpetrated by detainees on one another, and that persons of differing sexual orientation are particularly vulnerable. The Committee is also concerned by the lack of prompt and independent investigation of such acts and that appropriate measures to combat these abuses have not been implemented by the State party (arts. 16, 12, 13 and 14).

The State party should design and implement appropriate measures to prevent all sexual violence in all its detention centres. The State party should ensure that all allegations of violence in detention centres are investigated promptly and independently, perpetrators are prosecuted and appropriately sentenced and victims can seek redress, including appropriate compensation.

33. The Committee is concerned at the treatment of detained women in the State party, including gender-based humiliation and incidents of shackling of women detainees during childbirth (art. 16).

The State party should adopt all appropriate measures to ensure that women in detention are treated in conformity with international standards.

34. The Committee reiterates the concern expressed in its previous recommendations about the conditions of the detention of children, in particular the fact that they may not be completely segregated from adults during pretrial detention and after sentencing. The Committee is also concerned at the large number of children sentenced to life imprisonment in the State party (art. 16).

The State party should ensure that detained children are kept in facilities separate from those for adults in conformity with international standards. The State party should address the question of sentences of life imprisonment of children, as these could constitute cruel, inhuman or degrading treatment or punishment.

35. The Committee remains concerned about the extensive use by the State party's law-enforcement personnel of electroshock devices, which have caused several deaths. The Committee is concerned that this practice raises serious issues of compatibility with article 16 of the Convention.

The State party should carefully review the use of electroshock devices, strictly regulate their use, restricting it to substitution for lethal weapons, and eliminate the use of these devices to restrain persons in custody, as this leads to breaches of article 16 of the Convention.

36. The Committee remains concerned about the extremely harsh regime imposed on detainees in "supermaximum prisons". The Committee is concerned about the prolonged isolation periods detainees are subjected to, the effect such treatment has on their mental health, and that its purpose may be retribution, in which case it would constitute cruel, inhuman or degrading treatment or punishment (art. 16).

The State party should review the regime imposed on detainees in "supermaximum prisons", in particular the practice of prolonged isolation.

37. The Committee is concerned about reports of brutality and use of excessive force by the State party's law-enforcement personnel, and the numerous allegations of their ill-treatment of vulnerable groups, in particular racial minorities, migrants and persons of different sexual orientation which have not been adequately investigated (art. 16 and 12).

The State party should ensure that reports of brutality and ill-treatment of members of vulnerable groups by its law-enforcement personnel are independently, promptly and thoroughly investigated and that perpetrators are prosecuted and appropriately punished.

38. The Committee strongly encourages the State party to invite the Special Rapporteur on torture and other cruel, inhuman or degrading treatment or punishment, in full conformity with the terms of reference for fact-finding missions by special procedures of the United Nations, to visit Guantánamo Bay and any other detention facility under its de facto control.

39. The Committee invites the State party to reconsider its express intention not to become party to the Rome Statute of the International Criminal Court.

40. The Committee reiterates its recommendation that the State party should consider withdrawing its reservations, declarations and understandings lodged at the time of ratification of the Convention.

41. The Committee encourages the State party to consider making the declaration under article 22, thereby recognizing the competence of the Committee to receive and consider individual communications, as well as ratifying the Optional Protocol to the Convention.

42. The Committee requests the State party to provide detailed statistical data, disaggregated by sex, ethnicity and conduct, on complaints related to torture and ill-treatment allegedly committed by law-enforcement officials, investigations, prosecutions, penalties and disciplinary action relating to such complaints. It requests the State party to provide similar statistical data and information on the enforcement of the Civil Rights of Institutionalized Persons Act by the Department of Justice, in particular in respect to the prevention, investigation and prosecution of acts of torture, or cruel, inhuman or degrading treatment or punishment in detention

facilities and the measures taken to implement the Prison Rape Elimination Act and their impact. The Committee requests the State party to provide information on any compensation and rehabilitation provided to victims. The Committee encourages the State party to create a federal database to facilitate the collection of such statistics and information which assist in the assessment of the implementation of the provisions of the Convention and the practical enjoyment of the rights it provides. The Committee also requests the State party to provide information on investigations into the alleged ill-treatment perpetrated by law-enforcement personnel in the aftermath of Hurricane Katrina.

43. The Committee requests the State party to provide, within one year, information on its response to its recommendations in paragraphs 16, 20, 21, 22, 24, 33, 34 and 42 above.

44. The Committee requests the State party to disseminate its report, with its addenda and the written answers to the Committee's list of issues and oral questions and the conclusions and recommendations of the Committee widely, in all appropriate languages, through official websites, the media and non-governmental organizations.

45. The State party is invited to submit its next periodic report, which will be considered as its fifth periodic report, by 19 November 2011, the due date of the fifth periodic report.

DOCUMENT NO. 2

AGIZA v. SWEDEN

U.N. Committee Against Torture

Communication No. 233/2003, U.N. Doc. CAT/C/34/D/233/2003

May 20, 2005

CAT/C/34/D/233/2003
20 May 2005
Original: ENGLISH
COMMITTEE AGAINST TORTURE
Thirty-fourth session
2 - 20 May 2005

DECISION
Communication No. 233/2003
Submitted by: Mr. Ahmed Hussein Mustafa Kamil
Agiza (represented by counsel, Mr. Bo
Johansson, of the Swedish Refugee Advice Centre)
Alleged victim: The complainant
State party: Sweden
Date of complaint: 25 June 2003
Date of decision on admissibility: 19 May 2004
Date of present decision: 20 May 2005
* Made public by decision of the Committee against Torture.

Subject matter (merits) - expulsion of suspected terrorist on national security grounds from Sweden to Egypt following truncated procedure and receipt of diplomatic assurances Issues (merits) - procedural obligations inherent in article 3 - existence of real risk of torture upon expulsion given existence of diplomatic assurances and subsequent course of events - compliance with duty of co-operation with Committee Articles of the Convention - 3 and 22

On 20 May 2005, the Committee against Torture adopted the annexed draft as the Committee's Decision, under article 22, paragraph 7, of the

Convention in respect of communication No. 233/2003. The text of the Decision is appended to the present document.

[ANNEX]

Decision of the Committee against Torture under article 22 of the Convention against Torture and Other Cruel, Inhuman or Degrading Treatment or Punishment

Thirty-fourth session

Concerning

Communication No. 233/2003[1]

Submitted by: Mr. Ahmed Hussein Mustafa Kamil

Agiza (represented by counsel, Mr. Bo
Johansson, of the Swedish Refugee
Advice Centre)
Alleged victim: The complainant

State party: Sweden

Date of complaint: 25 June 2003

The Committee against Torture, established under Article 17 of the Convention against Torture and Other Cruel, Inhuman or Degrading Treatment or Punishment,

Meeting on 20 May 2005,

Having considered complaint No. 233/2003, submitted to the Committee against Torture by Mr. Ahmed Hussein Mustafa Kamil Agiza, under article 22 of the Convention against Torture and Other Cruel, Inhuman or Degrading Treatment or Punishment,

Having taken into account all information made available to it by the complainant and the State party,

Adopts the following decision:

Decision of the Committee Under Article 22, Paragraph 7, of the Convention

1.1 The complainant is Ahmed Hussein Mustafa Kamil Agiza, an Egyptian national born on 8 November 1962, detained in Egypt at the time of submission of the complaint. He claims that his removal by Sweden to Egypt on 18 December 2001 violated article 3 of the Convention. He is represented by counsel, who provides as authority to act a letter of authority issued by the complainant's father. The complainant himself, detained, is allegedly not allowed to sign any documents for external purposes without special

[1] The text of a separate opinion, dissenting in part, by Committee member Mr. Alexander Yakovlev is appended to the present document.

permission from the Egyptian State prosecutor, and according to counsel such a permit cannot be expected.

The Facts as Presented

2.1 In 1982, the complainant was arrested on account of his family connection to his cousin, who had been arrested for suspected involvement in the assassination of the former Egyptian President, Anwar Sadat. Before his release in March 1983, he was allegedly subjected to torture. The complainant, active at university in the Islamic movement, completed his studies in 1986 and married Ms. Hannan Attia. He avoided various police searches, but encountered difficulties, such as the arrest of his attorney, when he brought a civil claim in 1991 against the Ministry of Home Affairs, for suffering during his time in prison.

2.2 In 1991, the complainant left Egypt for Saudi Arabia on security grounds, and thereafter to Pakistan, where his wife and children joined him. After the Egyptian embassy in Pakistan refused to renew their passports, the family left in July 1995 for Syria under assumed Sudanese identities, in order to continue to Europe. This plan failed and the family moved to Iran, where the complainant was granted a university scholarship.

2.3 In 1998, the complainant was tried in Egypt for terrorist activity directed against the State before a "Superior Court Martial" in absentia, along with over one hundred other accused. He was found guilty of belonging to the terrorist group "Al Gihad", and was sentenced, without possibility of appeal, to 25 years' imprisonment. In 2000, concerned that improving relations between Egypt and Iran would result in his being returned to Egypt, the complainant and his family bought air tickets, under Saudi Arabian identities, to Canada, and claimed asylum during a transit stop in Stockholm, Sweden, on 23 September 2000.

2.4 In his asylum application, the complainant claimed that he had been sentenced to "penal servitude for life" in absentia on account of terrorism linked to Islamic fundamentalism,[2] and that, if returned, he would be executed as other accused in the same proceedings allegedly had been. His wife contended that, if returned, she would be detained for many years, as the complainant's wife. On 23 May 2001, the Migration Board sought the opinion of the Swedish Security Police on the case. On 14 September 2001, the Migration Board held a "major enquiry" with the complainant, with a further enquiry following on 3 October 2001. During of the same month, the Security Police questioned the complainant. On 30 October 2001, the Security Police advised the Migration Board that the complainant held a leading position in an organisation guilty of terrorist acts and was responsible for

[2] Counsel explains the variation with the actual sentence on the basis that a 25 year sentence amounted to the same as few could be expected to endure that length of time in prison.

the activities of the organisation. The Migration Board thus forwarded the complainant's case, on 12 November 2001, to the Government for a strength of the decision under chapter 7, section 11(2)(2), of the Aliens Act. In the Board's view, on the information before it, the complainant could be considered entitled to claim refugee status; however, the Security Police's assessment, which the Board saw no reason to question, pointed in a different direction. The balancing of the complainant's possible need for protection against the Security Police's assessment, thus had to be made by the Government. On 13 November 2001, the Aliens Appeals Board, whose view the Government had sought, shared the Migration Board's assessment of the merits and also considered that the Government should decide the matter. In a statement, the complainant denied belonging to the organisation referred to in the Security Police statement, arguing that one of the designated organisations was not a political organisation but an Arab-language publication. He also claimed that he had criticised Usama Bin Laden and the Afghan Taliban in a letter to a newspaper.

2.5 On 18 December 2001, the Government rejected the asylum applications of the complainant and of his wife. The reasons for these decisions are omitted from the text of this decision at the State party's request and with the agreement of the Committee. Accordingly, it was ordered that the complainant be deported immediately and his wife as soon as possible. On 18 December 2001, the complainant was deported, while his wife went into hiding to avoid police custody.

2.6 On 23 January 2002, the Swedish Ambassador to Egypt met the complainant at Mazraat Tora prison outside Cairo.[3] The same day, the complainant's parents visited him for the first time. They allege that they when they met him in the warden's office, he was supported by an officer and near breakdown, hardly able to shake his mother's hand, pale and in shock. His face, particularly the eyes, and his feet were swollen, with his cheeks and bloodied nose seemingly thicker than usual. The complainant allegedly said to his mother that he had been treated brutally upon arrest by the Swedish authorities. During the eight hour flight to Egypt, in Egyptian custody, he allegedly was bound by hands and foot. Upon arrival, he was allegedly subjected to "advanced interrogation methods" at the hand of Egyptian state security officers, who told him the guarantees provided by the Egyptian Government concerning him were useless. The complainant told his mother that a special electric device with electrodes connected to his body was utilized, and that electric shocks were utilized if he did not respond properly to orders.

[3] Counsel states that the following information concerning the complainant's whereabouts and well-being originates from Swedish diplomatic sources, the complainant's parents, a Swedish radio reporter and the complainant's Egyptian attorney.

2.7 On 11 February 2002, a correspondent for Swedish radio visited the complainant in prison. According to him, the complainant walked with difficulty but he could not see any sign of torture. In response to a question by counsel, the correspondent stated that he had explicitly asked the complainant if he had been tortured, and that he had replied that he could not comment. After the initial visit, the Ambassador or other Swedish diplomats were permitted to visit the complainant on a number of occasions. Counsel states that what can be understood from the diplomatic dispatches up to March 2003, is that the complainant had been treated "relatively well", and that he had not been subjected to torture even if the prison conditions were harsh.

2.8 On 16 April 2002, the complainant's parents again visited him. He allegedly told his mother that after the January visit further electric shocks had been applied, and that for the last ten days he had been held in solitary confinement. His hands and legs had been tied, and he had not been allowed to visit a toilet. At a following visit, he told his parents that he was still in solitary confinement but no longer bound. He was allowed to visit a toilet once a day, and the cell was cold and dark. With reference to a security officer, he was said to have asked his mother, "do you know what he does to me during the nights?" He had also been told that his wife would soon be returned to Egypt and that she and his mother would be sexually assaulted in his presence. Thereafter, the complainant's parents visited him once a month until July 2002 and then every fortnight. According to counsel, the information available is that he is held in a two square metre cell, which is artificially cooled, dark and without a mattress to sleep on. His toilet visits are said to be restricted.

2.9 In December 2002, the complainant's Egyptian lawyer, Mr. Hafeez Abu Saada, the head of an Egyptian human rights organization with knowledge of local conditions of detention and interrogation methods, met in Cairo with Mr. Thomas Hammarberg, head of the Olaf Palme International Centre. Mr. Abu Saada expressed his belief that the complainant had been subjected to torture.

2.10 On 5 March 2003, the Swedish Ambassador met the complainant with a human rights envoy from the Swedish Ministry of Foreign Affairs. The complainant allegedly stated for the first time that he had been subjected to torture. In response to the question as to why he had not mentioned this before, he allegedly responded, "It does no longer matter what I say, I will nevertheless be treated the same way".

The Complaint

3.1 Counsel claims that the reason that he lodged the complainant over one and a half years after the complainant's removal was that for a long period it was uncertain who was able to represent him. Counsel contends that the original intention had been for lawyer who had represented the complainant in domestic proceedings in Sweden to submit the complaint; "due to the circumstances", that lawyer found himself "unable to fulfill the commission" and transferred the case to present counsel "some months ago". Counsel adds that it had been difficult to obtain the complainant's personal consent to lodge a complaint.

3.2 As to the merits, counsel argues that the complainant's removal to Egypt by Sweden violated his right under article 3 of the Convention. He bases this proposition both on what was known at the time the complainant was expelled, as viewed in the light of subsequent events. He contends that it has been satisfactorily established that the complainant was in fact subjected to torture after his return.

3.3 Counsel argues that torture is a frequently used method of interrogation and punishment in Egypt, particularly in connection with political and security matters, and that accordingly the complainant, accused of serious political acts, was at substantial risk of torture. In counsel's view, the State party must have been aware of this risk and as a result sought to obtain a guarantee that his human rights would be respected. Counsel emphasizes, however, that no arrangements had been made prior to expulsion as to how the guarantees in question would be implemented after the complainant's return to Egypt. Counsel refers to the judgment of the European Court of Human Rights in Chahal v. United Kingdom,[4] where the Court found a guarantee provided by the Indian government to be, of its own, insufficient protection against human rights violations.

3.4 Subsequent events are said to bear out this view. Firstly, Amnesty International expressed concerns about the complainant's situation in communiqués dated 19 and 20 December 2001, 10, 22 January, and 1 February 2002. Secondly, the conclusions drawn by the State party as a result of its visits should be discounted because they took place in circumstances which were deficient. In particular, the visits were short, took place in a prison which is not the one where the complainant was actually detained, were not conducted in private and without the presence of any medical practitioners or experts. Thirdly, independent evidence tends to corroborate that torture did occur. Weight should be attached to the complainant's parents' testimony as, although supervised, not every word was recorded as it was with the official visits and there was opportunity for him to share sensitive information, especially when bidding his mother farewell. In the course of these visits, supervision lessened, with persons entering and leaving the room. Counsel argues it would not be in the parents' or the complainant's interests for them to have overrepresented the situation,

---

[4] Judgment of 15 November 1996.

as this would needlessly put him at risk of prejudicial treatment as well as distress the complainant's family still in Sweden. In addition, the parents, elderly persons without political motivation, would thereby be placing themselves at risk of reprisal.

3.5 Furthermore, the complainant's Egyptian lawyer is well qualified to reach his conclusion, after meeting with the complainant, that he had been tortured. Mr. Hammarberg, for his part, considers this testimony reliable. In advice dated 28 January 2003 provided by Mr. Hammarberg to counsel, the former considered that there was prima facie evidence of torture. He was also of the view that there were deficiencies in the monitoring arrangements implemented by the Swedish authorities, given that during the first weeks after return there were no meetings, while subsequent meeting were neither in private nor with medical examinations undertaken.

3.6 For counsel, the only independent evidence on the question, that of the radio correspondent's visit, confirms the above conclusions, as the complainant declined to answer a direct question as to whether he had been tortured. He would not have done this had he not feared further reprisals. The complainant also informed the Swedish Ambassador directly on 5 March 2003 that he had been subjected to torture, having by that point allegedly given up any hope that the situation would change.

3.7 Counsel concludes that the complainant's ability to prove torture has been very limited, though he has done his best to inform on his experiences in prison. He has been unable to present a full statement of his experiences or corroborative evidence such as medical reports.

The State Party's Submissions on the Admissibility and Merits of the Complaint

4.1 By submission of 5 December 2003, the State party contests both the admissibility and the merits of the complaint. It regards complaint as inadmissible (i) for the time elapsed since the exhaustion of domestic remedies, (ii) as an abuse of process, and (iii) as manifestly illfounded.

4.2 While accepting that neither the Convention not the Committee's case law prescribe a definitive timeframe within which a complaint must be submitted, the State party submits that in light of the content of Rule 107(f) of the Committee's rules of procedure, this cannot mean that a complaint could never be time-barred. The State party refers to the six month limit applicable to cases submitted to the European Court of Human Rights, including with respect to expulsion cases arising under article 3 of the European Convention, and the strong rationale of legal certainty for both complainants and States underlying that rule. The State party argues that this principle of legal certainty must be considered as one of the fundamental principles inherent in the international legal order. As the

Convention as well as the European Convention are both important parts of international human rights law, it would be natural for one regime to seek guidance from another on an issue on which the former is silent. In view of Rule 107(f) of the Committee's Rules,[5] therefore, a six-month limit could arguably serve as a point of departure for the Committee.

4.3 With respect to the present case, the State party argues that no convincing information has been provided for the delay of over one and a half years in submission of the complaint. As counsel derives his authority to act from the complainant's father rather than the complainant himself, there is no reason why this could not have been obtained at an earlier stage. Nor does it appear that any attempt was made shortly after expulsion to obtain authority to act from this or another relative, such as the complainant's wife in Sweden. The State party refers to the complaint submitted by the same counsel on behalf of the complainant's wife in December 2001,[6] where it was argued that her situation was so closely linked to that of the present complaint that it was impossible to argue her case without referring to his. The arguments advanced in her case show that counsel was well acquainted with the circumstances presently invoked, and he should not be allowed to argue that the delay was due to his involvement with the family's case until a much later stage. There is, in the State party's view, no reason why the present complainant could not have been included in the first complaint submitted in December 2001. Accordingly, the State party argues that in the interests of legal certainty, the time that has elapsed since exhaustion of domestic remedies is unreasonably prolonged, and the complaint is inadmissible pursuant to article 22, paragraph 2, of the Convention and Rule 107(f).

4.4 The State party also argues that the complaint discloses an abuse of the right of submission, disputing whether the complainant can be considered to have justifiable interest in having his complaint considered by the Committee. The factual basis of the current complaint is the same as that submitted on his wife's behalf in December 2001,[7] with the crucial issue in both cases relating to the guarantees issued by the Egyptian authorities prior to and for the purpose of the expulsion of the complainant and his family. In its decision on that case, after having assessed the value of the guarantees and finding no violation of the Convention, the Committee already dealt with the very issue raised by the present complaint. The issue should accordingly be considered res judicata.

[5] Rule 107(f) provides: "With a view to reaching a decision on the admissibility of a complaint, the Committee, its Working Group or a rapporteur designated under rules 98 or 106, paragraph 3, shall ascertain: . . . (f) That the time elapsed since the exhaustion of domestic remedies is not so unreasonably prolonged as to render consideration of the claims unduly difficult by the Committee or the State party."

[6] Hanan Ahmed Fouad Abd El Khalek Attia v. Sweden, Case No 199/2002, Decision adopted on 17 November 2003.

[7] Ibid.

4.5 Furthermore, within the framework of the proceedings concerning the complaint by the complainant's wife, the same extensive information has been submitted concerning his past activities, present whereabouts and conditions of detention. As both complaints were submitted by the same counsel, the present complaint places an unnecessary burden both on the Committee and the State party. Accordingly, the complainant does not have a demonstrable interest in having his complaint examined by the Committee. It should thus be regarded as an abuse of the right of submission and inadmissible pursuant to article 22, paragraph 2, of the Convention and Rule 107(b).[8]

4.6 Finally, the State party considers the complaint manifestly unfounded, as the complainant's claims fail to rise to the basic level of substantiation required in light of the arguments on the merits set out below. It should thus be declared inadmissible under article 22, paragraph 2, of the Convention and Rule 107(b).

4.7 On the merits, the State party sets out the particular mechanisms of the Aliens Act 1989 applicable to cases such as the complainant's. While asylum claims are normally dealt with by the Migration Board and, in turn, the Aliens Appeals Board, under certain circumstances either body may refer the case to the Government, while appending its own opinion. This constellation arises if the matter is deemed to be of importance for the security of the State or otherwise for security in general, or for the State's relations with a foreign power (chapter 7, section 11(2)(2), of the Act). If the Migration Board refers a case, it must first be forwarded to the Aliens Appeals Board which provides its own opinion on the case.

4.8 An alien otherwise in need of protection on account of a well-founded fear of persecution at the hand of the authorities of another State on account of a reason listed in the Convention on the Status of Refugees (under chapter 3, section 2, of the Act) may however be denied a residence permit in certain exceptional cases, following an assessment of that alien's previous activities and requirements of the country's security (chapter 3, section 4 of the Act). However, no person at risk of torture may be refused a residence permit (chapter 3, section 3 of the Act). In addition, if a person has been refused a residence permit and has had an expulsion decision issued against him or her, an assessment of the situation at the enforcement stage must be made to avoid that an individual is expelled to face, inter alia, torture or other cruel, inhuman or degrading treatment or punishment.

[8] Rule 107(b) provides: "With a view to reaching a decision on the admissibility of a complaint, the Committee, its Working Group or a rapporteur designated under rules 98 or 106, paragraph 3, shall ascertain: . . . (b) That the complaint is not an abuse of the Committee's process or manifestly unfounded."

4.9 The State party recalls UN Security Council Resolution 1373 of 28 September 2001, which enjoins all UN Member States to deny safe haven to those who finance, plan, support or commit terrorist acts, or themselves provide safe haven. The Council called on Member States to take appropriate measures, consistent with international human rights and refugee law, to ensure asylum seekers have not planned, facilitated, or participated in, terrorist acts. It also called upon Member States to ensure, in accordance with international law, that the institution of refugee status is not abused by perpetrators, organizers or facilitators of terrorist acts. In this context, the State party refers to the Committee's statement of 22 November 2001, in which it expressed confidence that responses to threats of international terrorism adopted by States parties would be in conformity with their obligations under the Convention.

4.10 The State party also recalls the interim report[9] submitted in July 2002 by the Special Rapporteur of the Commission on Human Rights on the question of torture and other cruel, inhuman or degrading treatment or punishment, submitted in accordance with resolution 56/143 of 19 December 2001. In his report, the Special Rapporteur urged States "to ensure that in all appropriate circumstances the persons they intend to extradite, under terrorist or other charges, will not be surrendered unless the Government of the receiving country has provided an unequivocal guarantee to the extraditing authorities that the persons concerned will not be subjected to torture or any other forms of ill-treatment upon return, and that a system to monitor the treatment of the persons in question has been put into place with a view to ensuring that they are treated with full respect for their human dignity" (paragraph 35).

4.11 As to the facts of the present case, the State party details the information obtained by its Security Police, which led it to regard the complainant as a serious security threat. At the State party's request, this information, while transmitted to counsel for the complainant in the context of the confidential proceedings under article 22 of the Convention, is not set out in the Committee's public decision on the present complaint.

4.12 The State party observes that on 12 December 2001, after referral of the case from the Migration and Aliens Appeals Boards, a state secretary of its Ministry of Foreign Affairs met with a representative of the Egyptian government in Cairo. At the State party's request and with the Committee's agreement, details of the identity of the interlocutor are deleted from the text of the decision. As the State party was considering to exclude the complainant from protection under the Refugee Convention, the purpose of the visit was to determine the possibility, without violating Sweden's

[9] A/57/173, 2 July 2002.

international obligations, including those arising under the Convention, of returning the complainant and his family to Egypt. After careful consideration of the option to obtain assurances from the Egyptian authorities with respect to future treatment, the State party's government concluded it was both possible and meaningful to inquire whether guarantees could be obtained to the effect that the complainant and his family would be treated in accordance with international law upon return to Egypt. Without such guarantees, return to Egypt would not be an alternative. On 13 December 2002, requisite guarantees were provided.

4.13 The State party then sets outs in detail its reasons for refusing, on 18 December 2001, the asylum claims of the complainant and his wife. These reasons are omitted from the text of this decision at the State party's request and with the agreement of the Committee.

4.14 The State party advises that the complainant's current legal status is, according to the Egyptian Ministries of Justice and Interior, that he presently serves a sentence for his conviction, in absentia, by a military court for, among other crimes, murder and terrorist activities. His family provided him with legal representation, and in February 2002, a petition for review of the case was filed with the President. By October 2002, this had been dealt with by the Ministry of Defence and would soon be handed to the President's office for decision. Turning to the monitoring of the complainant's situation after his expulsion, the State party advises that his situation has been monitored by the Swedish embassy in Cairo, mainly by visits approximately once every month. As of the date of submission, there had been seventeen visits.[10] On most occasions, visitors have included the Swedish Ambassador, and several on other visits a senior official from the Ministry of Foreign Affairs.

4.15 According to the embassy, these visits have over time developed into routine, taking place in the prison superintendent's office and lasting an average 45 minutes. At no time has the complainant been restrained in any fashion. The atmosphere has been relaxed and friendly, with the visitors and the complainant being offered soft drinks. At the end of the June 2002 visit, embassy staff observed the complainant in seemingly relaxed conversation with several prison guards, awaiting return to detention. At all times he has been dressed in clean civilian clothes, with well-trimmed beard and hair. He appeared to be well-nourished and not to have lost weight between visits. At none of the visits did he show signs of physical abuse or maltreatment, and he was able to move around without difficulty. At the request of

[10] These took place on 23 January, 7 March, 14 April, 27 May, 24 June, 22 July, 9 September and 4 November 2002, as well as 19 January, 5 March, 9 April, 14 May, 9 June, 29 July, 25 August, 30 September and 17 November 2003.

the Ambassador, in March 2002, he removed his shirt and undershirt and turned around, disclosing no sign of torture.

4.16 In the embassy's report of the first (January 2002) visit, the complainant did not seem to hesitate to speak freely, and told the Ambassador that he had no complaints as to his treatment in prison. Asked whether he had been subjected to any kind of systematic abuse, he made no claim to such effect. When asked during the April 2002 visit whether he had been in any way maltreated, he noted that he had not been physically abused or otherwise maltreated. During most visits he had complaints concerning his general health, concerning a bad back, gastric ulcer, kidney infection and thyroid gland, causing inter alia sleeping problems. He had seen a variety of internal and external medical specialists, and had had an MRI spinal examination, physiotherapy for his back and an X-ray thyroid gland examination. The X-ray revealed a small tumour for which he will undergo further tests. In August 2003, he expressed to the Ambassador, as he had done before, his satisfaction with the medical care received. At the November 2003 visit, he advised that a neurologist had recommended a back operation. He has received regular medication for various health problems.

4.17 During the May and November 2002 visits, the complainant remarked adversely about the general conditions of detention. He referred to the absence of beds or toilets in the cell, and that he was being held in a part of the prison for unconvicted persons. According to him, this generally improved after December 2002, when he was no longer kept apart from other prisoners and could walk in the courtyard. In January 2003, he was moved on health grounds to a part of the prison with a hospital ward. In March 2003, in response to a question, he said he was treated neither better nor worse than other prisoners; general prison conditions applied. At no subsequent visits did he make such complaints.

4.18 On 10 February 2002, that is at an early stage of detention, the Swedish national radio reported on a visit by one of its correspondents with the complainant in the office of a senior prison official. He was dressed in dark-blue jacket and trousers, and showed no external signs of recent physical abuse, at least on his hands or face. He did have some problems moving around, which he ascribed to a long-term back problem. He complained about not being allowed to read and about lack of a radio, as well as lack of permission to exercise.

4.19 Further issues that have been brought up regularly between the complainant and embassy staff are visits from family and lawyers. Following the June 2002 visit, a routine of fortnightly family visits appeared to have been established. At the time of submission this routine continued, though visits in May and June 2003 were restricted for security reasons.

The complainant remarked that he had only received two visits from his lawyer, in February and March 2002. He had not requested to see his lawyer as he considered it meaningless. This issue was raised in the embassy's follow-up meetings with Egyptian government officials, who affirmed that the complainant's lawyer is free to visit and that no restrictions apply.

4.20 As the complainant on several occasions and in reply to direct questions, stated he had not suffered abuse, the Ambassador concluded after the November 2002 visit that, although the detention was mentally trying, there was no indication that the Egyptian authorities had breached the guarantees provided. The State party details certain allegations subsequently made by the complainant and the actions it took in response thereto. At the request of the State party and with the Committee's agreement, details of these matters are not included in the text of this decision.

4.21 As to the application of the Convention, the State party observes that the present case differs from most article 3 complaints before the Committee in that the expulsion has already taken place. The wording of article 3 of the Convention however implies that the Committee's examination of the case must focus on the point in time when the complainant was returned to his country of origin. Events that have taken place or observations made thereafter may naturally be of interest in establishing whether the guarantees provided have been respected, and this bears on the assessment of the State party's Government that the complainant would not be treated contrary to the Convention was in fact correct. But while such developments are relevant, the State party maintains that the principal question in the current complaint is whether or not its authorities had reason to believe, at the time of the complainant's expulsion on 18 December 2001, that substantial grounds existed for believing him to be at risk of torture.

4.22 The State party refers to the Committee's constant jurisprudence that an individual must show a foreseeable, real and personal risk of torture. Such a risk must rise beyond mere theory or suspicion, but does not have to be highly probable. In assessing such a risk, a standard which is incorporated into Swedish law, the guarantees issued by the Egyptian government are of great importance. The State party recalls the Committee's decision on the complaint presented by the complainant's wife where the same guarantees were considered effective,[11] and refers to relevant decisions of the European organs under the European Convention on Human Rights.

4.23 In Aylor-Davis v. France (judgment of 20 January 1994), it was held that guarantees from the receiving country, the United States, were found to eliminate the risk of the applicant being sentenced to death. The death

[11] Ibid.

penalty could only be imposed if it was actually sought by the State prosecutor. By contrast, in Chahal v. United Kingdom, the Court was not persuaded that assurances from the Indian government that a Sikh separatist "would enjoy the same legal protection as any other Indian citizen, and that he would have no reason to expect mistreatment of any kind at the hand of the Indian authorities" would provide an adequate guarantee of safety. While not doubting the Indian government's good faith, it appeared to the Court that despite the efforts inter alia of the Indian government and courts to bring about reform, violations of human rights by members of the security forces in Punjab and elsewhere in India remained a recurrent problem. The case law thus suggests that guarantees may be accepted where the authorities of the receiving State can be assumed to have control of the situation.

4.24 Applying this test, the State party argues that the current case is more in line with Aylor-Davis. The guarantees were issued by a senior representative of the Egyptian government. The State party points out that if assurances are to have effect, they must be issued by someone who can be expected to be able to ensure their effectiveness, as, in the State party's view, was presently the case in light of the Egyptian representative's senior position. In addition, during the December 2001 meeting between the Swedish state secretary and the Egyptian official, it was made clear to the latter what was at stake for Sweden: as article 3 of the Convention is of absolute character, the need for effective guarantees was explained at length. The state secretary reaffirmed the importance for Sweden to abide by its international obligations, including the Convention, and that as a result specific conditions would have to be fulfilled in order to make the complainant's expulsion possible. It was thus necessary to obtain written guarantees of fair trial, that he would not be subjected to torture or other inhuman treatment, and that he would not be sentenced to death or executed. The trial would be monitored by the Swedish embassy in Cairo, and it should be possible to visit the complainant, even after conviction. Moreover, his family should not be subjected to any kind of harassment. It was made clear that Sweden found itself in a difficult position, and that Egypt's failure to honour the guarantees would impact strongly on other similar European cases in the future.

4.25 The State party expands on the details of these guarantees. They are omitted from the text of this decision at the request of the State party, and with the consent of the Committee. The State party points out that the guarantees are considerably stronger than those provided in Chahal and are couched much more affirmatively, in positive terms of prohibition. The State party recalls that Egypt is a State party to the Convention, has a constitutional prohibition on torture and acts of, or orders to torture, are serious felonies under Egyptian criminal law.

4.26 For the State party, it is of interest in assessing the complaint whether the guarantees have been and are being respected. It recalls the allegations of ill-treatment made by the complainant's mother, and subsequently by non-governmental organisations, including the mother's description of his physical condition at her first visit on 23 January 2002. The State party's Ambassador's visit the same day immediately followed the mother's visit, and the Ambassador observed no signs of physical abuse. As observed, he seemed to speak freely, made no complaints about torture, and in response to a direct question on systematic abuse in prison, made no claim to that effect. The State party thus argues the allegation of ill-treatment on that date has been effectively refuted by its Ambassador's observations.

4.27 The State party asserts that judging from the numerous reports provided by the Ambassador, embassy staff and the senior official of its Ministry of Foreign Affairs, the guarantees provided have proved effective vis-à-vis the complainant. Allegations made by him to the contrary have not been substantiated, and on numerous occasions, he confirmed to the Swedish Ambassador that he had not been tortured or ill-treated. The allegations of March 2003 were refuted by the Egyptian authorities. The complainant receives the medical care he requires as a result of his health problems, and legal assistance has been provided to him by his family. That his lawyer so far may not have taken sufficient action to achieve review of sentence is of no relevance to the current complaint. In addition, his family visits him regularly. On the whole, considering the inherent constraints of detention, the complainant appears to be in fairly good health. The State party concludes that as the allegations of torture have not been substantiated, they cannot form the basis of the Committee's assessment of the case. The State party also points out that the case has been widely reported in national media and has received international attention. The Egyptian authorities can be assumed to be aware of this, and are likely to ensure as a result he is not subjected to ill-treatment.

4.28 The State party recalls that in its decision on the complaint of the complainant's wife,[12] the Committee appeared to make a prognosis for her in the light of the information about the effectiveness of the guarantees regarding her husband, the present complainant, to whom she had linked her case solely on the basis of her relationship to him. The Committee declared itself "satisfied by the provision of guarantees against abusive treatment" and noted that they were "regularly monitored by the State party's authorities in situ." It went on to observe that Egypt "is directly bound properly to treat prisoners within its jurisdiction." In the State party's view, therefore, the Committee's conclusion that she had not made out

[12] Ibid.

a breach of article 3 in her complaint is of "essential importance" to the present complaint.

4.29 In conclusion, the State party argues that by obtaining the guarantees in question from the competent Egyptian official, it lived up to its commitments under the Convention while at the same time as fulfilling its obligations under Security Council Resolution 1373. Prior to expelling the complainant, appropriate guarantees were obtained from the official best placed to ensure their effectiveness. The guarantees correspond in content to the requirements of the Special Rapporteur (see paragraph 4.10 above), while a monitoring mechanism was put into place and has been functioning for almost two years. Therefore, the complainant has not substantiated his claims that the guarantees have, in practice, not been respected. Should the Committee come to another conclusion, the crucial question is what the State party's Government had reason to believe at the time of the expulsion. As the complainant has not substantiated his claim under article 3, his removal to his country of origin was not in breach of that provision.

Counsel's Comments on the State Party's Submissions

5.1 By letter of 21 January 2004, counsel disputed the State party's submissions both on admissibility and merits. On the State party's arguments concerning timely submission of the complaint, he argues that it was unclear for a long period who was entitled to represent the complainant. Counsel argues that his prior lawyer had been unable to arrange for a power of attorney to be signed prior to the complainant's rapid removal, and that the prior lawyer considered his responsibilities at an end once the complainant had been removed. Counsel argues that once the complainant had been removed and could not be consulted directly, it was necessary to obtain more information about his situation, before carefully evaluating, together with his parents, whether it would be productive to file a complaint on his behalf. Counsel argues that the circumstances in the complaint brought by the complainant's wife were "completely different", as she had remained in Sweden and thus an urgent communication was necessary in order to prevent removal. In the present case, the complainant had already been expelled, and there was no urgent need to submit the complaint before a careful evaluation of its substance. He also points out that the six-month limit for submission refers only to complaints presented under the European Convention, and that there is no difficulty in the existence of different treaty regimes. In any case, counsel argues that the issue of principle before the Committee in terms of the satisfactory protection afforded by diplomatic assurances is so important that it should consider the case rather than declare it inadmissible.

5.2 Counsel denies that the complaint constitutes an abuse of the right of submission. While conceding that many of the "basic factors" in the cases of the complainant and his wife are the same and that the circumstances "coincide to a considerable degree", the current complainant is the individual at most serious risk of torture. His wife, who by contrast based her claim simply as a close relative to a person sought for terrorist activities, is in a subsidiary position facing a less serious risk than her husband. As a result there are "major differences" between the two cases and the complaint should thus not be declared inadmissible on this ground. Counsel also rejects the characterisation of the case as manifestly ill-founded.

5.3 On the merits, counsel refers, for a general picture of the gross, flagrant and widespread use of torture by Egyptian authorities to reports of several human rights organizations. The human rights report of the Swedish Ministry of Foreign Affairs itself refers to frequent torture by Egyptian police, especially in terrorism-related investigations. Counsel argues that the complainant was not involved in any terrorist activities, and rejects any applicability of Security Council Resolution 1373. In any event, this resolution could not override other international obligations such as the Convention. Counsel denies that the complainant participated in terrorist activities, including through those organisations that the Security Police claimed he was involved in. In any case, allegations of involvement with terrorist organisations would only have served to heighten the existing interest of the Egyptian authorities in the complainant, an individual convicted of terrorist offences, and this aggravating circumstance exacerbating the risk of torture should have been considered by the State party prior to expelling him.

5.4 For counsel, the key issue is not whether a guarantee was given by a government official, but rather whether it can be implemented and, if so, how. The guarantee in question was obtained at short notice, vague in its terms and provided no details on how the guarantees would be given effect with respect to the complainant; nor did the Egyptian government provide, or the Swedish authorities request, any such information. Neither did the Swedish authorities conceive an effective and durable arrangement for monitoring, conducting the first visit over a month after the complainant's removal. This arrangement, coming shortly after the Committee had requested interim measures of protection with respect to the complainant's wife, appeared to be an ad hoc reaction rather than part of a properly conceived monitoring plan. Counsel reiterates his criticisms of the effectiveness of the monitoring arrangements, observing that standard routines in such cases applied by organisations such as the International Committee of the Red Cross had not been met. In addition, the Swedish authorities apparently did not seek to call any medical expertise, particularly after the complainant's direct allegation of torture in March 2003. Counsel contends that differences between the complainant's testimony to his parents on one hand, and to Swedish authorities, unknown to him and accompanied by Egyptian authorities, on the other, are explicable.

5.5 Counsel criticizes the Committee's decision on the complaint presented by the complainant's wife, as the information that her husband had suffered ill-treatment, was based on a variety of sources and could not be dismissed as unfounded. Counsel disputes the State party's interpretation of the jurisprudence of the European organs, viewing the content of the current guarantee and that offered by India in Chahal as "basically the same". He observes that the Court did not doubt the good faith of the Indian government, but regarded the fundamental problem as human rights violations committed at the operational level by the security forces. In the present case, similarly, even assuming the same good will at the political level on the part of Egyptian authorities such as the representative with whom the guarantees were agreed, the reality at the lower operational levels of the state security services and other authorities with whom the complainant was in contact is that torture is commonplace. The Aylor-Davis case, by contrast, is inapposite as the guarantee there was offered by a State the circumstances of which cannot be compared to those appertaining in Egypt.

5.6 With respect to the State party' statement that the Egyptian authorities rejected the allegations made by the complainant in March 2003, counsel observes that any contrary reaction would have been surprising, and that such refutation does not disprove the complainant's allegation. In counsel's view, the burden of proof to show ill-treatment did not occur rests with the State party, with the most effective capacity to present evidence and conduct appropriate supervision. Counsel submits that the State party has not discharged this burden.

5.7 While accepting that Egypt is a State party to the Convention, counsel observes that this formal act is regrettably no guarantee that a State party will abide by the commitments assumed. As to the prophylactic effect of media publicity, counsel argues that there was some coverage of the cases of the complainant and his wife around the time of the former's removal, but that thereafter interest has been limited. In any case, there is reason to doubt whether media coverage has any such protective effect, and even where coverage is intensive, its positive effect may be doubted.

5.8 Counsel submits that if the Committee were to accept guarantees such as those offered in the present case as sufficient protection against torture, one could not discount that large scale deportations could take place after some standard form of assurance provided by States with poor human rights records. At least in circumstances where there was a limited will and capability on the part of the removing state appropriately to monitor the consequences, the results could readily be wide scope for authorities of the receiving state to engage in and conceal torture and ill-treatment. As a result, counsel invites the Committee to find that there was (i) a violation by the State party of article 3 of the Convention at the time of the complainant's expulsion, in the light both of the information then available and of subsequent events, and (ii) that he has been subjected to torture after removal. Supplementary submissions by the parties

6.1 By letter of 20 April 2004, counsel advised that on 18 February 2004, the complainant met his mother in prison. He informed her that he had been threatened by interrogation officers that he could be killed or tortured, and the same day lodged a complaint that he had been tortured. On 19 February 2004, he was transferred to Abu-Zabaal prison some 50 kilometres from Cairo, against which he protested by hunger strike lasting 17 days. He was allegedly placed in a small punitive isolation cell measuring 1.5 square meters in unhygienic conditions, receiving a bottle of water a day. On 8 March 2004, representatives of the Swedish embassy visited him with unknown results. On 20 March 2004, following unsuccessful attempts by the complainant's mother to visit him, it was announced that no family visits would be permitted outside major holidays due to his status as a security prisoner with special restrictions. On 4 April 2004, he was returned to Masra Torah prison. On 10 April 2004, a retrial began before the 13th superior military court on charges of joining and leading an illegal group or organization and criminal conspiracy, to which the complainant pleaded not guilty. A representative of Human Rights Watch was admitted, but family, journalists and representatives of the Swedish embassy were not. The complainant's lawyer requested an adjournment in order that he could read the 2000 pages of charging material and prepare a defence. As a result, the trial was adjourned for three days, with the lawyer permitted only to make handwritten notes. In counsel's view, this information demonstrates that the complainant had been tortured in the past, has been threatened therewith and faces a considerable risk of further torture. It also shows he has been treated in cruel and inhumane manner as well as denied a fair trial.

6.2 By further letter of 28 April 2004, counsel advised that on 27 April 2004 the complainant had been convicted and sentenced to 25 years' imprisonment. He also contended that the court rejected a request from the complainant for a medical examination as he had been tortured in detention. In counsel's view, the complainant's statement to the court and the court's rejection of his request constitute a further clear indication that he had been subjected to torture.

7.1 By submission of 3 May 2004, the State party responded to counsel's letter of 20 April 2004. The State party advised that since the last (seventeenth) visit reported to the Committee on 5 December 2003, four further visits on 17 December 2003, 28 January 2004, 8 March 2004 and 24 March 2004 had taken place. The State party advised that from December 2003 to

January 2004, the complainant's situation remained broadly the same, with him taking up law studies. While complaining that his two cellmates disturbed peace and quiet required for study, he managed to prepare for examinations that took place in the facility in January 2004. The reportedly maximum security Abu-Zabaal facility to which he was transferred was said to be a more customary facility for prisoners sentenced to long terms. At the same time, the prison director advised that the complainant had been ordered to spend 15 days in isolation as a disciplinary sanction for having attempted to instigate a rebellion amongst Masra Torah inmates. The State party had obtained separate corroborating evidence that (i) the complainant had attempted to start a prison riot by "shouting words calling for disobedience against the instructions and regulation of the prison" and that (ii) restrictions had been imposed on correspondence and visiting rights, for a period of three months. The State party observed that the complainant was found guilty of one of the two offences with which he was charged, namely having held a leading position in, and being responsible for, the terrorist organization Islamic Al-Fath Vanguards. He was sentenced to life imprisonment, hard labour (abolished in 2003) not being imposed. He is currently in Masra Torah prison awaiting decisions as to future placement.

7.2 The State party maintained its earlier positions with respect to the admissibility of the complaint, as well as to the merits, that is, that the complainant has not substantiated his claims that the Egyptian authorities have not respected the guarantees in practice. It recalled that the crucial question is what the State party had reason to believe, in light of the guarantees given, at the time of the expulsion. The State party thus submitted that it has been in full conformity with its obligations under the Convention.

8.1 By letter of 3 May 2004, counsel argued that he had initially only been supplied with a redacted version of the diplomatic report supplied after the first ambassadorial meeting in 23 January 2002 with the complainant. Counsel contended that the full report had just been provided to him by a lawyer representing a third party deported at the same time as the complainant. Counsel contends that according to this report the complainant informed the Ambassador that he had been tortured (in the form of beating by prison guards) and subjected to cruel and degrading treatment (in the form of blindfolding, solitary confinement in a very small cell, sleep deprivation and refusal of prescribed medication). Counsel argued that the State party had not supplied this information to the Committee. Counsel further provided a report by Human Rights Watch critical of diplomatic assurances in this context,[13] as well as a statement dated 27 April 2004 of the

[13] Human Rights Watch: "Empty Promises: Diplomatic Assurances No Safeguard against Torture", April 2004, Vol.16 No. 4(D).

Egyptian Organization for Human Rights critical of the complainant's retrial.

8.2 By letter of 4 May 2004, counsel provided his translation of the diplomatic report described. After describing a forced posture during the air transport to Egypt, the complainant is said to have told the Ambassador at the first meeting, in the presence of Egyptian officials, that he had been "forced to be blindfolded during interrogation, kept in too narrow cells, 1.50 x 1.50 metres during the same period, lack of sleep due to supervision in cells, a delay of ten days before [he] once gets access to his anti-gastric drugs (after medical examination), that [he] had been beaten by prison guards during transport to and from interrogation and threats from interrogation offices that it could affect his family if he did not tell everything about his time in Iran". The Ambassador concluded that he could not evaluate the veracity of these statements, but did not understand the claim to be of any form of systematic, physical torture. Counsel viewed this newly-disclosed information as a clear indication that the complainant had been subjected to torture. Counsel also argued that the real reason that the complainant had been transferred to the Abu-Zaabal facility was because he had lodged a complaint of threatened torture. He also contended that the complainant was denied "real and fair possibilities" to prepare his defence and observed that the State party did not address issues arising from the complainant's trial.

8.3 By a further letter of 4 May 2004, counsel provided a statement of the same day by Human Rights Watch entitled "Suspected Militants Unfair Trial and Torture Claim Implicate Sweden", in which the complainant's retrial as well as the State party's monitoring arrangements were criticized. Counsel also provided a letter to him by a Human Rights Watch researcher purporting to confirm the contents of the unredacted first diplomatic report described above and concluding that there were credible allegations of ill-treatment.

8.4 By submission of 5 May 2004, the State party advised that it considered the Committee to be in a position to take a decision on the admissibility and, if necessary, the merits of the complaint on the basis of the Convention and the information before the Committee. Accordingly, it did not intend to make additional submissions beyond those already made on 3 May 2004. It observed in conclusion that counsel's letter of 4 May 2004 raised, inter alia, issues falling outside the scope of the Convention.

The Committee's admissibility decision:

9.1 At its 32nd session, the Committee considered the admissibility of the communication. The Committee ascertained, as it was required to do under article 22, paragraph 5 (a), of the Convention, that the same matter had not been and was not being examined under another procedure of international investigation or settlement.

9.2 On the State party's argument that the present complaint was an abuse of process which rendered it inadmissible, the Committee observed that the complaint submitted on behalf of the complainant's wife in order to prevent her removal had necessarily been filed with dispatch, and had concerned, at least at the time of the Committee's decision, the issue of whether at that point the circumstances were such that her removal would be a violation of article 3 of the Convention. In reaching the conclusion that removal of the complainant's wife would not breach article 3, the Committee had considered the chronology of events up to the time of its decision, a necessarily wider enquiry than that at issue in the present case, which was focused upon the situation of the complainant at the time of his expulsion in December 2001. Indeed, the Committee had observed in its decision on the original complaint that it was not being presented with the issue of whether the present complainant's removal itself breached article 3. The two complaints related to different persons, one already removed from the State party's jurisdiction at the time of submission of the complaint and the other still within its jurisdiction pending removal. In the Committee's view, the complaints were thus not of an essentially identical nature, and it did not consider the current complaint to be a simple re-submission of an already decided issue. While submission of the present complaint with greater dispatch would have been preferable, the Committee considered that it would be inappropriate to take so strict a view that would consider the time taken in obtaining authorization from the complainant's father as so excessively delayed as amounting to an abuse of process.

9.3 As to the State party inadmissibility argument grounded on Rule 107(f), the Committee observed that this Rule required the delay in submission to have made consideration of the case "unduly difficult". In the present case, the State party had had ready access to the relevant factual submissions and necessary argumentation, and thus, while the timing of submission of the two complaints may have been inconvenient, consideration of the present complaint could not be said to have been made unduly difficult by the lapse of 18 months from the date of the complainant's expulsion. The Committee thus rejected the State party's argument that the complaint is inadmissible on this ground.

9.4 The Committee noted that Egypt has not made the declaration provided for under article 22 recognizing the Committee's competence to consider individual complaints against that State party. The Committee observed, however, that a finding, as requested by the complainant, that torture had in fact occurred following the complainant's removal to Egypt (see paragraph 5.8), would amount to a conclusion that Egypt, a State party to the Convention, had breached its obligations under the Convention without it having had an opportunity to present its position. This separate claim against Egypt was thus inadmissible ratione personae.

9.5 In terms of the State party's argument that the remaining complaint was insufficiently substantiated, for purposes of admissibility, the Committee considered that the complainant had presented a sufficiently arguable case with respect to Sweden for it to be determined on the merits. In the absence of any further obstacles to the admissibility of the complaint advanced by the State party, the Committee accordingly was ready to proceed with the consideration of the merits.

9.6. Accordingly, the Committee against Torture decided that the complaint was admissible, in part, as set out in paragraphs 9.2 to 9.5 above. Supplementary submissions by the parties on the merits of the complaint

10.1 By letter of 20 August 2004, counsel for the complainant made additional submissions on the merits of the case, providing additional details on the complainant's retrial in April 2004. He stated that the complainant's defence counsel was only provided with copies of parts of the criminal investigation that had been conducted, despite a request to be able to photocopy the investigation records. When the trial was resumed on 13 April, the complainant was only able to speak to his counsel for about 15 minutes. The State called a colonel of the State Security Investigation Sector to testify against the complainant, to the effect that the complainant had had a leading position since 1980 in the Jamaa group, as well as links since 1983 with Ayman al Zawahiri, a central figure of the group. He further testified that the complainant had attended training camps in Pakistan and Afghanistan, and participated in weapons training sessions. Upon cross-examination, the colonel stated that the Jamaa leadership continually changes, that his testimony was based on secret information, that the sources thereof could not be revealed due to risks to their lives and that he (the colonel) had had a supplementary role in the investigation alongside other officers whom he did not know. According to counsel for the complainant, the court in its verdict of 27 April 2004 rejected the complainant's request for a forensic medical examination made during the trial, but referred to a medical examination report by the prison doctor which indicated that the complainant had suffered injuries in prison.

10.2 Counsel refers to a Swedish television broadcast of 10 May 2004 on entitled "Kalla Fakta", examining the circumstances of the expulsion of the complainant and another individual.[14] The programme stated that the two men had been handcuffed when brought to a Stockholm airport, that a private jet of the United States of America had landed and that the two men were handed over to a group of special agents by Swedish police. The agents stripped the clothes from the men's bodies, inserted suppositories of an unknown nature, placed diapers upon them and dressed them in

[14] Counsel has supplied a transcript of the programme.

black overalls. Their hands and feet were chained to a specially-designed harness, they were blindfolded and hooded as they were brought to the plane. Mr. Hans Dahlgren, State Secretary at the Foreign Ministry, stated in an interview that the Egyptian Government had not complied with the fair trial component of the guarantees provided.

10.3 According to counsel for the complainant, following this programme, the Swedish Foreign Ministry sent two senior representatives to Egypt to discuss with the Egyptian Government how the two deportees had been treated. Results of the meeting are not known apart from an Egyptian denial of maltreatment and that an investigation under Egyptian leadership, but with international participation and medical expertise, would be involved. Three separate investigations in Sweden have also resulted and are ongoing: (i) a proprio motu investigation by the Chief Ombudsman to determine whether the actions taken were lawful, (ii) a criminal investigation by the Stockholm public prosecutor, upon private complaint, on whether Swedish Security Police committed any crime in connection with the deportation, and (iii) an investigation by Parliament's Constitutional Committee into the lawfulness of the Swedish handling of the cases.

10.4 On 15 June 2004, the Aliens Appeals Board granted the complainant's wife and her five children permanent resident status in Sweden on humanitarian grounds. Later in June, the Egyptian Government through prerogative of mercy reduced the complainant's twenty-five year sentence to fifteen years' of imprisonment. According to counsel for the complainant, the complainant last met Swedish representatives in July 2004. For the first time, the meeting was wholly private. After the meeting, he met his mother and told her that prior to the meeting he had been instructed to be careful and to watch his tongue, receiving from an officer the warning "don't think that we don't hear, we have ears and eyes."

10.5 As at 20 August 2004, the date of the submissions, there was no information as to the announced inquiry in Egypt.[15] However, that day, the Swedish Minister of Foreign Affairs announced in a radio broadcast the receipt of a Note from the Egyptian government rejecting all allegations of the complainant's torture and considering an international inquiry unnecessary and unacceptable. The Minister of Foreign Affairs also considered there reason to be self-critical concerning the Swedish handling of the case.

---

[15] Counsel supplies a public statement by Amnesty International, dated 28 May 2004, entitled "Sweden: Concerns over the treatment of deported Egyptians" calling for an "international, wide-ranging, independent and impartial investigation " (EUR 42/001/2004), and, to similar effect, a statement by Human Rights Watch, dated 27 May 2004, entitled "Sweden: Torture Inquiry Must Be Under U.N. Auspices".

10.6 Counsel submits that the retrial fell patently short of international standards, being conducted in a military court with limited time and access available to the defence resulting in a conviction based on weak and insufficient evidence.[16] The failure to respect this portion of the guarantee, as conceded by State Secretary Dahlgren, raised of itself serious doubts as to the fulfillment of the remaining commitments. Counsel states that the complainant told his mother that he is irregularly sent to hospital for his back damage, there being no indication that he has been examined by a forensic physician. In counsel's view, the information already made known, coupled with the finding by the prison doctor that the complainant had suffered medical injuries (see paragraph 8.1, supra) and the refusal of the Egyptian authorities to allow an international investigation, together show that he has been subjected to torture. The burden to prove the contrary must rest upon the State party, with its commensurately greater resources and influence upon proceedings.

10.7 Reiterating his previous arguments, counsel contends that the complainant faced substantial risks of torture at the time of expulsion irrespective of the guarantees obtained from a country with a record such as Egypt. Counsel refers in this connection to a report on Sweden, dated 8 July 2004, of the Council of Europe, where criticism was expressed on the use of guarantees.[17] Alternatively, counsel argues that the steps taken to prevent and monitor the guarantees were insufficient. In addition to the arguments already raised, no detailed plans or programs featuring matters such as special orders on permissible interrogation techniques, confirmation that subordinate personnel were aware and would adhere to the guarantees or a post-expulsion treatment and trial plan were implemented.

11.1 By submission of 21 September 2004, the State party responded, observing that further visits since its last submissions of 3 May 2004 took place on 4 May, 2 June, 14 July and 31 August 2004. Each visit, excepting the most recent, took place in Masra Torah prison where the complainant appears to

---

[16] Counsel cites in support a public statement by Human Rights Watch, dated 4 May 2004, entitled "Sweden/Egypt: Suspected Militant's Unfair Trial and Torture Claims Implicate Sweden".

[17] Report by Mr. Alvaro Gil-Robles, Commissioner for Human Rights, on his Visit to Sweden (21-23 April 2003), CommDH(2004)13, stating, at paragraph 19: "The second point relates to the use of diplomatic assurances regarding the treatment of deported aliens in the countries to which they are returned. This example, which is not unique to Sweden, clearly illustrates the risks of relying on diplomatic assurances. The weakness inherent in the practice of diplomatic assurances lies in the fact that where there is a need for such assurances, there is clearly an acknowledged risk of torture and ill-treatment. Due to the absolute nature of the prohibition of torture or inhuman or degrading treatment, formal assurances cannot suffice where a risk nonetheless remains. As the UN Special Rapporteur on Torture has noted, such assurances must be unequivocal and a system to monitor such assurances must be in place. When assessing the reliability of diplomatic assurances, an essential criteria must be that the receiving state does not practice or condone torture or ill-treatment, and that it exercises effective control over the acts of non-state agents. In all other circumstances it is highly questionable whether assurances can be regarded as providing indisputable safeguards against torture and ill-treatment."

be serving sentence. The most recent visit took place at the Cairo university hospital. The State party refers to the complainant's improved legal situation, with the reduction to fifteen years' imprisonment subject, according to the complainant, to further reduction in the event of good behaviour. An assessment thereof is conducted automatically by the Egyptian Ministry for Interior Affairs. The complainant's health situation has also improved since May when he fell ill with pneumonia. Upon his return to Masra Torah prison on 4 April 2004, his previous treatments and medication were resumed. In late August 2004, he underwent surgery at the Cairo university hospital on spinal discs. The neurosurgeon involved informed the embassy on 31 August that the operation had taken five hours, involving microsurgery, but had been successful and without complications. According to the physician, the back problems were of a type which could befall anyone and had no apparent cause.

11.2 Concerning general conditions at Masra Torah prison, the complainant offered embassy staff no particular complaints when asked. Family visits have resumed upon his return to that prison. He was pleased to be informed of the permanent residence granted his wife and children, and has continued with his law studies and exams.

11.3 Following renewed allegations of ill-treatment by the complainant's counsel, his Egyptian lawyer and NGOs, the State party's Government made further investigative efforts. On 18 May 2004, it dispatched Ms. Lena Hjelm-Wallén, former Minister of Foreign Affairs and Deputy Prime Minister, as special envoy to Egypt, accompanied by the Director General for Legal Affairs of the Swedish Ministry for Foreign Affairs. The envoy met with the Egyptian Deputy Minister of Justice and the Minister in charge of the General Intelligence Service (GIS), voicing the State party's concerns over the alleged ill-treatment in the first weeks following the complainant's return to Egypt. She requested an independent and impartial inquiry on the allegations, including international medical expertise. The Egyptian Government dismissed the allegations as unfounded, but agreed to undertake an investigation. Subsequently, on 1 June 2004, the Swedish Minister of Foreign Affairs dispatched a letter to the Egyptian Minister in charge of the GIS, suggesting that in order for the Egyptian investigation to receive the widest possible international acceptance, it should be carried out with or by an independent authority, involving the judiciary and medical expertise, and preferably international expertise with recognized expertise in investigation of torture. She also professed willingness to allow a Swedish official, such as senior police officer or prosecutor, to assist. She added that it was crucial that the fight against terrorism be carried out with full respect for the rule of law and in conformity with international human rights obligations. In his answer of late July 2004, the responsible Egyptian Minister refuted the allegations of ill-treatment as unfounded, referring without detail to Egyptian investigations. While confirming the reduction of the complainant's sentence, he gave no direct answer to the Swedish request for an independent investigation.

11.4 The State party states that its Government is not content with the Egyptian response. In the process of considering possible further action, it is of the utmost importance that the Government receives a confirmation that such action will be in line with the complainant's own wishes, as further measures should not risk affecting his legal interests, safety or welfare adversely in any way. It is also necessary, in the circumstances, for the Egyptian Government to concur and co-operate in any further investigative efforts.

11.5 The State party reiterated its previous submissions based on a deficient retrial are outside the scope of the present case, concerned with whether the complainant's return to Egypt was in breach of the absolute ban on torture. It reiterates that the complainant has not substantiated his claim that he was ill-treated following return, and, thus, that the guarantees provided were not respected. The State party recalls that the crucial issue for decision is what its Government, in view of the guarantees received, had reason to believe at the time of the expulsion. Accordingly, the State party has complied with its obligations under the Convention, including article 3.

11.6 By letter of 16 October 2004, counsel responded to the State party's supplementary submissions, pointing out that the circumstances of the four visits from May to August 2004 described by the State party remained unclear but that it is likely that Egyptian officials were present and it would be difficult to speak freely. The situation may have been different for the hospital visit. Counsel criticises the State party for stating that it appeared that Masra Torah prison was the detention facility for sentence, arguing that as it is well known that the complainant was serving sentence at the Esquebahl Torah prison, the State party appeared to be ill-informed on the circumstances of his detention.

11.7 Counsel observes argues that the complainant's back condition was already diagnosed, as moderate, in Sweden. These problems deteriorated after his return and in 2003 he was brought to a Cairo hospital for examination, where he was recommended for surgery. Only a year later was "absolutely necessary" surgery actually carried out. He stayed for eleven days in hospital under supervision and received controlled visits from family. Although far from recovered, he was then returned to prison in an ordinary transport vehicle rather than an ambulance. Counsel argues that the State party knew of but neglected to tend to the complainant's medical condition for two and a half years, and in that time exposed him to treatment such as being kept in "very small" cells and with arms being tied behind the back. Apart from itself causing severe pain, such treatment seriously risked exacerbating his medical condition.

11.8 Counsel argues that the reduction in sentence does not affect how the complainant has been treated, is being and will be treated until release. As to law studies, it is not known whether and how the complainant has been able to pass any exams. Counsel rejects that there has been a significant improvement of the complainant's situation during the summer of 2004, conceding only that the situation is an improvement on that just after his return, arguing that as late as March 2004 the complainant was detained in a very small cell without adequate hygiene facilities and proper access to water. There remains a considerable risk the complainant will be subjected to torture or treatment approximating it. In any event, counsel argues that the complainant's present condition does not establish how he was treated in the past.

11.9 Counsel points out that the complainant's Egyptian attorney has lodged a request for review of verdict to the Highest State Security Court, on grounds that the trial Military Court misjudged the evidence, that the preliminary investigation was afflicted with serious shortcomings, that defence rights were violated at trial and that during the investigation the complainant had been subjected to violence and torture. The attorney has also lodged a special complaint with the Egyptian Minister of the Interior, the Chief Public Prosecutor and the Director-General of the Prison Institutions, alleging improper treatment of the complainant during his hospitalisation, including being chained to the bed and rendered immobile on medical grounds, and being returned to prison prior to recuperation.

11.10 Counsel argues that after the publicity generated by the television broadcast referred to in paragraph 10.2, supra, the State party shifted its position from a firm denial that torture had taken place to the "more reluctant position" shown by the measures it then took by way of dialogue with Egypt. Counsel points out Egypt's curt dismissal as unfounded of the allegations giving rise to the Swedish requests for an investigation, without so much as supplying any detail of the investigation allegedly conducted. This strongly suggests the complainant was in fact tortured, as Egypt would benefit significantly from being able to demonstrate to other countries, through an independent investigation showing the complainant had not been tortured, that Egypt could safely be entrusted with the return of sensitive prisoners and to abide by assurances given.

11.11 Counsel refers to the State party's apparent unwillingness to further press the Egyptian authorities, with the State party citing possible prejudices to the complainant's legal interests or welfare. This suggests the State party accepts, in contrast to its earlier view, that the complainant is at risk of external pressure in the event of an insistence on an independent investigation. In fact, the complainant, through his relatives, has repeatedly made known his desire for the fullest possible defence of his interests.

11.12 Counsel goes on to refer to relevant case law in national jurisdictions. In the case of Mr. Bilasi-Ashri, the Egyptian government refused to accept a detailed set of assurances, including post-return monitoring, requested by the Austrian Minister of Justice following a decision to that effect by an Austrian court of appeal. In the case of Ahmed Zakaev, a British extradition court found that a real risk of torture was not discounted by assurances given in open court by a Russian deputy minister overseeing prisons. Counsel argues that a similarly rigorous approach, with effective protection provided by the legal system, ought to have been followed in the complainant's case.

11.4 Counsel expands on the earlier reference to involvement of the United States of America in the complainant's case in paragraph 10.2, supra, referring to a book entitled "Chain of Command" by Seymour Hersh. This contended that "the Bromma action" (referring to the airport from which the complainant was removed) was carried out by members of the Special Access Program of the United States Department of Defense who were engaged in returning terrorist suspects to their countries of origin utilising "unconventional methods". It is said that the complainant's removal was one of the first operations carried out under this program and described by an operative involved as "one of the less successful ones". In counsel's view, this third State involvement at the removal stage in an anti-terrorism context should have confirmed what the State party already knew from its knowledge of the common use of torture in Egypt and the complainant's particular vulnerability, that is, that a real risk of torture existed at the time of his removal, in breach of article 3.

11.5 By further letter of 16 November 2004, counsel provided a copy of a Human Rights Watch report to the Committee entitled "Recent Concerns regarding the Growing Use of Diplomatic Assurances as an Alleged Safeguard against Torture". The report surveys recent examples of State practice in the area of diplomatic assurances by Germany, the United States of America, the Netherlands, the United Kingdom and Canada. The report argues that such assurances are increasingly viewed as a way of escaping the absolute character of nonrefoulement obligations, and are expanding from the anti-terrorism context into the area of refugee claims. It contends that assurances tend to be sought only from countries where torture is a serious and systematic problem, which thus acknowledges the real risk of torture presented in such cases.

11.6 In the light of national experience, the report concludes that assurances are not an adequate safeguard for a variety of reasons. Human rights protection is not amenable to diplomacy, with its tendency to untransparent process and to place the State to State relationship as the primary consideration. Such assurances amount to trusting a systematic abuser who otherwise cannot be trusted to abide by its international obligations. It also amounts to giving a systematic abuser a "pass" with respect to an individual case when torture is otherwise widespread. Finally, the effectiveness of post-return monitoring is limited by the undetectability of much professionally-inflicted torture, the absence of medical expertise from typical monitoring arrangements, the unwillingness of torture victims to speak out for fear of retribution, and the unwillingness of either the sending State or the receiving State to accept any responsibility for exposing an individual to torture.

11.7 In conclusion, the report refers to the October 2004 report to the General Assembly of the United Nations Special Rapporteur on Torture, who argued that, as a baseline, diplomatic assurances should not be resorted to in circumstances where torture is systematic, and that if a person is a member of a specific group that is routinely targeted and tortured, this factor must be taken into account. In the absence of either of these factors, the Special Rapporteur did not rule out the use of assurances provided that they reflect an unequivocal guarantee that is meaningful and verifiable.

12.1 By letter of 11 March 2005, the State party provided additional submissions on the merits of the complaint. It observed that the Swedish embassy in Cairo had continued to monitor the complainant's situation, with further visits taking place in Toraj prison on 3 October 2004, 21 November 2004, 17 January 2005 and 2 March 2005. The State party notes for the sake of clarity that there are several buildings on the prison grounds, one of which is called Masra and another Estekbal. The complainant has been detained, and visits have taken place, in both parts of the prison compound at different points in time.

12.2 With respect to his legal situation, the complainant stated that he had instructed his Egyptian lawyer to lodge a petition with the President of Egypt for a new trial in a civil court, invoking Egypt's undertaking prior to his expulsion from Sweden that he was to be given a fair trial. He had not met with the lawyer in person; his mother appeared to be the one giving instructions to the lawyer. According to the complainant, she had subsequently been informed by the lawyer that the petition had been lodged. However, the complainant was not very hopeful with regard to the outcome of such a petition.

12.3 Concerning the health situation, the complainant was recovering according to plan from the back surgery he underwent in August 2004 at the university hospital in central Cairo. Back at the Torah prison, he had spent some time in the prison hospital before returning to a normal cell. He had received physiotherapy treatment and a so-called MRI-examination, where his back had been x-rayed. He complained about the lack of further physiotherapy sessions which, he stated, had to be held at the hospital. This was due to the fact that the necessary equipment was not available in the prison. In order to further strengthen his back, he had been scheduled for special magnetic treatment.

12.4 With regard to the issue of the general conditions of detention, the State party observes that by March 2005 the complainant was placed in a cell of his own. He continued to receive visits from his mother, who brought him books, clothes and extra food. She also appeared to be providing him with information about his family in Sweden on a regular basis. However, he complained that his request to call his wife and children had been denied. Moreover, it was his intention to continue with his law studies. He had managed to pass further exams during the autumn.

12.5 In addition to the measures described in its last submissions to the Committee on 21 September 2004, the State party states that it had made further efforts to bring about an investigation into the ill-treatment allegedly suffered by the complainant at the hands of the Egyptian authorities during the initial stage of the detention. In a new letter of 29 September 2004 to the Egyptian Minister in charge of the GIS, the Swedish Minister of Foreign Affairs, Ms. Laila Freivalds, responded to the answer given by him in July of that year. Ms. Freivalds remarked that the letter she had received in July 2004 contained no information on the type of investigations that had been carried out by the Egyptian authorities and on which the Egyptian Minister's conclusions were based. She concluded, in her turn, that under the circumstances she did not exclude that she would have to revert to him on the same matter at a later stage.

12.6 In the course of the Swedish embassy's visit to the complainant on 3 October 2004, the question of the complainant's position in respect of further inquiries into the allegations of ill-treatment was raised again. When the issue had been raised with him for the first time (during the visit of 14 July 2004), the complainant's prison sentence had recently been reduced to 15 years and he was concerned that new investigations might have a negative impact on the chances of further reductions being made as a consequence of good behaviour on his part. On 3 October 2004, however, the complainant's position had changed. He then declared that he was in favour of an independent inquiry and said that he was willing to contribute to such an inquiry.

12.7 In view of the importance attached by the State party to the complainant's own wishes in this regard, the State party regarded the complainant's new position as making way for further measures on its part. Since the envisaged inquiry would naturally require the additional approval and cooperation of the Egyptian government, the Swedish Ambassador to Egypt was instructed on 26 October 2004 to raise this issue with the Egyptian Foreign Ministry at the highest possible level. The Ambassador consequently met with the Egyptian Minister of Foreign Affairs on 1 November 2004. The Ambassador conveyed the message that the Swedish Government continued to be concerned about the allegations that the complainant had been exposed to torture and other ill-treatment during the initial period following his return to Egypt. The need for a thorough, independent and impartial examination of the allegations, in accordance with the principle of the rule of law and in a manner that was acceptable to the international community, was stressed by the Ambassador. In response, the latter was informed of the Minister's intention to discuss the matter with the Minister in charge of the GIS. The Egyptian Minister of Foreign Affairs, however, anticipated two problems with regard to an international inquiry. Firstly, there was no tradition in Egypt when it came to inviting representatives of the international community to investigate domestic matters of this character. It would probably be viewed as an unwelcomed interference with internal affairs. Secondly, attempting to prove that ill-treatment had not occurred could pose a problem of a more technical nature, particularly in view of the fact that several years had passed since the ill-treatment allegedly took place.

12.8 As a follow-up to the meeting with the Minister of Foreign Affairs, the State party informs that its Ambassador met with the Undersecretary of State of the GIS on 22 November and 21 December 2004. During the first of these meetings, the undersecretary of state mentioned that Egypt was anxious to comply, as far as possible, with the Swedish Government's request for an inquiry. However, during the second meeting, the Ambassador was handed a letter by the Minister in charge of the GIS containing the Egyptian government's formal answer to the renewed Swedish request for an inquiry. The content of the letter was similar to that of the previous letter from the same Minister in July 2004. Thus, the allegations concerning ill-treatment of the complainant were again refuted as unfounded. Furthermore, no direct answer was provided to the request that an independent inquiry be conducted.

12.9 The matter was again brought up by Ms. Freivalds in connection with a visit to Stockholm on 15 February 2005 by the Egyptian Deputy Minister of Foreign Affairs responsible for multilateral issues. Ms. Freivalds informed the Egyptian Deputy Minister of the complainant's case and the allegations made regarding his ill-treatment. She stressed that it ought to be a common interest for Sweden and Egypt to look into those allegations and asked the Deputy Minister to use his influence with the Egyptian authorities in favour of the Swedish position. The Deputy Minister assured her that he would raise the issue upon his return to Cairo.

12.10 The State party also points out that the issue of an international inquiry was raised with the United Nations High Commissioner for Human Rights, Ms. Louise Arbour, when she visited Stockholm in December 2004. On that occasion, Ms. Freivalds made clear that the Swedish Government would welcome any efforts that might be undertaken by the High Commissioner to investigate the allegations that the complainant had been subjected to torture or other forms of ill-treatment while in detention in Egypt. The State party also observes that the investigation initiated by the Swedish Chief Parliamentary Ombudsman into the circumstances surrounding the execution of the Government's decision to expel the complainant from Sweden has not yet concluded.

12.11 The State party recalls that already in May 2004, counsel for the complainant provided the Committee with a written account of the embassy's report of its first visit on 23 January 2002 to the complainant after his return to Egypt. A copy of the report was submitted by counsel to the Committee in August 2004. In the State party's view, therefore, the Committee had thus been provided with all the information of relevance for its examination of the present case. Prior to explaining the fact that the report was not fully accounted for by the Government in its initial observations of 5 December 2003, the State party provides the following translation of the relevant portion of the Ambassador's report: "Agiza and [name of another person] had just been transferred to the Torah prison after having been interrogated for thirty days at the security service's facilities in another part of Cairo. Their treatment in the Torah prison was "excellent". However, they had a number of complaints that related to the time period between their apprehension in Sweden and the transfer to the Torah: excessive brutality on the part of the Swedish police when they were apprehended; forced to remain in uncomfortable positions in the airplane during the transport to Egypt; forced to be blindfolded during the interrogation period; detention in too small cells 1.5 x 1.5 meters during the same period; lack of sleep due to surveillance in the cells; a delay of ten days before Agiza, following a medical examination, had access again to his medication for gastric ulcer; blows from guards while transported to and from interrogation; threats from interrogator that there could be consequences for Agiza's family if he did not tell everything about his time in Iran etc. It is not possible for me to assess the veracity of these claims. However, I am able to note that the two men did not, not even on my direct questions, in any way claim that they had been subjected to any kind of systematic, physical torture and that they consider themselves to be well treated in the Torah prison."

12.12 The State party argues that it has been aware of difficulties experienced by the Committee in the past with regard to upholding respect for the confidentiality of its proceedings. For that reason, the State party formulated its submissions with great care when they involved the unveiling of information that has been classified under the Swedish Secrecy Act. For the State party, it was a question of balancing the need to reveal information in order to provide the Committee with the correct factual basis for the proper administration of justice, on the one hand, and the need to protect the integrity of Sweden's relations with foreign powers, the interests of national security and the security and safety of individuals, on the other.

12.13 The State party argues that its position in this regard should be seen against the background of the experience gained from the proceedings relating to the case of Hanan Attia.[18] In the State party's view, it became clear during those proceedings that the concerns in respect of confidentiality, which existed already at that time, were not unfounded. In that case, the Committee offered the State party in September 2002 the opportunity to withdraw its initial observations of 8 March 2002 and to submit a new version in view of the fact that the Committee could not guarantee that "any of the information submitted by the parties to the case would not be disclosed in any of its decisions or views on the merits of the case". Furthermore, in January 2003 counsel for Hanan Attia appended a briefing note from Amnesty International in London to his own observations, from which it was clear that counsel had made the State party's observations of 8 March 2002 available to Amnesty International.

12.14 The State party argues that its concerns with regard to the Committee's ability to uphold respect for the confidentiality of its proceedings were reflected in its repeated requests and comments concerning the confidentiality of the information that was in fact included in the initial observations of 5 December 2003 in the present case. However, in the light of the foregoing, the conclusion was drawn that only part of the classified information found in the Security Police's written opinion of 30 October 2001 to the Migration Board could be revealed. Another conclusion was that the information contained in the embassy's report from its first visit on 23 January 2002 to the complainant in detention should not be fully accounted for either. The reason for the latter conclusion was that it could not be ruled out that the information concerning ill-treatment provided by the complainant during the embassy's first visit would later be found in the public domain and thus become known to the Egyptian authorities.

12.15 The State party concludes that for these reasons not all the information that emerged at the embassy's first visit was revealed to the Committee.

[18] Op.cit.

If such unconfirmed information had been released at that stage, and with the indirect assistance of the Swedish Government, this could have resulted in reprisals against the complainant. The risk for reprisals was not deemed to be insignificant, irrespective of whether the information was correct or not. If the information regarding the complainant's ill-treatment was correct - although such treatment did not appear to amount to torture within the meaning of the Convention -, this would have meant that the diplomatic assurances had not had the intended effect to protect him against treatment in breach of Sweden's international obligations, including treatment prohibited under article 3 of the European Convention on Human Rights. In such a case, there was an apparent risk that the disclosure of the information would put the complainant at risk of further ill-treatment and maybe even of torture. On the other hand, if the disclosed information was incorrect, this could have had a negative impact on the relations between Sweden and Egypt. In turn, it could have led to problems as far as the embassy's monitoring efforts were concerned. In this situation, when the different risks involved were assessed, the conclusion was reached that the best course of action would be to await the report of the embassy's next visit.

12.16 The State party points out that according to the embassy's report from its second meeting with the complainant in the detention facility, there were at that time no indications of torture or other ill-treatment. However, even prior to the third visit on 14 April 2002, information was circulating to the effect that the complainant's mother had stated publicly that her son had been tortured after his return to Egypt. The embassy's report from the first visit on 23 January 2002 confirmed the information submitted by the complainant's mother, namely that the visit when she had allegedly noticed signs of ill-treatment on her son's body had been interrupted by the Swedish Ambassador's first visit. The fact that the Ambassador had reported that he had not been able to see any signs of physical abuse on that very same day led the State party to doubt the veracity of the claims made by the complainant's mother and affected its assessment of the credibility of the complainant's own information to the Ambassador the same day.

12.17 The State party observes that there was no new information from the complainant regarding ill-treatment during the following year and the view that the information submitted during the embassy's first visit had been incorrect gradually gained in strength. It was essential that the embassy's opportunities to carry out the monitoring on a regular basis were not hampered, which could have been the result if the State party had forwarded unconfirmed or incorrect information to the Committee already during the first months of 2002. Considering the situation in April 2002 when the contents of a letter by the complainant's mother became known, it was therefore, on balance, not deemed appropriate to supplement, at that time, the information already submitted by the State party regarding the embassy's first visit in its observations of 8 March 2002.

12.18 A different assessment was made by the State party when the complainant, on 5 March 2003, repeated his complaints about ill-treatment at the hands of the Egyptian authorities during the initial stages of his detention. The allegations were much more serious this time and included claims that he had been subjected to torture involving the use of electricity. The mere fact that the complainant came back more than a year later to what had allegedly occurred already at the beginning of the detention period contributed to the fact that a different assessment was made in March 2003. The allegations of torture were therefore immediately raised with representatives of the relevant Egyptian authorities, who refuted them categorically. The State party accounted for the information submitted by the complainant, and the Egyptian authorities' reactions to it, in its submissions to the Committee of 26 March 2003. It should be reiterated that the information in issue was considerably more serious than that provided by the complainant a year earlier and that it concerned the same time period.

12.19 The State party further contends that by March 2003 the reasons for confidentiality were not as weighty as before. Even if the information from the embassy's tenth visit on 5 March 2003 would have ended up in the public domain despite the fact that the proceedings before the Committee were confidential according to the applicable provisions in the Convention and the Committee's own rules of procedure, the damaging effects were no longer considered to be as serious as before. Following the State party's initial submissions to the Committee, information had already been in circulation that - if correct - amounted to a breach on the part of Egypt of the diplomatic assurances. Moreover, the issue of torture had already been raised with the Egyptian authorities in March 2003. Furthermore, the monitoring carried out by the embassy had been going on for more than a year by that time and had become routine for both the Egyptian authorities, the embassy and the complainant himself. It was thus no longer likely that there would be a negative impact on the monitoring so that it would be more difficult in the future to ensure the continued effectiveness of the assurances. The State party also stresses that the allegations made by the complainant during the first embassy visit did not amount, in its view, to torture within the meaning of the Convention. It is, however, clear that the ill-treatment complained of at that time would have amounted to inhuman and maybe also cruel treatment, had the allegations been substantiated.

12.20 The State party refers the Committee to the recent decision of the Grand Chamber of the European Court on Human Rights, on 4 February 2005, in the case of Mamatkulov et al. v. Turkey. This case concerned the applicants' extradition in March 1999 to Uzbekistan under a bilateral treaty with Turkey. Both applicants had been suspected of homicide, causing injuries to others by the explosion of a bomb in Uzbekistan and an attempted terrorist attack on the President of Uzbekistan. Following their extradition, they were found guilty of various offences and sentenced to twenty and eleven years' imprisonment respectively.

12.21 Before the European Court, the applicants claimed that Turkey had violated inter alia article 3 of the European Convention. In defence, Turkey invoked assurances concerning the two applicants given by the Uzbek authorities. According to those assurances, which were provided by the public prosecutor of the Republic of Uzbekistan, the applicants would not be subjected to acts of torture or sentenced to capital punishment. The assurances also contained the information that Uzbekistan was a party to the Convention against Torture and accepted and reaffirmed its obligation to comply with the requirements of the provisions of the Convention "as regards both Turkey and the international community as a whole". Officials from the Turkish embassy in Tashkent had visited the applicants in their respective places of detention in October 2001. They were reportedly in good health and had not complained about their prison conditions. Turkey also invoked medical certificates drawn up by military doctors in the prisons where the applicants were held.

12.22 The State party observes that the European Court assessed the existence of the risk primarily with reference to those facts which were known or ought to have been known to the State party at the time of the extradition, with information coming to light subsequent to the extradition potentially being of value in confirming or refuting the appreciation that had been made by the State party of the well-foundedness or otherwise of a complainant's fears. The Court concluded that it had to assess Turkey's responsibility under article 3 by reference to the situation that obtained on the date of the applicants' extradition, i.e. on 27 March 1999. While taking note of reports of international human-rights organisations denouncing an administrative practice of torture and other forms of ill-treatment of political dissidents and the Uzbek regime's repressive policy towards such dissidents, the Court furthermore stated that, although those findings described the general situation in Uzbekistan, they did not support the specific allegations made by the applicants in the case and required corroboration by other evidence. Against the background of the assurances obtained by Turkey and the medical reports from the doctors in the Uzbek prisons in which the applicants were held, the Court found that it was not able to conclude that substantial grounds existed at the relevant date for believing that the applicants faced a real risk of treatment proscribed by article 3 of the European Convention.

12.23 The State party invites the Committee to adopt the same approach. It points out that assurances similar to those in the case before the European Court were indeed obtained by the Swedish Government in the instant case. Although the guarantees given in this case did not refer to Egypt's obligations under the Convention against Torture, this is of no particular consequence since Egypt, like Uzbekistan, is in fact bound by the Convention. It is doubtful whether the value of assurances should be considered to be increased simply because they include a reference to a state's human rights obligations. The important factor must be that the State in issue has actually undertaken to abide by the provisions of a human rights convention by becoming party to it. The fact that Egypt was a party to the Convention against Torture was known to the State party when it obtained the diplomatic assurances in this case and subsequently decided to expel the complainant.

12.24 The State party goes on to argue that the assurances obtained in the present case must be regarded as carrying even more weight than those in the case against Turkey since they were issued by the person in charge of the Egyptian security service. It is difficult to conceive of a person better placed in Egypt to ensure that the diplomatic guarantees would actually have the intended effect, namely to protect the complainant against treatment in breach of Sweden's obligations under several human-rights instruments.

12.25 The State party acknowledges that no medical certificates have been invoked in the present case. However, the medical certificates obtained in the Turkish case had been issued by Uzbek military doctors working in the prisons where the applicants in that case were detained. In the State party's view, such certificates are of limited value in view of the fact that they had not been issued by experts who could be perceived as truly independent in relation to the relevant state authorities. Moreover, in the current case, the absence of corresponding medical certificates must reasonably be compensated by the monitoring mechanism put in place by the Swedish Government. To this date, almost thirty visits to the complainant in detention have been made by its embassy in Cairo. The visits have taken place over a period of time that amounts to over three years. This should be compared to the single visit by two officials from the Turkish embassy in Tashkent more than two and a half years after the extradition of the applicants in the case examined by the European Court.

12.26 By letter of 7 April 2005, counsel for the complainant made further submissions. As to his medical care, counsel argues that treatment following the complainant's surgery in August 2004 was interrupted prior to full recovery, and he was denied medical treatment in the form of microelectric stimulation that he required.

12.27 Counsel observes that in December 2004 and January 2005, the expulsion of the complainant and a companion case was debated in the Swedish parliament and media. The Prime Minister and the Minister of Immigration stated that the expellees were terrorists and their removal was necessary to prevent further attacks and deny safe haven. According to counsel, these statements were presented to the complainant by Egyptian officials during an interrogation. For counsel, this demonstrates that the Egyptian security services are still interrogating the complainant and seeking to extract information, exposing him to ongoing risk of torture.

12.28 Counsel provides the conclusions (in Swedish with official English summary) dated 22 March 2005 of the investigations of the Parliamentary Ombudsman into the circumstances of deportation from Sweden to Cairo, with an emphasis on the treatment of the expellees at Bromma Airport. According to the Ombudsman's summary, a few days prior to 18 December 2001 the Central Intelligence Agency offered the Swedish Security Police the use of an aircraft for direct expulsion to Egypt. The Security Police, after apparently informing the Minister of Foreign Affairs, accepted. At mid-day December 18, the Security Police was informed that American security personnel would be onboard the aircraft and they wished to perform a security check on the expellees. It was arranged for the check to be conducted in a police station at Bromma airport in Stockholm.

12.29 Immediately after the Government's decision in the afternoon of December 18, the expellees were apprehended by Swedish police and subsequently transported to Bromma airport. The American aircraft landed shortly before 9.00 p.m. A number of American security personnel, wearing masks, conducted the security check, which consisted of at least the following elements. The expellees had their clothes cut up and removed with a pair of scissors, their bodies were searched, their hands and feet were fettered, they were dressed in overalls and their heads were covered with loosely fitted hoods. Finally, they were taken, with bare feet, to the airplane where they were strapped to mattresses. They were kept in this position during the entire flight to Egypt. It had been alleged that the expellees were also given a sedative per rectum, which the Ombudsman was unable to substantiate during the investigation. The Ombudsman found that the Security Police had remained passive throughout the procedure. The Ombudsman considered that, given that the American offer was received only three months after the events of 11 September 2001, the Security Police could have been expected to inquire whether the American offer involved any special arrangements with regard to security. No such inquiry was made, not even when the Security Police had been informed of the fact that American security personnel would be present and wished to perform a security check. When the actual content of the security check became obvious as it was performed at Bromma airport, the attending Swedish police personnel remained passive.

12.30 In the Ombudsman's view, the investigation disclosed that the Swedish Security Police lost control of the situation at the airport and during the transport to Egypt. The American security personnel took charge and were allowed to perform the security check on their own. Such total surrender of power to exercise public authority on Swedish territory was, according to the Ombudsman, clearly contrary to Swedish law. In addition, at least some of the coercive measures taken during the security check were not in conformity with Swedish law. Moreover, the treatment of the expellees, taken as a whole, must be considered to have been inhuman and thus unacceptable and may amount to degrading treatment within the meaning of Article 3 of the European Convention for the Protection of Human Rights and Fundamental Freedoms. The Ombudsman emphasized that the inhuman treatment to which the expellees were subjected could not be tolerated. The Security Police should have decided to discontinue the expulsion proceedings and deserved severe criticism for its handling of the case.

12.31 Counsel observes that the Ombudsman declined to bring charges against any individuals, as it was not possible to hold any individual to account before a court. Counsel contends that, at least, the prolonged hooding amounted to torture, and that what occurred on the aircraft could also be formally imputed to Sweden. Counsel argues that in the prevailing atmosphere the State party ought to have been sceptical of American motives in offering to transport the expellees to Egypt and been reluctant to accept the Egyptian guarantees provided.

12.32 By letter of 12 April 2005, the State party also provided the summary of the Ombudsman's report, as "background information in full understanding that the execution of the Government's decision to expel the complainant from Sweden is not part of the case now pending before the Committee, which deals with the issue of the diplomatic assurances by Egypt with regard to the complainant."

12.33 By letter of 21 April 2005, counsel for the complainant submitted final remarks. He criticizes the modalities of the State party's most recent visits on the same basis as the earlier visits. As to medical care, the complainant has been re-examined twice at the facility that performed the 2004 surgery and may require further surgery. Concerning the proposed international investigation, counsel argues that the only reason for Egypt's refusal to cooperate lies in its breach of the guarantees provided.

12.34 Counsel rejects the State party's reasons for concealing part of the initial Ambassadorial report from the Committee, arguing that they can only be relevant to protect the complainant from Egyptian reprisals concerning his outspokenness as to the torture suffered. The complainant's statement was made in the presence of the prison warden and other officials, and the Ambassador raised the issue with the Ministry of Foreign Affairs. In any event, having already endured reprisals, there was nothing left for the State party to protect against in withholding information. Mistreatment of the author was already in the public domain through the complainant's mother and Amnesty International shortly after January 2002. Counsel argues that the State party's position also reflects "weak confidence" in the integrity of the Egyptian guarantees. Counsel also questions how national security could be affected by public knowledge of the complainant's allegations. In sum, the only plausible reason to conceal the information was to avoid inconvenience and embarrassment on the part of the State party.

12.35 Concerning his transmittal of information supplied in the context of the article 22 process to non-governmental organisations, counsel argues that at the time he saw no obstacle to doing so, neither the Convention nor the Committee's Rules proscribing, in his view, such a course. He did not intend to disseminate the information to the media or the broader public. Following the Committee's advice that complaint information was confidential, counsel argues his capacity to defend the complainant was significantly reduced, particularly given the disparity of resources available to the State party. In any event, the State party has shared other confidential intelligence information with the Committee, belaying its concerns that sensitive information would be inappropriately disseminated. Counsel argues that the conduct described is, contrary to the Ambassador's characterisation, torture as understood by the Committee, bearing in mind that the complainant may have been reluctant to disclose the totality of circumstances to the Ambassador and that more severe elements emerged through the testimony of his mother.

12.36 With respect to the European Court's decision in Mamatkulov et al., counsel seeks to distinguish the instant case. He emphasises however that in both cases the speed with which the removal was undertaken denied an effective exercise of a complaint mechanism, a circumstances that for the European Court disclosed a violation of article 34 of the European Convention. In counsel's view, the Mamatkulov Court was unable to find a violation of article 3 of the European Convention as, in contrast to the present case, there was insufficient evidence before the Court. A further distinction is that the treatment at the point of expulsion clearly pointed, in the current case, to the future risk of torture. Given the prophylactic purpose of article 3, it cannot be correct that an expelling State simply transfers, through the vehicle of diplomatic assurances, responsibility for an expellee's condition to the receiving State.

12.37 Finally, counsel supplies to the Committee a report, dated 15 April 2005, by Human Rights Watch, entitled "Still at Risk: Diplomatic Assurances no Safeguard against Torture", surveying the contemporary case law and experiences of diplomatic assurances and concluding that the latter are not effective instruments of risk mitigation in an article 3 context. Concerning the current case, Human Rights Watch argues that "there is credible, and in some instances overwhelming, evidence that the assurances were breached" (at 59).

Issues and Proceedings Before the Committee

Consideration of the Merits

13.1 The Committee has considered the merits of the complaint, in the light of all information presented to it by the parties, pursuant to article 22, paragraph 4, of the Convention. The Committee acknowledges that measures taken to fight terrorism, including denial of safe haven, deriving from binding Security Council Resolutions are both legitimate and important. Their execution, however, must be carried out with full respect to the applicable rules of international law, including the provisions of the Convention, as affirmed repeatedly by the Security Council.[19] Substantive assessment under article 3.

13.2 The issue before the Committee is whether removal of the complainant to Egypt violated the State party's obligation under article 3 of the Convention not to expel or to return a person to another State where there are substantial grounds for believing that he or she would be in danger of being subjected by the Egyptian authorities to torture. The Committee observes that this issue must be decided in the light of the information that was known, or ought to have been known, to the State party's authorities at the time of the removal. Subsequent events are relevant to the assessment of the State party's knowledge, actual or constructive, at the time of removal.

13.3 The Committee must evaluate whether there were substantial grounds for believing that the complainant would be personally in danger of being subjected to torture upon return to Egypt. The Committee recalls that the aim of the determination is to establish whether the individual concerned was personally at risk of being subjected to torture in the country to which he was returned. It follows that the existence of a consistent pattern of gross, flagrant or mass violations of human rights in a country does not as such constitute a sufficient ground for determining that a particular person was in danger of being subjected to torture upon his return to that country; additional grounds must exist to show that the individual concerned was

[19] Security Council Resolution 1566 (2004), at preambular paragraphs 3 and 6, Resolution 1456 (2003) at paragraph 6, and Resolution 1373 (2001) at paragraph 3(f).

personally at risk. Similarly, the absence of a consistent pattern of gross violations of human rights does not mean that a person could not be considered to be in danger of being subjected to torture in his or her specific circumstances.

13.4 The Committee considers at the outset that it was known, or should have been known, to the State party's authorities at the time of the complainant's removal that Egypt resorted to consistent and widespread use of torture against detainees, and that the risk of such treatment was particularly high in the case of detainees held for political and security reasons.[20] The State party was also aware that its own security intelligence services regarded the complainant as implicated in terrorist activities and a threat to its national security, and for these reasons its ordinary tribunals referred the case to the Government for a decision at the highest executive level, from which no appeal was possible. The State party was also aware of the interest in the complainant by the intelligence services of two other States: according to the facts submitted by the State party to the Committee, the first foreign State offered through its intelligence service an aircraft to transport the complainant to the second State, Egypt, where to the State party's knowledge, he had been sentenced in absentia and was wanted for alleged involvement in terrorist activities. In the Committee's view, the natural conclusion from these combined elements, that is, that the complainant was at a real risk of torture in Egypt in the event of expulsion, was confirmed when, immediately preceding expulsion, the complainant was subjected on the State party's territory to treatment in breach of, at least, article 16 of the Convention by foreign agents but with the acquiescence of the State party's police. It follows that the State party's expulsion of the complainant was in breach of article 3 of the Convention. The procurement of diplomatic assurances, which, moreover, provided no mechanism for their enforcement, did not suffice to protect against this manifest risk.

13.5 In light of this assessment, the Committee considers it appropriate to observe that its decision in the current case reflects a number of facts which were not available to it when it considered the largely analogous complaint of Hanan Attia,[21] where, in particular, it expressed itself satisfied with the assurances provided. The Committee's decision in that case, given that the complainant had not been expelled, took into account the evidence made available to it up to the time the decision in that case was adopted. The Committee observes that it did not have before it the actual report of mistreatment provided by the current complainant to the Ambassador at his first visit and not provided to the Committee by the State party

[20] See, among other sources, the Report of the Committee against Torture to the General Assembly (A/51/44), at paragraphs 180 to 222 and the Committee's Conclusions and Recommendations on the fourth periodic report of Egypt (CAT/C/CR/29/4, 23 December 2002).

[21] Op.cit.

(see paragraph 14.10 below); the mistreatment of the complainant by foreign intelligence agents on the territory of the State party and acquiesced in by the State party's police; the involvement of a foreign intelligence service in offering and procuring the means of expulsion; the progressively wider discovery of information as to the scope of measures undertaken by numerous States to expose individuals suspected of involvement in terrorism to risks of torture abroad; the breach by Egypt of the element of the assurances relating to guarantee of a fair trial, which goes to the weight that can be attached to the assurances as a whole; and the unwillingness of the Egyptian authorities to conduct an independent investigation despite appeals from the State party's authorities at the highest levels. The Committee observes, in addition, that the calculus of risk in the case of the wife of the complainant, whose expulsion would have been some years after the complainants, raised issues differing from to the present case.

Procedural Assessment Under Article 3

13.6 The Committee observes that the right to an effective remedy for a breach of the Convention underpins the entire Convention, for otherwise the protections afforded by the Convention would be rendered largely illusory. In some cases, the Convention itself sets out a remedy for particular breaches of the Convention,[22] while in other cases the Committee has interpreted a substantive provision to contain within it a remedy for its breach.[23] In the Committee's view, in order to reinforce the protection of the norm in question and understanding the Convention consistently, the prohibition on refoulement contained in article 3 should be interpreted the same way to encompass a remedy for its breach, even though it may not contain on its face such a right to remedy for a breach thereof.

13.7 The Committee observes that in the case of an allegation of torture or cruel, inhuman or degrading treatment having occurred, the right to remedy requires, after the event, an effective, independent and impartial investigation of such allegations. The nature of refoulement is such, however, that an allegation of breach of that article relates to a future expulsion or removal; accordingly, the right to an effective remedy contained in article 3 requires, in this context, an opportunity for effective, independent and impartial review of the decision to expel or remove, once that decision is made, when there is a plausible allegation that article 3 issues arise. The Committee's previous jurisprudence has been consistent with this view of

[22] See articles 12 to 14 in relation to an allegation of torture.

[23] See Dzemajl v. Yugoslavia, Case No 161/2000, Decision adopted on 21 November 2002, at paragraph 9.6.: "The positive obligations that flow from the first sentence of article 16 of the Convention include an obligation to grant redress and compensate the victims of an act in breach of that provision. The Committee is therefore of the view that the State party has failed to observe its obligations under article 16 of the Convention by failing to enable the complainants to obtain redress and to provide them with fair and adequate compensation."

the requirements of article 3, having found an inability to contest an expulsion decision before an independent authority, in that case the courts, to be relevant to a finding of a violation of article 3.[24]

13.8 The Committee observes that, in the normal course of events, the State party provides, through the operation of the Migration Board and the Aliens Appeals Board, for review of a decision to expel satisfying the requirements of article 3 of an effective, independent and impartial review of a decision to expel. In the present case, however, due to the presence of national security concerns, these tribunals relinquished the complainant's case to the Government, which took the first and at once final decision to expel him. The Committee emphasizes that there was no possibility for review of any kind of this decision. The Committee recalls that the Convention's protections are absolute, even in the context of national security concerns, and that such considerations emphasise the importance of appropriate review mechanisms. While national security concerns might justify some adjustments to be made to the particular process of review, the mechanism chosen must continue to satisfy article 3's requirements of effective, independent and impartial review. In the present case, therefore, on the strength of the information before it, the Committee concludes that the absence of any avenue of judicial or independent administrative review of the Government's decision to expel the complainant does not meet the procedural obligation to provide for effective, independent and impartial review required by article 3 of the Convention.

Frustration of Right Under Article 22 to Exercise Complaint to the Committee

13.9 The Committee observes, moreover, that by making the declaration under article 22 of the Convention, the State party undertook to confer upon persons within its jurisdiction the right to invoke the complaints jurisdiction of the Committee. That jurisdiction included the power to indicate interim measures, if necessary, to stay the removal and preserve the subject matter of the case pending final decision. In order for this exercise of the right of complaint to be meaningful rather than illusory, however, an individual must have a reasonable period of time before execution of a final decision to consider whether, and if so to in fact, seize the Committee under its article 22 jurisdiction. In the present case, however, the Committee observes that the complainant was arrested and removed by the State party immediately upon the Government's decision of expulsion being taken; indeed, the formal notice of decision was only served upon the complainant's counsel the following day. As a result, it was impossible for the complainant to consider the possibility of invoking article 22, let alone seize the

[24] Arkauz Arana v. France, Case No. 63/1997, Decision adopted on 9 November 1999, at paragraphs 11.5 and 12.

Committee. As a result, the Committee concludes that the State party was in breach of its obligations under article 22 of the Convention to respect the effective right of individual communication conferred thereunder.

The State Party's Failure to Co-operate Fully with the Committee

13.10 Having addressed the merits of the complaint, the Committee must address the failure of the State party to co-operate fully with the Committee in the resolution of the current complaint. The Committee observes that, by making the declaration provided for in article 22 extending to individual complainants the right to complain to the Committee alleging a breach of a State party's obligations under the Convention, a State party assumes an obligation to cooperate fully with the Committee, through the procedures set forth in article 22 and in the Committee's Rules of Procedure. In particular, article 22, paragraph 4, requires a State party to make available to the Committee all information relevant and necessary for the Committee appropriately to resolve the complaint presented to it. The Committee observes that its procedures are sufficiently flexible and its powers sufficiently broad to prevent an abuse of process in a particular case. It follows that the State party committed a breach of its obligations under article 22 of the Convention by neither disclosing to the Committee relevant information, nor presenting its concerns to the Committee for an appropriate procedural decision.

14. The Committee against Torture, acting under article 22, paragraph 7, of the Convention against Torture and Other Cruel, Inhuman or Degrading Treatment or Punishment, decides that the facts before it constitute breaches by the State party of articles 3 and 22 of the Convention.

15. In pursuance of rule 112, paragraph 5, of its rules of procedure, the Committee requests the State party to inform it, within 90 days from the date of the transmittal of this decision, of the steps it has taken in response to the Views expressed above. The State party is also under an obligation to prevent similar violations in the future. [Adopted in English, French, Russian and Spanish, the English text being the original version. Subsequently to be issued also in Arabic and Chinese as part of the Committee's annual report to the General Assembly.]

\- - - - - - -

Separate Opinion of Committee Member Mr. Alexander Yakovlev (Dissenting, in Part)

I respectfully disagree with the majority's finding on the article 3 issues. The Committee establishes, correctly, the time of removal as the key point in time for its assessment of the appropriateness, from the perspective of article, of the complaint's removal. As is apparent from the Committee's decision, the bulk of the information before it relates to events transpiring after expulsion, which can have little relevance to the situation at the time of expulsion. It is clear that the State party was aware of its obligations under article 3 of the Convention, including the prohibition on refoulement. Precisely as a result, it sought assurances from the Egyptian government, at a senior level, as to the complainant's proper treatment. No less an authority than the former Special Rapporteur of the Commission on Human Rights on Torture, Mr. van Boven, accepted in his 2002 report to the Commission on Human Rights the use of such assurances in certain circumstances, urging States to procure "an unequivocal guarantee . . . that the persons concerned will not be subjected to torture or any other forms of ill-treatment upon return" . This, which is precisely what the State party did, is now faulted by the Committee. At the time, the State party was entitled to accept the assurances provided, and indeed since has invested considerable effort in following-up the situation in Egypt. Whatever the situation may be if the situation were to repeat itself today is a question that need not presently be answered. It is abundantly clear however at the time that the State party expelled the complainant, it acted in good faith and consistent with the requirements of article 3 of the Convention. I would thus come to the conclusion, in the instant case, that the complainant's expulsion did not constitute a violation of article 3 of the Convention.

[signed]
Alexander Yakovlev

[Adopted in English, French, Russian and Spanish, the English text being the original version. Subsequently to be issued also in Arabic and Chinese as part of the Committee's annual report to the General Assembly.]

DOCUMENT NO. 3

ALLEGED SECRET DETENTIONS IN COUNCIL OF EUROPE MEMBER STATES

Council of Europe's Committee on Legal Affairs and Human Rights

January 22, 2006

Information Memorandum II

Rapporteur: Mr Dick Marty, Switzerland, Aliance of Liberals and Democrats for Europe

A. Introduction

1. First of all, it is necessary to set this work in context in terms of both facts and chronology (the latter being of some significance in this affair). I would stress that the allegations that are now receiving media coverage worldwide were already known and were condemned by the Council of Europe Parliamentary Assembly in a report on the "Lawfulness of detentions by the United States in Guantánamo Bay" presented by my colleague Kevin McNamara, to which I shall refer in this memorandum[1]. In his report he condemned the illegal practice of "extraordinary rendition" and recommended that Council of Europe member states *"ensure that their territory and facilities [were] not used in connection with practices of secret detention or rendition in possible violation of international human rights law"*[2].

2. At the time, the issue did not elicit the same media coverage as it is now receiving. We may well ask why it is only now that the allegations concerning secret detention centres in Europe are triggering a proper debate and public shock and indignation at the reports of ill-treatment and even torture in this connection. In countries that pride themselves in being

[1] See Doc.10497, report by the Committee on Legal Affairs and Human Rights (Rapporteur: McNamara) and Resolution 1433 (2005), on the *lawfulness of detentions by the United States in Guantánamo Bay.*
[2] Above-mentioned Resolution 1433 (2005), § 10.vii.

long-standing democracies that protect human rights, the revelation of these allegations should have sparked off reactions and categorical condemnation several months ago, and yet this was not the case, with a few exceptions, such as the article by the writer and journalist Stephen Grey ("United States: trade in torture", *Le Monde diplomatique,* April 2005) and the articles by Guido Olimpio in the *Corriere della Sera* and his book *Operazione Hotel California* (Feltrinelli, October 2005).

3. I am particularly struck by the fact that it is in the United States that the discussions first really took off. Following an article in *The Washington Post* and a report by *Human Rights Watch* (HRW) published in early November, the international media have reported allegations that the CIA is or was running a system of secret prisons, including prisons in certain "central and east European democracies". Numerous aircraft chartered by the CIA allegedly flew over, to and from European territory (benefiting, therefore, from airport facilities in Council of Europe member states) in order to transport suspects, completely illegally, to these secret centres.

4. Whereas *The Washington Post* did not mention any countries by name (further to an agreement entered into with the United States Government, which, to my mind, suggests that the reports are true), HRW expressly mentioned Poland and Romania. The press reports also quote denials by officials from Poland[3] and Romania, but also Latvia, the Czech Republic, Georgia, Armenia and Bulgaria.

5. Since then, recent further information has extended the list of countries allegedly concerned by the existence of secret detention centres. According to a fax from the Egyptian Ministry of European Affairs to the Egyptian Embassy in London, intercepted by the Swiss intelligence services, such centres existed in Romania, Bulgaria, Macedonia, Kosovo and Ukraine.

6. On 5 December 2005 ABC reported, in turn, the existence of secret prisons in Poland and Romania that had apparently been closed following *The Washington Posts* revelations. According to ABC, eleven suspects detained in these centres were then transferred to CIA facilities in North Africa. They were allegedly submitted to the harshest interrogation techniques (so-called "enhanced interrogation techniques"). I would point out that the ABC article confirming the use of secret detention camps in Poland and Romania by the CIA was available on the Internet for only a very short time before being withdrawn. This strikes me as a telling indication of the pressure put on the media in this affair (in this particular case, the pressure was apparently brought to bear direct by the CIA).

7. It would seem from confidential contacts that the information revealed by *The Washington Post,* HRW and ABC came from different sources,

[3] A denial that was firmly reiterated by President Aleksander Kwasniewski on 7 December 2005.

probably all well-informed official sources. This is clearly a factor that adds to the credibility of the allegations, since the media concerned have not simply taken information from one another.

8. In an interview broadcast by the American channel ABC on 29 November 2005, the Director of the United States Central Intelligence Agency, Porter Goss, did not deny the existence of CIA secret prisons in various parts of the world where people suspected of terrorism were held. He did, however, categorically deny that the United States used torture, while refusing to pass judgment on certain interrogation techniques used by its services.

9. On 5 December 2005, Condoleezza Rice, the American Secretary of State, made a statement addressed to Europeans in which she did not, at any point, deny the existence of the alleged centres, or of the flights transporting detainees, but reaffirmed the need to resort to "extraordinary renditions" in the context of efforts to counter terrorism. The only thing that Ms Rice categorically denied was the use of torture.

10. On 3 November Mr Friso Roscam Abbing, spokesman for Franco Frattini, Vice-President of the European Commission and Commissioner for Justice, Freedom and Security, said that the Commission would be seeking further information, on the grounds that such secret detention centres would be a violation of the founding principles of the European Union. On 4 November he said that the Commission had no reason to doubt the denials by the Polish and Romanian Governments. On 14 November Mr Frattini told the European Parliament that he welcomed the investigation initiated by the Council of Europe and that his departments would be following it closely. On 7 December 2005 Mr Frattini wrote to his colleagues Jacques Barrot and Benita Ferrero-Waldner asking them to support the requests the Committee on Legal Affairs and Human Rights of the Council of Europe Parliamentary Assembly had submitted to Eurocontrol and the European Union Satellite Centre (EUSC). On 28 November 2005 the British Foreign Secretary, Jack Straw, asked the American authorities, on behalf of the European Union, for explanations of the alleged stopovers in Europe of aircraft chartered by the CIA.

11. On 4 November Alvaro Gil-Robles, Council of Europe Commissioner for Human Rights, called for an investigation into the allegations.

12. The same day, the President of the Parliamentary Assembly, René van der Linden, asked the Committee on Legal Affairs and Human Rights, in a press release, to look into the allegations, stating that, if such detention centres did in fact exist, it would be a violation of the principles of both the European Convention on Human Rights and the European Convention for the Prevention of Torture.

13. Mention should also be made of the stand taken by the United Nations High Commissioner for Human Rights, Ms Louise Arbour, who said in an

article in *Le Monde* published on 7 December 2005 that secret detention was a form of torture in itself, for the person detained, who was at the mercy of the detaining authorities, and, worse still, for the families, who were faced with a situation that amounted to that of a missing person.

14. On 15 December the European Parliament agreed, in principle, to set up a temporary committee to investigate the alleged illegal transfer of detainees and the suspected existence of secret CIA detention facilities in the European Union and in candidate countries. On 12 January 2006 the European parliamentarians decided to go ahead and set up such a committee. On 18 January the European Parliament, sitting in Strasbourg, approved the mandate and membership suggested by the Conference of Presidents of the Political Groups for its temporary 46-member committee, which is to investigate the allegations of CIA prisons in Europe where persons suspected of terrorism have allegedly been detained and tortured. I am highly satisfied to note that the work of this committee explicitly reflects a continued desire to co-operate fully with our investigation.

15. In November and December 2005 the Committee on Legal Affairs and Human Rights was particularly active in connection with this affair. At its meeting on 7 November 2005, following President van der Linden's request, it discussed the matter, including the possibility of inviting the Secretary General of the Council of Europe to ask all Contracting Parties to the European Convention on Human Rights for information about the allegations, in accordance with the procedure provided for in Article 52 of the Convention. At the next meeting, on 22 November, I presented the information I had been able to obtain and my preliminary conclusions[4]. At its meeting on 13 December 2005 the committee:

- appointed me Rapporteur
- decided to ask the European Commission for Democracy through Law (Venice Commission) to prepare a legal opinion assessing the legality of secret detention in the light of Council of Europe member states' international obligations, in particular the European Convention on Human Rights and the European Convention for the Prevention of Torture, and expressed the wish that this opinion be submitted as soon as possible;
- instructed its Chair to submit to the Bureau a request for an urgent procedure debate on the allegations of secret detention in Council

[4] See document AS/Jur (2005) 52 rev 2, Information Memorandum presented by the Rapporteur. See also the statement *on alleged secret detention centres in Council of Europe member States* adopted by the Assembly's Standing Committee at its meeting in Bucharest on 25 November 2005 (Synopsis No.2005/130).

of Europe member states at the January 2006 part-session of the Assembly;

- extended the Rapporteur's mandate to visit the headquarters of the European institutions and make fact-finding visits to certain Council of Europe member states if he deemed it necessary;
- was informed by the Deputy Secretary General of the initiatives taken by the Secretary General in accordance with Article 52 of the ECHR.

16. On behalf of the Committee on Legal Affairs and Human Rights, I submitted a request to the Bureau for a debate under urgent procedure on the allegations of secret detention in Council of Europe member states at the January 2006 part-session of the Assembly. I was informed that, as the deadline for States' replies under the procedure set in motion under Article 52 ECHR was not until 21 February, the Assembly Bureau had decided, at its meeting on 9 January 2006, to suggest holding a current affairs debate, ie a debate without a report, which nevertheless leaves me free to submit this information memorandum to the Committee on Legal Affairs and Human Rights.

B. Steps Taken to Date

17. Following the Committee's meeting on 7 November, on 14 November 2005 requests for information were sent to the Polish and Romanian delegations to the Council of Europe Parliamentary Assembly and to the United States Permanent Observer to the Council of Europe.

18. On 21 November 2005, the Secretary General of the Council of Europe sent a request for information to the States Parties to the European Convention on Human Rights, in accordance with the procedure provided for in *Article 52*, asking them to reply by 21 February 2006 (see Appendix IV).

19. Letters were sent to the EU Satellite Centre and Eurocontrol on 29 November 2005, asking them to provide technical assistance with the preparation of the prospective report by forwarding certain information concerning flights and satellite pictures of certain sites, taken on different dates.

20. The Venice Commission, for its part, was informed at its meeting on 15 December 2005 of the request from the Committee on Legal Affairs and Human Rights for an opinion. It decided to instruct several of its members to start work on the matter (see Appendix III).

21. In a letter dated 10 January 2006, the Secretary of the Venice Commission informed me that work was already under way. The Venice Commission has instructed a working group comprising six eminent experts to draft an opinion for approval at its next plenary session, on 17 and 18 March 2006.

22. A questionnaire was forwarded to all the leaders of national delegations to the Parliamentary Assembly on 19 December 2005 so that the parliamentarians would put questions to their governments within their own parliaments, making use of their twofold mandate as national parliamentarians and members of the Assembly (see Appendix II).

23. On 5 January 2006, I met the prosecutor responsible for the Abu Omar case, Mr Armando Spataro, in Milan. He told me about one of the most comprehensive judicial inquiries so far carried out in Europe into a kidnapping carried out as part of an "extraordinary rendition" operation by the services of a foreign country.

24. I also had various meetings with NGO representatives and investigative journalists specialising in terrorism.

C. Criminal Investigations and Other Reactions

a. Council of Europe Member Countries

i. Overview

25. In two countries **(Italy** and **Germany)** judicial investigations have begun into "abduction" of persons subsequently transported to Guantànamo, Afghanistan and other detention centres by means of aircraft belonging to entities with hidden direct or indirect links to the CIA. The Italian prosecution service has even issued arrest warrants against CIA agents after the violent abduction of a Muslim, Abu Omar, in a Milan street in February 2003. The German judicial authorities are taking part in the investigation and have themselves begun investigating the case of a German citizen of Lebanese origin, Khaled al Masri. After being arrested by mistake in Macedonia he was reportedly taken to Kabul for interrogation[5]. Lastly, a **Spanish** judge is enquiring into whether the CIA used Son Sant Joan airport in Majorca as a base for transport of Muslim suspects, as announced by the Spanish minister of internal affairs, José Antonio Alonso, on 15 November 2005. The same aircraft as transported Abu Omar landed at least three times in Spain (and in other European countries).

26. The **Polish** Government ordered an enquiry into the alleged existence in Poland of secret CIA detention centres. The findings were to have been made known in December, but so far none have been published (although a parliamentary committee had been informed of these findings). On 21 December 2005, I wrote to the head of the Polish delegation to the

[5] A reporter working for the German television channel ZDF, Mr Brase, has passed onto me a certain amount of information and contact details of people involved locally, which I shall follow up in the next stages of my own enquiry.

Parliamentary Assembly, Mr Iwinski, asking him to let me have the findings as soon as possible.

27. On 6 December 2005, at the instigation of the opposition, the **Romanian** Parliament set up a commission to investigate the alleged existence of a secret detention centre on Romanian territory which the American secret services were said to have used for torture. A non-governmental human rights organisation (OADO—Organizaţia Pentru Apărarea Drepturilor Omului) sent specialists to all the places specifically mentioned in recent months as possible sites of secret detention centres. Their conclusions do not seem to provide any evidence of such centres. Traces of destroyed temporary structures are visible near Babadag training camp, Feteşti airbase and Mihail Kogălniceanu army base, but seemingly they were used in connection with international military exercises in the 2003–2005 period; American military personnel in transit were apparently accommodated there in May and June 2003. OADO stresses the absence of any basis for the allegations. On 20 January 2006 the head of the Romanian delegation to the Assembly wrote to me forwarding his delegation's replies to my 19 December 2005 questionnaire to heads of PACE delegations. The replies give general information about agreements between the United States and Romania on secret-service cooperation and NATO agreements. The bilateral agreement signed on 6 December 2005 (and not yet ratified) provides in its preamble that the parties are to respect national sovereignty, the United Nations Charter, human rights and their international obligations. The replies stress that no official Romanian authority was aware of any secret detention centre on Romanian territory. Nor have the Romanian authorities received any request for overflight of Romanian territory or use of Romanian airports by aircraft suspected of belonging to the CIA. They also state that military airfields have not been used by civil aircraft. The government has not asked for any further explanations, saying that it is satisfied with those given by Condoleezza Rice.

28. In the **United Kingdom** the NGO Liberty threatened the government with legal action for facilitating and colluding in use of torture if there was not an immediate enquiry into the very large number of flights and overflights by CIA-chartered planes and the possible use of certain United Kingdom airports. In reply to a parliamentary question on the subject, the United Kingdom foreign affairs minister, Jack Straw, stated in December 2005 that a thorough search of the relevant logs had not found any CIA request to use British airports in connection with transport of suspects. According to an internal memorandum dated December 2005, attributed to the private office of the foreign affairs minister and published by the *New Statesman* on 19 January 2006, the British Government intends to take the following approach to the problem: extraordinary renditions are usually illegal, but complete confidence should be placed in the assurances

provided by Ms Condoleezza Rise during her trip to Europe. The British press made a point of accusing the Government of duplicity. It remains to be seen whether the memorandum does indeed reflect the Government's official attitude. On 20 January I also received, from Mr Angus Robertson MP, a detailed report of numerous suspect movements of aircraft transiting through Scotland.

29. Further to questions to the government in the Bundestag from the leftwing and Liberal groups, the **German** Government asked the American authorities for information about CIA use, or not, of Frankfurt and Ramstein airports. In answer to most of the questions from the two groups, the government stated that it could provide replies only to the committee specially authorised to oversee the secret services. Asked whether the government or the German secret services knew of the existence of any secret detention centres on German or European territory, the government categorically denied any knowledge of such centres on national territory; with regard to the remainder of the question, it referred to its objection of principle that it was the special committee which had jurisdiction in the matter. In answer to a question from the leftwing group, the German air traffic safety office provided a detailed list of flights by two aircraft apparently chartered by the CIA which had landed at airports in Germany in 2002 and 2003, 137 and 146 times respectively and mainly at Frankfurt, Berlin and the US Ramstein base. However, the office was unable to provide the members of parliament with information as to the identity of any passengers. On 17 January 2006 the German members of parliament decided to set up a committee of enquiry to report back as soon as possible on the role of the intelligence services (BND) in Baghdad and on certain aspects of anti-terrorist action (including allegations of flights and overflights of German territory by CIA-chartered aircraft). Discussions are still under way as there seem to be misgivings in some political circles about setting up a committee that might undermine the operational capacity of the BND.

30. The **Armenian** parliamentary delegation forwarded to the head of internal security services the questionnaire which was sent on 19 December 2005 to heads of national delegations to the Parliamentary Assembly. The replies received shed no further light.

31. In response to parliamentary questions, the **Belgian** Government has launched an enquiry into flights and over-flights by CIA-chartered aircraft. So far, no stopover at a military airport has been discovered.

32. With regard to **Bosnia and Herzegovina,** their American lawyer[6] has sent me a detailed account of the case of six Bosnians abducted by American agents on Bosnian soil and taken to Guantànamo Bay, despite a Bosnia and

[6] Stephen H. Oleskey, of the law company WilmerHale.

Herzegovina Federal Supreme Court judgment ordering their release after police investigation had failed to uncover the slightest evidence against them. I shall be following developments in the case as part of my further investigations.

33. In a letter dated 19 January 2006, the leader of the **Cypriot** delegation to the Assembly forwarded to me his government's replies to the questionnaire I sent to the leaders of national delegations to the Assembly on 19 December 2005. The replies mention several landings in Cypriot airports, all of a technical nature (and therefore not subject to authorisation), of aircraft on the list forwarded to national delegations. The Cypriot Government states that it has no knowledge of secret detention centres on the part of national territory that is actually controlled by the Republic of Cyprus. It stresses that it is in its interests that full light should be shed on the matter and that it intends to use diplomatic channels to obtain explanations from the American authorities.

34. The **Danish** Government has asked the American authorities for explanations about CIA-chartered flights for alleged transport of prisoners over Danish territory.

35. The **Finnish** security services have reportedly asked the CIA for information about any passengers aboard a cargo plane which made a stop at Helsinki in 2003.

36. The **French** foreign affairs ministry has stated that it is checking with the civil aviation authorities on two flights which made stops in French territory and had apparently been chartered by the CIA.

37. In reply to a question from a European Parliament member, **Greece** is looking into the alleged existence of a secret prison at Souda naval base in Crete where persons suspected of involvement in the attacks on the London underground were allegedly subjected to violent interrogation by British agents.

38. The head of the **Irish** delegation to the Parliamentary Assembly informed me of the many questions to the government in the Irish Parliament, and of the replies received. In substance, the government expressed total condemnation of the practice of "extraordinary renditions" and stated that it had never authorised any overflights of Irish territory by chartered aircraft for that purpose.

39. The **Norwegian** Government apparently asked the American embassy for information about a plane which landed at Oslo on 20 July 2005 and was allegedly used by the American authorities for transport of suspected extremists.

40. The **Swedish** Government has instructed the relevant department and the civil aviation authority to look into flights to and from Swedish airports by United-States-registered aircraft since 2002.

ii. The More Detailed Cases of Italy and Switzerland

- **Italy**

41. At midday on 17 June 2003 an Egyptian citizen, Hassam Osama Mustafa Nasr, known as Abu Omar, was abducted in the middle of Milan. Thanks to an outstanding and tenacious investigation by the Milan judiciary and the DIGOS police services, Abu Omar's is undoubtedly the best known and best documented case of "extraordinary rendition"[7].

42. Via the military airbases at Aviano (Italy) and Ramstein (Germany) Abu Omar was flown to Egypt, where he was tortured before being released and re-arrested. To my knowledge no proceedings were brought against Omar in Egypt.

43. The Italian judicial investigation established, beyond all reasonable doubt, that the operation was carried out by the CIA (which has not issued any denials). The Italian investigators likewise established that the presumed leader of the abduction operation—who had worked as the American consul in Milan—was in Egypt for two weeks immediately after Omar was handed over to the Egyptian authorities. It may safely be inferred that he took part, in one way or another, in Omar's interrogation.

44. The proceedings instituted in Milan are concerned with 25 American agents, against 22 of whom the Italian authorities have issued arrest warrants.

45. Abu Omar was a political refugee. Suspected of Islamic militancy, he had been under surveillance by the Milan police and judicial authorities. As a result of the surveillance operation, the Italian police were probably on the point of uncovering an activist network operating in northern Italy. Abu Omar's abduction, as the Milan judicial authorities expressly point out, sabotaged the Italian surveillance operation and thereby dealt a blow to anti-terrorist action.

46. Is it conceivable or possible that an operation of that kind, with deployment of resources on that scale in a friendly country that was an ally (being a member of the coalition in Iraq), was carried out without the national authorities—or at least Italian opposite numbers—being informed? The Italian Government has denied having been informed. The presence on Italian territory of at least 25 foreign agents who abducted someone who had been granted political asylum and was already under police surveillance might have been expected, if not to create a diplomatic incident, then at least to trigger a sharp response from the national authorities. As far as

[7] I have met the prosecutor who headed the investigation, Armando Spataro, and was able to obtain as full information as confidentiality and procedural requirements permitted. The Abu Omar case is likewise described in the book, already referred to, by the *Corriere della Sera* journalist Guido Olimpio, *Operazione Hotel California*, Feltrinelli, October 2005.

I know, there was no such response. A further interesting point is that the Italian justice minister has so far not forwarded to the American authorities the Milan judicial authorities' requests for assistance and extradition.

47. Abu Omar's abduction is a perfect illustration of "extraordinary rendition". It is a clear indication that the method exists, together with complex logistic support in various parts of Europe and considerable deployment of personnel. It also plants doubts and raises the question of involvement of national authorities at one or other level.

- **Switzerland**

48. The methods used to counter the terrorist threat are also under debate in Switzerland.

49. In May 2002 an American citizen, José Padilla, was placed under close surveillance by the Swiss federal police and US agents when he flew into Zurich from Pakistan. Padilla was suspected of wanting to introduce a "dirty" bomb into the United States and explode it. Apparently the Swiss police even questioned him before he flew on to Chicago, where he was arrested. Since then Padilla has been in detention without any detailed charges being brought against him and is considered an "enemy combatant". It was only quite recently that he was handed over to the civil justice authorities to avoid the Supreme Court's ordering his release. Visiting Switzerland in June 2002, the United States justice minister, John Ashcroft, warmly congratulated the Swiss authorities on the valuable part they had played in Padilla's arrest. However, the case has sparked controversy in Switzerland, to such an extent that a parliamentary committee has begun an enquiry, for it would seem that the police co-operated closely with the American services without notifying the competent judge, or at any rate informed him after the event, when Padilla had already been arrested in the United States. If notification had been made in time—as procedure requires—Padilla would most likely have been arrested and handed over to the American authorities in accordance with the procedure laid down and with the safeguards which operate in cases of judicial assistance and extradition (which are not applied to so-called "enemy combatants"). My request to consult the parliamentary committee's report was refused on the justice ministry's advice, on the ground that the file contained material "concerning third parties and potentially harmful to relations with another country".

50. In June 2005 the Swiss press, in connection with what it called the "Guantànamo Express", mentioned several aircraft which had temporarily landed in Switzerland and were suspected of carrying prisoners. On a visit to the United States in late June 2005, the Swiss foreign affairs minister asked his opposite number for explanations. To date, and despite a repeat

request to the United States ambassador in Bern in December, no reply has been forthcoming from the American authorities.

51. The Egyptian Abu Omar, abducted by the CIA in Milan on 17 February 2003 (see the above section on Italy), was flown from the Italian base at Aviano to Ramstein in Germany, and then on to Cairo. The Italian judicial authorities have identified the aircraft used. The data, when compared with data held by Swiss air traffic control, indicate that he was flown through Swiss air space, which has prompted the federal prosecution authorities to institute an enquiry (the prosecution authorities at Zweibrücken, within whose jurisdiction the Ramstein base is located, have done likewise).

52. On 8 January the Swiss newspaper *Sonntagsblick* stated that, during the night of 11 to 12 November 2005, the Swiss intelligence services intercepted a fax from the Egyptian European affairs ministry to the Egyptian embassy in London referring to the existence of secret detention centres in Romania, Bulgaria, Ukraine, Macedonia and Kosovo. The newspaper published a copy of a Swiss departmental memorandum (in French) dated 14 November 2005 summarising the content of the original message intercepted (probably in Arabic). It was from the newspaper article that I discovered the content of the intercepted fax. Interception of the Egyptian fax has not been denied by the parties concerned. On the contrary the Swiss authorities are investigating the breach of official secrecy.

53. The foreign affairs minister stated in an interview published on 15 January 2006 that the Swiss authorities would co-operate with me "as far as possible".

B. Debate in North America

54. In the United States, the authorities' attitude in the war on terrorism and the controversial methods used by the CIA in that connection have also aroused controversy.

55. The CIA action programme set up after 11 September 2001 and known as the "GST programme", gives the CIA greatly enhanced powers (apparently comparable to those which existed during the cold war). It allows the CIA to arrest suspects with the help of foreign internal security services, hold them captive abroad, employ interrogation techniques (some of which are very widely regarded as possibly contravening the United States' international undertakings regarding prohibition of torture) and fly prisoners between countries[8].

---

[8] Dana Priest, "Covert CIA Program Withstands New Furor—Anti-Terror Efforts Continue to Grow", *The Washington Post*, 30 December 2005.

56. The facts as reported by several official sources point to higly controversial practices on the part of the American security services.

57. Several prominent figures have openly condemned the practices in question. One can but welcome the perseverance shown by Senator John McCain, who was himself a torture victim in Vietnam and who was responsible for an amendment to the 2006 defence expenditure bill expressly prohibiting cruel, inhuman and degrading treatment of foreign prisoners, whether in CIA hands, in the United States or abroad. The amendment is extremely significant in the context of my report, implying that such treatment was not hitherto prohibited by American law in the circumstances referred to. It also strikes me as fairly revealing that Vice-President Dick Cheney fought, unsuccessfully, to have the McCain amendment not apply to the CIA. However, we cannot be altogether confident of the effects the amendment will have—the press reports that President Bush seems to reserve the right to disregard the amendment in certain circumstances[9].

58. Similarly, extension of the Patriot Act was agreed to only after fierce debate and resistance in the Senate, and only for six months (during which period it is hoped to make its content more flexible). The fact is that a large number of senators regard the provisions of the Act, which was adopted in the wake of 11 September 2001 and is concerned, in particular, with empowering the FBI to secretly obtain information on telecommunications, as placing undue restrictions on citizens' rights and freedoms.

59. The uproar in the United States over telephone taps which President Bush has authorised, apparently without any legal basis whatever, can only reinforce that sentiment. The revelation by *The New York Times* has further fuelled present controversy.

60. Amnesty International (AI) expressed serious concern about the attitude adopted by the Canadian authorities. As suspect flights had been reported over the country, AI asked the authorities on 22 November 2005 to look into the matter. In an open letter to the Minister of Public Safety and Emergency Preparedness dated 18 January 2006, AI observes that there has still been no serious investigation into these allegations. We have no doubt that Canada, a permanent observer to the Assembly, will shed full light on the allegations.

D. Reminder: Anti-Terrorist Action Must Respect Human Rights

61. The Parliamentary Assembly has made its position very clear, which is that it shares "the United States' determination to combat international

[9] Charlie Savage, "Bush could bypass new torture ban—Waiver right is reserved", *The Boston Globe*, 4 January 2006.

terrorism and fully endorses the importance of detecting and preventing terrorist crimes, prosecuting and punishing terrorists and protecting human lives"[10].

62. Obviously that position is the only possible one and, as far as action on terrorism is concerned, requires close international co-operation, which, however, must be organised on the basis of clear, precise agreements and in compliance with agencies' powers and responsibilities.

63. "Rendition" of prisoners must be carried out in accordance with legal procedure, so that the prisoner is afforded all the legal guarantees to which he or she is entitled, including a fair trial within a reasonable time. In no case should it be made possible for a person to be returned or transferred "in reliance on 'diplomatic assurances' from countries known to engage in the systematic practice of torture and . . . unless the absence of a risk of ill-treatment is firmly established"[11].

64. It cannot be overemphasised that nothing and no one can justify waiving the principles of the rule of law and respect for human rights and that torture, in addition to being an unreliable way of obtaining information, is in any case absolutely prohibited.

65. As the Assembly has stated, "some human rights (such as the right to be protected from torture or inhuman treatment) are absolute, and should never be interfered with by state authorities, including internal security services."[12] Secret services' role, however fundamentally important to counter-terrorist action, clearly can never place such services above the law.

E. Preliminary Analysis of the Information Already Obtained

a. Awareness of Council of Europe Member States?

66. "Rendition" affecting Europe seems to have concerned more than a hundred persons in recent years[13]. Hundreds of CIA-chartered flights have passed through numerous European countries[14]. It is highly unlikely that European governments, or at least their intelligence services, were unaware.

[10] Resolution 1433(2005) on the lawfulness of detentions by the United States in Guantànamo Bay, §1.

[11] Idem, §8.x.

[12] Recommendation 1402(1999) on control of internal security services in Council of Europe member states, §4.

[13] Michael Scheuer, writing in *Die Zeit* of 29 December 2005, referred to "hundreds, but not thousands" of persons held by the United States in the context of "rendition".

[14] According to a list obtained from Germany's Office for Air Traffic Safety by the Left Party group in Germany, two aircraft linked to the CIA had landed at airports within Germany in 2002 and 2003, 137 and 146 times respectively. I dare not extrapolate the number of potentially suspect flights in all Council of Europe member states during the period under examination by the 40 aircraft allegedly linked to the CIA!

And a number of revelations have already been published by the press, especially in America, over the past few years. It is, to say the least, curious that media interest, especially in Europe, suddenly surged after the article in *The Washington Post* in early November 2005.

67. The statements made by Secretary of State, Condoleezza Rice, during and before her European visit of December 2005, and by her predecessor, Colin Powell, who said that the US had always respected the national sovereignty of its allies, are taken by some as both a reprimand and a warning: "stop being hypocritical", and "do you really want us to say what happened?".

68. In the case of Abu Omar it was obvious that the CIA acted without informing the Italian judicial and police authorities. The Milan public prosecutors explicitly state that the action taken by the American service, which they consider constituted a criminal offence, prevented them from competing investigations which they were conducting against Omar and which was on the verge of identifying a network of activists considered potentially dangerous. The Italians' meticulous and highly professional work had thus been undone by the unexpected intervention by CIA agents who, by abducting Abu Omar, had sabotaged a major anti-terrorist operation. This "rendition" is a glaring illustration of the fact that such actions, which infringe the principles of the rule of law, are not only unacceptable from the legal and ethical point of view but also ineffective, or indeed damaging to the fight against terrorism. This lack of cooperation with and confidence in the authorities officially mandated to fight crime is bound to have very serious consequences, challenging the very functioning of the law-based State and its democratic foundation. Similarly, we might add that the American authorities in Ramstein are refusing to co-operate with the German prosecutor responsible for the German strand of the Abu Omar case, on Washington's orders. It is difficult to believe that such an approach to relations between authorities in different countries can provide any valid basis for genuine cooperation among States endeavouring together to combat the worst threats facing us in modern times.

b. *Extraordinary Rendition* and Torture—a Link Known and Accepted?

69. Over the last few months, a number of former officials of the American intelligence services, some of whom had held responsible positions, have given interviews and provided many details of the resources used against actual and suspected terrorists. These statements, which have in fact been corroborated by indiscretions from officials still serving, clearly confirm that the current US Administration seems to start from the principle that the principles of the rule of law and human rights are incompatible with efficient action against terrorism. Even the laws of war, especially the Geneva Conventions, are not accepted or applied. The relocation of prison

camps to Guantanamo and elsewhere indicates that even American legal standards are seen as obstacles by the US Administration. "Extraordinary rendition" and secret detention facilitate the use of degrading treatment and torture. It is even the stated objective of such practices, as the following quotations would appear to confirm.

70. Mr Michael Scheuer, one of the architects of the "rendition" system further developed during the Presidency and with the agreement of Bill Clinton, formerly headed the CIA's Bin Laden unit. He stated in an interview with *Die Zeit*[15] that the CIA was within its rights to break all laws except American law. He expressed doubt as to the existence of secret prisons in eastern Europe, given the fact that the US had, in his opinion, sufficient capacity in other places, particularly in Iraq and Cuba.

71. In another interview, given to the *Sunday Herald* in October 2005, Mr Scheuer is reported to have said, on the subject of his knowledge of the use of torture, that he had no doubt about this and that the White House was more willing than the CIA itself to ignore the legal details ("to turn a blind eye to the legal niceties"). The CIA was aware that it would eventually have to take the blame ("The Agency always knew it would be left holding the baby for this one")[16].

72. As early as March 2005, in a CBS interview, Mr Scheuer had admitted knowing that suspects were tortured in Egypt, adding that it was "very convenient" finding "someone else to do your dirty work."[17]

73. Mr Robert Baer, a former CIA agent interviewed by British journalist Stephen Grey, is reported to have said: "If you want a serious interrogation, you send a prisoner to Jordan. If you want them to be tortured, you send them to Syria. If you want someone to disappear -never to see them again—you send them to Egypt."[18]

74. Mr Vincent Cannistraro, former head of counter-espionage in the CIA is reported to have said that a Guantánamo detainee suspected of belonging to Al-Qaeda and who was refusing to co-operate provided better information after being "rendered" to Egypt: "They promptly tore his fingernails out and he started to tell things."[19] Mr Cannistraro also reportedly said that Egyptian prisons were full of men without finger and toenails. "It's crude, but highly effective, although we could never condone it publicly.

---

[15] *Die Zeit*, 29 December 2005.

[16] Neil Mackay, "These two men are experts on rendition: one invented it, the other has seen its full horrors", *Sunday Herald* (Scotland), 16 October 2005, available at *http://www.sundayherald.com/52305*.

[17] Ibid.

[18] Stephen Grey, "America's Gulag", *The New Statesman*, 17 May 2004, available at *http://www.newstatesman.com/200405170016*.

[19] Knut Royce, "Mixed Reviews from Experts. Critics: Make Case on Deceit, Not Terror", *Newsday*, 6 February 2003.

The Egyptians and Jordanians are not that squeamish."[20] Lastly, he also said that only someone "deaf, dumb and blind" could believe that the Syrians did not used torture, despite their claims to the contrary.[21]

75. Some officials who have remained nameless have given even more direct evidence. A CIA member directly involved in "renditions", for instance, was quoted by *The Washington Post* back in December 2002 as saying "We don't kick the [expletive] out of them. We send them to other countries so they can kick the [expletive] out of them."[22]

76. "If you don't violate someone's human rights some of the time, you probably aren't doing your job": this was allegedly said by one official who had supervised the capture and transfer of alleged terrorists.[23]

77. Another official directly involved in "renditions" said that he knew the persons concerned would probably be tortured ("I . . . do it with my eyes open").[24]

78. Some officials of President Bush's administration have said that the CIA in practice uses a narrow definition of what amounts to "knowing" that a suspect has been tortured: "If we're not there in the room, who is to say?"[25]

79. Another case of rendition concerns a so-called Muslim militant in Canada, called Arar. Some American officials speaking on condition of anonymity are reported to have said that there was strong evidence that Mr Arar had long been associated with suspected Islamist militants in Canada. They reported that he had confessed under torture in Syria that he had received terrorist training in Afghanistan, and had given the names of his instructors and other details[26].

80. Others reportedly told *Time* that no American had been in the room in which the Syrians interrogated Mr Zammar. American officials in Damascus gave written questions to the Syrians, who passed back Zammar's answers. State Department officials appreciated this arrangement, which kept the American government out of any torture that the Syrians might use against

[20] Ian Bruce, "Middleman Reveals Al Qaeda Secrets", *The Herald* (Scotland), 17 October 2002.

[21] Shannon McCaffrey, "Canadian Sent to Syrian Prison Disputes U.S. Claims against Torture", Knight-Ridder, 1 August 2004.

[22] Dana Priest and Barton Gellman. "U.S. Decries Abuse but Defends Interrogations", *The Washington Post*, 26 December 2002, available at http://www.washingtonpost.com/ac2/wp-dyn/A37943—2002Dec25?language=printer; also see Doc. 10497, report of the Committee on Legal Affairs and Human Rights on the lawfulness of detentions by the United States in Guantánamo Bay, rapporteur Kevin McNamara.

[23] Ibid.

[24] Ibid.

[25] Ibid.

[26] Clifford Krauss, "Qaeda Pawn, U.S. Calls Him; Victim, He Calls Himself", *New York Times*, 18 November 2003.

him. Some State Department officials suspected that he had indeed been tortured[27].

81. In an interview with Dana Priest *(The Washington Post)* published in March 2005, another CIA official involved in "renditions" described other countries' "assurances" as "a farce,"[28] and admitted that it was widely understood that interrogation practices that would be illegal in the United States were being used[29]. In the same interview, he said that "They say they are not abusing them, and that satisfies the legal requirement, but we all know they do."[30]

82. It seems, furthermore, that the CIA's partners quite clearly understand the worse than ambiguous attitude it takes to the use of torture; one Arab diplomat from a country actively involved in anti-terror operations and sharing intelligence with the CIA reportedly said that it was unrealistic to believe that the CIA really wanted to verify the assurances given: "It would be stupid to keep track of them because then you would know what's going on [. . .] It's really more like 'Don't ask, don't tell.'"[31]

83. In this context, it can be noted that in May 2005 the U.N. Committee against Torture held that the 1984 U.N. Convention against Torture had been violated by Sweden with respect to the removal, to Egypt, of Ahmed Agiza and Mohammed al-Zari, back in December 2001 (see Agazi v. Sweden, CAT/C/34/D/233/2003 of 24 May 2005).

84. Another case concerning a certain Mr Mahdouh Habib, Australian citizen arrested in Pakistan in October 2002, is prompting debate in Australia, highlighting the legal difficulties arising out of the use of torture: "After promising for more than three years that it would charge Mr. Habib, the Bush administration told the Australians in January that it would not prosecute him because the C.I.A. did not want the evidence about Mr. Habib being taken to Egypt, and his allegations of torture, raised in court", Australian officials reportedly said[32].

85. Drawing on all this concordant information and evidence we can say that there is a great deal of coherent, convergent evidence pointing to the existence of a system of "relocation" or "outsourcing" of torture. Acts of torture, or severe violations of detainees' dignity through the administration of inhuman or degrading treatment, are carried out outside national territory and beyond the authority of the national intelligence services.

---

[27] Mitch Frank, "Help from an Unlikely Ally", *Time*, 1 July 2002.

[28] Dana Priest, "CIA's Assurances on Transferred Suspects Doubted", *The Washington Post*, 17 March 2005, available at *http://www.washingtonpost.com/wp-dyn/articles/A42072-2005Mar16.html*

[29] Ibid.

[30] Ibid.

[31] Ibid.

[32] Raymond Bonner, "Australians Uneasy About U.S. detainee case", *New York Times*, 10 April 2005.

Does this mean that torture is so easy to use in this day and age? Is it enough for one's own secret services not to be physically present at the place of interrogation and to pretend to have no official knowledge of this practice to state that the law is not being broken? In this context, the statements made by Mr Schäuble, Germany's new Minister for the Interior, appear at the very least highly debatable, if not alarming. He seems to consider that the use of information obtained by dubious means is acceptable, provided that the German services were not perpetrating acts of torture themselves.[33]

86. Did such pointers to the existence of "networked" torture really escape the notice of Council of Europe member states? What is, therefore, the share of responsibility of member states when their airport facilities are used to transport detainees to places where they will be subjected to torture, ie places—dare I say—of public notoriety ? Is there true co-operation between European states and the United States, or do the former display a respectable kind of duplicity?

87. These assumptions are obviously very serious, but all these questions require plain, honest answers. The opinion to be delivered by the Venice Commission in March 2006 will give us a clearer view of the legal consequences of these practices, including member States' responsibility in the light of the international treaties and the rules of general international law to which they are subject.

88. With specific reference to the awareness among member states' authorities of torture committed by their "partners" in the context of the fight against terrorism, we shall hear a personal account at our Committee's meeting of 24 January 2006 from Mr Craig Murray, former British Ambassador to Uzbekistan. The documents that he has already forwarded to me, and which led me to invite him to give his evidence, appear to be damning for the UK authorities, which seem to have knowingly continued to make use of information obtained under torture and supplied by the Uzbek intelligence services, thereby encouraging the practice of torture. Mr Murray was unable to persuade his authorities to cease doing so, and therefore resigned.[34]

89. Allegations have just been published to the effect that some German executive authorities had themselves, during co-operation with the American FBI, "outsourced" acts of torture, in collusion with the Lebanese and Syrian services. These allegations are currently being checked, and in

[33] Spiegel online, 16 December 2005; see also the opposite stance adopted by the President of the Constitutional Court, Mr Papier, in the *Handelsblatt*, 26 December 2005.

[34] See in this context the judgment of the House of Lords of 8 December 2005 confirming that information obtained under torture cannot be used in evidence before the courts.

the light of the statements quoted above such verification would appear necessary and urgent.

c. Secret Detention Centres

90. At this stage of the investigations, there is no formal, irrefutable evidence of the existence of secret CIA detention centres in Romania, Poland or any other country. Nevertheless, there are many indications from various sources which must be considered reliable, justifying the continuation of the analytical and investigative work. The information requested from the European Union Satellite Centre and from Eurocontrol should be supplied and evaluated in the very near future. The Egyptian message intercepted by the Swiss services, the authenticity of which is no longer in doubt, contains nothing very new, but it does nonetheless point to a different source regarding the existence of these centres. The Egyptian services have a reputation for efficiency, and there is a great deal of evidence to the effect that they have engaged in very active co-operation in carrying out these renditions.

d. Kosovo and Chechnya

91. Where Kosovo is concerned, the KFOR detention centre (Camp Bondsteel) is not "secret" in so far as its existence has been well-known for a long time now. Back in 2002 the Commissioner for Human Rights, Mr Gil-Robles, reported on his findings *in situ*. At the hearing with our committee on 13 December 2005 the Commissioner for Human Rights repeated that the Kfor detention centre had "many parallels with Guantanamo: prisoners arrested without recourse to any kind of judicial procedure or legal representation". Nor is Camp Bondsteel open for inspection by the Council of Europe's Committee for the Prevention of Torture (CPT), which has the right to inspect all places of detention in States Parties to the European Convention for the Prevention of Torture (including Serbia and Montenegro), and which has not hitherto obtained authorisation to visit. Negotiations are in progress with KFOR.

92. Where Chechnya is concerned, Mr Bindig's report, which is to be discussed in the plenary sitting of 25 January, reports on numerous cases of "enforced disappearances" and torture, as well as the existence of secret places of detention, all strongly criticised by the CPT in two public statements to which I referred in my December 2005 introductory memorandum, and which are still waiting to be given their due importance by the Committee of Ministers of the Council of Europe.

F. Looking Ahead to the Continuing Investigation

93. The replies from Eurocontrol and the European Union Satellite Centre would appear to be imminent, as the Romanian authorities have now

agreed supply satellite photographs of places located on their territory. We will not be able to pronounce on the importance and the scope of this information until a later juncture.

94. The factual elements secured to date, thanks *inter alia* to the action of the Council of Europe, have induced the European Parliament to set up a temporary special committee responsible for investigating any possible unlawful action taken in the context of the fight against terrorism in the European Union member or applicant States. This decision underscores the seriousness of the evidence secured so far. It is felicitous that other international institutions are also dealing with these issues, and the Council of Europe and its Rapporteur will obviously fully co-operate with them.

95. We should also mention the remarkable work being done by various NGOs and numerous investigatory journalists. Such journalists symbolise the commitment of a community which is determined to ascertain the truth and will not allow the fight against terrorism, which is absolutely vital, to justify using unspeakable methods, thereby raising the threat of a lapse into barbarity. Consequently, the officials who are well aware of the fact and who in all conscience cannot accept these methods, provide a major channel for ascertaining the truth. These officials face two contradictory imperatives, namely official secrecy and the ethical duty not to collude in acts infringing human dignity. In this context, whistle-blowing is the expression of civil commitment and courage, rather than an act of denunciation or betrayal.

96. The replies which the Council of Europe's member States must supply under the procedure set out in Article 52 of the European Convention on Human Rights must reach the Secretary General by 21 February 2006. These replies will provide additional material for assessing the situation.

97. Similarly, the legal opinion requested from the Venice Commission will be very important for the conclusions of the final report, particularly in terms of the Council of Europe member States' obligations under the European Convention on Human Rights in order to ensure that their territory, and even their airspace, are not misused, even by friendly and allied third states, for the purposes of human rights violations. National procedures for parliamentary supervision of intelligence services will have to be analysed and, where necessary, improved, in order to ensure that abuse cannot be perpetrated on the pretext of the confidentiality of current procedures. Parliamentarians must also analyse the repeated recourse by executives authorities to the concepts of "State secrecy" and "higher interests" in withholding information.

98. My experience as the Assembly's rapporteur on this particularly sensitive and substantial subject also makes me wonder about the resources at the Parliamentary Assembly's disposal for conducting this kind of inquiry.

When national procedures cannot appropriately deal with investigations into possible human rights violations which are more than individual cases (for which the European Court of Human Rights has jurisdiction) and which transcend borders, we are justified in wondering whether the current instruments are still equal to the task. Instead of one single member as Rapporteur with the support of the normal resources of the Committee's secretariat, already overwhelmed by other current reports, we might seriously consider whether setting up a true committee of inquiry, assisted by experts and holding more extensive investigatory powers, might not be a better solution and more able to deal with these new important challenges.

99. As we have said, no cogent evidence has yet emerged on the existence in Europe of detention camps like the one at Guantanamo Bay. On the other hand, it has been proved (and in fact never denied), that individuals have been abducted, deprived of their liberty and all rights, and transported to different destinations in Europe, to be handed over to countries in which they have suffered degrading treatment and torture. This is serious enough to justify the continuation of the Council of Europe's inquiries and strenuous efforts from all member States to ascertain the truth.

100. There is a heated public debate in America on the requisite resources for fighting terrorism. The fact that detention and interrogation centres have been relocated to other countries is proof that the authorities are fully aware that the methods used are incompatible with the American legal system. Europe must clearly and unambiguously declare that it refuses outright to tolerate such doings in its territory, or anywhere else.

101. It is equally unacceptable and appalling to ease one's conscience by delegating such tasks—illegal secret detention and use of torture—to third countries (which have long been the target of high-profile specific and repeated denunciations of very serious human rights violations and the lack of any kind of democratic control).

102. In fact, we must go beyond ascertaining the existence or non-existence of secret detention centres in Europe. The issue at stake is even more important than that. The current US Administration obviously considers that the traditional instruments of the democratic State governed by the rule of law—justice, constitutional guarantees of a fair trial, respect for human dignity—are inappropriate for facing up to the terrorist threat. Persons assumed to be terrorists are therefore arrested, interrogated, deported and detained without any rights or safeguards, thus accepting the concrete and inevitable risk of subjecting completely innocent people to such treatment (inside the CIA an internal inquiry is reportedly under way into several cases of individuals who were abducted, imprisoned and tortured, before it emerged that the wrong people had been targeted). Is Europe prepared

to accept such an approach? Can we really say that human rights are an obstacle to national security? Can there be any real security without respect for human dignity?

103. The safety and security of citizens and the fight against the terrorist threat are undeniable fundamental priorities for democracies and an immense challenge to the State founded on the rule of law. In a remarkable judgment handed down in June 2004, the US Supreme Court used the following very clear terms: "The point at issue in this case is nothing less than the essence of a free society. If this national is still attached to the ideals symbolised in its flag, it must not use the weapons of tyrants to resist an attack by the forces of tyranny". Frank, open dialogue between the institutions on both sides of the Atlantic is necessary, indeed absolutely vital, if we wish to implement the most effective means of combating the new threats facing us. This can only be achieved if one side answers the questions and the other is genuinely prepared to ask them.

* * *

Update: 23.01.06

On 23rd January 2006, the Rapporteur received information from both the EU Satellite Center and Eurocontrol. He will now undertake an analysis of the information (satellite pictures, flights records) provided.

Appendix I

Alleged Secret Detentions in Council of Europe Member States: Background Information

Rapporteur of the Committee on Legal Affairs and Human Rights (AS/Jur): Mr Dick Marty, Switzerland, ALDE (appointed 13.12.2005)

Rapporteur for opinion of the Political Affairs Committee: Mr Peter Schieder, Austria, SOC

- Mandate: Doc 10748, Reference 3153 of 25.11.2005
- Expiry date for adoption of the report: 25.11.2007

AS/Jur meeting on 7.11.2005:

- considered the possibility of asking the Standing Committee of the Assembly for an urgent procedure debate
- [provisionally] appointed its Chairperson, Mr Marty, as Rapporteur and instructed him to collect pertinent information and to present his conclusions at the next meeting
- authorised him, if he deemed it necessary, to make fact-finding visits to Poland and Romania in this context
- left it to him, if he deemed it necessary, to address a request for an urgent procedure debate to the President of the Assembly on behalf of the Committee
- invited the Secretary General of the Council of Europe to ask States Parties to the European Convention on Human Rights (ECHR) for information on this subject (Article 52)

14.11.2005:	Letters to US authorities (Observer to the CoE), and Polish and Romanian PACE Delegations, asking for information
17.11.2005:	Reply from Romanian PACE Delegation

AS/Jur meeting on 22.11.2005:

- considered and took note of an information memorandum (*AS/Jur (2005) 52 rev 2)* submitted by the Rapporteur, decided to declassify it and transmit it to the Bureau with a view to its public distribution at the Standing Committee's meeting in Bucharest on 25 November 2005
- held an exchange of views with Mrs Kathalijne Buitenweg, MEP (Netherlands, Group of the Greens), member of the Committee on Civil Liberties, Justice and Home Affairs of the European Parliament and Mr Emmanuel Crabit, Principal Administrator in the Directorate-General for Justice, Freedom and Security of the European Commission

- asked its Chairperson to table a motion for a resolution on alleged secret detention centres in Council of Europe member States and to propose to the President of the Assembly that the text be referred to the Committee on Legal Affairs and Human Rights for report as soon as possible (letter sent on 24.11.2005)

29.11.2005: Letters to Mr Frank Asbeck, Director of European Union Satellite Centre, and to Mr Victor Aguado, Director General of Eurocontrol, asking for their cooperation

5.12.2005: Letter from Eurocontrol, informing that they are seeking agreement of member states governing body

6.12.2005: Letter from US Ambassador (Observer to the CoE), enclosing public statement made by US Secretary of State on 5.12.2005

[7.12.2005: Letters from Mr Frattini, Vice-President of European Commission to Mrs Benita Ferrero-Waldner, European Commissioner, and to Mr Jacques Barrot, Vice-President of European Commission, asking for support for Mr Marty (concerning EU Satellite Centre and Eurocontrol respectively)]

9.12.2005: Interim provisional reply from EU Satellite Centre

12.12.2005: AS/Bur invited the national parliaments to cooperate fully with Mr Marty in the preparation of his report

AS/Jur meeting on 3.12.2005:

- held an exchange of views with Mrs Maud de Boer Buquicchio, Deputy Secretary General of the Council of Europe, Mr Alvaro Gil-Robles, Council of Europe Human Rights Commissioner, Mr Cem Özdemir, member of the European Parliament (Germany, Group of the Greens/European Free Alliance), and Mr Emmanuel Crabit, Principal Administrator in the Directorate-General for Justice, Freedom and Security of the European Commission
- heard a statement by the Rapporteur on developments on this issue since the last meeting,
- approved a public *statement by the Rapporteur*
- authorised the Rapporteur to go to the seats of the European institutions and to make fact-finding visits to certain Council of Europe member states if he deemed it necessary
- decided to ask the European Commission for Democracy through Law (Venice Commission) to prepare a legal opinion assessing the legality of secret detention in the light of Council of Europe member states' international obligations, in particular the European Convention on Human Rights and the European Convention for the Prevention of

Torture, and expressed the wish that this opinion be submitted as soon as possible

- asked its Chairperson to submit to the Bureau a request for an urgent procedure debate on «the alleged secret detentions in Council of Europe member states" during the Assembly's January 2006 part-session

14.12.2005:	Letter to Mr Brian Ross, Journalist ABC
14.12.2005:	Letter to Mr Lenn Downie, Editor, Washington Post
14.12.2005:	Letter from Mr Frank Asbeck, EU Satellite Centre, informing that the provision of satellite images is not part of the Centre's mission
15.12.2005:	Letter sent to the Venice Commission requesting a legal opinion (see Appendix III)
16.12.2005:	"Information Notice" (reply) from Polish Delegation
16.12.2005:	Letter sent to the President of the Assembly proposing an urgent procedure debate
19.12.2005:	Letters sent all PACE delegations, enclosing questions which MPs could put to their governments and a list of alleged flight patterns (see Appendix II)
21.12.2005:	Letter from Washington Post (Mr Downie), informing that it was not possible to disclose their sources
21.12.2005:	Follow-up letter to Mr Iwinski, Head of Polish PACE Delegation
22.12.2005:	Letter sent to Mr Javier Solana, SG of the Council of the European Union, asking him to authorise EU Satellite Centre cooperation
10.01.2006:	Letter from Venice Commission: adoption of its opinion foreseen on 17-18.03.2005
11.01.2006:	Reminder letter to Mr Victor Aguado, Director General of Eurocontrol + reminder e-mail from AS/Jur secretariat to Mr Solana's secretariat
16.01.2005:	Reminder messages sent to Mr Iwinski and Mr Ross (ABC)
19.01.2006:	Letter from ABC (on behalf of Mr Brian Ross) informing that it was not possible to disclose their sources, but that they could provide the video recording of the report of 5 December 2005 (to which Mr Marty replied that he would indeed appreciate receiving the video recording)
23.01.2006:	Information received from the EU Satellite Center and Eurocontrol

****

Secretariat contacts:

Mr Andrew DRZEMCZEWSKI, Head of the Secretariat

Tel: +33 3 88 41 23 26; Fax: +33 3 88 41 27 02; e-mail: andrew.drzemczewski@coe.int

Mr Günter SCHIRMER, Secretary

Tel: +33 3 88 41 28 09; Fax: +33 3 88 41 27 02; e-mail: guenter.schirmer@coe.int

Appendix II

Letter of 19 December 2005 from Mr Dick Marty, Chairperson of the Committee on Legal Affairs and Human Rights to the Chairpersons of the National Delegations

. . .

As you are no doubt aware, the Committee on Legal Affairs and Human Rights has instructed me to prepare a report on *"Alleged secret detention centres in Council of Europe member states"* (Doc 10748).

At its meeting in Paris on 13 December 2005, the Committee discussed the action taken on this issue in their national parliaments. I have been asked, at the request of members of the Committee, to prepare a list of pertinent questions which members of parliament could address to their governments. I would be grateful if you could forward this list to the members of your Parliament as soon as possible. The pressure thus brought to bear in national parliaments will reinforce that exerted by international organisations.

I would also be grateful if you could send me replies already given or to be given by your governments to these questions. This information will be extremely useful if the Assembly decides to follow the Committee's proposal to hold an urgent procedure debate on this matter during the January 2006 part-session.

Thanking you in advance for your cooperation, I remain,

. . .

[Enclosed with this letter was a list of alleged flight patterns of suspected CIA flights.]

Appendix to the letter:

Questions which members of the Parliamentary Assembly might put to their respective governments in their national parliament:

Secret services:

— Is the Government systematically informed of the activities of foreign secret services (in particular the CIA) on national territory?

— How does it supervise co-operation between the national secret services and those of partner countries? To what extent might the Government have *tolerated* certain illegal activities by foreign secret services on national territory by adopting a passive attitude?

— Are there any specific agreements with the USA on combating terrorism (possibly providing for the USA to have bases on national territory or even to carry out policing operations independently)?

Secret detention centres:

— Does the Government have any information regarding the existence of secret detention centres on national territory or elsewhere in Europe? If so, what information? Since when?

— Have the authorities been contacted by the authorities or secret services of other countries requesting permission for the (secret) detention and/or "rendition" of prisoners on national territory?

— Has the Government requested information from the American authorities regarding the alleged existence of secret detention centres in Europe? If so, what replies has it received to date?

Flights to, from or over national territory by CIA aircraft/transportation of prisoners:

— Does the Government know of any flights to, from or over national territory by aircraft chartered by the CIA or related agencies (outsourcing)? If so, since when, and how frequent have they been?

— Was permission requested from the Government or the competent authorities for the flights and overflights in question? If so, what was its/their response?

— What information must be provided in support of such requests? Must a list of passengers' names (always) be supplied?

— What implications do the NATO accords or other similar agreements have for the procedures for requesting permission for the alleged flights? Do these procedures only apply to military flights or can they be extended to civilian flights?

— Does the Government know of (or has it tolerated by adopting a passive attitude) the illegal transportation of prisoners on those flights? If so, since when has this been the case?

— What is the legal basis allowing prisoners to be transported *via* national territory by a third country? Has the Government ever authorised this kind of transportation? If so, what kind of assurances can it demand regarding the conditions under which these prisoners are held?

— Does the Government know of any landings on national territory of aircraft which may have carried such prisoners (eg on their way to the Guantanamo Bay base)? If so, please give details.

— Does the Government know of, or has it been passively or actively involved in, the carrying out of abductions by foreign secret services on national territory or that of other states? Have there been any judicial investigations into these cases? If so, what results have there been so far?

— Has the Government requested information from the American authorities regarding alleged flights to, from or over national territory by aircraft chartered by the CIA which may have been used for the illegal transportation of prisoners? If so, what replies has it received so far?

Appendix III

Letter of 15 December 2005 from Mr Dick Marty, Chairperson of the Committee on Legal Affairs and Human Rights to Mr Antonio La Pergola, President of the European Commission for Democracy through Law

. . .

As you are no doubt aware, I am preparing a report on "alleged secret detention centres in Council of Europe member states" (PACE Doc 10748 and document AS/Jur (2005) 52 rev 2, copies attached). In this context, I have been mandated by the Committee on Legal Affairs and Human Rights to request a Legal Opinion from the Venice Commission.

The Committee would appreciate receiving an Opinion with respect to the following two inter-related matters:

1. An assessment of the legality of secret detention in the light of Council of Europe member States' international law obligations, in particular the European Convention on Human Rights and the European Convention for the Prevention of Torture. In particular, to what extent is a State responsible if—actively or passively—it permits illegal detention or abduction by a third State or an agent thereof?

2. What are the legal obligations of Council of Europe member States, under human rights and general international law, regarding the transport of detainees by other States through their territory, including their airspace? What is the relationship between such obligations and possible countervailing obligations which derive from other treaties, including treaties concluded with non-member States?

Bearing in mind that my report is to be presented at the Assembly's session on 23- 27 January 2006, I would very much appreciate it if the said Legal Opinion, or at least an interim or provisional version thereof, could be provided to the Committee on Legal Affairs and Human Rights before the Assembly's January 2006 part-session.

. . .

Appendix IV

Communication of 21 November 2005 from the Secretary General of the Council of Europe to the Contracting Parties to the ECHR

Request for an explanation in accordance with Article 52 of the European Convention on Human Rights

The Secretary General of the Council of Europe,

Having regard to the Convention for the Protection of Human Rights and Fundamental Freedoms (hereafter referred to as "the Convention") and its Protocols;

Having regard also to the case law of the European Court of Human Rights which has given concrete expression to the rights and freedoms guaranteed thereunder and which has affirmed that the law and practice of the High Contracting Parties must comply with the provisions of the Convention and its additional Protocols;

Noting that there have been recent reports suggesting that individuals, notably persons suspected of involvement in acts of terrorism, may have been apprehended and detained, or transported while deprived of their liberty, by or at the instigation of foreign agencies, with the active or passive cooperation of High Contracting Parties to the Convention or by High Contracting Parties themselves at their own initiative, without such deprivation of liberty having been acknowledged;

Bearing in mind the fundamental importance of the safeguards contained in the Convention against arbitrary deprivation of liberty both in their own right and for the protection of the right to life and for upholding the absolute prohibition of torture or inhuman or degrading treatment or punishment;

Considering that, under Article 1 of the Convention, the High Contracting Parties shall secure to everyone within their jurisdiction the rights and freedoms guaranteed therein and that the participation, acquiescence or connivance of the authorities of a Contracting State in the acts of the agents of another State affecting Convention rights may engage the Contracting State's responsibility under the Convention and that such responsibility may also be engaged where that State's agents are acting *ultra vires* or contrary to instructions;

Considering also that unacknowledged deprivation of liberty raises serious questions concerning the effective implementation of, and compliance with, the Convention, notably its Articles 2, 3, 5, 6, 8, 13 and Article 2 of Protocol No. 4 to the Convention;

Acting on the basis of the powers conferred on him by virtue of Article 52 of the European Convention of Human Rights:

1. Requests the Governments of the High Contracting Parties to furnish an explanation of the manner in which their internal law ensures the effective implementation of the provisions of the Convention and its additional Protocols, as interpreted by the European Court of Human Rights, regarding the following specific issues:

- explanation of the manner in which their internal law ensures that acts by officials of foreign agencies within their jurisdiction are subject to adequate controls;
- explanation of the manner in which their internal law ensures that adequate safeguards exist to prevent unacknowledged deprivation of liberty of any person within their jurisdiction, whether such deprivation of liberty is linked to an action or an omission directly attributable to the High Contracting Party or whether that Party has aided or assisted the agents of another State in conduct amounting to such deprivation of liberty, including aid or assistance in the transportation by aircraft or otherwise of persons so deprived of their liberty;
- explanation of the manner in which their internal law provides an adequate response to any alleged infringements of Convention rights of individuals within their jurisdiction, notably in the context of deprivation of liberty, resulting from the conduct of officials of foreign agencies. In particular, explanation of the availability of effective investigations that are prompt, independent and capable of leading to the identification and sanctioning of those responsible for any illegal acts, including those responsible for aiding or assisting in the commission of such acts, and the payment of adequate compensation to victims;

In the context of the foregoing explanations, an explanation is requested as to whether, in the period running from 1 January 2002 (or from the moment of entry in force of the Convention if that occurred on a later date) until the present, any public official or other person acting in an official capacity has been involved in any manner—whether by action or omission—in the unacknowledged deprivation of liberty of any individual, or transport of any individual while so deprived of their liberty, including where such deprivation of liberty may have occurred by or at the instigation of any foreign agency. Information is to be provided on whether any official investigation is under way and/or on any completed investigation;

2. Requests that these explanations be provided by 21 February 2006.

DOCUMENT NO. 4

ALLEGED SECRET DETENTIONS AND UNLAWFUL INTER-STATE TRANSFERS OF DETAINEES INVOLVING COUNCIL OF EUROPE MEMBER STATES

Council of Europe's Committee on Legal Affairs and Human Rights

June 12, 2006

Summary

Our analysis of the CIA 'rendition' programme has revealed a network that resembles a 'spider's web' spun across the globe. The analysis is based on official information provided by national and international air traffic control authorities, as well as on other information. This 'web' is composed of several landing points, which we have subdivided into different categories, and which are linked up among themselves by civilian planes used by the CIA or military aircraft.

Analysis of the network's functioning and often individual cases allows us to make a number of conclusions both about human rights violations—some of which continue—and about the responsibilities of some Council of Europe Member states, which are bound by the European Convention on Human Rights and the European Convention for the Prevention of Torture.

The United States, an observer state of our Organisation, actually created this reprehensible network, which we criticise in light of the values shared on both sides of the Atlantic. But we also believe having established that it is only through the intentional or grossly negligent collusion of the European partners that this "web" was able to spread also over Europe.

Whilst hard evidence, at least according to the strict meaning of the word, is still not forthcoming, a number of coherent and converging elements indicate that secret detention centres have indeed existed and unlawful inter-state transfers have taken place in Europe. It is not intended to pronounce that the authorities of these countries are 'guilty' for having tolerated secret detention sites, but rather it is to hold them 'responsible' for failing to comply with the positive obligation to diligently investigate any serious allegation of fundamental rights violations.

The draft resolution and recommendation propose different measures so that terrorism can be fought effectively whilst respecting human rights at the same time.

A. Draft Resolution

1. The Council of Europe is both the point of reference and the guardian for human rights, democracy and respect for the rule of law in Europe. It draws its legal and moral authority from, *inter alia,* the common standards of human rights protection embodied in the European Convention on Human Rights (ECHR) and the European Convention on the Prevention of Torture (ECPT), to which all of its 46 member States subscribe.

2. The Parliamentary Assembly of the Council of Europe places human rights at the heart of its work. The Assembly must raise the alarm internationally whenever human rights are set aside, or when established standards of their application are undermined.

3. The Assembly reaffirms its absolute commitment to overcoming the threat of terrorism; but it must equally speak out in the strongest possible terms against the numerous and systematic human rights abuses committed in the pursuit of the so-called "war on terrorism". It considers that such violations play into the hands of the terrorists and ultimately serve to strengthen those who aim to destroy the established political, legal and social order.

4. The United States of America finds that neither the classic instruments of criminal law and procedure nor the framework of the laws of war (including respect for the Geneva Conventions) have been apt to address the terrorist threat. As a result, it has introduced new legal concepts, such as "enemy combatant" and "rendition", which were previously unheard of in international law and stand contrary to the basic legal principles that prevail on our continent.

5. Thus, across the world, the United States has progressively woven a clandestine "spider's web" of disappearances, secret detentions and unlawful inter-state transfers, often encompassing countries notorious for their use of torture. Hundreds of persons have become entrapped in this web, in some cases merely suspected of sympathising with a presumed terrorist organisation.

6. The "spider's web" has been spun out with the collaboration or tolerance of many countries, including several Council of Europe member States.

This co-operation, which took place in secret and without any democratic legitimacy, has spawned a system that is utterly incompatible with the fundamental principles of the Council of Europe.

7. The facts and information gathered to date, along with new factual patterns in the process of being uncovered, indicate that the key elements of this "spider's web" have notably included: a world-wide network of secret detentions on CIA "black sites" and in military or naval installations; the CIA's programme of "renditions", under which terrorist suspects are flown between States on civilian aircraft, outside of the scope of any legal protections, often to be handed over to States who customarily resort to degrading treatment and torture; and the use of military airbases and aircraft to transport detainees as human cargo to Guantanamo Bay in Cuba or to other detention centres.

8. The Assembly condemns the systematic exclusion of all forms of judicial protection and regrets that, by depriving hundreds of suspects of their basic rights, including the right to a fair trial, the United States has done a disservice to the cause of justice and has tarnished its own hard-won reputation as a beacon of the defence of civil liberties and human rights.

9. Some Council of Europe member States have knowingly colluded with the United States to carry out these unlawful operations; some others have tolerated them or simply turned a blind eye. They have also gone to great lengths to ensure that such operations remain secret and protected from effective national or international scrutiny.

10. This collusion with the United States of America by some Council of Europe member States has taken several different forms. Having carried out legal and factual analysis on a range of cases of alleged secret detentions and unlawful inter-state transfers, the Assembly has identified instances in which Council of Europe member States have acted in one or several of the following ways, wilfully or at least recklessly in violation of their international human rights obligations, as explained in the explanatory memorandum[1]:

10.1. secretly detaining a person on European territory for an indefinite period of time, whilst denying that person's basic human rights and failing to ensure procedural legal guarantees such as *habeas corpus;*

10.2. capturing a person and handing the person over to the United States, in the knowledge that such a person would be unlawfully transferred into a US-administered detention facility;

[1] See Doc . . .

10.3. permitting the unlawful transportation of detainees on civilian aircraft carrying out "renditions" operations, travelling through European airspace or across European territory;

10.4. passing on information or intelligence to the United States where it was foreseeable that such material would be relied upon directly to carry out a "rendition" operation or to hold a person in secret detention;

10.5. participating directly in interrogations of persons subjected to "rendition", or held in secret detention;

10.6. accepting or making use of information gathered in the course of detainee interrogations, before, during or after which the detainee in question was threatened or subjected to torture or other forms of human rights abuse;

10.7. making available civilian airports or military airfields as "staging points" or platforms for rendition or other unlawful detainee transfer operations, whereby an aircraft prepares for and takes off on its operation from such a point;

10.8. making available civilian airports or military airfields as "stopover points" for rendition operations, whereby an aircraft lands briefly at such a point on the outward or homeward flight, for example to refuel.

11. Attempts to expose the true nature and extent of these unlawful operations have invariably faced obstruction or dismissal, from the United States and its European partners alike. The authorities of most Council of Europe member States have denied their participation, in many cases without actually having carried out any inquiries or serious investigations.

12. In other instances such attempts have been thwarted on the grounds of national security or state secrecy. The Assembly takes the view that neither national security nor state secrecy can be invoked in such a sweeping, systematic fashion as to shield these unlawful operations from robust parliamentary and judicial scrutiny.

13. The Assembly highlights the widespread breach of the positive obligations of all Council of Europe member States to investigate such allegations in a full and thorough manner. It has now been demonstrated incontestably, by numerous well-documented and convergent facts, that secret detentions and unlawful interstate transfers involving European countries have taken place, such as to require in-depth inquiries and urgent responses by the executive and legislative branches of all the countries concerned.

14. While the Assembly has been seized in this instance with looking into allegations concerning very specific facts, it cannot ignore other allegations

surrounding the existence of other secret detention centres in Europe, apparently also set up in the context of the "war on terrorism". In particular, the Assembly expresses its deep concern at the continued reports of secret detentions in the North Caucasus. The European Committee for the Prevention of Torture issued a Public Statement on this subject in 2003, which was recently supplemented by new, detailed victim testimony and credible allegations from non-governmental organisations. Further serious investigation and analysis of secret detentions in the North Caucasus is clearly required.

15. The Assembly also regrets that detention centres in Kosovo were not accessible, until very recently, to the European Committee for the Prevention of Torture. The lack of access seems all the more unacceptable in light of the fact that the international community intervened in that region with the declared aim of restoring order, peace and the respect for human rights.

16. The Assembly's central objective is to prevent violations of the sort described in this resolution from occurring in the future.

17. The Assembly therefore commends the Secretary General of the Council of Europe for the swift and thorough use of his power of inquiry under Article 52 ECHR.

18. The Assembly calls upon the member States of the Council of Europe to:

18.1. undertake a critical review of the legal framework that regulates the intelligence services, with the dual objective of enhancing their efficiency and strengthening accountability mechanisms against abuse; clear regulations must also govern co-operation with foreign services and the activities of foreign services on national territory;

18.2. ensure that the laws governing state secrecy protect persons who disclose illegal activities of state organs (so-called "whistle-blowers") from disciplinary or criminal sanctions;

18.3. undertake a review of bilateral agreements signed between Council of Europe member States and the United States, particularly those on the status of US forces stationed in Europe and on the use of military and other infrastructures, to ensure that these agreements conform fully to applicable international human rights norms;

18.4. urge the United States to dismantle its system of secret detentions and unlawful inter-state transfers and to co-operate more closely with the Council of Europe in establishing common means of overcoming the threat of terrorism in line with international human rights standards and respect for the rule of law.

19. The Assembly also calls on the United States of America, which is an Observer State to the Council of Europe and Europe's long-standing ally in resisting tyranny and defending human rights and the rule of law, to:

19.1. send a strong message to the world by demonstrating that terrorism can be vanquished by lawful means, thereby proving the superiority of the democratic model founded on respect of human dignity;

19.2. co-operate more closely in identifying and employing the most effective means with which to prevent and suppress the terrorist threat in conformity with international human rights norms and the rule of law;

19.3. align its definitions of torture and other cruel, inhuman or degrading treatment with the definition used by the UN Committee Against Torture;

19.4. prohibit the transfer of persons suspected of involvement in terrorism to countries that practise torture and that fail to guarantee the right to a fair trial;

19.5. issue official apologies and award compensation to the victims of illegal detentions against whom no formal accusations, nor any court proceedings, have ever been brought;

19.6. refrain from prosecuting any officials, former officials or journalists who, by providing testimony or other information, have helped to bring to light the system of unlawful detentions and mistreatment.

20. The Assembly calls upon its Committee on Legal Affairs and Human Rights urgently to establish an ad hoc Sub-Committee to continue this inquiry into alleged secret detentions and unlawful inter-state transfers involving Council of Europe member States, in view of new facts that are still in the process of being uncovered.

21. The Assembly further urges its members to call for rigorous inquiries in their respective national parliaments, especially in those States from which no or insufficient information has been forthcoming.

22. The Assembly recognises, in the context of the present inquiry into secret detentions, that it lacks appropriate investigative powers akin to those provided to parliamentary inquiries in member States, including the powers to subpoena witnesses and compel disclosure of documents, and calls for consideration of this issue.

23. Finally, the Assembly expresses its appreciation to the relevant European Union institutions (European Commission, European Parliament and EU Satellite Centre), as well as to Eurocontrol, for their invaluable contributions

to this inquiry, whilst reiterating the Council of Europe's role as the guardian of human rights throughout Europe.

B. Draft Recommendation

1. The Parliamentary Assembly refers to its Resolution . . . (2006) on alleged secret detentions and unlawful inter-state transfers involving Council of Europe member states.

2. The Assembly also recalls its Resolution 1433 (2005) and its recommendation on the legality of the detention of persons by the United States in Guantanamo Bay.

3. The Assembly urges the Committee of Ministers to draft a recommendation to Council of Europe member States containing:

> common measures to guarantee more effectively the human rights of persons suspected of terrorist offences who are captured from, detained in or transported through Council of Europe member States; and
>
> a set of minimum requirements for "human rights protection clauses", for inclusion in bilateral and multilateral agreements with third parties, especially those concerning the use of military installations on the territory of Council of Europe member States.

4. The Assembly urgently requests that:

4.1. an initiative be launched on an international level, expressly involving the United States, an Observer to the Council of Europe, to develop a common, truly global strategy to address the terrorist threat. The strategy should conform in all its elements with the fundamental principles of our common heritage in terms of democracy, human rights and respect for the rule of law;

4.2. a proposal be considered, in instances where States are unable or unwilling to prosecute persons accused of terrorist acts, to bring these persons within the jurisdiction of an international court that is competent to try them. One possibility worth considering would be to vest such a competence in the International Criminal Court, whilst renewing invitations to join the Court to the United States and other countries that have not yet done so.

5. The Assembly finally recommends that the Committee of Ministers should consider means of improving the Council of Europe's ability to react rapidly and effectively to allegations of systematic human rights abuse involving several member States.

C. Explanatory memorandum

by Mr Dick Marty, Rapporteur

1. Are Human Rights Little More Than a Fairweather Option?

1.1. 11 September 2001

1. The tragedies that took place on 11 September 2001 undoubtedly marked the beginning of an important new chapter in the terrible, never-ending history of terrorism. It is a history of indiscriminate violence, instigated in order to create a climate of insecurity and fear with the intention of attacking the existing political and social system. For the first time, spectacular and extremely lethal acts struck highly symbolic targets at the very heart of the United States of America, the most powerful state in the world. Europe, for its part, already has a long and painful experience of terrorism, involving numerous victims and large-scale attacks, particularly in Italy[2], Germany, Spain, the United Kingdom, France and, more recently, Russia.

2. While the states of the Old World have dealt with these threats primarily by means of existing institutions and legal systems[3], the United States appears to have made a fundamentally different choice: considering that neither conventional judicial instruments nor those established under the framework of the laws of war could effectively counter the new forms of international terrorism, it decided to develop new legal concepts. The latter are based primarily on the *Military Order on the Detention, Treatment, and Trial of Certain Non-Citizens in the War against Terrorism* signed by President Bush on 13 November 2001[4]. It is significant that, to date, only one person has been summoned before the courts to answer for the 11 September attacks: a person, moreover, who was already in prison on that day, and had been in the hands of the justice system for several months[5]. By contrast, hundreds of other people are still deprived of their liberty, under American authority but outside the national territory, within an unclear normative framework. Their detention is, in any event, altogether contrary to the principles enshrined in all the international legal instruments dealing with respect for fundamental rights, including the domestic law of the

[2] More than 14 500 politically motivated acts of violence were recorded in Italy between 1969 and 1987, causing 419 deaths and 1181 casualties (Interior Ministry figures).

[3] We may recall the words of the former President of Italy, Sandro Pertini (albeit translated in paraphrased form): *"Italy can proudly say that it has defeated terrorism in the law courts, rather than resorting to "stadium justice"*.

[4] Regarding the various decisions taken by the American administration following the 11 September attacks, I refer readers to the excellent report by Kevin McNamara, *Lawfulness of Detentions by the United States in Guantanamo Bay,* accompanying the resolution and recommendation adopted by the PACE on 26 April 2005 (Doc 10497).

[5] The person in question is Zacarias Moussaoui, a French citizen of Moroccan descent, sentenced to life imprisonment by a Virginia grand jury on 3 May 2006; the jurors did not impose the death penalty sought by the federal prosecutors (thereby avoiding the trap set by the defendant, who clearly wished to be sentenced to death so as to appear a martyr). According to an American government document, now declassified, six important Al-Qaeda members directly involved in the organisation and funding of the 11 September attacks have apparently been captured by the United States. Although more heavily involved than Moussaoui, they have not been summoned before the American courts to answer for their actions (see also *Le Monde* of 22 April 2006).

United States (which explains the existence of such detention centres outside the country). The following headline appears to be an accurate summary of the current administration's approach: *No Trials for Key Players: Government prefers to interrogate bigger fish in terrorism cases rather than charge them*[6].

3. This legal approach is utterly alien to the European tradition and sensibility, and is clearly contrary to the European Convention on Human Rights and the Universal Declaration of Human Rights. Cicero's old adage, *inter arma silent leges,* appears to have left its mark even on international bodies supposed to ensure the rule of law and the fair administration of justice. It is frankly alarming to see the UN Security Council sacrificing essential principles pertaining to fundamental rights in the name of the fight against terrorism. The compilation of so-called "black lists" of individuals and companies suspected of maintaining connections with organisations considered terrorist and the application of the associated sanctions clearly breach every principle of the fundamental right to a fair trial: no specific charges, no right to be heard, no right of appeal, no established procedure for removing one's name from the list[7].

1.2. Guantanamo Bay

4. At Guantanamo Bay, on the island of Cuba, several hundred people are being detained without enjoying any of the guarantees provided for in the criminal procedure of a state governed by the rule of law or by the Geneva Conventions on the law of war. These people have been arrested in unknown circumstances, handed over by foreign authorities without any extradition procedure being followed, or illegally abducted in various countries by United States special services. They are considered "enemy combatants", according to a new definition introduced by the American administration[8].

5. The Parliamentary Assembly of the Council of Europe (PACE) has strongly criticised this state of affairs: on 26 April 2005, it unanimously adopted Resolution 1433 (2005) and Recommendation 1699 (2005) in which it urges the United States Government to put a stop to this situation and to ensure respect for the principles of the rule of law and human rights. It also concludes that *"the United States has engaged in the unlawful practice*

---

[6] Los Angeles Times of 4 May 2006.

[7] A motion raising the issue of the UN black lists (Doc 10856) has been referred to the PACE Committee on Legal Affairs and Human Rights, which will submit a report on the subject in the near future.

[8] Following an injunction by an American court, based on the provisions of press law, in April 2006 the Pentagon published, for the first time, a list of the names and nationalities of 558 people detained at Guantanamo. However, no details are given for some 140 people previously detained but no longer imprisoned at Guantanamo on that date. Furthermore, no outside body can confirm whether this list is actually comprehensive.

of secret detention". In its reply of 17 June 2005 (Doc 10585), the Committee of Ministers expresses *"its full support to all such efforts and to all efforts to obtain a prompt release or fair trial of persons detained at Guantanamo Bay by an independent and impartial court. It urges the United States Government to ensure that the rights of all detainees are ensured and that the principle of the rule of law is fully respected. For its own part, it expresses the determination of the member States to ensure that the rights of persons released and returned to their jurisdiction are fully respected"*. The Committee of Ministers has conveyed a message in these terms to the Government of the United States of America[9]. To our knowledge, no reply has been received to date.

6. The UN Committee against Torture has also called for the closure of the Guantanamo Bay detention facility in recent times, criticising its secret character and the denial of access to the ICRC[10].

1.3. Secret CIA Prisons in Europe?

7. This was the news item circulated in early November 2005 by the American NGO Human Rights Watch (HRW), the Washington Post and the ABC television channel. Whereas the Washington Post did not name specific countries hosting, or allegedly having hosted, such detention centres, simply referring generically to "eastern European democracies", HRW reported that the countries in question are Poland and Romania. On 5 December 2005, ABC News in turn reported the existence of secret detention centres in Poland and Romania, which had apparently been closed following the Washington Post's revelations. According to ABC, 11 suspects detained in these centres had been subjected to the harshest interrogation techniques (so-called "enhanced interrogation techniques') before being transferred to CIA facilities in North Africa.

8. It is interesting to recall that this ABC report, confirming the use of secret detention camps in Poland and Romania by the CIA, was available on the Internet for only a very short time before being withdrawn following the intervention of lawyers on behalf of the network's owners. The Washington Post subsequently admitted that it had been in possession of the names of the countries, but had refrained from naming them further to an agreement entered into with the authorities. It is thus established that considerable

---

[9] The United States has enjoyed observer status with the Committee of Ministers since 10 January 1996.

[10] See Press Release of the United Nations Office at Geneva, *CAT Concludes Thirty-Sixth* Session, 19 May 2006: "The Committee was concerned by allegations that the State party had established secret detention facilities, which were not accessible to the International Committee of the Red Cross. The Committee recommended that the United States cease to detain any person at Guantanamo Bay and that it close that detention facility, permit access by the detainees to judicial process or release them as soon as possible, ensuring that they were not returned to any State where they could face a real risk of being tortured"; available at: *http://www.unog.ch/unog/website/newsmedia.nsf/(httpNewsBvYear en)/5FBB9C351B9E70EBC1257173004EB4CE?O penDocument.*

pressure was brought to bear to ensure that these countries were not named. It is unclear what arguments prevailed on the media outlets in question to convince them to comply. What is certain is that these are troubling developments that throw into question the principles of the freedom and independence of the press. In this light, it is worth noting that just before the publication of the original revelations by the reporter Dana Priest in early November 2005, the Executive Editor of the Washington Post was invited for an audience at the White House with President Bush[11].

1.4. The Council of Europe's Response

9. The Council of Europe responded straight away. The President of the PACE immediately took a very firm position, and asked the Committee on Legal Affairs and Human Rights to look into the matter without delay. The latter did so at its meeting of 7 November 2005. The Secretary General of the Council, for his part, set in motion the procedure established by Article 52 of the European Convention on Human Rights (ECHR). The Committee on Legal Affairs and Human Rights also requested the Venice Commission to prepare an opinion on the international legal obligations and duties of Council of Europe member States in respect of secret detention facilities and inter-state transport of prisoners. Cooperation was likewise established with the Council of Europe's Human Rights Commissioner.

10. The European Union Commission, via its Vice-President Franco Frattini, expressed its full support for the Council of Europe. The EU Commission's support proved invaluable in obtaining the necessary information from Eurocontrol and the European Union Satellite Centre. The reference to named European countries suddenly aroused huge media interest. Yet these incidents—secret detentions and "renditions" -had already been attracting condemnation for some time, both from the PACE itself, *inter alia* through the aforementioned resolution and recommendation concerning Guantanamo Bay, the re-reading of which I cannot recommend highly enough, and in extremely detailed reports by NGOs, university professors and journalists known for their very painstaking work[12]. These revelations had met with curious indifference from the media, governments and political circles in general.

---

[11] This meeting, along with several similar instances, was reported in a column in the Washington Post at the end of 2005. Leonard Downie, the Executive Editor of the Washington Post, said: "*We met with them on more than one occasion . . . The meetings were off the record for the purpose of discussing national security issues in [Dana Priest's] story*". See Howard Kurtz, "Bush Presses Editors on Security", *The Washington Post*, 26 December 2005; available at http://www.washingtonpost.com/wp-dyn/content/article/2005/12/25/AR2005122500665_pf.html.

[12] These include the Human Rights Watch Breifing Paper of October 2004 entitled *The United States' 'Disappeared': The CIA's Long-Term Ghost Detainees;* and the Amnesty International report AMR 51/051/2006 of 5 April 2006, entitled *Below the radar: secret flights to torture and "disappearance"*, as well

1.5. European Parliament

11. Members of the European Parliament also became alarmed at the mounting evidence that European countries, or at least facilities located on European territory, had been the scene of systematic human rights violations. In early 2006, a 46-member Temporary Committee was set up and instructed to investigate the alleged existence of CIA prisons in Europe in which terrorist suspects had allegedly been detained and tortured[13].

12. I welcomed this initiative in my previous memorandum, considering it wholly consistent with the Council of Europe's desire to ascertain the truth. Co-operation with the Temporary Committee has been extremely satisfactory, both at the level of our respective secretariats and with its Chairman, Carlos Miguel Coelho, and rapporteur, Claudio Fava. I had the opportunity to address members of the European Parliament's committee during one of its first public hearings.

13. On 24 April 2006 the Temporary Committee presented its draft interim report, which confirmed strong indications of illegal actions carried out by the CIA in Europe. In its initial analysis, the report largely supported the observations we made in our own *Information Memorandum II* on 24 January 2006. The TDIP rapporteur Claudio Fava, in presenting his interim report, spoke of *"more than a thousand flights chartered by the CIA [that] have transited through Europe, often in order to carry out extraordinary renditions"*[14]. In a press conference, Mr Fava clarified that, according to information given to him in confidence by an intelligence source, *"30 to 50 people have been rendered by the CIA in Europe"* and that *"the CIA could not have carried out such renditions*

---

as numerous articles describing in detail the new techniques for fighting terrorism, such as *extraordinary renditions;* for instance, the articles in the *Corriere della Sera* by Paolo Biondani and Guido Olimpio, which the latter has compiled and edited in a well-researched book *(Operazione Hotel California,* Feltrinelli, 2005), along with articles by Stephen Grey *(America's Gulag,* The New Statesman, 17 May 2004; *US Accused of Torture Flights,* The Sunday Times, 14 November 2004; *Les Etats-Unis inventent la délocalisation de la torture,* Le Monde Diplomatique, April 2005); Alfred McCoy *(Cruel Science: CIA Torture and U.S. Foreign Policy,* New England Journal of Public Policy, Boston, 2004, an article subsequently expanded and published in book form, and also published in German under the title *Foltern und foltern lassen,* Zweitauseneins, 2005; *Torture by Proxy: International and Domestic Law Applicable to "Extraordinary Renditions",* report published in 2004 by the Committee on International Human Rights of the Association of the Bar of the City of New York and the Center for Human Rights and Global Justice, New York University School of Law, the conclusions of which could not be clearer: *"Extraordinary Rendition is an illegal practice under both domestic and international law, and that, consistent with U.S. policy against torture, the U.S. government is duty bound to cease all acts of Extraordinary Rendition, to investigate Extraordinary Renditions that have already taken place, and to prosecute and punish those found to have engaged in acts that amount to crimes in connection with Extraordinary Rendition."*

[13] Temporary Committee on the Alleged Use of European Countries by the CIA for the Transport and Illegal Detention of Prisoners (TDIP; *http://www.europarl.eu.int/comparl/tempcom/tdip/default_en.htm*).

[14] See *Le Monde,* 27 April 2006.

without the agreement of European states"[15]. The Temporary Committee proposes to continue its work[16].

1.6. Rapporteur or Investigator?

14. I have often been described as an "investigator", or even a "special investigator". It might be helpful to point out, therefore, that I do not enjoy any specific investigatory powers and, in particular, am not entitled to use coercive methods or to require the release of specific documents. My work has consequently consisted primarily of interviews and analysis. I submitted a set of questions to governments via their national parliamentary delegations, and asked the latter to take the debate to the national level. Parliamentary questions were thereby tabled in many states with a view to obtaining information from the various governments. Special parliamentary commissions of inquiry were set up in some countries. The work undertaken by a number of NGOs has proven invaluable and even, in many cases, more detailed and reliable than the information supplied by governments. A significant contribution was also made by many journalists investigating on the ground, often for months on end. I also received information entrusted to me only on the assurance that I would keep it confidential and protect my sources. The information thus received clearly cannot be presented as evidence; it did, however, point my research in certain more specific directions, and enables me to state with certainty that the search for the truth about what really happened to terrorist suspects in Europe will not end with the present report.

15. I received considerable assistance in this task from the head of the secretariat of the Committee on Legal Affairs and Human Rights and one of his colleagues—both of whom were already very busy with other tasks connected with the committee's operation and work with other rapporteurs—as well as from another young colleague who, in the end, was temporarily assigned specifically to this investigation (and whose help proved invaluable). I am extremely grateful to them for their outstanding competence and exceptional readiness to assist.

16. I was formally designated as Rapporteur on 13 December 2005. Within the Council of Europe it was considered that the report should be presented as quickly as possible. Taking into account the breadth and complexity of the subject, as well as the extremely modest means put at my disposal, I have certainly not been able to present a complete overview of the different

[15] See *Le Monde*, 18 May 2006.

[16] The draft resolution of the European Parliament, produced as an annex to the interim report, can be consulted at: *http://www.europarl.europa.eu/comparl/tempcom/tdip/interim report_en.pdf*. I should like to thank the Temporary Committee and its Rapporteur, Mr Fava, for having made it possible for a member of my team to join their visits to Macedonia and the United States.

aspects of what has really occurred. Moreover, we are still far from knowing all the details of "extraordinary renditions" and the conditions in which abducted persons have been detained and interrogated in Europe. It is thus highly likely that the Council of Europe should remain seized on this subject matter. Elements presently in the public domain—which are supplemented with new information as every week goes by—not only justify, but require that member States finally decide to open serious inquiries on the extent to which they were directly or indirectly implicated in such activities.

17. As I stated in my previous memorandum, serious consideration must be given to whether the Assembly should equip itself with other resources for dealing with such complex matters. Where investigations relate to possible human rights violations that are not confined to individual cases (for which the European Court of Human Rights has jurisdiction) and transcend borders, thereby sidestepping national procedures, one is justified in questioning the effectiveness of existing instruments. Instead of appointing a single member as rapporteur with the support of the normal resources of the Committee's secretariat, which is already overwhelmed by other reports in preparation, we might seriously consider whether setting up a proper commission of inquiry, assisted by experts and enjoying genuine investigatory powers, might not be a better solution for dealing with these new and important challenges.

18. We have tackled this problem with determination and a constant concern for objectivity, mindful of both the enormity of the task entrusted to me and the frankly derisory resources available and the risk of being manipulated. My aim was by no means to amass evidence for the purpose of condemning or stigmatising. On the contrary, I was guided by a desire to ascertain the truth in order to reaffirm the values the Council of Europe has always striven to uphold, and to guard against the repetition of such incidents.

1.7. Is this an Anti-American Exercise?

19. I consider this reproach, made fairly frequently when criticisms are voiced about violations of fundamental rights committed in the context of the fight against terrorism, downright ridiculous and wholly inaccurate. It overlooks the fact that the initial criticisms, relating to the establishment of the detention centre at Guantanamo Bay as well as the use of *extraordinary renditions* and torture, were first forcefully expressed by American journalists, NGOs and politicians, often thanks to detailed information released by sources within the administration, and indeed the intelligence services themselves. The debate has been, and in my view still is, considerably more heated in the United States than in Europe, at least in certain circles and media.

20. Moreover, the United States Supreme Court itself pointed out, in an extraordinary June 2004 judgment, that *"at stake in this case is nothing less than the essence of a free society. (. . .) For if this Nation is to remain true to the ideals symbolized by its flag, it must not wield the tools of tyrants even to resist an assault by the forces of tyranny"*[17]. This is a sharp reminder of the great democratic tradition of the United States and its exemplary commitment to human rights. The United States is, and remains, a deeply democratic country. Indeed, criticisms of some of the current administration's decisions also reflect a concern that a country which unquestionably serves as an example to the rest of the world is committing what we consider to be mistakes that not only violate fundamental principles, but also constitute a counterproductive anti-terrorism strategy.

1.8. Is there any Evidence?

21. It is paradoxical to expect bodies without any real investigatory powers—the Council of Europe and the European Parliament—to adduce evidence in the legal sense. Indeed, these European bodies have been prompted to undertake such investigations owing to a lack of willingness and commitment on the part of national institutions that could, and should, have completely clarified these allegations which from the outset did not appear to be totally unfounded.

22. At this stage there is no formal evidence of the existence of secret CIA detention centres in Poland, Romania or other Council of Europe member States, even though serious indications continue to exist and grow stronger. Nevertheless, it is clear that an unspecified number of persons, deemed to be members or accomplices of terrorist movements, were arbitrarily and unlawfully arrested and/or detained and transported under the supervision of services acting in the name, or on behalf, of the American authorities. These incidents took place in airports and in European airspace, and were made possible either by seriously negligent monitoring or by the more or less active participation of one or more government departments of Council of Europe member States.

23. In the light of the silence and obvious reluctance on the part of the bodies that could have provided the necessary information, it is legitimate to assume that there are more such cases than can be proven at present. In effect, the facts as would appear to be established today—and as will be illustrated throughout the report—as well as the total absence of serious inquiries by the national authorities concerned, implies, in my view, the reversal of the burden of proof: in such a situation it is incumbent on the Polish and Romanian authorities to conduct an independent and in-depth

[17] These are the words of Judge Sandra Day O'Connor in the case of Jose Padilla, judgement of the United States Supreme Court, 28 June 2004.

inquiry and to make public not only its results but also the method and the different stages of the enquiry[18]. Even if proof, in the classical meaning of the term, is not as yet available, a number of coherent and converging elements indicate that such secret detention centres did indeed exist in Europe. Such an affirmation does not pretend to be a judgment of a criminal court, necessitating "proof beyond reasonable doubt" in the Anglo-Saxon meaning of the term; it rather reflects a conviction based on a careful balance of probabilities, as well as logical deductions from clearly established facts. The intention is not to determine that the authorities of these countries are "guilty" for having tolerated secret detention sites, but rather to hold them "responsible" for failing to comply with the positive obligation to investigate serious allegations.

2. The Global "Spider's Web"19

24. The system of targeting, apprehending and detaining terrorist suspects, which forms the focus of this report, was not created overnight. Nor has it been built up from scratch in the wake of the terrorist attacks of 11 September 2001.

25. I have chosen to adopt the metaphor of a global "spider's web" as the *leitmotif for* my report. It is a web that has been spun out incrementally over several years, using tactics and techniques that have had to be developed in response to new theatres of war, new terms of engagement and an unpredictable threat.

26. The chief architect of the web, the United States of America, has long possessed the capacity to capture individual targets abroad and carry them to different parts of the world. Through its Central Intelligence Agency (CIA), the United States designed a programme known as "rendition" for this purpose in the mid-1990s. The CIA aimed to take terrorist suspects in foreign countries "off the streets" by transporting them back to other countries, usually their home countries, where they were wanted for trial, or for detention without any form of due process.

---

[18] Reversal of the burden of proof if the authorities concerned do not discharge their positive duty to investigate is not a new idea: Article 39 of the Rules of Procedure of the Inter-American Commission of Human Rights provides that *"The facts alleged in the petition, the pertinent parts of which have been transmitted to the State in question, shall be presumed to be true if the State has not provided responsive information during the maximum period set by the Commission under the provisions of Article 38 of these Rules of Procedure, as long as other evidence does not lead to a different conclusion"*. At the Council of Europe, this idea was applied in the Independent Experts' report to the Secretary General (by Mr Alkema and Mr Trechsel) on political prisoners in Azerbaijan (doc. SG/Inf (2001) 34 Addendum I), in which it was stated that the cases concerned had been submitted to the authorities for comments and observations and that, in the absence of substantive observations by the authorities, the experts had had to base their findings on plausible allegations from other sources (idem, p. 20).

[19] This section should be read in conjunction with the graphic map annexed to this explanatory memorandum, entitled: *The global "spider's web" of secret detentions and unlawful inter-state transfers.*

2.1. The Evolution of the Rendition Programme

27. During a recent mission to the United States, a member of my team came into contact with several "insider sources" in the US intelligence community. The most prominent such witness was Mr Michael Scheuer, who designed the original rendition programme in the 1990s under the Clinton Administration and remained employed by the CIA until November 2004[20]. Excerpts of Mr Scheuer's testimony are reflected verbatim in this report and, to the extent possible, have been substantiated or corroborated by a range of other source material in the account below.[21]

28. The strategic target of the CIA rendition programme has always been, and remains, the global terrorist network known as Al-Qaeda. In the conception of the United States, Al-Qaeda exists as a nebulous collection of "cells" in countries around the world, comprising "operatives" who perform various roles in the preparation of terrorist attacks. When the US National Security Council became alarmed, in 1995, at what appeared to be a serious prospect of Osama bin Laden acquiring weapons of mass destruction, it developed rendition, according to Scheuer and others, as a way of *"breaking down Al-Qaeda"*, *"taking down cells"* and *"incarcerating senior Al-Qaeda people"*.

29. Rendition was designed, at the outset of the programme at least, to fit within the United States' interpretation of its legal obligations[22]. The prerequisites for launching a rendition operation in the pre-9/11 period included:

- an "outstanding legal process" against the suspect, usually connected to terrorist offences in his country of origin;
- a CIA "dossier", or profile of the suspect, based on prior intelligence and in principle reviewed by lawyers;

---

[20] Mr Michael Scheuer was Chief of the Bin Laden Unit in the CIA Counter-Terrorism Center for four years, from August 1995 to June 1999. He then served for a further three years, from September 2001 to November 2004, as Special Advisor to the Chief of the Bin Laden Unit. He is recognised as one of the most important authorities on the evolution of rendition. Mr Scheuer graciously granted my representative a three-hour personal interview in Washington, DC in May 2006. Unlike many intelligence sources with whom my team spoke, he agreed to go "on the record", talking extensively about his first-hand operational experience of the rendition programme. A transcript of the interview is on file with the Rapporteur. Excerpts are cited in this report as follows: "Michael Scheuer, former Chief of the Bin Laden Unit in the CIA Counter-Terrorism Center".

[21] I also wish to recognise the valuable work of various non-governmental organisations and academic institutions in researching the evolution of rendition and to thank them for meeting with my team to relay their insights first-hand. In particular, the following groups have produced papers that I have consulted extensively: The Center for Human Rights and Global Justice at New York University School of Law, Human Rights First, Amnesty International, Human Rights Watch and Cage Prisoners.

[22] For further detail on the United States' interpretation of its international legal obligations, see the section below entitled *The point of view of the United States*, at heading 10.1.

- a "country willing to help" in the apprehension of the suspect on its territory; and
- "somewhere to take him after he was arrested".

30. The receiving countries were, as a matter of policy, only asked to provide diplomatic assurances to the United States that they would "treat the suspects according to their own national laws". After the transfer, the United States made no effort to assess the manner in which the detainees were subsequently treated[23].

31. Intelligence gathering, according to Scheuer, was not considered to be a priority in the pre-9/11 programme:

> *"It was never intended to talk to any of these people. Success, at least as the Agency defined it, was to get someone, who was a danger to us or our allies, 'off the street' and, when we got him, to grab whatever documents he had with him. We knew that once he was captured he had been trained to either fabricate or to give us a great deal of information that we would chase for months and it would lead nowhere. So interrogations were always a very minor concern before 9/11."*[24]

32. Several current Council of Europe member States are known to have co-operated closely with the United States in the operation of its rendition programme under the Clinton Administration[25]. Indeed, the United Kingdom Government has indicated to the Council of Europe[26] that a system of prior notification existed in the 1990s, whereby even intended stopovers or overflights were reported by the United States in advance of each rendition operation[27].

33. The act of "rendition" may not *per se* constitute a breach of international human rights law. It is worth noting that other States have also asserted their right to apprehend a terrorist suspect on foreign territory in order to

---

[23] In my *Information Memorandum II* in January, I quoted several former CIA agents who indicate that the United States knew some of the treatment of detainees would flout minimum standards of protection in international law. Mr Scheuer simply told my representative: *"I check my moral qualms at the door"*.

[24] Michael Scheuer, former Chief of the Bin Laden Unit in the CIA Counter-Terrorism Center, interview carried out by the Rapporteur's representative, *supra* note 19.

[25] See Jane Mayer, *Outsourcing Torture: The secret history of America's "extraordinary rendition" program,* in The New Yorker, 14 and 21 February 2005. Mayer refers to well-documented cases of rendition in which Croatia (1995) and Albania (1998) collaborated with the United States in apprehending suspects; at pages 109-110. Mr Scheuer gave a further example involving Germany, in which a suspect named Mahmood Salim, alias Abu Hajer, was arrested by Bavarian police.

[26] See Jack Straw, Secretary of State for Foreign and Commonwealth Affairs, *Written Ministerial Statement—Enquiries in respect of rendition allegations,* appended to the Response of the United Kingdom Government to the Request of the Secretary-General for an explanation in accordance with Article 52 ECHR, available at: *http://www.coe.int/T/E/Com/Files/Events/2006-cia/United-Kinqdom.pdf.*

[27] *Ibid.* Mr Straw states: "There were four cases in 1998 where the US requested permission to render one or more detainees through the UK or Overseas Territories. In two of these cases, records show the Government granted the request, and refused two others."

bring him to justice if the tool of international judicial assistance or cooperation did not attain the desired result[28].

34. The most prominent legal authorities in the United States, including its Supreme Court, have interpreted the object of the pre-9/11 rendition programme to be within the law[29]. Indeed, several human rights NGOs have assessed the original practice under the rubric of "rendition to justice", conceding that an inter-state transfer could be lawful if its object is to bring a suspect within a recognised judicial process respectful of human rights[30]. This indicator might in fact provide a legal benchmark against which unlawful inter-state transfers can be measured[31].

35. However, there has clearly been a critical deviation away from notions of justice in the rendition programme. In the wake of the 9/11 attacks, the United States transformed rendition into one of a range of instruments with which to pursue its so-called "war on terror". The attacks of 9/11 genuinely signalled something of a watershed in the United States approach to overcoming the terrorist threat[32]. This new "war on terrorism" was launched by the military intervention in Afghanistan in October 2001. At the same time new importance was attached to the collection of intelligence on persons suspected of terrorism. The CIA was put under pressure to play a more proactive role in the detention and interrogation of suspects rather than just putting them "behind bars". Without appropriate preparation, a global policy of arresting and detaining "the enemies" of the United States was—still according to Scheuer—improvised hastily. It was up to the lawyers to "legitimise" these operations, whilst the CIA and the American military became the principal supervisors and operators of the system[33].

---

[28] See US Secretary of State Condoleeza Rice, *Remarks upon her departure for Europe,* Andrews Air Force Base, 5 December 2005. Ms Rice refers to France's actions in the case of "Carlos the Jackal": "A rendition by the French government brought him to justice in France, where he is now imprisoned."

[29] See *United States v. Alvarez-Machain,* 504 U.S. 655 (1992), in which the Supreme Court upheld the jurisdiction of a US court to try a man brought to the US from Mexico by means of abduction rather than extradition. Case law on this matter dates back to the 1886 case of *Ker v. Illinois,* 119 U.S. 436 (1886), in which the Supreme Court said: "There is nothing in the Constitution that requires a court to permit a guilty person rightfully convicted to escape justice because he was brought to trial against his will."

[30] This concept of "rendition to justice" is discussed in greater detail in: Center for Human Rights and Global Justice, NYU School of Law, *Beyond Guantanamo: Transfers to Torture One Year after Rasul v. Bush,* 28 June 2005. I am also grateful to the staff of Human Rights First for their thorough explanations, in meetings, of the contemporary legal dilemmas faced in bringing terrorist suspects to justice.

[31] For a detailed analysis of the legal parameters of inter-state transfers, see Opinion No. 363/2005 of the European Commission for Democracy through Law (Venice Commission), available at: *http://www.venice.coe.int/docs/2006/CDL-AD(2006)009-e.asp.* See also the section below on the point of view of the Council of Europe, at heading 10.2.1.

[32] See Cofer Black, former Head of the CIA Counter-Terrorism Center, testimony before the House and Senate Intelligence Committees, *Hearings on Pre-9/11 Intelligence Failures,* 26 September 2002: "All you need to know is that there was a 'before 9/11' and an 'after 9/11'. After 9/11, the gloves came off."

[33] General Nicolo Pollari, the Director of the Italian Intelligance and Security Services (SISMI), testified before the European Parliament's TDIP Temporary Committee on 6 March 2003 that "the rules of the

36. Rendition operations have escalated in scale and changed in focus. The central effect of the post-9/1 1 rendition programme has been to place captured terrorist suspects outside the reach of any justice system and keep them there. The absence of human rights guarantees and the introduction of "enhanced interrogation techniques" have led, in several cases examined, as we shall see, to detainees being subjected to torture.

37. The reasons behind the transformation in the character of rendition are both political and operational. First, it is clear that the United States Government has set out to combat terrorism in an aggressive and urgent fashion. The executive has applied massive political pressure on all its agencies, particularly the CIA, to step up the intensity of their counter-terrorist activities. According to Scheuer, "after 9/11, we had nothing ready to go—the military had no plans, they had no response; so the Agency felt the brunt of the executive branch's desire to show the American people victories"[34].

38. Second, and more importantly, the key operational change has been the mandate given to the CIA to administer its own detention facilities. When it takes terrorist suspects into its custody, the CIA no longer uses rendition to transport them into the custody of countries where they are wanted. Instead, for the high-level suspects at least, rendition now leads to secret detention at the CIA's so-called "black sites"[35] in unspecified locations around the world. Rather than face any form of justice, suspects become entrapped in the spider's web.

2.2. Components of the Spider's Web

39. In addition to CIA "black sites", the spider's web also encompasses a wider network of detention facilities run by other branches of the United States Government. Examples reported in the public domain have included the US Naval Base at Guantanamo Bay and military prisons such as Bagram in Afghanistan and Abu Ghraib in Iraq. Although the existence of such facilities is known, there are many aspects of their operation that remain shrouded in secrecy too.

40. It should also be noted that "rendition" flights by the CIA are not the only means of transporting detainees between different points on the web. Particularly in the context of transfers to Guantanamo Bay, detainees

game have changed" in terms of international co-operation in the intelligence sector: "many security activities are now carried out on the borderline of legality, albeit within the legal framework".

[34] Michael Scheuer, former Chief of the Bin Laden Unit in the CIA Counter-Terrorism Center, interview carried out by the Rapporteur's representative, *supra* note 19.

[35] For an impressive account of CIA "black sites", see: Center for Human Rights and Global Justice, NYU School of Law, *Fate and Whereabouts Unknown: Detainees in the "War on Terror"*, 17 December 2005. The term "black sites" came into the public debate largely as a result of Dana Priest, *CIA Holds Terror Suspects in Secret Prisons*, Washington Post, 2 November 2005.

have been moved extensively on military aircraft[36], including large cargo planes. Accordingly military flights have also fallen within the ambit of my inquiry.

41. The graphic included in this report depicts only a small portion of the global spider's web. It consists of two main components.

42. First it illustrates the flights of both civilian and military aircraft, operated by the United States, which appear to be connected to secret detentions and unlawful inter-state transfers also involving Council of Europe member States. This inquiry is based on seven separate sets of data from Eurocontrol,[37] combined with specific information from about twenty national aviation authorities in response to my requests. In this way, we have obtained a hitherto unique database[38].

43. Second, it distinguishes four categories of aircraft landing points, which indicate the different degrees of collusion on the part of the countries concerned. These landing points have been placed into their respective categories as follows on the basis of the preponderance of evidence gathered[39]:

Category A: **"Stopover points"**
(points at which aircraft land to refuel, mostly on the way home)

Prestwick
Shannon
Roma Ciampino
Athens
Santa Maria (Azores)
Bangor
Prague

Category B: **"Staging points"**
(points from which operations are often launched—planes and crews prepare there, or meet in clusters)

Washington
Frankfurt

[36] See, *inter alia,* US Department of Defense documents released in response to a lawsuit under the *Freedom of Information Act* by Stephen H. Oleskey, Wilmer Hale LLP (copies of all disclosed documents on file with the Rapporteur). These materials shed light on the full extent to which military planes were used to transport detainees to Guantanamo Bay: in five consecutive missions in early January 2002 alone, nearly 150 detainees were transferred there (including out from European countries).

[37] Eurocontrol is the European Organisation for the Safety of Air Navigation. I am grateful to Eurocontrol's Director General, Mr Victor Aguado, and his staff for responding to my various enquires in such an efficient and collegial manner. See the section below, at heading 2.3.

[38] I sent a round of letters to the Heads of National Parliamentary Delegations on 31 March 2006 in which I asked specifically for information from their respective national aviation authorities.

[39] In this regard we have gathered detainee testimonies, exhibits placed before judicial and parliamentary enquiries, information obtained under *Freedom of Information* legislation, interviews with legal representatives and insider sources, the accounts of investigative journalists and research conducted by non-governmental organisations.

Adana-Incirlik
Ramstein
Larnaca
Palma de Mallorca
Baku

Category C: **"One-off pick-up points"**
(points from which, according to our research, one detainee or one group of detainees was picked up for rendition or unlawful transfer, but not as part of a systematic occurrence)

Stockholm-Bromma
Banjul
Skopje
Aviano
Tuzla

Category D: **"Detainee transfer / Drop-off points"**
(places visited often, where flights tend to stop for just short periods, mostly far off the obvious route—either their location is close to a site of a known detention facility or a *prima facie* case can be made to indicate a detention facility in their vicinity)

Cairo
Amman
Islamabad
Rabat
Kabul
Guantanamo Bay
Timisoara / Bucharest
Tashkent
Algiers
Baghdad
Szymany

2.3. Compiling a Database of Aircraft Movements

44. As we began our work in November 2005, various organisations and individuals in the non-governmental sector, especially investigative journalists and NGOs, sent us lists of aircraft suspected either of belonging to the CIA or of being operated on the CIA's behalf by bogus "front companies". The lists contained details such as the type of aircraft, the registered owner and operator, and the "N-number" by which an aircraft is identified. These lists are the result of painstaking efforts to piece together information that is publicly available on certain Internet sites, observations by "planespotters" and testimony from former detainees. We subsequently received from Eurocontrol "flight plans" regarding these planes, at least in

so far as the European air space is concerned, for the period between the end of 2001 and early 2005. The Eurocontrol data received in January and February 2006 include, on the one hand, the plans of flights foreseen (which can be changed even during a flight for different reasons) and, on the other hand, information that has been verified following a request for collection of route charges, and flight data obtained from aviation authorities in the United States and elsewhere.

45. The lists requested from Eurocontrol in our original correspondence were somewhat speculative, but knowingly so. It was important for the inquiry team, in conjunction with external experts and investigators familiar with the topic, to gain a sense of how CIA-related aircraft operate in relation to the thousands of other, non-CIA aircraft that use European airspace. In other words we sought to build a profile of the characteristics of CIA flights. Additionally we hoped that by casting our net widely, we would be able to identify planes never before connected to the CIA.

46. We subsequently reverted to Eurocontrol on several occasions to obtain additional flight records[40]. As our work has progressed, we have been able to narrow down the number of aircraft movements that are of interest to our work and develop our analysis into a more sophisticated, realistic measure of the extent of illegality in the CIA's clandestine flight operations.

47. Based on our initial analysis, we sent a series of one-off additional requests to certain national air traffic control bodies in order to obtain records of the flights actually made in their countries; we also asked for data on the movements of military aircraft, which are not covered by Eurocontrol.

48. I am happy to report that through this channel I received useful information from various state institutions in different Council of Europe member States, including from transport ministries, aeronautic authorities, airport operators and state airlines. In addition, I obtained official records from national parliaments directly, including papers lodged by ministries of defence in response to parliamentary questions[41]. All of these diverse sources have contributed to the database of aircraft movements relied upon in this report.

2.4. Operations of the Spider'S Web

49. We believe that we have made a significant step towards a better comprehension of the system of "renditions" and secret detention centres.

[40] Notably, in February 2006, I met with the staff of Eurocontrol for a very constructive briefing session.

[41] See, *inter alia,* the letter of the Rt. Hon Adam Ingram, UK Minister of State for the Armed Forces, in response to parliamentary questions in the House of Commons about the use of UK military airfields by US registered aircraft, dated 2 March 2006.

One observation must be made. We should not lose our sense of proportion. It would be exaggerated to talk of thousands of flights, let alone hundreds of renditions concerning Europe. On this point I share the views expressed by members of the US Department of State, who recently delivered a first-hand briefing in Washington, DC at which a member of my team was present[42]. We undermine our credibility and limit the possibility for serious discussion if we make allegations that are ambiguous, exaggerated or unsubstantiated[43]. Indeed, it is evident that not all flights of CIA aircraft participate in "renditions". As Mr John Bellinger pointed out:

> *"Intelligence flights are a manifestation of the co-operation that happens amongst us. They carry analysts to talk with one another, they carry evidence that has been collected . . . I'm sure the Director of Intelligence himself was personally on a number of those flights."*[44]

Mr Scheuer gave another explanation as to the purposes of such flights:

> *"There are lots of reasons other than moving prisoners to have aircrafts. It all depends on what you are doing. If you are in Afghanistan and you're supplying weapons to a commander that is working with Karzai's Government, then it could be a plane load of weapons. It could be food—the CIA is co-located with the US Military in bases around the country, so it could be rations.*
>
> *Also, we try to take care of our people as well as we can, so it's toiletries, it's magazines, it's video recorders, it's coffee makers. We even take up collections at Christmas, to make sure we can send out hundreds and hundreds of pounds of Starbucks Coffee. So out of a thousand flights, I would bet that 98% of those flights are about logistics!"*[45]

In fact it is precisely the remaining 2% that interests us.

50. In order to understand the notion of a "spider's web", what is important to bear in mind is not the overall numbers of flights[46]; but rather

---

[42] See John Bellinger, Chief Legal Advisor to the US Secretary of State, and Dan Fried, Assistant Secretary of State, Bureau of European and Eurasian Affairs; *Briefing to European Delegation during the visit of the TDIP Temporary Committee of the European Parliament to Washington, DC*, 11 May 2006 (transcript on file with the Rapporteur—hereinafter "Bellinger, *Briefing to European Delegation*" or "Fried, *Briefing to European Delegation*").

[43] *Ibid.* According to Mr Bellinger: "We have been trying, from Secretary Rice down, to engage in a real dialogue with our different partners in Europe, be it the EU, be it the Council of Europe. We know your concerns and we are interested in talking to you directly, but on the basis of fact and not mere hyperbole." According to Mr Fried: "If the charges are absurd, it becomes difficult to deal with the real problems of the legal regime and the legal framework in which we have to conduct this struggle."

[44] Bellinger, Briefing to European Delegation, supra note 41.

[45] Michael Scheuer, former Chief of the Bin Laden Unit in the CIA Counter-Terrorism Center, interview conducted by the Rapporteur's representative, *supra* note 19.

[46] Bellinger, *Briefing to European Delegation*, *supra* note 41: "There really is not evidence of this. There is not evidence of a thousand detainees; there's not evidence of a hundred detainees; there's not even evidence of ten detainees."

the nature and context of individual flights. Our research has covered ten case studies of alleged unlawful inter-state transfers, involving a total of seventeen individual detainees. In most of these cases it was possible to generate flight logs from the amalgamated official flight database referred to earlier. I have then matched those logs with the times, dates and places of the alleged transfer operations—according to victims themselves, lawyer's notes or other sources. Finally, where possible, I have corroborated this information with factual elements acquired from legal proceedings in Council of Europe member States or in the United States.

51. In translating these case studies into graphic representations, I resolved to trace each flight route not individually, but as part of a circuit. Each circuit begins and ends, where possible, at the aircraft's "home base" (very often Dulles Airport in Washington, DC) in the United States. Following these flight circuits helps to better understand the different categories of aircraft landings—simple stopovers for refuelling, staging points that host clusters of CIA aircraft or serve to launch operations, and detainee drop-off points. Despite being a fairly simple analytical technique, it has also helped discover some significant new information, which we present in the following sections.

2.5. Successive Rendition Operations and Secret Detentions

52. We believe we are in a position to state that successive CIA rendition operations have taken place in the course of the same, single flight circuit. Two of the rendition case studies examined in this report, both involving Council of Europe member States to differing degrees, belonged to the same clandestine circuit of abductions and renditions at different points of the spider's web. The information at our disposal indicates that the renditions of Binyam Mohamed and Khaled El-Masri were carried out by the same CIA-operated aircraft, within 48 hours of one another, in the course of the same 12-day tour in January 2004. This finding appears significant for a number of reasons. First, since neither man even knows of the other—Mr Mohamed is still detained at Guantanamo Bay and Mr El-Masri has returned to his home community near Ulm in the South of Germany—their respective stories can be used to lend credence to one another. My team has received direct or indirect testimony from each of them independently.

53. As they both allege having been subjected to CIA rendition, the fact that the same aircraft—operated by a CIA-linked company—carried out two transfers in such quick succession allows us to speak of the existence of a "rendition circuit" within the "spider's web".

54. It is also possible to develop a hypothesis as to the nature of some other aircraft landings belonging to the same renditions circuit.

Thus, for example, the landings which occurred directly before and directly after the El-Masri rendition bear the typical characteristics of rendition operations[47].

55. Our analysis of the rendition programme in the post-9/11 era allows us to infer that the transfer of other detainees on this rendition circuit must have entailed detainees being transferred out of Kabul to alternative detention facilities in different countries. Thus, drawing upon official flight data, the probable existence of secret detention facilities can be inferred in Algeria and, as we will see, in Romania.

2.6. Detention Facilities in Romania and Poland

2.6.1 The Case of Romania

56. Romania is thus far the only Council of Europe member State to be located on one of the rendition circuits we believe we have identified and which bears all the characteristics of a detainee transfer or dropoff point. The N313P rendition plane landed in Timisoara at 11.51 pm on 25 January 2004 and departed just 72 minutes later, at 1.03 am on 26 January 2004. I am grateful to the Romanian Civil Aeronautic Authority for confirming these flight movements[48].

57. It is known that detainee transport flights are customarily night flights, as is the case of the other rendition flights already documented. The only other points on this rendition circuit from which the plane took off at a similar hour of the morning were Rabat, Morocco (departure at 2.05 am) and Skopje, "the former Yugoslav Republic of Macedonia" (hereinafter "Macedonia") (departure at 1.30 am). In both of these cases, we possess sufficient indications to claim that when the plane left its destination, it was carrying a prisoner to a secret detention centre situated in Kabul.

58. We can likewise affirm that the plane was not carrying prisoners to further detention when it *left* Timisoara. Its next destination, after all, was Palma de Mallorca, a well-established "staging point", also used for recuperation purposes in the midst of rendition circuits.

---

47 See *Flight logs related to the successive rendition operations of Binyam Mohamed and Khaled El-Masri in January 2004*, reproduced in this report in the Appendix to the present document. The landings in question are at Algiers (Algeria) and Timisoara (Romania).

48 See *Information from the records of the Romanian Civil Aeronautic Authority and the Romanian Ministry of National Defence*, contained as Appenices to the letters sent to me by Gyorgy Frunda, Chairman of the Romanian delegation to PACE, dated 24 February 2006 and 7 April 2006. I wish to thank my colleague Mr Frunda for his outstanding efforts in gathering information from various Romanian authorities on my behalf.

59. There is documentation in this instance that the passengers of the N313P plane, using US Government passports[49] and apparently false identities[50], stayed in a hotel in Palma de Mallorca for two nights before returning to the United States. One can deduce that these passengers, in addition to the crew of the plane, comprised a CIA rendition team, the same team performing all renditions on this circuit.

60. The N313P plane stayed on the runway at Timisoara on the night of 25 January 2004 for barely one hour. Based on analysis of the flight capacity of N313P, a Boeing 737 jet, in line with typical flight behaviours of CIA planes, it is highly unlikely that the purpose of heading to Romania was to refuel. The plane had the capacity to reach Palma de Mallorca, just over 7 hours away, directly from Kabul that night—twice previously on the same circuit, it had already flown longer distances of 7 hours 53 minutes (Rabat to Kabul) and 7 hours 45 minutes (Kabul to Algiers).

61. It should be recalled that the rendition team stayed about 30 hours in Kabul after having "rendered" Khaled El-Masri. Then, it flew to Romania on the same plane. Having eliminated other explanations -including that of a simple logistics flight, as the trip is a part of a well-established renditions circuit—the most likely hypothesis is that the purpose of this flight was to transport one or several detainees from Kabul to Romania.

62. We consider that while all these factual elements do not provide definitive evidence of secret detention centres, they do justify on their own a positive obligation to carry out a serious investigation, which the Romanian authorities do not seem to have done to date.

2.6.2. The Case of Poland

63. Poland was likewise singled out as a country which had harboured secret detention centres.

64. On the basis of information obtained from different sources we were able to determine that persons suspected of being high level terrorists were transferred out of a secret CIA detention facility in Kabul, Afghanistan in late September and October 2003[51]. During this period, my official

[49] See Andrew Manreas, La investigacion halla en los vuelos de la CIA decenas de ocupantes con estatus diplomatico, in El Pais, Palma de Mallorca, 15 November 2005.

[50] See Matias Valles, journalist with Diario de Mallorca, *Testimony before the TDIP Temporary Committee of the European Parliament*, 20 April 2006. Valles researched a total of 42 names he had uncovered from the records of a hotel in Mallorca where the passengers of the N313P plane stayed. Many proved to be "false identities", apparently created using the names of characters from Hollywood movies such as *Bladerunner* and *Alien*. Valles confirmed that at least some of the persons who arrived back in Palma de Mallora from Romania after the rendition circuit were the same persons who had stayed in the hotel at a previous point on the circuit—thus indicating that the "rendition team" remained on the plane throughout its trip.

[51] My team has worked closely with Human Rights Watch to corroborate the available evidence of detainee movements out of Afghanistan. For an indication of the earlier analysis of this information,

database shows that the only arrival of CIA-linked aircraft from Kabul in Europe was at the Polish airport of Szymany. The flights in question, carried out by the well-known "rendition plane" N313P, bear all the hallmarks of a rendition circuit.

65. The plane arrived in Kabul, on 21 September 2003, from Tashkent, Uzbekistan. The axis between Tashkent and Kabul was well known for detainee transfers[52]. Still, according to information received, the most significant detainee movements at this time probably involved transfers *out of* Kabul. The explanation attributed by NGO sources and journalists who have investigated this period[53] is that the CIA required a more isolated, secure, controlled environment in which to hold its high-level detainees, due to the proliferation of both prison facilities and prisoners in Afghanistan arising from the escalating "war on terrorism".

66. Thus, the circuit in question continued on 22 September 2003, when the plane flew from Kabul to Szymany airport in Poland. On the same grounds given above for the case of Romania, one may deduce that this flight was a CIA rendition, culminating in a "detainee drop-off in Poland.

67. Szymany is described by the Chairman of the Polish delegation to PACE as a "former Defence Ministry airfield", located near the rural town of Szczytno in the North of the country. It is close to a large facility used by the Polish intelligence services, known as the Stare Kiejkuty base. Both the airport and the nearby base were depicted on satellite images I obtained in January 2006[54].

68. It is noteworthy that the Polish authorities have been unable, despite repeated requests, to provide me with information from their own national aviation records to confirm any CIA-connected flights into Poland. In his

see *Human Rights Watch Statement on US Secret Detention Facilities in Europe*, 7 November 2005, available at: *http://hrw.Org/enqlish/docs/2005/11/07/usint11995.htm.*

[52] See Craig Murray, former United Kingdom Ambassador to Uzbekistan, *Exchange of views with the Committee on Legal Affairs and Human Rights (AS/Jur)*, Strasbourg, 24 January 2006. The minutes reflect that Mr Murray spoke of "evidence of the CIA chartering flights to Uzbekistan, between Kabul and Tashkent, and of the use of torture by Uzbek agents, as well as evidence that the American and British authorities were willing to receive and use information obtained under torture by foreign agencies, the relevant decision having been taken at a high level". See also Don van Natta Jr, *Growing Evidence US Sending Prisoners to Torture Capital: Despite Bad Record on Human Rights, Uzbekistan is Ally*, New York Times, 1 May 2005, available at: *www,nytimes.com/2005/05/01/international/01renditions.html?ex=1272600000&en=932280de7e0c1048&ei=5088&partn er=rssnyt&emc=rss*

[53] For an excellent account of the motivations for moving detainees to secret locations, see James Risen, *State of War: The Secret History of the CIA and the Bush Administration*, Free Press, New York, 2006, at pages 29 to 31: "The CIA wanted secret locations where it could have complete control over the interrogations and debriefings, free from the prying eyes of the international media, free from monitoring by human rights groups, and, most important, far from the jurisdiction of the American legal system."

[54] See European Union Satellite Centre, information provided to the Rapporteur on 23 January 2006. For further information see the section below at heading 4.1.

letter of 9 May 2006, my colleague Karol Karski, the Chairman of the Polish delegation to PACE, explained:

> *"I addressed the Polish authorities competent in gathering the air traffic data, related to these aircraft numbers . . . I was informed that several numbers from your list were still not found in our flight logs' records. Being not aware about the source of your information connecting these flight numbers with Polish airspace, I am not able, [nor are] the Polish air traffic control authorities, to comment on the fact of missing them in our records."*[55]

69. Mr. Karski also made the following statement, which reflects the position of the Polish Government on the question of CIA renditions:

> *"According to the information I have been provided with, none of the questioned flights was recorded in the traffic controlled by our competent authorities—in connection with Szymany or any other Polish airport."*

70. The absence of flight records from a country such as Poland is unusual. A host of neighbouring countries, including Romania, Bulgaria and the Czech Republic have had no such problems in retrieving official data for the period since 2001. Indeed, the submissions of these countries, along with my data from Eurocontrol, confirm numerous flights into and out of Polish airports by the CIA-linked planes that are the subject of this report.

71. In this light, Poland cannot be considered to be outside the rendition circuits simply because it has failed to furnish information corroborating our data from other sources. I have thus presented in my graphic the suspected rendition circuit involving Szymany airport, in which the landing at Szymany is placed in the category of "detainee drop-off points.

72. According to records in our possession, the N313P plane remained at Szymany airport on 22 September 2003 for just 64 minutes. I can also confirm that the plane then flew from Szymany to Romania, where it landed, after a change of course, at Bucharest Baneasa airport. Here, as in the case of Timisoara above, the aircraft landing in Romania fits the profile of a "detainee drop-off.

73. It is possible that several detainees may have been transported together on the flight out of Kabul, with some being left in Poland and some being left in Romania. This pattern would conform with information from other sources, which indicated the simultaneous existence of secret prisons in these two Council of Europe member States[56].

---

[55] Letter sent to me by Karol Karski, Chairman of the Polish delegation to PACE, dated 9 May 2006.

[56] See, inter alia, Brian Ross and Richard Esposito, Sources Tell ABC News Top Al-Qaeda Figures Held in Secret CIA Prisons: 10 out of 11 Terror Leaders Subjected to "Enhanced Interrogation Techniques", ABC News, 5 December 2005, available at: *http://abcnews.qo.eom/WNT/lnvestiqation/story?id=1375123*.

74. This suspected rendition circuit continued after Romania by landing in Rabat, Morocco, which several elements point to as a location that harbours a detention facility[57]. It is conceivable that this landing may even have constituted a third "detainee drop-off in succession before the plane returned to the United States, via Guantanamo Bay.

75. As for Romania, I find that there is now a preponderance of indications, not to prove the existence of detention centres, but in any case to open a real in-depth and transparent inquiry. One can add that the sources at the origin of the publications by Human Rights Watch, The Washington Post and ABC News, referring to the existence of such centres in Romania and Poland, are multiple, concordant and particularly well informed, as they belong to the very services that have directed these operations.

2.7. The Human Impact of Rendition and Secret Detention

76. Rendition is a degrading and dehumanising practice; certainly for its victims, but also for those who perform the operations. This simple realisation has become clear to me and my team as we have met with various people whose lives have been indelibly changed by rendition.

77. Therefore, while it is necessary to analyse the global system that rendition has become, we should never lose sight of the human dimension, as this is at the core of the abuses.

78. I have considered the human impact of rendition in two ways: first, the systematic CIA practice of preparing a detainee to be transported on a rendition aircraft; and second, the grave and long-lasting psychological damage that extraordinary rendition inflicts upon its victims.

2.7.1. CIA Methodology—How a Detainee is Treated During a Rendition

79. The descriptions of rendition operations in this report reflect many different individual cases. These cases entail a diverse range of victims, being captured in and transferred to numerous different countries, spanning a time period of several years. The stories are recounted by both first- and second-hand witnesses, speaking various languages in various public and private forums. Some of the people subjected to rendition have since been released, while others are still detained in the custody of the United States or another country. In short, the cases appear to have little or no connection to one another.

80. Yet on the contrary there are striking parallels between several of these renditions, particularly as they relate to the CIA's methodology. It seems that in each separate case, rendition was carried out in an almost identical

[57] See the case study of Binyam Mohamed al Habashi at section 3.9 of this report.

manner. Collectively the cases in the report testify to the existence of an established *modus operandi* of rendition, put into practice by an elite, highly-trained and highly-disciplined group of CIA agents who travel around the world mistreating victim after victim in exactly the same fashion.

81. It falls to analyse this methodology through the lens of human rights, as they are enshrined in the European Convention on Human Rights (ECHR) and applied in the vast majority of the countries that share these values. Every individual, even those accused, or found guilty, of involvement in terrorism and other categories of serious crime, has the unqualified right not to be tortured or subjected to inhuman and degrading treatment or punishment. While state agents have the right to use force in carrying out their work, there are obviously strict limits on the extent to which restraining or coercive measures may be applied during the course of an arrest or transfer operation.

82. According to Michael Scheuer, the CIA intentionally puts security concerns ahead of the rights of the detainee during a rendition operation:

> *"Clearly your first priorities in those situations are to protect your officers. So the person would generally be shackled and restrained. And probably at least getting on to the plane and while it was on the ground, he was blindfolded.*
>
> *I would think that the locals who arrested him would probably be the ones who would handcuff and blindfold him. Then he would be put on the plane, prepared and tied into his seat, or however it happened, and be watched over by guards from the receiving country he was going back to."*[58]

83. I consider that no security measure justifies a massive and systematic violation of human rights and dignity. In the cases examined—whilst being conscious of dealing with possibly dangerous persons—the principle of proportionality was simply ignored and with it the dignity of the person. In several instances, the actions undertaken in the course of a "security check" were excessive in relation to security requirements[59] and may therefore constitute a violation of Article 3 ECHR[60]. While it does not appear to reach the threshold for torture[61], it may well be considered as inhuman or

[58] Michael Scheuer, former Chief of the Bin Laden Unit in the CIA Counter-Terrorism Center; interview carried out by Rapporteur's representative in Washington, DC, 12 May 2006 (transcript on file with the Rapporteur).

[59] Mr Scheuer appears to understate severity of the measures taken during a "security check". A further discrepancy with his description is that in most cases, as far as I can discern, American agents carry out the entire "security check" themselves. I have not received any account of European security police being directly involved in administering these coercive measures, although there was at least one Egyptian policeman involved in the transfer of Ahmed Agiza and Mohamed Alzery from Sweden.

[60] Article 3 ECHR states: "No one shall be subjected to torture or to inhuman or degrading treatment or punishment."

[61] I agree with the assessment of Sweden's Parliamentary Ombudsman, Mats Melin, on the threshold for torture: "It is clear that torture is a concept reserved for cases involving the intentional infliction

degrading, particularly in the extent to which it humiliates the person being rendered[62].

84. The "security check" used by the CIA to prepare a detainee for transport on a rendition plane was described to us by one source in the American intelligence community as a "twenty-minute takeout"[63]. His explanation was that within a very short space of time, a detainee is transformed into a state of almost total immobility and sensory deprivation. *"The CIA can do three of these guys in an hour. In twenty minutes they're good to go."*[64] An investigating officer for the Swedish Ombudsman was struck by the *"fast and efficient procedure"* used by the American agents[65], while the Swedish interpreter who witnessed the CIA operation at Bromma Airport said simply: *"It surprised me how the heck they could have dressed him so fast."*[66]

85. The general characteristics of this "security check" can be established from a host of testimonies as follows[67]:

i. it generally takes place in a small room (a locker room, a police reception area) at the airport, or at a transit facility nearby.

ii. the man is sometimes already blindfolded when the operation begins, or will be blindfolded quickly and remain so throughout most of the operation.

iii. four to six CIA agents perform the operation in a highly-disciplined, consistent fashion—they are dressed in black (either civilian clothes or special "uniforms'), wearing black gloves, with their full faces covered. Testimonies speak, variously, of *"big people in black*

of severe pain or grave suffering intended, for example, to obtain information to punish or intimidate." See Mats Melin, Parliamentary Ombudsman (Sweden), *A review of the enforcement by the Security Police of a Government decision to expel two Egyptian citizens,* Adjudication No. 2169-2004, dated 22 March 2005. Melin cites the judgement of the European Court of Human Rights (ECtHR) in *Salman v. Turkey,* 27 June 2000.

[62] In determining whether the standard for degrading treatment is met, the ECtHR takes account of whether it has been expressly *intended* to humiliate the individual in question, along with its effect on the individual's personality. In the context of a deprivation of liberty, the treatment must be in excess of the humiliation inherent in arrest or detention. See the judgement of the ECtHR in *Ocalan v. Turkey,* 12 March 2003.

[63] Confidential interview with a source in the US intelligence community who wished to remain anonymous; interview carried out in the United States by the Rapporteur's representative.

[64] ibid.

[65] See Office of the Parliamentary Ombudsman (Sweden), *Interview conducted with state official X of the Security Police (Säpo),* Case No. 2169-2004, 30 September 2004 (translated transcript on file with the Rapporteur—hereinafter "Interview with Swedish Säpo interpreter"); comment made at page 23.

[66] *Ibid,* observation made by the Säpo interpreter in answer to a question, at page 13.

[67] The person subjected to the "security check" is referred to generically as "the man", because we have not thus far heard of any cases in which it has happened to women. This overview contains aspects common to several renditions, while excerpts from individual testimonies are cited separately hereunder.

balaclavas,"[68] people *"dressed in black like ninjas,"*[69] or people wearing *"ordinary clothes, but hooded."*[70]

iv. the CIA agents *"don't utter a word when they communicate with one another"*[71], using only hand signals or simply knowing their roles implicitly,

v. some men speak of being punched or shoved by the agents at the beginning of the operation in a rough or brutal fashion[72]; others talked about being gripped firmly from several sides

vi. the man's hands and feet are shackled,

vii. the man has all his clothes (including his underwear) cut from his body using knives or scissors in a careful, methodical fashion; an eye-witness described how *"someone was taking these clothes and feeling every part, you know, as if there was something inside the clothes, and then putting them in a bag."*[73]

viii. the man is subjected to a full-body cavity search, which also entails a close examination of his hair, ears, mouth and lips.

ix. the man is photographed with a flash camera, including when he is nearly[74] or totally naked[75]; in some instances, the man's blindfold may be removed for the purpose of a photograph in which his face is also identifiable[76].

---

[68] See Bisher Al-Rawi, statement made to his lawyer during an interview at Guantanamo Bay (contained in unclassified attorney notes), submitted to the High Court of Justice in Case No. 2005/10470/05 through the *Witness Statement of Clive Stafford Smith* (hereinafter "Al-Rawi statement to lawyer"), at page 31.

[69] See Jamil El-Banna, statement made to his lawyer during an interview at Guantanamo Bay (contained in unclassified attorney notes), submitted to the High Court of Justice in Case No. 2005/10470/05 through the *Witness Statement of Clive Stafford Smith* (hereinafter "El-Banna statement to lawyer"), at page 40.

[70] See Interview with Swedish Säpo interpreter, *supra* note 85, at page 10.

[71] See Office of the Parliamentary Ombudsman (Sweden), *Interview conducted with Kjell Jönsson, Swedsh lawyer for Mohamed Alzery,* Case No. 2169-2004, September 2004 (translated transcript on file with the Rapporteur—hereinafter "Ombudsman's Interview with Swedish lawyer Jönsson"); at page 6.

[72] See Declaration of Khaled El-Masri in support of Plaintiff's Opposition to the United States' Motion to Dismiss, in *El-Masri v. Tenet et al,* Eastern District Court of Virginia in Alexandria, 6 April 2006 (hereinafter "El-Masri statement to US Court in Alexandria, 6 April 2006") at page 9: "As I was led into this room I felt two people violently grab my arms . . . They bent both my arms backwards. This violent motion caused me a lot of pain. I was beaten severely from all sides."

[73] See Interview with Swedish Säpo interpreter, *supra* note 65, at page 13.

[74] See Interview with Swedish Säpo interpreter, *supra* note 65, at page 13: "he wasn't naked, he had his underpants on; the upper body was undressed and then his picture was taken."

[75] See Binyam Mohamed Al-Habashi, statement made to his lawyer during an interview at Guantanamo Bay, contained in unclassified attorney notes of Clive A. Stafford Smith, dated 1 August 2005 (document on file with the Rapporteur -hereinafter "Binyam Mohamed statements to lawyer at Guantanamo"), at page 19: "there was a white female with glasses . . . One of them held my penis and she took digital pictures."

[76] See El-Masri statement to US Court in Alexandria, 6 April 2006, *supra* note 71, at page 9: "They took off my blindfold . . . As soon as it was removed, a very bright flashlight went off and I was temporarily blinded. I believe from the sounds that they had taken photographs of me throughout."

x. some accounts speak of a foreign object being forcibly inserted into the man's anus; some accounts speak more specifically of a tranquiliser or suppository being administered *per rectum*[77]—in each description this practice has been perceived as a grossly violating act that affronts the man's dignity.

xi. the man is then dressed in a nappy or incontinence pad and a loose-fitting *"jump-suit'* or set of overalls; *"they put diapers on him and then there is some handling with these handcuffs and foot chains, because first they put them on and then they are supposed to put him in overalls, so then they have to alternately unlock and relock them"*[78].

xii. the man has his ears muffled, sometimes being made to wear a pair of *"headphones"*[79]

xiii. finally a cloth bag is placed over the man's head, with no holes through which to breathe or detect light; they *"put a blindfold on him and after that a hood that apparently reaches far down on his body*[80].

xiv. the man is typically forced aboard a waiting aeroplane, where he may be *"placed on a stretcher, shackled"*[81], or strapped to a mattress or seat, or *"laid down on the floor of the plane and they bind him up in a very uncomfortable position that makes him hurt from moving"*[82].

xv. in some cases the man is drugged and experiences little or nothing of the actual rendition flight[83]; in other cases, factors such as the pain of the shackles or the refusal to allow him to drink water or use the toilet make the flight unbearable: *"this was the hardest moment in my life"*[84].

xvi. in most cases, the man has no notion of where he is going, nor the fate that awaits him upon arrival.

86. This manner of treating detainees has been heavily criticised by the lawyers of many of the persons subjected to rendition. In his testimony to the Swedish Ombudsman, Kjell Jönsson, the Swedish lawyer for

---

[77] See Ombudsman's Interview with Swedish lawyer Jönsson, *supra* note 70, at page 6: "they bend him forward and he can feel that something is being pushed up his rectum . . . after that he felt calmer and felt a muscle relaxation in all his body, but he was wide awake, so he was not sedated".

[78] See Ombudsman's Interview with Swedish lawyer Jönsson, *supra* note 70, at page 6.

[79] See El-Masri statement to US Court in Alexandria, 6 April 2006, *supra* note 71, at page 9. Also see reference to "earmuffs" in Al-Rawi statement to lawyer, *supra* note 67, at page 31; and reference to "earphones" in Binyam Mohamed statements to lawyer at Guantanamo, at page 5.

[80] See Ombudsman's Interview with Swedish lawyer Jönsson, *supra* note 70, at page 6.

[81] See Al-Rawi statement to lawyer, *supra* note 67, at page 31.

[82] See Ombudsman's Interview with Swedish lawyer Jönsson, *supra* note 70, at page 6.

[83] See El-Masri statement to US Court in Alexandria, 6 April 2006, *supra* note 71, at page 10: "They put something over my nose. I think it was some kind of anaesthaesia. It felt like the trip took about four hours, but I don't really remember. I was mostly unconscious for the duration".

[84] See Al-Rawi statement to lawyer, *supra* note 67, at page 31.

Mohamed Alzery[85], stated his concern that the measures taken before the rendition were disproportionate to the security needs: "from Alzery's point of view it would have been perfectly enough to ask him to co-operate and he would have done that just like he always has done before"[86].

87. Perhaps the most troubling aspect of this systematic practice, however, is that it appears to be intended to humiliate. Many accounts speak of these measures being taken despite "strong resistance", both physical and verbal, on the part of the detainee. The nudity, forced shackling "like an animal"[87] and being forced to wear nappies appear offensive to the notions of dignity held by the detainees. In my view it is simply not acceptable in Council of Europe member States for security services, whether European or foreign, to treat people in a manner that amounts to such "extreme humiliation"[88].

2.7.2. The Effects of Rendition and Secret Detention on Individuals and Families

88. In compiling this report, members of my team and I have met directly with several victims of renditions and secret detentions, or with their families. In addition, we have obtained access to further first-hand accounts from victims who remain detained, in the form of their letters or diaries, unclassified notes from their discussions with lawyers, and official accounts of visits from Embassy officials.

89. Personal accounts of this type of human rights abuse speak of utter demoralisation. Of course, the despair is greatest in cases where the abuse persists—where a person remains in secret detention, without knowing the basis on which he is being held, and where nobody apart from his captors knows about his exact whereabouts or wellbeing. The uncertainty that defines rendition and secret detention is torturous, both for those detained and those for whom they are "disappeared"[89].

90. Yet the ordeal continues long after a detainee is located, or even released and able to return home. Victims have described to us how they suffer from flashbacks and panic attacks, an inability to lead normal relationships and

---

[85] For more detail on the cases of Ahmed Agiza and Mohamed Alzery, please refer to the case study in the following section.

[86] See Ombudsman's Interview with Swedish lawyer Jönsson, *supra* note 70, at page 8.

[87] The detainee who made this statement asked that he remain anonymous.

[88] The words "extreme humiliation" are used in the Ombudsman's Interview with Swedish lawyer Jönsson, *supra* note 70, at page 8. In El-Masri statement to US Court in Alexandria, 6 April 2006, *supra* note 71, at page 9, he talks of "degrading and shameful" acts that left him feeling "terrified and utterly humiliated".

[89] See Louise Arbour, United Nations High Commissioner for Human Rights, *Human Rights: A casualty of the war on terror?;* Interview for UN World Chronicle No. 996, 7 December 2005 (transcript provided by UN Television, on file with the rapporteer): "Secret detention under these extreme conditions is an unacceptable treatment, both of the person detained and I would certainly suggest of members of their families [for whom], for all purposes, these people have disappeared."

a permanent fear of death. Families have been torn apart. On a personal level, deep psychological scars persist; and on a daily basis, stigma and suspicion seem to haunt anybody branded as "suspect" in the "war on terror". In short, links with normal society appear practically impossible to restore.

91. I salute the remarkable courage and resilience of those who have been held in secret detention and subsequently released, like Khaled El-Masri and Maher Arar. Both these men have spoken eloquently to us about what moves them to recount their experiences despite the obvious pain and trauma of doing so. From these words we must draw our own resolve to uncover the secret abuses of the spider's web and ensure that they never again be allowed to occur. From Mr El-Masri, "all I want is to know the truth about what happened to me and to have the American Government apologise for what it did"[90]; from Mr Arar, "the main purpose of talking about my torture is to prevent the same treatment from ever happening to another human being"[91].

3. Specific Examples of Documented Renditions

3.1. Khaled El-Masri

92. We spoke for many hours with Khaled El-Masri, who also testified publicly before the Temporary Committee of the European Parliament, and we find credible his account of detention in Macedonia and Afghanistan for nearly five months.

3.1.1. The Individual Account of Mr El-Masri

93. A summary of the unprecedented suffering endured by Mr El-Masri reads as follows:

94. [A]ccording to the statement of facts presented to the US District Court[92], Khaled El-Masri, a German citizen of Lebanese descent, travelled by bus from his home near Neu Ulm, Germany, to Skopje, Macedonia, in the final days of 2003. After passing through several international border crossings without incident, Mr El-Masri was detained at the Serbian-Macedonian border because of alleged irregularities with his passport. He was interrogated by Macedonian border officials, then transported to a hotel in Skopje. Subsequent to his release in May, 2004, Mr El-Masri was able to identify the hotel from website photographs as the Skopski Merak, and to identify

[90] Khaled El-Masri made this statement to me during our meeting in Strasbourg in April 2006.
[91] Maher Arar made this statement to my representative during their meeting in Brussels in March 2006.
[92] See El-Masri statement to US Court in Alexandria, 6 April 2006, *supra* note 71.

photos of the room where he was held and of a waiter who served him food. Over the course of three weeks, Mr El-Masri was repeatedly interrogated about alleged contacts with Islamic extremists, and was denied any contact with the German Embassy, an attorney, or his family. He was told that if he confessed to Al-Qaeda membership, he would be returned to Germany. On the thirteenth day of confinement, Mr El-Masri commenced a hunger strike, which continued until his departure from Macedonia. After 23 days of detention, Mr El-Masri was videotaped, blindfolded, and transported by vehicle to an airport.

95. There, he was beaten, stripped naked, and thrown to the ground. A hard object was forced into his anus. When his blindfold was removed, he saw seven or eight men, dressed in black and hooded. He was placed in a diaper and sweatsuit, blindfolded, shackled, and hurried to a plane, where he was chained spreadeagled to the floor. He was injected with drugs and flown to Baghdad, then on to Kabul, Afghanistan, an itinerary that is confirmed by public flight records. At some point prior to his departure, an exit stamp was placed in his passport, confirming that he left Macedonia on January 23, 2004.

96. Upon arrival in Kabul, Mr El-Masri was kicked and beaten and left in a filthy cell. There he would be detained for more than four months. He was interrogated several times in Arabic about his alleged ties to 9/11 conspirators Muhammed Atta and Ramzi Bin Al-Shibh and to other alleged extremists based in Germany. American officials participated in his interrogations. All of his requests to meet with a representative of the German government were refused.

97. In March, Mr El-Masri and several other inmates commenced a hunger strike. After nearly four weeks without food, Mr El-Masri was brought to meet with two American officials. One of the Americans confirmed Mr El-Masri's innocence, but insisted that only officials in Washington, D.C. could authorize his release. Subsequent media reports confirm that senior officials in Washington, including the CIA Director Tenet, were informed long before Mr El-Masri's release that the United States had detained an innocent man. Mr El-Masri continued his hunger strike. On the evening of April 10, Mr El-Masri was dragged from his room by hooded men and force-fed through a nasal tube.

98. At around this time, Mr El-Masri felt what he believed to be a minor earthquake. Geological records confirm that in February and April, there were two minor earthquakes in the vicinity of Kabul.

99. On May 16, Mr El-Masri was visited by a uniformed German speaker who identified himself as "Sam". "Sam" refused to say whether he had been sent by the German government, or whether the government knew about Mr El-Masri's whereabouts. Subsequent to his release, Mr El-Masri

identified "Sam" in a photograph and a police lineup as Gerhard Lehmann, a German intelligence officer.

100. On May 28, 2004, Mr El-Masri, accompanied by "Sam," was flown from Kabul to a country in Europe other than Germany. He was placed, blindfolded, into a truck and driven for several hours through mountainous terrain. He was given his belongings and told to walk down a path without turning back. Soon thereafter, he was confronted by armed men who told him he was in Albania and transported him to Mother Theresa Airport in Tirana. There, he was accompanied through customs and immigration controls and placed on a flight to Frankfurt.

101. Upon his return to Germany, Mr El-Masri contacted an attorney and related his story. The attorney promptly reported Mr El-Masri's allegations to the German government, thereby initiating a formal investigation by public prosecutors. Pursuant to their investigation, German prosecutors obtained and tested a sample of Mr El-Masri's hair, which proved consistent with his account of detention in a South-Asian country and deprivation of food for an extended period. That investigation, as well as a German parliamentary investigation of Mr El-Masri's allegations, is ongoing.

3.1.2. Elements of Corroboration for Mr El-Masri's Account

102. Mr El-Masri's account is borne out by numerous items of evidence, some of which cannot yet be made public because they have been declared secret[93], or because they are covered by the confidentiality of the investigation underway in the office of the Munich prosecuting authorities following Mr El-Masri's complaint of abduction.

103. The items already in the public domain are cited in the aforementioned memorandum[94] submitted to the Virginia court in which Mr El-Masri lodged his complaint:

- Passport stamps confirming Mr El-Masri's entry to and exit from Macedonia, as well as exit from Albania, on the dates in question;
- Scientific testing of Mr El-Masri's hair follicles, conducted pursuant to a German criminal investigation, that is consistent with Mr El-Masri's account that he spent time in a South-Asian country and was deprived of food for an extended period of time;

[93] The information in question appears in the report of the German Federal Government to the parliamentary committee monitoring the secret services (PKG); I was able to obtain from the chairman of that committee a "public" version of the report, which contains no particulars of individual cases. A version classified "confidential—for official use only" was handed to me by a journalist. This information enabled me to form a judgment as to the credibility of Mr El-Masri's account, but I have chosen to preserve the confidentiality of that report although, to be frank, I believe that the public should have access to this kind of information. To my knowledge, there is an even fuller version classified "secret", which I declined to obtain out of respect for German parliamentary procedure.

[94] See El-Masri statement to US Court in Alexandria, 6 April 2006, *supra* note 71.

- Other physical evidence, including Mr El-Masri's passport, the two t-shirts he was given by his American captors on departing from Afghanistan, his boarding pass from Tirana to Frankfurt, and a number of keys that Mr El-Masri possessed during his ordeal, all of which have been turned over to German prosecutors;
- Aviation logs confirming that a Boeing business jet owned and operated by defendants in this case, then registered by the FAA as N313P, took off from Palma, Majorca, Spain on January 23, 2004; landed at the Skopje airport at 8:51 p.m. that evening; and left Skopje more than three hours later, flying to Baghdad and then on to Kabul, the Afghan capital;
- Witness accounts from other passengers on the bus from Germany to Macedonia, which confirm Mr El-Masri's account of his detention at the border;
- Photographs of the hotel in Skopje where Mr El-Masri was detained for 23 days, from which Mr El-Masri has identified both his actual room and a staff member who served him food;
- Geological records that confirm Mr El-Masri's recollection of minor earthquakes during his detention in Afghanistan;
- Evidence of the identity of "Sam," whom Mr El-Masri has positively identified from photographs and a police line-up, and who media reports confirm is a German intelligence officer with links to foreign intelligence services;
- Sketches that Mr El-Masri drew of the layout of the Afghan prison, which were immediately recognizable to another rendition victim who was detained by the U.S. in Afghanistan;
- Photographs taken immediately upon Mr El-Masri's return to Germany that are consistent with his account of weight loss and unkempt grooming.

Numerous government inquiries, including the German prosecutors' investigation, a German parliamentary investigation, and various inter-governmental human rights inquiries, are almost certain to produce additional corroborating evidence.

3.1.3. The Role of "the Former Yugoslav Republic of Macedonia"

104. The role of "the former Yugoslav Republic of Macedonia" in the rendition of Khaled El-Masri has yet to be fully understood. The information collected on site by a member of my team appears to show a certain ambiguity in the Macedonian position. In effect, the Government of Macedonia has adopted an "official line" of complete negation, repeated in a rigid and stereotyped fashion.

105. I am indebted to the delegation from the European Parliament for arranging and administering an excellent programme of meetings with the highest-level representatives of the Macedonian Government and Parliament[95]. I share many of the reflections of my colleagues from the European Parliament in their review of these meetings, not least the sense of discomfort that in many areas the Macedonian authorities fell short of genuine transparency[96].

3.1.3.1. The Position of the Authorities

106. The "official line" of the Macedonian Government was first contained in a letter from the Minister of Interior, Ljubomir Mihajlovski, to the Ambassador of the European Commission, Erwan Fouere, dated 27 December 2005. In its simplest form, it essentially contains four items of information *"according to police records"*: first, Mr El-Masri arrived by bus at the Macedonian border crossing of Tabanovce at 4 pm on 31 December 2003; second, he was interviewed by *"authorised police officials"* who suspected *"possession of a falsified travel document"*; third, approximately five hours later, Mr El-Masri *"was allowed entrance"* into Macedonia, apparently freely; and fourth, on 23 January 2004, he left Macedonia over the border crossing of Blace into Kosovo.

107. Mr Mihajlovski restated exactly the same Government position in response to a parliamentary question in the Sobranie on 26 January 2006[97]. He cited *"official evidence of the Ministry of Interior"* and went on to describe the allegations as *"speculative and unfounded"*.

108. The President of the Republic, Branko Crvenkovski, set out a firm stance in the very first meeting with the European Parliament delegation, providing a strong disincentive to any official who may have wished to break ranks by expressing an independent viewpoint: *"Up to this moment, I would like to assure you that I have not come across any reason not to believe the official position of our Ministry of Interior. I have no additional comments or facts, from any side, to convince me that what has been established in the official report of our Ministry is not the truth."*

---

[95] The programme of meetings took place between 27 and 29 April 2006.

[96] President Branko Crvnekovski said in his opening remarks on 27 April 2006: "Macedonia is completely determined and open for co-operation with you. What I want to repeat is that we're completely prepared to establish the truth . . . Our joint task is to find out the truth and not to respond to the current public opinion or the positions of the media"; Siljan Avramovski, the former Head of the UBK, Macedonia's counter-intelligence service stated on 28 April: "We will provide maximum transparency and openness in our discussions". These were fairly typical of the sentiments expressed by all the officials who met with the delegation.

[97] Mr Slobodan Casule, a prominent opposition politician who met with the European delegation on 27 April 2006, posed the question. He said he sought clarification about the El-Masri case because he believes that *"such issues should be opened and closed within the Parliament"*.

109. On Friday 28 April the official position was presented in far greater detail during a meeting with Siljan Avramovski, who was Head of the UBK[98], Macedonia's main intelligence service, at the time of the El-Masri case. Avramovski stated that the UBK's "Department for Control and Professional Standards" had undertaken an investigation into the case and traced official records of all Mr El-Masri's contact with the Macedonian authorities. The further details as presented by Mr Avramovski[99] are summarized as follows:

> Mr El-Masri arrived on the Macedonian border on 31 December 2003, New Year's Eve. The Ministry of Interior had intensified security for the festive period and was operating a higher state of alert around the possible criminal activity. In line with these more intense activities, bus passengers were being subjected to a thorough security check, including an examination of their identity documents.
>
> Upon examining Mr El-Masri's passport, the Macedonian border police developed certain suspicions and decided to *"detain him"*. In order not to make the other passengers wait at the border, the bus was at this point allowed to continue its journey.
>
> The objective of holding Mr El-Masri was to conduct an interview with him, which (according to Avramovski) was carried out in accordance with all applicable European standards. Members of the UBK, the security and counter-intelligence service, are present at all border points in Macedonia as part of what is described as "Integrated Border Management and Security". UBK officials participated in the interview of Mr El-Masri.
>
> The officials enquired into Mr El-Masri's reasons for travelling into the country, where he intended to stay and whether he was carrying sufficient amounts of money. Avramovski explained: "I think these were all standard questions that are asked in the context of such a routine procedure—I don't think I need to go into further details".
>
> At the same time, Macedonian officials undertook a preliminary visual examination of Mr El-Masri's travel documents. They suspected that the passport might be faked or forged—noting in particular that Mr El-Masri was born in Kuwait, yet claimed to possess German citizenship.
>
> A further passport check was carried out against an Interpol database. The border point at Tabanovce is not linked to Interpol's network, so the information had to be transmitted to Skopje, from where an electronic request was made to the central Interpol database in Lyon. A UBK

[98] Uprava za Bezbednosti i Kontrarazuznavanje, or the Security and Counter-Intelligence Service.

[99] Meeting with Siljan Avramovski, now Deputy Director of UBK in the Ministry of Interior, 28 April 2006, transcript on file with the Rapporteur.

official in the Analytical Department apparently made this request using an electronic code, so the Macedonian authorities can produce no record of it. Mr El-Masri was made to wait on the border point while the Interpol search was carried out.

When it was established that there existed no Interpol warrant against Mr El-Masri and no further grounds on which to hold him[100], he was released. He then left the border point at Tabanovce, although Macedonian officials were not able to describe how. Asked directly about this point in a separate meeting, the Minister of Interior, Mr Mihajlovski said: *"we're not able to tell you exactly what happened to him after he was released because it is not in our interest after the person leaves the border crossing, we're not in a position to know how he traveled further"*[101].

The Ministry of Interior subsequently established, according to Avramovski, that Mr El-Masri had stayed at a hotel in Skopje called the "Skopski Merak". Mr El-Masri is said to have checked in on the evening of 31 December 2003 and registered in the Guest Book. He stayed for 23 nights, including daily breakfast, and checked out on 23 January 2004.

The Ministry then conducted a further check on all border crossings and discovered that on the same day, 23 January 2004, in the evening, Mr El-Masri left the territory of Macedonia over the border crossing at Blace, into the territory of Kosovo. When asked whether Mr El-Masri had received a stamp to indicate his departure by this means, Avramovski answered: *"Normally there should be a stamp on the passport as you cross the border out of Macedonia, but I can't be sure. UNMIK is also present on the Kosovo border and is in charge of the protocol on that side . . . My UBK colleague has just informed me that he has crossed the border at Blace twice in recent times and didn't receive a stamp on either occasion."*

Avramovski concluded his summary with the words: *"This is the truth of the case that has been exploited by the media—the so-called El-Masri case."*

110. In a separate meeting directly following Avramovski's briefing, Minister Mihajlovski retained the position and added very few further details. Both officials were keen to talk about the case as if it were a routine matter, one which only came to their attention when it was reported in the local and international press. They referred repeatedly to the media

[100] Avramovski stated that Macedonian border police decided for themselves that Mr El-Masri's passport was genuine, after an unspecified process or length of examination *"At our border points, expert members of the border police are qualified to assess whether a passport is counterfeit or not. When they decided that it was genuine, they took no further action. They did not inform the German Embassy; they didn't feel the need to request any documents against which to compare the passport."*

[101] Meeting with Ljubomir Mihajlovski, Minister of Interior, 28 April 2006, transcript on file with the Rapporteur.

"prejudice" and "pressure" against Macedonia. Mihajlovski even implied that there was a conspiracy theory at play, designed to discredit the country: *"Who is really behind all of this? This case is making so much damage to the country. If you can get a reason why it is happening, please send us a message; tell us."*

111. It seems clear that the Macedonian public has reacted negatively to the El-Masri affair. Most Macedonians feel aggrieved that their country has been given such a bad press and is associated with what is often portrayed as a manipulative operation. Many regard the international media interest as a thinly veiled attempt to discredit Macedonia's prospects for European integration. In reality, it seems that the Macedonian Government is itself responsible for this situation. More transparency, and a greater degree of preparedness genuinely to seek the truth, rather than locking themselves into a pre-established, dogmatic scheme, would have certainly avoided much criticism and suspicion.

3.1.3.2. Further Elements

112. The Government's official line is based on what Mr Avramovski called *"a reconstruction after the fact, based on information we established through documents and discussions"* with, *inter alia, "employees of the hotel"*. There is no doubt in my mind that the Ministry of Interior has put together a very thorough reconstruction of the case; just not an accurate one. Equally I accept that the Ministry has undertaken *"discussions"* with witnesses, including hotel employees; but I regard these as efforts to harmonise the official line, not to establish the truth.

113. One could, with sufficient application, begin to tease out discrepancies in the official line. For example, the Ministry of Interior stated that *"the hotel owner should have the record of Mr El-Masri's bill"*, while the hotel owner responded to several inquiries, by telephone and in person, by saying that the record had been handed over to the Ministry of Interior.

114. Contacts we were able to make with sources close to the administration and to the intelligence services have enabled us to obtain much more credible information, in order to better understand what really happened. We can consequently present a more coherent analysis of this case. For obvious reasons, the sources contacted locally wish to stay anonymous, at least for the time being.

115. The Government's public portrayal seems at first glance perfectly plausible. However, it ceases to be credible when it asserts that El-Masri was allowed to proceed freely from Tabanovce on the evening of 31 December 2003. In reality, that evening signalled the beginning of his five-month ordeal in secret detention ordered by the CIA.

116. What is not said in the official version is the fact that the Macedonian UBK routinely consults with the CIA on such matters (which, on a certain level, is quite comprehensible and logical). According to confidential information we received (of which we know the source), a full description of Mr El-Masri was transmitted to the CIA via its Bureau Chief in Skopje for an analysis similar to the one Avramovski says was undertaken by Interpol: did the person in question have contact with terrorist movements, in particular with Al Qaida? Based on the intelligence material about Khaled El-Masri in its possession—the content of which is not known to us—the CIA answered in the affirmative. The UBK, as the local partner organisation, was requested to assist in securing and detaining Mr El-Masri until he could be handed over to the CIA for transfer.

117. The UBK has an excellent reputation for its professionalism. It is well practiced in the conduct of clandestine surveillance and detention operations, having exploited its own network of "secret apartments" for decades[102]. Information obtained from our internal sources indicates that the UBK is equally skilled in working on behalf of the CIA.—we even learned of one previous collaborative operation between these services in the past, targeted at apprehending suspected Islamic terrorists. In the El-Masri case, according to our understanding, this co-operation was particularly efficient and the Macedonian services fulfilled the expectations of the CIA.

118. The choice of the Skopski Merak hotel as a detention site warrants comment. The Macedonian authorities have categorically denied that this hotel could have served as a place for detention, considering such a possibility as downright ridiculous. Avramovski said he could *"absolutely"* rule out the prospect of Mr El-Masri's being held there:

> *"Look, I can state this very specifically and decisively. The 31 December is New Year's Eve—that period is a holiday, there are always a lot of guests, many of them tourists, in the hotel to celebrate the New Year. There is not even a theoretical possibility [laughing] that a person could be detained in an open hotel, where there's a constant flow of people coming and going. There were many guests there at the time, including foreign nationals—it's a well-known, open hotel with a fine reputation in this city!"*

[102] The Macedonian Helsinki Committee for Human Rights has researched questions of secret detention and produced a variety of credible reports (copies of which are on file with the Rapporteur). In many cases, people are held in secret apartments to get them "out of the system" for an indefinite period of time, for the UBK to interrogate them and elicit confessions. Further still, in the notorious "Rastanski Lozja" case of March 2002, Macedonian police were said to have shot dead "seven members of a terrorist group" in what seemed like an act of summary exection. The Helsinki Committee wrote in its Annual Report of 2002: "the largest number of human rights violations was perpetrated by officers of the special units at the Ministry of Interior".

In fact, a busy place with this hotel's features lends itself very well to a clandestine operation, given that a top-floor room facing away from the street was used.

119. Whilst the operation was driven and directed by CIA agents, the Americans kept a very low profile throughout the operation in Macedonia. The CIA transmitted to UBK the questions to ask the suspect, without ever taking part in any interrogation.

120. Several of our interviewees told us—with varying degrees of knowledge—that German intelligence was informed of the fact that Mr El-Masri was in Macedonian custody in the days immediately following the arrest, but not about the operational details. Intelligence material from Germany was added to the dossier from which questions were later asked, both in Macedonia and in Afghanistan, by interrogators of various nationalities.

121. According to our insider sources in the intelligence community, whom we consider serious and well-informed, approximately 20 officials were involved overall on the Macedonian side, including "four or five" politically responsible persons in Government. Three teams of three agents rotated in the task of guarding and surveillance. Technicians and analysts helped to compile the record of the operation, which was a running log rather than a cumulative written report. An operational commander and a deputy marshalled the Macedonian agents and took responsibility for reporting to their liaisons in the CIA.

122. The period for which the Macedonians held Mr El-Masri in advance of his rendition—23 days—was abnormally long for any operation involving the CIA. Partner agencies and CIA officials alike prefer to keep the time between the initial arrest and the transfer to a CIA detention centre as short as possible[103].

123. The delay in this case appears to have been caused by logistical reasons, in particular related to the availability of an aircraft. A flight on an unusual route, from Skopje into the Middle East, had to be incorporated into an existing schedule for that month, which, as established above in the description of the newly-discovered rendition circuit, included other detainee transfers.

124. According to further eye-witness accounts from persons in the civil aviation sector, who described the presence and movements of the suspect rendition plane at Skopje airport that evening, the aircraft thought to have taken Mr El-Masri on board did not follow regular procedures. The manner in which the plane registered with ground staff and paid its

[103] See, for example, Michael Scheuer, former Chief of the Bin Laden Unit in the CIA Counter-Terrorism Center, interview carried out by the Rapporteur's representative, *supra* note 19.

"route charge" fees was highly unusual—as the Ministry of Interior himself confirmed, no passengers even left the plane to enter the terminal building and thus cross officially onto Macedonian territory. Instead the plane taxied into position at the far end of the runway, more than a kilometer from the terminal. A detail of armed Macedonian security police formed a lookout nearby, under strict instructions to face away from the plane itself. Asked whether such a measure was conventional for foreign aircraft, Minister of Interior Mihajlovski answered:

> *"No, no. Not at all. The plane is not Macedonian territory; if Spain sends us a plane, it's the territory of Spain. If there's a bomb on board we must come inside; but otherwise it's like a ship, a diplomatic territory".*

125. All these factual elements indicate that the CIA carried out a "rendition" of Khaled El-Masri. The plane in question had finished transferring another detainee just two days earlier and the plane was still on the same "rendition circuit". The plane and its crew had spent the interim period at Palma de Mallorca, a popular CIA staging point. The physical and moral degradation to which Mr El-Masri was subjected before being forced aboard the plane in Macedonia corresponds with the CIA's systematic "rendition methodology" described earlier in this report. The destination of the flight carrying Mr El-Masri, Kabul, forms a hub of CIA secret detentions in our graphic representation of the "spider's web".

126. All the indications are that the Macedonian authorities have decided to deny their part in the abduction of El-Masri, admitting only what has already been clearly proven and trying to conceal the rest. It is regrettable that the will is lacking to perform a true inquiry and that Parliament has not shown the initiative to take up the issue (as the German *Bundestag* has done in the same case). To this must be added the further accusations of the Macedonian Helsinki Committee for Human Rights. According to reports produced by this NGO, suspects were and still are interrogated and sometimes imprisoned and ill-treated for several days, outside the normal arrest and custody system[104], specifically in the "apartments" that had been widely used by the previous regime.

127. It is worth repeating that the analysis of all facts concerning this case points in favour of the credibility of El-Masri. Everything points in the direction that he was the victim of abduction and ill-treatment amounting to torture within the meaning of the term established by the case-law of the United Nations Committee against Torture. In addition, numerous indications support the conclusion that German services participated in a manner that still remains to be precisely established (not excluding the fact that

[104] My representative who travelled to Macedonia was able to see former "secret apartments", which are now closely supervised by NGOs defending human rights.

the same services were in the end instrumental in El-Masri's release; the latter told me that he considered "Sam" as his guardian angel, a kind of "life insurance')[105].

128. The detailed information with which El-Masri was confronted during his interrogations in Skopje and in Afghanistan included details of his private life in Neu-Ulm. It is hard to imagine that such information could have been obtained by foreign services without help from their German counterparts. For example, the interrogators in Afghanistan knew that El-Masri had met a certain Reda Seyam[106] at the *Multikulturhaus* and had agreed to get a car, which Seyam had just bought with his help and had registered in the name of El-Masri's wife in order to save on the cost of insurance. El-Masri assured me that he had shared this information only with Seyam and his wife. In addition, the same interrogators confronted him with bank details of money transfers between his bank in Neu-Ulm and an account in Norway[107]. Such bank details are not normally accessible to foreign services.

129. In my opinion, this detailed knowledge of Mr El-Masri's—real—life also rules out the theory that Mr El-Masri was the victim of mere mistaken identity[108], being confused with a person of the same (or similar) name, whose name appeared in the American Congressional report on the

[105] In a recent development, the BND was forced to admit that one of its agents had indeed heard about El-Masri's detention at the hands of the Macedonian services and his hand-over to the Americans as early as January 2004 in a civil service canteen in Skopje (see Spiegel-Online of 31 May and 1 June 2006). The German Minister of the Interior tried to play down the importance of this revelation by calling it a mere breakdown of communications, as the higher echelons of the BND had not been informed. Nonetheless it is interesting to note that the truthfulness of the content of this conversation was never called into question.

[106] According to a German source, Mr Seyam, a German national of Indonesian origin, had returned in an unbelievable manner from a stay in that country. He had allegedly been arrested by the Indonesian authorities who suspected him of involvement in the Bali bombing. He had been released for lack of evidence, and taken back to Germany by German agents, who had been sent in order to prevent Mr Seyam being "handed over" to the Americans, who were apparently already waiting. Mr Seyam then allegedly went to Neu-Ulm at the instigation of his German "rescuers", who recommended that he go to the *Multikulturhaus*. The latter, according to the source, was under observation by both the *Baden-Württemberg* services (who had "planted" an informer there in the person of Dr Yousif, an Islamic preacher at the centre and an old acquaintance of Mr Seyam) and those of neighbouring Bavaria who—not knowing that Yousif was working for *Baden-Württemberg*—regarded him as a "preacher of hate". It was in this Islamic cultural centre frequented by Mr El-Masri that the latter came to know Mr Seyam (against whom a judicial investigation had also been opened in Germany, and closed shortly afterwards for lack of evidence). The two men, both looking for housing for their large families, became friends.

[107] According to Mr El Hasri, these were money transfers relating to Norwegian customers in connection with his car sales activity.

[108] This appears to be the argument of the German government, in the context of the talks between Federal Chancellor Angela Merkel and American Secretary of State Condoleezza Rice (cf. the link to the record of the joint press conference by Mrs Merkel and Mrs Rice on 6 December 2005 [http://www.state.gov/secretary/rm/2005/57672;htm]. Mrs Merkel confirmed that she had spoken to Mrs Rice about the El-Masri case and said that the American government, the American administration, had admitted that the man had been taken by mistake and that the American administration did not deny in principle that this had occurred).

11 September attacks[109] as having travelled by train in Germany together with members of the "Hamburg cell" of the terrorists of 11 September, including one of the murderous pilots, Muhammad Atta[110].

130. As regards the identity of "Sam", who came and interrogated Mr El-Masri in Afghanistan and accompanied him back on the return flight to Europe, speaking German with a Northern accent, Mr El-Masri remains convinced that this is Mr Lehmann, an agent of the German *Bundeskriminalamt*. He had identified him with "100%" certainty on photographs and a videotape, and with "90%" certainty at a surprise police lineup on 22 February 2006[111].

131. Mr El-Masri has also been the victim of a defamatory campaign. The press service of the Baden-Württemberg Ministry of the Interior had indicated that El-Masri was a member of "Al Tawid", implying "Al Tawid al Jihad", a group belonging to Al Quaida and headed by Abu Musab al-Zarkawi. According to Mr Gnjidic, the confusion was deliberate: El-Masri did belong to a militant anti-Syrian party (a nationalist party of the left also including Islamist elements) called "Al Tawid", founded in 1982 and wound up in 1985 after the Syrian invasion. Whereas certain members were captured by the Syrians, El-Masri fled and sought political asylum in Germany, for precisely that reason. That group allegedly had absolutely nothing in common (except part of the name, which means "all-powerful god") with the terrorist group headed by al-Zarkawi. Mr El-Masri was again faced with this confusion at his hearing by the Temporary Committee of the European Parliament, where at least one EP deputy asked him to what other terrorist groups he belonged. As Mr El-Masri was still in a fragile psychological state, I find it particularly odious that he was also the subject of an article, with a photograph, in the local press[112] once again

---

109 Page 165.

110 Mr El Masri stated in our talks that he had not even been questioned about this train journey mentioned in the report on 11 September. In his written deposition to the Virginia court (Declaration of Khaled El-Masri in support of plaintiff's opposition to the United States' motion to dismiss [. . .] dated 6 April 2006, p. 13), he said that he was interrogated in Afghanistan also about his alleged association with important terrorists such as Muhammad Atta, Ramzi Bin Al-Shibh and other presumed extremists based in Germany.

111 To the surprise of El-Masri and his lawyer, Mr Gnjidic, the prosecutor's office immediately announced to the press that the identification of "Sam" had failed. Subsequently the magazine "Stern" unearthed a CIA agent of German origin, Thomas V., who spoke German with the "north German" accent detected in "Sam" by El-Masri, who had been posted in 2000 to the United States Consulate General in Hamburg and who might be "Sam". The Munich prosecutor in charge of the case, Mr Hofmann, now rules out the possibility of "Sam" being the same person as the federal agent Lehmann, believing that it is now almost fully established that he was present at the *Bundeskriminalamt* office in Berlin throughout May 2004. But Mr El-Masri and his German lawyer Gnjidic remain convinced that "Sam" is indeed Lehmann, and that the Thomas V. trail was intended mainly to exonerate the German services.

112 See Neu Ulmer Zeitug, Islamisten zieht es nach Ulm; Multi-Kultur-Leute treffen sichjetzt im Donautal—Welche Rolle spielt Khaled El-Masri? 15 March 2006.

insinuating his links with terrorist circles without any evidence whatsoever. He told us that he now hardly dares to leave his home.

132. The case of Khaled El-Masri is exemplary. Some aspects still require further investigation and it is for that reason that inquiries are ongoing in the *Bundestag's* Committee of Inquiry and by the Munich prosecutors. The story of El-Masri is the dramatic story of a person who is evidently innocent—or at least against whom not the slightest accusation could ever be made—who has been through a real nightmare in the CIA's "spider's web", merely because of a supposed friendship with a person suspected at some point in time of maintaining contacts with terrorist groups. El-Masri is still waiting for the truth to be established, and for an apology. His application to a court in the United States has been rejected, at least in the first instance: not because it seemed unfounded, but because the Government brought to bear so-called "national security" and "state secrecy" interests. This speaks for itself.

3.2. "The Algerian Six"

133. Six Bosnians of Algerian origin—four Bosnian citizens and two longstanding residents[113] were arrested in October 2001 by order of the Supreme Court of the Federation of Bosnia and Herzegovina and detained on remand. They were suspected of having planned bomb attacks on the American and British embassies.

134. The investigation, between October 2001 and January 2002, did not reveal any evidence linking these men to a terrorist plot. On 17 January 2002, the office of the federal prosecutor informed the investigating magistrate at the supreme court that he had no reason to keep the men in custody any longer. On that same day at about 3pm the investigating magistrate ordered the immediate release of the six men.

135. Again on the same day, at about 5pm, the Human Rights Chamber of Bosnia and Herzegovina issued an interim order, following an application lodged by four of the men[114]. The order, which had statutory force in Bosnia according to the Dayton peace accords, required the Government of Bosnia and Herzegovina to take all necessary steps to prevent the forcible deportation of the applicants from Bosnia and Herzegovina.

136. However, on the evening of 17 January 2002 the six men were arrested by Bosnian police officers, and handed over to members of the United

[113] Mustafa Ait Idir, Hadz Boudella, Lakhdar Boumediene, Saber Lahmar and Mohammed Nechle and Belkacem Bensayah.

[114] cf. Boudella, Boumediene, Nechle and Lahmar v. Bosnia and Herzegovina and the Federation of Bosnia and Herzegovina, Human Rights Chamber for Bosnia and Herzegovina, cases nos. CH/02/8679, CH/02/8690, CH/02/8691, Order for Provisional Measures and on the Organization of the Proceedings, 17 January 2001.

States military forces stationed in Bosnia and Herzegovina on the morning of 18 January. This is recorded as an established fact in a judgment of the Human Rights Chamber for Bosnia and Herzegovina of 4 April 2003[115]. The Chamber refers to a document of the Council of Ministers dated 4 February 2002, according to which members of the police forces of the Federation under the authority of the Federal Minister of the Interior and of forces of the Minister of the Interior of the Canton of Sarajevo handed the applicants over to the American forces at the Butmir base on 18 January at 6am.

137. According to the victims' evidence, transmitted by their lawyers[116], the six victims were handcuffed in uncomfortable positions and hooded so that they could not see the aircraft which they were forced to board, at a given time on 18 or 19 January 2002. According to the lawyers, official documents obtained in the course of the judicial proceedings in progress show that two aircraft were assigned to this operation[117], and that the aircraft which the six men were made to board was at the Tuzla military base. After a flight of several hours, the aircraft landed and the six men were made to disembark, at a place which they describe as very cold[118]. During the flights the men were beaten and tied up in uncomfortable positions. At the stopover -probably Incirlik—they were joined by other detainees, some of whom said they came from Afghanistan. The human cargo arrived at Guantanamo on 20 January 2002.

138. The six men have been prisoners at Guantanamo until the present time, that is to say for over four years.

139. The illegal nature of these detentions was recognised by the Human Rights Chamber for Bosnia[119]. In the three decisions, the Chamber invited the Government of Bosnia to assist the six men, including recourse to diplomatic and judicial means. In the decision of 4 April 2003 concerning Mr Ait Idir, the Chamber even ordered the Government of Bosnia to take

[115] Case no. CH/O2/9499, Bekasem Bensayah against Bosnia and Herzegovina and the Federation of Bosnia and Herzegovina (cf. in particular paras. 50 et 164).

[116] The international law firm Wilmer Hale, which supplied written documentation and oral testimony (Mrs Karin Matussek on 11 April 2006 to our committee, and Mr Steven Oleskey to the temporary committee of the European Parliament, on 25 April 2006.) My representative also met with four WilmerHale attorneys working on this case at their offices in Boston, USA in May 2006. I am grateful to this firm for its excellent cooperation.

[117] Two C-130 cargo planes bearing serial numbers UJM166301019 and UQU09Z10L019, one of which also used the American base at Ramstein in Germany for the purposes of this operation. The documents in question also show that the aircraft transporting the six men stopped over at the American base at Incirlik in Turkey.

[118] The six men think it might have been in Turkey, on the basis of what little they were able to see and hear.

[119] Afore-mentioned judgment of 4 April 2003 concerning Mr Bensayah and Mr Ait Idir; in a judgment of 11 October 2002, the Chamber had already decided the cases of the other four men (Boudellaa, Boumediene, Nechle and Lahmar against Bosnia and Herzegovina and the Federation of Bosnia and Herzegovina, cases nos. CH/02/8679, CH/02/8689, CH/02/8690, CH02/8691, decision of 11 October 2002).

all possible steps to secure the release of the applicant and his return home[120].

140. The Bosnian government has recognised its legal obligations but not complied with them.

141. In the Council of Ministers document cited by the Human Rights Chamber[121], the Government of Bosnia and Herzegovina admitted that the six men had been "handed over" to the American forces by the Bosnian authorities without extradition formalities being observed[122].

142. On 21 April 2004, the Human Rights Committee of the Parliament of Bosnia and Herzegovina exhorted the Bosnian executive to execute the decision of the Human Rights Chamber and start proceedings with the United States for the repatriation of the detainees. Its report was endorsed by the parliament chamber on 11 May 2004.

143. On 11 March 2005, the Minister of Justice confirmed that the Bosnian government had sent a letter to the American government requesting the return of the six men.

144. On 21 June 2005, the Bosnian Prime Minister Mr Adnan Terzic confirmed before the Parliamentary Assembly of the Council of Europe[123] the importance of this case as an indicator of democratic progress in Bosnia, and declared his willingness to identify the best way of ensuring the release of the six Bosnian citizens and former residents from Guantanamo, in accordance with Parliamentary Assembly Resolution 1433(2005).

145. Lastly, on 16 September 2005, the Bosnian parliament adopted a resolution inviting the Council of Ministers of Bosnia and Herzegovina to make contact with the American government in order to resolve the problem of the six men as rapidly as possible.

146. It is all the more surprising that, in spite of all these promising declarations, including that of the Prime Minister to the Parliamentary Assembly of the Council of Europe, there has been no government initiative aimed at the release of the six men.

---

120 Idem, para. 168.

121 Note 115 above.

122 The Human Rights Chamber, in the above-mentioned Bensayah judgment (note 114), explains in a relevant manner that the "handing over" of the applicant can in no way be deemed to constitute extradition. In particular, the note dated 17 January 2002 from the US embassy cannot be regarded as a request for extradition by the United States. In that note, the US embassy in Sarajevo informs the Government of Bosnia and Herzegovina that it is willing to take charge of the six Algerian citizens in question and offers to arrange for the physical transfer of these persons at a time and place suitable to both parties.

123 In reply to a question from our former colleague Kevin McNamara, following Resolution 1433 (2005) adopted by the Parliamentary Assembly on 26 April 2005, calling on all Council of Europe member States, including Bosnia and Herzegovina, to protect the rights of their citizens or residents detained at Guantanamo and to have them released and repatriated.

147. According to their lawyers[124], the American government has declared on several occasions that it is willing to enter into bilateral discussions with the governments of countries whose citizens are detained at Guantanamo in order to arrange their repatriation, subject to adequate security conditions. In the case of the six men in question, such measures would be unnecessary anyway, since the charges against them have already been investigated by the competent authorities and those investigations have shown that they are innocent. Nonetheless, the Bosnian government has apparently made no credible move to initiate negotiations in that direction[125].

148. The innocence of the men in question—which is in any event presumed, and is in no sense a condition for treating the suspects in accordance with legal rules—has just been strengthened by a report drawn up by the German military. This report, produced in decidedly unusual circumstances[126], which also aroused the interest of the German media and parliamentarians[127], concluded *inter alia* that the reasons for arresting the six men were "highly dubious"[128].

149. In my opinion, the case of the "Bosnian six" is another well documented example of the abduction of European citizens and residents by the American authorities with the active collusion of the authorities of a Council of Europe member state. The government of Bosnia and Herzegovina has the merit of no longer denying the fact that it handed over the six men to the American forces. According to information I have received[129], the Bosnian authorities acted under extraordinary pressure from the American embassy in Sarajevo, but the fact remains that they acted in violation of clear decisions by the Supreme Court and the Human

---

[124] Memorandum of 12 April 2006, addressed to the Temporary Committee of the European Parliament.

[125] See Matthew A. Reynolds, Acting Assistant Secretary, Legislative Affairs, US Department of State, letter to Senator James M. Jeffords, response to a requeset for information (copy on file with the Rapporteur), 15 June 2005: *"Although the Government of Bosnia and Herzegovina has made several inquiries regarding the condition of each detainee and has asked for their release, it has not indicated that it is prepared or willing to accept responsibility for them upon transfer."*

[126] German military personnel posed as journalists in order to conduct an interview with Mr Bensayah's wife, Mrs Anela Kobilica, on 17 June 2003. The report subsequently drawn up by the German military concluded that the grounds on which the six men were arrested and deported were *"highly dubious"* and that documents examined gave rise to the suspicion that at least some of the six had been *"subjected to an injustice"*.

[127] See, for example, *http://www.tagesschau.de/aktuell/meldungen/0,1185,OID5072374,00.html*. Journalists' associations protested vehemently at methods of investigation that involved intelligence agents masquerading as journalists, as this exposed real journalists to suspicion and possible reprisals.

[128] From a confidential source, I received a copy of this report, which, it was claimed, was deleted from the German military archives and never received by the German embassy in Sarajevo, to which it was said originally to have been addressed. See *Supplementary Intelligence Report*, 16 July 2003 (copy on file with the Rapporteur).

[129] See for example the Wilmer Hale memorandum of 12 April 2006, at page 3, supported by a wealth of documents given to us by Wilmer Hale, copies of which are all on file with the Rapporteur.

Rights Chamber ordering the release of these men. If the damage to the good human rights reputation of Bosnia and Herzegovina is to be repaired, official recognition of the facts is an important step in the right direction, but it must be followed as swiftly as possible with credible diplomatic intervention vis-a-vis the American government in order to secure the rapid repatriation of these six men, who have now been festering in Guantanamo Bay for over four years.

3.3. Ahmed Agiza and Mohammed Alzery (El Zari)

150. The case of the two Egyptian asylum-seekers "handed over" by the Swedish authorities to American agents who took them to Egypt, where they were tortured in spite of diplomatic assurances given to Sweden, is another very well documented case. It led to Sweden's being condemned by the United Nations Committee against Torture (UN-CAT)[130]. The Swedish authorities were also criticised for having attempted to conceal the facts from UN-CAT[131].

151. The affair was brought to public notice mainly by the "Kalla Fakta"[132] television programme, and research by the Swedish investigative journalists blew open the secret system of CIA aircraft transporting clandestine prisoners in the "war against terrorism". The aircraft used for this operation—a Gulfstream, number N379P—has become one of the most notorious "rendition" aircraft[133].

152. The behaviour of the Swedish secret police (Säpo) gave rise to a detailed investigation by the Swedish parliamentary ombudsman, Mats Melin[134].

---

130 United Nations Committee against Torture, decision of 20 May 2005, CAT/C/34/D/233/2003; see also United Nations Committee against Torture, Conclusions and recommendations of the Committee against Torture: Sweden. 06/06/2002, CAT/C/CR/28/6 (Concluding Observations/ Comments), and the Swedish reply (Comments by the Government of Sweden on the Concluding Observations of the Human Rights Committee (CCPR/CO/74/SWE) of 14 May 2003. In that reply (para. 16), the Swedish government said that in its opinion, the "assurances" given by Egypt were being and would continue to be fully respected, and that the government had received no information to cast doubt on that conclusion.

131 See "Kalla Fakta" (note 131 below), page 10: the Swedish reply to the final observations (note 129 above) seems to be contradicted by the first report of the Swedish Ambassador in Egypt, according to which Mr Agiza had spoken to him about the abuse and violence which he and Mr Alzery had suffered. According to "Kalla Fakta", the Swedish government had filed this information and refused to hand it to the United Nations. In its decision of 20 May 2005 (note 129 above, para. 13.10), UN-CAT notes that Sweden has not fulfilled its obligation to co-operate fully with the Committee, and has not made all the relevant and necessary information for resolving the case available to the Committee.

132 Translation of the title of the programme: "Cold facts"; a transcript of the broadcast of 22 November 2004 was provided to me by TV4.

133 Kalla Fakta has given an account of its research into the owner of N379P, Premier Executive Transport Services. Posing as potential clients, journalists satisfied themselves as to the governmental, clandestine nature of this firm (cf. transcript, note 131 above, pages 4-5).

134 See Mats Melin, Parliamentary Ombudsman (Sweden), *A review of the enforcement by the Security Police of a Government decision to expel two Egyptian citizens,* Adjudication No. 2169-2004, dated 22 March 2005. (Translated copy on file with the Rapporteur.)

The judicial authorities also examined the case and concluded that there were no grounds for a criminal prosecution against either the Swedish agents involved, or the pilot of the aircraft, or other American agents who were part of the team responsible for transporting Mr Agiza and Mr Alzery to Egypt[135].

153. In short, the facts occurred in the following manner: on 18 December 2001, Mr Agiza and Mr Alzery, Egyptian citizens seeking asylum in Sweden, were the subject of a decision dismissing the asylum application and ordering their deportation on grounds of security, taken in the framework of a special procedure at ministerial level. In order to ensure that this decision could be executed that same day, the Swedish authorities accepted an American offer to place at their disposal an aircraft which enjoyed special overflight authorisations[136]. Following their arrest by the Swedish police, the two men were taken to Bromma airport where they were subjected, with Swedish agreement, to a "security check" by hooded American agents.

154. The account of this *"check"* is especially interesting, as it corresponds in detail to the account given independently by other victims of "rendition", including Mr El-Masri. The procedure adopted by the American team, described in this case by the Swedish police officers present at the scene,[137] was evidently well rehearsed: the agents communicated with each other by gestures, not words. Acting very quickly, the agents cut Agiza's and Alzery's clothes off them using scissors, dressed them in tracksuits, examined every bodily aperture and hair minutely, handcuffed them and shackled their feet, and walked them to the aircraft barefoot.

155. The ombudsman condemns as degrading the way in which the detainees were treated from the time when they were taken charge of by the American agents until the end of the operation when the two men were handed to the Egyptian authorities. He does not consider that it constitutes torture for the purposes of Article 3 of the European Convention on Human Rights, but asks the question—though he does not answer it—whether the execution of the deportation order nonetheless violates Article 3. In any event, he finds that the operation was carried out in an inhuman and therefore unacceptable manner[138].

---

[135] *Ibid*, at page 3.

[136] An internal Säpo report seems to indicate that the American involvement was approved by the Ministry of Foreign Affairs; persons who attended the meeting with the minister and were questioned by the ombudsman have no recollection that this was mentioned.

[137] Owing to lack of space in the room made available to the Americans, the Swedish police were not able to observe everything. In particular, they did not see that (tranquillising) suppositories were administered and that diapers were affixed, as the detainees maintain, and as was done in other "renditions". See the earlier section of this report on the "Human Impact of Renditions and Secret Detentions".

[138] See the report by Mats Melin, *supra* note 134, page 23.

156. According to the ombudsman's findings, the Swedish officers, who were poorly led, lost control of the operation from the start of the American team's intervention. They ought to have intervened to put an end to the degrading treatment of the detainees, which was not justified on security grounds since the Swedish police had already carried out a body search on the detainees at the time of arrest.

157. Prior to deportation of the two men to Egypt, Sweden sought and obtained "diplomatic assurances" that they would not be subjected to treatment contrary to the anti-torture convention, would have fair trials and would not be subjected to the death penalty. The "assurances" were even backed up by a monitoring mechanism, regular visits by the Swedish Ambassador and participation by Swedish observers at the trial.

158. Developments in the case show that these "assurances" were not honoured. Mr Alzery's lawyer, Kjell Jönsson,[139] states that extremely grave acts of torture took place[140]. Although Mr Alzery was released from prison in October 2003, he is not allowed to leave his village without permission from the authorities. Mr Agiza was sentenced to 25 years imprisonment by a military court in a trial from which the Swedish observers were excluded for the first two days out of a total of four. Despite the fact that Mr Agiza complained of torture during his detention, which lasted over two years after his forced return to Egypt, and despite the fact that the prison doctor's report did record physical injuries sustained in prison, the military court did not act on the defence request for an independent medical examination[141].

159. The UN-CAT decision shows that the "diplomatic assurances", even with follow-up clauses attached, are not such as to prevent the risk of torture[142]. The deporting state therefore still bears responsibility.

160. All things considered, the Swedish case of Agiza and Alzery cannot be classed as "abduction" by the CIA. The two men were the subject of a Swedish deportation procedure following dismissal of the asylum application; that procedure was severely criticised by UN-CAT, and rightly so: the immediate execution of the decision deprived the two men of any

[139] Mr Jönsson testified before the Temporary Committee of the European Parliament on 23 March 2005; he spoke at great length with a member of my team during his visit to Brussels.

[140] Electric shock torture was used, with electrodes fixed to the most sensitive parts of the body, in the presence of a doctor who assesses what electrical charge the prisoner can survive. In order to prevent marks, the places affected are treated specially at the end of each torture session.

[141] A representative of Human Rights Watch observed the entire trial; the observed violations of the rights of the defence are listed in a HRW communique of 5 May 2005 (Sweden Implicated in Egypt's abuse of Suspected Militant—Egypt violated diplomatic promises of fair trial and no torture for terrorism suspect (http://hrw.org/english/docs/2004/05/05/egypt8530_txt.htm).

[142] Diplomatic assurances are not the focus of my mandate; here, nevertheless, are two very pertinent reports on the subject: Amnesty International, *"Diplomatic Assurances"—no protection against torture or ill-treatment*, report No. ACT 40/021/2005, 1 December 2005; and Human Rights Watch, *Still at Risk: "Diplomatic Assurances" No Safeguard against Torture*, Report No. 17, Vol. 3D, 17 April 2005.

possibility of appeal, including under the United Nations Convention against Torture—an appeal which moreover would have stood a good chance of success, in view of the risk of torture they faced in Egypt. Other criticisms directed at Sweden are the "slack" implementation of the follow-up clause relating to the assurances obtained prior to extradition[143], and above all the fact that Sweden did not send UN-CAT all the relevant information[144]. On the other hand, with regard to the ill-treatment of the prisoners at Bromma airport and in the aircraft, the reproach is aimed primarily at the United States. I share Mats Melin's view that such degrading and humiliating treatment is unacceptable.

161. Nonetheless, in my opinion it is for Sweden to clarify further the reasons and responsibilities: how was it that the Swedish officers present on the scene allowed their American counterparts to do as they wished, letting them take control of this operation while still on Swedish soil?

3.4. Abu Omar

162. At midday on 17 June 2003, Hassam Osama Mustafa Nasr, known as Abu Omar, an Egyptian citizen, was abducted in the middle of Milan. Thanks to an outstanding and tenacious investigation by the Milan judiciary and the DIGOS police services, Abu Omar's is undoubtedly one of the best-known and best-documented cases of "extraordinary rendition"[145]. Via the military airbases at Aviano (Italy) and Ramstein (Germany), Abu Omar was flown to Egypt, where he was tortured before being released and re-arrested. To my knowledge, no proceedings were brought against Abu Omar in Egypt. The Italian judicial investigation established beyond all reasonable doubt that the operation was carried out by the CIA (which has not issued any denials). The Italian investigators likewise established that the presumed leader of the abduction operation—who had also worked as the American consul in Milan—was in Egypt for two weeks immediately after Abu Omar was handed over to the Egyptian authorities. It may safely

[143] See the afore-mentioned HRW communique of 5 May 2005: the first visit Mr Agiza received from a Swedish diplomat was only five weeks after his arrival in Egypt, despite the fact that experience shows that torture and ill-treatment take place during the first days of detention. Furthermore, the Swedish diplomats, who were not trained to recognise signs of torture, apparently gave several days' notice of their visits, and all conversations were apparently monitored by the Egyptian warders.

[144] Sweden justifies the fact that it did not send its ambassador's first visit report, in which Mr Alzery's complaints of ill-treatment are recorded, for fear of reprisals against the detainees, given doubts about respect for confidentiality within UN-CAT. But in any case those complaints were known to the Egyptian authorities, who were represented during the ambassador's visit.

[145] I met the prosecutor heading the investigation, Armando Spataro, and was able to obtain as full information as confidentiality and procedural requirements permitted. The Abu Omar case is likewise described in the aforementioned book by Guido Olimpio, *Operazione Hotel California*, Feltrinelli, October 2005. The main documents in the judicial investigation have been collected and reproduced in a book by Guido Ruotolo and Vincenza Vasile: *Milano-Cairo. Viaggio senza ritorno. L'iman rapito in Italia dalla CIA*, Tullio Pironti Editore, 2005.

be inferred that he contributed, in one way or another, to Abu Omar's interrogation. The proceedings instituted in Milan concern 25 American agents, against 22 of whom the Italian judicial authorities have issued arrest warrants. Abu Omar was a political refugee. Suspected of Islamic militancy, he had been under surveillance by the Milan police and judicial authorities. As a result of the surveillance operation, the Italian police were probably on the verge of uncovering an activist network operating in northern Italy. Abu Omar's abduction, as the Milan judicial authorities expressly point out, sabotaged the Italian surveillance operation and thereby dealt a blow to the fight against terrorism. Is it conceivable or possible that an operation of this kind, with a deployment of resources on this scale in a friendly country that was an ally (being a member of the coalition in Iraq), was carried out without the Italian authorities—or at least the corresponding Italian officials—being informed? The Italian Government has denied having been informed. There has recently been a significant new development in the investigation by the Milan prosecuting authorities, however: an agent belonging to an elite *Carabinieri* unit has admitted taking part in Abu Omar's abduction as part of an operation co-ordinated by the military intelligence services (SISMI)[146]. But General Pollari, head of SISMI, had formally denied any SISMI participation in the abduction; he had even affirmed that he had only been informed of this episode after the abduction itself[147].

3.5. Bisher Al-Rawi and Jamil El-Banna

163. This case, which concerns two British permanent residents arrested in Gambia in November 2002 and transferred first to Afghanistan and from there to Guantanamo (where they still are), is an example of (ill-conceived) cooperation between the services of a European country (the British MI5) and the CIA in abducting persons against whom there is no evidence justifying their continued detention in prison and whose principal crime is to be on social terms with a leading Islamist, namely Abu Qatada.

164. The information made public to date[148] shows that the abduction of Messrs Al-Rawi and El-Banna was indeed motivated by information—partly erroneous—supplied by MI5.

---

[146] See Corriere della Sera and La Repubblica of 11 May 2006.

[147] Statement of General Pollari at the meeting of the TDIP on 6 March 2006.

[148] I wish to thank in particular my British colleague Andrew Tyrie, Chairman of the House of Commons All-Party Parliamentary Group (APPG) on renditions, who helped to arrange for two members of our committee secretariat to attend an APPG hearing with Mr Al-Rawi and Mr El Banna's lawyers and family. This hearing took place on 28 March 2006. I also thank the two men's American and British lawyers, Mr Brent Mickum and Ms Gareth Peirce, along with Mr Clive Stafford-Smith, the legal director of REPRIEVE, for the detailed information they provided for my inquiries.

165. Bisher Al-Rawi and Jamil El-Banna were arrested in Gambia on 8 November 2002. They intended to join Mr Al-Rawi's brother Wahab, a British citizen, and help him set up a mobile peanut processing plant. The British authorities were well aware of this business trip[149]. On 1 November, Messrs Al-Rawi and El-Banna left on their trip, but did not get very far. At Gatwick airport they were arrested by reason of a suspect item in Mr Al-Rawi's hand luggage.

166. On the same day, a first telegram from MI5 informed the CIA that the two men had been arrested under the 2000 anti-terrorist act. That telegram contained false information, including the statement that Mr Al-Rawi was an Islamist extremist, and that the search of his luggage had revealed that he was carrying a sort of improvised electronic device which could be used, according to preliminary investigations, as a component of a home-made bomb[150].

167. The two men spent 48 hours in police custody, until the police decided that the "suspicious device" was nothing other than a battery charger on sale in several electronic goods shops (Dixons, Argos, Maplins). Mr Al-Rawi explained this when he was arrested, but it had to be checked. The conclusion to the charger episode—that it was indeed a "harmless device"—was communicated to the Ministry of Foreign Affairs by MI5 in a telegram of 11 November 2002. Unfortunately, there is no evidence that this information was ever conveyed to the CIA. The allegations concerning this "device" reappeared in their "trial" before the CSRT (Combatant Status Review Tribunal)[151] as "evidence" that they were "enemy combatants".

168. Messrs Al-Rawi and El-Banna returned home on 4 November 2002 and reorganised their trip to Gambia for 8 November. Meanwhile, several telegrams were sent by MI5 to the Americans concerning the two men, informing them that they knew Abu Qatada and that Mr El-Banna was the latter's "financier". It is true that the two men knew Abu Qatada[152]. On the other hand, according to the lawyers, Mr Al-Rawi had helped MI5 to

[149] Mr El-Banna informed his lawyer that two MI5 agents had come to his home and told him that they knew all about his planned trip. In reply to his question as to whether everything was in order, they said yes and wished him good luck. Mr El-Banna's wife confirmed this visit at the APPG hearing on 28 March 2006.

[150] Telegram of 1 November 2002, made public on 27 March 2006, with other telegrams dated 4, 8 and 11 November and 6 December 2002; these documents are normally classified secret, but came into the public domain after being cited on 22 and 23 March 2006 at a public hearing in the Queens Bench Division of the High Court in London, before Lord Justice Latham and Mr Justice Tugendhat. The telegrams were also the subject of the APPG hearing on 27 March 2006. It is clear to their lawyers that not everything is said in the telegrams, which moreover refer to other communications, including telephone calls.

[151] See US Department of Defense, unclassified Combatant Status Review Tribunal (CSRT) transcripts disclosed in the matter of *El-Banna et al v. Bush,* in the US District Court of Columbia (copies of all transcripts on file with the Rapporteur), October 2004.

[152] At the APPG hearing on 27 March 2006, Mr El-Banna's wife explained that their "social" relations derived from the fact that the three men had family ties with Jordan.

prepare the non-violent arrest of Abu Qatada, and British agents had even thanked him for doing so[153].

169. On 8 November 2002, the day when the two men flew to Gambia, MI5 sent another telegram giving the flight details, including the departure of the delayed flight and the estimated arrival time. The telegram states that *"this message should be read in the light of earlier communications"*. In addition, the telegram of 8 November does not mention, as the earlier telegrams do, that this information *"must not be used as the basis of overt, covert or executive action"*.

170. At Banjul airport, Al-Rawi and El-Banna, accompanied by a collaborator, Mr El Janoudi, met Bisher Al-Rawi's brother Wahab, who had gone to Gambia one week before the others, and all four were arrested by Gambian agents. They were taken to a house outside Banjul. Mr Janoudi managed to telephone his wife in London, and another brother of Mr Al-Rawi, Numann, went to see his MP, Edward Davey, who informed the Foreign Ministry.

171. During the following days, according to Wahab's account, American agents were very present, but the detainees never saw a British official despite the fact that they asked to see a consular representative. Wahab stated at the APPG hearing that the CIA and Gambian officials repeatedly alluded to the fact that *"it is the British who have told us to arrest you"*. Mr El-Banna says he has continually been told the same thing during his subsequent detention at Guantanamo Bay:

> *"My interrogator asked me 'Why are you so angry at America? It is your Government, Britain, the MI5, who called the CIA and told them that you and Bisher were in The Gambia and to come and get you. Britain gave everything to us. Britain sold you out to the CIA'"*[154].

172. On 5 December 2002, after 27 days, Wahab was released and returned to the United Kingdom. Some days afterwards, on a Sunday, Bisher Al-Rawi and Jamil El-Banna were flown to Afghanistan in a military jet with over 40 seats. There were at least 7 or 8 American agents on board, including a female doctor. Through their lawyers, the two men gave a detailed account of their degrading and humiliating treatment, many details of which echo the treatment suffered by other victims of "renditions'[155].

173. At Kabul, they were taken in less than 15 minutes to the prison identified as the "Dark Prison". The description of the inhuman detention

---

[153] Al-Rawi's cooperation with MI5 is said also to be the reason for several visits by MI5 agents to Guantanamo. The lawyers presented details of these conversations in public as recounted by their clients (copy in file). MI5 has not officially recognised this cooperation, which Al-Rawi also claimed in his depositions to the CSRT.

[154] See El-Banna's statement to his lawyer, *supra* note 68.

[155] They were dressed in diapers, wore hoods without eye-holes, had their ears blocked up, their legs shackled and their hands painfully handcuffed behind their backs, and were denied access to toilets.

conditions in this prison[156], an important link in the CIA "spider's web", corresponds in many details to that given by other victims of "renditions" who were brought there. After two weeks in this sinister prison, the two men were transferred to Bagram by helicopter. At Bagram they were imprisoned and ill-treated for a further two months. The American interrogators allegedly offered Mr El-Banna large sums of money in exchange for false witness against Abu Qatada. When these offers failed to produce the expected result, the interrogators allegedly threatened to send him back for a year to the "Dark Prison", followed by 5 or 10 years in Cuba, and made shameful threats against his family living in London[157].

174. Finally, the two men were transported to Guantanamo, where they were again subject to inhuman treatment. Mr Al-Rawi says he received many visits from MI5 agents, the first of them in early autumn 2003, and that he was interrogated by ten or so different CIA agents. One of the MI5 agents, he says, even apologised to him. In January 2004, two British agents ("Martin" and "Mathew") asked him whether he would be willing to work for MI5 again. Mr Al-Rawi replied that he would, provided that this would serve the cause of peace. Several months later, a certain "Alex" with whom Mr Al-Rawi had worked in London came to see him at Guantanamo, accompanied by an "attractive female agent". However, at the time of his "trial" before the CSRT, the British authorities refused to send to Guantanamo the witnesses he named or simply to confirm his links with MI5, thereby condemning him to continuous detention—detention which continues to this day, having lasted almost four years in all.

175. The families of Messrs Al-Rawi and El-Banna and their lawyers at the London firm Birnberg, Peirce & Partners brought an action to oblige the British government to make representations to the United States through diplomatic channels in order to secure the release and repatriation of the two men as soon as possible. According to the latest information, the British government has acted along those lines with regard to Mr Al-Rawi, but not with regard to Mr El-Banna. The judgment at first instance, given in May 2006, dismissed the families' complaints.

176. In view of these highly disturbing facts, I find that the British authorities must shed light on this case in full. I welcome the fact that our colleague, Andrew Tyrie, has devoted much energy to this matter in order for truth to be established in this disturbing case. Meanwhile, the United Kingdom, even if it has no recognised legal obligation, must make good the consequences of the apparently very imprecise communication between

---

156 *"Diabolically"* loud music round the clock, total absence of light, rotten food, no possibility to wash or use a toilet, uncomfortable handcuffing and leg shackling, cold cells, inadequate clothing, and the frequent beating and trampling of prisoners.

157 I prefer not to quote this extremely upsetting testimony.

the MI5 and the American services. There is indeed little doubt that the arrest of the two men was largely triggered or at least influenced by the messages of November 2002, only part of which (the afore-mentioned telegrams) is public knowledge.

3.6. Maher Arar

177. Maher Arar, a Canadian citizen of Syrian origin, came to testify in public before the Temporary Committee of the European Parliament[158]. During a stopover on return from holiday in Tunisia, in September 2002, he was arrested at JFK airport in New York by American agents. After being detained in a high-security prison and interrogated for two weeks by the New York police, the FBI and the American immigration service, he was allegedly transported from New Jersey airport via Washington, Rome and Amman to a prison belonging to Syrian military intelligence[159]. He spent more than ten months there, during which he says he was tortured, abused and forced to make false confessions. During his stay in Syria, he says, he also heard the voice of a German prisoner being tortured. After a tenacious campaign by his wife, Mr Arar was able to have irregular contacts with Canadian diplomats posted in Syria. He says he has never been the subject of criminal charges in any country. Mr Arar stills suffers from post-traumatic stress syndrome following his terrible experience.

178. The American Government considers the "rendition" of Arar as a legitimate procedure in conformity with its immigration rules[160].

179. According to Mr Arar, the agents on board the aircraft never identified themselves, but he heard that they belonged to a *"special removal unit"*. In this specific case, the transfer of Mr Arar to Syria seems to be a well established example of the "outsourcing of torture", a practice mentioned publicly by certain American officials[161].

180. The question which interests us more particularly, in view of our mandate, is whether and if so, to what extent, the European states concerned (in particular Italy and Greece) were aware of the illegal transport of Mr Arar and perhaps even gave logistical support[162].

---

[158] Accompanied by his lawyer, he also had exhaustive talks with a member of the Committee's secretariat.

[159] This journey was retraced by a British investigative journalist, whose research is corroborated by data obtained by us from Eurocontrol and national air traffic control authorities. See *Flight logs related to the rendition of Maher Arar,* in the Appendix to this report.

[160] See Bellinger, *Briefing to European Delegation, supra* note XX: "With respect to Maher Arar, I can't comment on his case either. But I do know his case has gotten added to the list of so-called renditions, when in fact his removal was dealt with as an immigration matter, which is what all countries do when they find someone in their country and they don't want to prosecute them inside their countries. So he was expelled from the United States by order of an Immigration Court. I think that's a different situation. So this is not the same situation as these other cases."

[161] See the quotations reproduced in my information report of 22 January 2006.

[162] See Flight logs related to the rendition of Maher Arar, in the Appendix to this report.

181. Another question is the role of the Canadian authorities in the matter. This question is the subject of a very thorough investigation by a special commission[163].

182. The initial report of the investigator Stephen J. Toope was published on 14 October 2005[164]. Mr Toope, who has lengthy experience in working with torture victims, has convincingly established the truthfulness of Mr Arar's depositions, which he has compared with those of other former Syrian prisoners held in the same prison run by Syrian military intelligence (Far Falestin). His report, which also mentions the findings of specialist doctors whom Mr Arar consulted on his return, describes in detail Mr Arar's treatment in Syria, which he unhesitatingly regards as torture within the meaning of the United Nations Convention against Torture. However, that report does not cover the part played by the Canadian authorities in the matter. This point will be covered in the final report of the Commission, which is expected to be published by the end of the summer of 2006[165]. It is thus premature to draw any conclusions at this stage[166].

183. The working methods of this commission, a genuine commission of inquiry with real powers of investigation, empowered to take cognisance of classified information, strike me as very interesting. However, Mr Paul Cavalluzo, principal lawyer to the Commissioner, the Honourable Dennis O'Connor, has reportedly deplored the tendency of the Canadian authorities to use national security confidentiality; Mr Arar's lawyers, Lome Waldman et Marlys Edwardh, have accused the Government to "hide behind" official secrecy considerations.

3.7. Muhammad Bashmila and Salah Ali Qaru

184. The cases of Mr Bashmila and Mr Ali Qaru are described in an Amnesty International report[167] based on inquiries made on the spot and intensive

---

[163] Commission of inquiry into the action of Canadian officials in relation to Maher Arar, set up on 5 February 2004 *"to throw light on the actions of the Canadian authorities concerning the deportation and detention of Maher Arar"*. The commissioner heading the inquiry is the Honourable Dennis R. O'Connor, deputy chief judge of Ontario.

[164] Available on the commission's website: *www.commissionarar.ca*; the reports of experts/witnesses, the rules of procedure and—albeit greatly truncated—summaries of the hearings in camera are among other items also published on this website.

[165] See the communique of 11 April 2006, indicating that the delay (five months after the date originally planned) is "largely attributable to the process that was adopted to analyse reports in regard to the government's requests designed to protect certain information on grounds of confidentiality in connection with national security (CLSN)". The communique describes in detail the procedures followed where the government invokes CLSN, disputes on the matter being settled in the last resort by the federal court.

[166] See the "summaries of hearings in camera" (note 163 above), in particular para. 12 pp and 33. Given the provisional and incomplete nature of these summaries, I prefer not to comment in greater detail.

[167] Below the radar: secret flights to torture and "disappearance", 5 April 2006, AI Index: AMR 51/051/2006. My particular thanks go to Mrs Anne Fitzgerald for her co-operation with our committee's secretariat on this subject.

discussions with the victims. It is likely that they owe their recent release to Amnesty's commitment. The two men, who have never been accused of the slightest terrorist crimes, were arrested in Jordan and disappeared, as far as their families were concerned, into the American "spider's web" in October 2003[168]. According to AI's investigations, they were held in at least four secret American detention centres, probably in three different countries. The former detainees themselves say that they spent time in Djibouti, Afghanistan and—of particular interest to us—*"somewhere in eastern Europe"*. The exact location of the place where they spent the final 13 months from the end of April 2004 onwards remains unknown. The men gave a precise description of their place of detention, which has not yet been published in full[169], and of the route along which they were taken. Particularly intriguing is their return flight to Yemen on 5 May 2005, reportedly a non-stop flight lasting approximately seven hours. I wrote to the Yemeni authorities and asked where the plane had come from, and the arrival of the aircraft on that date with the two men on board was officially confirmed to me. Unfortunately, although I wrote again, I have not yet received the specific information requested. Since the aircraft concerned was probably a military one, the information obtained from Eurocontrol has also been unable to clarify this matter. We have been unable to locate a site corresponding to the description provided.

3.8. Mohammed Zammar

185. Mr Zammar, a German of Syrian origin, was suspected of having been involved in the "Hamburg cell" of Al Qaeda and had been under police surveillance for several years in Germany. After 11 September 2001, he had been the subject of a criminal investigation for "support for a terrorist organisation", but there was insufficient evidence to keep him in prison.

186. On 27 October 2001, he is reported to have left Germany for Morocco, where he spent several weeks. When he attempted to return to Germany, he was allegedly arrested by Moroccan officials at Casablanca airport early in December, and to have been questioned by Moroccan and American officials for over two weeks. Towards the end of December 2001, he is said to have been flown to Damascus, Syria, on a CIA-linked aircraft[170].

[168] AI's report (pp 9-16) gives a precise description of the sufferings of the victims and their families.

[169] Cf AI report (pp 13 and 14). One particularly interesting piece of information is a geographical deduction based on the prayer times provided, which were taken from an Internet site (islamicfinder.org). The time of the sunset prayer ranged from 4.30 to 8.45 pm (allowing for the change to summer time, which the whole of Europe uses, but not Afghanistan, Jordan or Pakistan). This corresponds to a location north of the 41st parallel, so well to the north of the Middle East, and very probably within a Council of Europe member state.

[170] The Eurocontrol data available to us does not enable us to confirm this flight, which took place between two non-European airports.

187. The case has received extensive press coverage[171], and there have been allegations that Mr Zammar's arrest in Morocco was facilitated through the provision of information by German services, that he was tortured by Syrian services and that he was questioned in Syria by German officials.

188. A detailed German government report to the *Bundestag*, a copy of which I have obtained[172], gives a balanced version of this affair.

189. Mr Zammar's arrest in Morocco was objectively facilitated by exchanges of information between the German services and their Dutch, Moroccan and also American counterparts. These exchanges of information about the travel plans of a person suspected of terrorist activities (the German government's report contains detailed information which seem to justify such suspicion) are part of normal international cooperation in the fight against terrorism. It cannot be deduced from the fact that the German services informed their colleagues of the dates on which Mr Zammar had flight reservations that it was their intention—or even that they suspected—that he would be arrested and held in violation of normal procedures. The facts date back to December 2001, well before the public revelations about the illegal practice of "rendition flights".

190. The German Ministry for Foreign Affairs and the Damascus and Rabat Embassies intervened several times, firstly to establish Mr Zammar's whereabouts, then to give him consular assistance during his detention in Syria. Syria refused any kind of consular intervention, on the basis of its non-recognition of his renunciation of Syrian nationality when he underwent naturalisation in Germany, a policy applied generally by Syria.

191. German officials did indeed question Mr Zammar in Syria. While Mr Zammar is said to have told his German interrogators that he had been beaten both in Morocco and in the early stages of his detention in Syria, but nothing supports the conclusion that this mistreatment related to the presence and intervention of the German agents. The German officials are reported to have found him in a good physical and psychological condition, although he had lost a considerable amount of weight. Relations

[171] Examples are the items published in the Washington Post on 12 and 19 June 2002 and 31 January 2003, in *Der Spiegel* in July 2002 and November 2005, and in Focus of 20 September 2002, and shown on *Kalla Fakta* (the fourth Swedish TV channel) on 22 November 2004.

[172] Following my request to the Chair of the *Bundestag* committee responsible for monitoring the special services, I received a copy of the public version of this report. I also received from an anonymous source a version classified "confidential/for official use only", of which I made responsible use, in the spirit of the decision taken by the Legal Affairs Committee at its meeting of 13 March 2006 on the receipt of confidential information. I was also offered a copy of an even more detailed version classified "secret", which I opted not to accept for ethical reasons. I place my trust in the members of the *Bundestag* to whom this document was addressed to take the necessary action on the basis thereof, including appropriate action to alert me to any fact reported in this version directly related to my terms of reference as rapporteur.

between Mr Zammar and his Syrian guards did not seem tense, although the German visitors did note a somewhat authoritarian relationship.

192. As indicated above, a *Bundestag* committee of inquiry is looking into the matter, and it is appropriate to await its results.

3.9. Binyam Mohamed Al Habashi

193. Binyam Mohamed al Habashi is an Ethiopian citizen who has held resident status in the United Kingdom since 1994. While many of his family members emigrated to the United States and became naturalised citizens there, Binyam moved to the UK as a teenager and claimed asylum. He spent seven years pursuing his education in London while his asylum application was considered in a protracted, ultimately unresolved process. He had problems with drugs and converted to Islam at the age of twenty.

194. Binyam is now detained at Guantanamo Bay and has been selected as one of the first group of ten prisoners to appear before a special United States Military Commission, probably later in 2006. We were able to view Binyam's diary, an account of the last five years of his life, and a series of letters he has written from Guantanamo. A member of my team was also able to hear first-hand testimony from members of his family and his legal representatives in the United Kingdom.

195. In treating Binyam's case in my report I shall avoid any reference to the charges he is likely to face before the Military Commission. Suffice to say that I regard such commissions generally as a flawed basis on which to prosecute allegations of the most serious nature, since the defendant's due process rights are severely impaired[173]. I do not consider these commissions to be fair hearings and I reiterate my position that the global effort to bring terrorist suspects to justice should depend primarily upon judicial remedies.

196. Of greatest concern in Binyam's case are the accounts of torture and other serious human rights violations which he says he has suffered. He speaks of being wounded all over his body with a scalpel and a razor blade, beaten unconscious and hung from the walls in shackles. He suffered gross physical injuries, including broken bones. He was constantly threatened with death, rape and electrocution.

197. It is difficult to say whether this account actually reflects reality. Let us just recall that some of these acts are included in what has been called "enhanced interrogation techniques", which have been developed by the

[173] Reference to the Executive Order that established Military Commissions for Guantanamo detainees, signed by President Bush in Oct / Nov 2001.

United States in the "war on terror"[174]. Furthermore many of the abuses described by Binyam bear striking similarities to the allegations of other detainees who have been held in the same detention facilities at various points over the last few years[175].

198. Binyam's case is an example for the very numerous detainees—most of whose names and whereabouts we do not know—who have become trapped in the United States' spider's web during the course of the "war on terror". Binyam has been subjected to two CIA renditions, a US military transfer to Guantanamo Bay and several other clandestine transfers by plane and helicopter. He has been held in at least two secret detention facilities, in addition to military prisons. During his illegal interrogations, he has been confronted with allegations that could only have arisen from intelligence provided by the United Kingdom.

199. Binyam's family told my representative that he disappeared in the summer of 2001. His close-knit family subsequently endured several years of desperate uncertainty about his whereabouts and well-being, only partially clarified by their first visit from FBI agents three years later, in 2004. Although they have received a handful of letters from him in Guantanamo, none of the family has been able to see or speak to Binyam for five years.

200. According to his testimony, Binyam travelled voluntarily to Afghanistan in 2001[176] and spent some time there, probably several months, before crossing into Pakistan and seeking to return to the UK. He was arrested by Pakistani officials at Karachi Airport on 10 April 2002 for attempting to travel on a false passport. Within ten days of his arrest, he was interrogated by American officials. Upon asserting his right to a lawyer, and later upon refusing to answer questions, American officers are alleged to have told him: *"The law has been changed. There are no lawyers. You can co-operate with us the easy way, or the hard way. If you don't talk to us, you're going to Jordan. We can't do what we want here, the Pakistanis can't do exactly what we want them to do. The Arabs will deal with you."*

201. The initial interrogations in Karachi involved Pakistani, American and British agents. Binyam was never accused of a particular crime and was told by MI6 agents that *"they checked out my story and said they knew I was a nobody"*. When he was discharged from Pakistani custody, however, he was not released. Instead, the Pakistani security services took him to a military airport in Islamabad and handed him over to the United States.

---

[174] Reference to some of the many documents on interrogation techniques obtained by the ACLU in its series of applications under the Freedom of Information Act.

[175] In this regard, see the Human Rights Watch reports on Temara in Morocco, plus a range of NGO and detainee accounts from the Dark Prison in Kabul.

[176] Binyam told his lawyer that he wanted to travel to Afghanistan to see the Taliban with his own eyes and decide *"whether it was a good Islamic country or not"*. He also wanted to get away from a social life in London that revolved around drug use.

202. Binyam testifies that he underwent his first rendition on 21 July 2002. He was set upon by unidentified people *"dressed in black, with masks, wearing what looked like Timberland boots"*. He describes how they *"stripped [him] naked, took photos, put fingers up [his] anus and dressed [him] in a tracksuit. [He] was shackled, with earphones, and blindfolded"*, before being forced onto an aircraft and flown to Morocco. Official flight records obtained by this inquiry show that the known rendition plane, N379P, took off from Islamabad on 21 July 2002 and flew to Rabat, Morocco.

203. Binyam has described various secret detention facilities in which he was held in Morocco, including one prison that was submerged *"almost underground'* and one more sanitary place in which he was apparently placed to recover from injuries sustained from his torture. Between July 2002 and January 2004 Binyam was tortured on numerous occasions by a team of interrogators and other officials, most of whom were Moroccan. Some of the officials wore masks, while others did not; at least one interrogator, who identified herself as a Canadian, is thought to have been an American CIA agent.

204. It appears that the object of the torture was to break Binyam's resistance, or to destroy him physically and psychologically, in order to extract confessions from him as to his involvement in terrorist activities. In addition to the sustained abuse and threats, the torturers used information, apparently obtained from intelligence sources, to indicate to Binyam that they knew a lot about him. Much of the personal information–including details of his education, his friendships in London and even his kickboxing trainer -could only have originated from collusion in this interrogation process by UK intelligence services.

205. Binyam has described his ill-treatment in Morocco to his lawyer in several phases: an initial "softening up"; a routine "circle of torture"; and eventually a "heavy" abuse involving mental torment and the infliction of physical injury. In the first few weeks of his detention he was repeatedly suspended from the walls or ceilings, or otherwise shackled, and brutally beaten: *"They came in and cuffed my hands behind my back. Then three men came in with black ski masks that only showed their eyes . . . One stood on each of my shoulders and the third punched me in the stomach. The first punch . . . turned everything inside me upside down. I felt I was going to vomit. I was meant to stand, but I was in so much pain I'd fall to my knees. They'd pull me back up and hit me again. They'd kick me in the thighs as I got up. They just beat me up that night . . . I collapsed and they left. I stayed on the ground for a long time before I lapsed into unconsciousness. My legs were dead. I could not move. I'd vomited and pissed on myself."*

206. At its worst, the torture involved stripping Binyam naked and using a doctor's scalpel to make incisions all over his chest and other parts of his

body: *"One of them took my penis in his hand and began to make cuts. He did it once and they stood for a minute, watching my reaction. I was in agony, crying, trying desperately to suppress myself, but I was screaming. They must have done this 20 to 30 times, in maybe two hours. There was blood all over. They cut all over my private parts. One of them said it would be better just to cut it off, as I would only breed terrorists."*

207. Eventually Binyam began to co-operate in his interrogation sessions in an effort to prevent being tortured: *"They said if you say this story as we read it, you will just go to court as a witness and all this torture will stop. I could not take any more . . . and I eventually repeated what they read out to me. They told me to say I was with bin Laden five or six times. Of course that was false. They continued with two or three interrogations a month. They weren't really interrogations—more like trainings, training me what to say."*

208. Binyam says he was subjected to a second rendition on the night from 21 to 22 January 2004. After being cuffed, blindfolded and driven for about 30 minutes in a van, he was offloaded at what he believes was an airport. Again, Binyam's description matches the "methodology" of rendition described earlier in this report: *"They did not talk to me. They cut off my clothes. There was a white female with glasses–she took the pictures. One of them held my penis and she took digital pictures. When she saw the injuries I had, she gasped. She said: 'Oh my God, look at that'."*

209. The second rendition of Binyam Mohamed took place within the "rendition circuit" that I have identified in this inquiry. The aircraft N313P, operated on behalf of the CIA, is shown in my official data to have flown from Rabat to Kabul in the early hours of 22 January 2004. Two days later, as part of the same circuit, the same plane flew back to Europe and was used in the rendition of Khaled El-Masri[177].

210. Binyam Mohamed's ordeal continued in Kabul, Afghanistan, where he was held in the facility he refers to as "The Prison of Darkness"[178] for four months. Detention conditions in this prison amount to inhuman and degrading treatment. In addition, forcing prisoners to remain in painful positions, sleep alteration, sensory deprivation and other recognised "enhanced interrogation techniques"[179] are known to be deployed there routinely by the United States military and its partners. At various times, Binyam was chained to the floor with his arms suspended above his head, had his head knocked against the wall and describes *"torture by music"*,

[177] References to the sections on rendition circuits and the individual case of El-Masri.

[178] Many other accounts in the file of the Rapporteur refer to this facility as the "Dark Prison" or the "Disco Prison".

[179] These so-called "enhanced interrogation techniques", which are considered acceptable in the context of some interrogations by the Americans, were exposed by the ACLU in its application under the *Freedom of Information Act*. In particular, these techniques are enumerated in a document from the FBI, available at *www.aclu.org*.

involving the sounds of loud rap and heavy metal, thunder, planes taking off, cackling laughter and horror sounds that amounted to a *"perpetual nightmare"*.

211. Up until his transfer by helicopter to Bagram at the end of May 2004, Binyam was not allowed to see daylight. He was persistently interrogated and told about terrorist plots and activities in which he was accused of involvement. He was subjected to irregular eating patterns and *"weird'* sessions with psychiatrists.

212. In a detention facility at Bagram Air Base, Afghanistan, Binyam was forced to write out a lengthy statement prepared by the Americans. The content of the statement is unknown to us. Binyam has told his lawyers that he wrote and signed this document in a state of complete mental disarray: *"I don't really remember [what I wrote], because by then I just did what they told me. Of course, by the time I was in Bagram I was telling them whatever they wanted to hear."*

213. The case of Binyam Mohamed is sufficient grounds for an urgent and decisive change of course in the international effort to overcome terrorism. The Council of Europe is duty-bound to ensure that secret detentions, unlawful inter-state transfers and the use of torture are absolutely prohibited and never resorted to again.

214. It remains to be seen whether a Military Commission process will decide for or against Binyam Mohamed. The only certain legacy of this case is the deeply disturbing recognition that a human being has, in his own words, been completely dehumanised: *"I'm sorry I have no emotion when talking about the past, 'cause I have closed. You have to figure out all the emotional part; I'm kind of dead in the head."*

4. Secret Places of Detention

215. After the publication of allegations by the Washington Post and Human Rights Watch,[180] we centred our search on certain sites in Poland and Romania.

4.1. Satellite Photographs

216. We obtained from the European Union Satellite Centre (EUSC) in Torrejon a number of satellite photographs of the sites concerned,[181] some taken at different times. We studied these with the assistance of an independent expert.

---

180 See para. 7 above.

181 The following sites were captured in the satellite photographs: Cataloi, Fetesti and Mihail Kogalniceanu in Romania; and Szczytno / Szymany in Poland.

217. These photographs do not constitute conclusive evidence. With the expert's help, we were able to identify several specific locations at a civil airport and a secret services base (in Poland) and at military airfields (in Romania) which would be very suitable for the secret detention of persons flown in from abroad. There are however hundreds of equally favourable locations throughout Europe. As the EUSC did not have available, for most of the places concerned, sequences of photographs which would have shown whether physical structures (huts, fences, watchtowers, and so on) had been altered (added or dismantled) at certain relevant times, the satellite photographs do not enable us to reach any conclusions with a high degree of certainty.

218. On the other hand, they did enable us to request certain clarifications from the Polish and Romanian delegations. All the replies we received, in my opinion, show a lack of transparency and genuine willingness to co-operate in the authorities concerned[182].

4.2. Documented Aircraft Movements

219. As we showed above, the information received from Eurocontrol and certain national air traffic control authorities, confirmed by witnesses' accounts, makes it possible to be sure that certain flights were made between known detention centres and the suspected places in Poland and Romania. The geographical position of these places making them unlikely to be used for refuelling, the period spent on the ground in these places by these aircraft, and in particular the fact that the landings in question belong to well-established "rendition circuits'[183], allow us to suspect that they are or were places of detention which form part of the "spider's web" referred to above.

4.3. Witnesses' Accounts

220. Accounts given by witnesses to Amnesty International[184] make it look very likely that a relatively large place of detention had to be located in a European country, without any more detail.

[182] In Poland's case, we detected, at an airfield said not to have been used for military purposes since the end of World War II, a very well-maintained double fence around a structure identified as containing munitions bunkers. Our question as to the reason for keeping this double fence in perfect condition did not receive a convincing reply. Where Romania is concerned, the authorities first stated that the construction works at the airbases concerned were merely being carried out to maintain existing infrastructure; only when the question was raised again, backed up by the only single-site photo sequence available to us, clearly showing the building of a new hangar and an extension of the aircraft parking area, did the Romanian authorities confirm that some new building had also been done.

[183] See para. 52 above.

[184] See para. 184 above, the case of Mr Bashmila and Mr Ali Qaru.

221. A journalist working for German television[185] interviewed a young Afghan in Kabul who said that he had been held in Romania. This witness, very frightened and unwilling to give direct evidence to a member of my team, was reported to have been told by a guard to whom he had complained about his conditions of detention that he was lucky in fact to be in Romania.

222. Let us recall also—as mentioned in my note of January 2006[186]—that according to a fax sent by the Egyptian Ministry for European Affairs to the Egyptian Embassy in London and intercepted by Swiss intelligence services, such centres had existed in Romania, Bulgaria, Macedonia, Kosovo and in Ukraine.

223. Both sources from inside the CIA referred to by the Washington Post, ABC and HRW are said to have named Poland and Romania, but without indicating specific places[187].

4.4. Evaluation

224. Whilst to date no evidence, in the formal sense of the term, has come to light, many coherent and convergent elements provide a basis for stating that these secret CIA detention centres have indeed existed in Europe, and we have seen that several indicators point at these two countries. As explained above, even if these elements do not constitute evidence, they are sufficiently serious to reverse the burden of proof: it is now for the countries in question to address their "positive obligations" to investigate, in order to avoid endangering the credibility of their denials.

5. Secret Detentions in the Chechen Republic

225. Although massive violations of human rights in Chechnya began and were denounced long before the American "spider's web" was woven, it is regrettable and worrisome to observe that the two principal world powers cite the fight against terrorism as a reason to abandon the principle of respect for fundamental rights. This creates a mechanism of "reciprocal justification" and sets a deplorable example for other states.

226. It is hardly possible to speak of secret detention centres in Council of Europe member States without mentioning Chechnya. Mr Rudolf Bindig's very recent report also notes not only numerous cases of forced disappearance and torture, but also the existence of secret places of detention.

---

185 Ashwin Raman, one of the makers of an ARD documentary shown on the ARD channel on 1 March and on SWF on 8 March 2006.

186 Information note dated 22 January 2006, para. 5 and 52.

187 *Ibid*, see para. 7.

5.1. The Work of the European Committee for the Prevention of Torture (CPT)

227. The situation in Chechnya, where unofficial places of detention are concerned, has already been roundly criticised by the CPT in two public declarations to which I referred in my memoranda of December 2005 and January 2006[188]. The positions expressed therein could not be clearer, but the Committee of Ministers of the Council of Europe has not yet given them the attention they deserve. During a very recent visit to the region, in May 2006, a CPT delegation again had grounds to believe that locations which might serve as unofficial places of detention were in the region[189].

5.2. Damning Recent Accounts by Witnesses

228. Aaron Rhodes, Executive Director of the International Helsinki Federation for Human Rights (IHF), sent me an open letter dated 12 May 2006[190] accompanied by a report compiled by the IHF, with the help of Russian non-governmental organisations active in the region, containing damning accounts by the victims of secret detention and torture, often followed by enforced disappearance, in the North Caucasus region. Many of these cases were attributed to the *Kadyrovtsi*, the militia under the direct command of the current Prime Minister of the Chechen Republic, Ramzan Kadyrov. According to several of these accounts, some places used as unofficial places of detention were in Tsentoroy, the village where the Kadyrov family originated.[191]

229. Concern about our Organisation's credibility means that these allegations deserve to be investigated in the same way as the violations committed by American services, especially as the Chechen Republic is on the territory of a member state of the Council of Europe.

6. Attitude of Governments

230. It has to be said that most governments did not seem particularly eager to establish the alleged facts. The body of information gathered makes it unlikely that European states were completely unaware of what, in the

[188] See the two Public Declarations concerning the Chechen Republic, CPT/Inf (2001) 15 and CPT/Inf (2003) 33, available at: *http://www.cpt.coe.int/documents/rus/2001-07-10-enq.htm* and *http://www.cpt.coe.int/documents/rus/2003-33-inf-eng.htm*

[189] Cf. CPT press release: *http://www.cpt.coe.int/documents/rus/2006-05-09-eng.htm*. Exceptionally, a CPT visit was interrupted when access to the village of Tsentoroy (Khosi-Yurt), south-east of Gudermes, was denied on 1 May 2006; the visit resumed the next day, when the delegation gained access to the village early in the afternoon.

[190] See the letter entitled: *"Secret prisons in Europe should be of concern to the Council of Europe"*, authored by Aaron Rhodes, IHF; 12 May 2006; *http://www.ihf-hr.org/documents/doc summarv.php?sec id=3&d id=4249*.

[191] See note 82 above.

context of the fight against international terrorism, was happening at some of their airports, in their airspace or at American bases located on their territory. Insofar as they did not know, they did not want to know. It is inconceivable that certain operations conducted by American services could have taken place without the active participation, or at least the collusion, of national intelligence services. If this were the case, one would be justified in seriously questioning the effectiveness, and therefore the legitimacy, of such services. The main concern of some governments was clearly to avoid disturbing their relationships with the United States, a crucial partner and ally. Other governments apparently work on the assumption that any information learned via their intelligence services is not supposed to be known[192].

231. The most disturbing case—because it is the best documented—is probably that of Italy. As we have seen, the Milan prosecuting authorities and police have been able, thanks to a remarkably competent and independent investigation, to reconstruct in detail the *extraordinary rendition* of the imam Abu Omar, abducted on 17 February 2003 and transferred to the Egyptian authorities. The prosecuting authorities have identified 25 persons responsible for this operation mounted by the CIA, and have issued arrest warrants against 22 of them. The then Justice Minister in fact used his powers to impede the judicial authorities' work: as well as delaying forwarding requests for judicial assistance to the American authorities, he categorically refused to forward the arrest warrants issued against 22 American citizens[193]. Worse still: the same Justice Minister publicly accused the Milan judiciary of attacking the terrorist hunters rather than the terrorists themselves[194]. Furthermore, the Italian Government did not even consider it necessary to ask the American authorities for explanations regarding the operation carried out by American agents on its own national territory, or to complain about the fact that Abu Omar's abduction ruined an important anti-terrorism operation being undertaken by the Milan judiciary and police. As I stated in my January 2006 memorandum, it is unlikely that the Italian authorities were not aware of this large-scale CIA operation. As mentioned in chapter 3.4 above, the investigation in progress shows that Italian officials directly took part in Abu Omar's abduction and that the intelligence services were involved.

232. In an effort to be impartial, I shall also discuss the example of my own country, Switzerland. As we shall see, a number of aircraft described as

[192] Some states' legislation expressly prohibits them from using or releasing information gathered by their intelligence services. This is the case in Hungary, for example.

[193] Article 4 of the extradition treaty between the United States and Italy also provides for the extradition of each country's own nationals. It should be added, however, that warrants issued by the Italian judiciary are enforceable in EU countries, as European arrest warrants do not have to be forwarded by the Ministry via diplomatic channels.

[194] ANSA agency, 27 February 2006, widely published in the Italian press.

suspect and mentioned in the questionnaires sent to the member States landed in Geneva (and Zurich, as Amnesty International investigations subsequently showed). The United States did not respond to the Swiss authorities' requests for explanations for several months. A few hours before the annual clearance for aircraft flying on behalf of the American Government to overfly Swiss territory was due to expire, an American official apparently gave a Swiss Embassy representative in Washington verbal assurances that the United States had respected Switzerland's sovereignty and had not transported prisoners through Swiss airspace, thus simply reiterating the statement made by Ms Rice in Brussels on 5 December 2005. This assurance was very belated and, above all, not particularly credible in the light of the established facts: the Italian judicial authorities have established, on the basis of some very convincing evidence, that Abu Omar, abducted in Milan on 17 February 2003, was flown the same day from the Aviano base to the base at Ramstein in Germany, passing through Swiss airspace; this flight has been confirmed, moreover, by Swiss air traffic controllers. The Italian investigation also established that the head of the Milan operation stayed in Switzerland. The Swiss Government deliberately ignored these allegations[195]—despite their detailed and clearly serious nature—and settled for that vague, somewhat informal response from an official. It has taken a formalistic position, claiming that it did not have any evidence and, under international law, had to rely on the principle of trust. It clearly wished to renew the overflight clearance, which it quickly did without asking any further questions. The Confederal Prosecutor's Office has nevertheless opened a preliminary investigation to establish whether there have been violations of the law under Swiss jurisdiction in the Abu Omar case. At the same time, the Military Prosecutor's Office has begun an investigation aimed at identifying and punishing the perpetrator(s) of the leak which allowed the publication of the Egyptian fax intercepted by the intelligence services. The journalists who published this are also being prosecuted, on the basis of rules whose compatibility with the principles of the freedom of the press in a democratic system seems highly doubtful. A revelation made these days rekindles the criticism directed at the authorities accused of servile obedience towards the United States: according to press reports, based on apparently well-informed sources, the Swiss authorities are said to have deliberately failed to execute an international arrest warrant brought by the Italian judicial authorities following the abduction of Abu Omar in February 2003. Robert Lady, the head of the detail wanted by the police, who was at the time in charge of the CIA in

[195] The Swiss federal prosecuting authorities have, however, instituted a preliminary investigation into these allegations.

Milan holding the title and status of Consul of the United States, is said to have stayed in Geneva very recently; the police had been ordered to merely carry out discrete surveillance.

233. The principle of trust has also been invoked by other governments. This is the case with Ireland, for example: the government has stated that there was no reason to investigate the presence of American aircraft, since the United States had given assurances[196]. In Germany, the government and the ruling parties opposed—ultimately in vain—the establishment of a parliamentary commission of inquiry, despite the significant questions being raised about the role of the intelligence services, particularly in the case of the abduction of El-Masri. Lastly, in November 2005 I sent a request for information to the United States Ambassador (an observer to the Council of Europe). The Ambassador responded by sending me the public statement made by the American Secretary of State on 5 December 2005. In particular, the latter stated that the United States had not violated the sovereignty of European states, that "renditions" had saved human lives and that no prisoners had been transported for the purpose of torture[197]. European ministers, meeting in the framework of NATO, hastened to declare themselves satisfied with these assurances[198]. Or almost[199].

234. It should be pointed out that some governments have deliberately assisted in "renditions". This is especially well established with regard to Bosnia and Herzegovina, which has rendered six persons to the American forces outside of any legal procedure, as established by the national judicial authorities, as we have noted above. This certainly deserves to be stressed and welcomed. It is true that the Government of Bosnia and Herzegovina was regrettably not particularly determined, but it should not be forgotten that this young republic had been strongly pressured by a great power present on its territory. We have already criticised the Macedonian authorities, which have locked themselves up in categorical denial without having carried out any serious enquiry. Sweden has also rendered two asylum seekers to American operatives for "rendition" to the

[196] We would not see any reason to because we have received categorical assurances from the US that they are not using Shannon in this way (Irish Examiner, 22 February 2006).

[197] The United States does not transport, and has not transported, detainees from one country to another for the purpose of interrogation using torture (statement of 5 December 2005).

[198] The German Foreign Minister, Mr Steinmeier, emphasised the need for such clarification, because, he said, *we should not diverge from one another on the interpretation of international law* (AP 8 December 2005).

[199] Only Bernard Bot, the Dutch Foreign Affairs Minister, considered the American explanations "inadequate"; Scandinavian diplomats also protested against the American services' use of "methods on the edge of legality". On the whole, however, the Europeans, headed by Britain's Jack Straw, kept a low profile so as not to offend the "iron lady" of American diplomacy. (Le Figaro of 8 December 2005).

Egyptian authorities, as formally condemned by the UN Committee against Torture. The Swedish authorities, despite this international condemnation and parliamentary requests to this effect have yet to commence a proper inquiry into these facts[200].

235. When the previous memoranda, which set out interim summaries, were published, criticisms were voiced that the evidence referred primarily to NGO reports and accounts related in the press. It should be pointed that without the work undertaken by these organisations and the investigations of competent and tenacious journalists, we would not today be talking about this affair—which, nobody can now dispute, has some basis in fact. Indeed, governments did not spontaneously or autonomously take any real action to seek evidence for the allegations, despite their serious and detailed nature. Critics included those who, given their existing or previous positions and responsibilities, could have helped to establish the truth. Furthermore, it is shocking that some countries put pressure on journalists not to publish certain news items (I have mentioned the cases of the ABC and the *Washington Post)* or prosecuted them for publishing documents deemed confidential[201]. Such zeal would have been better employed in seeking to ascertain the truth—a fundamental requirement in a democracy—and prosecuting those guilty of perpetrating or tolerating any kind of abuse, such as illegal abductions or other acts contrary to human dignity.

236. The American administration's attitude to the questions being raised in Europe about the CIA's actions was, once again, clearly illustrated during the fact-finding visit to the United States by a delegation from the European Parliament's Temporary Committee (TDIP): no or few replies were given to the numerous questions. I have already discussed the response to my request from the United States Ambassador to the Council of Europe (3.1.4). It is obvious that if the American authorities did not constantly raise the objection of secrecy for national security reasons, it would be far easier to establish the truth. We find that today, this secrecy is no longer justified. In a free and democratic society, it is far more important to establish the truth on numerous allegations of serious human rights violations, many of which are proven to a large extent.

200 As condemned by the Council of Europe's Commissioner for Human Rights in his statement on "fight against terrorism by legal means" published on the Council of Europe's website on 3 April 2006.

201 In particular, this is what happened to the two Swiss journalists who, in early January 2006, published the content of the Egyptian fax, intercepted by Swiss intelligence services, mentioning the existence of detention centres in Eastern Europe. The two journalists have published a book outlining the circumstances by which they came into possession of the document: Sandro Brotz, Beat Jost, *CIA-Gefängnisse in Europa—Die Fax-Affäre und ihre Folgen,* Orell Füssli, 2006.

7. Individual cases: judicial proceedings in progress

7.1. A Positive Example: the Milan Public Prosecutor's Office (Abu Omar Case)

237. In this case, the Italian judicial authorities and police have shown great competence and remarkable independence in the face of political pressures. Their competence and independence was already proven during the tragic years stained with blood by terrorism. The Milan public prosecutor's office was able to reconstitute in detail a clear case of "rendition" and a regrettable example of the lack of international cooperation in the fight against terrorism[202]. As I have already said[203], the Italian judicial authorities have brought international arrest warrants against 22 American officials. In addition, the ongoing investigation seems to be in the process of showing that operatives belonging to the Italian services have participated in the operation.

7.2. A Matter Requiring Further Attention: the Munich (El-Masri case) and Zweibrucken (Abu Omar Case) Public Prosecutors' Offices

238. The German justice system gave its attention to the Abu Omar and El-Masri cases in terms of criminal proceedings for abduction against persons unknown. In the first-named case, normal co-operation took place with the Milan public prosecutor's office. As I have already stated, in my memorandum of January 2006, the Zweibrucken public prosecutor's office came up against a total lack of co-operation by the American authorities, who refused to provide any information on what had happened at the Ramstein base.

239. Where the second case is concerned, I have already[204] given some information showing that certain serious investigative measures have already been taken and that more remains to be done, especially in relation to the witnesses named by El-Masri and to clarification of the possible role played by the various German intelligence services.

7.3. Another Matter Requiring Further Attention: the Al Rawi and El Banna Case

240. Where the case of Al Rawi and El Banna is concerned, the British justice system has had to deal with an application by the families of the persons concerned attempting to force the UK government to intercede with the US government to obtain the release of both men, who are still

[202] I talked to Chief Prosecutor Mr Spataro for several hours and I wish to thank him for being so generous with his time.
[203] In para. 162.
[204] In para. 103.

held at Guantanamo Bay. It was in the framework of this procedure that the telegrams proving that the MI5 was involved in the two men's arrest in Gambia came into the public domain. After proceedings had begun, the UK authorities agreed to intercede on Mr Al Rawi's behalf, but not on that of his fellow detainee, Mr El Banna, although he had been arrested for the same reasons with the assistance of the UK services. In May 2006, the action was dismissed by the court of first instance.

241. In view of the circumstances which have led up to the arrest of these two men, one may think that the UK government is under at least a moral and political obligation to do everything in its power to actively intercede to secure their release from Guantanamo so that they can return to the country.

7.4. Sweden: What Next in the Agiza and Alzery Case?

242. Sweden was condemned by the UN Committee against Torture in respect of the case of Mr Agiza and Mr Alzery, which led to an investigation by the parliamentary ombudsman, Mr Mats Melin. He noted that a preliminary investigation by the judicial authorities had culminated in the termination of the proceedings[205].

243. According to some criticisms, which do not appear unfounded, different aspects of the case need further investigation. This disguised extradition, without any possibility of appeal and judicial scrutiny, and the ill-treatment at Bromma airport, still on the ground, under the eyes of Swedish officials, as well as the incomplete information provided to UN-CAT are serious matters which require that the whole truth be exposed.

7.5. Spain

244. The Palma de Mallorca public prosecutor's office has begun an investigation following the transmission of a *Guardia Civil* file containing the names of the passengers on the aircraft which took off from the local airport bound for Skopje, where they were most likely joined by Mr El-Masri and flown on to Afghanistan[206].

7.6. Mr El-Masri's Complaint in the United States

245. With the assistance of the American Civil Liberties Union[207], Mr El-Masri has taken judicial action in Alexandria, in Virginia, seeking

---

[205] See above, para. 152

[206] I have in my possession a copy of this list, but I have no information on the states concerned.

[207] I should like to thank the ACLU for making detailed documentation about this case available to me.

compensation from the CIA. On 19 May 2006, his complaint was rejected by the court of first instance, without a ruling on the merits of his application, as the court accepted the US government's argument that continuation of the proceedings would have jeopardised national security. In the course of the trial, the CIA's secret methods would indeed become the subject of discussions before the court.

8. Parliamentary Investigations

246. As long ago as January, I called on national parliaments to put questions to their governments and to begin inquiries, where appropriate, to clarify the role of European governments in this affair. A large number of questions were indeed raised in the parliaments of numerous Council of Europe member States, which is very gratifying. Unfortunately, the government replies were almost without exception vague and inconclusive. The German and UK parliaments were particularly active, whereas parliamentary reactions in three of the main countries concerned by the allegations that are the subject of this report (Poland, Romania and "the former Yugoslav Republic of Macedonia") were particularly feeble, if not inexistent.

8.1. Germany

247. Opposition MPs in Germany, although few in number since the recent elections, have put numerous questions to their government[208]. The replies were very general in every case[209]. The government systematically hid behind the responsibility of the parliamentary monitoring committee *(parlamentarisches Kontrollgremium,* known as the PKG) for dealing with matters relating to the activities of the secret services. A number of questions relating to the subject of this report have effectively been discussed within the PKG, but the government's detailed report to this very select group, which works in very carefully maintained secrecy, was classified "secret". The chair of the committee, Mr Rottgen (CDU), in response to my request, sent me the "public" version of this report, which is, frankly, not very informative and does not mention the individual cases raised by the media. The government attempted to avoid setting up a committee of inquiry by sending all members of the *Bundestag* a more informative version, classified "confidential", which contains some information about

[208] I should like to thank not only our Committee colleague Sabine Leutheusser-Schnarrenberger (Liberal), but also Mr Stroebele (Green party), for the information they have regularly supplied to me on this subject.

[209] The same is true of the replies given by other governments questioned by members of their parliaments, such as those of Belgium, the United Kingdom, Sweden and Ireland.

some of the aforementioned individual cases[210]. At the insistence of the three opposition parties, a committee of inquiry has nevertheless been set up, and it started work in May[211]. Its mandate includes investigation of the allegations of collusion between the German authorities and the CIA in the case of Mr El-Masri. In short, the *Bundestag* has been highly active, urged on by the opposition parties in particular.

8.2 The United Kingdom

248. Our work regarding the United Kingdom benefited greatly from the efforts of a variety of interlocutors, whom I should like to salute in this report.[212] The United Kingdom parliament has not yet established a formal inquiry into possible British participation in abuses committed by the United States in the course of the "war on terror", but there have been several noteworthy parliamentary initiatives designed to broaden the public debate and encourage greater openness.

249. Late last year, one of the UK Parliament's standing committees, the Joint Committee on Human Rights (JCHR), launched an inquiry into UK Compliance with the United Nations Convention against Torture. As part of its mandate the Committee examined several issues of relevance to this inquiry, including the use of diplomatic assurances and the practice of "extraordinary rendition".

250. The JCHR held a series of evidentiary sessions, featuring Ministers of the United Kingdom Government[213] as well as representatives of non-governmental organisations[214]. Members of my team, on a visit to London in March 2006, met with a Committee Specialist of the JCHR and attended its evidentiary session with the UK Minister of State for the Armed Forces, Rt. Hon. Adam Ingram. In its report on UK Compliance with UNCAT published on 26 May 2006[215], the JCHR recognised the *"growing calls for an independent public inquiry"* in the UK, but ultimately decided that such

[210] The names of persons were represented by initials. See note 92 above in respect of my approach to the "confidential" and "secret" versions of this report.

[211] I have been invited to address this committee in the near future.

[212] In this regard, I should like to make particular mention of the London-based non-governmental organisation REPRIEVE, which has supported my team by providing contacts, research insights and materials relating to the cases they work on.

[213] For example, on 6 March 2006 the JCHR heard evidence from the Solicitor General and Minister of State in the Department for Constitutional Affairs, Harriet Harman, along with other officials from her department. An uncorrected transcript of the session is available online at: *http://www.publications.parliament.uk/pa/it200506/itselect/itriqhts/uc701-iii/uc70102.htm*

[214] On 21 November 2005 the JCHR heard evidence from Human Rights Watch, Amnesty International and REDRESS. An uncorrected transcript of the session is available online at: *http://www.publications.parliament.uk/pa/it200506/itselect/itrights/uc701-i/uc70102.htm*

[215] The full report is available online at: *http://www.publications.parliament.uk/pa/it200506/itselect/itrights/185/18502.htm*: a full record of oral and written evidence was published in a separate volume, available at: *http://www.publications.parliament.uk/pa/it200506/itselect/itrights/185/185-ii.pdf*.

an inquiry would be *"premature"* until the Government's own inquiries have been given a chance to publish the *"detailed information required"*.

251. In the meantime an ad-hoc body known as the "All-Party Parliamentary Group (APPG) on Extraordinary Renditions" has engaged Members of the UK Parliament belonging to all political parties. On Tuesday 28 March, members of my team attended the APPG's information session on the cases of Bisher Al-Rawi and Jamil El-Banna[216], which featured testimony from both men's legal representatives, MPs and family members. This session stimulated considerable media interest in the case and coincided with the public release of government telegrams passed on to the CIA in advance of the men's rendition. I wish to thank the Chairman of the APPG, Mr Andrew Tyrie MP, along with his dedicated staff, for their valuable support.

8.3. Poland: a Parliamentary Inquiry, Carried Out in Secret

252. A parliamentary inquiry into the allegations that a "secret prison" exists in the country has been conducted behind closed doors in Poland. Promises made beforehand notwithstanding, its work has never been made public, except at a press conference announcing that the inquiry had not found anything untoward. In my opinion, this exercise was insufficient in terms of the positive obligation to conduct a credible investigation of credible allegations of serious human rights violations.

8.4. Romania and "the Former Yugoslav Republic of Macedonia": No Parliamentary Inquiry

253. To my knowledge, no parliamentary inquiry whatsoever has taken place in either country, despite the particularly serious and concrete nature of the allegations made against both. What is more, the committee which supervises the secret services in "the former Yugoslav Republic of Macedonia" ceased operations three years ago[217], and this is particularly worrying in a country where the secret services not so very long ago played a particularly important and controversial role.

9. Commitment to Combating Terrorism

9.1. Fight Against Terrorism: An Absolute Necessity

254. The fight against terrorism is unquestionably a priority for every government and, above all, for the international community as a whole. The use of terror, previously employed primarily as a weapon against

[216] See to the section of the report that treats these cases, at 3.5 above.

[217] Response of the Parliament of the former Yugoslav Republic of Macedonia (Sobranie) to the questionnaire of the TDIP Temporary Committee of the European Parliament. Available at: *www.statewatch.orq/'rendition*.

individual governments, has increasingly become a means of attacking a political and social model, and indeed a lifestyle and civilisation represented by large parts of the planet. Terrorism has taken on a clear international connotation in recent years, and it too has taken advantage of the tremendous technological progress made in the fields of arms, telecommunication and mobility. It is consequently vital to co-ordinate the fight against terrorism at the international level.

255. It has to be said, however, that there are still significant deficiencies in such co-ordination, and that it too often depends on the goodwill, but also the arbitrary nature, of intelligence services. An understanding of this phenomenon, its structures, the resources at its disposal and its leaders is essential in order to deal with the terrorist threat successfully. Intelligence services consequently play an important and irreplaceable role. That role must, however, be specified and delimited within a well-defined institutional framework consistent with the principles of the rule of law and democratic legitimacy. This also calls for effective supervisory mechanisms; the evidence under consideration has highlighted alarming flaws in such mechanisms. It is a well-known fact that the various American and European intelligence services have set up working groups and exchanged information. This initiative can only be welcomed. The events of recent years show, however, that international co-ordination is still seriously inadequate. The Milan imam's abduction is emblematic in this regard: the operation by CIA agents ruined the efforts of the Italian judiciary and police, who were involved in a major anti-terrorism investigation targeting precisely the Milan mosque.[218]

256. The governments' very replies and especially their silence are a telling indication that intelligence services appear increasingly to work outside the scope of proper supervisory mechanisms. The way in which American services were able to operate in Europe, carrying out several hundred flights and transporting illegally arrested persons without any scrutiny, can only point to the participation or collusion of several European services—or, alternatively, incredible incompetence, a scenario which, frankly, is difficult to envisage. Indeed, everything seems to indicate that the American services were given considerable latitude and allowed to act as they saw fit, even though it would have been impossible not to be aware that their methods were incompatible with national legal systems and European standards relating to respect for human rights[219]. Such passivity

[218] This fact was expressly confirmed by Milan's Deputy Public Prosecutor, during his hearing before the European Parliament's Temporary Committee in Brussels on 23 February 2006.

[219] In an interview with the German magazine *Die Zeit* on 29 December 2005, Mr Michael Scheuer, former head of the CIA's "Bin Laden" unit and one of the architects of the "rendition" system further developed during Bill Clinton's presidency and with his agreement, stated that the CIA was within its rights to break all laws except American law. See also Michael Scheuer, former Chief of the Bin Laden Unit in the CIA Counter-Terrorist Centre, *supra* note 19.

on the part of European governments and administrative departments is disturbing, and such a careless, laissez-faire attitude unworthy.

257. The Council of Europe has already had the opportunity to voice clearly its concern *about certain practices that have been adopted, particularly in the fight against terrorism, such as the indefinite imprisonment of foreign nationals on no precise charge and without access to an independent tribunal, degrading treatment during interrogations, the interception of private communications without subsequently informing those concerned, extradition to countries likely to apply the death penalty or the use of torture, and detention or assault on the grounds of political or religious activism, which are contrary to the European Convention on Human Rights (ETS n° 5) and the protocols thereto, the European Convention for the Prevention of Torture and Inhuman or Degrading Treatment or Punishment (ETS n° 126), and the Framework Decision of the Council of the European Union*[220].

9.2. The Strength of Unity and of the Law

258. The Parliamentary Assembly has already expressed its views very clearly: it unreservedly shares *the United States' determination to combat international terrorism and fully endorses the importance of detecting and preventing terrorist crimes, prosecuting and punishing terrorists and protecting human lives*[221] This determination must also be shared by all of Europe. Back in 1986, the Assembly regretted *the procrastination of European states in reacting multilaterally to the terrorist threat, and the absence up to the present time of a coherent and binding set of co-ordinated measures adopted by common consent*[222]. Despite the intervening years and the spectacular development of this threat, no significant progress has really been made. It is more necessary than ever to extend this *coherent and binding set of co-ordinated measures* to Europe and to other parts of the world, starting with the United States. The approach of simply leaving the United States to it and pretending not to know what is happening, in many cases even on one's own territory, is unacceptable. Only the adoption of a joint strategy by all the countries concerned can successfully counter the new threats, such as terrorism and organised crime. If, as the United States believes, existing legal instruments are no longer adequate to counter the new threats, the situation must be analysed and discussed on a joint basis.

259. It is highly likely that existing resources and arrangements will have to be adapted in order to combat international terrorism effectively. This is

[220] Recommendation 1713 (2005) of the PACE on Democratic oversight of the security sector in member States.

[221] Resolution 1433 (2005), on Lawfulness of detentions by the United States in Guantanamo Bay, § 1.

[222] Resolution 863 (1986) on the European response to international terrorism, § 3.

the view held by the United States Government, in particular[223]. Police investigation tools and the rules of criminal procedure clearly need to take into account the development of more serious forms of crime. However, such adaptation calls for multilateral consultation, presupposing dialogue, debate or even a frank and open confrontation, which clearly have yet to take place. On the contrary, the states of the European Union have just issued a particularly negative signal: giving in to what appears to be a nationalist reflex, in late April 2006 they turned down a Commission proposal to step up judicial and police co-operation under the Schengen Agreement[224].

260. Efforts to combat impunity are undoubtedly a crucial element in the fight against terrorism. It is unfortunate that the American administration has systematically opposed the establishment of a universal jurisdiction, refusing to ratify the Rome agreement on the establishment of the International Criminal Court[225]. Handing over terrorist suspects (without, moreover, any verification of the substance of the accusations by a judicial authority) to states one knows, or must presume, will not respect fundamental rights, is unacceptable. Relying on the principle of trust and on diplomatic assurances given by undemocratic states known not to respect human rights is simply cowardly and hypocritical.

261. The American administration states that *rendition* is a vital tool in the fight against international terrorism[226]. We consider that *renditions* may be acceptable, and indeed desirable, only if they satisfy a number of very specific requirements (which, with a few exceptions[227], has not been the case in any of the known *renditions* to date). If a state is unable, or does not wish, to prosecute a suspect, it should be possible to apply the following principle: no person genuinely suspected of a serious act of terrorism should feel safe anywhere in the world. In such cases, however, the person in question may be handed over only to a state able to provide all the guarantees of a fair trial, or—even better—to an international jurisdiction, which in my view should be established as a matter of urgency.

262. The UN High Commissioner for Human Rights, Louise Arbour, has publicly criticised the practice of handing over detainees—outside the scope

[223] The captured terrorists of the 21st century do not fit easily into traditional systems of criminal or military justice, which were designed for different needs. We have had to adapt. (Ms Rice, statement of 5 December 2005).

[224] See, for instance, Le Figaro of 28 April 2006.

[225] See, for example, Resolution 1336 (2003) on *Threats to the International Criminal Court.*

[226] Rendition is a vital tool in combating transnational terrorism (Ms Rice, in her statement of 5 December 2005).

[227] In particular, this applies to the case of the terrorist Carlos, which was mentioned by Ms Rice. She appears to forget, however, that Carlos was abducted in Sudan, where he enjoyed total impunity and was transported to France, where he was judged according to a procedure consistent with the European Convention on Human Rights.

of the justice system—to countries known to use torture, while demanding assurances that these prisoners will not be ill treated. She added that secret detention was a form of torture[228].

263. Abandoning or relativising human dignity and fundamental human rights is utterly inconceivable. All of history shows that arbitrary decisions, contempt for human values and torture have never been effective, have failed to resolve anything and, ultimately, have led only to a subsequent exacerbation of violence and brutality. In the end, such abuses have served only to confer a sense and appearance of legitimacy on those who attack institutions. In fact, giving in to this temptation concedes a major initial victory to the very people attacking our values. Furthermore, attempting to focus solely on security aspects, as is the case at present -with an outcome that is more than questionable—plays into the hands of the terror lords. It is imperative for a global anti-terrorism strategy to consider political and social aspects. Above all, we must be mindful of the strength of the values of the society for which we are fighting[229]. Benjamin Franklin inevitably comes to mind, and his approach seems more relevant than ever: *they that can give up essential liberty to attain a little temporary security deserve neither liberty nor safety*[230].

264. Legality and fairness by no means preclude firmness, but confer genuine legitimacy and credibility on a state's inevitable preventive actions. In this respect, some of the international community's attitudes are disturbing. I have already mentioned the unacceptable practice involving the application of UN Security Council sanctions on the basis of black lists. Another example is the situation in Kosovo, where the international community intervened to restore peace, justice and democracy: the inhabitants of this region are still the only people in Europe—with the exception of Belarus—not to have access to the European Court of Human Rights; its prisons are a virtual black hole, not open for inspections or monitoring by the Committee for the Prevention of Torture. In the name of what legitimacy, and with what credibility, is this same international community entitled to lecture Serbia? *Examples are more effective than threats* (Corneille).

[228] Le Monde of 9 December 2005.

[229] A judgment of the Israeli Supreme Court, called to rule on an alleged breach of the principle of equality following the distribution of gas masks on the West Bank during the Gulf War, contains the following remarkable passage written by the President of the Court, Aaron Barak, himself a survivor of the Kovnus ghetto in Lithuania: *"When the guns speak, the Muses fall silent. But when the guns speak, military commands must comply with the law. A society that wishes to be able to confront its enemies must above all be mindful that it is fighting for values worth protecting. The rule of law is one of those values"*; in: Aaron Barak, *Democrazia, Terrohsmo e Corti di giustizia*, Giurisprudenza Costituzionale, 2002, 5, p. 3385.

[230] Quoted just recently by Heinrich Koller, Kampf gegen Terrorismus—Rechstaatlichen Grundlagen und Schranken, conference held in Zurich on 19 January 2006 before the Schweizeriche Helsinki Vereinigung fur Demokratie, Rechtsstaat und Menschenrechte.

10. Legal Perspectives

10.1. The Point of View of the United States

265. In May 2006 the United States sent its first state delegation to the United Nations Committee against Torture (UN CAT) since the Bush Administration came to power. The delegation was headed by the Chief Legal Advisor to the Department of State, Mr John Bellinger.

266. Mr Bellinger oversaw the presentation of a 184-page submission to UN CAT, in which the United States set out its "exhaustive written responses" to most of the Committee's list of issues. The United States should certainly be commended for this level of engagement, notwithstanding that its policy regarding secret detentions and intelligence activities remained, for the most part, at a firm *"no comment."*[231]

267. There can have been few more opportune times at which to engage Mr Bellinger on discussion of pertinent legal issues than in the week of his return from the UN CAT to Washington, DC. In a briefing lasting about one hour[232], Mr Bellinger and his colleague Dan Fried, Assistant Secretary of State for European Affairs, provided us with a range of valuable perspectives, which I think it worthwhile to indicate in this report as the best contemporary first-hand portrayal of the US legal position.

268. Mr Bellinger made clear on several occasions that a programme of renditions remains a key strand of United States' foreign policy: *"As Secretary Rice has said, we do conduct renditions, we have conducted renditions and we will not rule out conducting renditions in the future."*

269. He was very decisive, however, in drawing a distinction between the original meaning of rendition and the popular, media-driven notion of Extraordinary Rendition:

> *"To the extent that extraordinary rendition—as I have seen it defined—means the intentional transfer of an individual to a country, expecting or intending that they will be mistreated, then the United States does not do extraordinary renditions to begin with. The United States does not render people to other countries for the purpose of being tortured, or in the expectation that they will be tortured."*

270. Dan Fried used the briefing to explain some of the underlying considerations for the United States in pursuit of its "war on terror":

> *"We are attempting to keep our people safe; we are attempting to fight dangerous terrorist groups who are active and who mean what they say about destroying us. We are trying to do so in a way consistent with our values and our international*

---

[231] See the CAT submission of the United States and the newly-published comments of the Committee (at page 4) on secret detentions, available at *www.usmission.ch*.

[232] Detailed notes of the meeting with Mr Bellinger and transcripted comments are on file with the Rapporteur.

legal obligations. Doing all of those things in practice is not easy, partly because—as we've discovered as we've gotten into it—the struggle we are in does not fit neatly either into the criminal legal framework, or neatly into the law of war framework."

271. With regard to the question of fitting into legal frameworks, I find it particularly noteworthy that the United States does not see itself bound to satisfy anyone's interpretation of international law but its own. Mr Bellinger continually expressed this view: *"We have to comply with our legal obligations. None of this can be done in an illegal way. We think from our point of view that we comply with all the legal obligations we have."*

272. Similarly, in one of his longer explanations, Mr Bellinger defended the United States' record in the eyes of its European partners:

"For those who say we're not following our international obligations in certain cases, I have to say that sometimes it comes down to a disagreement on what the obligation is.

With regard to Article 3 of CAT, this is a technical issue. The obligation under Article 3 of the Convention Against Torture requires a country not to return, expel or refouler an individual. For more than a decade, the position of the US Government, and our courts, has been that all of those terms refer to returns from, or transfers out from the United States.

So we think that Article 3 of the CAT is legally binding upon us with respect to transfers of anyone from the United States; but we don't think it is legally binding outside the United States.

Similarly the Senate of the United States and our courts for more than ten years have taken a position that the words 'substantial grounds' means 'more likely than not'. If we transfer a person from one point outside the United States to another point outside the United States then, as a policy matter, if we think there are substantial grounds to believe that the individual will be tortured or mistreated, we follow the same rules. I think it is a reasonable position for our courts to have set—that 'substantial grounds' means 'more likely than not'.

What I can say, though, is that there are different legal regimes between the European Court of Human Rights and our courts, and you can't 'beat up' our courts and our Senate based on some things that they said ten years ago as how they interpret the law.

You may wish that the ECtHR interpretation of the CAT was the same position that we have here, but it is not. We do, though, take our legal obligations seriously. And there needs to be a recognition that there may be different interpretation of the terms, but nonetheless the United States still takes our legal obligations seriously—and we do that."

Mr Bellinger's interpretation also serves to explain why a detention facility like Camp Delta is situated at Guantanamo Bay, in Cuba, and not in the desert of Arizona. The United States' formalistic and positivist approach shocks the legal sensibilities of Europeans, who are rather influenced by "teleological" considerations. In other words, the European approach is to opt for an interpretation that affords maximum protection to the values on which the legal rule is based.

273. Mr Bellinger was predictably reluctant to discuss the legal issues surrounding any of the cases of rendition that are alleged to have occurred, including the case studies treated in this report. He cited a considered policy on the part of the US Government to refrain from commenting:

> *"We have thought seriously about whether we can answer specific questions publicly and say that there were one, two, or three renditions and where they went through. But we have concluded that, due to the nature of intelligence activities, we simply cannot get into the business of confirming or denying specific questions—as much as we would like to. I'm not going to confirm or deny whether there have been any renditions that have gone through Europe at all."*

274. The United States Government is always prepared, however, to explain the "hard choices" it feels it has to make to protect its citizens[233]. Mr Bellinger, for his part, described a hypothetical *"policy dilemma"* based loosely on a real-life scenario, where a member of Al-Qaeda is captured at the Kenyan border, *"trying to enter the country but the Kenyans don't want him there"*. The captive is known to be wanted by *"some other country such as Egypt, Pakistan or Jordan"* and the United States has an aircraft it could use to render him back. Mr Bellinger concluded his briefing by characterising the choice:

> *"If the choice is between letting a person go who's suspected of involvement in terrorism, or taking them back to their country of nationality, or some other country where they're wanted—then that's your choice, because there's no extradition treaty and you obviously don't want us to put more people in Guantanamo.*
>
> *If the choice is whether the person will disappear and be let go, or the country of his nationality or some other country wants him back, and the US is able to provide that—what should be done? That's your choice.*
>
> *The United States says there are cases where in fact rendition might make sense."*

10.2. The Point of View of the Council of Europe

10.2.1. The European Commission for Democracy Through Law (Venice Commission)

275. The legal issues raised by the facts examined in this report, from the point of view of the Council of Europe, have been set out clearly and

[233] See Secretary Rice's remarks upon her departure for Europe, Andrews Air Base, 5 December 2005: "Protecting citizens is the first and oldest duty of any government. Sometimes these efforts are misunderstood. I want to help all of you understand the hard choices involved, and some of the responsibilities that go with them."

precisely by the Venice Commission, whom the Committee on Legal Affairs and Human Rights had asked for a legal opinion in December 2005[234].

276. In its conclusion, the Venice Commission stresses the responsibility of the Council of Europe's member States to ensure that all persons within their jurisdiction enjoy internationally agreed upon fundamental rights (including the right to security of the person, freedom from torture and the right to life), even in the case of persons who are aboard an aircraft that is simply transiting through its airspace[235]. The Venice Commission also confirms that the obligations arising out of the numerous bilateral and multilateral treaties in different fields such as collective self-defence, international civil aviation and military bases, *"do not prevent States from complying with their human rights obligations"*[236].

277. In reply to the specific questions asked by the Committee on Legal Affairs and Human Rights, the Venice Commission has drawn the following conclusions:

"As regards arrest and secret detention

a) Any form of involvement of a Council of Europe member State or receipt of information prior to an arrest within its jurisdiction by foreign agents entails accountability under Articles 1 and 5 of the European Convention on Human Rights (and possibly Article 3 in respect of the modalities of the arrest). A State must thus prevent the arrest from taking place. If the arrest is effected by foreign authorities in the exercise of their jurisdiction under the terms of an applicable Status of Forces Agreement (SOFA), the Council of Europe member State concerned may remain accountable under the European Convention on Human Rights, as it is obliged to give priority to its jus cogens obligations, such as they ensue from Article 3.

b) Active and passive co-operation by a Council of Europe member State in imposing and executing secret detentions engages its responsibility under the European Convention on Human Rights. While no such responsibility applies if the detention is carried out by foreign authorities without the territorial State actually knowing it, the latter must take effective measures to safeguard against the risk of disappearance and must conduct a prompt and

---

234 Opinion on the International Legal Obligations of Council of Europe Member States in Respect of Secret Detention Facilities and Inter-State Transport of Prisoners, adopted by the Venice Commission at its 66th Plenary Session (Venice, 17-18 March 2006) on the basis of comments by Mssrs Iain Cameron (Substitute Member, Sweden), Pieter van Dijk (Member, the Netherlands), Olivier Dutheillet de Lamothe (Member, France), Jan Helgesen (Member, Norway), Giorgio Malinverni (Member, Switzerland) and Georg Nolte (Substitute Member, Germany)—opinion no. 363/2005, CDL-AD(2006)009.

235 cf. Opinion cited above, paras. 143–146.

236 Ibid., para. 156. See EU Network of Independent Experts on Fundamental Rights, Opinion No. 3-2006 on "The Human Responsibilities of the EU Member States in the Context of the CIA Activities in Europe ('Extraordinary Renditions'), 25 May 2006, at page 7. The Network reaches the same conclusion on the basis of Article 6(1) EU.

effective investigation into a substantiated claim that a person has been taken into unacknowledged custody.

c) *The Council of Europe member State's responsibility is engaged also in the case where its agents (police, security forces etc.) co-operate with the foreign authorities or do not prevent an arrest or unacknowledged detention without government knowledge, acting ultra vires. The Statute of the Council of Europe and the European Convention on Human Rights require respect for the rule of law, which in turn requires accountability for all form of exercise of public power. Regardless of how a State chooses to regulate political control over security and intelligence agencies, in any event effective oversight and control mechanisms must exist.*

d) *If a State is informed or has reasonable suspicions that any persons are held incommunicado at foreign military bases on its territory, its responsibility under the European Convention on Human Rights is engaged, unless it takes all measures which are within its power in order for this irregular situation to end.*

e) *Council of Europe member States which have ratified the European Convention for the Prevention of Torture must inform the European Committee for the Prevention of Torture of any detention facility on their territory and must allow it to access such facilities. Insofar as international humanitarian law may be applicable, States must grant the International Committee of the Red Cross permission to visit these facilities.*

As regards inter-state transfers of prisoners

f) *There are only four legal ways for Council of Europe member States to transfer a prisoner to foreign authorities: deportation, extradition, transit and transfer of sentenced persons for the purpose of their serving the sentence in another country. Extradition and deportation proceedings must be defined by the applicable law, and the prisoners must be provided appropriate legal guarantees and access to competent authorities. The prohibition to extradite or deport to a country where there exists a risk of torture or ill-treatment must be respected.*

g) *Diplomatic assurances must be legally binding on the issuing State and must be unequivocal in terms; when there is substantial evidence that a country practices or permits torture in respect of certain categories of prisoners, Council of Europe member States must refuse the assurances in cases of requests for extradition of prisoners belonging to those categories.*

h) *The prohibition to transfer to a country where there exists a risk of torture or ill-treatment also applies in respect of the transit of prisoners through the territory of Council of Europe member States: they must therefore refuse to allow transit of prisoners in circumstances where there is such a risk.*

As regards overflight

i) *If a Council of Europe member State has serious reasons to believe that an airplane crossing its airspace carries prisoners with the intention of transferring them to countries where they would face ill-treatment in violation of Article 3 of the European Convention on Human Rights, it must take all the necessary measures in order to prevent this from taking place.*

j) *If the state airplane in question has presented itself as a civil plane, that is to say it has not duly sought prior authorisation pursuant to Article 3 c) of the Chicago Convention, the territorial State must require landing and must search it. In addition, it must protest through appropriate diplomatic channels.*

k) *If the plane has presented itself as a state plane and has obtained overflight permission without however disclosing its mission, the territorial State cannot search it unless the captain consents. However, the territorial State can refuse further overflight clearances in favour of the flag State or impose, as a condition therefor, the duty to submit to searches; if the overflight permission derives from a bilateral treaty or a Status of Forces Agreement or a military base agreement, the terms of such a treaty should be questioned if and to the extent that they do not allow for any control in order to ensure respect for human rights.*

l) *In granting foreign state aircraft authorisation for overflight, Council of Europe member States must secure respect for their human rights obligations. This means that they may have to consider whether it is necessary to insert new clauses, including the right to search, as a condition for diplomatic clearances in favour of State planes carrying prisoners. If there are reasonable grounds to believe that, in certain categories of cases, the human rights of certain passengers risk being violated, States must indeed make overflight permission conditional upon respect of express human rights clauses. Compliance with the procedures for obtaining diplomatic clearance must be strictly monitored; requests for overflight authorisation should provide sufficient information as to allow effective monitoring (for example, the identity and status (voluntary or involuntary passenger) of all persons on board and the destination of the flight as well as the final destination of each passenger). Whenever necessary, the right to search civil planes must be exercised.*

m) *With a view to discouraging repetition of abuse, any violations of civil aviation principles in relation to irregular transport of prisoners should be denounced, and brought to the attention of the competent authorities and eventually of the public. Council of Europe member States could bring possible breaches of the Chicago Convention before the Council of the International Civil Aviation Organisation pursuant to Article 54 of the Chicago Convention.*

n) *As regards the treaty obligations of Council of Europe member States, the Commission considers that there is no international obligation for them to allow irregular transfers of prisoners or to grant unconditional overflight rights, for the purposes of combating terrorism. The Commission recalls that if the breach of a treaty obligation is determined by the need to comply with a peremptory norm (jus cogens), it does not give rise to an internationally*

> *wrongful act, and the prohibition of torture is a peremptory norm. In the Commission's opinion, therefore, States must interpret and perform their treaty obligations, including those deriving from the NATO treaty and from military base agreements and Status of Forces Agreements, in a manner compatible with their human rights obligations."*

10.2.2 The Secretary General of the Council of Europe (Article 52 ECHR)

278. The Secretary General has made use of his power of enquiry under Article 52 ECHR as rapidly and as completely as possible. In his report dated 28 February 2006,[237] the Secretary General takes a clear position as regards member States' responsibilities:

> *"The activities of foreign agencies cannot be attributed directly to States Parties. Their responsibility may nevertheless be engaged on account of either their duty to refrain from aid or assistance in the commission of wrongful conduct, acquiescence and connivance in such conduct, or, more generally, their positive obligations under the Convention. In accordance with the generally recognised rules on State responsibility, States may be held responsible of aiding or assisting another State in the commission of an internationally wrongful act. There can be little doubt that aid and assistance by agents of a State Party in the commission of human rights abuses by agents of another State acting within the former's jurisdiction would constitute a violation of the Convention. Even acquiescence and connivance of the authorities in the acts of foreign agents affecting Convention rights might engage the State Party's responsibility under the Convention. Of course, any such vicarious responsibility presupposes that the authorities of States Parties had knowledge of the said activities."*[238]

As regards the result of the Secretary General's request for information, the report of 28 February concludes in a preliminary fashion that *"all forms of deprivation of liberty outside the regular legal framework need to be defined as criminal offences in all States Parties and be effectively enforced. Offences should include aiding and assisting in such illegal acts, as well as acts of omission (being aware but not reporting), and strong criminal sanctions should be provided for intelligence staff or other public officials involved in such cases. However, the most significant problems and loopholes revealed by the replies concern the ability of competent authorities to detect any such illegal activities and take resolute action against them. Four main areas are identified where further measures should be taken at national, European and international levels:*

- *— the rules governing activities of secret services appear inadequate in many States; better controls are necessary, in particular as regards activities of foreign secret services on their territory;*

[237] SG/Inf (2006)5, available at the Council of Europe's website (http://www.coe.int).

[238] ibid., para. 23; see also the excellent analysis of the case law of the European Court of Human Rights regarding member States' "positive obligations" in paras. 24-30

— *the current international regulations for air traffic do not give adequate safeguards against abuse. There is a need for States to be given the possibility to check whether transiting aircraft are being used for illegal purposes. But even within the current legal framework, States should equip themselves with stronger control tools;*

— *international rules on State immunity often prevent States from effectively prosecuting foreign officials who commit crimes on their territory. Immunity must not lead to impunity where serious human rights violations are at stake. Work should start at European and international levels to establish clear human rights exceptions to traditional rules on immunity;*

— *mere assurances by foreign States that their agents abroad comply with international and national law are not enough. Formal guarantees and enforcement mechanisms need to be set out in agreements and national law in order to protect ECHR rights."*[239]

279. In this context, the Secretary General, referring to my memorandum of 21 January 2006, was worried about the fact that some countries have not replied, or have not replied completely, to his question concerning the involvement of any public official in such deprivation of liberty or transport of detainees, and whether any official investigation is under way or has been completed. Consequently, the Secretary General has asked additional questions to some countries. The replies are not yet in the public domain.

11. Conclusion

280. Our analysis of the CIA "rendition" programme has revealed a network that resembles a "spider's web" spun across the globe. The analysis is based on official information provided by national and international air traffic control authorities, as well as other information including from sources inside intelligence agencies, in particular the American. This "web", shown in the graphic,[240] is composed of several landing points, which we have subdivided into different categories, and which are linked up among themselves by civilian planes used by the CIA or military aircraft.

281. These landing points are used for various purposes that range from aircraft stopovers to refuel during a mission to staging points used for the connection of different "rendition circuits" that we have identified and where "rendition units" can rest and prepare missions. We have also marked the points where there are known detention centres (Guantanamo Bay,

239 *Ibid.*, p. 1 (non-official executive summary).

240 See graphic annex to this report: "The global "spider's web" of secret detentions and unlawful inter-state transfers".

Kabul and Baghdad . . .) as well as points where we believe we have been able to establish that pick-ups of rendition victims took place.

282. In two European countries only (Romania and Poland), there are two other landing points that remain to be explained. Whilst these do not fall into any of the categories described above, several indications lead us to believe that they are likely to form part of the "rendition circuits'[241]. These landings therefore do not form part of the 98% of CIA flights that are used solely for logistical purposes[242], but rather belong to the 2% of flights that concern us the most. These corroborated facts strengthen the presumption -already based on other elements—that these landings are detainee drop-off points that are near to secret detention centres.

283. Analysis of the network's functioning and of ten individual cases allows us to make a number of conclusions both about human rights violations—some of which continue—and about the responsibilities of some Council of Europe member States.

284. It must be emphasised that this report is indeed addressed to the Council of Europe Member states. The United States, an observer state of our Organisation, actually created this reprehensible network, which we criticise in light of the values shared on both sides of the Atlantic. But we also believe to have established that it is only through the intentional or grossly negligent collusion of the European partners that this "web" was able to spread also over Europe.

285. The impression which some Governments tried to create at the beginning of this debate—that Europe was a victim of secret CIA plots—does not seem to correspond to reality. It is now clear—although we are still far from having established the whole truth—that authorities in several European countries actively participated with the CIA in these unlawful activities. Other countries ignored them knowingly, or did not want to know.

286. In the draft resolution, which sums up this report's conclusions, I have not directly named the countries responsible simply because there is not enough room in such a text to adequately develop the nuances of each individual case. In addition, we only know part of the truth so far, and other countries may still turn out to be implicated in light of future research or revelations. This explanatory note, however, explains the discovered facts in far greater detail. Finally, the purpose of this report is not to attribute "grades" to different member States, but to try to understand what really happened throughout Europe and to stop certain violations shown from reoccurring in future. I would add that a key element seems to be the urgent need to improve the international response to the threat of terrorism.

[241] See paragraph 51 above.

[242] See paragraph 49 above (quoting Michael Scheuer, architect of the rendition programme).

This response presently appears today as largely inadequate and insufficiently coordinated.

287. Whilst hard evidence, at least according to the strict meaning of the word, is still not forthcoming, a number of coherent and converging elements indicate that secret detention centres have indeed existed and unlawful inter-state transfers have taken place in Europe. I do not set myself up to act as a criminal court, because this would require evidence beyond reasonable doubt. My assessment rather reflects a conviction based upon careful examination of balance of probabilities, as well as upon logical deductions from clearly established facts. It is not intended to pronounce that the authorities of these countries are "guilty" for having tolerated secret detention sites, but rather it is to hold them "responsible" for failing to comply with the positive obligation to diligently investigate any serious allegation of fundamental rights violations.

288. In this sense, it must be stated that to date, the following member States could be held responsible, to varying degrees, which are not always settled definitively, for violations of the rights of specific persons identified below (respecting the chronological order as far as possible):

— Sweden, in the cases of Ahmed Agiza and Mohamed Alzery;

— Bosnia-Herzegovina, in the cases of Lakhdar Boumediene, Mohamed Nechle, Hadj Boudella, Belkacem Bensayah, Mustafa Ait Idir and Saber Lahmar (the "Algerian six");

— The United Kingdom in the cases of Bisher Al-Rawi, Jamil El-Banna and Binyam Mohamed;

— Italy, in the cases of Abu Omar and Maher Arar;

— "The former Yugoslav Republic of Macedonia", in the case of Khaled El-Masri;

— Germany, in the cases of Abu Omar, of the "Algerian six", and Khaled El-Masri;

— Turkey, in the case of the "Algerian six".

289. Some of these above mentioned states, and others, could be held responsible for collusion—active or passive (in the sense of having tolerated or having been negligent in fulfilling the duty to supervise) -involving secret detention and unlawful inter-state transfers of a non specified number of persons whose identity so far remains unknown:

— Poland and Romania, concerning the running of secret detention centres;

— Germany, Turkey, Spain and Cyprus for being "staging points" for flights involving the unlawful transfer of detainees;

— Ireland, the United Kingdom, Portugal, Greece and Italy for being "stopovers" for flights involving the unlawful transfer of detainees.

290. Other States should still show greater willingness and zeal in the quest for truth, as serious indications show that their territory or their airspace might have been used, even unbeknownst, for illegal operations (the example of Switzerland was cited in this context).

291. The international community is finally urged to create more transparency in the places of detention in Kosovo, which to date qualify as "black holes" that cannot even be accessed by the CPT. This is frankly intolerable, considering that the international intervention in this region was meant to restore order and lawfulness.

292. With regards to these extremely serious allegations, it is urgent—that is the principal aim of this report—that all Council of Europe member States concerned finally comply with their positive obligation under the ECHR to investigate. It is also crucial that the proposals in the draft resolution and recommendation are implemented so that terrorism can be fought effectively whilst respecting human rights at the same time.

ANNEX

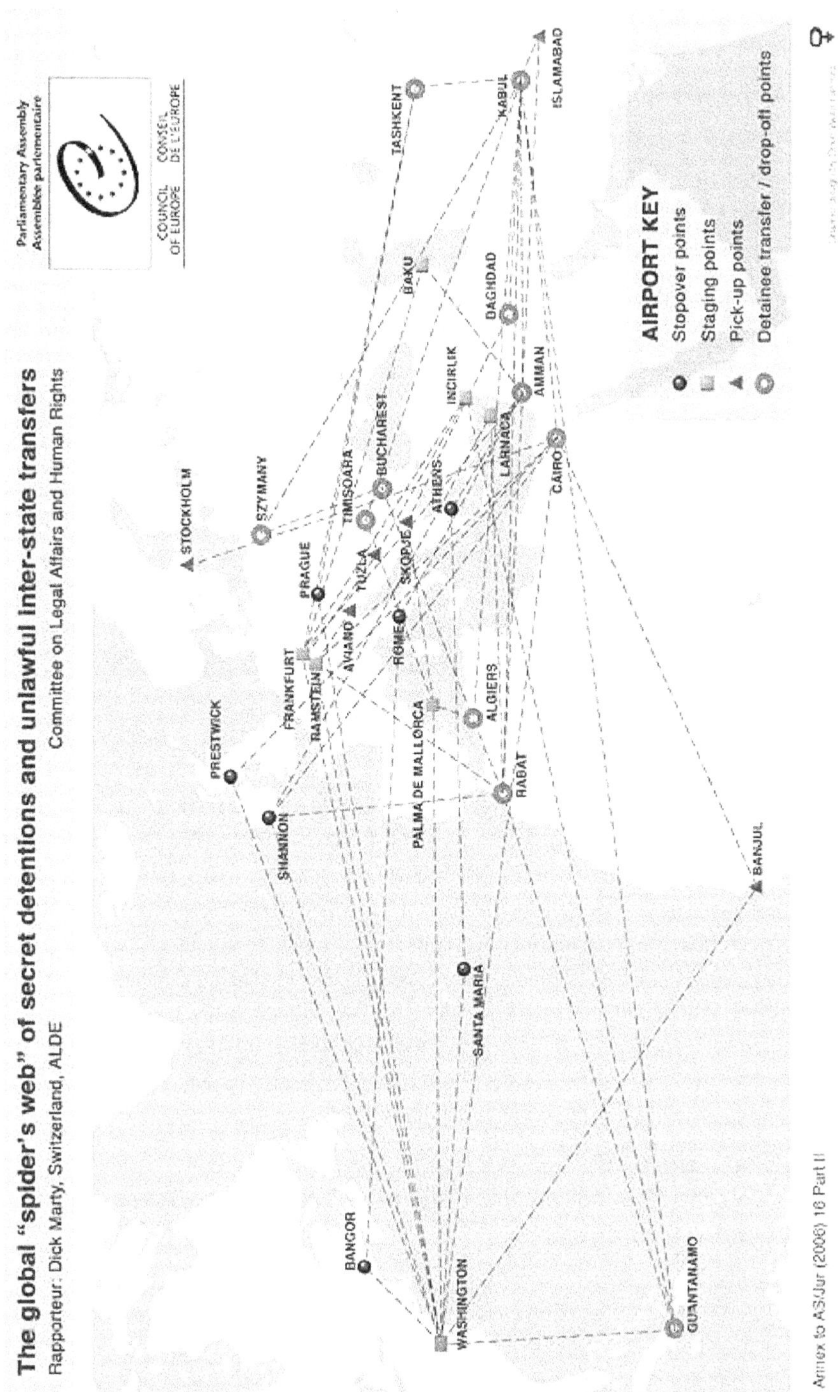

Figure 1: The global "spider's web" of secret detentions and unlawful inter-state transfers

Annex

Reporting committee: Committee on Legal Affairs and Human Rights

Reference to committee: Doc 10748 and Reference No 3153 of 25 November 2005

Draft resolution and draft recommendation unanimously adopted by the Committee on 7 June 2006

Members of the Committee: Mr Dick **Marty** (Chairperson), Mr Erik **Jurgens,** Mr Eduard Lintner, Mr Adrien Severin (Vice-Chairpersons), Mrs Birgitta Alhqvist, Mr Athanasios Alevras, Mr Rafis Aliti, Mr Alexander Arabadjiev, Mr Miguel Arias, Mr Birgir Ármannsson, Mr Josë Luis Arnaut, Mr Abdülkadir Ateş, Mr Jaume **Bartumeu Cassany,** Mrs Meritxell Batet, Mrs Soledad Becerril, Mrs Marie-Louise **Bemelmans-Videc,** Mr Giorgi Bokeria, Mrs Olena Bondarenko, Mr Erol Aslan Cebeci, Mrs Pia Christmas-Møller, Mr Boriss **Cilevičs,** Mr Domenico Contestabile, Mr András Csáky, Mrs Herta **Däubler-Gmelin,** Mr Marcello Dell'Utri, Mrs Lydie Err, Mr Jan Ertsborn, Mr Václav **Exner,** Mr Valeriy Fedorov, Mr György **Frunda,** Mr Jean-Charles Gardetto, Mr Jószef Gedei, Mr Stef Goris, Mr Valery **Grebennikov,** Mrs Gultakin Hajiyeva, Mrs Karin Hakl, Mr Nick Harvey, Mr Michel **Hunault,** Mr Rafael **Huseynov,** Mrs Fatme Ilyaz, Mr Kastriot Islami, Mr Sergei Ivanov, Mr Tomáš Jirsa, Mr Antti Kaikkonen (alternate: Mr Kimmo **Sasi),** Mr Uyriy Karmazin, Mr Karol Karski, Mr Hans Kaufmann (alternate: Mr Andreas **Gross),** Mr Nikolay Kovalev, Mr Jean-Pierre Kucheida, Mrs Darja Lavtižar-Bebler, Mr Andrzej Lepper, Mrs Sabine Leutheusser-Schnarrenberger, Mr Tony Lloyd, Mr Humfrey Malins, Mr Andrea Manzella, Mr Alberto Martins, Mr Tito Masi, Mr Andrew McIntosh, Mr Murat Mercan, Mr Philippe Monfils, Mr Philippe Nachbar, Mr Tomislav Nikolić, Ms Ann Ormonde, Mr Rino Piscitello, Mrs Maria Postoico, Mr Christos **Pourgourides,** Mr Jeffrey Pullicino Orlando, Mr Martin Raguž, Mr François Rochebloine, Mr Armen Rustamyan, Mr Michael Spindelegger, Mrs Rodica Mihaela Stănoiu, Mr Christoph Strasser, Mr Petro Symonenko, Mr Vojtech **Tkáč,** Mr Øyvind **Vaksdal,** Mr Egidijus **Vareikis,** Mr Miltiadis Varvitsiotis (alternate: Mrs Elsa **Papadimitriou),** Mrs Renate Wohlwend, Mr Krysztof Zaremba, Mr Vladimir Zhirinovsky, Mr Zoran Žižić, Mr Miomir Žužul

N.B.: The names of the members who took part in the meeting are printed in **bold** *Secretariat of the Committee:* Mr Drzemczewski, Mr Schirmer, Ms Heurtin, Mr Simpson

DOCUMENT NO. 5

OPINION ON THE INTERNATIONAL LEGAL OBLIGATIONS OF COUNCIL OF EUROPE MEMBER STATES IN RESPECT OF SECRET DETENTION FACILITIES AND INTER-STATE TRANSPORT OF PRISONERS

The Venice Commission

March 17, 2006

INTRODUCTION

1. By a letter of 15 December 2005, Mr Dick Marty, chairperson of the Committee on Legal Affairs and Human Rights of the Parliamentary Assembly of the Council of Europe, requested an opinion of the Commission in respect of the following inter-related matters:

a) An assessment of the legality of secret detention centres in the light of the Council of Europe member States' international law obligations, in particular the European Convention on Human Rights (ECHR) and the European Convention for the Prevention of Torture. In particular, to what extent is a State responsible if—actively or passively—it permits illegal detention or abduction by a third State or an agent thereof?

b) What are the legal obligations of Council of Europe member States, under human rights and general international law, regarding the transport of detainees by other States through their territory, including the airspace ? What is the relationship between such obligations and possible countervailing obligations which derive from other treaties, including treaties concluded with non-member States ?

2. A working group was set up, which was composed of the following members: Mr Iain Cameron, Mr Pieter van Dijk, Mr Olivier Dutheillet de Lamothe, Mr Jan Helgesen, Mr Giorgio Malinverni and Mr Georg Nolte. It was assisted by Ms Simona Granata-Menghini, Head of the Constitutional Co-operation Division.

3. Two working meetings were held in Paris,on 13 January and on 27 and 28 February 2006.

4. The Working Group sought the assistance of the NATO Legal Services and requested clarifications in relation to certain matters of military law as well as certain documents. Regrettably, the Commission was not provided with either of them.

5. The Working Group availed itself of the valuable assistance of the International Civil Aviation Organisation (ICAO), whose Legal Bureau provided documentation about the interpretation of certain provisions of the Chicago Convention on International Civil Aviation. The Commission wishes to express its appreciation and gratitude for the co-operation of the ICAO.

6. The present study was discussed within the Sub-Commissions on International Law and on Democratic Institutions in the course of a joint meeting on 16 March 2006, and was subsequently adopted by the Commission at its 66th Plenary Session (Venice, 17-18 March 2006).

7. The present opinion does not aim, nor does it have the ambition to assess the facts in relation to the current allegations about the existence of secret detention facilities in Europe or about the transport of detainees by the CIA through the territory (including the airspace) of certain European States. This is not the task of the Venice Commission. It is instead the object of the report that is in the process of being prepared by the PACE Legal Affairs Committee.

8. This opinion does not aim at identifying the pertinent internal law and practice of the Council of Europe member-States either. On 21 November 2005, the Secretary General of the Council of Europe decided to use his power of inquiry under Article 52 of the ECHR and invited the Council of Europe member States to furnish an explanation of the manner in which their internal law ensures the effective implementation of the ECHR in relation to secret detention and transport of detainees. On 28 February 2006, the Secretary General presented his report based on the replies submitted by all member States (See the Secretary General's report under Article 52 ECHR on the question of secret detention and transport of detainees suspected of terrorist acts, notably by or at the instigation of foreign agencies, SG/Inf (2006)5).

9. The aim of this opinion is to provide a reply to the questions put by PACE Legal Affairs Committee, and thus to identify the obligations of Council of Europe member States under public international law in general and under human rights law in particular, in respect of the irregular transport, extradition, deportation or detention of prisoners. In order to be able to do so, the Commission deems that it is necessary to outline at the outset the basic rules under international law, human rights law, humanitarian law and air law (Section I) in respect of detention and inter-State transport of prisoners. The Commission will subsequently proceed with the identification of the specific obligations of Council of Europe member States in these areas (Section II), and will then answer the questions put by PACE (Conclusions).

SECTION I: THE LEGAL REGIME

A. General principles

a. Regular inter-State transfers of prisoners

10. Under international law and human rights law, there are four situations in which a State may lawfully transfer a prisoner to another State: deportation, extradition, transit and transfer of sentenced persons for the purposes of serving their sentence in another country.

11. *Deportation* is the expulsion from a country of an alien whose presence is unwanted or deemed prejudicial. A person against whom a deportation decision has been taken by an administrative authority must have the possibility of applying to a competent authority[1], preferably a court[2]. Deportation is only possible on the specific grounds indicated by the pertinent national law.

12. *Extradition* is a formal procedure whereby an individual who is suspected to have committed a criminal offence and is held by one State is transferred to another State for trial or, if the suspect has already been tried and found guilty, to serve his or her sentence.

13. Extradition is a process to which both international and national law apply. While extradition treaties may provide for the transfer of criminal suspects or sentenced persons between States, domestic law determines under what conditions and according to which procedure the person concerned is to be surrendered in accordance with such treaties. Extradition legislation varies significantly among the different European countries, notably as concerns the incorporation of treaties into national law, procedural guarantees, especially the respective role of the executive and the judiciary in the extradition process, and the proof (and assurances) required for extradition.

---

[1] Article 1, Protocol 7 to the ECHR (Procedural safeguards relating to expulsion of aliens) provides:

> "1. An alien lawfully resident in the territory of a State shall not be expelled therefrom except in pursuance of a decision reached in accordance with law and shall be allowed: a to submit reasons against his expulsion, b to have his case reviewed, and c. to be represented for these purposes before the competent authority or a person or persons designated by that authority.
>
> 2. An alien may be expelled before the exercise of his rights under paragraph 1.a, b and c of this Article, when such expulsion is necessary in the interests of public order or is grounded on reasons of national security."

Similarly, Article 13 of the International Covenant on Civil and Political Rights provides:

> "An alien lawfully in the territory of a State Party to the present Covenant may be expelled therefrom only in pursuance of a decision reached in accordance with law and shall, except where compelling reasons of national security otherwise require, be allowed to submit the reasons against his expulsion and to have his case reviewed by, and be represented for the purpose before, the competent authority or a person or persons especially designated by the competent authority."

[2] European Court of Human Rights, Klass and others v. Federal Republic of Germany judgment of 24 October 1979, § 55.

14. In Council of Europe member States, extradition laws must take into consideration, or be interpreted in conformity with constitutional provisions guaranteeing human rights and international human rights treaties and humanitarian law.

15. The 1957 European Convention on Extradition[3] requires, like most bilateral extradition treaties nowadays, respect for the principles of *ne bis in idem* and speciality. It also forbids extradition to a country where the death penalty would be carried out. The same is true if the extraditing State has "substantial grounds for believing that a request for extradition for an ordinary criminal offence has been made for the purpose of prosecuting or punishing a person on account of his race, religion, nationality or political opinion, or that that person's position may be prejudiced for any of these reasons". In addition, the *nulla poena* principle has to be respected.[4]

16. The 1977 European Convention on the Suppression of Terrorism[5] was adopted with a view to eliminating or restricting the possibility for the requested State of invoking the political nature of an offence in order to oppose an extradition request in respect of terrorist acts. Under this Convention, for extradition purposes, certain specified offences shall never be regarded as "political" (Article 1) and other specified offences may not be regarded as such (Article 2), notwithstanding their political content or motivation. There is no obligation, and even a prohibition to extradite, however, if the requested State has substantial grounds for believing that the request for extradition has been made for the purpose of prosecuting or punishing a person on account of his race, religion, nationality or political opinion or that the position of the person whose extradition is requested may be prejudiced for any of these reasons.

17. *Transit* is an act whereby State B provides facilities for State A to send a prisoner through its territory.

18. Transit is regulated by bilateral and multilateral treaties, *inter alia* Article 21 of the European Convention on Extradition, which provides:

> *1. Transit through the territory of one of the Contracting Parties shall be granted on submission of a request by the means mentioned in Article 12, paragraph 1,*

[3] ETS no. 24. The European Council Framework Decision 2002/584/JHA of 13 June 2002 on the European arrest warrant and the surrender procedures between Member States simplifies and speeds up the procedure of extradition between EU member States, by requiring each national judicial authority (the executing judicial authority) to recognise, ipso facto, and with a minimum of formalities, requests for the surrender of a person made by the judicial authority of another Member State (the issuing judicial authority). As of 1 July 2004, it has replaced for the EU member States the 1957 European Extradition Convention and the 1978 European Convention on the suppression of terrorism as regards extradition; the agreement of 26 May 1989 between 12 Member States on simplifying the transmission of extradition requests; the 1995 Convention on the simplified extradition procedure; the 1996 Convention on extradition and the relevant provisions of the Schengen agreement.

[4] Article 7 ECHR.

[5] ETS no. 90.

provided that the offence concerned is not considered by the Party requested to grant transit as an offence of a political or purely military character having regard to Articles 3 and 4 of this Convention.

2. Transit of a national, within the meaning of Article 6, of a country requested to grant transit may be refused.

3. Subject to the provisions of paragraph 4 of this article, it shall be necessary to produce the documents mentioned in Article 12, paragraph 2.

4. If air transport is used, the following provisions shall apply:

a when it is not intended to land, the requesting Party shall notify the Party over whose territory the flight is to be made and shall certify that one of the documents mentioned in Article 12, paragraph 2.a exists. In the case of an unscheduled landing, such notification shall have the effect of a request for provisional arrest as provided for in Article 16, and the requesting Party shall submit a formal request for transit;

b when it is intended to land, the requesting Party shall submit a formal request for transit.

5. A Party may, however, at the time of signature or of the deposit of its instrument of ratification of, or accession to, this Convention, declare that it will only grant transit of a person on some or all of the conditions on which it grants extradition. In that event, reciprocity may be applied.

6. The transit of the extradited person shall not be carried out through any territory where there is reason to believe that his life or his freedom may be threatened by reason of his race, religion, nationality or political opinion.

19. Although the wording of Article 21 § 4 a) indicates that States need to "notify" a transit flight, State practice on this matter may vary, and indeed some States do not appear to require notification of transit of a prisoner by air over their territory, when no landing is planned[6].

20. European Council Directive no. 2003/110/EC of 25 November 2003 on assistance in cases of transit for the purposes of removal by air[7], underlines that "member States are to implement this Directive with due respect for human rights and fundamental freedoms" and that "in accordance with the applicable international obligations, transit by air should be neither requested nor granted if in the third country of destination or of transit the third-country national faces the threat of inhumane or humiliating

[6] The Explanatory report on the European Convention on Extradition underlines that different approaches were taken by the different States as to whether the transport of a person on board of a ship or aircraft of the nationality of a country other than the requesting or requested Parties was to be considered as transit through the territory of that country. This question was left to be settled in practice (see Explanatory Report on Article 21, at http:/conventions.Council of Europe.int/treaty/en/reports/htlm/024.htm).

[7] OJ L, 321, 6.12.2003, p. 26.

treatment, torture or the death penalty, or if his life or liberty would be at risk by reason of his/her race, religion, nationality, membership of a particular social group or political conviction". Pursuant to Article 4 of the Directive,

> *"1. The request for escorted or unescorted transit by air and the associated assistance measures under Article 5(1) shall be made in writing by the requesting Member State. It shall reach the requested Member State as early as possible, and in any case no later than two days before the transit. This time limit may be waived in particularly urgent and duly justified cases.*
>
> *2. The requested Member State shall inform the requesting Member State forthwith of its decision within two days. This time limit may be extended in duly justified cases by a maximum of 48 hours. Transit by air shall not be started without the approval of the requested Member State.*
>
> *Where no reply is provided by the requested Member State within the deadline referred to in the first subparagraph, the transit operations may be started by means of a notification by the requesting Member State.*
>
> *Member States may provide on the basis of bilateral or multilateral agreements or arrangements that the transit operations may be started by means of a notification by the requesting Member State."*

21. Under this Directive, with respect to any request for transit, the requesting member State must provide the requested member State with information about the third-country national to whom the transit request relates, flight details and further information about the state of health of the person and possible public order concerns.

22. The text of an Agreement on Extradition between the European Union and the USA was finalised in 2003; however, this agreement has, so far, not entered into force in respect of any EU member-State[8]. It provides that a EU member State may authorise transportation through its territory of a person surrendered to the US by a third State, or by the US to a third State. A request for transit shall be made through the diplomatic channel and shall contain a description of the person being transported and a brief description of the facts of the case. Authorization is not required when air transportation is used and no landing is scheduled on the territory of the transit State (which does not change the obligations of member States of the Council of Europe under human rights treaties, see below, para. 147); if an unscheduled landing occurs, the State on whose territory the landing takes place may require a request for transit.

[8] The specific human rights obligations for Council of Europe member States in respect of extradition treaties, including this agreement, will be dealt with below (see paras 137-153).

23. States may enter into agreements concerning the *transfer of sentenced persons* for the purpose of serving their sentence in their country of origin. Such procedures are not relevant for this opinion.

b. Irregular inter-State transfers of prisoners[9]

24. A transfer is unlawful or irregular when the government of State B transfers a person from State B to the custody of State A, against his or her consent, in a procedure not set out in law (i.e. not extradition, deportation, transit or transfer with a view to sentence-serving).

25. The kidnapping of a person by agents of State A on the territory of State B and his or her removal to State A or to a third State is a violation of State B's territorial sovereignty and therefore an internationally wrongful act which engages the international responsibility of State A[10].

26. Under general international law (see para. 37 below), in such a case State A has to make "full reparation for the injury caused by the internationally wrongful act" at the request of the injured State, which, in this case, would include the return of the person in question. The rights of the person in question vis-à-vis State A depend upon the latter's law, on the applicable human rights obligations.

27. Irregular transfers may take place with the acquiescence of the territorial government. This type of situation raises a human rights issue. For a *Rechtsstaat*, it will also raise the issues of governmental responsibility for acts of its organs and services and of parliamentary control over government.

28. Another form of irregular transfer happens where some section of the public authorities in State B (police, security forces etc.) transfers a person from State B but not in accordance with a procedure set out in law, or even contrary to domestic law. This, in turn, may take the form of official participation in the transfer (arresting and handing over), or facilitating a kidnapping (actively, or passively—not preventing a kidnapping which it was known would occur). The security/police action may occur with or without government knowledge.

29. If there is no legal basis for an active measure (arrest, handing over etc) under national law, then there will be in such cases a breach of national law on arrest, and consequently also a breach of Article 5 of the European Convention on Human Rights. This situation also raises the issue of

[9] In the context of the present opinion, the term "prisoner" means "anyone deprived of their liberty by State authorities".

[10] European Court of Human Rights, Stocké v. Germany judgment of 12 October 1989, Series A no. 199, opinion of the Commission, p. 24, § 167.

governmental control over the security/police services, and parliamentary control over the government (see below, §§ 38-43).

30. As regards the terminology used to refer to irregular transfer and detention of prisoners, the Venice Commission notes that the public debate frequently uses the term "rendition". This is not a term used in international law. The term refers to one State obtaining custody over a person suspected of involvement in serious crime (e.g. terrorism) in the territory of another State and/or the transfer of such a person to custody in the first State's territory, or a place subject to its jurisdiction, or to a third State. "Rendition" is thus a general term referring more to the result—obtaining of custody over a suspected person—rather than the means. Whether a particular "rendition" is lawful will depend upon the laws of the States concerned and on the applicable rules of international law, in particular human rights law. Thus, even if a particular "rendition" is in accordance with the national law of one of the States involved (which may not forbid or even regulate extraterritorial activities of state organs), it may still be unlawful under the national law of the other State(s). Moreover, a "rendition" may be contrary to customary international law and treaty or customary obligations undertaken by the participating State(s) under human rights law and/or international humanitarian law.

31. The term "extraordinary rendition" appears to be used when there is little or no doubt that the obtaining of custody over a person is not in accordance with the existing legal procedures applying in the State where the person was situated at the time.

c. International co-operation in the fight against terrorism

32. General international law allows States to cooperate in the transport of detainees, provided that such transport is carried out in full respect of human rights and other international legal obligations of the States concerned. Numerous international treaties confirm this rule.

33. As movement around the world becomes easier and crime takes on a larger international dimension, it is increasingly in the interest of all nations that terrorist crimes be prevented and that persons who are suspected of having committed a very serious crime and are suspected to have acted from abroad or who have fled abroad should be brought to justice. Conversely, the establishment of safe havens for persons who are preparing terrorist crimes or who are suspected of having committed a serious crime would not only result in danger for the State harbouring the protected person but also tend to undermine the foundations of extradition[11].

[11] European Court of Human Rights, Soering v. the United Kingdom judgment of 7 July 1989, p. 35, § 89.

34. The European Convention on Human Rights does not, in principle, prevent cooperation between States, within the framework of extradition treaties or in matters of deportation, for the purpose of bringing suspects of serious crimes to justice, provided that it does not interfere with any of the rights or freedoms recognised in the ECHR[12].

35. The Council of Europe has produced several international instruments and recommendations relating to the fight against terrorism, including three international treaties dealing with suppression of terrorism[13], prevention of terrorism[14] and money laundering and terrorist financing[15], and three recommendations of the Committee of Ministers to member States relating to special investigation techniques; protection of witnesses and collaborators of justice; and questions of identity documents which arise in connection with terrorism[16].

36. An additional set of standards aimed specifically at safeguarding human rights and fundamental freedoms has been produced after 2001, namely the Guidelines on Human Rights and the Fight Against Terrorism (2002), a Policy Recommendation on Combating Racism While Fighting Terrorism (2004), the additional Guidelines on the Protection of Victims of Terrorist Acts (2005) and a Declaration on Freedom of expression and information in the media in the context of the fight against terrorism (2005).

d. Some observations on State responsibility

37. When a State commits, through its agents acting in their official capacity, an internationally wrongful act, it incurs responsibility and "is under an obligation to make full reparation for the injury caused by the internationally wrongful act" at the request of the injured State (see Article 31 para. 1 of the International Law Commission (ILC)'s Articles on State Responsibility).

38. With respect to the imputability of an international wrong, the question arises of whether and to what extent a State incurs responsibility when its agents have *ultra vires* consented expressly or impliedly by rendering assistance, to acts of a foreign State infringing its territorial sovereignty (see above, paras. 27 and 29).

---

[12] European Court of Human Rights, Stocké v. Germany, 12 October 1989, Series A no. 199, opinion of the Commission, p. 24, § 169.

[13] European Convention on the Suppression of Terrorism, ETS 90.

[14] European Convention on the Prevention of Terrorism, ETS No. 196.

[15] European Convention on laundering, search, seizure and confiscation of the proceeds from crime and on the financing of terrorism, ETS No. 198.

[16] Recommendation Rec(2005)10 of the Committee of Ministers to member States on "special investigation techniques" in relation to serious crimes including acts of terrorism; Recommendation REC(2005)09 of the Committee of Ministers to member States on the protection of witnesses and collaborators of justice; Recommendation Rec(2005)07 of the Committee of Ministers to member States on identity and travel documents and the fight against terrorism.

39. *Ultra vires* acts usually bind the State for the purposes of State responsibility (Article 7, ILC Articles on State Responsibility).

40. Consent to carry out activities which otherwise would be internationally wrongful renders them lawful, unless these activities are contrary to *jus cogens* (see para. 42 below). However, consent to an interference with sovereignty must be validly given (Article 20, ILC Articles on State Responsibility). In this context, Article 46 of the Vienna Convention of the Law of Treaties is pertinent. It provides that:

> *1. A State may not invoke the fact that its consent to be bound by a treaty has been expressed in violation of a provision of its internal law regarding competence to conclude treaties as invalidating its consent unless that violation was manifest and concerned a rule of its internal law of fundamental importance.*
>
> *2. A violation is manifest if it would be objectively evident to any State conducting itself in the matter in accordance with normal practice and in good faith.*

41. In the opinion of the Commission, if a public authority of a State would give a permission to the representative of another State to arrest and/or transfer a person against his will from the territory of that State and it is clear that this would be outside of the ordinary (judicial, administrative) procedures for such arrest/transfer, such permission would be a manifest violation of a rule of internal law of fundamental importance in any State under the rule of law. Such permission could therefore not be invoked by the other State as valid consent.

42. Even where such permission does not result in the conclusion of or accession to a treaty, the Law of Treaties insofar reflects the general principle of good faith.[17] This principle is "one of the most basic principles governing the creation and performance of legal obligations"[18]. The giving of a permission is comparable to the conclusion of a treaty insofar as the validity of consent is concerned. In any case, the validity of any consent as a circumstance precluding wrongfulness in international law is limited by the rule enunciated in Article 26 of the ILC Articles on State Responsibility:

> *"Nothing in this Chapter precludes the wrongfulness of any act of a State which is not in conformity with an obligation arising under a peremptory norm of general international law."*

43. A norm is of peremptory character (*jus cogens*) when it "is accepted and recognized by the international community of States as a whole as a norm

---

[17] See *Müller/Kolb*, Article 2(2), MN. 16, in: Simma (ed.), The Charter of the United Nations—A Commentary, Oxford, 2nd ed. 2002).

[18] Border and Transborder Armed Actions, Nicaragua v. Honduras, Jurisdiction of the Court and Admissibility of the Application, ICJ Rep. 1988, 69, 105, para. 105.

from which no derogation is permitted" (Article 53 of the Vienna Convention of the Law of Treaties). These norms include, *inter alia*, the prohibitions of genocide, aggression, crimes against humanity, slavery, piracy and torture.[19]

44. In order to be considered wrongful, an act must be inconsistent with an international obligation of the State which commits it. For Council of Europe member States, in the present context, the obligation in question stems directly from the European Convention on Human Rights, namely from the obligation not to expose anyone to the risk of treatment contrary to Article 3, the obligation to prevent any detention in breach of Article 5 and the obligation to investigate into any substantiated claim that an individual has been taken into unacknowledged custody. These obligations may be breached by a State also by merely but knowingly letting its territory be used by a third State in order to commit a breach of international law.

45. For a State knowingly to provide transit facilities to another State may amount to providing assistance to the latter in committing a wrongful act, if the former State is aware of the wrongful character of the act concerned. Under general international law (see Article 16 ILC Articles on State Responsibility) "a State which aids or assists another State in the commission of an internationally wrongful act by the latter is internationally responsible for doing so if: (a) that State does so with knowledge of the circumstances of the internationally wrongful act; and (b) the act would be internationally wrongful if committed by that State."

46. The consequences of irregular transfers and secret detentions from the viewpoint of human rights law for Council of Europe member States will be examined below (see paras. 137-153).

B. Human rights law

a. The rights at issue

47. Council of Europe member States are committed to respecting fundamental rights, as defined by a number of international treaties, both at the universal level (including the 1966 International Covenant on Civil and Political Rights ("ICCPR"), and the 1987 UN Convention against Torture and Other Cruel, Inhuman or Degrading Treatment or Punishment; and at the European level, *in primis* the European Convention on Human Rights, but also the European Convention for the Prevention of Torture and Inhuman or Degrading Treatment or Punishment).

[19] See ICTY, Prosecutor v. Furundzija, International Legal Materials 38 (1999) 317, at p. 349; further references in: Andreas Paulus, Jus Cogens in a Time of Hegemony and Fragmentation, Nordic Journal of International Law 74 (2005) 297-334 (at p. 306).

48. With respect to the matters which form the object of the present opinion, the fundamental rights which are at issue are primarily the right to liberty and security of person and the ban on torture and other inhuman or degrading treatments or punishments.

i) Liberty and security of person

49. Article 5 ECHR protects the right to liberty and security of person. Although this right is not absolute (see the authorized deprivations of liberty under paragraph 1 a) to f) of Article 5), a person may only be detained on the basis of and according to procedures set out by the law, and the law in question must be consistent with recognised European standards, that is *inter alia* with the (other) provisions of the ECHR. In addition, paragraph 4 of Article 5 provides for all forms of deprivation of liberty allowed under that article, that the detainee "shall be entitled to take proceedings by which the lawfulness of his detention shall be decided speedily by a court and his release ordered if the detention is not lawful" (*habeas corpus*).

50. Detention must be lawful and in accordance with a procedure prescribed by law: in the European Court of Human Rights' view, the requirement of lawfulness means that both domestic law and the ECHR must be respected. The possible reasons for detention are exhaustively enumerated in Article 5 (1) ECHR. Paragraph 1 (c) of Article 5 permits "the lawful arrest or detention of a person effected for the purpose of having committed an offence or when it is reasonably considered necessary to prevent his committing an offence or fleeing after having done so", while paragraph (f) of Article 5 permits "the lawful arrest or detention of a person to prevent his effecting an unauthorised entry into the country or of a person against whom action is being taken with a view to deportation or extradition." A detention for any reason other than those listed in Article 5 § 1 is unlawful and thus a violation of a human right.

51. As regards extradition arrangements between States, when one is a party to the ECHR and the other is not, the rules established by an extradition treaty or, in the absence of any such treaty, the cooperation between the States concerned are also relevant factors to be taken into account for determining whether the arrest was lawful. The fact that a person has been handed over as a result of cooperation between States does not in itself make the arrest unlawful or give rise to an issue under Article 5. However, for the member States of the Council of Europe the provisions of the extradition treaty or the practice of cooperation cannot justify any deviation of their obligations under the ECHR; for those States the decisive factor is whether the extradition is according to domestic law and respects the State's obligations under the ECHR.

52. The ECHR contains no provisions concerning the exact circumstances in which extradition may be granted, or the procedure to be followed before

extradition may be granted. Subject to its being the result of cooperation between the States concerned and provided that the legal basis for the order for the suspect's arrest is an arrest warrant issued by the authorities of the suspect's State of origin, even an atypical extradition cannot as such be regarded as being contrary to the ECHR[20]. This being said, it has also to be stressed that several rights and freedoms protected by the ECHR, may be relevant in the case of extradition and will have to be respected, the most important being Articles 2 and 3, and in some circumstances Articles 5 and 6.

53. Article 5 must be seen as requiring the authorities of the territorial State to take effective measures to safeguard against the risk of disappearance and to conduct a prompt effective investigation into a substantiated claim that a person has been taken into custody and has not been seen since[21].

ii) Torture, inhuman and degrading treatment or punishment

54. Torture is prohibited by Article 3 ECHR, Article 7 ICCPR, the European Convention for the Prevention of Torture and Inhuman or Degrading Treatment or Punishment and the UN Convention against Torture and other Cruel, Inhuman or Degrading Treatment or Punishment. It is defined as "any act by which severe pain or suffering, whether physical or mental, is intentionally inflicted on a person for such purposes as obtaining from him or a third person information or a confession, punishing him for an act he or a third person has committed or is suspected of having committed, or intimidating or coercing him or a third person, or for any reason based on discrimination of any kind, when such pain or suffering is inflicted by or at the instigation of or with the consent or acquiescence of a public official or other person acting in an official capacity. It does not include pain or suffering arising only from, inherent in or incidental to lawful sanctions."[22]

55. The crucial distinction between "torture", "inhuman treatment" and "degrading treatment" lies in the degree of suffering caused.

56. "Inhuman treatment" is such treatment which causes severe suffering, mental or physical, which, in the particular situation, is unjustifiable. Unlike torture, inhuman treatment does not need to be intended to cause suffering.[23] In its judgment in Irelandv. United Kingdom[24], the European Court of Human Rights held that the so-called "five techniques" were inhuman treatment. This decision has sometimes been misunderstood to

[20] European Court of Human Rights, Öcalan v. Turkey judgment [GC] of 12 May 2005.
[21] European Court of Human Rights, Kurt v. Turkey judgment of 25 May 1988, § 124.
[22] Article 1 of the Convention against Torture and Other Cruel, Inhuman or Degrading Treatment or Punishment.
[23] European Court of Human Rights, Ireland v. UK judgment of 18 January 1978, § 167.
[24] European Court of Human Rights, Ireland v. UK judgment, § 167.

mean that the same or similar techniques would not amount to torture. However, in the *Selmouni* case the Court later clarified that, since the Convention is a "living instrument which must be interpreted in the light of present-day conditions", acts which were classified in the past as "inhuman and degrading treatment" could be classified as torture in future.[25] The Court stated that "the increasingly high standard being required in the area of the protection of human rights and fundamental liberties correspondingly and inevitably requires greater firmness in assessing breaches of the fundamental values of democratic societies."[26]

57. "Degrading treatment" is treatment which grossly humiliates or debases a person before others or drives him to act against his will or conscience. Although causing less suffering than torture or inhuman treatment, it must attain a minimum level[27]. It too does not need to be intended to cause suffering.

58. The prohibition of torture and inhuman or degrading treatment or punishment enshrines one of the most fundamental values of democratic societies. As the European Court of Human Rights has stated on many occasions, even in the most difficult circumstances, such as the fight against terrorism and organised crime, the ECHR prohibits in absolute terms torture and inhuman or degrading treatment or punishment. Unlike most of the substantive clauses of the ECHR and of Protocols Nos. 1 and 4, Article 3 makes no provision for limitations and no derogation from it is permissible under Article 15 § 2, not even in the event of a public emergency threatening the life of the nation.

59. Article 2, paragraph 2, of the UN Convention against Torture and Other Cruel, Inhuman or Degrading Treatment or Punishment ("the UN Convention against Torture") expressly States that "No exceptional circumstances whatsoever, whether a State of war or a threat of war, internal political instability or any other public emergency, may be invoked as a justification of torture."

60. The European Convention for the Prevention of Torture and Inhuman and Degrading Treatment ("ECPT") establishes the European Committee for the Prevention of Torture and Inhuman or Degrading Treatment or Punishment ("CPT") which, "by means of visits, examines the treatment of persons deprived of their liberty with a view to strengthening, if necessary, the protection of such persons from torture and from inhuman or degrading treatment or punishment." Pursuant to Article 2 of this Convention, CPT can visit any place on the territory of member States where a person is deprived of their liberty (i.e. including military bases, non-official

[25] European Court of Human Rights Selmouni v. France judgment of 29 July 1999, § 101.
[26] European Court of Human Rights, Selmouni v. France judgment, § 101.
[27] European Court of Human Rights, Tyrer v. United Kingdom judgment of 25 April 1978, § 29.

detention centres such as the offices of the intelligence service or a particular police department - drugs, anti-terrorism - if CPT believes that persons are being held/interviewed in these offices).

61. Member Statesof the ECHR not only have the obligation not to torture but also the duty to prevent torture.[28] In addition they have an obligation of investigation. Under this obligation Member States must assure an efficient, effective and impartial investigation.[29] As soon as the authorities receive substantiated information giving rise to the suspicion that torture or inhuman or degrading treatment has been committed, a duty to investigate arises whether and in which circumstances torture has been committed.

b. Scope of the duty of Council of Europe member States to secure human rights

62. Under Article 1 of the ECHR, "The High Contracting Parties shall secure to everyone *within their jurisdiction* the rights and freedoms defined in Section I of this Convention"[30]. According to the European Court of Human Rights, the notion of "jurisdiction" is primarily territorial. It does, however, exceptionally extend to certain other cases, such as acts of public authority performed abroad by diplomatic or consular representatives of the State, or by an occupying force; acts performed on board vessels flying the State flag or on aircraft or spacecraft registered there.

63. There is a presumption that jurisdiction is exercised by the State throughout its territory. States may also be held accountable for human rights violations occurring outside their territory in certain situations[31].

64. Article 2 of the International Covenant on Civil and Political Rights provides that a State Party undertakes to "respect and to ensure to all individuals within its territory and subject to its jurisdiction the rights recognized in the present Covenant."

65. The term "jurisdiction" under the International Covenant on Civil and Political Rights is comparable to the same term under the European

[28] European Court of Human Rights, Z v. United Kingdom judgment of 10 May 2001; A. v. the United Kingdom judgment of 23 September 1998, § 22.

[29] European Court of Human Rights, Caloc v. France judgment of 20 July 2000.

[30] Article 2 of the UN Convention against Torture and Other Cruel, Inhuman or Degrading Treatment or Punishment similarly States that "Each State Party shall take effective legislative, administrative, judicial or other measures to prevent acts of torture in any territory under its jurisdiction." See para. 146.

[31] See European Court of Human Rights, Issa v. Turkey judgment of 6 November 2004, §§ 71-74; International Court of Justice, Advisory Opinion on legal consequences of the construction of a wall in the occupied Palestinian territory, 9 July 2004, §109. See also the views adopted by the Human Rights Committee on 29 July 1981 in the cases of Lopez Burgos v. Uruguay and Celiberti de Casariego v. Uruguay, nos. 52/1979 and 56/1979, at §§ 12.3 and 10.3 respectively. See Inter-American Commission on Human Rights, Coard v. US, Case 10.951, Report No. 109/99, 29 September 1999, § 37, and Alejandre Cuba, Case 11.589, Report No. 86/99 29 September 1999, § 23.

Convention on Human Rights. It is also not limited to territorial jurisdiction. The Human Rights Committee has held, for example, that communications by persons who were kidnapped by agents in a neighbouring States are admissible, reasoning that States Parties are responsible for the actions of their agents on foreign territory[32]. The Human Rights Committee also clarified in its General Comment no. 31 that "a State Party must respect and ensure the rights laid down in the Covenant to anyone within the power or effective control of that State Party, even if not situated within the territory of the State Party."[33]

66. The duty of State parties under Article 1 ECHR to "secure" to everyone within their jurisdiction "the rights and freedoms . . . of this Convention" is not limited to the duty of state organs not to violate these rights themselves. This duty also includes positive obligations to protect individuals against infringements of their rights by third parties, be they private individuals or organs of third States operating within the jurisdiction of the State party concerned (see para. 146 below). The European Court of Human Rights has, in particular, recognized positive obligations which flow from the prohibition of torture and inhuman treatment, the right to life, and the right to freedom and security. Such positive obligations include duties to investigate, especially in the case of disappeared persons, and to provide for effective remedies.

c. Limitations on the competence to transfer prisoners imposed by human rights obligations

67. The international condemnation of torture has a clear impact on extradition and deportation. Article 3 of the UN Convention against Torture prevents States Parties from "expelling, returning ("refouler") or extraditing a person to another State where there are substantial grounds for believing that he would be in danger of being subjected to torture"[34].

68. The ECHR does not guarantee a right not to be extradited or deported. Nor is there a right to political asylum. Extradition and deportation are not

[32] Lopez Burgos, No 52/ 1979, § 12.3; Celiberti, No 56/1979, § 103.3; Persons who have fled abroad are not prevented by Art 2 (1) from submitting an individual communication, No 25/1978, § 7.2; No. 74/1980, § 4.1; No. 110/1981, § 6; States parties are responsible for violations of the Covenant by foreign diplomatic representatives, No 31/1978; No 57/1979; Nr 77/1980, No 106/1981; No 108/1981; No. 125/1982.

[33] HRC General Comment 31, § 10.

[34] See Also Article 33 (Prohibition of expulsion or return ("refoulement")) of the 1951 UN Convention relating to the Status of Refugees. In 1990, the United Nations General Assembly sought to ensure that human rights would receive full respect in the extradition process when it gave approval to the UN Model Treaty on Extradition which excludes extradition not only if there are substantial grounds for believing that the person will be prosecuted or punished in the requesting State on account of his race, religion, nationality, ethnic origin, political opinion, sex or status, or subjected to torture or cruel inhuman or degrading treatment or punishment, but also "if that person has not received or would not receive the minimum guarantees in criminal proceedings as contained in the International Covenant on Civil and Political Rights".

per se in breach of Article 3 of the ECHR. Nonetheless, extradition or deportation may run counter to provisions of the ECHR. According to the *Soering* doctrine of the European Court of Human Rights, a State may be held responsible for a violation of Articles 2 and 3, in flagrant cases also of possible violations of Articles 5 and 6 ECHR, if its decision, permission or other action has created a real risk of a violation of these rights by the State to which the prisoner is to be transferred.[35] It is of no relevance in such case whether the State on whose territory the violation will or could ultimately take place is also bound by the ECHR[36].

69. Under what circumstances a State may be deemed to have known about a "real risk of a violation" is to be determined in each separate case. Indeed, the establishment of the responsibility of a State in respect of an extradition or deportation inevitably involves an assessment of conditions in the requesting or receiving country against the standards of Article 3 ECHR. Nonetheless, the responsibility of the requesting or receiving country, whether under general international law, under the ECHR or otherwise, is not decisive for the liability of the extraditing State under the ECHR. Such liability may have been incurred by the latter member State by reason of its having taken action which has as a direct consequence the exposure of an individual to ill-treatment prohibited by Article 3 ECHR[37].

70. In the Agiza case, the UN Committee against Torture found a violation of article 3, as Sweden, at the time of the complainant's removal to Egypt, knew or should have known that Egypt resorted to consistent and widespread use of torture against prisoners, and therefore that the complainant was at a real risk of torture. In the opinion of the Committee, the procurement of diplomatic assurances, which, moreover, had no effective mechanism for enforcement, did not suffice to protect against this risk[38].

71. In the Mamatkulov case, the European Court of Human Rights accepted that assurances leading to extradition/deportation can take away the real risk of torture, even when the follow-up procedures were not extensive[39]. However, the assessment of diplomatic assurances in this case should not be overestimated. The Court merely took "formal cognizance of the diplomatic notes from the Uzbek authorities that have been produced by the Turkish Government"[40]. Moreover, there was no substantiated evidence in the individual case that the people in question had in fact been tortured.

[35] European Court of Human Rights, Soering v. the United Kingdom judgment of 7 July 1989; Chahal v. United Kingdom judgment, of 15 November 1996, § 80.
[36] Soering judgment, § 86.
[37] Soering judgment, §§ 89-91.
[38] Ahmed Hussein Mustafa Kamil Agiza v. Sweden, Decision CAT/C/34/D/233/2003, 24 May 2005.
[39] European Court of Human Rights, Mamatkulov and Askerov v. Turkey judgment [GC] of 4 February 2005.
[40] European Court of Human Rights, Mamatkulov and Askerov judgment, § 76.

Finally, according to the European Court of Human Rights, the existence of the risk must be assessed "primarily with reference to those facts which were known or ought to have been known to the Contracting Stateat the time of the expulsion."[41]

d. Derogations

72. Under Article 15 ECHR, a Contracting State may derogate from certain of its obligations under the ECHR "in time of war or other public emergency threatening the life of the nation. Among these "derogable" obligations are also those laid down in Articles 5 and 6; but, under paragraph 2 of Article 15, not those laid down in Articles 2, except in respect of deaths resulting from lawful acts of war, or from Articles 3, 4 (paragraph 1) and 7[42]. However, a State may apply Article 15 only if and to the extent that a war or other public emergency threatening the life of the nation presents itself in that very same State, and the derogating measures are "strictly required by the exigencies of the situation" and "are not inconsistent with its other obligations under international law". When such a situation pertains, it is imperative for the State in question to make a formal derogation under Article 15 ECHR[43]. Moreover, in case of such derogation, the third paragraph of Article 15 requires that the State concerned keep the Secretary General of the Council of Europe fully informed of the measures that it has taken and the reasons therefore.

73. Article 4(1) of the International Covenant on Civil and Political Rights is expressed in terms very similar to those of article 15(1)[44].

---

[41] European Court of Human Rights, Cruz Varas and others v. Sweden judgment of 20 March 1991, § 75, Mamatkulov and Askerov judgment, § 69; Vilvarajah and others v. UK judgment of 30 October 1991, § 107.

[42] See e.g. European Court of Human Rights, Aksoy v. Turkey judgment of 18 December 1996, § 62.

[43] See European Court of Human Rights, Isayeva v. Russian Federation judgment of 24 February 2005, § 191; ICJ, Advisory Opinion on the Legal Consequences of the Construction of a Wall in the Occupied Palestinian Territory Advisory Opinion of 9 July 2004, para. 127 ("The Court notes that the derogation so notified concerns only Article 9 of the International Covenant on Civil and Political Rights, which deals with the right to liberty and security of person and lays down the rules applicable in cases of arrest or detention. The other Articles of the Covenant therefore remain applicable not only on Israeli territory, but also on the Occupied Palestinian Territory").

[44] Article 4(1) ICCPR has led to the formulation by the United Nations, Economic and Social Council, U.N. Sub-Commission on Prevention of Discrimination and Protection of Minorities, of the so-called Siracusa Principles on the Limitation and Derogation of Provisions in the International Covenant on Civil and Political Rights, Annex, UN Doc E/CN.4/1984/4 (1984). In paras 39-40, under the heading "Public Emergency which Threatens the Life of the Nation", it is said: "39. A State party may take measures derogating from its obligations under the International Covenant on Civil and Political Rights pursuant to Article 4 (hereinafter called 'derogation measures') only when faced with a situation of exceptional and actual or imminent danger which threatens the life of the nation. A threat to the life of the nation is one that: (a) affects the whole of the population and either the whole or part of the territory of the State, and (b) threatens the physical integrity of the population, the political independence or the territorial integrity of the State or the existence or basic functioning of institutions indispensable to ensure and protect the rights recognised in the Covenant. 40. Internal conflict and unrest that do not constitute a grave and imminent threat to the life of the nation cannot justify derogations under Article 4".

74. In its Resolution 1271, adopted on 24 January 2002, the Parliamentary Assembly of the Council of Europe resolved (para 9) that: "In their fight against terrorism, Council of Europe members should not provide for any derogations to the European Convention on Human Rights". It also called on all member States (para 12) to "refrain from using Article 15 to limit the rights and liberties guaranteed under its Article 5."

75. In its 2002 Guidelines on human rights and the fight against terrorism, the Committee of Ministers of the Council of Europe reiterated that member States "may never, and whatever the acts of the person suspected of terrorist activities, or convicted of such activities, derogate from the right to life as guaranteed by these international instruments, from the prohibition against torture or inhuman or degrading treatment or punishment, from the principle of legality of sentences and of measures, nor from the ban on the retrospective effect of criminal law."[45]

76. In its General Comment no 29/2001 on Article 4 of the International Covenant on Civil and Political Rights, the UN Human Rights Committee observed (in para 3) that "On a number of occasions the Committee has expressed its concern over States parties that appear to have derogated from rights protected by the Covenant, or whose domestic law appears to allow such derogation, in situations not covered by article 4."

77. In the era of "global terrorism" it has been put to debate whether fundamental human rights as they are discussed in this opinion or the extent of possible derogations from them should be reinterpreted. Recent decisions by several domestic courts in Europe and beyond, however, have confirmed that the existing rights and standards are, in principle, appropriate for the current situation of the fight against global terror.[46] It is also the Commission's opinion that no such reinterpretation is necessary or warranted.

C. International Humanitarian law

78. At present, International Humanitarian Law has only limited relevance for the question of the law applicable to extraordinary transfers of prisoners and secret detention on the territory or through the airspace of

[45] Guidelines of the Committee of Ministers of the Council of Europe on human rights and the fight against terrorism, 11 July 2002, article XV.

[46] House of Lords, Judgments - A (FC) and others (FC) (Appellants) v. Secretary of State for the Home Department (Respondent) (2004)A and others (Appellants) (FC) and others v. Secretary of State for the Home Department (Respondent) (Conjoined Appeals), [2005] UKHL 71; House of Lords, Judgments - A (FC) and others (FC) (Appellants) v. Secretary of State for the Home Department (Respondent), [2004] UKHL 56; Bundesverfassungsgericht, Aviation Security Act, 1 BvR 357/05; Israeli Supreme Court, Public Committee Against Torture in Israel v. The State of Israel et al., Case HCJ 5100/94; Israeli Supreme Court, The Center for the Defense of the Individual v. The Commander of IDF Forces in the West Bank, Case HCJ 3278/02; Israeli Supreme Court, Marab v. The Commander of IDF Forces in the West Bank, Case HCJ 3239/02; see also US Supreme Court, Rasul v. Bush, Case No. 03-334, 542 US 466 (2004) 321 F.3d 1134.

member States of the Council of Europe. International Humanitarian Law applies during "armed conflict" and it distinguishes between international and non-international armed conflicts. "Armed conflict" in the sense of International Humanitarian Law refers to protracted armed violence between States or between governmental authorities and/or organised armed groups within a State.[47] "State practice indicates that banditry, criminal activity, riots, sporadic outbreaks of violence and acts of terrorism do not amount to an armed conflict."[48] This means, for example, that the organised hostilities in Afghanistan before and after 2001 have been an "armed conflict" which was at first a non-international armed conflict, and later became an international armed conflict after the involvement of US troops. On the other hand, sporadic bombings and other violent acts which terrorist networks perpetrate in different places around the globe and the ensuing counter-terrorism measures, even if they are occasionally undertaken by military units, cannot be said to amount to an "armed conflict" in the sense that they trigger the applicability of International Humanitarian Law.

79. The Venice Commission considers that counter-terrorist measures which are part of what has sometimes been called "war on terror" are not part of an "armed conflict" in the sense of making the regime of International Humanitarian Law applicable to them. It considers that further reflection is necessary to consider whether any additional instrument may be needed in the future to meet or anticipate the novel threats to international peace and security.[49]

80. International Humanitarian Law thus only applies to such transports of prisoners through the territory and/or airspace of the member States of the Council of Europe if such prisoners have been arrested/captured in the context of an "armed conflict" as explained above. This would be the case, for example, if a prisoner was captured in an area of Afghanistan in which organized fighting takes place at the time of the arrest. In this case his or her transfer or detention would be covered by International Humanitarian Law irrespective of where he or she is transferred to or detained in Europe. If, on the other hand, persons are transported or detained who have been arrested in the territory of a State where no armed conflict takes place, or in an area in which no armed conflict takes place, International Humanitarian Law does not apply. In such cases human rights law fully applies.

81. Even in those limited cases in which International Humanitarian Law applies (in the context of extraordinary transport of prisoners) this body of

[47] See Prosecutor v. Tadic (1996) 105 ILR 419, 488.

[48] The Manual of the Law of Armed Conflict, UK Ministry of Defence, Oxford (OUP) 2004, no. 3.5.1 (at p. 31).

[49] See Venice Commission's opinion on possible need to further develop the Geneva Convention, CDL-AD(2003)018, § 87.

law does not apply exclusively. As a general rule, human rights law applies at all times, whether in times of peace or concurrently in situations of armed conflict, to all persons subject to a State's authority and control ("jurisdiction"). However, once an armed conflict has begun, human rights law is normally partly superseded by International Humanitarian Law, which contains rules specifically regulating the behaviour of parties to an armed conflict. For example, human rights law does not specifically take account of the regime of belligerent occupation. This means that the rules of the Hague Regulations and the Fourth Geneva Convention of 1949 largely serve as *lex specialis*. However, as the Commission has previously pointed out[50], human rights law's non-derogable rules and those rules which have not been derogated from in accordance with the derogation mechanism provided for under the relevant treaty instrument are also applicable in situations of armed conflict.

82. Under the 1949 Geneva Conventions, persons who are arrested by a power in the course of an international armed conflict are protected either as prisoners of war (hereinafter "POW") (Article 4 GCIII) or as other "protected persons" (all persons, in particular civilians, who are not nationals of the detaining Power or are not protected by other Conventions, Article 4 GCIV). The plain wording of Article 4 (1) and (4) GC IV makes it clear that there should be no category of persons that would remain unprotected. As the Commission has pointed out before, even those persons who do not fulfil the nationality requirements of Article 4 GC IV are protected by customary international humanitarian law, as it has been given expression in Article 75 of the First Additional Protocol of 1977 to the Geneva Conventions.

83. Persons who are suspected to be members of an international terrorist network, such as Al-Qaeda, and who have been arrested in connection with an armed conflict, will fall either into the category of other "protected persons" or into the category of POWs.

84. As far as the Fourth Geneva Convention, the First Additional Protocol and customary international humanitarian law apply, all protected persons, including terrorist suspects, must be treated according to the rules laid down in Articles 27-78 GCIV and the minimum requirements of Article 75 of the First Additional Protocol. This has been confirmed in recent years by national courts.[51]

[50] Opinion on the possible need for further development of the Geneva Conventions, CDL-AD(2003)018, § 56.

[51] See Supreme Court of Israel, HCJ 7015/02, Ajuri v. The Commander of the IDF Forces in the West Bank, in: Judgments of the Supreme Court of Israel—Fighting Terrorism within the Law, http://www.mfa.gov.il/MFA/Government/Law/Legal±Issues±and±Rulings/Fighting±Terrorism±within±the±Law±2-Jan-2005.htm, at pp. 144-178.

85. In the case that suspected members of international terrorist networks qualify as POWs, their transfer would be regulated by the Third Geneva Convention (see in particular Articles 12 and 46-48).

D. General principles of civil aviation

86. International air law has a codified framework in the Convention on International Civil Aviation (commonly referred to as the "Chicago Convention"), signed in Chicagoon 7 December 1944.

87. The Chicago Convention sets out in Article 1 the principle that every State has complete and exclusive sovereignty over the airspace above its territory, that is to say above the land areas and territorial waters adjacent thereto.

88. Article 4 of the Chicago Convention provides that: *"Each contracting State agrees not to use civil aviation for any purpose inconsistent with the aims of this Convention"*.

89. The Chicago Convention sets out the regime for civil aircraft and civil aviation. According to Article 3 (a), such regime does not apply to State aircraft.

90. Under the Convention, aircraft "used in military, customs and police services" are deemed to be state aircraft (Article 3(b)). This presumption, however, is not irrebuttable[52]. Moreover, aircraft engaged in other state activities such as coast guard and search and rescue could also be either state aircraft or civil aircraft in the sense of the Convention.[53]

91. It has generally been admitted[54] that, in case of doubt, the status of an airplane as "civil aircraft" or "state aircraft" will be determined by the

---

[52] The Secretariat of the ICAO Council stated that "the predominant view is that all such other aircraft [performing State services other than military, police and customs] would in fact be considered as falling within the scope of the Convention". In the study, it is recalled that under the Paris Convention of 1919 all State aircraft other than military, customs and police aircraft were treated as private aircraft and subjected to all the provisions of the Paris Convention (see Doc. C-WP/9835 of 22/09/1993, Secretariat Study on "Civil/State aircraft" presented by the Secretary General at the ICAO Council 140th Session, § 5.2).

[53] In Germany, for example, certain flights performing state functions, such as transports of high government officials or humanitarian/disaster relief flights are referred to as "civil State flights" (zivile Staatsflüge) and are regarded as civil flights in the sense of the ICAO Convention (but not necessarily in the sense of general public international law), see Bericht der Bundesregierung (Offene Fassung) gemäß Anforderung des Parlamentarischen Kontrollgremiums vom 25. Januar 2006 zu den Vorgängen im Zusammenhang mit dem Irakkrieg und der Bekämpfung des Internationalen Terrorismus, at http://www.bundesregierung.de/Anlage965868/Bericht±der±Bundesregierung±-±offene±Fassung.pdf., at pp. 62-67.

[54] ICAO Secretariat Study on "Civil/State Aircraft" LC/29-WP/2-1, Pellet, Dailler, Droit International Public, LGDJ, 7è edition, 2002, pp. 1250; Combacau (J.), Sur (S), Droit international Public, Montchristien, 5è édition, 2001, p. 473; "Status of military aircraft in international law", address at the Third International Law Seminar of 28 August 1999, by Professor Michael Milde, formerly the head of the legal bureau of the International Civil Aviation Organisation, at: http:// www.mindef.gov.sg/dmg/ls/Il399.doc; Diederiks-Verschoor, Introduction to air law, Kluwer, pp. 30 and following.

function it actually performs at a given time[55]. As a general rule, "aircraft are recognised as state aircraft when they are under the control of the State and used exclusively by the State for state intended purposes"[56]. Accordingly, the same airplane can be considered to be "civil aircraft" and "state aircraft" on different occasions.

92. Civil aircraft that are not engaged in scheduled international air services of a State party to the Chicago Convention[57] are entitled to make flights into or in transit non-stop across the territory of another State party and to make stops for non-traffic purposes without the necessity of obtaining prior permission and subject to the right of the State flown over to require landing. The authorities of each State party have the right, without unreasonable delay, to search aircraft of the other State party on landing or departure, and to inspect the certificates and other documents prescribed by the Chicago Convention (Article 16).

93. State aircraft do not enjoy the overflight rights of civil aircraft. According to Article 3 (c), state aircraft are not permitted to fly over or land in foreign sovereign territory otherwise than with express authorisation of the State concerned, and in harmony with the terms of such authorisation. Such authorisation must be given by special agreement "or otherwise"; the practice of States indicates that the preferred form is a bilateral or multilateral agreement between the States concerned, valid for a given period of time, one year for example, or general permissions, or "ad hoc" permissions properly obtained through the diplomatic channels. In the latter case, the diplomatic notes are to be submitted to the competent authorities - to the Ministry of Foreign Affairs, for example - prior to the operation of the flight and usually contain *inter alia* the name of the foreign air operator, the type of aircraft and its registration and identification, the proposed flight routing (including last point of departure outside the State, the first point of entry, the date and time of arrival, the place of embarkation or disembarkation abroad of passengers or freight), the purpose of the flight (number of passengers and their names).

[55] In the case of a civil aircraft (B-737, MisrAir flight 2843 from Cairo to Tunis) carrying, on the basis of charter by the Government, suspected terrorists out of the country under Military Police escort and intercepted and forced to land in Italy by the US military based in Italy, the US Government, in a letter to the International Federation of Air Line Pilots Association, stated: "It is our view that the aircraft was operating as a state aircraft at the time of interception. The relevant factors - including exclusive State purpose and function of the mission, the presence of armed military personnel on board and the secrecy under which the mission was attempted - compel this conclusion". This case, quoted in ICAO document LC/29-WP/2-1, pp. 11-12, was cited by Professor Milde, see above, footnote 54. See also A. Cassese, Terrorism, Politics and Law, the Achille Lauro case, Polity Press, p. 39.

[56] Diederiks-Verschoor, Introduction to air law, Kluwer, pp. 30 § 12. See also footnote 52.

[57] Status of ratifications of the Chicago Convention available at: http://www.ICAO.int/ICDB/HTML/English/Representative%20Bodies/Council/Working%20Papers%20by%20Session/163/c.163.wp.11641.en/C.163.WP.11641.ATT.EN.HTM

94. If "state aircraft" enter the foreign sovereign air space without a proper authorisation, they may be:

— intercepted for purposes of identification;

— directed to leave the violated air space;

— directed to land for the purpose of further investigation/prosecution;

— forced to land for further investigation/prosecution[58].

95. Under customary international law[59], state aircraft enjoy immunity from foreign jurisdiction in respect of search and inspection. Accordingly, they cannot be boarded, searched or inspected by foreign authorities, including host State's authorities, without the captain's consent. However, because state aircraft need authorisation to enter another State's airspace, the extent of their immunity is conditioned on such an authorisation pursuant to Article 3 (c) of the Chicago Convention[60].

96. A mere operational air traffic control clearance for the flight is not sufficient to satisfy the requirement for permission under Article 3 (c)[61], unless this corresponds to an accepted practice.

97. Article 3bis para. b) of the Chicago Convention provides that:

> *[E]very State, in the exercise of its sovereignty, is entitled to require the landing at some designated airport of a civil aircraft flying above its territory without authority or if there are reasonable grounds to conclude that it is being used for any purpose inconsistent with the aims of this Convention; it may also give such aircraft any other instructions to put an end to such violations. For this purpose, the contracting States may resort to any appropriate means consistent with relevant rules of international law, including the relevant provisions of this Convention, specifically paragraph a) of this Article[62]. Each contracting State agrees to publish its regulations in force regarding the interception of civil aircraft.*

98. The flag State of the violating aircraft is internationally responsible for the infraction; the consequences of such responsibility would impact on

---

58 See M. Milde, "Status of military aircraft in international law", address at the Third International Law Seminar of 28 August 1999, op. cit.

59 The United Nations Convention on Jurisdictional Immunities of States and their Property, signed on 1 March 2004, provides in its Article 3 § 3 that "The present Convention is without prejudice to the immunities enjoyed by a State under international law with respect to aircraft or space objects owned or operated by the State".

60 See Pellet, Dailler, Droit International Public, op. cit., p. 1252; A. Cassese, Terrorism, Politics and Law, op. cit., p. 39.

61 See "Status of military aircraft in international law", address at the Third International Law Seminar of 28 August 1999, by Professor Michael Milde, formerly the head of the legal bureau of the International Civil Aviation Organisation, at: http:// www.mindef.gov.sg/dmg/ls/I1399.doc.

62 Para. a) of Article 3bis of the Chicago Convention provides that " The contracting States recognize that every State must refrain from resorting to the use of weapons against civil aircraft in flight and that, in case of interception, the lives of persons on board and the safety of aircraft must not be endangered. This provision shall not be interpreted as modifying in any way the rights and obligations of States set forth in the Charter of the United Nations.

the overall relations of the States concerned and can range from the duty to apologise, a promise to penalise the individuals responsible, a promise not to repeat the infraction and so on, to more severe sanctions.

99. Pursuant to Article 54 of the Chicago Convention, any action which may be considered as an infraction, breach, violation or infringement of the Convention is potentially subject to action by the Council of the International Civil Aviation Organisation (ICAO) under Article 54 (j) or (k). For example, a contracting State which by its action contravenes the principle in Article 1 that every State has complete and exclusive sovereignty over the airspace above its territory, can be considered committing an infraction of the Convention. A similar conclusion could be drawn in respect of a State which by its action disregards the scope of "territory" given in Article 2; or whose regulations for State aircraft do not show "due regard for the safety of navigation of civil aircraft" (Article 3 (d)); or which uses weapons against civil aircraft in flight contrary to Article 3 *bis*; or which uses civil aviation for any purpose inconsistent with the aims of the Chicago Convention (Article 4). Infractions may be brought before the Council by a Contracting State or a group of Contracting States.

100. As long as an airplane is in the air and not on the ground, persons on board are subject to the concurrent jurisdiction of both the national State of the airplane and the territorial State[63]. In this context, it should be noted that Article 4 of the Convention on Offences and Certain other Acts Committed on Board Aircraft (the Tokyo Convention)[64], to which practically all Council of Europe member States are party, provides that:

> *"A Contracting State which is not the State of registration may not interfere with an aircraft in flight in order to exercise its criminal jurisdiction over an offence committed on board except in the following cases:*
>
> *(a) the offence has effect on the territory of such State;*
>
> *(b) the offence has been committed by or against a national or permanent resident of such State;*
>
> *(c) the offence is against the security of such State;*
>
> *(d) the offence consists of a breach of any rules or regulations relating to the flight or manoeuvre of aircraft in force in such State;*

[63] For Germanysee Schönke/Schröder, Strafgesetzbuch, 26th ed. 2001, Vor §§ 3-7, para. 30, and § 153 c Strafprozessordnung (Law on Criminal Procedure), according to which the Public Prosecutor *may* abstain from prosecuting a crime which has been committed by a foreigner in a foreign aircraft; this provision presupposes that full jurisdiction over foreign aircraft in flight exists and only gives the Prosecutor a discretionary power not to exercise this jurisdiction, see Meyer-Goßner, Strafprozessordnung, 48th ed. 2005. See also, e.g. Males (French Cour de Cassation, 29 June 1972, 27 June 1973, 73 ILR 698), Public Prosecutor v. Janos V. Austrian Supreme Court 17 May 1972, 71 ILR 229, Air India v. Wiggens, UK House of Lords, 3 July 1980, 77 ILR 276), US v. Georgescu, 723 F. Supp. 912 (1989).

[64] Tokyo,14 September 1963, UNTS 704.

(e) the exercise of jurisdiction is necessary to ensure the observance of any obligation of such State under a multilateral international agreement."

101. This provision does not limit the jurisdiction of the territorial State but only the exercise of its right to interfere with an aircraft in flight. In the first place, serious offences of abduction, torture etc. certainly have "effect" on the territorial state. Where the conditions of a prisoner on a plane do not in themselves constitute inhuman or degrading treatment, all acts involved in transferring by air a prisoner to a place where he or she runs a real risk of being tortured may not necessarily be criminal offences in the territorial State. This will depend upon how the relevant offences and inchoate offences (preparation, conspiracy etc.) are formulated in the law in the territorial State (e.g. whether the acts in question constitute a continuing offence of abduction) and that State's rules on extraterritorial crime, in particular, whether the deliberate handing over of a person to extraterritorial torture is an offence. It should be stressed however that the obligations of a Council of Europe member State to ensure protection of human rights (see above, paras. 62-67, and below para. 146) are not limited simply to enforcing its criminal law. Thus, it is not decisive that, in a particular case, a territorial State may not, in fact, make all acts involved in transfer punishable, or exercise jurisdiction over these. In addition, according to subparagraph (e) of Article 4 of the Tokyo Convention, the limitation of the exercise of the right of the territorial State to interfere with an aircraft in flight does not apply when "the exercise of jurisdiction is necessary to ensure the observance of any obligation of such State under a multilateral international agreement", such as the European Convention of Human Rights. Therefore, if the positive obligations arising under the ECHR require a member State of the Council of Europe to investigate possible violations of human rights committed in an aircraft in flight through its airspace, this member State is not barred by the Tokyo Convention to interfere with this aircraft in flight.

102. The question arises in this context of what would be the status of an airplane registered in the flag State as civil aircraft but carrying out "State functions" (such as special missions for the transport of prisoners) which entered the airspace of another State without seeking a specific authorisation or without following the applicable procedures for State aircraft.

103. In the opinion of the Venice Commission, state aircraft can only claim immunity inasmuch as they make their state function known to the territorial State through the appropriate channels. If the public purpose was not declared in order to circumvent the requirement of obtaining the necessary permission(s), then the State will be estopped from claiming State aircraft status[65] and the airplane will be deemed to be civil and thus falling within the

[65] ICJ judgment on the North Sea Continental Shelf Cases (Federal Republic of Germany v Denmark; Federal Republic of Germany v Netherlands) [1969] ICJ Reports 4 at 26 (§ 30).

scope of application of the Chicago Convention, including its Article 16 providing for the territorial State's right to search and inspection. The territorial State could request the airplane to land and could proceed to search and inspection and take the necessary measures to put an end to possible violations it might identify[66]. In addition, the flag State would face international responsibility for the breach of Article 4 of the Chicago Convention and of customary international law.

104. The relations between air law and human rights law will be analysed below (see paras 144-152).

E. Military bases

105. The lawfulness of the presence of the armed forces of one State on the territory of another State in peacetime is contingent on the consent of the host State. The initial decision to admit the force may take the form of a bilateral or multilateral treaty, often defence agreements. There follows a decision by the receiving State granting the use of facilities on its soil, which is normally done through a further agreement.

106. A State does not abandon its sovereignty when it consents to the presence of foreign armed forces on its territory. It guarantees the enjoyment of the privilege of user of its territory accorded to the sending State; it retains however the right to regulate this privilege within the framework of the applicable treaties and agreements. It follows that the sending State acquires various powers pertaining to the operation of its defence forces on a territory that remains subject to the sovereignty of the host State. The sending State may lawfully claim in or over the territory of the receiving State, only those rights and powers that are connected directly with the establishment and operation of, and access to, the sites at which the foreign forces and installations are located. The principle of sovereignty dictates that any further rights and powers can derive only from an express grant by the receiving States. In particular, the extent of the right for the receiving State to search a foreign military base on its territory depends on the terms of the defence agreement or of the "Status-of-forces agreement" (SOFA)[67].

107. SOFAs between the host State and a State stationing military forces in the host State define the legal status of the sending State's personnel and property in the territory of the host State. They are usually an integral part of

[66] See ICAO Secretariat Study on "Civil/State Aircraft" LC/29-WP/2-1; Council Working paper C-WP/10588 Misuse of Civil Aviation (Request from Cuba).

[67] For example, the agreement of 26 July 1962 between Italy and the Supreme Commander of the NATO on the specific conditions of settling and operation on the Italian territory of the present or future international military General Quarters provides at Article 4 that the Italian Government accepts that the moveable and immoveable property of the General Quarters is immune from search.

the overall military bases agreements that allow the sending State's military forces to operate within the host State[68].

108. Foreign armed forces whose admission has been consented to by the receiving State are, as a rule, not subject to the normal immigration controls and entry formalities applicable to foreign nationals. The NATO-SOFA agreement provides that "members of a force shall be exempted from passport and visa regulations and immigration inspection on entering or leaving the territory of a receiving State. They shall also be exempt from the regulations of the receiving State on the registration and control of aliens"[69]. This waiver of entry procedures is counter-balanced by the requirement for members of the force, to present on demand, whether on entry or at any time thereafter, identification and an individual or collective movement order certifying the status of the individual as a member of a force[70]. The receiving State has a discretion whether to require a movement order to be countersigned by its authorised representatives. Exemption from entry formalities is made conditional on compliance with the formalities established by the receiving State relating to the entry and departure of a force or the members thereof.

109. The sending State must have access to the base and, where it has more than one base on the territory of the same State, it must be allowed movement between them. To deny access would amount to a derogation from the grant made by the host State. It is therefore common for military base agreements to authorise the sending State to have access to its forces and to the ports or airfields which it has been accorded in the host State. This authorisation is essential, as in relation to public vessels and aircraft there is no right of access under customary international law. It is, however, often the practice in bilateral treaties for entry to the ports of the receiving State to be subject to "appropriate notification under normal conditions" made to the authorities of the latter[71].

68 SOFAs are normally bilateral; there exists in addition a multilateral SOFA with NATO members, the NATO Status of Forces Agreement (SOFA) of 19 June 1951 (Agreement between the Parties to the North Atlantic Treaty Regarding the Status of their Forces, http://www.nato.int/docu/basictxt/b510619a.htm). Pursuant to Article VII of the NATO SOFA, when only the sending State's law is violated, the sending State has the power to exercise sole criminal jurisdiction. When only the receiving State's law is violated, the receiving State has the power to exercise sole criminal jurisdiction. When a crime violated the laws of both countries, there is concurrent criminal jurisdiction: the receiving State maintains primary jurisdiction except for offences committed solely against the property or security or member of the sending State force, or for offences arising out of any act or omission done by the sending State service member in the performance of official duty. In all other cases, the receiving State has the primary right to exercise jurisdiction. In cases of concurrent jurisdiction, the receiving State may relinquish jurisdiction through waiver requests from the sending State.

69 Article III.1.

70 Article III.2.

71 This is usual, for instance, in US treaty practice. See John Woodcliffe, "The peacetime use of foreign military installations under modern international law", Martinus Nijhoff, 1992, p. 144.

110. The sending State does not benefit from an unrestricted freedom of movement within, and overflight of, the receiving State, unless such rights are expressly granted in a base agreement. In any case, the national and international law that is applicable to military bases cannot, and does not claim to, diminish the obligations and responsibilities of the member States of the Council of Europe under human rights treaties.

F. Article V of the NATO Treaty[72]

111. Article V is the core clause of the Washington Treaty, NATO's founding charter. It states that an armed attack against one Ally shall be considered an attack against them all. In response to an invocation of Article 5, each Ally determines, in consultation with other Allies, how it can best contribute to any action deemed necessary to restore and maintain the security of the North Atlantic area, including by the use of armed force.

112. Article V was first invoked on 12 September 2001 immediately following the 11 September terrorist attacks against the United States. The invocation was initially provisional, pending determination that the attacks were directed from abroad. This was confirmed on 2 October 2001, after US officials presented findings on investigations into the attacks to the North Atlantic Council, concluding that the Al-Qaeda terrorist network was responsible.

113. On 4 October 2001, the Allies agreed on a series of measures to assist the US-led campaign against Al-Qaeda and related terrorism[73]. These include enhanced intelligence sharing and cooperation, blanket over-flight clearances in accordance with the necessary air traffic arrangements and national procedures, and access to ports and airfields for US and other Allied craft for operations against terrorism.

114. In application of this agreement, certain NATO member-States granted US (and NATO member States') aircraft either blanket over-flight clearances for certain time-periods, or overflight rights upon request[74].

115. Article V of the North Atlantic Treaty does not contain an obligation for member States of the Council of Europe to allow irregular transfers of prisoners or to grant blanket overflight rights, for the purposes of fighting against terrorism. That treaty provision at most contains an obligation to take measures, including cooperation and consent, into consideration; but leaves any decision as to concrete measures to the appreciation of the State

---

72 There is a similar provision in the Treaty on Collective Security of the Commonwealth of Independent States (CIS). Two Council of Europe member States, Russia and Armenia, are currently party to this treaty.

73 The Commission has not been able to see the text of this agreement.

74 See US Department of Defense, Fact Sheet of 7 June 2002, International contributions to the War against terrorism, at http://www.defenselink.mil/news/Jun2002/d20020607contributions.pdf.

concerned of the necessity of such measures in order to restore and maintain security. In addition, neither Article 5 of the North Atlantic Treaty nor any Agreements in execution thereof can, or claim to, diminish the obligations and responsibilities of member States of the Council of Europe under human rights treaties.

SECTION II—THE INTERNATIONAL LEGAL OBLIGATIONS OF COUNCIL OF EUROPE MEMBER STATES

A. Council of Europe Member States' Obligations in Respect of Arrests by Foreign Authorities on Their Territory

116. A State party to the European Convention on Human Rights is presumed to exercise its jurisdiction over its whole territory. Any arrest of a person by foreign authorities on the territory of a Council of Europe member State without the agreement of this member State is a violation of its sovereignty and is therefore contrary to international law. In addition, the now defunct European Commission of Human Rights has stated that "an arrest made by the authorities of one State on the territory of another State, without the prior consent of the State concerned, does not only involve the State responsibility vis-à-vis the other State, but also affects that person's individual right to security under Article 5 § 1".[75]

117. The European Court of Human Rights has clearly expressed how the responsibility of a Council of Europe member State is engaged in relation to the arrest of an individual on its territory by foreign authorities: irrespective of whether the arrest amounts to a violation of the law of the State in which the suspect has been arrested, the responsibility of the host State is engaged unless it can be proved that the authorities of the State to which the applicant has been transferred have acted extra-territorially and without consent, and consequently in a manner that is inconsistent with the sovereignty of the host State[76].

118. Any form of involvement of the Council of Europe member State or receipt of information prior to the arrest taking place entails responsibility under Articles 1 and 5 ECHR (and possibly Article 3 in respect of the modalities of the arrest). A State must thus prevent the arrest from taking place, unless the arrest is effected by the foreign authorities in the exercise of their jurisdiction under the terms of an applicable SOFA (see footnote 68 above).

---

[75] European Court of Human Rights, Stocké v. Germany judgment of 12 October 1989, Series A no. 199, opinion of the Commission, p. 24, § 167.

[76] European Court of Human Rights, Öcalan v. Turkeyjudgment, § 90.

119. The responsibility of the Council of Europe member States is engaged also in the case that some section of its public authorities (police, security forces etc.) has co-operated with the foreign authorities or has not prevented an arrest *without government knowledge*. This situation raises the question of governmental control over the security/police services, and possibly, if the applicable national law so foresees, of parliamentary control over the government.

120. Different European States exercise different systems for political insight into, and control over, the operations of the security and intelligence services, depending upon constitutional structure, historical factors etc. Different mechanisms exist for ensuring that particularly sensitive operations are subject to approval and/or adequate control. Meaningful government accountability to the legislature is obviously conditioned upon meaningful governmental control over the security and intelligence services[77]. Where the law provides for governmental control, but this control does not exist in practice, the security and intelligence services risk becoming a "State within a State". Where, on the other hand, the law provides for a degree of distance between government ministers and officials and the day-to-day operations of the security and intelligence services, but government ministers in fact exercise influence or even control over these operations, then the phenomenon of "deniability" can arise. In such a case, the exercise of power is concealed, and there is no proper accountability. The Statute of the Council of Europe and the ECHR require respect for the rule of law which in turn requires accountability for *all* exercises of public power. Independently of how a State chooses to regulate political control over security and intelligence agencies, in any case effective oversight and control mechanisms must exist to avoid these two problems.[78]

B. Council of Europe Member States' Obligations in Respect of Alleged Secret Detention Facilities

121. The term "secrecy" can have different meanings. In the context of the present opinion, the problematic aspect of the secrecy of detention lies in the first place in the impact which such secrecy has on the prisoner's defence rights under Articles 5[79] and 6 ECHR. In addition, prolonged secret detention may impinge on Article 3[80] and on other aspects of Article 6 ECHR.

[77] Internal Security Services In Europe, Report adopted by the Venice Commission at its 34th Plenary meeting, 7 March 1998 CDL-INF(1998)006e).

[78] European Court of Human Rights, Klass and others v. Federal Republic of Germany judgment of 6 September 1978, § 75 in connection with § 71; Leander v. Sweden judgment of 26 March 1987, § 84.

[79] European Court of Human Rights, Kurt v. Turkey judgment of 25 May 1998, § 121.

[80] Inter-American Court of Human Rights, Velasquez Rodrigues case, 29 July 1988, § 187 and Suarez Rosero case, 12 November 1997, §§ 90-91. UN Human Rights Committee, Polay Campos v. Peru, Communication 577/1994, 6 November 1997, §§ 8.4, 8.6 and 8.7. See also European Court of Human Rights, Ocalan v. Turkey judgment of 12 March 1993, §§ 31-232.

122. For a State to provide facilities to another State to conduct voluntary interviews with suspects on its territory is, in principle, not in violation of international law. On the contrary, it is a feature of most modern Mutual Assistance Treaties. It depends upon the territorial States' constitutional and administrative rules on the exercise of public power whether this can go so far as involuntary interrogation. Some States will not allow any but their own officials to exercise public power on their territory. Others make exceptions by treaty rules[81].

123. The territorial State retains its full jurisdiction within the meaning of Article 1 ECHR over any place on its territory where such interviews take place, including any ad hoc detention facilities:: that State is therefore responsible for any infringement of the ECHR in relation to any suspect treated in violation of Articles 3 and 5, e.g. any prisoners who may be held incomunicado there. The modalities of the interrogation and detention, and of treatment given, need to comply with the standards of the European Convention on Human Rights.

124. *Incomunicado* detention, that is detention without the possibility of contacting one's lawyer and of applying to a court, is clearly not "in accordance with a procedure prescribed by law" of any of the member States of the Council of Europe, if alone because the detention is not subject to judicial review. For the detainee, it is not possible to exercise his entitlement to *habeas corpus* guaranteed by Article 5, paragraph 4. The unlike possibility that such a detention is "in accordance with a procedure prescribed by law" under the law of the foreign State by whose authorities the detention was ordered and executed, is irrelevant for the issue of the responsibility under the European Convention on Human Rights of the State on whose territory it takes place.

125. If and in so far as *incomunicado* detention takes place, is made possible or is continued on the territory of a member State of the Council of Europe, in view of its secret character that detention is by definition in violation of the European Convention on Human Rights and the applicable domestic law of that State.

126. Active and passive co-operation by a Council of Europe member State in imposing and executing secret detentions engages its responsibility under the European Convention on Human Rights. The European Court of Human Rights has ruled that "the acquiescence or connivance of the authorities of a Contracting State in the acts of private individuals which violate the Convention rights of other individuals within its jurisdiction may engage the State's responsibility under the Convention"[82]. This is even more true in respect of acts of agents of foreign States.

---

[81] The Schengen Treaty, for example.

[82] European Court of Human Rights, Ilascu and others v. Moldovaand Russia judgment of 8 July 2004, § 318.

127. While no such responsibility applies if the detention is carried out by foreign authorities without the territorial State actually knowing it, the territorial State must take effective measures to safeguard against the risk of disappearance and must conduct a prompt and effective investigation into a substantiated claim that a person has been taken into unacknowledged custody.

128. The possible obligation by a Council of Europe member State under bilateral or multilateral treaties to co-operate in prosecution measures does not affect or diminish this State's obligation not to allow or contribute to secret detention on its territory.

129. As the European Court of Human Rights has pointed out[83], the opinion of the State under whose authority the detention is decided and executed concerning the issue of whether the detention is in violation of fundamental rights is not conclusive for the question of whether cooperation engages responsibility of a member State of the Council of Europe under the European Convention on Human Rights; only the relevant provisions of the latter Convention, as interpreted by the European Court of Human Rights, are decisive. This means, for instance, that the opinion which has been put forward in certain quarters with respect to the US Government that "cruel and unusual punishment", if applied outside US territory, does not violate the US Constitution, is of no relevance whatsoever for the question of responsibility of member States under the European Convention on Human Rights. It also means that the individual opinion of specific Governments, or of certain public persons, about possible limits to the absolute character of the scope of the prohibition of torture are not relevant either. In addition to the interpretation given by the European Court of Human Rights concerning the absolute character of the prohibition of torture, Article 2, paragraph 2, of the UN Convention against Torture and Other Cruel, Inhuman or Degrading Treatment or Punishment expressly states that there is no room whatsoever and under any circumstances to justify torture

130. If a State is informed or has reasonable grounds to suspect that any persons are held *incomunicado* at foreign military bases on its territory, despite its limited jurisdiction over foreign military bases, its responsibility under the European Convention on Human Rights is still engaged, unless it takes all measures which are within its power in order for this irregular situation to end.

131. As a rule, a State cannot search foreign military bases on its territory unless this is allowed under the relevant treaties or unless the host State is authorised by the sending State to do so. However, the right to detain

[83] European Court of Human Rights, Chahal v. United Kingdom judgment of 15 November 1996.

non-military personnel does not fall under the ordinary rights and powers that are connected directly with the establishment and operation of the sites at which the foreign forces and installations are located (see para. 106 above), unless the site falls under the jurisdiction of the sending State under the applicable SOFA, such as the NATO-SOFA (see footnote 68 above).

132. The host State is therefore entitled and even obliged to prevent, and react to such abuse of its territory. It could exercise its powers in respect of registration and control of aliens, and demand identification and movement orders of those present on the military base in question. Access to such military bases, assuming that it had been freely granted under the military base agreement, would require notification under normal conditions. In addition, appropriate diplomatic channels can be used in order to protest against such practice.

133. The case might arise that some section of the public authorities of the Council of Europe member State (police, security forces etc.) is informed and tolerates, or fails to prevent or even co-operates in the maintenance of secret detentions without government knowledge. While this situation raises the already mentioned constitutional issue of control over security forces, the State remains responsible under the European Convention on Human Rights.

134. States which have ratified the European Convention for the Prevention of Torture have the obligation to co-operate with the Committee for the Prevention of Torture and to provide it with a list of all the detention centres which are present on their territory. CPT must have access to all and any of these detention centres. Failure by a State to inform CPT of any detention facility can be seen as a lack of co-operation within the meaning of Article 3 ECPT[84], which, if not clarified appropriately, can result in procedures towards a public statement under Art 10(2)[85].

135. As concerns international humanitarian law, the Geneva Conventions (Articles 126 of GCIII and 143 GCIV) grant the International Committee of the Red Cross "permission to go to all places where prisoners of war or protected persons may be, particularly to places of internment, imprisonment and labour", and "access to all premises occupied by" them, including "the places of departure, passage and arrival of prisoners who are being transferred". Responsibility could arise in this respect too.

---

[84] Article 3 ECPT provides: "In the application of this Convention, the Committee and the competent national authorities of the Party concerned shall co operate with each other." See also Article 8 § 2 (b) ECPT.

[85] Article 10 § 2 ECPT provides: "If the Party fails to co-operate or refuses to improve the situation in the light of the Committee's recommendations, the Committee may decide, after the Party has had an opportunity to make known its views, by a majority of two thirds of its members to make a public Statement on the matter."

136. Insofar as detention can be "secret" vis-à-vis the national authorities, the Commission considers that a State is exempted from responsibility only if and as long as it does not have any knowledge of a detention carried out by foreign agents in breach of its territorial sovereignty. However, if any branch of the State is involved in or informed about the detention, irrespective of their acting *ultra vires*, the responsibility of the State as a subject of international law is engaged (see paras. 38-43 above).

C. Council of Europe Member States' Obligations in Respect of Inter-State Transfers of Prisoners

137. There are only four legal ways of transferring a prisoner to foreign authorities: deportation, extradition, transit and transfers of sentenced persons for the purpose of their serving the sentence in their country of origin.

138. Extradition and deportation proceedings must be specified by the applicable law, and the prisoners must be given access to the competent authorities. In addition, extradition and deportation proceedings cannot be carried out where substantial grounds have been shown for believing that the person in question, if expelled, would face a real risk of being subjected to treatment contrary to Article 3 of the ECHR and of the UN Convention against Torture in the receiving country. In these circumstances, Article 3 implies the obligation not to expel the person in question to such a country.

139. In this context, it is worth underlining that Council of Europe member States are under an obligation to prevent prisoners' *exposure to the risk* of torture: the violation does not depend on whether the prisoner is eventually subjected to torture.

140. The assessment of the reality of the risk must be carried out very rigorously. The risk assessment will depend upon the circumstances, meaning both the rights which risk being violated and the situation in the receiving State. The diplomatic assurances which are usually provided by the requesting State in order to exclude human rights breaches in its territory after the extradition or deportation is carried out may be appropriate as concerns risks of application of the death penalty[86] or for fair trial violations, because such risks can in most instances be monitored satisfactorily. On the other hand, as regards the risk of torture, monitoring is impracticable in the vast majority of conceivable cases, especially bearing in mind the fact that, even after conviction in a criminal case, a State may torture a prisoner for the

[86] And is indeed required: see European Court of Human Rights, Nivette v. Francejudgment of 3 July 2001, in which the European Court of Human Rights found that extradition to a State imposing the death sentence violated Protocol 6.

purpose of obtaining information. At the same time, it is impracticable to have a "life-long" responsibility for people who are removed out of the country.

141. This situation raises the question of the value of diplomatic assurances[87]. In the Venice Commission's view, the acceptance of such assurances is in principle the expression of the necessary good faith and mutual trust between friendly States, although, as far as assurances may be regarded as acceptable in principle (see para. 142 below), the terms of the diplomatic assurances need to be unequivocal (for instance, a reference to "torture" or to "inhuman or degrading treatment" should be interpreted within the meaning given to these terms by the ECtHR, the CAT and the HR Committee) and need to reflect the scope of the obligation by which the State which issues them is legally bound.

142. However, this general mutual trust must not prevail over the accurate examination of each specific situation, particularly if there are precedents or even patterns of violation of previously accepted assurances[88]. For example, an important difference between the situation in the Mamatkulov case (see para. 71 above) and later ones is that recent experience has shown that the risk of torture seems to be greater than what was known before, despite assurances. In the Commission's view, under these circumstances the room for accepting guarantees against torture is reduced significantly. Where there is substantial evidence that a country practices or permits torture in respect of certain categories of prisoners, guarantees may not satisfactorily reduce this risk in cases of requests for extradition of prisoners belonging to those categories.

143. The requirement of not exposing any prisoner to the real risk of ill-treatment also applies in respect of the transit of prisoners through the territory of Council of Europe member States: member States should therefore refuse to allow transit of prisoners in circumstances where there is such a risk.

144. The situation may arise that a Council of Europe member State has serious reasons to believe that the mission of an airplane crossing its airspace is to carry prisoners with the intention of transferring them to countries where they would face ill-treatment.

---

[87] The Council of Europe Steering Committee on Human Rights (CDDH) has set up a Group of Specialists with the task of "reflection on the issues raised with regard to human rights by the use of diplomatic assurances in the context of expulsion procedures; and consider the appropriateness of a legal instrument, for example a recommendation on minimum requirements/standards of such diplomatic assurances, and, if need be, present concrete proposals".

[88] See European Committee for the Prevention of Torture and Inhuman and Degrading Treatment, 15th General Report on the CPT's activities, §§39-40, at http://www.cpt.coe.int/en/annual/rep-15.htm.

145. If such an airplane does not require landing, as long as the plane is in the air, all persons on board are subject to the jurisdiction of both the flag State and the territorial State. In the Commission's view, Council of Europe member States' responsibility under the European Convention on Human Rights is engaged if they do not take the preventive measures which are within their powers. In addition, their responsibility for aiding another State to commit an unlawful act would be at issue. It follows, in the Commission's view, that the territorial State is entitled to, and must take all possible measures in order to prevent the commission of human rights violations in its territory, including in its air space.

146. There are obviously practical difficulties involved in securing the effective enjoyment of Convention rights in aircraft transiting a Council of Europe member State's airspace or military base for foreign forces on its territory. Without prejudice to the wider question of how such difficulties can affect the scope of a State's obligations to secure generally the rights under the Convention, the case-law of the European Court of Human Rights makes it clear that the State's duty to secure the most elementary rights at issue in the present case (right to security of person; freedom from torture and right to life) continues to apply, regardless of acquiescence or connivance[89].

147. The territorial State possesses a different course of action in respect of the suspect airplane, depending on its status.

148. If the state airplane in question has presented itself as if it were a civil plane, that is to say it has not duly sought prior authorisation pursuant to Article 3 c) of the Chicago Convention, it is in breach of the Chicago Convention: the territorial State may therefore require landing. The airplane having failed to declare its State functions, it will not be entitled to claim State aircraft status and subsequently not be entitled to immunity: the territorial State will therefore be entitled to search the plane pursuant to Article 16 of the Chicago Convention and take all necessary measures to secure human rights. In addition, it will be entitled to protest through appropriate diplomatic channels.

149. If the plane has presented itself as a State plane and has obtained overflight permission without however disclosing its mission, the territorial State can contend that the flag State has violated its international obligations. The flag State could thus face international responsibility. The airplane however will, in principle, be entitled to immunity according to general international law and to the applicable treaties: the territorial State will therefore be unable to search the plane, unless the captain consents.

[89] See European Court of Human Rights, Ilascu and others v. Moldova and the Russian Federation, judgment of 8 July 2004, § 318, Riera Blume and others v. Spain judgment of 14 October 1999 (final 14/01/2000) §§ 34-35; Gongadze v. Ukraine, judgment of 8 November 205, § 165.

150. However, the territorial State may refuse further overflight clearances in favour of the flag State or impose, as a condition therefore, a duty to submit to searches. If the overflight permission derives from a bilateral treaty or a SOFA or a military base agreement, the terms of such treaty might be questioned if and to the extent that they do not allow for any control in order to ensure respect for human rights, or their abuse might be advanced. In this respect, the Venice Commission recalls that the legal framework concerning foreign military bases on the territory of Council of Europe member States must enable the latter to exercise sufficient powers to fulfil their human rights obligations.

151. While mutual trust and economic and military co-operation amongst friendly States need to be encouraged, in granting foreign state aircraft authorisation for overflight, Council of Europe member States must secure respect for their human rights obligations. This means that they may have to consider whether it is necessary to insert new clauses, including the right to search, as a condition for diplomatic clearances in favour of State planes carrying prisoners. If there are reasonable grounds to believe that, in certain categories of cases, the human rights of certain passengers risk being violated, States must indeed make overflight permission conditional upon respect of express human rights clauses. Compliance with the procedures for obtaining diplomatic clearance must be strictly monitored; requests for overflight authorisation should provide sufficient information as to allow effective monitoring (for example, the identity and status (voluntary or involuntary passenger) of all persons on board and the destination of the flight as well as the final destination of each passenger). Whenever necessary, the right to search civil planes must be exercised.

152. With a view to discouraging repetition of abuse, any violations of civil aviation principles in relation to irregular transport of prisoners should be denounced, and brought to the attention of the competent authorities and eventually of the public. Council of Europe member States could bring possible breaches of the Chicago Convention before the Council of the International Civil Aviation Organisation pursuant to Article 54 of the Chicago Convention.

153. As regards the treaty obligations of Council of Europe member States, the Commission considers that there is no international obligation for them to allow irregular transfers of prisoners to or to grant unconditional overflight rights, for the purposes of fighting terrorism. In the Commission's opinion, therefore, States must interpret and perform their treaty obligations, including those deriving from the NATO treaty and from military base agreements and SOFAs, where these are applicable, in a manner compatible with their human rights obligations. As regards notably the NATO treaty, the Commission stresses that this principle is expressed in Article 7 according

to which "[t]his Treaty does not affect, and shall not be interpreted as affecting in any way the rights and obligations under the Charter [of the United Nations] of the Parties which are members of the United Nations." Even if NATO member states have undertaken obligations concerning irregular transfer or unconditional overflight, the Commission recalls that if the breach of a treaty obligation is determined by the need to comply with a peremptory norm (*jus cogens*), it does not give rise to an internationally wrongful act. As underlined above (para. 43), the prohibition of torture is a peremptory norm.

Conclusions

154. Council of Europe member States are under an obligation to fight terrorism, but in doing so they must safeguard human rights.

155. Council of Europe member States are under an international legal obligation to secure that everyone within their jurisdiction (see para. 146 above) enjoy internationally agreed fundamental rights, including and notably that they are not unlawfully deprived of their personal freedom and are not subjected to torture and inhuman and degrading treatment, including in breach of the prohibition to extradite or deport where there exists a risk of torture or ill-treatment. This obligation may also be violated by acquiescence or connivance in the conduct of foreign agents. There exists in particular a positive duty to investigate into substantiated claims of breaches of fundamental rights by foreign agents, particularly in case of allegations of torture or unacknowledged detention.

156. Council of Europe member States are bound by numerous multilateral and bilateral treaties in different fields, such as collective self-defence, international civil aviation and military bases. The obligations arising out of these treaties do not prevent States from complying with their human rights obligations. These treaties must be interpreted and applied in a manner consistent with the Parties' human rights obligations. Indeed, an implied condition of any agreement is that, in carrying it out, the States will act in conformity with international law, in particular human rights law.

157. The Venice Commission considers that there is room to interpret and apply the different applicable treaties in a manner that is compatible with the principle of respect for fundamental rights. Council of Europe member States must do so. For example, the search of a state airplane which has presented itself as a civil aircraft is allowed under the Chicago Convention and must be effected whenever there are reasonable grounds to suspect that the plane may be used to commit human rights breaches. The relevant inter-state practice must be changed and adapted to this obligation,

without however frustrating the legitimate aims pursued by the treaties in question. Diplomatic measures may also need to be taken.

158. To the extent that this due interpretation and application of the existing treaties in the light of human rights obligations is not possible, Council of Europe member States must take all the necessary measures to renegotiate and amend the treaty provisions to this effect.

159. In reply to the questions put by the Legal Affairs Committee of the Parliamentary Assembly of the Council of Europe, the Venice Commission has reached the conclusions listed below:

As regards arrest and secret detention

a) Any form of involvement of a Council of Europe member State or receipt of information prior to an arrest within its jurisdiction by foreign agents entails accountability under Articles 1 and 5 of the European Convention on Human Rights (and possibly Article 3 in respect of the modalities of the arrest). A State must thus prevent the arrest from taking place. If the arrest is effected by foreign authorities in the exercise of their jurisdiction under the terms of an applicable Status of Forces Agreement (SOFA), the Council of Europe member State concerned may remain accountable under the European Convention on Human Rights, as it is obliged to give priority to its *jus cogens* obligations, such as they ensue from Article 3.

b) Active and passive co-operation by a Council of Europe member State in imposing and executing secret detentions engages its responsibility under the European Convention on Human Rights. While no such responsibility applies if the detention is carried out by foreign authorities without the territorial State actually knowing it, the latter must take effective measures to safeguard against the risk of disappearance and must conduct a prompt and effective investigation into a substantiated claim that a person has been taken into unacknowledged custody.

c) The Council of Europe member State's responsibility is engaged also in the case where its agents (police, security forces etc.) co-operate with the foreign authorities or do not prevent an arrest or unacknowledged detention *without government knowledge*, acting *ultra vires*. The Statute of the Council of Europe and the European Convention on Human Rights require respect for the rule of law, which in turn requires accountability for *all* form of exercise of public power. Regardless of how a State chooses to regulate political control over security and intelligence agencies, in any event effective oversight and control mechanisms must exist.

d) If a State is informed or has reasonable suspicions that any persons are held *incomunicado* at foreign military bases on its territory, its responsibility under the European Convention on Human Rights is engaged, unless it takes all measures which are within its power in order for this irregular situation to end.

e) Council of Europe member States which have ratified the European Convention for the Prevention of Torture must inform the European Committee for the Prevention of Torture of any detention facility on their territory and must allow it to access such facilities. Insofar as international humanitarian law may be applicable, States must grant the International Committee of the Red Cross permission to visit these facilities.

As regards inter-state transfers of prisoners

f) There are only four legal ways for Council of Europe member States to transfer a prisoner to foreign authorities: deportation, extradition, transit and transfer of sentenced persons for the purpose of their serving the sentence in another country. Extradition and deportation proceedings must be defined by the applicable law, and the prisoners must be provided appropriate legal guarantees and access to competent authorities. The prohibition to extradite or deport to a country where there exists a risk of torture or ill-treatment must be respected.

g) Diplomatic assurances must be legally binding on the issuing State and must be unequivocal in terms; when there is substantial evidence that a country practices or permits torture in respect of certain categories of prisoners, Council of Europe member States must refuse the assurances in cases of requests for extradition of prisoners belonging to those categories.

h) The prohibition to transfer to a country where there exists a risk of torture or ill-treatment also applies in respect of the transit of prisoners through the territory of Council of Europe member States: they must therefore refuse to allow transit of prisoners in circumstances where there is such a risk.

As regards overflight

i) If a Council of Europe member State has serious reasons to believe that an airplane crossing its airspace carries prisoners with the intention of transferring them to countries where they would face ill-treatment in violation of Article 3 of the European Convention on Human Rights, it must take all the necessary measures in order to prevent this from taking place.

j) If the state airplane in question has presented itself as a civil plane, that is to say it has not duly sought prior authorisation pursuant to Article 3 c) of the Chicago Convention, the territorial State must require landing and must search it. In addition, it must protest through appropriate diplomatic channels.

k) If the plane has presented itself as a state plane and has obtained overflight permission without however disclosing its mission, the territorial State cannot search it unless the captain consents. However, the territorial State can refuse further overflight clearances in favour of the flag State or impose, as a condition therefor, the duty to submit to searches; if the overflight permission derives from a bilateral treaty or a Status of Forces Agreement or a military base agreement, the terms of such a treaty should be questioned if and to the extent that they do not allow for any control in order to ensure respect for human rights.

l) In granting foreign state aircraft authorisation for overflight, Council of Europe member States must secure respect for their human rights obligations. This means that they may have to consider whether it is necessary to insert new clauses, including the right to search, as a condition for diplomatic clearances in favour of State planes carrying prisoners. If there are reasonable grounds to believe that, in certain categories of cases, the human rights of certain passengers risk being violated, States must indeed make overflight permission conditional upon respect of express human rights clauses. Compliance with the procedures for obtaining diplomatic clearance must be strictly monitored; requests for overflight authorisation should provide sufficient information as to allow effective monitoring (for example, the identity and status (voluntary or involuntary passenger) of all persons on board and the destination of the flight as well as the final destination of each passenger). Whenever necessary, the right to search civil planes must be exercised.

m) With a view to discouraging repetition of abuse, any violations of civil aviation principles in relation to irregular transport of prisoners should be denounced, and brought to the attention of the competent authorities and eventually of the public. Council of Europe member States could bring possible breaches of the Chicago Convention before the Council of the International Civil Aviation Organisation pursuant to Article 54 of the Chicago Convention.

n) As regards the treaty obligations of Council of Europe member States, the Commission considers that there is no international obligation for them to allow irregular transfers of prisoners or to grant unconditional overflight rights, for the purposes of combating terrorism.

The Commission recalls that if the breach of a treaty obligation is determined by the need to comply with a peremptory norm (*jus cogens*), it does not give rise to an internationally wrongful act, and the prohibition of torture is a peremptory norm. In the Commission's opinion, therefore, States must interpret and perform their treaty obligations, including those deriving from the NATO treaty and from military base agreements and Status of Forces Agreements, in a manner compatible with their human rights obligations.

160. The Venice Commission hopes that this opinion will assist the Committee on Legal Affairs and Human Rights of the Parliamentary Assembly of the Council of Europe in the completion of the inquiry into these matters. The Commission also hopes that this opinion will assist the Secretary General of the Council of Europe in his ongoing inquiry under Article 52 of the European Convention on Human Rights. The Commission is ready to pursue its reflection on these matters, if so requested.

DOCUMENT NO. 6

OPINION NO. 3-2006: THE HUMAN RIGHTS RESPONSIBILITIES OF THE EU MEMBER STATES IN THE CONTEXT OF THE C.I.A. ACTIVITIES IN EUROPE

The E.U. Network of Independent Experts on Fundamental Rights

May 25, 2006

I. Introduction

By a letter dated April 7th, 2006, the European Commission (DG Justice, Freedom and Security) requested from the EU Network of Independent Experts on Fundamental Rights an opinion on the question of the alleged CIA activities in Europe (extraordinary renditions) within the Framework of the NATO or the bilateral SOFA ('status of forces') agreements (ref. DG JLS/C3/AG/bh/D(2006) 4783). This in turn followed a request to the vice-president of the European Commission, Mr Frattini, from the Chairman of the Temporary Committee on the alleged use of European countries by the CIA for the transportation and illegal detention of prisoners (TDIP Temporary Committee), Mr Carlos Coelho, dated March 29th, 2006 (ref. D(2006)1731).

It will be recalled that, following reports by *The Washington Post* that the CIA had been holding and interrogating al Qaeda captives at secret facilities in Eastern Europe, part of a global covert prison system established after the 11 September 2001, attacks, and allegations by Human Rights Watch that CIA airplanes had been traveling from Afghanistan in 2003 and 2004 to airfields in Poland and Romania, a number of initiatives have been taken, both within the Council of Europe and within the European Union. On 2 November 2005, the President of the Parliamentary Assembly of the Council of Europe, Mr van der Linden, asked the Committee on Legal Affairs and Human Rights of the Parliamentary Assembly to look into these allegations. The chair of the Committee on Legal Affairs and Human Rights, Mr Dick Marty, was appointed as rapporteur. The Committee recalled the Resolution 1433(2005) of the Parliamentary Assembly on the legality of the detention of persons by the United States in Guantanamo Bay, in which it called upon the Member States to 'ensure that their territory and facilities [were] not used in connection with practices of secret detention or rendition in possible violation of international human rights law' (para. 10, vii).

By a letter of 15 December 2005, Mr Dick Marty, chairperson of the Committee on Legal Affairs and Human Rights of the Parliamentary Assembly of the Council of Europe, requested an opinion of the European Commission for Democracy through Law (the Venice Commission), which the Venice Commission delivered on 18 March 2006.[1] The Venice Commission was asked to provide an 'assessment of the legality of secret detention centres in the light of the Council of Europe member States' international law obligations, in particular the European Convention on Human Rights (ECHR) and the European Convention for the Prevention of Torture', and identify in particular, the extent to which a State may be 'responsible if—actively or passively—it permits illegal detention or abduction by a third State or an agent thereof'. It also was asked 'what are the legal obligations of Council of Europe member States, under human rights and general international law, regarding the transport of detainees by other States through their territory, including the airspace', and what the relationship is 'between such obligations and possible countervailing obligations which derive from other treaties, including treaties concluded with non-member States'.

Acting under Article 52 of the European Convention on Human Rights, the Secretary General of the Council of Europe requested the Governments of the High Contracting Parties to the Convention to furnish, by 21 February 2006, an explanation of the manner in which their internal law ensures the effective implementation of the provisions of the Convention and its additional Protocols, as interpreted by the European Court of Human Rights, regarding the following specific issues: explanation of the manner in which their internal law ensures that acts by officials of foreign agencies within their jurisdiction are subject to adequate controls; explanation of the manner in which their internal law ensures that adequate safeguards exist to prevent unacknowledged deprivation of liberty of any person within their jurisdiction, whether such deprivation of liberty is linked to an action or an omission directly attributable to the High Contracting Party or whether that Party has aided or assisted the agents of another State in conduct amounting to such deprivation of liberty, including aid or assistance in the transportation by aircraft or otherwise of persons so deprived of their liberty;

[1] Opinion no. 363 / 2005, of the Venice Commission, on the international legal obligations of Council of Europe Member States in respect of secret detention facilities and inter-State transport of prisoners, adopted by the Venice Commission at its 66th Plenary Session (Venice, 17-18 March 2006), CDL-AD(2006)009.

explanation of the manner in which their internal law provides an adequate response to any alleged infringements of Convention rights of individuals within their jurisdiction, notably in the context of deprivation of liberty, resulting from the conduct of officials of foreign agencies. In particular, the Member States of the Council of Europe were requested to explain how effective investigations that are prompt, independent and capable of leading to the identification and sanctioning of those responsible for any illegal acts, including those responsible for aiding or assisting in the commission of such acts, and the payment of adequate compensation to victims, were provided for. In the context of the foregoing explanations, an explanation was requested as to whether, in the period running from 1 January 2002 (or from the moment of entry in force of the Convention if that occurred on a later date) until the present, any public official or other person acting in an official capacity has been involved in any manner—whether by action or omission—in the unacknowledged deprivation of liberty of any individual, or transport of any individual while so deprived of their liberty, including where such deprivation of liberty may have occurred by or at the instigation of any foreign agency. Information is to be provided on whether any official investigation is under way and/or on any completed investigation. All the Member States of the Council of Europe had responded to this inquiry within the deadline or within days following the deadline. The results were presented on March 1st, 2006.

The European Parliament's Committee on Civil Liberties, Justice and Home Affairs, has also been acting on this issue. On 15 December 2005 the European Parliament decided to set up a temporary committee to investigate the alleged illegal transfer of detainees and the suspected existence of secret CIA detention facilities in the European Union and in candidate countries (hereafter referred to as 'TDIP Temporary Committee'). After the formal decision was adopted on 12 January 2006 to set up such committee, the European Parliament, on 18 January 2006, approved the mandate and membership suggested by the Conference of Presidents of the Political Groups for its temporary 46-member committee, which is to investigate the allegations of CIA prisons in Europe where persons suspected of terrorism have allegedly been detained and tortured.

It is in this context that the Network of independent experts on fundamental rights has been requested to focus on the examination of two questions. The first question relates to the alleged CIA activities in Europe within the framework of the NATO or the bilateral SOFA ('status of forces') agreements. The TDIP Temporary Committee asks if the existing multilateral (NATO) or bilateral (SOFA) agreements to which the EU Member States are parties could have been applied in a way that has legitimated or tolerated the alleged abuses which are the subject of the work of the TDIP Temporary Committee. The second question relates to the implementation by the

EU Member States of the prohibition of torture under international law and the control mechanisms which are established to ensure the application of this international norm.

This opinion therefore has a limited scope. It seeks to answer the two questions identified by the TDIP Temporary Committee of the European Parliament, without examining the broader context in which the opinion is requested from the Network of independent experts on fundamental rights. Moreover, this opinion will build on preexisting inquiries, and has made full use of the information available from those inquiries. In particular, the second part of the opinion (II.), which addresses the first question submitted by the TDIP Temporary Committee, relies both on the independent findings of the Network of independent experts, and on the opinion delivered by the Venice Commission, which has been referred to above. The third part of the opinion (III.), which addresses the second question submitted by the TDIP Temporary Committee, is based on a variety of sources, including in particular the individual contributions of the independent experts of the Network, the reports of the EU Member States to the Committee against torture created under the 1984 UN Convention against Torture and Other Cruel, Inhuman or Degrading Treatment and Punishment, and the answers of the EU Member States, provided as Member States of the Council of Europe, to the inquiry of the Secretary General of the Council of Europe acting under Article 52 of the European Convention on Human Rights. A final paragraph (IV.) contains a limited set of conclusions and recommendations.

Mr Martin Scheinin, a member of the Network of independent experts, also UN Special Rapporteur on human rights and counterterrorism, has prepared the draft of part II of the opinion with his team, on the basis of the Opinion no. 363/2005 of the Venice Commission and on all the information the Network has received on this issue. Mr Manfred Nowak, a member of the Network of independent experts, also UN Special Rapporteur on torture and other cruel, inhuman or degrading treatment or punishment, has prepared the initial draft of this part of the opinion, with the assistance of his team. On the basis of the reports prepared by Messrs Scheinin and Nowak, the coordinator of the Network, Mr. Olivier De Schutter, prepared the final text of this opinion, which was sent to all experts of the network for comments, corrections or additions before being finalized.

II. The Alleged CIA Activities in Europe (Extraordinary Renditions) within the Framework of the NATO or the Bilateral SOFA ('Status of Forces') Agreements

1. Introduction

The purpose of this part of the opinion is to evaluate the NATO or the bilateral SOFA ('status of forces') agreements through the prism of fundamental and human rights. The focus is on 'extraordinary renditions' within the framework of these agreements. By 'rendition' is meant a situation in which one State obtains custody over a person suspected of involvement in serious crime (e.g. terrorism) in the territory of another State and/or the transfer of such a person to custody in the first State's territory, or a place subject to its jurisdiction, or to a third State. Whether a particular "rendition" is lawful will depend upon the laws of the States concerned and on the applicable rules of international law, in particular human rights law. By "extraordinary rendition" is meant any occasion on which there is little or no doubt that the obtaining of custody over a person is, for one reason or another, not in accordance with the existing legal procedures applying in the State where the person was situated at the time.[2]

Extraordinary rendition is thus a general term referring to any particular "rendition" which is not, for one reason or another, in accordance with the law. In practice, extraordinary renditions may involve multiple layers of human rights violations. Firstly, victims of rendition may be arrested and detained illegally; others may be abducted; yet others may be denied access to any legal process, including the ability to challenge the decision to transfer them because of the risk of torture. In addition, there may be a link between renditions and enforced disappearances. A person who has been illegally detained in one country and illegally transported to another may subsequently "disappear". Finally, a victim of rendition may be subjected to torture and other ill-treatment.

The Network underlines that the present opinion does not aim to establish, nor does it have the ambition to assess the facts in relation to the existence of secret detention facilities in Europe or about the transport of detainees by the CIA through the territory (including the airspace) of certain European States.

The Network also recalls that it bases all its reports and opinions, including the present opinion, on the Charter of Fundamental Rights of the European Union. Article 51 of the Charter of Fundamental Rights limits the scope of application of the Charter to the institutions of the Union and to the Member States only in their implementation of Union law. However, the Charter constitutes a catalogue of common values of the Member States of the Union. In that respect, the Charter may be taken into account in the understanding of Article 6(1) EU, to which Article 7 EU refers. In conformity with

[2] According to the Venice Commision, the term "extraordinary rendition" is used in public debate "when there is little or no doubt that the obtaining of custody over a person is not in accordance with the existing legal procedures applying in the State where the person was situated at the time." Opinion no. 363 / 2005, paragraph 31. Amnesty International uses the term "rendition" to describe "the transfer of individuals from one country to another, by means that bypass all judicial and administrative due process." See Report 51/051/2006, 5 April 2006, *USA: Below the radar: Secret flights to torture and 'disappearance'* (05/04/06).

its mandate, the Network considers the Charter as the most authoritative embodiment of these common values, on which its evaluation therefore may be based.

The Charter, as an instrument for the protection of human rights, should be interpreted and applied in accordance with the general principles of the international law of human rights. It has been the consistent practice of the Network to read the Charter in accordance with the rights guaranteed in instruments adopted in the field of human rights in the framework of the United Nations, the International Labour Organisation and the Council of Europe, including the findings of bodies set up within the framework of these instruments.

In accordance with this practice, the Network has relied essentially adopting this opinion, on the opinion no. 363/2005 of the Venice Commission of 17 March 2006 which provides an in-depth analysis of the matter through the prism of European and international human rights law, as well as international law in general. The present opinion by the Network does not seek to be exhaustive on the domains covered by the opinion of the Venice Commission. On the contrary, the Network has decided to underscore particular topics, which are felt to be of particular importance in the evaluation of the NATO or the bilateral SOFA ('status of forces') agreements through the prism of fundamental and human rights law. Moreover, even on the issues covered, the present opinion does not repeat all the findings and descriptions found in the opinion of the Venice Commission, where they are detailed.

Section 2 describes the legal framework under the NATO or the Bilateral SOFA ('status of forces') Agreements. Section 3 addresses the question how the human rights obligations of the EU Member States limit and shape the application of the NATO and the Bilateral SOFA agreements, in particular with reference to the alleged CIA activities (extraordinary renditions). Section 4 concludes that the requirements of fundamental and human rights, as derived from the EU Charter of Fundamental Rights and the international law of human rights, should be taken into account in the application of the NATO and the Bilateral SOFA agreements as these requirements limit the nature and scope of Member State obligations which may derive from the NATO or the bilateral SOFA ('status of forces') agreements. The obligations arising out of these treaties should not be seen as preventing Member States from complying with their human rights obligations. On the contrary, the Network emphasizes that these treaties must be interpreted and applied in a manner consistent with the Member States' human rights obligations under international law, and with their status as Member States of the Union bound to comply with certain common values referred to in Article 6(1) EU. Indeed, an implied condition of any agreement is that, in carrying it out, the Member States will act in conformity with international law, in particular human rights law.

2. The Essentials of the NATO or the Bilateral the 'Status-of-Forces Agreements' (SOFAs)

a) General Remarks

The lawfulness of the presence of the armed forces of one State on the territory of another State in peacetime is contingent on the consent of the host State. The consent of the host State is normally expressed in a two-stage procedure as follows: first, the initial decision to admit the forces takes the form of a bilateral or multilateral treaty, often defence agreements; second, the receiving State makes a concrete decision in which the use of facilities on its soil is granted. This second decision is usually made through a further agreement between the two States concerned.

The 'Status-of-forces agreements' (SOFAs) between the host State and a State stationing military forces in the host State define the legal status of the sending State's personnel and property in the territory of the host State. They form an integral part of the overall military bases agreements that allow the military forces of the sending State to operate within the host State.

SOFAs are usually bilateral. Bilateral SOFAs usually form an integral part of the overall military bases agreements that allow the sending State's military forces to operate within the host State. In addition, there exists a multilateral SOFA between NATO members, the NATO Status of Forces Agreement (SOFA) of 19 June 1951 (Agreement between the Parties to the North Atlantic Treaty Regarding the Status of their Forces).[3]

The United States has concluded some 90 SOFAs. The EU Member States are party to a SOFA with the United States *either* on the basis of their membership in NATO[4], *or* as States participating in Partnership for Peace (PfP)[5]. The 'Agreement among the States Parties to the North Atlantic Treaty and the other States Participating in the Partnership for Peace regarding the Status of their Forces' and the Additional Protocol thereto, both done at Brussels on 19 June 1995, make applicable to the Contracting States the NATO Status of Forces Agreement, including the so-called Paris Protocol

---

[3] See http://www.nato.int/docu/basictxt/b510619a.htm, 13 April 2006.

[4] The following 19 EU Member States are parties to the NATO: Belgium, Czech Republic, Denmark, Estonia, France, Germany, Greece, Hungary, Italy, Latvia, Lithuania, Luxembourg, Netherlands, Poland, Portugal, Slovakia, Slovenia, Spain and United Kingdom.

[5] The formal basis for the Partnership for Peace is the Framework Document (done at Brussels, on 10 January 1994), which sets out specific undertakings for each Partner country. The following EU Member States feature as Partnership for Peace (PfP) countries: Austria, Finland, Ireland and Sweden.

(the Status of International Military Headquarters set up pursuant to the North Atlantic Treaty, done at Paris, August 28, 1952). These agreements have been complemented by the Further Additional Protocol to the Agreement among the States Parties to the North Atlantic Treaty and the Other States Participating in the Partnership for Peace regarding the Status of Their Forces, done at Brussels, 19 December 1997.

b) The Scope and Essential Content of SOFAs

SOFAs between the host State and a State stationing military forces in the host State define the legal status of the sending State's military and civilian personnel, including their dependents, when such personnel are present in any such territory in connection with their official duties or, in the case of dependents, the official duties of their spouse or parent. SOFAs also define the legal status of the sending State's property in the territory of the host State. As already noted, they usually form an integral part of the overall military bases agreements that allow the sending State's military forces to operate within the host State.

In more detail, SOFAs regulate immigration requirements, documentation, the use of uniform, possession of arms, as well as a general requirement for those employed by the sending Contracting Party to comply with the laws of the receiving State. Typically, SOFAs guarantee a privileged position to the sending State's military and civilian personnel, including their dependents, insofar as entry formalities are concerned. Accordingly, foreign armed forces whose admission has been consented to by the receiving State are not, as a rule, subject to the normal immigration controls and entry formalities applicable to foreign nationals. For instance, Article III. 1 of the NATO-SOFA agreement provides that "members of a force shall be exempted from passport and visa regulations and immigration inspection on entering or leaving the territory of a receiving State. They shall also be exempt from the regulations of the receiving State on the registration and control of aliens". However, this waiver of entry procedures is counterbalanced by the requirement under Article III.2 that members of the force must present on demand identification, whether on entry or at any time thereafter, and an individual or collective movement order certifying the status of the individual as a member of a force. The receiving State enjoys discretion whether to require a movement order to be countersigned by its authorised representatives. Exemption from entry formalities is also made conditional on compliance with the formalities established by the receiving State relating to the entry and departure of a force or the members thereof.

It is common for SOFAs to authorize the sending State to have access to its forces and to the ports or airfields which it has been accorded in the host State. This authorisation is essential, as in relation to public vessels and aircraft there is no right of access under customary international law. It is, however, often the practice in bilateral treaties for entry to the ports of the receiving State to be subject to "appropriate notification under normal conditions" made to the authorities of the latter. Even more importantly, the sending State does not benefit from an unrestricted freedom of movement within, and overflight of, the receiving State, unless such rights are expressly granted in a base agreement. Finally, as this opinion will emphasize below, the national and international law that is applicable to military bases cannot, and does not claim to, diminish the obligations and responsibilities of the EU Member States under Union law and human rights treaties.

The rules on jurisdiction are stipulated in Art. VII of the NATO SOFA. The distribution of jurisdiction between the sending State and the receiving State is typically as follows: When only the sending State's law is violated, the sending State has the power to exercise sole criminal jurisdiction. When only the receiving State's law is violated, the receiving State has the power to exercise sole criminal jurisdiction. When a crime violated the laws of both countries, there is concurrent criminal jurisdiction: the receiving State maintains primary jurisdiction except for offences committed solely against the property or security or member of the sending State force, or for offences arising out of any act or omission done by the sending State service member in the performance of official duty. In all other cases, the receiving State has the primary right to exercise jurisdiction. In cases of concurrent jurisdiction, the receiving State may relinquish jurisdiction through waiver requests from the sending State.

As a result of the regime thus established, the military authorities of the sending State as a rule shall have the right to exercise within the receiving State all criminal and disciplinary jurisdiction on the basis of the law of the sending State. As a rule, too, the receiving State cannot search foreign military bases on its territory unless this is allowed under the relevant treaties or unless the host State is authorised by the sending State to do so. This may constitute an obstacle to the effective exercise by the receiving State of its jurisdiction, in particular in order to enforce its domestic law where offences against that law are committed on such military bases.

The rules recalled above however do not result in a situation where an EU Member State is unable to ensure that there does not exist extraordinary rendition or associated practice, such as enforced disappearance, torture or other ill-treatment and incommunicado and secret detention in military bases within the framework of SOFAs. Such a conclusion would be entirely inappropriate, due to two distinct, yet inter-related reasons.

First, the receiving State does not abandon its sovereignty altogether when it consents to the presence of foreign armed forces on its territory. While it admits the enjoyment of the privilege of use of its territory accorded to the sending State, it nonetheless retains the right to regulate this privilege within the framework of applicable treaties and agreements. Therefore, the sending State acquires various powers pertaining to the operation of its defence forces on a territory that remains subject to the sovereignty of the host State. The sending State may lawfully claim in or over the territory of the receiving State, only those rights and powers that are connected directly with the establishment and operation of, and access to, the sites at which the foreign forces and installations are located. The principle of sovereignty of the territorial State dictates that any further rights and powers can derive only from an express grant by the receiving State. In particular, the extent of the right for the receiving State to search a foreign military base on its territory depends on the concrete terms of the defence agreement or of the "Status-of-forces agreement" (SOFA).

Second, SOFAs may not, nor do they claim to, diminish the obligations and responsibilities of the EU Member States under human rights treaties. The EU Member States must interpret and perform their treaty obligations, including those deriving from the NATO treaty and from military base agreements and SOFAs, where these are applicable, in a manner compatible with their human rights obligations. Moreover, EU Member States remain accountable under the European Convention on Human Rights and other human rights treaties binding upon them even if extraordinary rendition or associated practices are effected by foreign authorities in the exercise of their (alleged) jurisdiction under the terms of an applicable SOFA.

The following section elaborates further on these observations.

3. Human Rights Obligations of the EU Member States within the Framework of SOFAs

a) The Applicability of the International Law of Human Rights to SOFAs

EU Member States are committed to respecting fundamental rights, as defined by a number of international treaties, both at the universal level (including the 1966 International Covenant on Civil and Political Rights ("ICCPR"), and the 1984 UN Convention against Torture and Other Cruel, Inhuman or Degrading Treatment or Punishment) and at the European level, in particular the 1950 European Convention on Human Rights, but also the 1987 European Convention for the Prevention of Torture and Inhuman or Degrading Treatment or Punishment.

With respect to the matters which form the object of the present opinion, the human rights which are at issue are primarily the right to liberty and security of the person and the ban on torture and other inhuman or degrading treatment or punishment. The opinion by the Venice Commission discusses these rights in detail and obviates the necessity of recapitulation.[6]

The basic argument that human rights law should be respected within the framework of SOFAs is based on the following well-established considerations in human rights law and public international law in general. The Network would recall, in terms which closely follow the opinion by the Venice Commission, the following principles on State responsibility and human rights law.

1. In accordance with general principles of international law, any good faith application of a human rights instrument entails a general obligation to prevent violations thereof. Reasonable and appropriate measures must be taken to avoid breaches of human rights. Hence, if there is a real risk that the adoption and subsequent implementation of a certain treaty would lead to violations of human rights, then effective respect for human rights requires the elimination of such a danger.
2. Where contracting parties fail to take human rights properly into account, or where a treaty leads to infringements of human rights whether or not such violations could be anticipated when the treaty was concluded, the parties concerned can be held responsible for such violations: the obligation to secure the enjoyment of human rights and fundamental freedoms continues to exist after the conclusion of a treaty with third parties. This is in conformity with the rule expressed in Article 30 of the Vienna Convention on the Law of Treaties of 23 May 1969, entitled 'Application of successive treaties relating to the same subject-matter' (see, specifically, Article 30 § 4, b)).[7] The European Court of Human Rights has ruled that Article 1 ECHR, which requires the States Parties to secure for everyone within their jurisdiction the rights and freedoms defined in the Convention, "makes no distinction as to the type of rule or measure concerned". The Court has also insisted that Article 1 ECHR "does not exclude any part of the member States' 'jurisdiction' from scrutiny under the Convention. It is, therefore, with respect to their 'jurisdiction' as a whole—which is often exercised in the first place through the Constitution—that the States Parties are called on to show compliance with the Convention". This necessarily entails that a State party

[6] See Opinion no. 363/2005 of the Venice Commission, paragraphs 49-61.

[7] As explained by Special Rapporteur Fitzmaurice: "Since anything that some of the parties to a treaty do *inter se* under another treaty is clearly *res inter alios acta*, it cannot in law result in any formal diminution of the obligation of these parties under the earlier treaty, or affect juridically the rights or position of the other parties, which remain legally intact and subsisting" (G. Fitzmaurice, Third Report, *ILC Yearbook* (1958), vol. II, p. 43).

to the Convention is also bound by its provisions when it is exercising its 'jurisdiction' under a certain treaty—and irrespective of whether the other State involved is party to the Convention. Where certain States parties to the European Convention on Human Rights have agreed to create between themselves an international organisation in particular, the Court has emphasized that the Convention 'does not exclude the transfer of competences to international organisations provided that Convention rights continue to be "secured". Member States' responsibility therefore continues even after such a transfer'.[8] A State Party to the European Convention on Human Rights is therefore considered by the European Court of Human Rights to retain Convention liability in respect of treaty commitments subsequent to the entry into force of the Convention.[9]

3. The duty of the States Parties to secure for everyone within their jurisdiction the rights and freedoms defined in the Convention also includes positive obligations to protect individuals against infringements of their rights by third parties, be they private individuals or organs of third States operating within the jurisdiction of the State party concerned.[10] The European Court of Human Rights has, in particular, recognized positive obligations which flow from the prohibition of torture and inhuman treatment, the right to life, and the right to freedom and security. Such positive obligations include duties to investigate, especially in the case of disappeared persons, and to provide for effective remedies.

4. These considerations are even more compelling in situations involving a serious risk that a person would be subjected to the death penalty, torture or inhuman or degrading treatment or punishment. The European Court of Human Rights has stated on many occasions, even in the most difficult circumstances, such as the fight against terrorism and organised crime, that the ECHR prohibits in absolute terms torture and inhuman or degrading treatment or punishment. Unlike most of the substantive clauses of the ECHR and of Protocols Nos. 1 and 4, Article 3 makes no provision for limitations and no derogation from it is permissible under Article 15 § 2, not even in the event of a public emergency threatening the life of the nation. In this context, it is also worth underlining that Council of Europe Member States are under an obligation to prevent prisoners'

---

[8] Eur. Ct. HR (GC), *Matthews v. the United Kingdom* (Appl. N° 24833/94) judgment of 18 February 1999, § 32.

[9] Eur. Ct. HR (GC), *Bosphorus Hava Yolları Turizm ve Ticaret Anonim irketi v. Ireland* (Appl. N° 45036/98) judgment of 30 June 2005, § 154.

[10] See, inter alia, Eur. Ct. HR (GC), *Ilascu and Others v. Moldova and Russia* (Appl. N° 48787/99), judgment of 8 July 2004, para. 330-331.

exposure to the risk of torture: the violation does not depend on whether the prisoner is eventually subjected to torture. The assessment of the reality of the risk must be carried out on a case-by-case basis and very rigorously.

b) Member States' Human Rights Obligations in Respect of Extraordinary Renditions Within the Framework of the Nato or the Bilateral Sofa ('Status of Forces') Agreements

General remarks

Member States may face practical difficulties in securing the effective enjoyment of human rights in military bases for foreign forces on their territory. Without prejudice to the wider question of how such difficulties can affect the scope of a Member State's obligations to secure human rights, the Network emphasizes that the case-law of the European Court of Human Rights makes it clear that the State has a duty to secure the most elementary rights at issue (right to security of person; freedom from torture and from inhuman or degrading treatments and right to life), regardless of acquiescence or connivance.

In its concluding observations, the Venice Commission noted that the obligations arising out of such multilateral and bilateral treaties as SOFAs do not prevent States from complying with their human rights obligations. These treaties must be interpreted and applied in a manner consistent with the Parties' human rights obligations.

The Venice Commission emphasized that an implied condition of any agreement is that, in carrying it out, the States will act in conformity with international law, in particular human rights law. The Venice Commission also felt that there is room to interpret and apply the different applicable treaties in a manner that is compatible with the principle of respect for fundamental rights. It insisted that this is an obligation for all Council of Europe member States. To highlight this point, the Venice Commission made a reference to the search of a state airplane which has presented itself as a civil aircraft. The Commission noted that such a search is allowed under the Chicago Convention and must be effected whenever there are reasonable grounds to suspect that the plane may be used to commit human rights breaches. The Commission also noted that the relevant inter-state practice must be changed and adapted to this obligation, without however frustrating the legitimate aims pursued by the treaties in question. Diplomatic measures may also need to be taken. Finally, the Commission observed that to the extent that this due interpretation and application of the existing treaties in the light of human rights obligations is not possible, Council of Europe member States must take all the necessary measures to renegotiate and amend the treaty provisions to this effect.

While sharing these observations by the Venice Commission, the Network would recall the limited value which, in its view, may be afforded to diplomatic assurances provided by the State with whom the receiving State is bound by a 'status of forces' agreement or by a treaty containing clauses of a similar nature. This question is examined hereunder in greater detail.

The Network also notes that it is important to keep close track of how the Member States of the European Union will observe their human rights obligations within the framework of SOFAs.

Specific issues

In its opinion, the Venice Commission highlighted the following issues of particular concern: arrest and secret detention, inter-state transfers of prisoners and overflight. Regarding these issues, the Venice Commission reached the following conclusions which deserve to be quoted here in their entirety.

As regards arrest and secret detention, the Venice Commission reached the following conclusions:

> a) Any form of involvement of a Council of Europe member State or receipt of information prior to an arrest within its jurisdiction by foreign agents entails accountability under Articles 1 and 5 of the European Convention on Human Rights (and possibly Article 3 in respect of the modalities of the arrest). A State must thus prevent the arrest from taking place. If the arrest is effected by foreign authorities in the exercise of their jurisdiction under the terms of an applicable Status of Forces Agreement (SOFA), the Council of Europe member State concerned may remain accountable under the European obligations, such as they ensue from Article 3.
>
> b) Active and passive co-operation by a Council of Europe member State in imposing and executing secret detentions engages its responsibility under the European Convention on Human Rights. While no such responsibility applies if the detention is carried out by foreign authorities without the territorial State actually knowing it, the latter must take effective measures to safeguard against the risk of disappearance and must conduct a prompt and effective investigation into a substantiated claim that a person has been taken into unacknowledged custody.
>
> c) The Council of Europe member State's responsibility is engaged also in the case where its agents (police, security forces etc.) co-operate with the foreign authorities or do not prevent an arrest or unacknowledged detention without government knowledge, acting ultra vires. The Statute of the Council of Europe and the European Convention on Human Rights require respect for the rule of law, which in turn requires accountability for all form of exercise of public power. Regardless of

how a State chooses to regulate political control over security and intelligence agencies, in any event effective oversight and control mechanisms must exist.

d) If a State is informed or has reasonable suspicions that any persons are held incommunicado at foreign military bases on its territory, its responsibility under the European Convention on Human Rights is engaged, unless it takes all measures which are within its power in order for this irregular situation to end.

e) Council of Europe member States which have ratified the European Convention for the Prevention of Torture must inform the European Committee for the Prevention of Torture of any detention facility on their territory and must allow it to access such facilities. Insofar as international humanitarian law may be applicable, States must grant the International Committee of the Red Cross permission to visit these facilities.

As regards inter-state transfers of prisoners, the Venice Commission reached the following conclusions:

f) There are only four legal ways for Council of Europe member States to transfer a prisoner to foreign authorities: deportation, extradition, transit and transfer of sentenced persons for the purpose of their serving the sentence in another country. Extradition and deportation proceedings must be defined by the applicable law, and the prisoners must be provided appropriate legal guarantees and access to competent authorities. The prohibition to extradite or deport to a country where there exists a risk of torture or ill-treatment must be respected.

g) Diplomatic assurances must be legally binding on the issuing State and must be unequivocal in terms; when there is substantial evidence that a country practices or permits torture in respect of certain categories of prisoners, Council of Europe member States must refuse the assurances in cases of requests for extradition of prisoners belonging to those categories.

h) The prohibition to transfer to a country where there exists a risk of torture or ill-treatment also applies in respect of the transit of prisoners through the territory of Council of Europe member States: they must therefore refuse to allow transit of prisoners in circumstances where there is such a risk.

As regards overflight, the Venice Commission reached the following conclusions:

i) If a Council of Europe member State has serious reasons to believe that an airplane crossing its airspace carries prisoners with the intention of transferring them to countries where they would face ill-treatment in violation of Article 3 of the European Convention on Human Rights, it must take all the necessary measures in order to prevent this from taking place.

j) If the state airplane in question has presented itself as a civil plane, that is to say it has not duly sought prior authorisation pursuant to Article 3 c) of the Chicago Convention, the territorial State must require landing and must search it. In addition, it must protest through appropriate diplomatic channels.

k) If the plane has presented itself as a state plane and has obtained overflight permission without however disclosing its mission, the territorial State cannot search it unless the captain consents. However, the territorial State can refuse further overflight clearances in favour of the flag State or impose, as a condition therefore, the duty to submit to searches; if the overflight permission derives from a bilateral treaty or a Status of Forces Agreement or a military base agreement, the terms of such a treaty should be questioned if and to the extent that they do not allow for any control in order to ensure respect for human rights.

l) In granting foreign state aircraft authorisation for overflight, Council of Europe member States must secure respect for their human rights obligations. This means that they may have to consider whether it is necessary to insert new clauses, including the right to search, as a condition for diplomatic clearances in favour of State planes carrying prisoners. If there are reasonable grounds to believe that, in certain categories of cases, the human rights of certain passengers risk being violated, States must indeed make overflight permission conditional upon respect of express human rights clauses. Compliance with the procedures for obtaining diplomatic clearance must be strictly monitored; requests for overflight authorisation should provide sufficient information as to allow effective monitoring (for example, the identity and status (voluntary or involuntary passenger) of all persons on board and the destination of the flight as well as the final destination of each passenger). Whenever necessary, the right to search civil planes must be exercised.

m) With a view to discouraging repetition of abuse, any violations of civil aviation principles in relation to irregular transport of prisoners should be denounced, and brought to the attention of the competent authorities and eventually of the public. Council of Europe member States could bring possible breaches of the Chicago Convention before the Council of the International Civil Aviation Organisation pursuant to Article 54 of the Chicago Convention.

n) As regards the treaty obligations of Council of Europe member States, the Commission considers that there is no international obligation

> for them to allow irregular transfers of prisoners or to grant unconditional overflight rights, for the purposes of combating terrorism. The Commission recalls that if the breach of a treaty obligation is determined by the need to comply with a peremptory norm (jus cogens), it does not give rise to an internationally wrongful act, and the prohibition of torture is a peremptory norm. In the Commission's opinion, therefore, States must interpret and perform their treaty obligations, including those deriving from the NATO treaty and from military base agreements and Status of Forces Agreements, in a manner compatible with their human rights obligations.

The Network concurs in these conclusions by the Venice Commission insofar as issues of arrest and secret detention, inter-state transfers of prisoners and overflight may take place within the framework of SOFAs. In particular, the Network emphasises that the Member States of the European Union are not obliged to allow extraordinary renditions under SOFAs. The Network thus strongly warns against the tendency of thinking that the obligations arising out of these treaties would somehow prevent Member States from complying with their human rights obligations. The case is totally the opposite: these treaties must always be interpreted and applied in a manner consistent with the Member States' human rights obligations. In particular, the Member States are under the absolute duty to secure the most elementary rights at issue, i.e. the right to liberty and security of the person, freedom from torture and other inhuman treatment, and the right to life.

Although the Venice Commission does not exclude the use of diplomatic assurances, it has emphasized that 'when there is substantial evidence that a country practices or permits torture in respect of certain categories of prisoners, Council of Europe member States must refuse the assurances in cases of requests for extradition of prisoners belonging to those categories'. In a different context, the Network has underscored (in its Conclusions relating to the year 2005 (Concl. 2005, pp. 157-161); see also Concl. 2005, p. 81) that 'diplomatic assurances' cannot be a substitute for a verification, on a case-to-case basis, that a person facing the threat of removal (for instance in cases of extradition, expulsion or after being denied asylum, but also in situations where a person is under the jurisdiction of the host State and faces the threat of being removed from the territory by agents of a foreign State) will not be subjected to a real risk of torture, to other forms of inhuman or degrading treatment or punishment or to the death penalty, and that the security of that person will not be threatened. This position, which has been clearly expressed by the Special Rapporteur on Torture of the United Nations Commission on Human Rights to the General Assembly, is shared by international jurisdictions and the human rights treaties bodies. The Network relied in particular on the position adopted on 20 May 2005 by the UN Committee against Torture (CAT)[11]. The Network also recalls the statement made by the Council of Europe Commissioner for Human Rights, Alvaro Gil-Robles, in July 2004, according to which: "The weakness inherent in the practice of diplomatic assurances lies in the fact that where there is a need for such assurances, there is clearly an acknowledged risk of torture or ill-treatment. Due to the absolute nature of the prohibition of torture or inhuman or degrading treatment, formal assurances cannot suffice where a risk nonetheless remains"[12]. As the Special Rapporteur of the UN Commission on Human Rights on torture and other cruel, inhuman or degrading treatment or punishment, Mr. Manfred Nowak[13] took the view that States 'cannot resort to diplomatic assurances as a safeguard against torture and ill-treatment where there are substantial grounds for believing that a person would be in danger of being subjected to torture or ill-treatment upon return'[14]. The Network of Independent Experts considers that, in the view of the status of the international norm prohibiting torture and of the absolute and unconditional character of this prohibition, this is the only acceptable position under international law.

III. The Protection from Torture and other Forms of Cruel, Inhuman or Degrading Treatment in E.U. Member States

1. Introduction

The second part of the opinion deals with the question on how protection from torture and other cruel, inhuman or degrading treatment is ensured in the E.U. Member States. The context in which an answer to this question is requested from the Network should be recalled.

On 15 February 2006, five special procedures of the United Nations Human Rights Commission published a joint report on the situation of detainees at Guantanamo Bay,[15] in which they conclude, *inter alia,* that international human rights law is applicable in Guantanamo Bay, that the continuing detention of all persons held there amounts to arbitrary detention in violation of article 9 ICCPR, that the US Government violates the right to a fair trial before an independent tribunal as provided for by article 14 ICCPR,

[11] UN Doc. CAT/C/34/D/233/2003, 20 May 2005, p. 34. The *Agiza* case in which this position was adopted is referred to hereunder in broader detail.

[12] Report by Mr. Alvaro Gil-Robles, Commissioner for Human Rights, on His Visit to Sweden, 21-23 April 2004, Council of Europe, document CommDH(2004)13, 8 July 2004, para. 9.

[13] Manfred Nowak is also the expert for Austria of the EU Network of Independent Experts on Fundamental Rights and the main author of part III of this opinion.

[14] UN doc. A/60/316, 30 August 2005, at para. 51-52.

[15] The UN Report on the „Situation of detainees at Guantanamo Bay" was submitted jointly by the Chairperson of the Working Group on Arbitrary Detention and the Special Rapporteurs on the independence of judges and lawyers, on torture, on freedom of religion and on the right to health: See UN Doc. E/CN.4/2006/120 of 5 February 2006.

and that the detention facilities at Guantanamo Bay should therefore be closed without further delay by either releasing the detainees or charging them before an independent court for crimes which they allegedly committed. In the joint report, the five experts also express their 'utmost concern' about the 'attempts by the United States Administration to redefine torture in the framework of the struggle against terrorism in order to allow certain interrogation techniques that would not be permitted under the internationally accepted definition of torture'. These independent experts added that 'the confusion with regard to authorized and unauthorized interrogation techniques over the last years is particularly alarming. The interrogation techniques authorized by the Department of Defense, particularly if used simultaneously, amount to degrading treatment in violation of article 7 of ICCPR and article 16 of the convention against Torture. If in individual cases, which were described in interviews, the victim experienced severe pain or suffering, these acts amounted to torture as defined in article 1 of the Convention. Furthermore, the general conditions of detention, in particular the uncertainty about the length of detention and prolonged solitary confinement, amount to inhuman treatment and to a violation of the right to health as well as a violation of the right of detainees under article 10(1) ICCPR to be treated with humanity and with respect for the inherent dignity of the human person. The excessive violence used in many cases during transportation, in operations by the Initial Reaction Forces and force-feeding of detainees on hunger strike must be assessed as amounting to torture as defined in article 1 of the Convention against Torture'. The experts also noted that 'force-feeding of competent detainees violates the right to health as well as the ethical duties of any health professionals who may be involved'.[16]

It follows that the EU Member States are under an obligation to prohibit the removal from persons under their jurisdiction to Guantanamo Bay, or to any other location where such persons risk being subjected to torture or to forms of treatment which are considered cruel, inhuman or degrading under international law.[17] Article 19(2) of the EU Charter of Fundamental

[16] Ibid, paras. 83 to 88 and 94.

[17] The Network has also emphasized in its Conclusions relating to the year 2005 (pp. 143-144) that there exists an absolute prohibition on returning a person to a State where he or she risks being sentenced to death. This prohibition can be inferred from the undertaking of the Member States of the European Union with regard to Article 6 of the International Covenant on Civil and Political Rights, as interpreted by the United Nations Human Rights Committee (Human Rights Committee, *Judge v. Canada*,communicationn°829/1998,finalviewsof20October2003,ONUdoc.CCPR/C/78/D/829/1998 (2003)). The Member States of the European Union have all ratified Protocols Nos. 6 and 13 to the European Convention on Human Rights. Consequently, they are States that have abolished the death penalty within the meaning of Article 6(2) of the International Covenant on Civil and Political Rights. Moreover, the European Court of Human Rights has also considered that 'it cannot be ruled out that an issue might exceptionally be raised under Article 6 of the Convention by [a decision to return a person] in circumstances where the [returnee] has suffered or risks suffering a flagrant denial of justice in the requesting country' (Eur. Ct. HR, *S. Einhorn v. France*, dec. of 16 October 2001

Rights states that 'No one may be removed, expelled or extradited to a State where there is a serious risk that he or she would be subjected to the death penalty, torture or other inhuman or degrading treatment or punishment'. This provision restates Article 3 of the European Convention for the Protection of Human Rights and Fundamental Freedoms (1950). It should be read also in accordance with the requirements formulated by Article 7 of the International Covenant on Civil and Political Rights (1966), by Article 3 of the Convention against Torture and Other Cruel, Inhuman or Degrading Treatment and Punishment (1984) (CAT) and by Article 33 of the Convention relating to the Status of Refugees (1951). These provisions impose an absolute prohibition on removing a person to a territory where that person runs a real risk of being subjected to forms of treatment which amount to torture or to cruel, inhuman or degrading treatment or punishment.

The European Parliament should clearly reiterate its support for this fundamental guarantee provided under the international law of human rights. In the case of *Ramzy v. the Netherlands* (Appl. N° 25424/05), currently pending before the European Court of Human Rights, the Governments of Lithuania, Portugal, Slovakia and the United Kingdom, who have been given leave to intervene in support of the Dutch government's position, are taking the view that suspected terrorists might be expelled in conditions which, if the persons concerned did not represent such a serious threat to the community of the expelling State, would be in violation of Article 3 ECHR. While these governments do not challenge the absolute nature of the prohibition in Article 3 against a Contracting State itself subjecting an individual to Article 3 ill-treatment, they insist however that, 'the context of removal involves assessments of risk of ill-treatment, and needs to afford proper weight to the fundamental rights of the citizens of Contracting States who are threatened by terrorism'; that 'it is necessary and appropriate for all the circumstances of a particular case to be taken into account in deciding whether or not a removal in the situation set out above is, or is not, compatible with the Convention—national security considerations cannot simply be dismissed as irrelevant in this context'.[18] These governments are asking the European Court of Human Rights to overrule the *Chahal v. the United Kingdom* judgment it delivered on 15 November 1996, where the Court clearly identified an *absolute* prohibition to expel, extradite, or return a person to a State where he or she would be facing a serious risk of torture or of treatment or punishment contrary to Article 3 ECHR,

(Appl. No. 71555/01), § 32 (citing the judgment of the Court in *Soering v. the United Kingdom* of 7 July 1989, p. 45, § 113, and, *mutatis mutandis, the Drozd and Janousekv. France and Spain judgment* of 26 June 1992, Series A no. 240, p. 34, § 110; Eur. Ct. HR (GC), *Mamatkulov and Askaraov v. Turkey* (Appl. n° 46827/99 and 46951/99) judgment of 4 February 2005, § 88).

[18] Observations of the governments of Lithuania, Portugal, Slovakia and the United Kingdom, presented to the European Court of Human Rights in the case of *Ramzy v. the Netherlands,* 21 November 2005.

explicitly dismissing as without relevance the seriousness of the offences committed by that individual or the threat that person would represent for the national security of the expelling State. In its conclusions and recommendations relating to the year 2005, the Network expresses its deep concern about this attempt to move the clock of human rights backwards.

The question addressed to the Network of Independent Experts concerns the legal and practical measures which the EU Member States have adopted in order to ensure that they comply with their obligation, clearly stipulated under international law, to protect persons under their jurisdiction from being removed to locations where they run a real risk of being torture or subjected to cruel, inhuman or degrading treatments and punishments.

In order to gather accurate information in this regard the Network undertook a survey of the 25 E.U. Member States. For each State, the experts sought to answer the following questions:

1) Is torture a crime under the domestic law in your country as required by Art. 4 CAT? Please provide the relevant text including the penalty.
2) How has the principle of non-refoulement in relation to torture (Art. 3 CAT) been implemented in domestic law? Please provide the relevant texts in all laws relating to expulsion/extradition/deportation/transit and transfer of sentenced persons.
3) Does your domestic law provide for any independent national mechanisms to visit places of detention as foreseen in the Optional Protocol to the UN Convention Against Torture?
4) Are there any places of detention in your country where the CPT and/or national monitoring bodies entrusted to carry out visits to places of detention have no access? In particular, are there any military bases of the United States/NATO where people might be detained without any possibility of domestic bodies to monitor possible torture practices?
5) Are there any domestic investigations carried out in relation to CIA rendition flights? If so, can you provide us with the results of these investigations?
6) Does your domestic law provide for the possibility of searching civil or State aircrafts landing on your territory (e.g. for the purpose of re-fuelling) in case of suspicion that these aircrafts carry detainees and/or that these persons might be subjected to torture, cruel, inhuman or degrading treatment? Does your domestic law provide for any possibility to prevent these aircrafts to continue transporting

detainees to countries where there exists a substantial risk of being subjected to torture?

7) Do you know of any cases after 11 September 2001 in which the authorities of your country have actively participated in CIA rendition flights?

8) Do you know of any cases after 11 September 2001 in which the authorities of your country have taken action to prevent CIA rendition flights and/or to protect CIA detainees against torture, cruel, inhuman or degrading treatment, including the principle of non-refoulement?

Questions 1 to 3 concern the legal framework within the Member States in respect to the protection from torture and cruel, inhuman or degrading treatment and punishments, the legal protection against *refoulement*, i.e. provisions that guarantee that no individual is sent to a country where he or she might face a substantial risk of being tortured, and the existence of national mechanisms authorised to inspect places of detention within the Member States. This legal framework is addressed in section 2 of this part of the opinion.

Question 4 asks whether factually there are places, such as foreign military bases, within the EU Member States where the CPT and/or national monitoring mechanisms have no access. The first part of the opinion has focused on the legal background. Section 3 in this part of the opinion examines the practical question of whether the EU Member States have adopted all the necessary measures which ensure an adequate protection of all persons under their jurisdiction from the risk of being detained and removed in conditions which would violated the norms of international law which Article 19(2) of the EU Charter of Fundamental Rights recapitulates.

Finally, questions 5 to 8 are particularly concerned with CIA rendition or "extraordinary rendition" flights within the airspace of the Member States of the European Union and on its airfields. This question is addressed in Section 4 of this part of the opinion.

The answers of the independent experts to the questions cited above form the basis of this part of the opinion. They were completed by other sources of information, such as the respective State reports to the UN Committee Against Torture and the CAT Committee's concluding observations and recommendations, the Report of the Council of Europe Secretary General following the use of his powers under Article 52 ECHR as referred to above and the national contributions to this report, results of investigations or opinions by specifically established mechanisms of the Council of Europe as well as the European Parliament, reports from non-governmental organisations and media sources.

2. The Legal Framework Applicable to Torture and the Protection From *Refoulement*

a) Torture as a crime under domestic law

Article 4 CAT obliges the States parties to make torture a crime under domestic law, which should be made punishable with adequate sanctions.

> 1. Each State Party shall ensure that all acts of torture are offences under its criminal law. The same shall apply to an attempt to commit torture and to an act by any person which constitutes complicity or participation in torture.
>
> 2. Each State Party shall make these offences punishable by appropriate penalties which take into account their grave nature.

The definition of torture under domestic law should reflect the definition given in Article 1 CAT, according to which torture is "any act by which severe pain or suffering, whether physical or mental, is intentionally inflicted on a person for such purposes as obtaining from him or a third person information or a confession, punishing him for an act he or a third person has committed or is suspected of having committed, or intimidating or coercing him or a third person, or for any reason based on discrimination of any kind, when such pain or suffering is inflicted by or at the instigation of or with the consent or acquiescence of a public official or other person acting in an official capacity". Those issuing an order to carry out torture are guilty of complicity or participation in the sense of article 4(1). Attempted torture should also be made punishable.

With regard to Article 4(2), while the Committee Against Torture as a whole did not comment on the appropriate level of sentences for torture, based on individual opinions of members, it is possible to conclude that the range within which such sentences for the offence of torture should fall would be somewhere between 6 and 20 years of imprisonment.[19]

The analysis of the replies given by the independent experts shows that the E.U. Member States are far from conforming to their obligations under Article 4 CAT. Member States fall largely into two main categories: States whose criminal laws explicitly make torture a crime and States who do not. In the former category one can make a division between States, where the definition satisfies the criteria set out by CAT (or is even broader) and where the sanctions correlate to the severe nature of the crime and States where this is not the case.

[19] See references in C. Ingelse, *The UN Committee Against Torture: An Assessment*, Chapter 11, § 3.1.2.

Category 1. Those States whose criminal laws explicitly make torture a crime include Belgium, Cyprus, Czech Republic, Estonia, France, Germany, Greece, Ireland, Luxembourg, Malta, the Netherlands, Portugal, the Slovak Republic, Spain and the United Kingdom.

However, within this category, in order for these States to comply with the requirements of Article 4(1) CAT, there must be a definition of torture in national legislation which complies with the criteria set out in Article 1 CAT and "adequate sanctions" as laid down in Article 4(2). It is unfortunate to note that, based on the responses of the independent experts and on the findings of the Committee Against Torture in the State reporting procedure, it would appear that some of those Member States whose criminal laws do explicitly make torture a crime, have either failed to incorporate a definition of torture altogether, do not adequately incorporate or at least not with the requisite amount of clarity, the definition of torture in their national legislation. This makes it also difficult to establish whether or not the penalties provided for are appropriate in the given circumstances.

For instance, while explicitly criminalising acts of torture, the **Netherlands** has failed to adopt a definition of torture.[20] In relation to **Estonia,** the Committee Against Torture pointed out that the definition of torture contained in Article 122 of the Penal Code as "continuous physical abuse or abuse which causes great pain" did not make adequately plain that *mental* suffering was also encompassed within the definition and therefore did not comply fully with Article 1 of the Convention. The Committee noted that, according to the delegation, Article 122 protects physical as well as mental health, but it was of the opinion that the wording of the article might lead to restrictive interpretations as well as confusion.[21] It recommended that the State party incorporate into the Penal Code a definition of the crime of torture that fully and clearly responded to Article 1 of the Convention.[22] While welcoming the possible direct applicability, under the Estonian Constitution, of the definition of torture set out in Article 1 of the Convention,[23] the Committee expressed concern that Article 1 of the Convention has not yet been directly applied by magistrates, and that the direct application of international human rights treaties, although possible in theory, is not widely practised in the courts.[24] The CAT pointed out in April 2006, that the **French** Criminal Code does not contain a definition of torture that is in conformity with Article 1 of the Convention, "an omission that can lead to confusion and adversely affect the collection of relevant data". It recommended that "a distinction be drawn between acts

[20] A/55/44, paras.181-188.
[21] CAT/C/CR/29/5, §C5(b). 23rd December 2002.
[22] CAT/C/CR/29/5, §D6(a).
[23] UN Doc. CAT/C/CR/29/5, B 4 (c).
[24] UN Doc. CAT/C/CR/29/5, C 5 (a).

of torture committed by or at the instigation of or with the consent or acquiescence of a public official or any other person acting in an official capacity, and acts of violence in the broad sense committed by non-State actors".[25]

Category 2: Those States whose criminal laws do not explicitly make torture a crime include Austria, Denmark, Finland, Hungary, Latvia, Lithuania, Poland, Slovenia, and Sweden

All States of the second category prefer to rely on traditional offence definitions, such as assault, ill-treatment or abuse of power provision in their criminal codes.

Defining and criminalising torture is important for a number of reasons which have been stressed by the Committee Against Torture in the State reporting procedure. Firstly, in explicitly making torture a specific offence as opposed to the traditional offence definitions, such as ill-treatment or abuse of power, with more severe penalties for public officials, a State party reinforces the moral abhorrence of the use of torture and acknowledges it as a threat to the very foundation of democracy.[26] At the same time such incorporation makes it easier to collect statistical data on the incidence of torture within each country and to compare implementation and practices across countries.[27] After ratification of the CAT many States continue to be opposed to changing their criminal codes. Taking **Austria** as an example, during the consideration of the Austrian report in 2005, Austria had argued that the existing provisions of the Penal Code were effective in preventing torture and that to introduce a special provision including the definition from the Convention in Austrian legislation would lead to duplication.[28] Another reason given by Austria for not having incorporated in its domestic legislation a definition of torture in line with that of the Convention was that it considered that its compliance with various national and international provisions afforded a higher degree of protection.[29] Mr. El Masry, Country Rapporteur drew attention to the fact that the present legal system in Austria recognised three different definitions of torture, which caused confusion and led to problems in data collection noting that a lack of conformity in the definition of torture could undermine efforts to eliminate that practice.[30] The Chairperson added that the purpose and circumstances of torture had an impact not only on the type of penalty imposed, but also on the application of universal jurisdiction. The latter was not compulsory but could be lawful in certain situations and the Committee attached great importance to information on State practice in

[25] UN Doc. CAT/C/FRA/CO/3.
[26] UN Doc. CAT/C/SR.415.
[27] UN Doc. CAT/C/SR.534, §19.
[28] UN Doc. CAT/C/SR.679, §7.
[29] UN Doc. CAT/C/SR.679, §55.
[30] Mr. El Masry, Country Raaporteur, UN Doc. CAT/C/SR.679, §20.

that connection with a view to combating impunity for international crimes.[31] **Denmark** is of the opinion that this was "legally unnecessary and only had symbolic value" preferring that torture be covered by provisions on violence and threats. In **Finland** torture is indirectly made a crime in domestic law under the provisions in the Penal Code related to assault and grave assault. The Committee reiterated its recommendation in 2006 that Finland enact specific legislation criminalizing torture in all its forms, as defined in Article 1 CAT.[32] In **Hungary** torture is also only indirectly covered by a set of rules regarding coercion, violation of personal freedom, kidnapping, malfeasance in office, abuse of authority, mistreatment in official proceedings, unlawful detention, and crimes against the person and sexual morality. **Latvia** only mentions torture as an aggravating factor to other crimes such as intentional serious bodily injury and intentional moderate bodily injury. In **Lithuania** torture falls under the provision in the Criminal Code on "injury, torture or other cruel, inhuman or degrading treatment of persons protected under international humanitarian law" and "serious health impairment". Although the Criminal Code of **Slovenia** refers to torture, it is not made a crime and remains undefined.[33] Finally, torture in **Sweden** is encompassed under the crime of assault. In 2002 the Committee recommended that Sweden incorporate in its domestic law the definition of torture set out in Article 1 of the Convention, and should characterise acts of torture and cruel, inhuman and degrading treatment as specific crimes, punishable by appropriate sanctions.[34]

Finally, turning to Article 4(2) and the question of adequate sanctions, bearing in mind the individual opinions of the Committee against Torture in its state reporting procedure, the Network would conclude a sentence of 2 years such as the case in **Austria** for maltreatment of a prisoner by a law enforcement agent would be too lenient whereas, a sentence of life imprisonment as provided for in, for instance, **Greece, Ireland, Luxembourg, the Netherlands** and the **United Kingdom,** would be too serious.[35]

b) The Principle of Non-Refoulement Under Domestic Law

According to Article 3(1) CAT "No State Party shall expel, return ("refouler") or extradite a person to another State where there are substantial grounds for believing that he would be in danger of being subjected to torture." According to Article 3(2), "For the purpose of determining whether there are such grounds, the competent authorities shall take into account all relevant considerations including, where applicable, the existence in the State

[31] UN Doc. CAT/C/SR.679, §50.
[32] UN Doc. CAT/C/SR/34/FIN.
[33] UN Doc. CAT/C/CR/30/4.
[34] UN Doc. CAT/C/CR/28/6.
[35] UN Doc. CAT/C/SR.234, §41, 51 and 76.

concerned of a consistent pattern of gross, flagrant or mass violations of human rights."

Specific provisions must exist in domestic law preventing expulsion, return (refoulement) and extradition to a country where there is a danger of torture being inflicted.[36] If there is no specific provision in domestic law then Article 3 must be directly applicable if the Convention is to be complied with.[37] Legal measures should also be taken to implement Article 3(2) which requires that the competent authorities take into account relevant considerations, including the existence in the State concerned of a consistent pattern of gross violations of human rights.[38]

The EU Member States' domestic systems in general contain various provisions regarding **expulsion** (a legal sanction against non-citizens), **extradition,** (on request of another State that wishes to exercise its jurisdiction over the person concerned), **deportation** (of aliens whose asylum claims were not successful), **return** (of an alien at the border of a State), and **transit** or **transfer** of indicted persons by foreign authorities.

Refoulement of asylum-seekers whose claim to asylum has been rejected.

Generally, it must be noted that the majority of EU Member States foresee non-refoulement provisions in their laws on asylum and the treatment of aliens that comply with the UN Convention relating to the Status of Refugees of 1951 (Refugee Convention). According to this convention no person shall be deported or returned to a country where he or she has a "well-founded fear of being persecuted for reasons of race, religion, nationality, membership of a particular social group or political opinion".

Other forms of removal

Article 3 CAT is much wider than the provisions contained in the Refugee Convention, which only apply to asylum seekers and refugees.[39] A person could very well not be persecuted for reasons of race, religion, nationality, membership of a particular social group or political opinion and still be at risk of torture.[40] The Committee has confirmed on a number of occasions, the absolute nature of Article 3[41]. Article 3 should be applicable to all aliens

[36] UN Docs. CAT/C/SR.26, §34; CAT/C/SR.34, §24; CAT/C/SR.34, §37; CAT/C/SR.34, §72; CAT/C/SR.52, §19; CAT/C/SR.59, §24; CAT/C/SR.61, §74; CAT/C/SR.77, §35; CAT/C/SR.79, §40CAT/C/SR.90, Add.1, §44; CAT/C/SR.91, §54; CAT/C/SR.92, §51; CAT/C/SR.93, §26; CAT/C/SR.98, §44; CAT/C/SR.158, §66; CAT/C/SR.195, §9; CAT/C7SR.164, §53; CAT/C/SR.166, §39; CAT/C/SR.169, §71.

[37] UN Docs. CAT/C/S/SR.26, §23; CAT/C/SR.26, §29; CAT/C/SR.65. §19. CAT/C/SR.89, §58; CAT/C/SR.92, §51; CAT/C/SR.93, §45; CAT/C/SR.108, §30; CAT/C/SR.145, §30; CAT/C/SR.168, §48.

[38] UN Doc. CAT/C/SR.93, §37.

[39] UN Docs. CAT/C/SR.13, §27; CAT/C/SR.12, §27; CAT/C/SR.52, §6; CAT/C/SR.65, §60; CAT/C/SR.79, §10.

[40] UN Docs. CAT/C7SR.65, §60; CAT/C/SR.91, § 54.

[41] UN Doc. CAT/C/SR.77, § 26.

not only to refugees[42] but also to others without such status[43] and including those who have not requested asylum[44]. Common criminals cannot be excluded from the application of Article 3[45] nor can those persons considered to be "threats to national security"[46]. Because of these differences the Network would like to reiterate that it is not sufficient for EU Member States to refer to general non-refoulement clauses under refugee and asylum laws in order to comply with Article 3 CAT.

A number of States claim that an explicit provision regarding the prohibition of expulsion/extradition/deportation in the case where the person concerned faces a serious risk of being tortured is not necessary as their laws generally oblige all public officials to act in accordance with their Constitutions, which often foresee a prohibition of torture, and international agreements, like the ECHR, the CAT, and the ICCPR. For example, in **Austria** the ECHR has the status of constitutional law and is directly applicable to any act of a public official. Also in **Belgium,** judges must apply Article 3 ECHR when deciding on expulsion or extradition and Article 3 CAT is applicable in cases where the authorities wish to return a foreigner at the border. According to the **Greek** Constitution, Article 3 CAT is directly applicable in cases of expulsion/extradition/deportation/transfer. Apart from this general constitutional rule the only explicit norm in Greek laws relates to the judicial expulsion of minors, according to which the deciding tribunal must take into consideration the serious risk to life, physical integrity or personal or sexual liberty of the minor in the country of return.[47] Regarding deportation, the **Maltese** Immigration Act refers to Malta's international obligations in cases of deportation. All other forms of return are governed by the direct applicability of the ECHR. No specific reference to the principle of non-refoulement in the sense of Article 3 CAT can be found in **Portuguese** laws. However, the Portuguese authorities are expressly obliged to apply international human rights treaties when cooperating with other States in criminal matters, like in extradition procedures.[48] The **Slovenian** Constitution establishes that extradition of aliens shall only be permitted in accordance with international treaties.

While general provisions linking the legality of any public act to the application of international obligations are desirable, the Network is of the opinion that such general clauses alone do not seem to be sufficient to guarantee a high degree of protection against torture in the receiving countries. They should be reinforced by specific provisions, not only at the

[42] UN Doc. CAT/C/SR.28, § 77.
[43] UN Doc. CAT/C/SR.63, § 37.
[44] UN Doc. CAT/C/SR.52, § 62.
[45] UN Doc. CAT/C/SR.32, § 15.
[46] UN Docs. CAT/C/SR.12, §21; CAT/C/SR.126, § 51.
[47] Article 74 of the Greek Criminal Code.
[48] Law 144/99, of 31 August, on International Cooperation on Criminal Matters.

constitutional level, in order to raise the awareness of the public authorities who have to implement expulsion/extradition/deportation decisions. Indeed, this is linked in a way to the positive obligation under Article 3 CAT to ensure that public officials have been made aware of their obligations and received special training or instructions on their Article 3 related obligations[49]; border police in particular should be trained in order to recognise torture victims and to ensure that bona fide victims are not sent back.[50] Immigration officials carrying out refugee status reviews should also receive training on their obligations under the Convention.[51]

Expulsion for reasons of public order. Some countries foresee a clear prohibition of expulsion as a criminal sanction against non-citizens in cases where the person concerned faces a valid threat that he or she will be subjected to torture. These countries include the **Czech Republic, Germany, Ireland** and **Lithuania.** In certain countries, such a prohibition is only made explicit with regard to certain categories of persons, such as persons who were granted subsidiary or temporary protection under refugee law **(Cyprus)** or persons who have obtained the status of refugee **(Hungary).**

Extradition. Extradition, i.e. the handing over of a person on request of another State that wishes to exercise its jurisdiction over this person or for execution of a court sentence, is explicitly prohibited in **Ireland** if there are substantial grounds for believing that the extradited person is in danger of being subjected to torture. The same is true in **Lithuania** and **Luxembourg.** Other countries have specific provisions regarding the inadmissibility of extradition of asylum seekers, refugees or persons under temporary protection, like **Cyprus, Hungary** and **Latvia. Estonian, Germany,** and **Polish** laws also provide for specific provisions that an extradition request is inadmissible if this cooperation is "in contradiction with general principles of the law, like the main international obligations" (Estonia), or the outcome of such cooperation is "patently incompatible with the law" (Germany), or if it would "contravene the law" (Poland).

The prohibition on extraditing persons to countries where they face the death penalty and corresponding domestic provisions are often quoted by Member States.[52] For example, in the absence of written guarantees, the laws of **Austria, Belgium, Denmark, Estonia, Finland, Hungary, Portugal,** the **Slovak Republic** and the **United Kingdom** provide for a prohibition of extradition in cases where the person would face the death penalty in the requesting State. At the same time, some States have legislation prohibiting extradition if there is a real risk that the person concerned will be subjected

---

49 CAT/C/SR.195, §9.

50 CAT/C/SR.12, §37; CAT/C/SR.10, §24; CAT/C7SR.13, §25; CAT/C/SR.126, §37; CAT/C/SR.197, §23.

51 CAT/C/SR.91, §22.

52 See Eur. Ct. HR, *Soering v. the United Kingdom,* judgment of 7 July 1989, Series A, n° 161.

to a flagrant breach of the right to a fair trial as guaranteed by Article 6 ECHR (e.g. the **Netherlands).** While welcome, standing alone, such provisions can not be deemed sufficient to cover a Member State's obligations under Article 3 CAT.

A problematic issue in regard to extradition is if it is left to the discretion of a governmental Minister to decide whether an extradition shall be permitted or not, like in the case of the **Slovak Republic.** Even though it can be argued that the respective Minister is also bound by international human rights treaties in his decision the Committee Against Torture has noted that under the CAT, States parties are not allowed any discretion in regard to Article 3 CAT.[53]

Deportation of foreigners without legal status in E.U. Member States is mainly governed by principles of the Refugee Convention. Nevertheless, a number of E.U. Member States make the risk of torture in the country of origin an explicit reason for inadmissibility of deportation, like the **Czech Republic, Finland, Germany, Hungary, Ireland, Poland** and **Sweden.** In addition to the prohibition of deportation, some States consider the risk of torture a reason for granting subsidiary or temporary protection, "alternative status", or providing the aliens in question with a residence permit, like **Cyprus, Denmark, Latvia,** and the **Netherlands.**

The **Czech** Law amending the Aliens/Asylum Act provides that a person can be deported regardless of the risk of torture if he or she is a danger to security or has been convicted for a serious crime. The Network reiterates in that respect the absolute nature of Article 3, which has been recalled in the introductory section of this part of the opinion.[54] Common criminals cannot be excluded from the application of Article 3[55] nor can those persons considered to be "threats to national security".[56]

Transit or transfer of persons. Finally, the provisions regulating transit or transfer of persons in the E.U. Member States seldom take into account a risk of torture when providing permission to transit or transfer. Only the general rule of direct application of international treaties apply in a number of States (see above), or there is a general prohibition of cooperation in criminal matters if it contravenes domestic laws and principles (**Estonia, Germany, Poland**). In the **Slovak Republic** bilateral agreements with Poland, Hungary, Slovenia and Austria contain specific clauses on

[53] UN Doc. CAT/C/SR.91, § 17.
[54] See also UN Doc. CAT/C/SR.77, §26.
[55] UN Doc. CAT/C/SR.32, §15.
[56] UN Doc. CAT/C/SR.12, §21; CAT/C/SR.126, §51.

this matter. In **Spain,** the transit of a sentenced person can only be effected in a manner which "respects the dignity and rights of the individuals"[57].

c) National Monitoring Mechanisms

The Optional Protocol to the United Nations Convention Against Torture (OPCAT)[58] foresees the establishment of a system of regular visits by independent international and national bodies to places of detention in order to prevent torture and other forms of ill-treatment. All States parties have an obligation to create or, if it already exists, to maintain such a national system within one year after the entry into force of the OPCAT or, once it is in force[59], one year after the ratification or accession. The OPCAT sets out specific guarantees and safeguards which must be respected by States parties in order to guarantee the effective and independent functioning of these bodies and to ensure that they will be free from undue interference. For instance, States must make available the necessary resources. States are left free to establish the form that these mechanisms will take whilst at the same time paying due regard to the Paris Principles.[60]

Denmark, Malta, Poland, Spain, Sweden and the **United Kingdom** have ratified OPCAT. The following EU Member States have neither signed, nor ratified OPCAT: **Germany,**[61] **Greece, Hungary, Ireland, Latvia, Lithuania, the Slovak Republic** and **Slovenia.** Other EU Member States have signed but not ratified OPCAT: **Austria, Belgium, Cyprus, Czech Republic, Estonia, Finland, France, Italy, Luxembourg, the Netherlands** and **Portugal.**

The EU member States can be divided into three categories:

- Firstly, those Member States who explicitly provide for national monitoring mechanisms in their domestic laws and who already have functioning national mechanisms which largely comply with the requirements of OPCAT. These countries include; The **Czech Republic, Denmark, Finland, Latvia,** the **Netherlands, Poland, Portugal, Slovenia, Sweden** and the **United Kingdom.** This opinion

[57] Article 18 of the Law 1/1979 of 26 September.

[58] The Optional Protocol was adopted on 18 December 2002 at the fifty-seventh session of the General Assembly of the United Nations by resolution A/RES/57/199.

[59] OPCAT currently has 18 ratifications. It will enter into force on the thirtieth day after the date of deposit with the Secretary-General of the United Nations of the twentieth instrument of ratification or accession.

[60] See Part IV OPCAT on national preventive mechanisms http://www.ohchr.org/english/law/cat-one.htm. See also, the Principles relating to the Status of National Institutions (Paris Principles) http://www.ohchr.org/english/law/parisprinciples.htm.

[61] On 26 April 2006, the federal government of Germany expressed its intention to sign OPCAT. The ratification is intended for 2007.

cannot be taken as a definitive judgement on compliance or non compliance with OPCAT however as concerns have been expressed regarding, for instance, the possible limited human resources available to certain national mechanisms (e.g. **Czech Republic, Poland, Slovenia**).

- Secondly, those EU Member States which do have national monitoring mechanisms but where these mechanisms do not largely comply with the provisions of OPCAT for one or more than one of the following reasons; there is no explicit provision establishing the monitoring mechanism in domestic law; the monitoring mechanism is not functionally independent; it cannot visit all places of detention; it is only reactive in nature. These countries include the following; **Austria, Belgium, Cyprus, Estonia, France, Greece, Ireland, Lithuania, Malta and the Slovak Republic.**
- Thirdly, those Member States which do not have such monitoring mechanisms. These countries include; **Germany, Hungary, Luxembourg** and **Spain.** It should be noted that Germany and Spain are currently in the process of setting up such a national body.

3. Access of the CPT and National Monitoring Bodies to Places of Detention

Based on the information which the Network has received, the following EU Member States do not have US/NATO military bases on their territory and there have been no instances in which the CPT or a national monitoring body[62] has asked for, but been refused access to, any places of detention: **Austria, Cyprus (government controlled area), Czech Republic, Estonia, Finland, France, Ireland, Latvia, Lithuania, Luxembourg, Malta, Poland, Portugal, Slovak Republic, Slovenia, Sweden.**

As far as the Network is aware, in the following countries, which do have US/NATO military bases on their territory, neither the CPT nor the national monitoring bodies have had access to these facilities; **Belgium, Denmark[63],**

[62] Where one exists, see preceding section, c).

[63] The only United States military base within the Danish Kingdom is the Thule Air base in Greenland. The main basis for the American presence in Greenland today is the 1951 Agreement on the Defense of Greenland. It follows from the amended Agreement that the provisions on jurisdiction of the NATO Status of Forces Agreement (NATO SOFA) apply. According to the 1951 Agreement "The Government of the United States of America shall have the right to exercise exclusive jurisdiction over those defense areas in Greenland", the CPT and/or national monitoring bodies will therefore not be able to access the Thule Air Base, since the areas are not within Danish jurisdiction. The provisions of the NATO Status of Forces Agreement are not seen to alter this point of departure.

Germany[64], **Greece, Hungary, the Netherlands, Spain**[65], and the **United Kingdom.**[66]

In the cases of the above countries, to the knowledge of the Network, there have been no instances where the CPT or, where applicable, the national monitoring body has been refused access to any other place of detention. In the absence of any information to the contrary, the Network can therefore presume that the CPT has never asked for access to US/ NATO military bases in EU Member States.

4. "Extraordinary Renditions"

The following paragraphs are concerned with the practice of CIA rendition flights and their legal as well as factual impact on Member States of the European Union. The main focus is put on what became known as "extraordinary renditions", i.e. transfers of detainees which are not in accordance with the law.[67] "Extraordinary renditions" infringe on various national and international laws, like the Convention on International and Civil Aviation of 7 December 1944 (Chicago Convention) and other bilateral aviation agreements, the principle of sovereignty and domestic laws regulating the

[64] In premises made available by the Federal Republic of Germany to the armed forces of foreign states signatory to the Agreement between the Parties to the North Atlantic Treaty regarding the Status of their Forces (NATO Status of Forces Agreement) of 19 June 1951 and to the Agreement to Supplement the Agreement between the Parties of the North Atlantic Treaty regarding the Status of their Forces with respect to Foreign Forces stationed in the Federal Republic of Germany (Supplementary Agreement to the NATO Status of Forces Agreement) of 3 August 1959 for their executive use, the military police of the force have in principle the right to exercise police powers (Article VII, paragraph 10 (a), NATO Status of Forces Agreement). However, without prejudice to the above-mentioned provisions, the German police are entitled to exercise their authority within such accommodation to the extent that the public order and safety of the Federal Republic of Germany are jeopardized or violated (Article 28 of the Supplementary Agreement to the NATO Status of Forces Agreement).

[65] There are four NATO military bases in Spain: Rota (Cádiz), Morón (Sevilla), Cartagena (Murcia) et Torrejón de Ardoz (Madrid). Other military bodies are connected with NATO operations.

[66] The following bases/facilities/ United States bases are publicly acknowledged to exist in the United Kingdom: Beck Row Family Hsg, Yildenhall, US Air Force; Eriswell Family Hsg Annex, Eriswell, US Air Force; Ipswich Storage Site, Ipswich, US Air Force; JMF St Mawgan, St Mawgan, US Navy; Lynn Wood Family Hsg, Thetford, US Air Force; NAVACT London UK, London, US Navy; Newmarket Fam Hsg Anx No 3, Newmarket, US Air Force; RAF Alconbury, Alconbury, US Air Force;RAF Barford St John Transmitter Annex, Barford St John, US Air Force; RAF Bicester, Bicester, US Air Force; RAF Chelveston Fam Hsg Anx, Rushden, US Air Force; RAF Croughton, Croughton, US Air Force; RAF Digby, Lincolnshire*; RAF Fairford, Fairford, US Air Force;RAF Feltwell, Feltwell, US Air Force; RAF Fylingdales*; RAF Hythe, US Army; RAF Lakenheath, Lakenheath, US Air Force RAF Leuchars, Scotland*; RAF Mildenhall, Mildenhall, US Air Force; RAF Mildenhall Storage Annex, Mildenhall, US Air Force; RAF Mildenhall Waste Annex, Mildenhall, US Air Force RAF Molesworth, Thrapston, US Air Force; RAF Molesworth Storage Anx No 12, Molesworth, US Air Force; RAF Oakhanger*; RAF Shepherds Grove Family Hsg Annex, Stanton, US Air Force; RAF Upwood, Upwood, US Air Force; RAF Welford Ammo Stor Area, Newbury, US Air Force. In addition it is claimed at http://www.kelebekler.com/occ/bas_gb.htm that there are some 31 installations for which no further details are available—although it does not list those marked* and the United States has two bases in British Indian Ocean Territory: Diego Garcia, Diego Garcia, US Navy; Diego Garcia, Diego Garcia, US Air Force and one at RAF Ascension Island, Ascension Island in the Atlantic Ocean.

[67] For the definition of "extraordinary rendition" see the introductory section to part II of this opinion.

legality of activities of foreign agents on the host State's territory, and, most importantly, a number of human rights provisions, including the right to personal liberty, freedom of movement and the prohibition of arbitrary expulsion, the right to a fair trial and, finally, the right not to be subjected to torture or other forms of cruel, inhuman or degrading treatment or to be brought to a country where there are substantial grounds for believing that the personal risk to be tortured is high (principle of non-refoulement).[68]

The concept of "extraordinary rendition" is not new[69] and was practiced already before 11 September 2001. After the attacks, media reports of such flights increased in the course of the "war on terror" and occasionally certain EU Member States were mentioned in the context of rendition flights.[70] In early 2005, the media and NGOs started to point out that the problem of "extraordinary rendition" was not only an issue that concerned the United States of America but that European States played a role in at least condoning this illegal practice by giving permission to the use of their airspace and airports.[71] As has been recalled in the introduction to this opinion, after reports emerged about United States' secret places of detention within Europe[72], the Council of Europe and the European Union reacted by setting up investigative mechanisms in order to clarify the involvement of European States and to reiterate their legal obligations in this respect. In addition to detailed media reports[73] and well-researched contributions from non-governmental organisations[74], official reports and opinions were prepared by the Council of Europe's Committee on Legal Affairs and Human Rights[75], the Council of Europe's Secretary-General[76], the

---

[68] Some scholars see the decisive difference between "ordinary" and "extraordinary" rendition precisely in the fact that suspected terrorists are being transferred to locations where they may be tortured in order to obtain information from them. See Association of the Bar of the City of New York, Center for Human Rights and Global Justice, Torture by Proxy: International and Domestic Law Applicable to "Extraordinary Renditions", 2004, available at: *www.abcny.org, www.nyuhr.org* (Torture by Proxy).

[69] See Center for Human Rights and Global Justice, *Beyond Guantánamo: Transfers to Torture One Year after Rasul v. Bush,* NYU School of Law, New York, 2005, pp. 19 ff. (Beyond Guantánamo).

[70] See for example the case of *Mohammed Al-Zery and Ahmed Agiza v. Sweden,* Decision of the UN Committee against Torture of 20 May 2005, or the case of Abu Omar, who was kidnapped by the CIA in Milan, Italy, and deported to Egypt.

[71] See for example Stephen Grey and Andrew Buncombe, Britain Accused Over CIA's Secret Torture Flights, The Independent, 10 February 2005.

[72] Dana Priest, CIA Holds Terror Suspects in Secret Prisons, Washington Post, 2 November 2005.

[73] See for example The Guardian, CIA Rendition Flights, available at *www.guardian.co.uk/usa/rendition.*

[74] See for example Beyond Guantánamo, cited above; Amnesty International, United States of America. Below the radar: Secret flights to torture and 'disappearance', AI Index: AMR 51/051/2006 of 5 April 2006 (Below the radar), Human Rights Watch, Statement on U.S. Secret Detention Facilities in Europe, 7 November 2005, available at http://hrw.org/english/docs/2005/1 1/07/usint1 1995.htm.

[75] Council of Europe, Parliamentary Assembly, Committee on Legal Affairs and Human Rights, Alleged secret detentions in Council of Europe member states, Information Memorandum II by Rapporteur Dick Marty, 22 January 2006 (Information Memorandum II).

[76] Council of Europe, Secretary General's report under Article 52 ECHR on the question of secret detention and transport of detainees suspected of terrorist acts, notably by or at the instigation of foreign agencies, 28 February 2006 (Article 52 ECHR Report).

Venice Commission[77], and the European Parliament's Temporary Committee on the alleged use of European countries by the CIA[78].

These reports make two issues regarding rendition flights perfectly clear. Firstly, there is proof that "extraordinary rendition" flights have taken place and that the CIA used an estimated 1,000 times European airspace and on various occasions European airports with aircraft declared to be civilian flights in violation of the Chicago Convention since 2001.[79] According to Mr. Dick Marty, "rendition affecting Europe seems to have concerned more than a hundred persons in recent years. Hundreds of CIA-chartered flights have passed through numerous European countries."[80]

Secondly, as the Council of Europe Secretary-General has pointed out, "virtually none of our Member States have proper legislative and administrative measures to effectively protect individuals against violations of human rights committed by agents of friendly foreign security services operating on their territory"[81].

Whereas the preceding sections in this part of the opinion were mainly concerned with the domestic legal framework of the EU Member States regarding torture and non-refoulement as well as the existence of national mechanisms for the prevention of torture, this section specifically deals with CIA rendition flights, the legal provisions governing such flights and investigations or other forms of action taken by the E.U. Member States in connection with allegations of "extraordinary rendition".

a) National Investigations into CIA Rendition Flights

Investigations into alleged violations of various international and domestic norms have been conducted on different levels. In a broader understanding of the term "investigation" the Network also takes into account requests for clarification through diplomatic channels as well as parliamentary hearings on this issue within the Member States.

In December 2005, the UK Presidency on behalf of the European Union officially requested clarifications from the United States Government. Additionally, a number of governments of the EU Member States have

[77] Council of Europe, European Commission for Democracy through Law (Venice Commission), Opinion no. 363/2005 on the International Legal Obligations of Council of Europe Member States in Respect of Secret Detention Facilities and Inter-State Transport of Prisoners, 17 March 2006.

[78] European Parliament, Temporary Committee on the alleged use of European countries by the CIA for the transport and illegal detention of prisoners, Draft Interim Report by Rapporteur Giovanni Claudio Fava, 24 April 2006 (Fava Report).

[79] Dan Bilefsky, EU inquiry links 1,000 flights to CIA, International Herald Tribune, 27 April 2006. Fava Report, cited above, para. 14.

[80] Information Memorandum II, cited above, para. 66.

[81] Notes for the press conference given by Terry Davies, Secretary-General of the Council of Europe, on 12 April 2006, available at: *www.coe.int/T/E/Com/Files/PA-Sessions/April-2006/20060412 Speaking-notes sg.asp*.

entered into bilateral communications with the respective US embassies in their country. Such consultations were initiated by **Austria, Finland, Germany, Ireland, Malta, Netherlands, Portugal** and **Spain.** In response, United States Secretary of State, Ms Condoleezza Rice, on her visit to Europe assured the Governments that the United States of America did adhere to international as well as national laws in the "war on terror", and in particular to the obligation not to torture.[82] A vast majority of Member States regarded these assurances given by the United States sufficient and did not conduct any other forms of investigations. For example, the Government of **Ireland** "are satisfied that they are entitled under the Convention [the European Convention on Human Rights] to rely on clear and explicit factual assurances given by the Government of a friendly state, on a matter which is within the direct control of that Government"[83].

Other forms of investigation have been carried out for instance in **Luxembourg,** where the Ministry of Foreign Affairs together with the Ministry of Transport are investigating two landings of two suspect aircraft in November 2005 and January 2006. However, the Network did not receive further information on these investigations. Also **Malta** indicated that the Ministry of Foreign Affairs was conducting investigations but no details of the results were conveyed to the Network. In addition, a Maltese MEP raised a Parliamentary Question before the European Parliament in relation to CIA rendition flights. Again, consequences or results of this inquiry remain unknown. Moreover, the **Dutch** Parliament has posed questions to members of the Government in this regard. The **Portuguese** Government has contacted the national technical services and after receiving all the relevant documentation concluded that there was no evidence that any aircraft of the type prescribed by the press, which would violate national and/or international law, used Portuguese airspace.

In the more narrow understanding of the term "investigations", i.e. criminal investigations, the Network comes to the conclusion that in the majority of EU Member States no official criminal investigations into the issue of alleged illegal CIA flights have been initiated. These countries include: **Belgium, Cyprus, Czech Republic, Denmark, Estonia, Finland, France, Greece,**[84] **Ireland, Latvia, Lithuania, Malta, Netherlands, Poland, Portugal, Slovak Republic** and **Slovenia.** In a number of cases the Governments and/or public prosecutors found that there was not enough evidence to officially launch investigations or that, according to the Governments,

---

[82] In the course of time the United States Government repeatedly made statements to this effect. See also second periodic report to the UN Committee Against Torture by the United States of America, UN Doc. CAT/C/48/Add.3/Rev.1 of 13 January 2006, Paras. 4-7.

[83] Article 52 ECHR Report, referred to above, Appendix, Reply of the Government of Ireland.

[84] Although it must be noted that Greek authorities were investigating into an alleged abduction of seven Greek men by British security forces. See BBC News, Greece to probe abduction claims, 13 December 2005, available at *http://news.bbc.co.uk/go/pr/fr/-/2/hi/europe/4526502.stm.*

no allegations had been made in this regard or that they were not aware of such illegal practices.

Such statements are completely contradictory to the existence of vast and well-founded information regarding allegations of "extraordinary rendition" flights in Europe. Or, as the European Parliament's Temporary Committee Rapporteur, Giovanni Claudio Fava, put it in his Draft Interim Report, "The European Parliament considers it implausible, on the basis of the testimonies and documents received to date, that certain European governments were not aware of the extraordinary rendition activities taking place on their territory and in their airspace or airports" (para. 8).

The latest report of Amnesty International on "extraordinary rendition" alone names 15 out of the 25 EU Member States in a comprehensive list of countries where CIA flights had landed in the past years.[85] Additionally, national NGOs and media consistently report on the use of the national airspace and airports by undeclared CIA flights, as for example in **Denmark,** where the Danish branch of Amnesty International has reported on twelve such incidents.

A small number of EU Member States have carried out further investigations, like **Austria** in the case of one overflight, **Hungary** in the case of two landings of one aircraft, and **Sweden,** where the Government has instructed the relevant departments and civil aviation authority to look into flights to and from Swedish airports by US registered aircraft since January 2002.

In the case of the **United Kingdom,** the Greater Manchester Police Chief only recently confirmed that he will investigate "extraordinary rendition" flights. These investigations, however, will only cover the territories of England and Wales, but not Scotland, where Amnesty International has spotted a substantive number of landings.

So far, only **Germany, Italy,** and **Spain** have initiated official criminal investigations into specific cases, which will be summarised briefly. In **Germany,** the public prosecution office in Zweibrücken and the Munich I public prosecution office have each launched an investigation on suspicion of unlawful deprivation of liberty. The first case concerns the alleged abduction of Abu Omar, an Egyptian citizen, by CIA agents in Milan, Italy and is investigated by the German authorities because of allegations that his "extraordinary rendition" flight to Egypt, where he has been allegedly tortured, stopped over at the United States military airbase in Ramstein, Germany. In the second case, the alleged abduction of the German citizen Khaled El Masri in Macedonia, no allegations of involvement of an EU

[85] Below the radar, referred to above. The report names Cyprus, Czech Republic, Estonia, Finland, France, Germany, Greece, Ireland, Italy, Malta, Netherlands, Poland, Portugal, Spain and the United Kingdom.

Member State were made. In both cases findings are not yet available. The case investigated by the **Italian** authorities also concerns the alleged kidnapping of Abu Omar by 13 CIA agents in Milan. In **Spain,** investigations were or still are undertaken regarding various landings of aircraft supposedly chartered by the CIA on airports in Palma de Mallorca, Ibiza and the Canary Islands.

Despite the fact that "extraordinary rendition" flights violate numerous international and national laws and that the alleged acts of abducting suspected terrorists, depriving them of their liberty without judicial control and, most of all, transporting them to countries where there are substantial grounds to believe that they will be tortured, constitute, directly or indirectly[86], criminal acts in all Member States of the European Union, and although a substantial number of these States seem to be affected by allegations of CIA rendition flights, the number of criminal investigations is very low. If anything at all, States rather take recourse to inquiries through diplomatic channels and seem to find the assurances given sufficient.

It should be emphasized however that States are under an obligation to promptly and effectively investigate alleged violations of laws, and generally to take appropriate steps to ensure respect for human rights within their jurisdiction. This implies in the present context that the EU Member States are now more than ever under an obligation to be more vigilant regarding future use of their airspace and airports by US private flight, in particular if the companies and aircraft numbers are on one of the published "black lists", but also to carry out investigations into alleged incidents of past "extraordinary renditions" in their airspace and on their territory.

With regard to proper investigations into past incidents, the Network holds the opinion that at least in those EU Member States that have been named in recent reports it is important to initiate independent investigations into all landings of US registered aircraft since 2001 in order to verify the accuracy of the NGO and media reports, as is currently done in **Sweden.**

b) Legal Means to Search Aircraft

All 25 EU Member States are States parties to the Chicago Convention of 1944, which regulates civil aviation. A number of provisions of this convention are relevant in the context of this opinion, in particular Article 1 (every State has exclusive and complete sovereignty over the airspace above its territory), Article 3 (b) (no State aircraft of a contracting State shall fly over the territory of another State or land thereon without authorisation) and Article 3bis (b) (the contracting States recognise that every State, in the

[86] See above questions 1 and 2.

exercise of its sovereignty, is entitled to require the landing at some designated airport of a civil aircraft flying above its territory without authority or if there are reasonable grounds to conclude that it is being used for any purpose inconsistent with the aims of the convention). These provisions have been relied on extensively in the discussion of the alleged misuse of civil aviation by the CIA transporting detainees either to the United States or to third countries.

This section deals specifically with the legal means of the EU Member States to search civil aircraft[87]once it is landed and prevent it from continuing transport if detainees are found on board who face a substantial risk of being tortured in the countries of destination or whose human rights risk otherwise being violated. In this respect, Article 16 of the Chicago Convention is of particular interest as it states that "the appropriate authorities of each of the contracting States shall have the right, without unreasonable delay, to search aircraft of the other contracting States on landing and departure". This provision does not elaborate specific reasons for such a search and leaves it to the States parties to regulate the details of this right. And indeed, a number of EU Member States have based national legislation on this provision. However, as shown by the Network's survey, States that do make use of the right to search are doing so mainly for reasons of customs, public order and security.

For instance, **Finland's** Frontier Guard Act provides border guards with the authority to stop and search vehicles entering the territory. Its Aviation Act foresees a possibility to prohibit the departure of an aircraft for reasons of public order and safety. According to the Civil Aviation Code of **France,** the Minister responsible for civil aviation or any person authorised by the Minister can carry out inspections of all aircraft landed on airfields located on French territory in order to ensure that they conform to security and safety standards. The Aviation Code of **Greece** foresees the possibility of provisionally preventing an aircraft from continuing its journey by ministerial order in case of violation of said code; the code, however, deals mainly with security and customs and does not contain a specific provision in regard to torture or other human rights violations committed on board. The Regulations of the Organisation of the Airspace of **Lithuania** provides that the Minister of Defence can authorise the search of an aircraft if there is suspicion that it carries illegal cargo. Also the **Maltese** Airports and Civil Aviation (Security) Act provides for searches for security reasons. In **Portugal,** the National Institute of Civil Aviation can immobilise an aircraft if security questions are at stake. The more detailed provision of the

[87] State aircraft is generally exempted from searches due to immunity provisions. However, State aircraft is subject to specific authorisation and it is a prerogative of State sovereignty to grant such authorisation.

Slovakian Civil Aviation Act grants the airport operator, who is responsible for safety and public order, the right to request explanations related to safety of life and health of persons, search any place, identify persons and arrest persons if necessary. Searches of vehicles for customs reasons are also foreseen in the State Border Supervision Act of **Slovenia.**

According to the Network's survey, a substantial number of EU Member States apply as a general rule the right and obligation of the authorities to search any premises where there is suspicion that a crime is being committed or was committed. Most of these provisions foresee that a police or security officer can enter and search the premises if there is imminent danger and the matter bears no delay. Otherwise, judges have the authority to issue a search warrant. Although, as noted above, not all EU Member States have made torture a crime under their domestic criminal laws and the CAT does not oblige the States to criminalise a violation of the principle of non-refoulement in relation to torture but rather to establish legal safeguards against the transfer of a person to a country where he or she faces torture, illegal deprivation of liberty is a crime in every Member State, and unauthorised activities by foreign State agents are prohibited in all States. Moreover, under Article 5 of the European Convention on Human Rights, the States parties to that instrument are under a positive obligation to protect the liberty of all persons under their jurisdiction. The European Court of Human Rights has recently noted that

> Any conclusion to the effect that this was not the case would not only be inconsistent with the Court's case-law, notably under Articles 2, 3 and 8 of the Convention. It would, moreover, leave a sizeable gap in the protection from arbitrary detention, which would be inconsistent with the importance of personal liberty in a democratic society. The State is therefore obliged to take measures providing effective protection of vulnerable persons, including reasonable steps to prevent a deprivation of liberty of which the authorities have or ought to have knowledge (see, *mutatis mutandis, Z and Others v. the United Kingdom* [GC], no. 29392/95, § 73, ECHR 2001-V, and *Ila_cu and Others v. Moldova and Russia* [GC], no. 48787/99, §§ 332-352 and 464, ECHR2004-VII).[88]

EU Member States that fall in the category of States authorising the respective authorities to search any premises, including landed aircraft, if there is suspicion or evidence that an illegal act under their respective criminal laws is or was committed, include: **Austria, Belgium, Denmark, Cyprus** (if the crime in question is punishable with more than two years imprisonment), **Netherlands** (the Royal Constabulary may inspect any aircraft that landed on Dutch territory if there is suspicion of a criminal act),

[88] Eur. Ct. HR (3d sect.), *Storck v. Germany* (Appl. N° 61603/00), judgment of 16 June 2005 (final on 16 September 2005), § 102.

the **Slovak Republic** (the Act on Police Corps empowers police officers to prevent the departure of any means of transport and carry out an examination if there is suspicion that a crime was committed; according to the Code of Criminal Procedure, a prosecutor can order the inspection of "other areas", i.e. places not for accommodation, and a police officer can enter any place if the entry is necessary in order to protect life and health, or rights and freedoms of persons), **Slovenia** and **Spain.** Within the same category falls the current opinion of the **United Kingdom** House of Lords, according to which: "If the aircraft is on the ground, the control authorities—the police, customs and immigration—already have a variety of powers to enter, take evidence and make arrests. For civil aircraft, the police could board an aircraft in the UK if they had reasonable suspicion that certain crimes were being committed within UK jurisdiction under UK law."[89]

This latter position reflects the general attitude adopted within the EU Member States. However, there are obvious practical difficulties with the implementation of such general provisions. As illustrated by the non-existence of such interventions or searches,[90] the authorities responsible have so far not seen the need to search United States civil aircraft with a view to crimes possibly committed on board. It remains to be seen whether these general rules for searches of premises will be applied more vigorously in the future, now that more and more evidence of criminal acts possibly committed on US civil aircraft comes to light and the authorities cannot simply refer to a lack of suspicion any longer. This is particularly true in case one of the airplanes known to be chartered by the CIA through private front companies landed on the national territory of an EU Member State. To rely on other services, like customs and air safety authorities, to notify the police in case they by chance encounter a suspicious situation during their routine inspections, as is the practice for instance in the **Netherlands,** is simply not enough.

Some EU Member States provide for more specific regulations in this regard. In **Belgium,** the law on air navigation foresees that the Executive could take any measure necessary to ensure compliance with obligations resulting from international treaties with regard to aircraft, its crew and its route. However, so far no such measures have been taken in regard to compliance with the CAT. Hungary's laws provide for the possibility of searching foreign aircraft only in case of suspicion that a crime is under commission or has been committed on the aircraft and that this illegal act is a crime under universal jurisdiction, which would be the case with the crime of torture but not with illegal deprivation of liberty. According to

[89] Statement by Lord Davies of Oldham (Deputy Chief Whip in the House of Lords), House of Lords, 28 March 2006.

[90] The opinion returns to the question hereunder.

the Aviation Law Act of **Poland,** the responsible State organs may call on a civil aircraft to change its course, land or perform other orders (including searches) if there are justified concerns that the aircraft is being used for illegal activities.

The Network's survey revealed that in fact only in **Ireland** Section 2 of the Criminal Justice (United Nations Convention Against Torture) Act implies the power to search aircraft suspected of being used to facilitate torture of individuals. Again, this is not an explicit provision regarding the matter. However, the Irish Minister of Foreign Affairs has indicated that this power exists and that it would be exercised if sufficient evidence was presented to the appropriate authorities.[91]

Although many of the domestic provisions listed above can be interpreted in a manner that includes searches for persons illegally deprived of their liberty, ill-treated on board of an aircraft or brought to countries where they face torture, no explicit provision in this regard exists throughout the European Union. Due to the relative novelty of this issue, it is not surprising that countries do not foresee such specific provisions. However, if national authorities are hesitant to make use of their powers implied in general provisions, either a specific change of legislation should be considered or the Governments should issue a clear policy that requires the respective authorities to firmly comply with the principle of legality also in regard to civil aviation.

In the opinion of the Network it is inadequate to state that so far no need has arisen to investigate into past landings or to routinely search U.S. civil aircraft at present and in the future because of a lack of suspicion while at the same time issuing blanket permissions to these aircraft without closely looking at the flight route or specifications of the aircraft, information that has to be provided also by civil aircraft in accordance with International Civil Aviation Organization (ICAO) rules. If an airplane with a registration number listed on the "black list" of aircraft, operated by a company known to be a front company for the CIA, with route Guantánamo Bay via, for example, Shannon, Ireland or Ramstein, Germany to Mitiga, Libya asks overflight clearance or landing permission for technical maintenance, then this should be enough suspicious information to justify a search of the aircraft.

However, such extreme cases cannot be considered the norm. Therefore, and in the light of current developments, the Network recommends that EU Member States should start to think about introducing a system of routine searches of civil aircraft by the responsible authorities in order to check compliance with international aviation regulations, like the

[91] Irish Times, 24 December 2005, p. 11.

Chicago Convention, issues of sovereignty as well as compliance with international and national human rights standards. Routine searches relating to customs regulations as well as security checks are already for a long time standard procedures and rigid searches for smuggled drugs, weapons or other goods are constantly on the agenda within the EU Member States. Now it is time to make routine searches relating to alleged severe human rights violations also a standard procedure in accordance with the States' positive obligations to protect human rights under their jurisdiction.

There is the possibility that in many cases the national authorities will not find a detainee on board, who is illegally detained and/or brought to a country where he/she faces a risk of being tortured. Also, it might turn out that the aircraft is indeed only used for a civil flight according to its declaration and in accordance with international law. However, the United States of America have repeatedly assured the international community that they did not violate national or international legal obligations in the "war on terror" and that they have nothing to hide. Therefore, there is no reason to believe that a routine search of aircraft should result in any kind of diplomatic or political consequences.

c) Involvement of National Authorities

The independent experts were asked whether they had knowledge of any cases after 11 September 2001 in which the authorities of their country have actively participated in CIA rendition flights. The information received on this question coincides to a large part with the official replies by the Member States to the Council of Europe's Secretary-General acting under his powers of Article 52 ECHR. In the cases of **Austria, Belgium, Cyprus, Czech Republic, Denmark, Estonia, Finland, France, Germany, Greece, Hungary, Latvia, Luxembourg, Malta, Netherlands, Portugal, Slovenia** and the **United Kingdom** the official statements by the Governments read that no public official or any other person acting in an official capacity has been involved in any manner—whether by action or omission—in rendition flights or that the Government had no knowledge of such an involvement. Neither is the Network aware of any information to the contrary.

However, as for example the Government of the **United Kingdom** has pointed out, under the current arrangements United States aircraft does not need clearance to use UK military airfields and no passenger lists have to be provided.[92] Therefore, the Government is not necessarily in a position to know whether their authorities are—unknowingly—involved in illegal

[92] Evidence of Harriet Harman (Minister of State, Department of Constitutional Affairs) to the parliamentary Joint Committee on Human Rights on UK compliance with the UN Convention Against Torture, 6 March 2006.

activities such as "extraordinary rendition" flights. This might also be the case in other E.U. Member States.

Although the Government of **Ireland** in its reply to the request of the Council of Europe Secretary-General has answered the question regarding any kind of involvement by Irish public officials clearly in the negative, the Network would point out that the Government has shown itself to be cognisant of the fact that six aircraft, believed to have been chartered by the CIA, landed and took off on 43 separate occasions from Shannon Airport since 11 September 2001[93].

Regarding **Italy,** the Government has stated that Italian authorities were certainly not involved in what they call "flying prisons" and denied governmental knowledge previous to the abduction of Abu Omar in Milan by CIA agents. However, the Council of Europe's Rapporteur Dick Marty asked whether it was "conceivable or possible that an operation of that kind, with deployment of resources on that scale in a friendly country that was an ally, was carried out without the national authorities being informed."[94]

Even though **Lithuania** has omitted to answer the respective question by the Council of Europe Secretary-General, the Network has received information that the Government has noted that the Ministry of Justice has neither received any request from the competent United States institutions to transport an arrested or sentenced person via the territory nor do they have information about the transportation by air without scheduled landings. The Government has underlined that it has no information about any landing on its territory of an aircraft with a prisoner on board.

Poland appears not to have answered the Council of Europe request in a satisfying manner. In particular, the Secretary-General criticised in his report that the Government has elided his question regarding transport of detainees through Polish territory. However, the Network has no additional information on any kind of involvement of Polish public officials.

The same criticism applies to the **Slovak Republic,** where the Government has given no reply regarding transport and has in general been unclear in its response regarding the involvement of Slovakian authorities in cases of illegal deprivation of liberty. At this stage, the Network is not aware of any publicly available information according to which there might have been any cases in which the State authorities of the Slovak Republic were involved in illegal transports of detainees in cooperation with the CIA. However, the Network observes that a possible collaboration of Slovakian authorities with the CIA in rendition flights has neither been

[93] Irish Times, 14 December 2005, p. 6.
[94] Information Memorandum II, referred to above, para. 46.

confirmed nor explicitly disproved by representatives of the competent State authorities.

Despite numerous allegations in **Spanish** domestic media regarding the landings of CIA rendition flights on airports of Palma de Mallorca, Barcelona, and the Canary Islands, and the fact that the Procurator of the Balearics lightened the controls of US aircraft shortly before the war in Afghanistan and declared that the passengers of these aircraft were to be considered diplomatic personnel, the Spanish Government insists that there has been no involvement whatsoever by Spanish officials in CIA rendition flight. A journalist of the newspaper "Diario de Mallorca", who published a report on more than 100 CIA aircraft landings on Spanish territory, stated in a public hearing before the European Parliament that in his opinion it was impossible that the Spanish authorities did not have any notice of this vast amount of air traffic. The governmental reply to the Article 52 ECHR investigation by the Council of Europe only referred to ongoing criminal investigations in this regard.

Finally, the Network notes that **Sweden** replied to the Council of Europe Secretary-General that, according to his question, *since 1 January 2002* there had been no involvement of Swedish public authorities in "unacknowledged deprivation of liberty [. . .] of any individual by or at the instigation of a foreign agency". However, in December 2001, two Egyptian men, Mohammed Al-Zery and Ahmed Agiza, had been arrested by Swedish police officers and handed over to the Egyptian authorities. The men were transported to Egypt, where they were subjected to torture. Following a communication filed before the Committee Against Torture, Sweden was found to have violated Article 3 of the CAT[95]. It will be noted that the Swedish Government had based its decision to proceed with the expulsion in December 2001 on a so-called 'diplomatic assurances' of fair treatment from the Egyptian authorities upon the return of Messrs Al-Zery and Agiza. The Committee nevertheless came to the conclusion that Sweden had violated Article 3 of the UN Convention against Torture and Cruel, Inhuman or Degrading Treatment or Punishment. In the view of CAT, the applicant had credibly alleged that he would be under a risk of torture after his forcible return to Egypt. The Committee stressed that assurances of the kind that has been given to the Swedish authorities could not protect Agiza from the risk of torture he faced upon return: "the procurement of diplomatic assurances, which, moreover, provided no mechanism for their enforcement, did not suffice to protect against this manifest risk"[96]. The Committee against Torture also pointed out that it "should have been known, to the

[95] Case of *Mohammed Al-Zery and Ahmed Agiza v. Sweden*, UN Doc. CAT/C/34/D/233/2003, 20 May 2005.

[96] UN Doc. CAT/C/34/D/233/2003, 20 May 2005, p. 34.

State party's authorities at the time of the complainant's removal that Egypt resorted to consistent and widespread use of torture against detainees, and that the risk of such treatment was particularly high in the case of detainees held for political and security reasons". Finally, the Committee made the observation that the applicant's retrial in an Egyptian military tribunal in April 2004 was deemed unfair by the Swedish authorities themselves.

d) Domestic Action Taken to Prevent CIA Rendition Flights

The independent experts were asked whether they knew of any cases after 11 September 2001 in which the authorities of their country have taken action to prevent CIA rendition flights and/or to protect CIA detainees against torture, cruel, inhuman or degrading treatment, including the principle of non-refoulement. The answers indicate that no such action was ever taken within any of the EU Member States, or that information of such action was unavailable. The same conclusions may be drawn from the replies of the EU Member States to the inquiry of the Council of Europe Secretary-General under the powers attributed to him by Article 52 ECHR. No indication can be found that any of the States has taken action in this regard, either by ordering or forcing an aircraft to land or by preventing it from carrying on after a stopover. Only in the case of **Spain** does there exist a report that the airport's technical services employees had routinely carried out maintenance tasks on US civil aircraft during which they had entered the planes. Reportedly, they had found nothing suspicious on board of the aircraft.[97] However, these routine inspections were conducted for technical security reasons and not in relation to any allegations of torture, ill-treatment or illegal deprivation of liberty of a person on board.

Regrettably, it seems highly unlikely that EU Member States will start to order US civil aircraft to land in order to be searched or prevent them from departure. However, such implications should be no excuse for the Member States to look away, condone illegal activities or even actively participate in them. On the contrary, in the light of all the information revealed by different sources and detailed lists of aircraft, which have been used in the past to transport persons suspected of terrorism, Member States cannot simply refer to the lack of sufficient evidence in order to get active.

A first step would be not to grant blanket or automatic overflight clearances to US aircraft declared as private flights. Meanwhile, political pressure should be applied on the United States not to circumvent the Chicago Convention by allowing State agencies like the CIA to charter

[97] Article 52 ECHR Report, referred to above, Appendix, Reply of the Government of Spain, pp. 15-16.

private aircraft.[98] To the knowledge of the Network, no explanation has been provided by the United States so far, why the CIA has resorted to the use of private aircraft in circumvention of international aviation laws. This question should be posed to the US Government, regardless of whether detainees have been illegally transported or not. The adherence to human rights obligations should be the main focus of EU Member States dealing with this issue. But additionally, it is also in the interest of the Member States to ensure that other States parties to the Chicago Convention do apply its provisions and thereby respect States' sovereignty. If political and diplomatic means turn out to be insufficient to put an end to the misuse of civil aviation regulations States should have the legal means (as well as the political will) to resort to routine searches of US aircraft.

In this context the Network recommends the holding of a high level conference between the United States, the European Union and its Member States in order to clarify the matter.

Additionally, the Network recommends that the Union should give a clear sign to accession States that participation in illegal activities like "extraordinary rendition" flights and detention on secret places will not be tolerated.

IV. Conclusions and Recommendations

- The European Parliament should clearly reaffirm its commitment to uphold the absolute character of the prohibition to expel, extradite, or return a person to a territory where that person runs a real risk of being subjected to torture or to cruel, inhuman or degrading treatment, or of being sentenced to the death penalty or to a trial in flagrant violation of the requirements of a fair trial. It should also express its position that the EU Member States cannot resort to diplomatic assurances as a safeguard against torture and ill-treatment where there are substantial grounds for believing that a person would be in danger of being subjected to torture or ill-treatment upon return.
- In accordance with their obligation under Article 4 CAT, all Member States of the European Union should make torture a crime under domestic law and provide for adequate sanctions. The provisions

[98] The exercise of diplomatic and political pressure may constitute one means through which a State party to the European Convention on Human Rights may fulfil its positive obligation to protect the rights and freedoms the Convention recognizes. See Eur. Ct. HR (GC), *Ilascu and Others v. Moldova and Russia*, at §§ 330-331 (referring to the positive obligation under Article 1 of the Convention of the defending State to "take the diplomatic, economic, judicial or other measures that it is in its power to take and are in accordance with international law to secure to the applicants the rights guaranteed by the Convention").

should contain a definition of torture that reflects the definition of Article 1 CAT.

- The principle according to which no individual should be subjected to a risk of torture or of cruel, inhuman or degrading treatment or punishment should be implemented in domestic laws through specific provisions within all laws governing expulsion, extradition, deportation, return, transfer or transit of persons by all Member States of the European Union.
- All Member States of the European Union should sign and ratify the Optional Protocol to the Convention against Torture (OPCAT) and accordingly establish independent national mechanisms to monitor places of detention. Due regard to the "Paris Principles" should be taken in the establishment of such mechanisms, in particular as regards their independency and legal status.
- The CPT and national monitoring bodies should be granted access to any place of detention within the Member States of the European Union, including foreign military bases.
- Effective and independent investigations into past incidents of CIA rendition flights over the territory of the Member States of the European Union or landings of such aircraft on airfields of Member States should be promptly carried out. In particular those Member States that have been named in recent reports should initiate independent investigations into all landings of United States aircraft since 2001.
- Introduction of specific legislation with regard to searches of civil aircraft in case of suspicion of human rights violations committed on board should be considered in all Member States of the European Union. A system of routine searches of United States civil aircraft in this respect would be desirable.
- No blanket or automatic overflight or landing clearances should be granted to United States civil or State aircraft.
- The European Union and its Member States should request assurances from the United States that United States public officials will not abuse international civil aviation regulations and will respect the principle of sovereignty. Where in the past such incidents have taken place, the European Union should request an explanation from the United States Government.
- A clear signal should be given to European Union accession States that participation in illegal activities like "extraordinary rendition" flights and detention on secret places will not be tolerated by the European Union.

DOCUMENT NO. 7

REPORT ON THE ALLEGED USE OF EUROPEAN COUNTRIES BY THE CIA FOR THE TRANSPORTATION AND ILLEGAL DETENTION OF PRISONERS

European Parliament

2006/2200(INI)

January 30, 2007

Motion for a European Parliament Resolution

on the alleged use of European countries by the CIA for the transportation and illegal detention of prisoners

(2006/2200(INI))

The European Parliament,

— having regard to its resolution of 15 December 2005 on the presumed use of European countries for the transportation and illegal detention of prisoners by the CIA[1],

— having regard to its decision of 18 January 2006 setting up a Temporary Committee on the alleged use of European countries by the CIA for the transportation and illegal detention of prisoners[2],

— having regard to its resolution of 6 July 2006 on the alleged use of European countries by the CIA for the transportation and illegal detention of prisoners, adopted midway through the work of the Temporary Committee[3],

— having regard to the delegations which the Temporary Committee sent to the Former Yugoslav Republic of Macedonia, the United

[1] *Texts Adopted*, P6_TA(2005)0529.
[2] *Texts Adopted*, P6_TA(2006)0012.
[3] *Texts Adopted*, P6_TA(2006)0316.

States, Germany, the United Kingdom, Romania, Poland and Portugal,

— having regard to the hearings, numbering no fewer than 130, held by the Temporary Committee in the course of its meetings, delegation missions and confidential interviews,

— having regard to all the written contributions received by the Temporary Committee or to which it has had access, particularly the confidential documents forwarded to it (in particular by the European Organisation for the Safety of Air Navigation (Eurocontrol) and the German Government or which it has obtained from various sources,

— having regard to its resolution of 30 November 2006 on the progress made in the EU towards the Area of freedom, security and justice (AFSJ) (Articles 2 and 39 of the EU Treaty)[4], notably its paragraph 3,

— having regard to its resolution of 13 June 2006 on the situation of prisoners at Guantánamo[5],

— having regard to Rule 175 of its Rules of Procedure,

— having regard to the report of the Temporary Committee on the alleged use of European countries by the CIA for the transportation and illegal detention of prisoners (A6-0020/2007),

A. whereas, in its resolution of 6 July 2006, Parliament decided that 'the Temporary Committee would continue its work for the remainder of its established twelve-month term, without prejudice to the provisions of Rule 175 of its Rules of Procedure on the possibility of extending the term',

B. whereas, in adopting its resolution of 22 November 1990 on the Gladio affair[6], it drew attention, more than 16 years ago, to the existence of clandestine operations involving intelligence services and military organisations without adequate democratic control,

C. whereas the Member States cannot circumvent the requirements imposed on them by European Community (EC) and international law by allowing other countries' intelligence services, which are subject to less stringent legal provisions, to work on their territory; whereas, in addition, the operations of intelligence services are consistent with fundamental rights only if adequate arrangements exist for monitoring them,

[4] *Texts Adopted*, P6_TA-PROV(2006)0525.
[5] *Texts Adopted*, P6_TA(2006)0254.
[6] OJ C 324, 24.12.1990, p. 201.

D. whereas the principle of the inviolability of human dignity is enshrined in international human rights law, notably in the preamble to the Universal Declaration of Human Rights and the preamble to and Article 10 of the International Covenant on Civil and Political Rights, and whereas that principle is guaranteed by the jurisprudence of the European Court of Human Rights; whereas this principle appears in most Member States' constitutions, as well as in Article 1 of the Charter of Fundamental Rights of the European Union[7] and whereas that principle should not be undermined, even for the purposes of security, in times of peace or war,

E. whereas the principle of inviolability of human dignity underlies every other fundamental right guaranteed by international, European and national human rights instruments, in particular the right to life, the right to freedom from torture and inhuman or degrading treatment or punishment, the right to liberty and security, the right to protection in the event of removal, expulsion or extradition and the right to an effective remedy and to a fair trial,

F. whereas extraordinary rendition and secret detention involve multiple violations of human rights, in particular violations of the right to liberty and security, the freedom from torture and cruel, inhuman or degrading treatment, the right to an effective remedy, and, in extreme cases, the right to life; whereas, in some cases, where rendition leads to secret detention, it constitutes enforced disappearance,

G. whereas the prohibition of torture is a peremptory norm of international law *(jus cogens)* from which no derogation is possible and the obligation to protect against, investigate and sanction torture is an obligation owed by all states *(erga omnes)*, as provided by Article 5 of the Universal Declaration of Human Rights, Article 7 of the International Covenant on Civil and Political Rights, Article 3 of the European Convention for the Protection of Human Rights and Fundamental Freedoms (ECHR) and the related case law, Article 4 of the Charter of Fundamental Rights, and national constitutions and laws; whereas specific conventions and protocols on torture and monitoring mechanisms adopted at the European and international level demonstrate the importance attached to this inviolable norm by the international community; whereas the use of diplomatic assurances is incompatible with this obligation,

H. whereas in democracies in which the respect for the rules of law is inherent, the fight against terrorism cannot be won by sacrificing or limiting the very principles that terrorism seeks to destroy, notably, the protection of human rights and fundamental freedoms must never be compromised;

[7] OJ C 364, 18.12.2000, p. 1.

whereas terrorism can and must be fought by legal means and must be defeated while respecting international and national law,

I. whereas the United States (US) administration's strategy to combat terrorism has made use of pervasive instruments to monitor sensitive data relating to European citizens, such as the Passenger Names Record (PNR) agreement, and to monitor bank details through the Society for Worldwide Interbank Financial Telecommunication (Swift) network,

J. whereas on 6 September 2006, US President George W. Bush confirmed that the Central Intelligence Agency (CIA) was operating a secret detention programme outside the United States,

K. whereas President George W. Bush said that the vital information derived from the extraordinary rendition and secret detention programme had been shared with other countries and that the programme would continue, which raises the strong possibility that some European countries may have received, knowingly or unknowingly, information obtained under torture,

L. whereas the Temporary Committee has obtained, from a confidential source, records of the informal transatlantic meeting of European Union (EU) and North Atlantic Treaty Organisation (NATO) foreign ministers, including US Secretary of State Condoleezza Rice, of 7 December 2005, confirming that Member States had knowledge of the programme of extraordinary rendition, while all official interlocutors of the Temporary Committee provided inaccurate information on this matter,

M. whereas the Temporary Committee has obtained, from a confidential source, records of meetings of the Council's Working Party on Public International Law (COJUR) and Transatlantic Relations Working Party (COTRA) with senior representatives of the US Department of State during the first half of 2006 (notably on 8 February and 3 May 2006), while it was provided by the Council Presidency only with a summarised version of these documents; whereas the documents sent by the Council to Parliament concerning those meetings in answer to Parliament's specific request, were incomplete summaries of the proceedings with essential parts missing,

N. whereas the information on these meetings was not notified to Parliament and absolute secrecy was maintained in relation to their proceedings,

O. whereas, in the present resolution, 'European countries' should be understood as meaning Member States and candidate and associate countries, as outlined in the mandate of the Temporary Committee adopted on 18 January 2006,

1. Recalls that terrorism represents one of the main threats to the security of the European Union and that it must be fought with lawful and coordinated efforts by all European governments, in close collaboration with

international partners and notably with the United States, along the lines of the strategy defined at United Nations (UN) level; underlines that the fight against terrorism must be fought on the basis of, and in order to protect, our common values of democracy, the rule of law, human rights and fundamental freedoms; furthermore stresses that all the work carried out by the Temporary Committee is intended to make a contribution towards the development of clear and focused measures in the fight against terrorism, which are commonly accepted and respect national and international law;

2. Considers that after 11 September 2001, the so-called 'war on terror' -in its excesses- has produced a serious and dangerous erosion of human rights and fundamental freedoms, as noted by the outgoing UN Secretary-General Kofi Annan;

3. Is convinced that the rights of the individual and full respect for human rights contribute to security; considers it necessary that in the relationship between the need for security and the rights of individuals, human rights must always be fully respected, ensuring that suspected terrorists are tried and sentenced while due process is observed;

4. Emphasises that the positive obligation to respect, protect and promote human rights is binding, regardless of the legal status of the individual concerned, and that any discrimination among EU nationals, residents of Member States or any other person entitled to protection from, or otherwise under the jurisdiction of, the Member States must be avoided;

5. Recalls that the purpose of this resolution, based on the report of the Temporary Committee, is to determine responsibilities for the facts that it has been able to examine on the one hand and to consider ways of preventing any repetition of the abuses and violations perpetrated in connection with measures against terrorism on the other;

6. Notes the statement made by US President George W. Bush on 6 September 2006, according to whom "a small number of suspected terrorist leaders and operatives captured during the war have been held and questioned outside the United States, in a separate programme operated by the CIA" and that many of the persons who had been detained there, had subsequently been transferred to Guantánamo and it is strongly suspected that other prisoners are still held in secret places of detention; notes the report of the Federal Bureau of Investigation (FBI) of 2 January 2007 mentioning 26 testimonies of mistreatment in Guantánamo since 11 September 2001;

7. Deplores, in this context, the inability of the Council—due to the opposition of certain Member States—to adopt conclusions in response to that statement at the General Affairs and External Relations Council of 15 September 2006, and requests that the Council adopt them urgently,

to dissipate any doubt as to the Member State governments' cooperation with and connivance in the extraordinary rendition and secret prisons programme in the past, present and future;

8. Calls on the Council and the Member States to issue a clear and forceful declaration calling on the US Administration to put an end to the practice of extraordinary arrests and renditions, in line with the position of Parliament;

9. Deplores the fact that the governments of European countries did not feel the need to ask the US administration for clarifications regarding the existence of secret prisons outside US territory;

10. Notes the statements by the legal adviser to the US State Department at a meeting on 3 May 2006 with representatives of the Member States meeting within the Council, according to which, in carrying out the extraordinary rendition programme, whose existence he confirmed, the sovereignty of the countries concerned had always been fully respected; notes that this remark was subsequently confirmed at the meeting with the Temporary Committee delegation which visited Washington;

11. Thanks the former CIA agents who agreed to cooperate with the Temporary Committee, particularly at certain confidential meetings at which they confirmed that the extraordinary rendition programme had already begun during the 1990s;

12. Welcomes the announcement by the new majority established by the elections to the US Senate that it will investigate the CIA's extraordinary rendition programme; notes that this is further confirmation of the relevance of the work of the Temporary Committee;

13. Denounces the lack of cooperation of many Member States, and of the Council of the European Union towards the Temporary Committee; stresses that the behaviour of Member States, and in particular the Council and its Presidencies, has fallen far below the standard that Parliament is entitled to expect;

14. Believes that the serious lack of concrete answers to the questions raised by victims, non-governmental organisations (NGOs), the media and parliamentarians has only strengthened the validity of already well-documented allegations;

15. Stresses the serious and rigorous work undertaken by the judicial authorities of Italy, Germany and Spain concerning the allegations which fall within the remit of the Temporary Committee, and invites the judicial authorities in other Member States to act similarly on the basis of the substantial information made available by the Temporary Committee;

16. Encourages the national parliaments of European countries to continue or launch thorough investigations, in the ways they consider

most appropriate and efficient, into these allegations, including by setting up parliamentary committees of inquiry;

17. Pays tribute to the world press, in particular the US journalists who were the first to disclose the abuses and breaches of human rights related to extraordinary rendition, thus demonstrating the great democratic tradition of the US press; also recognises the efforts and good work undertaken by several NGOs on these matters, in particular Statewatch, Amnesty International and Human Rights Watch;

18. Recognises that some information in this report, including the existence of secret CIA prisons, comes from official or unofficial US sources, demonstrating the vitality and self-policing inherent in the US democracy;

19. Expresses its profound gratitude to all victims who had the courage to share their very traumatic experiences with the Temporary Committee;

20. Calls on all European countries to refrain from taking any action against officials, former officials, journalists or others who, by providing testimony or other information, either to the Temporary Committee or to other investigating bodies, have helped shed light on the system of extraordinary rendition, illegal detention and the transportation of terrorism suspects;

21. Reiterates its call on the Council, as expressed in its resolution of 6 July 2006, to adopt a common position ruling out the acceptance of mere diplomatic assurances from third countries as a basis for any legal extradition provision, where there are substantial grounds for believing that individuals would be in danger of being subjected to torture or ill-treatment;

Cooperation with EU Institutions and International Organisations

22. Deplores the failure by the Council and its Presidency to comply with their obligations to keep Parliament fully informed of the main aspects and basic choices of the common foreign and security policy (CFSP) and of work carried out in the field of police and judicial cooperation in criminal matters pursuant to Articles 21 and 39 of the Treaty on European Union;

23. Stresses, in this context, that it is wholly unacceptable that the Council should first have concealed and then, at Parliament's request, only supplied piecemeal information on the regular discussions held with senior officials of the US Administration, asserting that this was the only available version; furthermore denounces the fact that the Council also referred to the request by the government of a third country that the information remain confidential;

24. Points out that these shortcomings of the Council implicate all Member State governments since they have collective responsibility as members of the Council;

25. Is outraged by the proposal which was to have been made by the then Council Presidency to set-up a joint "framework" with the US on standards for the rendition of terrorism suspects, as confirmed by those who took part in the meeting of the Council's Working Party on Public International Law (COJUR) and the Transatlantic Relations Working Party (COTRA) with senior representatives of the US Department of State held in Brussels on 3 May 2006;

26. Calls for the disclosure of the results of the discussions conducted with the United States, according to Gijs de Vries, on the definitions of "rendition" and "extraordinary rendition";

27. Takes note of the fact that the Secretary-General (and High Representative for the Common Foreign and Security Policy (CFSP)) of the Council of the European Union, Javier Solana, reaffirmed that Member States must ensure that any measures they take to combat terrorism comply with their obligations under international law; expresses its concern about the omissions in the statements made to the Temporary Committee by the Secretary-General, regarding the Council's discussions and knowledge of the methods used by the United States in its campaign against terrorism; deplores the fact that he was unable to supplement the evidence already in the possession of the Temporary Committee; asks him to declare all facts and discussions that are within his knowledge and to promote a European foreign policy and an international anti-terrorism strategy that respect human rights and fundamental freedoms;

28. Questions the real substance of the post of EU Counter-terrorism Coordinator occupied by Gijs de Vries, since he was unable to give satisfactory answers to the questions raised by the Temporary Committee; is of the opinion that a revision and strengthening of his competences and powers, as well as the increased transparency and monitoring of his activities by Parliament must be undertaken in the near future, so as to enhance the European dimension of the fight against terrorism;

29. Deplores the refusal by the Director of the European Police Office (Europol), Max-Peter Ratzel, to appear before the Temporary Committee, particularly because it has emerged that liaison officers, in particular for the US intelligence services, were seconded to the Office; requests that he provide Parliament with comprehensive information concerning the role of those liaison officers, their tasks, the data to which they had access and the conditions for such access;

30. Thanks Commission Vice-President Franco Frattini for his cooperation with the work of the Temporary Committee and encourages the Commission to step up its work in the context of the continuing efforts to ascertain the truth and find ways of preventing any repetition of the facts analysed by the Temporary Committee;

31. Welcomes, in particular, the commitment shown by Vice-President Frattini to launching a Euro-Atlantic cooperation framework in the fight against international terrorism, with harmonised rules on the protection of human rights and fundamental freedoms;

32. Thanks Eurocontrol, and notably its Director, for its excellent cooperation and for the very useful information which it shared with the Temporary Committee;

33. Appreciates the close cooperation which it has maintained with the Council of Europe, particularly its Parliamentary Assembly and its Secretary-General, and encourages the Committee on Legal Affairs and Human Rights—and its Chairman, Senator Dick Marty—to continue its work; endorses the recommendations made to the Committee of Ministers by the Secretary-General, Terry Davis; stresses the convergence of the findings of the two committees to date;

34. Expresses its deep concern with the refusals of the former and current Secretaries-General of NATO, Lord Robertson and Jaap de Hoop Scheffer, to appear before the Temporary Committee or with that organisation's rejection of its request for access to the decision taken by the North Atlantic Council on 4 October 2001 concerning the implementation of Article 5 of the North Atlantic Treaty following the attacks on the United States on 11 September 2001; reiterates its request to make the document public and at least to provide information on its contents, its past and current implementation, whether it still remains into force and whether CIA flights have operated within its framework;

35. Thanks the special rapporteurs of the United Nations, Manfred Nowak (on torture) and Martin Scheinin (on the promotion and protection of human rights in connection with counter-terrorism measures) for their contributions to the work of the Temporary Committee, while regretting that it was not possible for the High Commissioner for Human Rights, Louise Arbour, to meet it; thanks the European Network of Experts on Human Rights and notably its Co-ordinator, Olivier De Schutter, for their contribution to the works of the Temporary Committee;

Information Analysed by the Temporary Committee

Extraordinary Rendition and the Misuse of Airspace and Airports

36. Recalls that the programme of extraordinary rendition is an extra-judicial practice which contravenes established international human rights standards and whereby an individual suspected of involvement in terrorism is illegally abducted, arrested and/or transferred into the custody of US officials and/or transported to another country for interrogation which, in the majority of cases, involves *incommunicado* detention and torture;

37. Deplores the fact that the families of the victims are kept in complete ignorance of the fate of their relatives;

38. Underlines, not withstanding an intended confusion created by some US representatives in private and public speeches, that extraordinary rendition is a wholly different practice from one that has been used by some European countries only in very exceptional circumstances, namely the detention or reception into custody in third countries of individuals formally accused of very serious crimes, in order to transfer them to European soil in order to face criminal charges before a court with all the legal guarantees of a judicial system;

39. Condemns extraordinary rendition as an illegal instrument used by the United States in the fight against terrorism; condemns, further, the acceptance and concealing of the practice, on several occasions, by the secret services and governmental authorities of certain European countries;

40. Condemns any participation in the interrogation of individuals who are victims of extraordinary rendition, because it represents a deplorable legitimisation of that type of illegal procedure, even where those participating in the interrogation do not bear direct responsibility for the kidnapping, detention, torture or ill-treatment of the victims;

41. Considers that the practice of extraordinary rendition has been shown to be counterproductive in the fight against terrorism and that extraordinary rendition in fact damages and undermines regular police and judicial procedures against terrorism suspects;

42. Stresses that at least 1 245 flights operated by the CIA flew into European airspace or stopped over at European airports between the end of 2001 and the end of 2005, to which should be added an unspecified number of military flights for the same purpose; recalls that, on one hand, there may have been more CIA flights than those confirmed by the investigations carried out by the Temporary Committee, while, on the other hand, not all those flights have been used for extraordinary rendition;

43. Regrets that European countries have been relinquishing their control over their airspace and airports by turning a blind eye or admitting flights operated by the CIA which, on some occasions, were being used for extraordinary rendition or the illegal transportation of detainees, and recalls their positive obligations arising out of European Court of Human Rights case law, as reiterated by the European Commission for Democracy through Law (Venice Commission);

44. Is concerned, in particular, that the blanket overflight and stopover clearances granted to CIA-operated aircraft may have been based, inter alia, on the NATO agreement on the implementation of Article 5 of the North Atlantic Treaty, adopted on 4 October 2001;

45. Recalls that Article 1 of the Convention on International Civil Aviation (the Chicago Convention) sets out the principle that contracting States have complete and exclusive sovereignty over the airspace above its territory, and accordingly does not imply any exclusion from the States' full responsibility for the observance of human rights within their territory, including the airspace above it;

46. Emphasises that the CIA has been using civil aviation rules to bypass the legal obligations for state aircraft, including those operated by the military and the police, as provided in the Chicago Convention; recalls that Article 4 of the Chicago Convention provides that: "Each contracting State agrees not to use civil aviation for any purpose inconsistent with the aims of this Convention";

47. Confirms, in view of the additional information received during the second part of the proceedings of the Temporary Committee, that it is unlikely that certain European governments were unaware of the extraordinary rendition activities taking place in their territory;

48. Stresses that the Temporary Committee's working documents Nos 7 and 8[8] provide strong evidence of the extraordinary renditions analysed by the committee, as well as of the companies linked to the CIA, the aircraft used by the CIA and the European countries in which CIA aircraft made stopovers;

Italy

49. Deplores the fact that the representatives of the current and former Italian Governments who are or were responsible for the Italian secret services declined the invitation to appear before the Temporary Committee;

50. Condemns the extraordinary rendition by the CIA of the Egyptian cleric Abu Omar, who had been granted asylum in Italy and who was abducted in Milan on 17 February 2003, transferred from Milan to the NATO military base of Aviano by car, and then flown, via the NATO military base of Ramstein in Germany, to Egypt, where he has been held *incommunicado* and tortured ever since;

51. Condemns the active role played by a carabinieri marshal and certain officials of the Italian military security and intelligence services (SISMI) in the abduction of Abu Omar, as shown by the judicial investigation and the evidence collated by Milan's Public Prosecutor Armando Spataro;

52. Concludes, and deplores the fact, that General Nicolò Pollari, former Director of the SISMI, concealed the truth while appearing before the Temporary Committee on 6 March 2006, when he stated that Italian agents

[8] Reference numbers: PE 380.593v04-00 and PE 380.984v02-00.

had played no part in any CIA kidnapping and that the Italian intelligence services were not aware of the plan to kidnap Abu Omar;

53. Considers it very likely, in view of the involvement of its secret services, that the Italian Government of the day was aware of the extraordinary rendition of Abu Omar from within its territory;

54. Thanks Public Prosecutor Spataro for his testimony to the Temporary Committee, applauds the efficient and independent investigations he carried out in order to shed light on the extraordinary rendition of Abu Omar and fully endorses his conclusions and the decision to bring to judgment 26 US nationals, CIA agents, seven senior officials of the SISMI, an ROS carabiniere and the assistant editor of the 'Libero' daily newspaper; welcomes the opening of the proceedings at the Milan Court;

55. Regrets that the abduction of Abu Omar jeopardised Public Prosecutor Spataro's investigation into the terrorist network to which Abu Omar was connected; recalls that had Abu Omar not been illegally seized and transported to another country, he would have faced a regular and fair trial in Italy;

56. Takes note that the testimony provided by General Pollari is inconsistent with a number of documents found on SISMI premises and confiscated by Milan prosecutors; considers that such documents show that the SISMI was regularly informed by the CIA about the detention of Abu Omar in Egypt;

57. Deeply regrets the systematic misleading, among others, of Milan prosecutors by the SISMI board with the aim of jeopardising the investigation into the extraordinary rendition of Abu Omar; is extremely concerned about the fact that the SISMI board appeared to be working to a parallel agenda, and about the lack of appropriate internal and governmental controls; requests the Italian Government to remedy this situation urgently by establishing enhanced parliamentary and governmental controls;

58. Condemns the fact that Italian journalists investigating the extraordinary rendition of Abu Omar were illegally pursued, that their telephone conversations were tapped and their computers were confiscated; stresses that testimonies from those journalists have been of the utmost benefit to the work of the Temporary Committee;

59. Criticises the length of time it took for the Italian Government to decide to remove from office and replace General Pollari;

60. Regrets that a document on US-Italian cooperation in the fight against terrorism, which would have assisted the investigation into the extraordinary rendition of Abu Omar, was classified by the former Italian Government and that the current government has confirmed the classified status of this document;

61. Urges the Italian Minister of Justice to process, as soon as possible, the requests for extradition of the 26 US nationals referred to, for the purpose of standing trial in Italy;

62. Condemns the extraordinary rendition of Italian citizen Abou Elkassim Britel, who was arrested in Pakistan in March 2002 by the Pakistani police and interrogated by US and Pakistani officials, and subsequently rendered to the Moroccan authorities and imprisoned in the detention facility 'Temara', where he remains detained; emphasises that the criminal investigations in Italy against Abou Elkassim Britel were closed without any charges being brought;

63. Regrets that, according to the documentation provided to the Temporary Committee by Abou Elkassim Britel's lawyer, the Italian Ministry of Internal Affairs was at the time in 'constant cooperation' with foreign secret services concerning the case of Abou Elkassim Britel following his arrest in Pakistan;

64. Urges the Italian Government to take concrete steps in order to obtain the immediate release of Abou Elkassim Britel and Abu Omar so that proceedings against the latter can be prosecuted in the Court of Milan;

65. Deeply regrets that Italian territory was used by the CIA to make a stopover during the flight that was used to carry out the extraordinary rendition of Maher Arar, who gave testimony to the Temporary Committee, from the United States to Syria, via Rome;

66. Notes the 46 stopovers made by CIA-operated aircraft at Italian airports and expresses serious concern about the purpose of those flights which came from or were bound for countries linked with extraordinary rendition circuits and the transfer of detainees; deplores the stopovers at Italian airports of aircraft which have been shown to have been used by the CIA on other occasions for the extraordinary rendition of, Bisher Al-Rawi, Jamil El-Banna, Abou Elkassim Britel, Khaled El-Masri, Binyam Mohammed, Abu Omar and Maher Arar and for the expulsion of Ahmed Agiza and Mohammed El Zari;

The United Kingdom

67. Deplores the manner in which the UK Government, as represented by its Minister for Europe, cooperated with the Temporary Committee; is extremely surprised at the letter of the Minister sent to Parliament's President,

68. Thanks the All-Party Parliamentary Group on Extraordinary Renditions (APPG), comprising members of the House of Commons and the House of Lords, for its work and for providing the Temporary Committee delegation to London with a number of highly valuable documents;

69. Condemns the extraordinary rendition of Bisher Al-Rawi, an Iraqi citizen and resident of the United Kingdom, and Jamil El-Banna, a Jordanian citizen and resident of the United Kingdom, who were arrested by Gambian authorities in Gambia in November 2002, turned over to US agents, and flown to Afghanistan and then to Guantánamo, where they remain detained without trial or any form of judicial assistance;

70. Points out that the telegrams from the UK security service MI5 to an unspecified foreign government which were released to the Chairman of the APPG, Andrew Tyrie, suggest that the abduction of Bisher Al-Rawi and Jamil El-Banna was facilitated by partly erroneous information supplied by the UK security service;

71. Criticises the unwillingness of the UK Government to provide consular assistance to Bisher Al-Rawi and Jamil El-Banna on the grounds that they are not UK citizens;

72. Condemns the multiple extraordinary rendition of Binyam Mohammed, Ethiopian citizen and resident of the United Kingdom; points out that Binyam Mohammed has been held in at least two secret detention facilities, in addition to military prisons;

73. Is deeply disturbed by the testimony of Binyam Mohammed's lawyer, who gave an account of the most horrific torture endured by his client to the official delegation of the Temporary Committee to the United Kingdom;

74. Emphasises that the former UK Secretary of State for Foreign and Commonwealth Affairs, Jack Straw, conceded in December 2005 that UK intelligence officials met Binyam Mohammed when he was arrested in Pakistan; points out in this respect that some of the questions put by the Moroccan officials to Binyam Mohammed appear to have been inspired by information supplied by the UK;

75. Condemns the extraordinary rendition of UK citizen Martin Mubanga, who met the official delegation of the Temporary Committee to the United Kingdom, and who was arrested in Zambia in March 2002 and subsequently flown to Guantánamo; regrets the fact that Martin Mubanga was interrogated by British officials at Guantánamo, where he was detained and tortured for four years without trial or any form of judicial assistance and then released without charge;

76. Thanks Craig Murray, former UK Ambassador to Uzbekistan, for his very valuable testimony to the Temporary Committee on the exchange of intelligence obtained under torture and for providing a copy of the legal opinion of Michael Wood, former legal advisor to the UK Foreign and Commonwealth Office;

77. Is outraged by Michael Wood's legal opinion, according to which 'receiving or possessing' information extracted under torture, in so far as there is no direct participation in the torture, is not per se prohibited by the UN Convention against Torture and other Cruel, Inhumane or Degrading Treatment or Punishment; expresses its outrage at any attempt to obtain information by means of torture, regardless of who is involved;

78. Expresses serious concern about the 170 stopovers made by CIA-operated aircraft at UK airports, which on many occasions came from or were bound for countries linked with extraordinary rendition circuits and the transfer of detainees; deplores the stopovers at UK airports of aircraft which have been shown to have been used by the CIA, on other occasions, for the extraordinary rendition of Bisher Al-Rawi, Jamil El-Banna, Abou Elkassim Britel, Khaled El-Masri, Binyam Mohammed, Abu Omar and Maher Arar and for the expulsion of Ahmed Agiza and Mohammed El Zari;

Germany

79. Acknowledges the good cooperation on the part of the German Government by providing restricted documents to the Chairman and the rapporteur of the Temporary Committee; regrets, on the other hand, that no representative of the German Government was able to appear before the Temporary Committee;

80. Welcomes the excellent work of the German Parliament inquiry committee and expresses its full support for the continuation of that committee's work;

81. Thanks Munich Public Prosecutor Martin Hofmann for his testimony to the Temporary Committee and applauds all ongoing judicial inquiries in Germany;

82. Deplores the fact that German authorities at least had knowledge of the illegal abduction of German citizen Khaled El-Masri, who gave testimony to the Temporary Committee, and requests the German Parliament inquiry committee to examine further and clarify the role of German agents in this case;

83. Condemns the extraordinary rendition of Turkish citizen and resident of Germany Murat Kurnaz, who gave testimony to the Temporary Committee and who was arrested in Pakistan in November 2001, transferred to the US units across the border in Afghanistan by the Pakistani police on no legal basis and with no judicial assistance, and finally flown to Guantánamo at the end of January 2002, from where he was released on 24 August 2006 without charge, having been tortured in all the locations where he had been held;

84. Points out that, according to confidential institutional information, the German Government did not accept the US offer, made in 2002, to release Murat Kurnaz from Guantánamo; notes that on many occasions since 2002, Murat Kurnaz's lawyer was told by the German Government that it was impossible to open negotiations with the US Government on his release because Murat Kurnaz was a Turkish citizen; notes that all investigations concluded, as early as the end of October 2002, that Murat Kurnaz posed no terrorist threat;

85. Regrets the fact that Murat Kurnaz was interrogated twice, in 2002 and in 2004, by German officials at Guantánamo, where he was detained subject to neither formal charge nor trial and without judicial assistance; regrets the fact that German officials denied him any assistance and were only interested in questioning him;

86. Fully supports the investigation launched by the public prosecutor in Potsdam, transferred to the Public Prosecutor in Tübingen/Karlsruhe on 25 October 2006, into unknown perpetrators in order to establish whether Murat Kurnaz was ill-treated in Afghanistan by German soldiers belonging to the Kommando Spezialkräfte (KSK), the German army's special operational forces, before being sent to Guantánamo;

87. Notes that during his interrogations Murat Kurnaz was confronted with details from his personal life; notes that this gives rise to the suspicion that even before he left the country Murat Kurnaz was the subject of surveillance of a closeness which can normally only be provided by domestic intelligence services;

88. Appreciates the German Government's initiative in January 2006 which led to the release of Murat Kurnaz;

89. Condemns the extraordinary rendition of the German citizen Mohammed Zammar, arrested without formal charge on 8 December 2001 at Casablanca airport in Morocco and detained and tortured in Morocco and Syria;

90. Notes that, according to a confidential institutional source, on 26 November 2001 the German Federal Criminal Police Office provided details of Mohammed Zammar's whereabouts to the US Federal Bureau of Investigation (FBI), and that this facilitated Mohammed Zammar's arrest;

91. Points out that, subsequently to a meeting between the officials of the German Federal Chancellery and Syrian intelligence officials in July 2002, German prosecutors dropped charges against several Syrian citizens in Germany while the Syrian authorities allowed German officials to meet Mohammed Zammar in the Syrian prison Far' Falastin, as also confirmed by a confidential institutional source; regrets that Mohammed Zammar was interrogated by German agents in that prison;

92. Calls on the German Bundestag's First Committee of Inquiry, in the context of the forthcoming expansion of its remit, to investigate the case which recently came to light involving the illegal rendition of the Egyptian national Abdel-Halim Khafagy, who had long been resident in Germany; Abdel-Halim Khafagy was probably arrested in Bosnia and Herzegovina in September 2001 on suspicion of being a terrorist and abducted to a prison on the US 'Eagle Base' military base in Tuzla, where he was severely mistreated and detained under inhumane conditions;

93. Is deeply concerned at information contained in an unclassified document made available to the Temporary Committee which shows that the illegal rendition of at least six Algerians from Tuzla via Incirlik to Guantánamo was planned at the US European Command (USEUCOM) military base near Stuttgart; calls on the German Bundestag to investigate without delay whether those alleged renditions involved breaches of the Forces Status Agreement or other agreements or treaties concluded with US military forces on German territory, whether further illegal renditions were planned by USEUCOM and whether German liaison officers were involved in any way;

94. Expresses serious concern about the 336 stopovers made by CIA-operated aircraft at German airports that on many occasions came from or were bound for countries linked with extraordinary rendition circuits and the transfer of detainees; deplores the stopovers in Germany of aircraft which have been shown to have been used by the CIA, on other occasions, for the extraordinary renditions of Bisher Al-Rawi, Jamil El-Banna, Abou Elkassim Britel, Khaled El-Masri, Binyam Mohammed, Abu Omar and Maher Arar and for the expulsionof Ahmed Agiza and Mohammed El Zari; is particularly concerned that one of the flights referred to was destined for Guantánamo; strongly encourages the German authorities further to investigate that flight;

95. Notes the allegations concerning the temporary detention and mistreatment of suspected terrorists at the US military prison in Mannheim-Blumenau, welcomes the investigations opened by the Federal Public Prosecutor's Office and hopes that the German Bundestag and/or the competent committee of inquiry will investigate this case more closely;

Sweden

96. Takes note of the position of the Swedish Government expressed in the letter transmitted to the Temporary Committee by its Foreign Minister Carl Bildt; regrets that no representative of the government was able to appear before the Temporary Committee in order to hold an exchange of views on its position;

97. Condemns the fact that Sweden's expulsion in December 2001 of Mohammed El-Zari and Ahmed Agiza, Egyptian nationals who were seeking asylum in Sweden, was based solely on diplomatic assurances from the Egyptian Government, which did not provide effective safeguards against torture; also acknowledges that the Swedish government hindered them from exercising their rights in accordance with the European convention, by not informing their lawyers until before they had arrived in Cairo; deplores the fact that the Swedish authorities accepted an US offer to place at their disposal an aircraft which benefited from special overflight authorisation in order to transport the two men to Egypt;

98. Deplores the fact that the Swedish security police lost control over the enforcement of the expulsion of Ahmed Agiza and Mohammed El-Zari to Egypt, outside the rule of law, by remaining passive during the degrading treatment of the men by US agents at Bromma airport;

99. Underlines that the decision of the expulsion was taken at the highest executive level, from which no appeal was possible;

100. Fully endorses the UN Human Rights Committee's decision of 6 November 2006 in which it found that Sweden had breached the absolute ban on torture; similarly endorses a separate ruling by the UN Committee against Torture of 20 May 2005, which concluded that Sweden had violated the UN Convention against Torture and other Cruel, Inhuman or Degrading Treatment or Punishment and stated that "procurement of diplomatic assurances (from Egypt), which, moreover, provided no mechanism for their enforcement, did not suffice to protect against this manifest risk";

101. Thanks the Swedish Chief Parliamentary Ombudsman, Mats Melin, for his testimony to the Temporary Committee and applauds his investigation which concluded that the Swedish security service and airport police "were remarkably submissive to the American officials" and "lost control of the enforcement", resulting in the ill-treatment of Ahmed Agiza and Mohammed El-Zari, including physical abuse and other humiliation, at the airport immediately before they were transported to Cairo;

Austria

102. Notes the written explanations given on behalf of the Austrian Government but regrets that the Austrian Government did not consider it appropriate to appear before the Temporary Committee in order to hold an exchange of views about its position;

103. Notes that the persons referred to in the following paragraphs, Masaad Omer Behari and Gamal Menshawi, are individuals who did not and still do not have Austrian citizenship, whose freedom of movement was unrestricted; notes that the two men left Austria voluntarily and without

undergoing checks by the Austrian authorities, and that they were arrested by foreign agencies, outside Austrian territory and outside the area of influence of the Austrian authorities, with no Austrian involvement; notes that, accordingly, these are clearly not cases of rendition of persons to foreign authorities;

104. Condemns the fact that Masaad Omer Behari, a Sudanese citizen and resident of Austria since 1989 who gave testimony to the Temporary Committee, was abducted at Amman airport on 12 January 2003 on his way back to Vienna from Sudan;

105. Deplores the fact that Masaad Omer Behari was later illegally secretly detained in a prison close to Amman run by the Jordan General Intelligence Department, without trial orlegal assistance, and that he was tortured and ill-treated there until 8 April 2003, when he was released without charge; recalls that a judicial procedure was started by the Austrian authorities against Masaad Omer Behari in September 2001, which was subsequently closed in August 2002, without charge;

106. Deplores the fact that, according to Masaad Omer Behari's statement to the Temporary Committee, there may have been cooperation between the US, Austrian and Jordanian authorities in respect of his case;

107. Condemns the abduction of Egyptian citizen and resident of Austria, Gamal Menshawi, who was arrested on his way to Mecca at Amman airport in February 2003, and later brought to Egypt where he was secretly detained until 2005 without trial or legal rights; recalls that no allegations have ever been made against Gamal Menshawi in Austria;

108. Regrets that, having considered the above paragraphs, neither a special nor a parliamentary inquiry was carried out in Austria into the possible involvement of the Austrian authorities in the two cases referred to; urges the Austrian Parliament to start appropriate inquiries as soon as possible;

Spain

109. Welcomes the declaration of good cooperation with the Temporary Committee of the Spanish Government, in particular, the testimony given to the Temporary Committee by its Minister for Foreign Affairs; regrets, nevertheless, that the Spanish Government ultimately did not authorise the Director of the Spanish Intelligence Services to appear before the Temporary Committee, several months after having been requested to do so;

110. Thanks the Chief Prosecutor Javier Zaragoza and Prosecutor Vicente González Mota of the *Audiencia Nacional* for their testimony to the Temporary Committee and applauds their investigations into the use of Spanish airports for the transit of CIA aircraft within the context of the programme

of extraordinary rendition; encourages the prosecutors to investigate further the stopovers of the aircraft involved in the extraordinary rendition of Khaled El-Masri;

111. Applauds the investigative journalism of Diario de Mallorca, which played an important role in revealing the transit of CIA aircrafts through the Balearic Island airports and the identification of their crews;

112. Recalls the words of Chief Prosecutor Zaragoza that "there was no obstacle, objection or trouble from the Spanish Government side in the investigations by the *Audiencia Nacional*";

113. Calls on the Spanish authorities to take all necessary steps to allow Spanish citizen Mustafa Setmariam Nasarwho, abducted in Syria in October 2005 and rendered to US agents, to face a fair trial before competent judicial authorities;

114. Expresses serious concern about the 68 stopovers made by CIA-operated aircraft at Spanish airports that on many occasions came from or were bound for countries linked with extraordinary rendition circuits and the transfer of detainees; deplores the stopovers in Spain of aircraft which have been shown to have been used by the CIA in other countries for the extraordinary rendition of Ahmed Agiza, Mohammed El-Zari, Bisher Al-Rawi, Jamil El-Banna, Abou Elkassim Britel, Khaled El-Masri, Binyam Mohammed, Abu Omar and Maher Arar, according to the legal investigations under way in Spain and Italy; is particularly concerned that, of the above flights, three originated from or were destined for Guantánamo; strongly encourages the Spanish Prosecutors further to investigate those flights;

Portugal

115. Welcomes the meeting in Lisbon with the Portuguese Minister of Foreign Affairs and the fact that the Portuguese Government supplied documents and explanations; regrets that the Portuguese authorities were unable or reluctant to answer all the questions raised by the Temporary Committee delegation in Portugal;

116. Asks the Portuguese authorities to investigate the case of Abdurahman Khadr, allegedly carried on board the Gulfstream IV N85VM from Guantánamo to Tuzla in Bosnia and Herzegovina on 6 November 2003, with a stopover in Santa Maria on the Azores Islands on 7 November 2003; calls on the Portuguese authorities to examine this case and those of other possible victims transported via Portugal with a view to determining whether there should be compensation for violations of human rights;

117. Welcomes the establishment of the inter-ministerial working group on 26 September 2006 and the entry into force, on 13 October 2006,

of a regulation stipulating that lists of the names of crew members and passengers on private flights must be submitted to the Portuguese frontier authorities;

118. Deplores the fact that the former Minister of Defence, Paulo Portas, and the former Minister of the Interior, António Figueiredo Lopes, declined invitations to meet the delegation of the Temporary Committee;

119. Notes that some of the 91 stopovers made in Portugal enabled the CIA and US military bodies to carry out the extraordinary rendition of Bisher Al-Rawi, Jamil El-Banna, Khaled El-Masri, Binyam Mohammed and Abu Omar and for the expulsion of Ahmed Agiza and Mohammed El Zari; is particularly concerned that of those flights, at least three originated from or were destined for Guantánamo; notes that the aircraft involved in the rendition of Maher Arar and Abou Elkassim Britel made stopovers in Portugal on their return flights;

120. Expresses deep concern at an additional list that the Temporary Committee has obtained, the authenticity of which the Portuguese Government has not denied, which indicates that, in addition to the 91 stopovers made, aircraft from a number of countries, travelling to or from Guantánamo, made 17 stopovers (including three contained in Eurocontrol lists) at the Portuguese airports of Lajes and Santa Maria between 11 January 2002 and 24 June 2006;

Ireland

121. Welcomes the testimony given to the Temporary Committee by the Irish Minister for Foreign Affairs on behalf of the Irish Government as well as his unequivocal criticism of the process of extraordinary rendition; notes the fact, however, that he failed to answer all the questions in relation to the concerns that Irish airports may have been used by CIA aircraft travelling to or from extraordinary rendition missions (as in the case of Abu Omar);

122. Thanks the Irish Human Rights Commission (IHRC) for its testimony to the Temporary Committee and endorses its view which considers that acceptance by the Irish government of diplomatic assurances do not fulfil Ireland's human rights obligations, which oblige the government actively to seek to prevent any actions that could in any way facilitate torture or ill-treatment in Ireland or abroad; regrets the decision of the Irish Government not to follow the IHRC's advice on this matter to date; notes that there is continuing dialogue between the IHRC and the Irish Government;

123. Expresses serious concern about the 147 stopovers made by CIA-operated aircraft at Irish airports that on many occasions came from or were bound for countries linked with extraordinary rendition circuits and

the transfer of detainees; deplores the stopovers in Ireland of aircraft which have been shown to have been used by the CIA, on other occasions, for the extraordinary rendition of Bisher Al-Rawi, Jamil El-Banna, Abou Elkassim Britel, Khaled El-Masri, Binyam Mohammed, Abu Omar and Maher Arar and for the expulsion of Ahmed Agiza and Mohammed El Zari;

124. Notes the absence of Irish parliamentary scrutiny of either Irish or foreign intelligence services and the potential that this creates for abuse;

125. Considers, that, in the absence of a system of random searches, a ban should be imposed on all CIA-operated aircraft landing in Ireland;

126. Urges the Irish Government, in view of the findings of the Temporary Committee, to agree to launch a parliamentary inquiry into the use of Irish territory as part of the CIA rendition circuit;

Greece

127. Expresses serious concern about the 64 stopovers made by CIA-operated aircraft at Greek airports that on many occasions came from or were bound for countries linked with extraordinary rendition circuits and the transfer of detainees; deplores the stopovers in Greece of aircraft which have been shown to have been used by the CIA, on other occasions, for the extraordinary rendition of Ahmed Agiza, Mohammed El-Zari, Bisher Al-Rawi, Jamil El-Banna, Abou Elkassim Britel, Khaled El-Masri, Binyam Mohammed and Maher Arar;

Cyprus

128. Expresses serious concern about the 57 stopovers made by CIA-operated aircraft at Cypriot airports that on many occasions came from or were bound for countries linked with extraordinary rendition circuits and the transfer of detainees; deplores the stopovers in Cyprus of aircraft which have been shown to have been used by the CIA, on other occasions, for the extraordinary rendition of Ahmed Agiza, Mohammed El-Zari, Bisher Al-Rawi, Jamil El-Banna, Abou Elkassim Britel, Khaled El-Masri, Binyam Mohammed and Abu Omar;

Denmark

129. Welcomes the cooperation received from the Danish authorities, while regretting that no representative of the government considered it appropriate to appear before the Temporary Committee;

Belgium

130. Calls on the Belgian Government to disclose the results of all investigations that have taken place and deplores the fact that Belgium did not

conduct a thorough investigation concerning the use of Belgian airports and the Belgian airspace by aircraft clearly involved in the extraordinary rendition programme or the transport of detainees;

131. Notes the statements of the President of the Belgian Senate Anne-Marie Lizin and refers to the conclusions of the report of the Belgian Senate which deplore the lack of cooperation by the Belgian intelligent services and the Belgian authorities;

Turkey

132. Expresses its serious concern about the failure of the Turkish authorities to extend diplomatic protection to their national Murat Kurnaz and about the absence of any step to secure his release from the prison at Guantánamo;

133. Regrets that, on the contrary, the same authorities used the illegal detention of their national to interrogate him at Guantánamo;

134. Deplores the silence of the Turkish authorities concerning the use of their territory for the stopover of an aircraft which had taken to Guantánamo the six nationals of or residents in Bosnia and Herzogovina, of Algerian origin, who were illegally arrested in Bosnia and Herzegovina;

Former Yugoslav Republic of Macedonia

135. Emphasises that a delegation of the Temporary Committee was received in Skopje in April 2006 by the President of the Republic, members of the government and several officials and thanks them for the welcome given to the delegation; notes, however, a lack of thorough investigation into the Khaled El-Masri case by the authorities of the Former Yugoslav Republic of Macedonia;

136. Condemns the extraordinary rendition of the German citizen Khaled El-Masri, abducted at the border-crossing Tabanovce in the Former Yugoslav Republic of Macedonia on 31 December 2003, illegally held in Skopje from 31 December 2003 to 23 January 2004 and then transported to Afghanistan on 23-24 January 2004, where he was held until May 2004 and subjected to degrading and inhuman treatment;

137. Urges the Council and its High Representative for the CFSP to shed full light on the fact that the EU police mission (PROXIMA) was incorporated into the Ministry of Interior of the Former Yugoslav Republic of Macedonia and was involved in the work of the Macedonian Security and Counter-Espionage Service (DBK) at the time when Khaled El-Masri was handed over to the CIA; would like to know if it is true that the Council questioned the EU staff involved in the PROXIMA mission so as to evaluate the level of information in their possession regarding the case of Khaled

el Masri; if appropriate, asks the Council to provide Parliament with a full account of the investigation;

138. Fully endorses the preliminary findings of Munich Public Prosecutor Martin Hofmann that there is no evidence on the basis of which to refute Khaled El-Masri's version of events;

139. Deeply regrets the fact that the authorities of the Former Yugoslav Republic of Macedonia failed to follow up the recommendations made by the Temporary Committee in its interim report of 6 July 2006;

140. Points out again that the Former Yugoslav Republic of Macedonia authorities are expected to carry out investigations; urges the newly elected national parliament of the Former Yugoslav Republic of Macedonia to set up a committee of inquiry as soon as possible to deal with the case of Khaled El-Masri and to cooperate fully with the ongoing inquiry of the German Parliament;

Bosnia and Herzegovina

141. Welcomes the fact that the Government of Bosnia and Herzegovina is the only European government that does not deny its participation in the extraordinary rendition of four citizens of and two residents in Bosnia and Herzegovina, all of Algerian origin, and stresses that the Government of Bosnia and Herzegovina is the only European government to have accepted formal responsibility for its illegal actions; regrets, however, that the steps undertaken by the Government of Bosnia and Herzegovina have not yet resulted in the release of the six men from Guantánamo;

142. Condemns the extraordinary rendition of those six men, who were abducted in Sarajevo on 17 January 2002, turned over to US soldiers and then flown to Guantánamo, where they remain detained without trial or legal guarantees;

143. Takes note of the testimony given to the Temporary Committee by Wolfgang Petritsch, former High Representative of the international community in Bosnia and Herzegovina, and by Michèle Picard, former President of the Human Rights Chamber of Bosnia and Herzegovina, which stated that representatives of the international community in Bosnia and Herzegovina were given adequate notice of the imminent handing-over of the men referred to the US forces before events unfolded; condemns in this respect the Member States for their lack of action;

144. Regrets the fact that the international community as represented in Bosnia and Herzegovina turned a blind eye when the decisions of the Supreme Court and the Human Rights Chamber of Bosnia and Herzegovina ordering the release of the men from custody were not implemented;

145. Points out that, according to the information that the Temporary Committee received from the lawyers of the six men, the authorities of Bosnia and Herzegovina were subject to unprecedented pressure from the US Government, which threatened to close its embassy, withdraw all staff and cease diplomatic relations with Bosnia and Herzegovina unless the Government of Bosnia and Herzegovina immediately arrested the six men on terrorism charges;

146. Notes that Wolfgang Petritsch confirmed that the United States put considerable pressure on the authorities of Bosnia and Herzegovina and the international community not to interfere in the renditions and that the commander of the international NATO-led Stabilisation Force in particular rejected any questioning of his activities since he acted in his capacity as US military officer;

Other European Countries

147. Is concerned about the stopovers made by CIA-operated aircraft in other European countries' airports and expresses serious concern about the purpose of those flights which came from or were bound for countries linked with extraordinary rendition circuits and the transfer of detainees; encourages the authorities of those European countries to launch adequate investigations into this matter;

Secret Detention Facilities

148. Welcomes the investigations carried out into the existence of secret detention facilities in Europe by Human Rights Watch, the Washington Post and American Broadcasting Company News (ABC News);

149. Recalls that some journalists at the Washington Post and ABC News, as they confirmed to the Temporary Committee, were put under pressure not to name the eastern European countries, namely Poland and Romania, where there were said to have been secret detention facilities;

150. Emphasises that the concept of "secret detention facility" includes not only prisons, but also all places where somebody is held *incommunicado,* such as private apartments, police stations or hotel rooms, as in the case of Khaled El-Masri in Skopje;

151. Is deeply concerned that, in some cases, temporary secret detention facilities in European countries may have been located at US military bases;

152. Calls for the appropriate implementation of bilateral agreements, Status of Forces Agreements and military base agreements (between Member States and third countries) to ensure the monitoring of respect for human rights and, where appropriate, for a review and renegotiation of

those agreements to this effect; stresses that, according to the Venice Commission, the legal framework of foreign military bases on the territory of Council of Europe's Member States must enable them to exercise sufficient powers to fulfil their human rights obligations;

153. Points out in this regard the allegations concerning the US Coleman Barracks in Mannheim, Germany, and calls on both the judiciary and the German Bundestag's inquiry Committee to investigate this case further;

154. Regrets that there may have been a lack of control over US military bases by host European countries; recalls, however, that the ECHR provides that all State parties are bound to exercise jurisdiction over their whole territory, including foreign military bases;

155. Recalls that the ECHR also provides that every case of detention must be lawful and must be the result of proceedings prescribed by law, whether national or international;

156. Recalls that imposing or executing or allowing directly or indirectly secret and illegal detentions, which are instruments resulting in people's 'disappearance', per se constitute serious violations of human rights and that the active or passive involvement in such secret and illegal detentions by a European country renders that county responsible under the ECHR;

Romania

157. Welcomes the excellent hospitality and good cooperation extended by the Romanian authorities to the Temporary Committee, including meetings with members of the Romanian Government, as well as the establishment of an ad hoc inquiry committee of the Romanian Senate;

158. Notes, however, the reluctance on the part of the Romanian authorities to investigate thoroughly the existence of secret detention facilities on its territory;

159. Regrets that the report issued by the Romanian inquiry committee was entirely secret except for its conclusions, included in Chapter 7, categorically denying the possibility that secret detention facilities could be hosted on Romanian soil; regrets that the Romanian inquiry committee heard no testimony from journalists, NGOs, or officials working in airports, and has not yet provided the Temporary Committee with the report contrary to its commitment to do so; regrets that taking these elements into consideration, the conclusions drawn in the Romanian inquiry committee's report appear premature and superficial; takes note, however, of the intention expressed by the Chairwoman of the inquiry committee to the Temporary Committee delegation to consider the conclusions provisional;

160. Regrets the lack of control of the Gulfstream aircraft with Registration Number N478GS that suffered an accident on 6 December 2004 when

landing in Bucharest; recalls that the aircraft took off from Bagram Air Base in Afghanistan, and that its seven passengers disappeared following the accident; appreciates, however, the good cooperation of the Romanian authorities in handing over the report on the accident to the Temporary Committee;

161. Is deeply concerned to see that Romanian authorities did not initiate an official investigation process, as any democratic country should have done, into the case of a passenger on the aircraft Gulfstream N478GS, who was found carrying a Beretta 9 mm Parabellum pistol with ammunition;

162. Expresses serious concern about the 21 stopovers made by CIA-operated aircraft at Romanian airports, which on many occasions came from or were bound for countries linked with extraordinary rendition circuits and the transfer of detainees; deplores the stopovers in Romania of aircraft which have been shown to have been used by the CIA, on other occasions, for the extraordinary rendition of Bisher Al-Rawi, Jamil El-Banna, Abou Elkassim Britel, Khaled El-Masri, Binyam Mohammed and Abu Omar and for the expulsion of Ahmed Agiza and Mohammed El Zari; is particularly concerned that, of the flights referred to, two originated from or were destined for Guantánamo; strongly encourages the Romanian authorities further to investigate those flights;

163. Is extremely concerned that the Romanian authorities may have lacked control over US activities in the military base at Kogalniceanu airport;

164. Cannot exclude, based only on the statements made by Romanian authorities to the Temporary Committee delegation to Romania, the possibility that US secret services operated in Romania on a clandestine basis and that no definitive evidence has been provided to contradict any of the allegations concerning the running of a secret detention facility on Romanian soil;

Poland

165. Deplores the glaring lack of cooperation by the Polish Government with the Temporary Committee, in particular when receiving the Temporary Committee delegation at an inappropriate level; deeply regrets that all those representatives of the Polish Government and Parliament who were invited to do so, declined to meet the Temporary Committee;

166. Believes that this attitude reflected an overall rejection on the part of the Polish Government of the Temporary Committee and its objective to examine allegations and establish facts;

167. Regrets that no special inquiry committee has been established and that the Polish Parliament has not conducted an independent investigation;

168. Recalls that on 21 December 2005, the Special Services Committee held a private meeting with the Minister Coordinator of Special Services and the heads of both intelligence services; emphasises that the meeting was conducted speedily and in secret, in the absence of any hearing or testimony and subject to no scrutiny; stresses that such an investigation cannot be defined as independent and regrets that the committee released no documentation, save for a single final statement in this regard;

169. Expresses serious concern about the 11 stopovers made by CIA-operated aircraft at Polish airports that on many occasions came from or were bound for countries linked with extraordinary rendition circuits and the transfer of detainees; deplores the stopovers in Poland of aircraft which have been shown to have been used by the CIA, on other occasions, for the extraordinary rendition of Bisher Al-Rawi, Jamil El-Banna, Abou Elkassim Britel, Khaled El-Masri and Binyam Mohammed and for the expulsion of Ahmed Agiza and Mohammed El Zar;

170. Regrets that following the hearings carried out by the Temporary Committee delegation in Poland, there was confusion and contradictory statements were made about the flight logs for those CIA flights, which were first said not to have been retained and then said to have probably been archived at the airport and finally claimed to have been sent by the Polish Government to the Council of Europe; acknowledges that in November 2006, the Szymany Airport's management provided the Temporary Committee with partial information on flight logs;

171. Thanks the former manager of the Szymany airport, for the valuable testimony given before the Temporary Committee; notes the fact that during 2006 he or she was questioned in the framework of a late enquiry concerning the CIA flights, immediately after his or her testimony was made public;

172. Takes note that, according to different sources, several high-value detainees who had been held secretly in Afghanistan in 2003 were transferred out of the country in September and October 2003; underlines with concern that a Boeing 737 with Registration Number N313P, used by the CIA for ascertained renditions, flew from Kabul to Szymany airport on 22 September 2003 and was then directed to Guantánamo;

173. Recalls that, concerning the landing of the aircraft referred to at Szymany airport, seven staff on board were joined by five passengers and that no customs control was carried out on those passengers;

174. Takes note of the declarations made by Szymany airport employees, and notably by its former manager, according to which:

- in 2002, two Gulfstream jets, and in 2003, four Gulfstream jets with civilian registration numbers were parked at the edge of the airport and did not enter customs clearance;

— orders were given directly by the regional border guards about the arrivals of the aircraft referred to, emphasising that the airport authorities should not approach the aircraft and that military staff and services alone were to handle those aircraft and only to complete the technical arrangements after the landing;

— according to a former senior official of the airport, no Polish civilian or military staff were permitted to approach the aircraft;

— excessive landing fees were paid in cash—usually between EUR 2 000 and EUR 4 000;

— one or two vehicles waited for the arrival of the aircraft;

— the vehicles had military registration numbers starting with "H", which are associated with the intelligence training base in nearby Stare Kiejkuty;

— in one case, a medical emergency vehicle belonging either to the police academy or the military base was involved;

— one airport staff member reported following the vehicles on one occasion and seeing them heading towards the intelligence training centre at Stare Kiejkuty;

175. Acknowledges that shortly after, and in accordance with, President George W. Bush's statements on 6 September 2006, a list of the 14 detainees who had been transferred from a secret detention facility to Guantánamo was published; notes that 7 of the 14 detainees had been referred to in a report by ABC News, which was published nine months previously on 5 December 2005 but was withdrawn shortly thereafter from ABC's webpage, listing the names of twelve top Al Qaeda suspects held in Poland;

176. Encourages the Polish Parliament to establish a proper inquiry committee, independent of the Government and capable of carrying out serious and thorough investigations;

177. Regrets that Polish human rights NGOs and investigative journalists have faced a lack of cooperation from the government and refusals to divulge information;

178. Considers that in the light of the above circumstantial evidences, it is not possible to acknowledge that secret detention centres were based in Poland;

179. Notes with concern that the official reply of 10 March 2006 from Under-Secretary of State Witold Waszykowski to Terry Davis indicates the existence of secret cooperation agreements, initialled by the two countries' secret services themselves, which exclude the activities of foreign secret services from the jurisdiction of Polish judicial bodies;

Kosovo (Under UN Security Council Resolution 1244)

180. Expresses deep concern over the fact that the European Committee for the Prevention of Torture and Inhuman or Degrading Treatment or Punishment (CPT) obtained access to NATO-run detention facilities in Kosovo only in July 2006;

181. Regrets the refusal of NATO to provide evidence on the allegations of illegal detention of terrorist suspects in the prison run by the NATO-led peacekeeping force in Kosovo (KFOR) at Camp Bondsteel, the only detention facility in Europe where CPT inspectors were not allowed unlimited access until very recently;

182. Points out in this respect that the testimony given to the Temporary Committee by the former Kosovo Ombudsman, Marek Antoni Nowicki, confirmed that from July 1999, inmates were frequently detained at Camp Bondsteel, subject only to a decision by the Commander of KFOR and subject to no judicial decision or any form of other external control; recalls that from 2000 to 2001, a number of people were detained also following administrative decisions of the Special Representative of the UN Secretary-General and that, according to official data available, 23 people were imprisoned at Camp Bondsteel for a short period of time by the KFOR Commander in connection with violent events in Kosovo in spring 2004;

Other Relevant Information Collected by the Temporary Committee

183. Points out that the Temporary Committee came across information—including the direct testimony of Murat Kurnaz—about the interrogation of Guantánamo detainees carried out by agents of Member State governments; emphasises that those interrogations were aimed at collecting information from individuals illegally detained, which is clearly in contradiction with the public condemnation of Guantánamo, as expressed at both EU and Member State level on several occasions;

184. Encourages the Member States involved to launch adequate investigations into this matter;

Recommendations

Political Recommendations

185. Considers it necessary that those European countries that have started inquiries and investigations at governmental, parliamentary and/or judicial level on matters within the remit of the Temporary Committee should conduct their work as speedily as possible and make public the results of the investigations;

186. Urges European countries in relation to which serious allegations have been made regarding active or passive cooperation with extraordinary rendition and that have not undertaken governmental, parliamentary and/or judicial investigations to commence such proceedings as soon as possible; recalls that, according to the case law of the European Court of Human Rights, there is a positive obligation on Member States to investigate allegations of and sanction human rights violations in breach of the ECHR;

187. Calls for the closure of Guantánamo and for European countries immediately to seek the return of their citizens and residents who are being held illegally by US authorities;

188. Considers that all European countries that have not done so should initiate independent investigations into all stopovers made by civilian aircraft carried out by the CIA, at least since 2001, including those cases already analysed by the Temporary Committee;

189. Expects to be kept fully informed on all developments concerning all the above-mentioned procedures;

190. Calls on European countries to compensate the innocent victims of extraordinary rendition and to ensure that they have access to effective and speedy compensation, including access to rehabilitation programmes, guarantees that there will be no repetition of what happened as well as appropriate financial compensation;

191. Asks the Commission to undertake an evaluation of all anti-terrorist legislation, in the Member States and of both formal and informal arrangements between Member State and third-country intelligence services, from a human rights perspective, to review legislation where international or European human rights bodies considers that it could lead to breach of human rights and to present proposals for actions in order to avoid any repetition of the matters under the remit of the Temporary Committee;

192. Considers it necessary to review by limiting and restrictively defining the exceptions that flow from the notion of 'State secret', also in the framework of the impending review of Regulation 1049/01[9], as well as the adoption of common principles by the EU institutions as regards the treatment of confidential information, to avoid abuses and deviations that are more and more unacceptable in modern democratic States and that contradict human rights obligations; deems it necessary to establish specific mechanisms to allow for access to secret information by parliaments and judges, as well as for the release of the information after a certain period of time;

[9] Regulation (EC) No 1049/2001 of the European Parliament and of the Council of 30 May 2001 regarding public access to European Parliament, Council and Commission documents (OJ L 145, 31.5.2001, p. 43).

193. Notes the recent creation of a High-Level Working Group composed of representatives of the Commission, the Council and US governmental representatives of the Justice Ministry and the Homeland Security, which constitutes the political framework for EU-US dialogue on security matters, including differences in the approach to terrorism as well as the concerns raised by the Temporary Committee; deems it necessary to associate in this High-Level Working Group the European Parliament and the US Congress, as well as to publish its agendas, minutes, documents examined and decisions taken, in order to ensure and increase its democratic legitimacy and transparency;

194. Encourages European countries when they conduct military operations in third countries to:

- ensure that any detention centre established by their military forces is subject to civilian and judicial supervision and that *incommunicado* detention is not permitted;
- take active steps to prevent any other authority from operating detention centres which are not subject to political and judicial oversight or where *incommunicado* detention is permitted;

Legal Recommendations

195. Considers that the powers of Parliament's temporary inquiry committees should be reinforced and the inter-institutional decision governing the exercise of Parliament's right of inquiry be amended accordingly;

196. Considers that Parliament should be adequately involved when the Community or the Union adopt measures affecting civil rights and liberties;

197. Calls for the establishment of an adequate and structured system of cooperation between Parliament and competent bodies of the United Nations and the Council of Europe when dealing with matters related to internal security of the European Union;

198. Calls for enhanced cooperation with national parliaments in order to share all information related to the fight against international terrorism;

199. Underlines the importance of a common definition of 'terrorism'; believes that the United Nations is the most suitable organisation to define the concept;

Secret Services

200. Fully endorses the conclusions of the Secretary-General of the Council of Europe, Terry Davis, about the lack of oversight and judicial control

mechanisms in respect of security services, as expressed in the "Follow-up to the Secretary General's reports under Article 52 ECHR" and expects his recommendations to be duly taken into consideration; calls on Member States to provide adequate and effective parliamentary monitoring (by establishing oversight committees with appropriate powers to access documents and budgetary information) and legal supervision over their secret and intelligence services and the formal and informal networks of which they are part;

201. Considers it necessary to enhance the Conference of the Oversight Committees on the Intelligence bodies of the Member States, in which Parliament should be fully involved;

202. Considers that all European countries should have specific national laws to regulate and monitor the activities of third countries' secret services on their national territories, to ensure a better monitoring and supervision also of their activities, as well as to sanction illegal acts or activities, notably in violation of human rights;

203. Considers the reinforcement of cooperation between the secret and security services of Member States to be highly desirable, either on a multilateral basis, preferably within an EU framework, or on a bilateral basis, provided that a legal framework for it is created ensuring full democratic parliamentary and judicial control and human rights are respected and protected at all times;

204. Urges the Council and the Member States to establish as a matter of priority a system for the democratic monitoring and control over the joint and coordinated intelligence activities at EU level; proposes an important role for Parliament in this monitoring and control system;

Air Traffic

205. Urges the Member States to ensure that Article 3 of the Chicago Convention, which excludes state aircraft from the scope of the Convention, is properly implemented in order that all military and/or police aircraft fly over or land on another State's territory only if they have prior authorisation;

206. Calls on Member States to take adequate measures to ensure that overflight clearances for military and/or police aircraft should be granted only if accompanied by guarantees that human rights will be respected and monitored;

207. Considers it necessary to enforce effectively, both at EU and national level, the Tokyo Convention on Offences and Certain Other Acts Committed on Board Aircraft so that the exercise of jurisdiction is used to ensure the observance of any obligation under a multilateral international agreement,

in particular concerning the protection of human rights, and that, when appropriate, inspections on board should be undertaken;

208. Calls on the Commission to adopt adequate legislative proposals on transport safety, as provided for in Article 71 EC Treaty, taking into account the recommendations included in this resolution;

209. Recalls the Community competence in the field of transport, and notably transport security; asks the Commission, therefore, to take immediate action to ensure that the recommendations made by the Secretary-General of the Council of Europe as well as by Parliament are implemented;

210. Calls on the Commission to consider adopting rules on the use, monitoring and management of European airspace, on the use of EU airports and on the monitoring of non-commercial aviation;

International Conventions and Agreements

211. Urges the Member States that have not yet done so to complete as soon as possible ratification of the 2003 EU-US Extradition Agreement, while taking adequate steps to avoid wrongly interpreting Article 12 of the Agreement, thereby ensuring that its scope does not extend beyond formal extradition and does not legitimise extraordinary renditions;

212. Calls on European countries to support the rapid adoption by the UN General Assembly of the International Convention for the Protection of All Persons Against Enforced Disappearance, adopted on 29 June 2006 by the UN Human Rights Council;

213. Believes that, in providing for the adequate interpretation and enforcement of the UN Convention Against Torture, all European countries should ensure that their definition of torture is in accordance with Article 1 of the Convention and that, moreover, the obligations relating to the prohibition of torture are also fulfilled with respect to other acts of cruel, inhuman, degrading treatment referred to in Article 16 of the Convention; considers that all European countries should ensure that Article 3 of the Convention is properly enforced, in particular in relation to the activities of their secret services;

214. States that, given that the protection against *refoulement* is higher under the ECHR than under the Convention against Torture, European countries should ensure in any event the protection afforded by the ECHR; recalls, in this context, that the principle of *non-refoulement* is also recognised by the Court of Justice of the European Communities;

215. Calls on all European countries to sign and ratify the Optional Protocol to the Convention Against Torture and establish independent national mechanisms to monitor places of detention; emphasises the need to ensure

that all such procedures used by the different international conventions on human rights are compatible;

216. Takes the view that the CPT should be granted access without delay or obstruction to any place of detention within the European countries, including foreign military bases, and provided with all relevant information concerning such detention, and that, to this end, any bilateral agreements that restrict the access of the CPT should be revised;

217. Urges all European countries to comply with the provisions of the Rome Statute of the International Criminal Court;

218. Believes that the European Union should encourage all third countries to become party to the Optional Protocol to the Convention against Torture and to the Convention on Enforced Disappearances;

219. Asks European countries to establish clear rules that provide for the possibility of State immunity being waived where illegal actions violate human rights;

Administrative Recommendations (at EU Level)

220. Takes the view that all internal services within the Council (inter alia, the Policy Unit and the Joint Situation Centre) and the Commission (the Crisis Management and Conflict Prevention Unit in the Directorate-General for External Relations and relevant services in the Directorate-General for Justice, Freedom and Security), should be strengthened in the framework of the implementation of the EU Security Strategy and the counter-terrorism strategy in close cooperation with all Member States, and that their cooperation with each other, as well as with Member States, be clearly regulated and data protection be ensured; considers that Parliament should be involved fully in this regard by granting it oversight powers similar to those of national parliamentary oversight committees, and that the Court of Justice be granted competence in this area; underlines that the competence of the EU in the field of combating terrorism should be significantly strengthened;

EU Relations with Third Countries

221. Urges the European Union to stress in its contacts with third countries that the appropriate legal framework for governing the international fight against terrorism is criminal law and international human rights law;

222. Stresses the necessity of political dialogue with the US, as well as with other strategic partners of the European Union, on security matters in order to combat terrorism effectively and by legal means;

223. Calls on the European Union to recall that the full application of the 'democratic clause' is fundamental in its relations with third countries,

especially those with which it has concluded agreements; calls on Egypt, Jordan, Syria and Morocco to provide clarity on their role in the extraordinary renditions programme;

224. Strongly believes that it is necessary to promote within the UN framework codes of conduct for all security and military services based on respect for human rights, humanitarian law and democratic political control, similar to the 1994 Code of Conduct on Politico-Military Aspects of Security of the Organisation for Security and Cooperation in Europe;

Final Conclusions

225. Stresses, in view of the powers it was provided with and of the time which it had at its disposal, and the secret nature of the investigated actions, that the Temporary Committee was not put in a position fully to investigate all the cases of abuses and violations falling within its remit and that its conclusions are therefore not exhaustive;

226. Recalls the principles and values on which the European Union is based, as provided in Article 6 of the Treaty on European Union, and calls on the EU institutions to meet their responsibilities in relation to Article 7 of the Treaty on European Union and all other relevant provisions of the Treaties, and to take all appropriate measures in the light of the conclusions of the work of the Temporary Committee, the facts revealed in the course of the Temporary Committee's investigation and any other facts that may emerge in the future; expects the Council to start hearings and commission an independent investigation without delay, as foreseen in Article 7, and, where necessary, to impose sanctions on Member States in case of a serious and persistent breaches of Article 6, including where a violation of human rights has been declared by an international body but no measure has been taken to redress the violation;

227. Believes that the principle of loyal cooperation enshrined in the Treaties—which requires Member States and the EU institutions to take measures to ensure the fulfilment of their obligations under the Treaties, such as the respect of human rights, or resulting from action taken by the EU institutions, such as ascertaining the truth about alleged CIA flights and prisons, and to facilitate the achievement of EU tasks and objectives—has not been respected;

228. Recalls that in light of European Court of Human Rights case law, a signatory State bears responsibility for the material breach of the provisions of the ECHR, and therefore also of Article 6 of the Treaty on the European Union, not only if its direct responsibility can be established beyond reasonable doubt, but also by failing to comply with its positive obligation to conduct an independent and impartial investigation into reasonable allegations of such violations;

229. Notes the reports by reputable media operators that extraordinary rendition, illegal detention, and systematic torture involving many people is continuing, and considering the declaration by the current US Government that the use of extraordinary rendition and secret places of detention will be continued; therefore calls for an EU-US counterterrorism summit to seek an end to such inhumane and illegal practices, and to insist that cooperation with regard to counter-terrorism is consistent with international human rights and anti-torture treaty obligations;

230. Instructs its Committee on Civil Liberties, Justice and Home Affairs, where necessary in cooperation with the Committee on Foreign Affairs, notably its Sub-Committee on Human Rights, to follow up politically the proceedings of the Temporary Committee and to monitor the developments, and in particular, in the event that no appropriate action has been taken by the Council and/or the Commission, to determine whether there is a clear risk of a serious breach of the principles and values on which the European Union is based, and to recommend to it any resolution, taking as a basis Articles 6 and 7 of the Treaty on European Union, which may prove necessary in this context;

231. Calls on its Secretary-General to publish, at least in compliance with Regulation 1049/2001, all the documents received, produced and examined, as well as the records of the proceedings of the Temporary Committee on the Internet as well as in any other appropriate manner and calls on the Secretary-General to ensure that the developments in fields falling within the remit of the Temporary Committee after its disbandment are monitored;

0 0

0

232. Instructs its President to forward this resolution to the Council, the Commission, the governments and parliaments of the Member States, of the candidate Member States and the associated countries, and to the Council of Europe, NATO, the United Nations and the Government and two Houses of Congress of the United States, and to request them to keep Parliament informed of any development that may take place in the fields falling in the remit of the Temporary Committee.

Explanatory Statement

This final report is the outcome of one year of intense work directly involving 46 Members from all political groups, with the support of secretariat officials and political group staff.

The following figures give some idea of the volume and complexity of the work carried out:

- 33 committee meetings (i.e. more than 110 hours of official meetings);
- 10 meetings of the Bureau and with political group coordinators;
- 7 official committee delegation visits (Former Yugoslav Republic of Macedonia, United States, Germany, United Kingdom, Romania, Poland and Portugal);
- evidence given by some 200 persons, both in committee and during missions;
- 19 extraordinary renditions considered (with four victims of renditions giving evidence directly);
- some 700 amendments tabled to both provisional and final versions of the resolution;
- thousands of pages of documentation received and analysed by the committee.

All the documents produced (reports, working documents, minutes and transcripts of meetings, official delegation reports, etc.) and the documents received (with the exception of confidential documents) will be made public.

All the committee's work (the facts analysed, the evidence given and the documents received) is covered in nine *working documents*, the purpose of which is to elucidate and flesh out the political conclusions set out in the final resolution. The rapporteur feels it would useful to go briefly over the three working documents that were produced last, namely:

- Working document No 7[10], which provide a fuller picture of the individual extraordinary renditions considered by the committee, setting out details of the CIA flights used to transfer detainees. The flight data supplied by Eurocontrol provide incontrovertible evidence of extraordinary renditions. In particular, they reveal a pattern of

[10] PE 380.593.

systematic and deliberate illegal behaviour, with extraordinary rendition circuits involving the repeated use of European airports as stopovers or staging points for illegal missions conducted by US intelligence services for the purpose of abducting terrorist suspects.

- Working document No 8[11], which contains an analysis of the shell companies and aircraft used by the CIA for the 1 245 flights which our committee was able to reconstruct in minute detail, from the types of aircraft used to the airports of departure and arrival, flight times, stopovers and, in particular, the 'suspicious locations', i.e. the places of departure or origin in which the temporary commission was able to establish the existence of detention centres at which the use of torture was common practice.
- Working document No 9[12], which contains a country-by-country overview of the information gathered by our committee on the extraordinary renditions, the alleged secret detention centres and the role of national authorities.

It should be emphasised that, behind the rigorous exposition of incidents, facts and responsibilities in the report lie the stories of individual human beings, many of whom have -following years of detention—been recognised as being totally innocent of the charges brought against them. These are men deprived of their most basic rights and in many cases forced to undergo degrading and humiliating treatment. It should be remembered that we were only able to address the plight of these victims of extraordinary renditions because their cases had become public knowledge. It is to be feared that many others may have suffered the same fate but escaped the notice of history (and this committee).

Finally, as further reading to this explanatory statement and the political conclusions set out in the two reports, the rapporteur has attached the following documents:

1. An overview of all the activities of the TDIP temporary committee (Annex 1).
2. A list of all the persons who gave evidence before the committee or during an official delegation mission (Annex 2).
3. A document providing details on cooperation afforded to our committee by individual European countries (Annex 3).
4. A list of all those who declined an invitation to meet the committee (Annex 4).

[11] PE 380984.
[12] PE 382.420.

To wind up, the rapporteur considers it his duty to point out that his final report and all the documents and analyses he has produced are the fruit of collective effort involving a large number of Members from all political groups, in what were difficult circumstances. A special mention should go to the members of the committee secretariat and the staff working directly for the rapporteur, as well as to all other EP secretariat and political group staff involved in the arduous work performed over the past year. Our thanks go to each and every one of them.

Annex 1: TDIP Committee events

DATE	TIME	INSTITUTION-PLACE	SUBJECT	
15 December 2005—Thursday		European Parliament (EP) -Strasbourg (STR)	**Plenary sitting 1:**	Resolution on presumed use of European countries by the CIA for the Transportation and Illegal Detention of Prisoners -TDIP-(P6_TA-PROV(2005)0529
EF PLENARY -Jan. (from 16 to 19) 18 January 2006—Wednesday	12h00—13h00	EP—STR	**Plenary sitting 2:**	Decision setting up a temporary committee on TDIP (P6_TA-PROV(2006)0012
24 January 2006—Tuesday	08h30	Council of Europe -Strasbourg	**Parliamentary Assembly 1:**	Meeting of the Committee on Legal Affairs and Human Rights (Point 1 of the Agenda: *Alleged secret detentions in Council of Europe member states)* and debate in plenary of the Parliamentary Assembly. Follow-up by the TDIP secretariat
26 January 2006—Thursday	09h00-10h00	EP—Bruxelles (BXL)	**TDIP Committee 1:**	Constituent meeting (election of chairman, *Carlos COELHO* and vice-chairmen, *Baroness Sarah LUDFORD, Giorgos DIMITRAKOPOULOS, Cem OZDEMIR*)
01 February 2006—Wednesday	18h45—20h00	EP—BXL	**Steering group 1:**	Provisional calendar of meetings and planning of the provisional report up to June 2006; Opening and transparency of proceedings; List of personalities/institutions to be invited; Committee delegations; Background information, specific studies, expertise

DATE		TIME	INSTITUTION-PLACE	SUBJECT	
08 February 2006—Wednesday		18h45—20h00	EP—BXL	**Steering group 2:**	Agreement on a working programme to be adopted by the Committee on 13 February 2006
EP PLENARY—Feb (from 13 to 16)	13 February 2006—Monday	19h00—21h00	EP—STR	**TDIP Committee 2:**	*Franco FRATTINI*, Vice-President of the European Commission; Adoption of the calendar of meetings and of the TDIP working programme until 30 June 2006; presentation by *Giovanni Claudio FAVA*, rapporteur
	14 February 2006—Tuesday	14h30—15h00	EP—STR	**Press conference 1:**	*Carlos COELHO*, chairman and *Giovanni Claudio FAVA*, rapporteur: Start of the committee proceedings
23 February 2006—Thursday		9h00—12h00	EP-BXL	**TDIP Committee 3:**	*Joanne MARINER*, Human Rights Watch; *Anne FITZGERALD*, Amnesty International; *Tony BUNYAN*, Statewatch
		15h00—18h30			*Armando SPATARO*, Prosecutor (Milan); *Dick MARTY*, Council of Europe
		19h30		**Working meal 1 (dinner):**	Hosted by Carlos COELHO, (Bureau and coordinators) with *Dick MARTY*, Council of Europe
6 March 2006—Monday		15 h00—17h30	EP-BXL	**TDIP Committee 4:**	*Generale Nicolò POLLARI*, Italian Intelligence and Security Services (in camera); *Anne-Marie LIZIN*, President of the Senate of Belgium; *Jean Claude DELEPIERE*, Chairman of the Permanent Committee R
		17h30—18h30		**Steering group 3:**	Treatment of confidential information; Organisation of TDIP Committee work

EP PLENARY—March (from 13 to 16)	13 March 2006—Monday	11h45- 13h00	Council of Europe -Paris	**Parliamentary Assembly 2:**	Meeting of the Committee on Legal Affairs and Human Rights (Point 7 of the Agenda: *Alleged secret detentions in Council of Europe member states)* with the participation of *Giovanni Claudio FAVA*, rapporteur
		21h00-22h30	EP—STR	**TDIP Committee 5:**	*Khaled EL MASRI* (German citizen), alleged victim and his lawyer, *Manfred GNJIDIC*
21 March 2006—Tuesday		15h00—18h00	EP-BXL	**TDIP Committee 6:**	*Stephen GREY*, journalist (free lancer); *Guido OLIMPIO* and *Paolo BIONDANI*, journalists from *Il corriere della sera* (IT)
		18h00—19h00		**Steering group 4:**	Delegations to FYROM and USA; Programme of future Committee meetings; Organisation of TDIP Committee meetings
23 March 2006—Thursday		15h00—18h00	EP-BXL	**TDIP Committee 7:**	*Maher ARAR* (Canadian citizen) alleged victim and his lawyers, *Lorne WALDMAN* and *Marlys EDWARDH*; *Kjell JÖNSSON*, lawyer of Mohammed EL-ZARY (Egyptian citizen) alleged victim
EP PLENARY—April (from 3 to 6)	3 April 2006—Monday	21h00-22h15	EP-STR	**TDIP Committee 8:**	Preparation of the draft interim report (2006/2027 (INI))
		22h15—22h35		**Steering group 5:**	Delegations to FYROM and USA; Treatment of confidential information ('Eurocontrol')
11 April 2006—Tuesday		from 8h30	Council of Europe -STR	**Parliamentary Assembly 3:**	Meeting of the Committee on Legal Affairs and Human Rights (Point 4 of the Agenda: *Alleged secret detentions in Council of Europe member states)* Follow-up by the TDIP secretariat

DATE	TIME	INSTITUTION-PLACE	SUBJECT	
20 April 2006—Thursday	9h30—12h30	EP-BXL	**TDIP Committee 9:**	*Craig MURRAY*, former UK ambassador to Uzbekistan; *Gijs DE VRIES*, EU's Counter-Terrorism Coordinator
	15h00—18h30			*Matías VALLES*, journalist from "Diario de Mallorca"; *Edward HORGAN*, former UN peacekeeper and Retired Commandant of the Irish Army
24 April 2006—Monday	13h00	EP-BXL	**Working meal 2 (lunch):**	Hosted by chairman COELHO with Thomas HAMMARBERG, CoE's Human Rights Commissioner
25 April 2006—Tuesday	15h00—18h30	EP-BXL	**TDIP Committee 10:**	Examination of the draft interim report; *Stephen H. OLESKEY*, Counsel for six citizens of Bosnia and Herzegovina imprisoned at Guantanamo Bay; *Srdjan DIZDAREVIC*, President of the Helsinki Committee for Human Rights in Bosnia and Herzegovina; *Michele PICARD*, former President of the Human Rights Chamber of Bosnia Herzegovina
26 April 2006—Wednesday	11h00-12h00	EP-BXL	**Press conference 2:**	*Carlos COELHO*, chairman and *Giovanni Claudio FAVA*, rapporteur: Presentation of the draft interim report (2006/2027 (INI))
27 April 2006—Thursday	15h00—18h30	EP-BXL		**TDIP Committee:** (cancelled because of the delegation to Skopje)

27 April 2006—Thursday (afternoon) / 29 April 2006—Saturday (morning)	***	Skopje (FYROM)	**Delegation TDIP 1: Skopje (FYROM)** Sylvia-Yvonne KAUFMANN [acting chair], Giovanni Claudio FAVA, Wolfgang KREISSL-DÖRFLER, Raül ROMEVA I RUEDA, Ryszard CZARNECKI	*Erwan FOUÉRÉ*, Head of the European Commission delegation and EU Special Representative; *Bancko CRVENKOVSKI*, President of the Republic; *Radmila SEKERINSKA*, Deputy Prime Minister; *Slobodan CASULE*, Member of the Parliament; *Siljan AVRAMOVSKI*, Deputy Director of the Security and counter-Intelligence Directorate; *Ljubomi MIHAILOVSKI*, Minister of Interior; *Ljupco JORDANOVSKI*, President of the Assembly; *Karolina RISTOVA-ASTERUD*, President of the Parliament's EU Affairs Committee; *Tenta ARIFI*, President of the Parliament's Foreign Affairs Committee; *Ganka SAMOILOVSKA CVETANOVA*, Member of Parliament; *Mirjana NAJCEVSKA*, President of the Macedonian Helsinki Committee; *Esad RAHIC*, President of the Parliamentary Committee for Defence and Security; *Stojan ANDOV*, President of the Human Rights Parliamentary Committee; *Zvonimir JANKULOVSKI*, Security expert
28 April 2006—Friday	19h30—20h00	Skopje (FYROM)	**Press conference 3:**	*Sylvia-Yvonne KAUFMANN*, acting chairwoman and *Giovanni Claudio FAVA*, rapporteur: Outcome of the delegation to FYROM
02 May 2006—Tuesday	14h30	EP-BXL		Informal meeting between *Javier SOLANA* and the Steering group
	15h00—18h30	EP-BXL	**TDIP Committee 11:**	*Javier SOLANA*, EU High Representative for the CFSP; *Alvaro GIL-ROBLES*, Council of Europe's former Human Rights Commissioner
04 May 2006—Thursday	9h30—12h30	EP-BXL	**TDIP Committee 12:**	Exchange of views on the draft interim report (2006/2027 (INI)); *Manfred NOWAK*, United Nations Special Rapporteur on Torture
	15h00—18h30			*Mats MELIN*, Swedish Chief Parliamentary Ombudsman

DATE	TIME	INSTITUTION-PLACE	SUBJECT	
	12h30—13h15	EP-BXL	**Press conference 4:**	*Sylvia-Yvonne KAUFMANN*, acting chairwoman and *Giovanni Claudio FAVA*, rapporteur: Outcome of the delegation to FYROM
08 May 2006—Monday (evening) / 12 May 2006—Friday (morning)	***	Washington (USA)	**Delegation TDIP 2: Washington (USA)** Carlos COELHO, Baroness Sarah LUDFORD, Cem ÖZDEMIR, Giovanni Claudio FAVA, Jas GAWRONSKI, Jose-Ingnacio SALAFRANCA SÁNCHEZ-NEYRA, Wolfgang KREISSL-DÖRFLER, Giulietto CHIESA, Jean LAMBERT, Giusto CATANIA, Konrad SZYMANSKI, Miroslaw PIOTROWSKI, Roger HELMER)	*John BRUTON*, Head of the European Commission Delegation; *Scott HORTON*, Chair of the committee on International Law; *Margaret L. SATTERTHWAITE*, Assistant Professor of Clinical Law and Faculty Director; *Barbara OLSHANSKY*, Director and Counsel (Guantanamo Global Justice Initiative); *Elisa MASSIMINO*, Director of the Washington, D.C. Office (Human Rights First); *Angela COLAIUTA*, Center for Victims of Torture, *John BRADSHAW*, Open Society Policy Center, Smita BARUAH, Physicians for Human Rights, *Jumana MUSA*, Advocacy Director for Domestic Human Rights and International Justice; *Jonathan SIFTON*, Counterterrorism Researcher, *Jennifer DASKAL*, US Advocacy Director; Representative *Robert WEXLER* (D-Florida); *Dan FRIED*, Assistant Secretary of State, *John BELLINGER*, Department of State's Legal Adviser; *Steven M. WATT*, Staff Attorney *Ann BEESON*, Associate Legal Director, *Chris ANDERS*, Legislative Counsel; Senator *Arlen SPECTER* (R) Pennsylvania; Senator *Richard DURBIN* (D) Illinois; Congressman *Ed MARKEY* (D) Massachusetts; *James WOOLSEY* (Former CIA Director 1993-1995); *David RIVKIN*, *Olivier GUITTA* and *Sally McNAMARA* from the American Legislative Exchange Council; *Morton H. HALPERIN*, *Lawrence J. KORB*, *Peter RUNDLET* and *Ken GUDE* from the Center for American Progress; *Eva NOWOTNY*, Austrian Ambassador to the USA representing the EU Council's Presidency

11 May 2006—Thursday	17h30—18h15	Commission Delegation Washington (USA)	**Press conference 5:**	*Carlos COELHO*, chairman and *Giovanni Claudio FAVA*, rapporteur: Outcome of the delegation to USA
EP PLENARY—May (from 15 to 18) 15 May 2006—Monday	21h00-22h30	EP-STR	**TDIP Committee 13:**	Exchange of views on the Research Note on the international law concerning the prohibition of torture presented by a representative of the Legal Service of the EP; Report on the TDIP committee delegation to USA (Washington, 8 to 12 May 2006)
16 May 2006—Tuesday	12h00			Deadline for *submission of the amendments* to the draft interim report (Committee's Secretariat)
17 May 2006—Wednesday	11h00-11h30		**Press conference 6:**	*Carlos COELHO*, chairman and *Giovanni Claudio FAVA*, rapporteur: Outcome of the delegation to USA
30 May 2006—Tuesday	15h00—18h30	EP-BXL	**TDIP Committee 14:**	Exchange of views on the study of the EU Network of Independent Expertise with Olivier DE SCHUTTER; Exchange of views on the amendments to the draft interim report (2006/2027 (INI));
01 June 2006—Thursday		EP—BXL		**TDIP Committee:** (cancelled by a committee decision)
07 June 2006—Wednesday	from 09h00	Council of Europe -Paris	**Parliamentary Assembly 4:**	Meeting of the Committee on Legal Affairs and Human Rights (Point 3 of the Agenda: *Alleged secret detentions in Council of Europe member states: Consideration of a draft report and vote on a draft resolution and a draft recommendation)*

DATE		TIME	INSTITUTION-PLACE	SUBJECT	
EP PLENARY -June (from 12 to 15)	12 June 2006—Monday	19h00—20h30	EP—STR	**TDIP Committee 15**	Vote of motion for a interim resolution (2006/2027 (INI)) midway through the TDIP work
	13 June 2006—Tuesday	15h00-15h30		**Press conference 7:**	*Carlos COELHO*, chairman and *Giovanni Claudio FAVA*, rapporteur: Outcome of the vote on the interim resolution in the Committee
21 June 2006—Wednesday		15h00	EP-BXL	**Meeting with rapporteur 1:**	Brian JOHNSON-THOMAS, expert on arms trade
		18h45—20h15		**Steering group 6:**	Informal exchange of views on eventual programme of work for the second semester of the year
27 June 2006—Tuesday		from 10h00	Council of Europe -Paris	**Parliamentary Assembly 5:**	Plenary of the Parliamentary Assembly, 3rd part of 2006 Ordinary Session (Point 2 of the Agenda: *Alleged secret detentions in Council of Europe member states; Statement by Franco FRATTINI, Vice-President of the European Commission; Statement by Giovanni Claudio FAVA, rapporteur; vote on Legal Affairs and Human Rights Committee's report)*
EP PLENARY -July (from 3 to 6)	03 July 2006—Monday	21h00-22h30	EP—STR	**TDIP Committee 16:**	Exchange of views with *Dick MARTY*, Council of Europe
	05/06 July 2006	13h15—13h45		**Plenary sitting 3:**	Debate(5 July) and vote(6 July) of the resolution (2006/2027 (INI)) midway through TDIP work
				Press conference 8:	*Carlos COELHO*, chairman and *Giovanni Claudio FAVA*, rapporteur: Outcome of the vote on the resolution just adopted in Plenary (6 July)

10 July 2006—Monday	15h00—18h00	EP-BXL	**TDIP Committee 17:**	Working programme for the second half of the year; Munich prosecutor *Martin HOFMANN* (Germany) in charge of the El-Masri case
	18h00—18h30		**Steering group 7:**	Delegations to Germany, United Kingdom, Romania and Poland
PLENARY -September I (from 4 to 7) 4 September 2006—Monday	21h00-22h30	EP-STR	**TDIP Committee 18:**	*Carlo BONINI*, journalist from La Repubblica (IT)
14 September 2006—Thursday	09h00—12h30	EP-BXL	**TDIP Committee 19:**	*Bernhard DOCKE*, Partner of Dr. Hannover and Partner Bremen, Lawyer of Murat KURNAZ; *Gül PINAR*, Lawyer of Mohammed ZAMMARS's family; *Francesca LONGHI*, Lawyer of Abou ELKASSIM BRITEL, Italian citizen
	14h00—15h00		**Steering group 8:**	State of play of TDIP Committee working programme (hearings and delegations); Preparation of TDIP Committee final recommendations
	15h00—18h30		**TDIP Committee 19:**	*Marek Antoni NOWICKI*, Former Kosovo Ombudsman (2000 -2005); *Miguel Angel MORATINOS*, Minister for Foreign Affairs of Spain

DATE	TIME	INSTITUTION-PLACE	SUBJECT	
19 September 2006—Tuesday	***	Berlin (Germany)	**Delegation TDIP 3: Berlin (GERMANY)** Carlos COELHO, (chairman), Giovanni Claudio FAVA, Jas GAWRONSKI, Wolfgang KREISSL-DÖRFLER, Alexander ALVARO, Cem ÖZDEMIR, Sylvia Yvonne KAUFMANN	*Hans-Martin TILLACK*, Stern Magazine; *Ferdinand MUGGENTHALER and Susanne BAUMANN*, Amnesty International; Members of the Bundestag's Inquiry Committee: *GROHE Hermann, HARTMANN Michael, HUBINGER Anette, JUNG Johannes, KASTER Bernhard, KAUDER Siegfried Kauder, KOHLER Kristina, KONIGSHAUS Hellmut, MAYER Stephan, MOGG Ursula, NACHTWEI Winfried, NESKOVIC Wolfgang, OPPERMANN Thomas, PAU Petra, STADLER Max and STRÖBELE Hans-Christian*
20 September 2006—Wednesday	12h00	EP-BXL	**Meeting with rapporteur 2:**	*Francis GAINCHE*, Adviser to the Director of the Central Flow Management (EUROCONTROL)
EP PLENARY -September II (from 25 to 28) 25 September 2006—Monday	21h00-22h30	EP-STR	**TDIP Committee 20:**	*Hans BORN*, Senior fellow, Geneva Centre for the Democratic Control of Armed Forces (DCAF)

02 October 2006—Monday	16h15—17h00	EP-BXL	**TDIP Committee 21:**	Exchange of views on the delegation to Berlin; Projection of the film "CIA: Guerre secrete en Europe"
	17h00—18h30		**Steering group 9:**	Treatment of confidential information; State of play of TDIP Committee working programme (hearings and delegations)
03 October 2006—Tuesday	09h00—12h30		**TDIP Committee 21:**	*Víctor AGUADO*, Director General of the European Organisation for the Safety of Air Navigation (EUROCONTROL); *Martin SCHEININ*, United Nations Special Rapporteur for promotion and protection of Human rights while countering terrorism
04 October 2006-Wednesday (morning) 06 October 2005—Friday (evening)	***	London (United Kingdom)	**Delegation TDIP 4: London (UNITED KINGDOM)** Sarah LUDFORD, [acting chair], Giovanni Claudio FAVA, Jas GAWRONSKI, Wolfgang KREISSL-DÖRFLER,, Jean LAMBERT, Giusto CATANIA, Miroslaw PIOTROWSKI	*Wahab El-Rawi*, brother of Bisher al-Rawi; *Clive Stafford Smith*, lawyer for Bisher al-Rawi, Jamil El-Banna and Binyam Mohamed; *Gareth Peirce*, lawyer for Bisher al-Rawi and Jamil El-Banna; *Brent Mickum*, US lawyer of Bisher al Rawi and Jamil El-Banna; *Rt Hon Michael Ancram MP*, Member of the Intelligence and Security Committee; *Martin Mubanga*; *Louise Christian*, lawyer of Martin Mubanga; *Eric Metcalfe*, representative from Justice; *Gareth Crossman*, representative from Liberty; *Anne Fitzgerald*, representative from Amnesty International; Ian Cobain and Richard Norton-Taylor, journalists from "The Guardian"; Stephen GREY, free-lance journalist; *Mike Gapes MP*, Chairman of the Foreign Affairs Committee (House of Commons); *Rt Hon Geoff Hoon MP*, Minister for Europe, Foreign and Commonwealth Office; *Andrew Tyrie MP*, Chairman of the All-Party Parliamentary Group on extraordinary rendition, comprising members of the House of Commons and House of Lords

DATE	TIME	INSTITUTION-PLACE	SUBJECT	
06 October 2006—Friday	11h00-12h00	Commission Delegation London (United Kingdom)	**Press conference 9:**	*Sarah LUDFORD*, acting chair and *Giovanni Claudio FAVA*, rapporteur: Outcome of the delegation to London
09 October 2006—Monday	15h00—18h30	EP-BXL	**TDIP Committee 22:**	*Armando SPATARO*, Prosecutor (Milano)
10 October 2006—Tuesday	09h00—12h30			*Otmar LAHODINSKY*, Journalist and European editor of Austria's weekly magazine "Profil"; *Masaad Omer BEHARI*, Alleged victim of Sudanese origin, living in Vienna
17 October 2006—Tuesday (morning) 19 October 2006—Thursday (evening)	***	Bucharest (Romania)	**Delegation TDIP 5: Bucharest (ROMANIA)** Carlos COELHO, (chairman), Giovanni Claudio FAVA, Sarah LUDFORD, Cem OZDEMIR, Frieda BREPOELS, Ana GOMES, Willy MEYER, Ryszard CZARNECKI	*Tapio SAARELA*, Finnish Ambassador representing the EU Council's Presidency; *Jonathan SCHEELE*, Head of the European Commission delegation; *Adrian Cosmin VIERITA*, Secretary of State for EU affairs, Ministry for Foreign Affairs; *Norica NICOLAI*, Senator, Chairwoman of the Special Inquiry Committee of the Romanian Senate; *Teodor MELESCANU*, Vice-president of the Romanian Senate; *Radu STROE*, Chairman of the Parliamentary Committee for the Oversight of the Romanian Intelligence Services; *Romeo RAICU*, Chairman of the Romanian Foreign Intelligence Service Oversight Parliamentary Committee; *Renate WEBER*, Chair of the Open Society Foundation; *Diana-Olivia CALINESCU*, Executive Director APADOR—CH (Romanian Helsinki Committee); *Calin COSMACIUC*, Journalist, Evenimentul Zilei; *Dan VULCAN*, Former chief inspector, Department of Civil Aviation, Ministry of Transport; *Catalin RADU*, Chief inspector,

				Department of Civil Aviation, Ministry of Transport; *Sergiu Tudor MEDAR*, National Security Adviser, Presidential Administration; *Anghel ANDREESCU*, Secretary of State for public order and security; *George MAIOR*, Head of the Romanian Intelligence Service; *Radu TIMOFTE*, Former Head of the Romanian Intelligence Service; *Maria IONESCU*, Editor in chief at "Observator de Constanta" newspaper; *Cristian RADU and Stefan CANDEA*, Romanian Centre for Investigative Journalism; *Alison MUTLER*, Associated Press Writer; *Mihaela DANGA*, Deputy Director at the Centre for Independent Journalism; *Ioan TALPES*, Senator, Member of the Committee for National Security and Defence; *Gheorghe FULGA*, Former Head of the Romanian External Intelligence Services
19 October 2006—Thursday	11h23-12h00	Commission Delegation Bucharest (Romania)	**Press conference 10:**	*Carlos COELHO*, chairman and *Giovanni Claudio FAVA*, rapporteur: Outcome of the delegation to Bucharest
EP PLENARY -October (from 23 to 26) 23 October 2006—Monday	19h00—19h30	EP-STR	**TDIP Committee 23:**	Exchange of views on the delegation to Romania (Bucharest)
	19h30—20h30		**Steering group 10:**	Treatment of confidential information; State of play of TDIP Committee working programme (hearings and delegations)

DATE	TIME	INSTITUTION-PLACE	SUBJECT	
08 November 2006—Tuesday (morning) 10 November 2006—Thursday (evening)	***	Warsaw (Poland)	**Delegation TDIP 6: Warszawa (POLAND)** Carlos COELHO, (chairman), Giovanni Claudio FAVA, Jas GAWRONSKI, Giulietto CHIESA, Sophia IN'T VELD, Cem OZDEMIR, Giusto CATANIA, Konrad SZYMANSKI, Boguslaw ROGALSKI, Ryszard CZARNECKI	*Jarosław GIZIŃSKI*, Journalist, Newsweek Polska; *Paweł WROŃSKI*, Journalist, Gazeta Wyborcza; *Marek Antoni NOWICKI*, President, Helsinki Foundation for Human Rights; *Marek PASIONEK*, Undersecretary of State in the Chancellery of the Prime Minister; *Adam KRZYKOWSKI*, Journalist, Public TV Olsztyn; *Jarosław JURCZENKO*, Chairman of the Board, Szczytno/Szymany Airport; *Marek KSIĄŻEK*, Journalist from the region of Szczytno (free lance); *Zbigniew SIEMIĄTKOWSKI*, former Head of the Foreign Intelligence Agency (AW) (2002 -2004); *Jerzy KOS*, former Chairman of the Board, Szczytno/Szymany Airport.
10 November 2006—Friday	13h30—14h00	Commission Delegation Warsaw (Poland)	**Press conference 11:**	*Carlos COELHO*, chairman and *Giovanni Claudio FAVA*, rapporteur: Outcome of the delegation to Warsaw

EP PLENARY—November (from 13 to 16) 13 November 2006—Monday	19h00—20h30	EP-STR	**TDIP Committee 24:**	*Terry DAVIS*, Council of Europe's Secretary General
20 November 2006—Monday	15h00—18h30	EP-BXL	**TDIP Committee 25:**	*Wolfgang PETRITSCH*, former United Nations High Representative in Bosnia and Herzegovina; *Javier ZARAGOZA* and *Vicente GONZALEZ MOTA*, Spanish prosecutors
22 November 2006—Wednesday	09h00—12h30	EP-BXL	**TDIP Committee 26:**	*Murat KURNAZ*, victim; *Bernhard DOCKE*, Partner of Dr. Hannover and Partner Bremen, Lawyer of Murat KURNAZ
23 November 2006—Thursday	15h00—18h30	EP-BXL	**TDIP Committee 27:**	*Mariola PRZEWŁOCKA*, Former director of Szczytno/Szymany Airport (Poland)
28 November 2006—Tuesday	15h00—18h30	EP-BXL	**TDIP Committee 28:**	*Maurice MANNING*, president of the Irish Human Rights Commission and *Suzanne EGAN*, Commissioner of the Irish Human Rights Commission; presentation of the final report by *Giovanni Claudio FAVA*, rapporteur
28 November 2006—Tuesday	18h30—20h00	EP-BXL	**Steering group 10:**	TDIP Temporary Committee delegation to Lisbon, 6 December 2006
29 November 2006—Wednesday	15h30—16h00	EP-BXL	**Press conference 12:**	*Giovanni Claudio FAVA*, rapporteur: presentation of draft final report

	DATE	TIME	INSTITUTION-PLACE	SUBJECT	
	30 November 2006—Thursday	15h00—18h30	EP-BXL	**TDIP Committee 29:**	*Dermot AHERN*, Irish Minister for Foreign Affairs; *Gerald STABEROCK*, International Commission of Jurists
	06 December 2006—Wednesday	****	Lisbon (Portugal)	**Delegation TDIP 7: Lisbon (PORTUGAL)** Carlos COELHO, (chairman), Sarah LUDFORD, Frieda BREPOELS, Wolfgang KREISSL-DÖRFLER, Raúl ROMEVA, Ana Maria GOMES	*Luis AMADO*, Minister for Foreign Affairs, *Micael PEREIRA* and *Ricardo LOURENÇO*, journalists from "Expresso", *Maria Helena FALEIRO DE ALMEIDA*, Director of Economic Regulation of Instituto Nacional de Aviação Civil (INAC), *Fernando CARVALHO*, Administrator of Navegação Aérea de Portugal (NAV), *Manuel JARMELA PALOS*, Director of Serviço de Estrangeiros e Fronteiras (SEF), *heads of political groups*.
EP PLENARY -December (from 11 to 14)	12 December 2006—Tuesday	13h00—22h00	Mannheim (Germany)	**Fact finding mission 1:** Cem OZDEMIR, Vice-President	*Wolf-Dieter DIETRICH*, prosecutor; *Peter WRIGHT*, peace activist; Mr. *RÄBOCK* and Mr. *SCHINDLER*, witnesses (Coleman BARRACKS)
	14 December 2006—Thursday	10h00-11h00	EP-STR	**TDIP Committee 30:**	Exchange of views on the draft final report

	18 December 2006—Monday	12h00	EP-BXL		Deadline for submission of the amendments to the draft final report (Committee's Secretariat)
	18 December 2006—Monday	15h00—18h30	EP-BXL	**TDIP Committee 31:**	Exchange of views on the delegation to Lisbon (Portugal); Exchange of views on the draft final report (continuation from the previous meeting)
	19 December 2006—Tuesday	09h00—12h30	EP-BXL	**TDIP Committee 31:**	*Franco FRATTINI*, Vice-President of the European Commission
EP PLENARY—January (15 to 18)	15 January 2007—Monday	19h00—20h30	EP-STR	**TDIP Committee 32:**	Exchange of views on the amendments to the draft final report
	23 January 2007—Tuesday	09h00—12h30	EP-BXL	**TDIP Committee 33:**	Vote of the motion for a resolution (2006/2200 (INI))
	23 January 2007—Tuesday	14h30—15h00	EP-BXL	**Press conference 13:**	*Carlos COELHO*, chairman and Giovanni *Claudio FAVA*, rapporteur: Outcome of the vote on the motion for a resolution as adopted by TDIP Committee
EP PLENARY -February (12 to 15)	13 February 2007—Tuesday	15h00—17h30	EP-STR	**Plenary sitting 4:**	Debate on the resolution on the outcome of TDIP work
EP PLENARY -February (12 to 15)	15 February 2007—Wednesday	Midday	EP-STR	**Plenary sitting 5:**	Vote of the resolution
EP PLENARY -February (12 to 15)	15 February 2007—Wednesday	After vote	EP-STR	**Press conference 14:**	Outcome of the vote on the resolution concluding TDIP work in Plenary

Annex 2:

Meetings in the Framework of the Committee's Work

No	Name	Function	Country/ Institution	Date of the meeting	Place of the meeting	Remarks
EU Institutions						
1	**FRATTINI Franco**	Vice-President	European Commission	19 December 2006	Brussels	Hearing
				13 February 2006	Strasbourg	
2	**BRUTON John**	Head of the European Commission delegation	European Commission	08 May 2006	Washington	Delegation
3	**SCHEELE Jonathan**	Head of the European Commission delegation	European Commission	17 October 2006	Bucharest	Delegation
4	**FOUÉRÉ Erwan**	Head of the European Commission delegation and EU Special Representative	FYROM	27 April 2006	Skopje	Delegation
5	**SOLANA Javier**	EU High Representative for the CFSP	Council of the European Union	02 May 2006	Brussels	Hearing
6	**DE VRJIES Gijs**	EU's Counter-terrorism Coordinator	Council of the European Union	20 April 2006	Brussels	Hearing
7	**SAARELA Tapio**	Finnish Ambassador to Romania representing the EU Council's Presidency	European Union Council's Presidency	17 October 2006	Bucharest	Delegation
8	**NOWOTNY Eva**	Austrian Ambassador to the USA representing the EU Council's Presidency	European Union Council's Presidency	08 May 2006	Washington	Delegation

Governments						
1	**AVRAMOVSKI Siljan**	Deputy Director of the Security and Counter-Intelligence Directorate	FYROM	28 April 2006	Skopje	Delegation
2	**CRVENKOVSKI Branko**	President of the Republic	FYROM	27 April 2006	Skopje	Delegation
3	**MIHAILOVSKI Ljubomir**	Minister of Interior	FYROM	28 April 2006	Skopje	Delegation
4	**SEKERINSKA Radmila**	Deputy Prime Minister	FYROM	27 April 2006	Skopje	Delegation
5	**AHERN Dermot**	Minister for Foreign Affairs	Ireland	30 November 2006	Brussels	Hearing
6	**POLLARI Nicolò**	Head of the Italian Intelligence and Security Services	Italy	06 March 2006	Brussels	Hearing
7	**PASIONEK Marek**	Undersecretary of State at the Chancellery of the Prime Minister	Poland	09 November 2006	Warsaw	Delegation
8	**SIEMIĄTKOWSKI Zbigniew**	Former Head of the Foreign Intelligence Agency (AW)	Poland	10 November 2006	Warsaw	Delegation
9	**AMADO Luis**	Minister for Foreign Affairs	Portugal	05 December 2006	Lisbon	Delegation
10	**CARVALHO Fernando**	Administrator of Navegação Aérea de Portugal (NAV)	Portugal	05 December 2006	Lisbon	Delegation
11	**FALEIRO DE ALMEIDA Maria Helena**	Director of Economic Regulation of Instituto Nacional de Aviação Civil (INAC)	Portugal	05 December 2006	Lisbon	Delegation

No	Name	Function	Country/ Institution	Date of the meeting	Place of the meeting	Remarks
12	**JARMELA PALOS Manuel**	Director of Serviço de Estrangeiros e Fronteiras (SEF)	Portugal	05 December 2006	Lisbon	Delegation
13	**ANDREESCU Anghel**	Secretary of State for public order and security	Romania	18 October 2006	Bucharest	Delegation
14	**FULGA Gheorghe**	Former Head of the Romanian External Intelligence Service	Romania	19 October 2006	Bucharest	Delegation
15	**MAIOR George**	Head of the Romanian Internal Intelligence Service	Romania	18 October 2006	Bucharest	Delegation
16	**MEDAR Sergiu Tudor**	National Security Adviser, Presidential Administration	Romania	18 October 2006	Bucharest	Delegation
17	**RADU Catalin**	Chief Inspector, Department of Civil Aviation, Ministry of Transport	Romania	18 October 2006	Bucharest	Delegation
18	**ROMERO**	Deputy Director of the Romanian Internal Intelligence Service	Romania	18 October 2006	Bucharest	Delegation
19	**TIMOFTE Radu**	Former Head of the Romanian Internal Intelligence Service	Romania	18 October 2006	Bucharest	Delegation
20	**VIERITA Adrian Cosmin**	Secretary of State for EU affairs, Ministry for Foreign Affairs	Romania	17 October 2006	Bucharest	Delegation
21	**VULCAN Dan**	Former Chief Inspector, Department of Civil Aviation, Ministry of Transport	Romania	17 October 2006	Bucharest	Delegation

22	**MORATINOS Miguel Angel**	Minister for Foreign Affairs	Spain	14 September 2006	Brussels	Hearing
23	**HOON Geoff**	Minister for Europe, Foreign and Commonwealth Office	United Kingdom	05 October 2006	London	Delegation
24	**BELLINGER John**	Department of State Legal Adviser Office	USA	11 May 2006	Washington	Delegation
25	**FRIED Dan**	Assistant Secretary of State, Bureau of European and Eurasian Affairs	USA	11 May 2006	Washington	Delegation
26	**WOOLSEY James**	Former CIA Director	USA	12 May 2006	Washington	Delegation
National Parliaments						
1	**DELEPIÈRE Jean-Claude**	Chairman of the Permanent Committee R	Belgium	06 March 2006	Brussels	Hearing
2	**LIZIN Anne-Marie**	President of the Senate of Belgium	Belgium	06 March 2006	Brussels	Hearing
3	**ANDOV Stojan**	President of the Human Rights Parliamentary Committee	FYROM	28 April 2006	Skopje	Delegation
4	**ARIFI Teuta**	President of the Foreign Affairs Committee	FYROM	28 April 2006	Skopje	Delegation
5	**CASULE Slobodan**	Member of Parliament (Former Minister of Foreign Affairs)	FYROM	27 April 2006	Skopje	Delegation
6	**JORDANOVSKI Ljupco**	President of the Parliament	FYROM	28 April 2006	Skopje	Delegation

No	Name	Function	Country/ Institution	Date of the meeting	Place of the meeting	Remarks
7	**RAHIC Esad**	President of the Parliamentary Committee for Defence and Security	FYROM	28 April 2006	Skopje	Delegation
8	**RISTOVA-ASTERUD Karolina**	President of the Parliament's EU Affairs Committee	FYROM	28 April 2006	Skopje	Delegation
9	**SAMOILOVSKA CVETANOVA Ganka**	Member of the Parliament's EU Affairs and Foreign Affairs Committees	FYROM	28 April 2006	Skopje	Delegation
10	**GROHE Hermann**	1st Committee of Inquiry of the German Bundestag	Germany	19 September 2006	Berlin	Delegation
11	**HARTMANN Michael**	Vice-Chairman, 1st Committee of Inquiry of the German Bundestag	Germany	19 September 2006	Berlin	Delegation
12	**HUBINGER Anette**	1st Committee of Inquiry of the German Bundestag	Germany	19 September 2006	Berlin	Delegation
13	**JUNG Johannes**	1st Committee of Inquiry of the German Bundestag	Germany	19 September 2006	Berlin	Delegation
14	**KASTER Bernhard**	1st Committee of Inquiry of the German Bundestag	Germany	19 September 2006	Berlin	Delegation
15	**KAUDER Siegfried Kauder**	Chairman, 1st Committee of Inquiry of the German Bundestag	Germany	19 September 2006	Berlin	Delegation
16	**KOHLER Kristina**	1st Committee of Inquiry of the German Bundestag	Germany	19 September 2006	Berlin	Delegation

17	**KONIGSHAUS Hellmut**	1st Committee of Inquiry of the German Bundestag	Germany	19 September 2006	Berlin	Delegation
18	**MAYER Stephan**	1st Committee of Inquiry of the German Bundestag	Germany	19 September 2006	Berlin	Delegation
19	**MOGG Ursula**	1st Committee of Inquiry of the German Bundestag	Germany	19 September 2006	Berlin	Delegation
20	**NACHTWEI Winfried**	1st Committee of Inquiry of the German Bundestag	Germany	19 September 2006	Berlin	Delegation
21	**NESKOVIC Wolfgang**	1st Committee of Inquiry of the German Bundestag	Germany	19 September 2006	Berlin	Delegation
22	**OPPERMANN Thomas**	1st Committee of Inquiry of the German Bundestag	Germany	19 September 2006	Berlin	Delegation
23	**PAU Petra**	1st Committee of Inquiry of the German Bundestag	Germany	19 September 2006	Berlin	Delegation
24	**STADLER Max**	1st Committee of Inquiry of the German Bundestag	Germany	19 September 2006	Berlin	Delegation
25	**STRÖBELE Hans-Christian**	1st Committee of Inquiry of the German Bundestag	Germany	19 September 2006	Berlin	Delegation
26	**MELESCANU Teodor**	Vice president of the Romanian Senate and Member of the Special Inquiry Committee	Romania	17 October 2006	Bucharest	Delegation
27	**NICOLAI Norica**	Senator, Chairwoman of the Special Committee of the Romanian Parliament	Romania	17 October 2006	Bucharest	Delegation

No	Name	Function	Country/ Institution	Date of the meeting	Place of the meeting	Remarks
28	**RAICU Romeo**	Chairman of the Romanian Foreign Intelligence Service Oversight Parliamentary Committee	Romania	17 October 2006	Bucharest	Delegation
29	**STROE Radu**	Chairman of the Parliamentary Committee for the Oversight of the Romanian Intelligence Services	Romania	17 October 2006	Bucharest	Delegation
30	**TALPES Ioan**	Senator, Member of the Committee for National Security and Defence	Romania	19 October 2006	Bucharest	Delegation
31	**MELIN Mats**	Chief Parliamenary Ombudsman	Sweden	04 May 2006	Brussels	Hearing
32	**ANCRAM Hon Michael**	MP, Member of the Intelligence and Security Committee	United Kingdom	04 October 2006	London	Delegation
33	**GAPES Mike**	Chairman of the Foreign Affairs Committee	United Kingdom	04 October 2006	London	Delegation
34	**TYRIE Andrew**	MP, Chairman of the All-Party Parliamentary Group on extraordinary rendition	United Kingdom	05 October 2006	London	Delegation
35	**DURBIN Richard**	Senator	USA	12 May 2006	Washington	Delegation
36	**HORTON Scott**	Chair of the Committee on International Law, House of Representatives	USA	09 May 2006	Washington	Delegation

37	**MARKEY Edward**	Member of House of Representatives	USA	12 May 2006	Washington	Delegation
38	**SPECTER Arlen**	Senator	USA	12 May 2006	Washington	Delegation
39	**WEXLER Robert**	Member of House of Representatives	USA	10 May 2006	Washington	Delegation
Judiciary						
1	**HOFMANN Martin**	Prosecutor, Munich	Germany	10 July 2006	Brussels	Hearing
2	**DIETRICH Wolf-Dieter**	Prosecutor, Mannheim	Germany	12 December 2006	Mannheim	Fact finding mission
3	**SPATARO Armando**	Senior Prosecutor, Milan	Italy	23 February 2006 09 October 2006	Brussels	Hearing
4	**GONZALEZ MOTA Vicente**	Prosecutor of Audencia Nacional	Spain	20 November 2006	Brussels	Hearing
5	**ZARAGOZA Javier**	Chief Prosecutor of Audiencia Nacional	Spain	20 November 2006	Brussels	Hearing
Council of Europe						
1	**DAVIS Terry**	Secretary General	Council of Europe	13 October 2006	Strasbourg	Hearing
2	**GIL-ROBLES Alvaro**	Former Commissioner for Human Rights	Council of Europe	02 May 2006	Brussels	Hearing
3	**HAMMARBERG Thomas**	Commissioner for Human Rights	Council of Europe	24 April 2006	Brussels	Working lunch

No	Name	Function	Country/ Institution	Date of the meeting	Place of the meeting	Remarks
4	**MARTY Dick**	Chairman of Legal Affairs and Human Rights Committee/ Rapporteur on alleged secret detentions of the Parliamentary Assembly	Council of Europe (Parliamentary Asembly)	23 February 2006	Brussels	Hearing
				03 July 2006	Strasbourg	
International organisations						
1	**AGUADO Victor**	Director General	Eurocontrol	03 October 2006	Brussels	Hearing
2	**GAINCHE Francis**	Adviser to the Director of the Central Flow Management	Eurocontrol	20 September 2006	Brussels	Rapporteur
3	**NOWICKI Marek Antoni**	Former Kosovo Ombudsman (2000-2005)& President of the Helsinki Foundation for Human Rights (Poland)	Kosovo	14 September 2006	Brussels	Hearing
			Poland	09 November 2006	Warsaw	Delegation
4	**NOWAK Manfred**	UN Special Rapporteur on Torture	United Nations	04 May 2006	Brussels	Hearing
5	**SCHEININ Martin**	UN Special Rapporteur for Promotion and Protection of Human Rights while Countering Terrorism	United Nations	03 October 2006	Brussels	Hearing
6	**PETRITSCH Wolfgang**	Former UN High Representative	United Nations: Bosnia & Herzegovina	20 November 2006	Brussels	Hearing

7	**PICARD Michèle**	Former President of Human Rights Chamber	United Nations / Council of Europe: Bosnia & Herzegovina	25 April 2006	Brussels	Hearing
Victims						
1	**BEHARI Masaad Omer**	Resident in Austria of Sudanese origin	Austria	10 October 2006	Brussels	Hearing
2	**ARAR Maher**	Canadian citizen	Canada	23 March 2006	Brussels	Hearing
3	**EL MASRI Khaled**	German citizen	Germany	13 March 2006	Strasbourg	Hearing
4	**KURNAZ Murat**	German resident of Turkish origin	Germany	22 November 2006	Brussels	Hearing
5	**MUBANGA Martin**	British and Zambian citizen	United Kingdom	04 October 2006	London	Delegation
Lawyers						
1	**OLESKEY H. Stephen**	Counsel for Six citizens of Bosnia and Herzegoina imprisoned at Guantanamo Bay	Bosnia & Herzegovina	25 April 2006	Brussels	Hearing
2	**EDWARDH Marlys**	Lawyer of Maher ARAR	Canada	23 March 2006	Brussels	Hearing
3	**WALDMAN Lorne**	Lawyer of Maher ARAR	Canada	23 March 2006	Brussels	Hearing

No	Name	Function	Country/ Institution	Date of the meeting	Place of the meeting	Remarks
4	**DOCKE Bernhard**	Lawyer of Murat KURNAZ	Germany	14 September 2006	Brussels	Hearing
				22 November 2006		
5	**GNJIDIC Manfred**	Lawyer of Khaled EL MASRI	Germany	13 March 2006	Strasbourg	Hearing
6	**PINAR Gül**	Lawyer of Mohammed ZAMMARS's family	Germany	14 September 2006	Brussels	Hearing
7	**LONGHI Francesca**	Lawyer of Abou ELKASSIM BRITEL	Italy	14 September 2006	Brussels	Hearing
8	**JÖNSSON Kjeff**	Lawyer of MOhammed EL-ZARY (Egyptian citizen), alleged victim	Sweden	23 March 2006	Brussels	Hearing
9	**CHRISTIAN Louise**	Lawyer of Martin MUBANGA	United Kingdom	04 October 2006	London	Delegation
10	**MICKUM Brent**	US lawyer of Bisher AL-RAWI and Jamil EL-BANNA	United Kingdom	04 October 2006	London	Delegation
11	**PEIRCE Gareth**	Lawyer for Bisher AL-RAWI and Jamil EL-BANNA	United Kingdom	04 October 2006	London	Delegation
12	**STAFFORD SMITH Clive**	Lawyer for Bisher AL-RAWI, Jamil EL-BANNA and Mohamed BINYAM	United Kingdom	04 October 2006	London	Delegation

NGOs						
1	**FITZGERALD Anne**	Senior Research Policy Adviser	Amnesty International	23 February 2006	Brussels	Hearing
				04 October 2006	London	Delegation
2	**DIZDAREVIC Srdjan**	President of the Helsinki Committee for Human Rights	Bosnia & Herzegovina	25 April 2006	Brussels	Hearing
3	**NAJCEVSKA Mirjana**	President of the Macedonian Helsinki Committee	FYROM	28 April 2006	Skopje	Delegation
4	**BAUMANN Susanne**	Amnesty International Germany	Germany	19 September 2006	Berlin	Delegation
5	**MUGGENTHALER Ferdinand**	Amnesty International Germany	Germany	19 September 2006	Berlin	Delegation
6	**DASKAL Jennifer**	US Advocacy Director	Human Rights Watch	10 May 2006	Washington	Delegation
7	**MARINER Joanne**	Director of Terrorism and Counterterrorism Program	Human Rights Watch	23 February 2006	Brussels	Hearing
8	**SIFTON John**	Counterterrorism Researcher	Human Rights Watch	10 May 2006	Washington	Delegation
9	**STABEROCK Gerald**	Director of the Global Security and the Rule of Law Programme	International Commission of Jurists	30 November 2006	Brussels	Hearing
10	**CALINESCU Diana-Olivia**	Executive Director APADOR-CH (Romanian Helsinki Committee)	Romania	17 October 2006	Bucharest	Delegation

No	Name	Function	Country/ Institution	Date of the meeting	Place of the meeting	Remarks
11	**WEBER Renate**	Chair of the Open Society Foundation	Romania	17 October 2006	Bucharest	Delegation
12	**BUNYAN Tony**	Director	Statewatch	23 February 2006	Brussels	Hearing
13	**CROSSMAN Gareth**	Representative from Liberty NGO	United Kingdom	04 October 2006	London	Delegation
14	**METCALFE Eric**	Representative from Justice NGO	United Kingdom	04 October 2006	London	Delegation
15	**BARUAH Smita**	Physicians for Human Rights	USA	10 May 2006	Washington	Delegation
16	**BRADSHAW John**	Open Society Policy Center	USA	10 May 2006	Washington	Delegation
17	**COLAIUTA Angela**	Center for Victims of Torture	USA	10 May 2006	Washington	Delegation
18	**GUDE Ken**	Associate Director, International Rights and Responsibilities Program, The Center for American Progress	USA	12 May 2006	Washington	Delegation
19	**MASSIMINO Elisa**	Human Rights First, Director at the Washington office	USA	09 May 2006	Washington	Delegation
20	**MUSA Jumana**	Advocacy Director for Domestic Human Rights and International Justice	USA	10 May 2006	Washington	Delegation

21	**OLSHANSKY Barbara**	Director and Counsel of the Guantanamo Global Justice Initiative	USA	09 May 2006	Washington	Delegation
Journalists						
1	**LAHODYNSKY Otmar**	Journalist and European Editor of Austria's weekly magazine *Profil*	Austria	10 October 2006	Brussels	Hearing
2	**TILLACK Hans-Martin**	Journalist from *Stern Magazin*	Germany	19 September 2006	Berlin	Delegation
3	**BIONDANI Paolo**	Journalist from *Il Corriere della Sera*	Italy	21 March 2006	Brussels	Hearing
4	**OLIMPIO Guido**	Journalist from *Il Corriere della Sera*	Italy	21 March 2006	Brussels	Hearing
5	**BONINI Carlo**	Journalist from *La Repubblica*	Italy	04 September 2006	Strasbourg	Hearing
6	**GIZIŃSKI Jarosław**	Journalist from *Newsweek Polska*	Poland	08 November 2006	Warsaw	Delegation
7	**KRZYKOWSKI Adam**	Journalist from public TV *Olsztyn*	Poland	09 November 2006	Warsaw	Delegation
8	**KSIĄŹEK Marek**	Journalist from the region of Szczytno (free lance)	Poland	09 November 2006	Warsaw	Delegation
9	**WROŃSKI Paweł**	Journalist form *Gazeta Wyborcza*	Poland	09 November 2006	Warsaw	Delegation
10	**LOURENCO Ricardo**	Journalist from *Expresso*	Portugal	05 December 2006	Lisbon	Delegation

No	Name	Function	Country/ Institution	Date of the meeting	Place of the meeting	Remarks
11	**PEREIRA Micael**	Journalist from *Expresso*	Portugal	05 December 2006	Lisbon	Delegation
12	**CANDEA Stefan**	Romanian Center for Investigative Journalism	Romania	18 October 2006	Bucharest	Delegation
13	**RADU Cristian**	Romanian Center for Investigative Journalism	Romania	18 October 2006	Bucharest	Delegation
14	**COSMACIUC Calin**	Journalist from the *Evenimentul Zilei*	Romania	17 October 2006	Bucharest	Delegation
15	**DANGA Mihaela**	Deputy Director at the Center for Independent Journalism	Romania	19 October 2006	Bucharest	Delegation
16	**IONESCU Maria**	Editor in chief at Observator de Constanta newspaper	Romania	18 October 2006	Bucharest	Delegation
17	**MUTLER Allison**	Associated Press Writer	Romania	18 October 2006	Bucharest	Delegation
18	**VALLES Matias**	Journalist from *Diario de Mallorca*	Spain	20 April 2006	Brussels	Hearing
19	**COBAIN Ian**	Journalist from *The Guardian*	United Kingdom	05 October 2006	London	Delegation
20	**NORTON-TAYLOR Richard**	Journalist from *The Guardian*	United Kingdom	05 October 2006	London	Delegation
21	**GREY Stephen**	Journalist free lance	United Kingdom	21 March 2006	Brussels	Hearing
				04 October 2006	London	Delegation

Academics and research						
1	**BORN Hans**	Senior Fellow of the Geneva Centre for the Democratic Control of Armed Forces (DCAF)	(DCAF) Geneva	25 September 2006	Strasbourg	Hearing
2	**JANKULOVSKI Zvonimir**	Security expert, (Former FYROM Ambassador to the Council of Europe)	FYROM	29 April 2006	Skopje	Delegation
3	**DE SCHUTTER Olivier**	Coordinator or the EU Network of Independent Experts	Network of Independent Experts on Fundamental Rights	30 May 2006	Brussels	Hearing
4	**ANDERS Chris**	Legislative Counsel, American Civil Liberties Union	USA	11 May 2006	Washington	Delegation
5	**BEESON Ann**	Associate Legal Director, American Civil Liberties Union	USA	11 May 2006	Washington	Delegation
6	**GUITTA Olivier**	Consultant, The American Legislative Exchange Council	USA	12 May 2006	Washington	Delegation
7	**HALPERIN Morton H.**	Senior Fellow and Director of the Security and Peace Initiative, The Center for American Progress	USA	12 May 2006	Washington	Delegation
8	**KORB Lawrence J.**	Senior Fellow, The Center for American Progress	USA	12 May 2006	Washington	Delegation
9	**McNAMARA Sally**	International Relations Project Director, The American Legislative Exchange Council	USA	12 May 2006	Washington	Delegation

No	Name	Function	Country/ Institution	Date of the meeting	Place of the meeting	Remarks
10	**RIVKIN David**	Partner, Baker & Hostetler LLP, The American Legislative Exchange Council	USA	12 May 2006	Washington	Delegation
11	**RUNDLET Peter**	Vice President for National Security, The Center for American Progress	USA	12 May 2006	Washington	Delegation
12	**SATTERTHWAITE Margaret L.**	Assistant Professor of Clinical Law & Faculty of New York University School of Law	USA	09 May 2006	Washington	Delegation
13	**WATT Steven M.**	Staff Attorney, American Civil Liberties Union	USA	11 May 2006	Washington	Delegation
Others						
1	**EGAN Suzanne**	Commissioner of the Irish Human Rights Commission	Ireland	28 November 2006	Brussels	Hearing
2	**MANNING Maurice**	President of the Irish Human Rights Commission	Ireland	28 November 2006	Brussels	Hearing
3	**HORGAN Edward**	Former UN peacekeeper and Retired Commandant of the Irish Army	Ireland	20 April 2006	Brussels	Hearing
4	**RÄBOCK**	Witness (Coleman BARRACKS)	Mannheim	12 December 2006	Mannheim	Fact finding mission
5	**SCHINDLER**	Witness (Coleman BARRACKS)	Mannheim	12 December 2006	Mannheim	Fact finding mission

6	**WRIGHT Peter**	Peace activist	Mannheim	12 December 2006	Mannheim	Fact finding mission
7	**JURCZENKO Jarosław**	Chairman of the Board, Szczytno/Szymany Airport	Poland	09 November 2006	Warsaw	Delegation
8	**KOS Jerzy**	Former Chairman of the Board, Szczytno/Szymany Airport	Poland	10 November 2006	Warsaw	Delegation
9	**PRZEWŁOCKA Mariola**	Former Director of Szczytno/ Szymany Airport	Poland	23 November 2006	Brussels	Hearing
10	**AL-RAWI Wahab**	Brother of Bisher AL-RAWI	United Kingdom	04 October 2006	London	Delegation
11	**MURRAY Craig**	Former Ambassador to Uzbekistan	United Kingdom	20 April 2006	Brussels	Hearing
12	**JOHNSON-THOMAS Brian**	Expert on arms trade	United Kingdom	21 June 2006	Brussels	Rapporteur

Annex 3:

Table Summarizing Cooperation of the Governments with the TDIP Committee

Country	Reaction from Permanent Representatives to the TDIP invitation for cooperation (Chairman's letter of 22.02.2006)	Meetings[1]	Declinations to requests for meetings[2]	Useful elements provided to the TDIP
Austria	In reply general cooperation with the TDIP was declared.	None	Ursula PLASSNIK, Minister for Foreign Affairs	None
Belgium	No written reaction[3]	No request for a meeting	N/A	Belgian authorities provided logistical support for facilitating the movements of TDIP invitees.
Bulgaria	No written reaction	No request for a meeting	N/A	None
Croatia	No written reaction	No request for a meeting	N/A	None
Cyprus	In reply, an information that the invitation was received.	No request for a meeting	N/A	None
Czech Republic	No written reaction	No request for a meeting	N/A	None

[1] Please refer for more details to annex 2 of the Explanatory Statement
[2] Please refer for more details to annex 4 of the Explanatory Statement
[3] TDIP Secretariat received a copy of a letter dated 10.03.2006 of Foreign Minister De Gucht to other Ministers concerned and to Parliament requesting cooperation with TDIP

Denmark	In reply general cooperation with the TDIP was declared.	None	Fleming HANSEN, Minister of Transportation	• A copy of Government's reply to Council of Europe was sent, • A copy of detailed dossier prepared for the Danish Parliament with large amount of technical data about flights was provided by Government to the TDIP.
Estonia	No written reaction	No request for a meeting	N/A	None
Finland	No written reaction	No request for a meeting	N/A	None
France	In reply general cooperation with the TDIP was declared.	No request for a meeting	N/A	None
Germany	No written reaction	None	Frank-Walter STEINMEIER, Minister for Foreign Affairs Klaus-Dieter FRITSCHE, Coordinator of Intelligence Services Ernst UHRLAU[1], President of BND	None
Greece	In reply: • General cooperation with the TDIP was declared, • A brief summary of national investigation was provided.	No request for a meeting	N/A	• A copy of Government's reply to Council of Europe was sent, • After a request of the TDIP, Government provided transcripts of parliamentary activities and a brief summary of preliminary investigations of "the Pakistani case" (17.11.2006).

[1] Mr Fritsche and Mr Uhrlau are high officials

Country	Reaction from Permanent Representatives to the TDIP invitation for cooperation (Chairman's letter of 22.02.2006)	Meetings	Declinations to requests for meetings	Useful elements provided to the TDIP
Hungary	In reply general cooperation with the TDIP was declared.	No request for a meeting	N/A	None
Ireland	In reply general cooperation with the TDIP was declared.	Dermot AHERN, Minister for Foreign Affairs	Rory BRADY[1], Attorney General	A copy of Governments reply to Council of Europe was sent.
Italy	In reply a further cooperation with the TDIP was declared (after meeting with general Pollari).	Nicolò POLLARI, Head of SISMI[2]	Enrico MICHELI, Secretary of State responsible for intelligence services	None
Latvia	No written reaction	No request for a meeting	N/A	None
Lithuania	No written reaction	No request for a meeting	N/A	None
Luxembourg	In reply general cooperation with the TDIP was declared.	No request for a meeting	N/A	A copy of Government's reply to Council of Europe was sent.
Malta	No written reaction	No request for a meeting	N/A	None
Netherlands	In reply general cooperation with the TDIP was declared.	No request for a meeting	N/A	None

[1] Mr Brady is a high official
[2] General Pollari is a high official

Poland	In reply general cooperation with the TDIP was declared.	Marek PASIONEK[1], Undersecretary of State at the Chancellery of the Prime Minister	Andrzej LEPPER, Deputy Prime Minister Anna FOTYGA, Minister of Foreign Affairs Radosław SIKORSKI, Minister of National Defence Zbigniew WASSERMANN, Minister Coordinator of Special Services	Copies of Government's replies to Council of Europe were sent.
Portugal	No written reaction	Luis AMADO, Minister for Foreign Affairs	None	After requests of the TDIP Chairman and of TDIP Member Ana Maria Gomes, Government provided a copy of Portugal's reply to Council of Europe (07.07.2006) and vast but not complete explanations and information about CIA flights (18.09.2006, 13.10.2006, 12.12.2006, 12.01.2007 and 16.01.2007).
Romania	In reply general cooperation with the TDIP was declared.	Anghel ANDREESCU, Secretary of State for public order and security Adrian Cosmin VIERITA, Secretary of State for EU affairs	Vasile BLAGA, Minister for Internal Affairs Mihai-Razvan UNGUREANU, Minister for Foreign Affairs	• Copy of Government's reply to Council of Europe was sent, • Confidential report of Romanian Border Police on accident of a CIA plane was provided to the TDIP delegation by Government.

[1] Mr Pasionek is a high official

Country	Reaction from Permanent Representatives to the TDIP invitation for cooperation (Chairman's letter of 22.02.2006)	Meetings	Declinations to requests for meetings	Useful elements provided to the TDIP
Slovakia	No written reaction	No request for a meeting	N/A	None
Slovenia	No written reaction	No request for a meeting	N/A	None
Spain	In reply general cooperation with the TDIP was declared.	Miguel Angel MORATINOS, Minister for Foreign Affairs	Alberto SAIZ CORTES, Secretary of State, Director of CNI	None
Sweden	In reply: General cooperation with the TDIP was declared and a summary of national investigation was provided.	None	Carl BILDT, Minister for Foreign Affairs	None
Country	**Reaction from Permanent Representatives to the TDIP invitation for cooperation** (Chairman's letter of 22.02.2006)	**Meetings**	**Declinations to requests for meetings**	**Useful elements provided to the TDIP**
Turkey	No written reaction	No request for a meeting	N/A	None

United Kingdom	No written reaction	HOON Geoff, Minister for Europe	Margaret BECKETT, Secretary of State for Foreign and Commonwealth Affairs Des BROWNE, Secretary of State for Defence John REID, Secretary of State for the Home Office Douglas Alexander, Secretary of State for Transport and Secretary of State for Scotland Elisa MANNINGHAM-BULLER, Director General of Security Service (MI5) John SCARLET[8], Chief of the Secret Intelligence Service (MI6)	None

[1] Ms Manningham-Buller and Mr Scarlet are high officials

Annex 4:

List of People Who Declined the TDIP Committee's Invitations for Meetings

• COUNCIL OF THE EUROPEAN UNION

Javier SOLANA, *Secretary General and High Representative CFSP*
Reason given for not meeting the Committee:
Mr Solana **met with the TDIP Committee on 2nd May 2006** and agreed to meet once more. **The second invitation of the Committee was turned down** by Mr Solana as he has found some comments in the draft report of the TDIP Committee as *"unjust and erroneous."*[13]

Erkki TUOMIOJA, *President of the EU Council*
No reason given for not meeting the Committee: *"I would like to underscore the importance attached to and the continued cooperation given by the Presidency and the Secretary-General/High Representative to your Committee's work even if I am not able to appear before your Committee."*[14]

• AUSTRIA

Ursula PLASSNIK, *Minister for Foreign Affairs*
According to State Secretary Hans Winkler, who replied on her behalf: *"Es liegen zu diesen Vorgängen keine weiteren Erkenntnisse vor, sodass keine weiteren Auskünfte erteilt werden können. Ein persönliches Erscheinen vor dem Ausschuss erscheint angesichts dieser Sachlage nicht erforderlich."*[15]

• DENMARK

Fleming HANSEN, *Minister of Transportation*
Reason given for not meeting the Committee:
All information available about the TDIP issues was sent to the Danish Parliament and has been forwarded to the EP.[16]

• GERMANY

Frank-Walter STEINMEIER, *Minister for Foreign Affairs*
Reason given for not meeting the Committee:
Open in principle to meet but did not want to come before the Bundestag's Inquiry Committee would have finished dealing with the el-Masri case.[17]

[13] Letter of 14 December 2006 to EP President Josep Borrell.
[14] Letter of 29 November 2006 to TDIP Chairman Carlos Coelho.
[15] Letter of 13 December to TDIP Chairman Carlos Coelho.
[16] Letter of 8 November 2006 to TDIP Chairman Carlos Coelho.
[17] Letter of 30 November 2006 to TDIP Chairman Carlos Coelho.

Klaus-Dieter FRITSCHE, *Coordinator of Intelligence Services*
Ernst UHRLAU, *President of BND*
Reason given for not meeting the Committee:
Not allowed to meet by Government.[18]

• **IRELAND**

Rory BRADY, *Attorney General*
Reason given for not meeting the Committee:
No authorisation from Government.

• **ITALY**

Enrico MICHELI, *Secretary of State responsible for intelligence services*
Reason given for not meeting the Committee:
Busy agenda.

BIANCO Enzo, *Chairman of the Committee for Intelligence and Security Services and for State Secret*
Reason given for not meeting the Committee:
Busy agenda.

Gianni LETT *A, former Secretary of State responsible for intelligence services*
Reason given for not meeting the Committee:
Mr Letta would not come, as the Secretary in office (Micheli) had refused.

• **POLAND**

Andrzej LEPPER, *Deputy Prime Minister*
Reason given for not meeting the Committee:
Mr Lepper initially confirmed and afterwards another representative of Government was singled out to meet the TDIP delegation.

Anna FOTYGA, *Minister of Foreign Affairs*
Reason given for not meeting the Committee:
No information on the TDIP issues.[19]

Radosław SIKORSKI, *Minister of National Defence*
Reason given for not meeting the Committee:
Mr Sikorski initially confirmed and afterwards claimed busy agenda.

Zbigniew WASSERMANN, *Minister Coordinator of Special Services*
Reason given for not meeting the Committee:
Mr Wassermann seconded his deputy Under-Secretary Marek Pasionek[20] as the representative of Government.[21]

---

[18] Letter of 21 November 2006 of Minister Thomas de Maizière to TDIP Chairman Carlos Coelho.
[19] Letter of 16 October 2006 of Director Jarosław Lindenberg to TDIP Secretariat.
[20] Mr Pasionek is not a member of Government but a civil servant.
[21] Letter of 31 October 2006 to TDIP Chairman Carlos Coelho.

Marek BIERNACKI, *MP, Chairman of Special Services Committee of the Sejm*
Reason given for not meeting the Committee:
Mr Biernacki initially confirmed a meeting and afterwards informed that he had no information on TDIP issues and refused to meet.[22]

Jerzy SZMAJDZIŃSKI, *MP, former Minister of National Defence (2001—2005)*
Reason given for not meeting the Committee:
Busy agenda.

Andrzej BARCIKOWSKI, *former Head of the Internal Security Agency (ABW) 2002—2005*
Reason given for not meeting the Committee:
The law on national secrets forbids Mr Barcikowski to discuss the TDIP issues.

Mariusz HARAF, *Commander of Border Guards responsible for controls at the Szymany airport*
Reason given for not meeting the Committee:
Mr Haraf initially confirmed and later informed that the TDIP shall seek an authorisation for the meeting from Minister for Internal Affairs.

Sylwester LATKOWSKI, *film director and journalist (free lance)*
Reason given for not meeting the Committee:
Only an independent film would allow him to express his point of view on the TDIP issues without being misinterpreted.

Paweł SMOLEŃSKI, *Journalist from Gazeta Wyborcza*
Reason given for not meeting the Committee:
Mr Smolenski initially confirmed and later claimed busy agenda.

Tomasz STAROWIEYSKI, *former Chairman of the Board of the Szczytno/ Szymany Airport owner (2004—2006)*
Reason given for not meeting the Committee:
Mr Starowieyski claimed that he could not devote the whole day for travelling to Warsaw and meeting the TDIP delegation.

• PORTUGAL

Luis A. FONSECA DE ALMEIDA, *President of National Institute for Civil Aviation (INAC)*
Reason given for not meeting the Committee:
Mr Fonseca singled out Director Falerio de Almeida to represent the Institute, as he was not its President anymore at the time of the meeting.

[22] Letter of 27 October 2006 to TDIP Chairman Carlos Coelho.

Carlos GONCALVES DE COSTA, *President of Conselho de Administração da NAV*
Reason given for not meeting the Committee:
Mr Gonçalves singled out Mr Carvalho to represent the NAV as his agenda was busy.

Antonio FIGUEIREDO LOPES, *former Minister for Home Affairs*
Paulo PORTAS, *former Minister for Defence*
Reason given for not meeting the Committee:
Current Government's representatives would meet the TDIP delegation and no information on the TDIP issues.

• ROMANIA

Vasile BLAGA, *Minister of Internal Affairs*
Reason given for not meeting the Committee:
Busy agenda—Secretary of State Vierita singled out to deputise Mr Blaga.

Mihai-Razvan UNGUREANU, *Minister of Foreign Affairs*
Reason given for not meeting the Committee:
Busy agenda—Secretary of State Andreescu singled out to deputise Mr Ungureanu.

• SPAIN

Alberto SAIZ CORTES, *Secretary of State, Director of CNI*
Reason given for not meeting the Committee:
Another representative of Government was singled out to meet the delegation.

• SWEDEN

Carl BILDT, *Minister for Foreign Affairs*
Reason given for not meeting the Committee:
Busy agenda.[23]

• UNITED KINGDOM

Margaret BECKETT, *Secretary of State for Foreign and Commonwealth Affairs*
Reason given for not meeting the Committee:
Ms Beckett claimed busy agenda and singled out Minister Hoon to deputise her.

[23] Letter of 7 December 2006 to TDIP Chairman Carlos Coelho.

Des BROWNE, *Secretary of State for Defence*
John REID, *Secretary of State for the Home Office*
Douglas Alexander, *Secretary of State for Transport and Secretary of State for Scotland*
No reasons given for not meeting the Committee. Officials representing the Home Office, Ministry of Defence and the Department of Transport were present during the meeting with Minister Hoon.[24]

Elisa MANNINGHAM-BULLER, *Director General of Security Service (MI5)*
John SCARLET, *Chief of the Secret Intelligence Service (MI6)*
Irfan SIDDIQ, *member of the Diplomatic Service*
Reason given for not meeting the Committee:
No authorisation for a meeting from Government.

Richard DEARLOVE, *former Head of MI6*
Michael WOOD, *former Legal Adviser of the Foreign & Commonwealth Office*
No reasons given for not meeting the Committee.[25]

• FORMER YUGOSLAV REPUBLIC OF MACEDONIA

Aleksandar BOZINOVSKI, *Journalist of Vreme newspaper*
Reason given for not meeting the Committee:
Logistical problems.

• COUNCIL OF EUROPE

Christos ROZAKIS, *Vice-President of the European Court of Human Rights*
Reason given for not meeting the Committee:
No authorisation from the ECHR.

• UNITED STATES OF AMERICA

Condoleezza RICE, *Secretary of State*
Reason given for not meeting the Committee:
Government decided that Assistant Secretary of State Daniel Fried would represent it.

Pat ROBERTS, *Chairman of the Select Committee on Intelligence of US Senate*
Reason given for not meeting the Committee:
Mr Roberts' policy of confidentiality does not allow him to discuss the TDIP issues.

Jim *BINGAMAN, Senator* ***Sam BROWNBACK,*** *Senator*
Jo Ann DAVIS, *Member of House of Representatives*

---

[24] Letter of 11 September 2006 of Minster Geoff Hoon to TDIP Head of Secretariat.
[25] Letter of 27 July 2006 of Minster Margaret Beckett to TDIP Head of Secretariat.

Russell FEINGOLD, *Senator*
Jane HARMAN, *Member of House of Representatives*
Pete HOEKSTRA, *Member of House of Representatives*
Darrell ISSA, *Member of House of Representatives*
John KERRY, *Senator*
Tom LANTOS, *Member of House of Representatives*
John Patrick LEAHY, *Senator*
Carl LEVIN, *Senator*
John McCAIN, *Senator*
Nancy PELOSI, *Member of House of Representatives*
John D. ROCKEFELLER, *Senator*
Christopher SHAYS, *Member of House of Representatives*
Chris SMITH, *Member of House of Representatives*
Porter J. GOSS, *CIA Director*
Tyler DRUMHELLER, *former CIA agent*
Michael SCHEUER, *former CIA agent*
No reason given for not meeting the Committee.

Colin POWELL, *former Secretary of State*
Reason given for not meeting the Committee:
No authority to discuss the topic.

Dana PRIEST, *Journalist of Washington Post*
Reason given for not meeting the Committee:
No permission for a meeting from her editors.

BAER Bob, *former CIA agent* ***Richard CLARKE,*** *former CIA agent*
Reasons given for not meeting the Committee:
Busy agenda.

- **EGYPT**

Montasser AL-ZAYAT, *Lawyer of Abu OMAR*
Reason given for not meeting the Committee:
Mr Al-Zayat initially confirmed and afterwards refused to meet without giving any reason.

Hossam EL-HAMALAWY, *Journalist*
Reason given for not meeting the Committee:
No authorisation from his publisher.

- **OTHERS**

Louise ARBOUR, *UN High Commissioner for Refugees*
Reason given for not meeting the Committee:
Busy agenda.

Jaap DE HOOP SCHEFFER, *Secretary General of NATO*
Reason given for not meeting the Committee:
No intention to meet.

Jakob KELLENBERGER, *President of International Red Cross*
Reason given for not meeting the Committee:
The IRC's policy of confidentiality.

George ROBERTSON, *former Secretary General of NATO*
Reason given for not meeting the Committee:
Busy agenda.

Michael STEINER, *former Head of UN Interim Administration Mission in Kosovo*
Reason given for not meeting the Committee:
Mr Steiner claimed that authorisation of both UN Secretary General and German Foreign Minister would be needed to meet the TDIP Committee.

Procedure

Title	The alleged use of European countries by the CIA for the transportation and illegal detention of prisoners
Procedure number	2006/2027(INI)
Committee responsible Date authorisation announced in plenary	TDIP 18.1.2006
Committee(s) asked for opinion(s) Date announced in plenary	
Rapporteur(s) Date appointed	Giovanni Claudio Fava 26.1.2006
Previous rapporteur(s)	
Discussed in committee	14.12.2006 18.12.2006 15.1.2007
Date adopted	23.1.2007
Result of final vote	+ 28
	17
	0 3
Members present for the final vote	Alexander Alvaro, Frieda Brepoels, Kathalijne Maria Buitenweg, Giusto Catania, Carlos Coelho, Simon Coveney, Giorgos Dimitrakopoulos, Giovanni Claudio Fava, Jas Gawronski, Ana Maria Gomes, Ignasi Guardans Cambó, Sylvia-Yvonne Kaufmann, Magda Kósáné Kovács, Wolfgang Kreissl-Dörfler, Barbara Kudrycka, Sarah Ludford, Marian-Jean Marinescu, Claude Moraes, Józef Pinior, Mirosław Mariusz Piotrowski, Hubert Pirker, Bogusław Rogalski, Luca Romagnoli, Eoin Ryan, José Ignacio Salafranca Sánchez-Neyra, György Schöpflin, Inger Segelström, Hannes Swoboda, Konrad Szymański, Charles Tannock, Elena Valenciano Martínez-Orozco, Jan Marinus Wiersma
Substitute(s) present for the final vote	Panayiotis Demetriou, Proinsias De Rossa, Roger Helmer, Erna Hennicot-Schoepges, Jeanine Hennis-Plasschaert, Sajjad Karim, Helmut Kuhne, Jean Lambert, Henrik Lax, Bill Newton Dunn, Rihards Pīks, Marie-Line Reynaud, Bogusław Sonik, Josef Zieleniec
Substitute(s) under Rule 178(2) present for the final vote	Panagiotis Beglitis, Philip Bushill-Matthews, Pasqualina Napoletano, Neil Parish.
Date tabled	30.1.2007
Comments (available in one language only)	

B. REPORTS FROM NATIONAL JURISDICTIONS

COMMENTARY

COMMENTARY ON REPORTS FROM INTERNATIONAL BODIES

[*Commentary for Document 8*] Canada: The Arar Inquiry

In September 2002, Syrian-born Canadian citizen Maher Arar was in transit through John F. Kennedy Airport in New York City on his way home to Canada from a family vacation. Arar was taken into custody by officials from the Federal Bureau of Investigation and the then Immigration and Naturalization Service.[1] Arar's requests for a lawyer were initially dismissed on the ground that he was not a U.S. citizen. Later, although Arar was allowed access to a lawyer, U.S. authorities contrived to contact the lawyer so late in the process that the lawyer could take no action to remedy Arar's situation. Based on evidence supplied by the Canadian intelligence services about Arar's alleged connections to terrorist groups, U.S. officials questioned Arar and threatened him with transfer to Syria. Arar protested that he would be tortured if moved to Syria. Nevertheless, then-Acting Attorney General Larry Thompson ordered his dispatch to Syria. Arar was detained in Syria for ten months. He alleges that during this time he was repeatedly beaten, tortured, and kept in a shallow grave. In part due to the intercession of the Canadian government, Arar was eventually released. The Syrian Ambassador to Washington has since stated that it does not have, and never has had, evidence linking Arar to any terrorist group.[2]

Under intense public pressure, the Canadian government initiated an inquiry led by a respected former Supreme Court Justice into the circumstances of Arar's detention and transfer, and in particular the role played by Canadian intelligence agencies. The detailed overview of that report is included in this volume. This commission confirmed Arar's accusations of torture in Syrian hands. It also explored the cause of his transfer to Syria. It found that after the September 11 attacks Canadian and U.S. officials had met and agreed to improve intelligence cooperation with what was known as a "free-flow-of-information agreement." That agreement abandoned

---

[1] This agency has since been folded into the Department of Homeland Security.

[2] See Frederick A.O. Schwarz and Aziz Z. Huq, *Unchecked and Unbalanced: Presidential Power in a Time of Terror* 98-99 (New Press: 2007).

numerous official protocols that had retarded or impeded information sharing in the past. Soon afterwards, Arar came to the attention of the Royal Canadian Mounted Police when he was observed meeting with Abdullah Almalki, the target of a terrorist investigation. The meeting prompted an investigation of Arar during which Canadian officials shared information with U.S. authorities pursuant to the earlier free-flow-of-information agreement. As extensively documented by the Commission of Inquiry, much of the information on Arar turned out to be inaccurate and misleading. It was this very information that led the Immigration and Naturalization Service to conclude that Arar was a member of al Qaeda and to wrongfully deport him to Syria. Subsequent to the publication of the Commission's report, Arar was awarded $9.75 million in compensation by the Canadian government for his ordeal.[3]

[*Commentary for Document 9*] **Italy: The Milan Indictments**

At or around midday on June 17, 2003, an Egyptian national Hassam Osama Mustafa Nasr (known as "Abu Omar") was abducted from the streets of Milan. Abu Omar was transported via the American military air force bases at Aviano and Ramstein to Egypt. After being detained in the Tora prison on the outskirts of Cairo without criminal charge and subjected to interrogation measures that may have constituted torture under Article 3 of the Convention against Torture, he was released. At the time, Abu Omar had been under surveillance by Italian police. The seizure disrupted their ongoing criminal investigation. As a result, an Italian magistrate named Armando Spataro commenced an investigation into what under Italian law was the illegal kidnapping and detention of an Italian resident. As part of this inquiry, Spataro issued arrest warrants against 22 alleged agents of the CIA.

The request for custodial measures (i.e., pretrial detention) lodged by Spataro is reproduced in part here. The indictment provides a glimpse into the realities of extraordinary rendition and the difficult of investigating (let alone prosecuting) its instigators. The document begins with a recitation of the evidence concerning Abu Omar's seizure and transfer. It traces Abu Omar's path to Egyptian custody, and then documents the ample cell-phone records—apparently left by CIA operatives involved in the capture from which Spataro was able to reconstruct the rendition. It is thus a fascinating, and almost unique, glimpse into the operation of an actual rendition.

Although the Italian Justice Ministry declined Spataro's request for extradition filings against 22 alleged CIA agents, the Italian prosecutor

[3] Ian Austen, Canada Will Pay $9.75 Million to Man Sent to Syria and Tortured, *New York Times*, Jan. 27, 2007, at A5.

nonetheless pressed ahead with criminal trials in absentia of the US agents. In November 2009, Spataro obtained convictions against 23 U.S. officials. Judge Oscar Magi handed an eight-year sentence to Robert Seldon Lady, a former C.I.A. base chief in Milan, and five-year sentences to the 22 other Americans, including an Air Force colonel and 21 C.I.A. operatives. Three other Americans including Jeffrey Castelli, a former C.I.A. station chief in Rome, secured diplomatic immunity. The Obama Administration expressed disappointment at the verdicts. In an interview published in *Il Giornale,* Mr. Lady, the former C.I.A. Milan station chief said, "Of course it was an illegal operation. But that's our job. We're at war against terrorism."[4]

[*Commentary for Documents 10 and 11*] **The United Kingdom: Parliamentary inquiries**

The United Kingdom Parliament's Joint Committee on Human Rights addressed extraordinary rendition in its nineteenth report published in 2005. The relevant section of that report is included in this compilation. The report begins its analysis of the issue by noting the contrast between the British government's claim that no rendition flights have used U.K. air space and the existence of evidence that clearly repudiated that claim. The report also notes that police forces whose jurisdictions included airports where rendition flights may have stopped have begun investigations, but that these inquiries have petered out.

More interesting is the Joint Committee's discussion of the 1944 Chicago Convention on International Civil Aviation, which echoes in some ways the analysis of the Venice Commission. The terms of the Chicago Convention impinge on extraordinary rendition in two ways. First, "state" aircraft require prior authorization to use UK airspace, which may be conditioned as the country sees fit. That is, this generally applicable civil aviation treaty provided a vehicle for registering disapproval of American rendition policy. Second, the joint committee report identified Article 3 of the Chicago Convention as a source of power to order any craft to land and to search that craft for evidence of illegal activity.

In tandem, these elements of the Chicago Convention create tools for a government committed to resisting any form of complicity with American rendition policy to eliminate such complicity. The joint committee thus makes it clear that the British government's claim of non-involvement can be operationalized as a binding legal commitment. Whether the practical resources or political will necessary for enforcing such a decision exists in the United Kingdom or any other country is, of course, a separate question.

---

[4] See Rachel Donadio, Italy Convicts 23 Americans for C.I.A., Renditions, *New York Times*, November 5, 2009.

Responding to this perceived gap in the law enforcement fabric, an informal group called the All Party Parliamentary Group on Extraordinary Renditions, led by the Conservative Member of Parliament Andrew Tyrie, formed in 2005 to consider possible reform measures. A section of the resulting report is included in this volume. According to this report, the critical "gap in the UK criminal structure" is that "there has been a failure to prosecute, or to provide the tools to prosecute, behaviour that has occurred, which is abhorrent and which needs to be remedied." Although the parliamentary group identified concerns with both the content of the law and its implement, its recommendations target the substance of the law. Hence, it proposes a series of new criminal prohibitions. Most interestingly, it suggests a new offence of failing to prevent the transfer of an individual, without his consent, to or from the United Kingdom (or any of its overseas territories) from or to another State without lawful excuse.

[*Commentary for Document 12*] **Sweden: Ombudsman's Inquiry**

As described above, the Swedish government was implicated in extraordinary rendition policy through the case of Ahmed Agiza and Mohammed al-Zari, two Egyptian asylum seekers who were transferred back to Egypt, apparently at the behest of or with the substantial cooperation of the U.S. government, notwithstanding the fact they risked torture there. The CAT Committee issued one formal communication about their case. But an internal inquiry within Sweden also sought to probe the decisional processes of the Swedish government rather than the international law questions.

On March 22, 2005, the Chief Parliamentary Ombudman, Mats Melin issued a report in which he expressed "extremely grave criticism" of the Swedish Security Police. Melin singled out the fact that those police had allowed the management of the transfer to be shifted to U.S. hands. As a consequence, Melin found, Agiza and al-Zari were subject to "degrading" and "inhuman" treatment by the foreign officials who handled them and moved them into an airplane at the Swedish point of departure (Bromma Airport). Nevertheless, Melins noted, the relevant prosecuting entity with jurisdiction over the matter had determined that it lacked grounds to initiate any criminal action against the agents. He did, however, stress that the Security Police's own internal procedural directives already barred non-Swedish officials from the "exercise" of their powers while in Sweden. Drawing attention to this rule, Malin sought to limit the chance that another such incident would happen in the future.

While Melins identified flaws in police internal management—in particular the absence of any clear chain of command or allocation of responsibility among the officers involved—he did not inquiry into the adequacy of justifications for the expulsion order (and in particular the Swedish government's apparent reliance on "diplomatic assurances" from the Egyptian government). Specifically, Melins did not conduct a detailed inquiry into why the Swedish government had reversed their initial position that Agiza and al-Zari were entitled to protection under refugee law. Melin noted that it was the Foreign Minister who made the decision, and at the time of the decision, an American offer to facilitate transportation of the two men was on the table. This question of when and how a government abrogates the normal, legally mandated procedures of its immigration law is more consequential, however, than the question of how to manage the physical handling of transferred prisoners.

[*Commentary for Document 13*] **Ireland: Diplomatic protests**

Eire has not played a significant role in extraordinary rendition with the exception of possible fly-overs of aircraft bearing subjects of extraordinary rendition. Perhaps as a consequence its government has a relatively free hand in denouncing that policy. Included in this volume is a letter from Dermont Ahern, Minister for Foreign Affairs for the republic, to the Irish Human Rights Commission expressing his government's "complete opposition" to renditions to torture; the statement also claims that the Irish government has gone to "great lengths" to "raise our concerns at the very highest levels of the US government."

DOCUMENT NO. 8

REPORT OF THE EVENTS RELATING TO MAHER ARAR: ANALYSIS AND RECOMMENDATIONS: COMMISSION OF INQUIRY INTO THE ACTIONS OF CANADIAN OFFICIALS IN RELATION TO MAHER ARAR

September 19, 2006

1. Background

Maher Arar is a Canadian citizen. He is married and has two children. He has a Bachelor of Engineering in Computers from McGill University and a Master's degree in Telecommunications from the University of Quebec's *Institut national de la recherche scientifique.*

On September 26, 2002, while passing through John F. Kennedy International Airport in New York, Mr. Arar was arrested and subsequently detained by American officials for 12 days. He was then removed against his will to Syria, the country of his birth, where he was imprisoned for nearly a year. While in Syria, Mr. Arar was interrogated, tortured and held in degrading and inhumane conditions. He returned to Canada after his release on October 5, 2003. Not surprisingly, the effects of this ordeal on Mr. Arar have been devastating and he and his family continue to suffer to this day.

Mr. Arar has never been charged with any offence in Canada, the United States or Syria. Indeed, although RCMP officers conducting a terrorism-related investigation were interested in interviewing Mr. Arar, they did not consider him a suspect or a target of that investigation. They wished to interview him as a witness because of his associations with certain other individuals. I have heard evidence concerning all of the information collected about Mr. Arar in Canadian investigations, and there is nothing to indicate that Mr. Arar committed an offence or that his activities constitute a threat to the security of Canada.

There was a great deal of media coverage of Mr. Arar's case in the later stages of his imprisonment in Syria and even more after his return to Canada. Concerns were raised about the role Canadian officials might have played in relation to his detention in the United States, his removal to Syria and his imprisonment and treatment in that country. In response to mounting public pressure, the Government of Canada called this public inquiry and I was appointed Commissioner.

The Inquiry mandate is divided into two parts. The first, referred to as the Factual Inquiry, requires me to investigate and report on the actions of Canadian officials in relation to Mr. Arar. The second, the Policy Review, directs me to make recommendations concerning an independent, arm's-length review mechanism for the RCMP's activities with respect to national security. Given the different nature of the two parts, I established a separate process for each. This report pertains only to the Factual Inquiry.

The Factual Inquiry process was thorough and comprehensive, and I am satisfied that I have been able to examine all the Canadian information relevant to the mandate. Over 70 government officials were called as witnesses, and the government produced approximately 21,500 documents, of which some 6,500 were entered as exhibits. The process was complex because of the need to keep some of the relevant information confidential, to protect national security and international relations interests. I received some of the evidence in closed, or *in camera,* hearings and am unable to refer to some of the evidence heard in those hearings in the public version of this report. However, I am pleased to say that I am able to make public all of my conclusions and recommendations, including those based on *in camera* evidence.

2. Organization and Content of Report

The Factual Inquiry Report is presented in two parts. The first part, which you are now reading, contains my analysis of the different aspects of the evidence and all of my conclusions (chapters I through VII), a description of the Inquiry process (Chapter VIII) and my recommendations arising from the evidence I heard during the Inquiry (Chapter IX).

I have written the analysis in such a way as to avoid disclosing information that is subject to national security confidentiality. For that reason, I sometimes leave out detail. For example, I occasionally refer to times generally, rather than specifically, and I do not always identify individuals or agencies. I am nonetheless satisfied that the lack of detail does not mislead the reader about what occurred. Moreover, I have been careful to ensure that my conclusions are based on an assessment of all of the evidence, regardless of whether or not it may be publicly disclosed.

The second part of my Report presents the detailed factual background, based on the evidence I received during the hearings. There are two versions of the factual background. One, which may not be disclosed publicly, is a summary of all of the evidence, including that which is subject to national security confidentiality. The other is a public version, from which I have removed those parts of the evidence that, in my opinion, may not be disclosed publicly for reasons of national security confidentiality.

A good deal of evidence in the Inquiry was heard *in camera*. As it turns out, I have included a significant amount of *in camera* evidence in the public version. However, because of the amount of evidence not heard in public and not readily available to the public, I considered it important to prepare a more extensive summary of the evidence than might have been the case in a public inquiry in which all of the hearings were open to the public and all transcripts of evidence are readily available.

This Report is based primarily on the evidence of Canadian officials. The governments of the United States, Jordan and Syria declined my invitation to give evidence or otherwise participate in the hearings. Despite their failure to participate, I have for the most part been able to determine what actually happened and reach the conclusions required by the mandate. In a few instances, however, I have been hampered by the lack of evidence of officials of these other countries. I point these instances out in the Report.

In addition, I have not heard the evidence of Mr. Arar. For reasons of fairness, it was not deemed appropriate for Mr. Arar to testify before the release of the Report, the idea being that the Report would provide the maximum amount of disclosure of information to him about what had occurred. I have indicated to him that, if he wishes, he may apply to me to testify in the future. Should he do so, I will consider his request at that time. I do occasionally point out in the Report that Mr. Arar's evidence might shed additional light on a particular event or conclusion. In the main, however, I do not think that I was limited in any significant way by not hearing Mr. Arar's evidence.

3. Scope of my Mandate and the Issue of Causation

An Order in Council sets out the mandate for the Inquiry. The parts relevant to the Factual Inquiry read as follows:

(a) to investigate and report on the actions of Canadian officials in relation to Maher Arar, including with regard to

(i) the detention of Mr. Arar in the United States,

(ii) the deportation of Mr. Arar to Syria via Jordan,

(iii) the imprisonment and treatment of Mr. Arar in Syria,

(iv) the return of Mr. Arar to Canada, and

(v) any other circumstance directly related to Mr. Arar that the Commissioner considers relevant to fulfilling this mandate. . . .[1]

There are two purposes to this part of the mandate: to investigate and report fully on the matters described in the mandate; and to make recommendations with respect to matters that are disclosed in the evidence. In order to fulfill these purposes, it is necessary that I make findings of fact and, in some circumstances, assess those facts and make evaluations about what happened and why.

Government counsel and counsel for certain RCMP officers have argued that I should not make any negative or critical findings with respect to their clients unless I am able to find as a fact that the actions of their clients "caused or contributed to" what happened to Mr. Arar. They have contended that, because the American and Syrian authorities declined to testify at the Inquiry, there is no evidence about what caused American officials to detain and remove Mr. Arar to Syria or what caused the Syrian authorities to imprison and torture him. They have submitted that, absent findings that link actions of their clients to Mr. Arar's fate as described in the mandate, I am not permitted to make findings of misconduct—negative or critical comments—in relation to their clients.

I do not accept this argument. It invokes an overly technical and legalistic approach to the Inquiry and is based on an unduly narrow interpretation of the mandate. The mandate, by its terms, is not limited to examining actions that can be established to have caused Mr. Arar's fate; rather, it directs me to consider actions of Canadian officials "in relation to Mr. Arar." The use of the phrase "in relation to" suggests a broader investigation and report than one focused solely on the "causes" of what happened to Mr. Arar.

Moreover, the mandate is not limited to examining the events set out in subparagraphs i) to iv). The list is preceded by the word "including" and, in subparagraph v), the mandate directs that I also examine "any other circumstance directly related to Mr. Arar that [I consider] relevant to fulfilling the mandate."

I agree with those who argue that a public inquiry should not be turned into a fault-finding exercise. Indeed, in preparing this report, I have avoided making unnecessary negative or critical comments about individuals or agencies. That said, I have found it necessary in some instances to make comments that may be viewed as negative or critical in order to fully report on what occurred. In addition, I thought it necessary, in several places in

[1] Order in Council P.C. 2004–48, Appendix 1(A).

the Report, to point to the shortcomings, as I viewed them, in what Canadian officials did or did not do in relation to Mr. Arar, for purposes of making the recommendations contained in Chapter IX. I discuss this issue of causation further in Chapter VIII.

4. Summary of Main Conclusions

The following are my main conclusions, presented under four headings that reflect the different stages examined: information sharing prior to Mr. Arar's detention, Mr. Arar's detention in New York and removal to Syria, his imprisonment and mistreatment in Syria, and the period after his return to Canada.

4.1 Information Sharing Prior to Mr. Arar's Detention

- The RCMP provided American authorities with information, including the entire database from the aforementioned terrorism investigation, in ways that did not comply with RCMP policies requiring screening for relevance, reliability and personal information. Some of the information related to Mr. Arar.
- The RCMP provided American authorities with information about Mr. Arar that was inaccurate, portrayed him in an unfairly negative fashion and overstated his importance in the RCMP investigation.
- The RCMP provided American authorities with information about Mr. Arar without attaching written caveats,[2] as required by RCMP policy, thereby increasing the risk that the information would be used for purposes of which the RCMP would not approve, such as sending Mr. Arar to Syria.
- The RCMP requested that American authorities place lookouts for Mr. Arar and his wife, Monia Mazigh, in U.S. Customs' Treasury Enforcement Communications System (TECS). In the request, to which no caveats were attached, the RCMP described Mr. Arar and Dr, Mazigh as "Islamic Extremist individuals suspected of being linked to the Al Qaeda terrorist movement."[3] The RCMP had no basis for this description, which had the potential to create serious consequences for Mr. Arar in light of American attitudes and practices at the time.
- Project A-O Canada was the front-line investigative unit in the RCMP that conducted the investigation in which Mr. Arar was a person of interest, and it was that unit that provided information about Mr. Arar

[2] "Caveats" are written restrictions on the use and further dissemination of shared information.
[3] Exhibit C-30, Tab 44.

to American agencies. The RCMP, as an institution, gave Project A-O Canada unclear and, in some instances, misleading direction concerning the manner in which information should be shared, and failed to properly oversee the Project's investigation, including its information-sharing practices.

- CSIS did not share any information about Mr. Arar with the American authorities prior to his detention in New York and removal to Syria.

4.2 Detention in New York and Removal to Syria

- There is no evidence that Canadian officials participated or acquiesced in the American authorities' decisions to detain Mr. Arar and remove him to Syria.
- It is very likely that, in making the decisions to detain and remove Mr. Arar, American authorities relied on information about Mr. Arar provided by the RCMP.
- While Mr. Arar was being detained in New York on September 26, 2002, the RCMP provided the U.S. Federal Bureau of Investigation (FBI) with information about him, some of which portrayed him in an inaccurate and unfair way.
- Without the evidence of the American authorities, I am unable to conclude what role, if any, the TECS lookout requested by the RCMP played in the American decisions to detain Mr. Arar and remove him to Syria.
- During Mr. Arar's detention in New York, consular officials with the Canadian Department of Foreign Affairs and International Trade (DFAIT)[4] took reasonable steps to provide Mr. Arar with consular services, including addressing the possibility that he might be sent to Syria.

4.3 Imprisonment and Mistreatment in Syria

- Mr. Arar arrived in Syria on October 9, 2002 and was held incommunicado until October 22, 2002. In the intervening period, he was interrogated and tortured.
- I am unable to conclude whether or not Canadian officials could have obtained Mr. Arar's release from Syrian imprisonment at an earlier

[4] Changes were made to the structure and organization of Foreign Affairs and International Trade over recent years. Prior to and during Mr. Arar's ordeal, it was a single entity (DFAIT). In 2004, two separate departments (Foreign Affairs and International Trade) were created. Recently, the two departments were reintegrated. In this report, I refer to DFAIT or Foreign Affairs, as appropriate.

point in time. However, there is cause for serious concern in regard to a number of actions taken by Canadian officials during Mr. Arar's imprisonment, including some that could have had an effect on the time taken to release Mr. Arar:

— On receiving a summary of a statement made by Mr. Arar while in Syrian custody in early November 2002, DFAIT distributed it to the RCMP and CSIS without informing them that the statement was likely a product of torture. That statement became the basis for heightened suspicion in some minds about Mr. Arar's involvement in terrorism. That was unfair to him.

— In November 2002, CSIS received information about Mr. Arar from the Syrian Military Intelligence (SMI) and did not do an adequate reliability assessment as to whether the information was likely the product of torture. Indeed, its assessment was that it probably was not.

— In January 2003, the RCMP, acting through the Canadian Ambassador, sent the SMI questions for Abdullah Almalki, the subject of the relevant investigation and also in Syrian custody. This action very likely sent a signal to Syrian authorities that the RCMP approved of the imprisonment and interrogation of Mr. Almalki and created a risk that the SMI would conclude that Mr. Arar, a person who had some association with Mr. Almalki, was considered a serious terrorist threat by the RCMP.

— In March and April 2003, DFAIT failed to take steps to address the statement by Syrian officials that CSIS did not want Mr. Arar returned to Canada.

— In May and June 2003, the RCMP and CSIS were not supportive of a DFAIT initiative to send the Syrians a letter conveying that Canada spoke with one voice in seeking Mr. Arar's release.

— From time to time, DFAIT distributed reports of consular visits with Mr. Arar to the RCMP and CSIS. Ostensibly, this was done to seek assistance for Mr. Arar. However, DFAIT failed to make that purpose clear or to ensure that the reports were used only for that purpose.

— On several occasions, there was a lack of communication among the Canadian agencies involved in Mr. Arar's case. There was also a lack of a single, coherent approach to efforts to obtain his release.

— DFAIT consular officials took reasonable steps to obtain consular access to Mr. Arar throughout his imprisonment in Syria.

4.4 After Mr. Arar's Return to Canada

- Following Mr. Arar's return, reports were prepared within government that had the effect of downplaying the mistreatment or torture to which Mr. Arar had been subjected.
- Both before and after Mr. Arar's return to Canada, Canadian officials leaked confidential and sometimes inaccurate information about the case to the media for the purpose of damaging Mr. Arar's reputation or protecting their self-interests or government interests.
- When briefing the Privy Council Office and senior government officials about the investigation regarding Mr. Arar, the RCMP omitted certain key facts that could have reflected adversely on the Force.

5. Summary Analysis

In the sections that follow, I provide an overview of the analysis on which I have based my conclusions concerning the actions of Canadian officials in relation to Mr. Arar, again broken down by stage.

5.1 Pre-Detention

5.1.1 Formation of Project A-O Canada

Project A-O Canada was the investigative unit of the RCMP that conducted the investigation that in time involved Maher Arar. Created in the aftermath of the September 11, 2001 terrorist attacks on the United States, the Project was directed to carry out an investigation, centred in Ottawa, into the activities of Abdullah Almalki, a person suspected of being associated with al-Qaeda. The Project was also charged with investigating any leads about the threat of a second wave of attacks after the events of 9/11. In the months that followed, the scope of the Project's investigation expanded to include new information that it received about other individuals and activities.

During the Inquiry, two issues arose with respect to the formation of Project A-O Canada. First, there was some suggestion that, in the wake of 9/11, the RCMP had been thrust back into the national security field and that, as a law enforcement agency, it inappropriately had become involved in investigations within the mandate of CSIS, Canada's civilian security intelligence agency. I will comment on this suggestion only as it relates to Project A-O Canada.

In late September and early October 2001, CSIS transferred to the RCMP prime responsibility for a number of investigations, which subsequently led to the creation of Project A-O Canada. I have no reason to believe that the transfer of this investigation was inappropriate. CSIS witnesses testified that investigations were selected for transfer when they were found suitable for continued investigation by a law enforcement agency. By that, they meant that there had to be a sufficient nexus to criminal activity to engage the RCMP's mandate to either prevent, or prosecute the commission of, criminal offences. That said, I did not review all of the information about the previous CSIS investigations. To do so would have been an enormous task and well beyond my mandate. However, there was nothing in the evidence that I did hear about the Project A-O Canada investigation that raised a concern in my mind that the investigation that eventually involved Mr. Arar should not have been transferred to the RCMP.

I hasten to point out that one should not read into my comments a conclusion that Abdullah Almalki, the subject of that investigation, has committed any offence or is a threat to Canada's national security. On the contrary, Mr. Almalki, who has been the subject of investigation for a considerable period of time, has never been charged with any offence and is presumed to be innocent of any criminal activity.

The second issue with respect to the formation of Project A-O Canada had to do with the training and experience of its members. The officers assigned to Project A-O Canada were, in the view of their superiors, among the best investigators available. Many of them had extensive experience with large and complicated investigations involving financial transactions. Others had a wide array of skills of value to the investigative team. The major shortcoming was that, with few exceptions, the officers assigned to Project A-O Canada, including the Project managers, lacked experience and training in conducting national security investigations and in addressing human rights and cultural sensitivity issues that might arise in such investigations.

While I accept that, given the circumstances immediately after 9/11, the RCMP had no choice but to form the Project team as it did, it was incumbent upon the RCMP to ensure that the Project received clear direction and proper oversight with respect to the unique aspects of a national security investigation that fell outside the previous experience of the great majority of the officers. In this regard, the RCMP failed completely, particularly in the critically important area of information sharing with American agencies.

The officers of Project A-O Canada were given little guidance. They were largely left on their own. Even more troubling, the directions the RCMP did provide about how information should be shared with the American agencies were unclear and misleading. As events developed, the Project provided those agencies with information about Mr. Arar that was inaccurate and unfairly prejudicial to him. The information was provided in contravention of RCMP policy requiring that information be screened for relevance, reliability and personal information before being shared and that written caveats be attached to control the use to which the information is put.

5.1.2 Early Investigative Steps

Mr. Arar first came to the attention of Project A-O Canada as a result of a meeting he had with Abdullah Almalki at Mango's Café in Ottawa on October 12, 2001. I am satisfied that, based on the information available to them, the Project members had reasonable grounds to conduct surveillance of this meeting. This was a routine and proper investigative step and was not the result of racial profiling.

I am also satisfied that, as a result of the meeting at Mango's Café, the Project properly considered Mr. Arar to be a person of interest in its investigation. While the meeting might have been innocent, there were aspects of it that reasonably raised the investigators' antennae. Messrs. Almalki and Arar were seen walking together in the rain and conversing for 20 minutes. Given that Mr. Almalki was a target of the investigation, it was reasonable for the Project to investigate Mr. Arar, about whom it had no information at the time.

The investigators conducted background searches on Mr. Arar using public source information. The process included obtaining copies of Mr. Arar's rental application and tenancy agreement from his landlord's management company. The emergency contact given on Mr. Arar's rental application was Mr. Almalki.

Mr. Arar's counsel questioned whether obtaining the rental documents had been proper, given that there had been no search warrant or even the basis for obtaining one. I conclude that there was nothing improper in Project A-O Canada obtaining these documents without a warrant. The officers asked for the documents and the property manager, who had a proprietary interest in them, produced them. There was no compulsion, and the property manager did not suggest that Mr. Arar had a privacy interest in any information in the documents.

5.1.3 Border Lookouts

Towards the end of October 2001, Canada Customs[5] placed border lookouts for Mr. Arar and his wife, Dr. Mazigh, at the request of Project A-O Canada. The lookouts were intended to ensure that Mr. Arar and

[5] I refer to "Canada Customs" frequently throughout this report. Prior to December 12, 2003, Canadian customs operations came under the Customs branch of the Canada Customs and Revenue Agency (CCRA). They have since come under the Canada Border Services Agency (CBSA). This change in organizational structure is not significant for the purposes of my report.

Dr. Mazigh would undergo both primary and secondary examinations when entering Canada. Any person entering Canada may be subjected to a secondary examination; however, when there is a lookout, the front-line Customs officers must refer the person for a secondary examination.

I am satisfied that Project A-O Canada had sufficient reason at the time to request a lookout for Mr. Arar. In any investigation, it is important to determine the role, if any, of persons associated with the subject of the investigation, in this case Mr. Almalki. By then, Mr. Arar was properly a person of interest to the investigators, who were aware that he had met with Mr. Almalki at Mango's Café and that he had listed him as an emergency contact on his rental application, indicating they might have close ties.

There is a reduced expectation of privacy at the border when any person is entering Canada, and secondary examinations are frequently conducted where search warrants cannot be obtained. In the circumstances, requesting a lookout for Mr. Arar was an appropriate investigative step.

Once a lookout request is received, it falls to Canada Customs to decide whether there are "reasonable grounds" for issuing the lookout. For the same reasons I conclude it was reasonable for Project A-O Canada to request a lookout for Mr. Arar, I am satisfied that Canada Customs had reasonable grounds for issuing it.

That said, the lookout for Mr. Arar was designated a "terrorism" lookout. According to a Canada Customs bulletin, that designation is used when someone is suspected of being a member, associate or sympathizer of a known terrorist organization. Mr. Arar did not meet these criteria. He was not suspected of being a member of a terrorist organization and should not have been labelled in this fashion in the lookout. To do so was unfair to Mr. Arar, who was merely a person of interest. It is essential that precise and accurate language be used when describing an individual's role in a terrorism-related investigation, particularly in these times of heightened concern about public safety and national security. Labels have a way of sticking to individuals, reputations are easily damaged and when labels are inaccurate, serious unfairness to individuals can result.

In regard to Dr. Mazigh, I conclude that there was no basis for the RCMP to request a lookout for her and no basis for Canada Customs to place the lookout. The important distinction between Mr. Arar and Dr. Mazigh is the factual connection with Mr. Almalki. Mr. Arar was a person of interest because of his association with Mr. Almalki, but the RCMP had no information suggesting a link between Dr. Mazigh and Mr. Almalki. While it may make sense to include the spouse of a suspect in a lookout because that person might be involved in the suspect's activities, that rationale does not extend to the spouse of someone who is merely a person of interest and not suspected of any wrongdoing, such as Mr. Arar.

Further, the lookout for Dr. Mazigh, as for Mr. Arar, was a "terrorism" lookout. Labelling Dr. Mazigh in this fashion was inaccurate. It was wrong and very unfair to her.

At the same time Project A-O Canada requested Canada Customs lookouts for Mr. Arar and Dr. Mazigh, it also requested U.S. border lookouts for them. U.S. Customs has a computer system called the Treasury Enforcement Communications System (TECS), which provides lookout information on suspect individuals, businesses, vehicles, aircraft and vessels.

U.S. authorities declined the invitation to testify at the Inquiry. According to my understanding of the system, organizations around the world may submit requests to have individuals placed on a TECS lookout, and RCMP officers routinely make such requests. However, I have little information about how American agencies would have used the Project A-O Canada request and what the consequences might have been for Mr. Arar and Dr. Mazigh in the post-9/11 environment in the United States.

There was no RCMP policy or directive laying down the criteria for submitting foreign lookout requests. It appears, however, that making such requests was considered a normal investigative step at the time. In Chapter IX, I recommend that the RCMP develop guidelines for submitting lookouts to foreign countries, giving specific consideration to the use to be made of the lookouts and the potential impact of the lookouts on the civil liberties of the individuals affected. It is important that the RCMP have policies that set out the circumstances under which such potentially important steps as requesting a foreign border lookout should be taken.

In regard to the U.S. lookout for Dr. Mazigh, it is clear that the RCMP should not have requested such a lookout, for the same reason that it should not have requested a Canadian lookout.

One aspect of the Canadian and American lookout requests that is highly alarming is the most unfair way in which Project A-O Canada described Mr. Arar and Dr. Mazigh. The requests indicated they were part of a "group of Islamic Extremist individuals suspected of being linked to the Al Qaeda terrorist movement,"[6] a description that was inaccurate, without any basis, and potentially extremely inflammatory in the United States in the fall of 2001. I discuss the language used in this letter in more detail below, in my comments on Project A-O Canada's information-sharing practices.

---

[6] Exhibit C-30, Tab 44.

5.1.4 Canada Customs Secondary Examinations

Canada Customs carried out three secondary examinations that warrant comment: two of Mr. Arar, on November 29 and December 20, 2001, and one of Dr. Mazigh, on November 14, 2002.

During Mr. Arar's secondary examinations, officials photocopied documents found in his possession. With the exception of some teaching materials, those documents related to Mr. Arar's travel and personal identification. I am satisfied that, in copying these documents, Canada Customs officials acted in accordance with the *Customs Enforcement Manual* and relevant Enforcement Bulletin as they existed then. There was nothing of a particularly private nature about the travel and personal information obtained from the documents. The one possible exception to this conclusion involves the teaching materials, on which I cannot comment without hearing from Mr. Arar. I also conclude that, under the *Customs Act,* Customs officials had the authority to provide the RCMP with the information copied from Mr. Arar's documents.

During the December 20, 2002 secondary examination, apart from copying documents found in Mr. Arar's possession, Customs officials seized Mr. Arar's computer and personal digital assistant (PDA) for non-payment of duties and then copied information from those devices that was accessible without the use of a password. Based on the description of what occurred set out in a report by the Customs official who conducted the secondary examination, I find that Canada Customs had authority to seize the articles for non-payment of duties.[7]

I am also satisfied that the Customs officials who copied information from Mr. Arar's computer and PDA believed, reasonably in the circumstances, that they were authorized to do so. However, I do not have sufficient information to determine whether in fact they had the authority under the *Customs Act* to conduct those examinations or whether such examinations breached Mr. Arar's privacy rights under the *Canadian Charter of Rights and Freedoms.* I would need the evidence of Mr. Arar as a starting point.

As I have indicated, Dr. Mazigh should not have been the subject of the lookout that triggered her secondary examination on November 14, 2002. The examination therefore should not have taken place. Moreover, Canada Customs uploaded the profiles of Dr. Mazigh and her children, who were travelling with her, into the Intelligence Management System (IMS), an automated facility for reporting and compiling intelligence information on targets known or suspected to be potential border risks. While the uploaded information was basic information obtained from the travel itinerary and

[7] This is one instance where I might arrive at a different conclusion if Mr. Arar were to testify.

identification documents of Dr. Mazigh and her children, it should not have been uploaded into the IMS, as Dr. Mazigh and her children were not known or suspected to be potential border risks.

5.1.5 Information Sharing With American Agencies

I want to start the discussion about information sharing by making it clear that nothing in this report should be taken to indicate that Canadian agencies should not share information with American agencies. On the contrary, I strongly endorse the importance of information sharing. Sharing information across borders is essential for protecting Canada's national security interests, in that it allows more complete and accurate assessments of threats to our security. The importance of information sharing has increased in the post-9/11 era, when it is clear that the threats that need to be addressed are globally-based and not confined within national borders. However, information must be shared in a principled and responsible manner. There is good reason for the RCMP's written policies governing information sharing. Those policies make sense and it is important that they be followed.

The most significant problems arising from the Project A-O Canada investigation pertained to information sharing with the United States. Unfortunately, the RCMP gave Project A-O Canada unclear and even misleading directions on how to share information with the American agencies primarily responsible for terrorist activities in the U.S. and then failed to adequately oversee the Project's practices in that regard. As a result, Project A-O Canada did not comply with RCMP policies with regard to screening information and attaching caveats to information provided to other agencies.

5.1.5.1 RCMP Policies

As indicated above, the RCMP has policies requiring that information to be shared with other agencies be screened for relevance, reliability and personal information and that caveats be attached.

The RCMP has a legitimate concern, indeed a responsibility, to ensure that information it provides to other agencies is accurate and appropriate for sharing in the particular circumstances; hence the need for screening.

It is also important that the RCMP control, to the extent it is able, the use to which information provided to other agencies may be put. Written caveats are used by the RCMP and other agencies that share information to try to prevent recipient agencies from further disseminating information or using it for purposes of which they do not approve. While such caveats do not guarantee protection against unacceptable use, common sense tells us that they should significantly reduce the risk.

The fact that Project A-O Canada did not attach written caveats to the information about Mr. Arar provided to American agencies increased the risk that those agencies would use the information for purposes unacceptable to the RCMP, such as removing him to Syria.

5.1.5.2 Original Arrangement

Immediately after the events of 9/11, the RCMP, CSIS, and the American agencies primarily responsible for terrorist activities in the U.S. met to discuss the threat of another terrorist attack and the need for increased co-operation and coordination among the agencies, including the sharing of information in "real time," that is, in a prompt manner. In making its information-sharing arrangement, the RCMP did not intend to deviate from existing policies requiring that information be screened before being shared and that caveats be attached to any documents provided to other agencies.

The senior officer with the Criminal Intelligence Directorate (CID) at RCMP Headquarters discussed the arrangement with senior officers in the various divisions, including those at "A" Division in Ottawa. They in turn discussed it with Project A-O Canada managers. Instructions connected with the information-sharing arrangement were passed down the RCMP chain of command by word of mouth. Those involved now have varying recollections about what was intended and what instructions were given.

In the end, the Project managers had a very different understanding of the arrangement than what was intended by the senior CID officers. According to their testimony, they understood that "caveats were down"—in other words, notwithstanding RCMP policy, there was no need to attach written caveats to documents being shared with the other partner agencies. However, in their minds, there was an implicit understanding that the information would be used for intelligence purposes only. Further, the Project managers understood that all information obtained by the Project could be transferred to the "partners to the agreement," that is, CSIS and the American partner agencies, without screening the information for relevance, reliability or personal information, pursuant to RCMP policy.

Project A-O Canada also understood that it could share information received from one party to the arrangement with the other parties without the consent of the originator, even if caveats had been attached by the originator. This was another departure from RCMP policy not intended by senior CID officers. Moreover, CSIS, which was a party to the original arrangement, did not believe there had been such an arrangement or agreement.

As a result of these understandings, Project A-O Canada provided a large amount of information to the American agencies in a manner that contravened RCMP policies and was very different from what had been intended by senior CID officers. These highly alarming practices began shortly after the start of the Project's investigation in October 2001 and continued until the summer of 2002, when officers with CID took steps to bring the Project's information-sharing practices into line with RCMP policy.

The most serious incident in this regard in the period leading up to Mr. Arar's detention in New York occurred in April 2002, when Project A-O Canada provided the American agencies with its entire investigative database, in the form of three compact discs (CDs), without screening the information beforehand or attaching written caveats.

These failures should never have occurred. It was incumbent upon the RCMP and its senior officers to ensure that Project A-O Canada received clear and accurate direction with regard to how information was to be shared and to exercise sufficient oversight to rectify any unacceptable practices. Indeed, there was an especially strong need for direction and oversight because of the lack of training and experience in national security investigations of most of the Project A-O Canada members, including the managers.

5.1.5.3 Inaccurate Information

Project A-O Canada supplied the American agencies with a good deal of inaccurate information about Mr. Arar, some of which was inflammatory and unfairly prejudicial to him.

As mentioned above, in its request for U.S. border lookouts, Project A-O Canada described Mr. Arar and his wife as Islamic extremists suspected of being linked to the al-Qaeda movement. Everyone who testified accepts that this description was wrong and should not have been given to the Americans. There was no basis for such an assertion. The request was sent to U.S. Customs in late October 2001, but it was also given directly to the American agencies five months later, in April 2002. The potential consequences of labelling someone an Islamic extremist in post-9/11 America are enormous.

Prior to Mr. Arar's detention in New York on September 26, 2002, Project A-O Canada provided documents to the American agencies that variously described Mr. Arar as a suspect, a target, a principal subject of its investigation, a person with an "important" connection to Mr. Almalki, a person directly linked to Mr. Almalki in a diagram titled "Bin Laden's Associates: Al Qaeda Organization in Ottawa," and a business associate or a close associate of Mr. Almalki.

These descriptions were either completely inaccurate or, at a minimum, tended to overstate Mr. Arar's importance in the Project A-O Canada investigation. I repeat that Project A-O Canada's view was that Mr. Arar was never a suspect—he was merely a person of interest. While it might be that, in meetings, the Project's officers communicated this actual view of Mr. Arar's status in the investigation, there was no justification for the improper and unfair labels attached to him in written documents. Written labels, particularly when no caveats are attached, have a way of sticking to an individual and then spreading to others and becoming the accepted fact or wisdom. Threats of terrorism understandably arouse fear and elicit emotional responses that, in some cases, lead to overreaction. The need for accuracy and precision when sharing information in terrorist investigations cannot be overstated. This is especially so when the information is contained in a document that, rightly or wrongly, carries an air of authority. Statements made by police officers tend to be taken at face value.

In addition to unfairly labelling Mr. Arar, Project A-O Canada provided U.S. agencies with some factually inaccurate information about him. For example, it passed on erroneous notes taken by RCMP officers during an interview with Abdullah Almalki's brother that indicated that the brother had said Mr. Arar had a business relationship with Abdullah Almalki, when in fact the brother had indicated that he wasn't sure whether Mr. Arar had a business relationship with his brother. Further, a report supplied to the Americans about the meeting at Mango's Café erroneously stated that Mr. Arar had travelled from Quebec to meet Mr. Almalki, giving an unfounded sense of importance to the meeting.

In a presentation to American authorities in May 2002, Project A-O Canada provided information that tended to link Mr. Arar to certain other individuals who were suspects in the investigation. That information turned out to be inaccurate. At the same time, the Project informed the American authorities that Mr. Arar had refused to be interviewed by it in January 2002. That was also incorrect. Mr. Arar had actually agreed to be interviewed, but subject to conditions recommended by his counsel, which Project A-O Canada had found unacceptable. The statement about the refusal to be interviewed had the potential to arouse suspicion, especially among law enforcement officers, that Mr. Arar had something to hide.

While Project A-O Canada might have provided the American authorities with a good deal of accurate information, there is no excuse for its sharing of inaccurate or imprecise information. I do not accept the arguments made by some that the inaccuracies were minor or hair-splitting. In my view, they were not. During the Inquiry, investigators frequently emphasized the need to share all relevant information, even seemingly insignificant details, with other agencies, as one never knows what importance information may have in the overall picture being pieced together. A series of relatively minor details, when taken together, can create a picture of someone who is heavily involved in illegal activities. This rationale for sharing information highlights the importance of accuracy and precision in the details being shared. If details are important, they should be accurate.

I accept that the members of Project A-O Canada did not intend to provide inaccurate information to American authorities. However, proper screening would have prevented most, if not all, of the inaccuracies. In any event, this is an instance where the Project members' lack of training and experience in national security investigations appears to have played a part.

5.1.6 Role of RCMP Headquarters

Project A-O Canada provided CID at RCMP Headquarters with a considerable amount of information about its investigation on an ongoing basis. It routinely supplied daily situation reports describing the investigative steps taken, and Project officers met periodically with CID officers to inform them about the investigation.

Nonetheless, there were a number of serious failures of communication between the Project and CID, the most important being the misunderstanding about how information should be shared with other agencies, discussed above. Ultimately, it was the responsibility of the RCMP as an institution to ensure that information was shared properly and in accordance with established policies. It failed to discharge that responsibility.

There was another problem with communications between Project A-O Canada and senior RCMP officers. During its investigation, the Project provided senior officers at "A" Division and CID at RCMP Headquarters with essentially the same information it gave the American agencies, which, as described above, was sometimes inaccurate in regard to Mr. Arar and tended to unfairly overstate his importance in the Project investigation. Later, when Mr. Arar was in Syrian custody, these inaccuracies might have played a role in the RCMP's institutional responses to requests for assistance in obtaining his release. I discuss this issue below.

More generally, I observe that, given that Project A-O Canada had few officers with experience or training in national security investigations, I would have expected CID to exercise more, rather than less, oversight. That did not happen. While CID, like other units of the RCMP, might have been burdened with an increased workload in the aftermath of 9/11, it would not have been terribly time-consuming to ensure that Project A-O Canada received clear instructions with regard to information sharing and the need to comply with RCMP policies.

5.2 Detention in New York and Removal to Syria

5.2.1 Canadian Investigators

On September 26, 2002, Mr. Arar arrived at John F. Kennedy International Airport in New York on a flight from Zurich, Switzerland. He had started his trip in Tunisia and was connecting though New York on his way to Montreal. Upon his arrival at the airport in New York, he was detained by American authorities.

Mr. Arar is a citizen of both Canada and Syria. On October 7, 2002, the Regional Director of the U.S. Immigration and Naturalization Service (INS) issued an order finding Mr. Arar to be a member of al-Qaeda and directing his removal from the United States. On October 8, Mr. Arar, still in American custody, was flown to Jordan. A short time later, he was driven to Syria, where he was imprisoned for almost a year.

The RCMP had several communications with members of the American agencies about Mr. Arar shortly before and during the time he was detained in New York. Three of those communications are noteworthy.

Prior to Mr. Arar's arrival in New York on September 26, 2002, the FBI contacted Project A-O Canada to inform it of the American authorities' intention to question Mr. Arar and deny him entry into the United States, and to ask whether the RCMP had any questions it wanted put to Mr. Arar while he was in New York. The same day, the Project faxed the FBI a list of questions for Mr. Arar. I conclude that Project A-O Canada did not act improperly in sending the questions. At the time, the Canadian officers believed Mr. Arar would be denied entry to the United States and promptly sent back to Zurich. There was a legitimate investigative reason for sending the questions, as Mr. Arar was a person of interest in the Project's investigation and might have information as a witness that would further the investigation. Moreover, the Project members believed that the American authorities would extend a person in Mr. Arar's position similar protection to that provided by Canadian law.

However, in sending the questions, Project A-O Canada included information about Mr. Arar that was inaccurate and portrayed him in an unfair way. It indicated that Mr. Arar had been in the vicinity of Washington, D.C. on September 11, 2001, which was false. This information could have unfairly raised a suspicion about Mr. Arar's connections. Also, a concluding section of the fax stated that Mr. Arar had declined to be interviewed in January 2002 and, soon after, had suddenly left Canada for Tunisia. There are a number of problems with this information. Mr. Arar did not decline an interview. He agreed to be interviewed, subject to certain conditions. He did not leave Canada soon after the interview request. He left five months later. There is no evidence that he left "suddenly." Linking these inaccurate pieces of information together painted an incorrect and potentially inflammatory picture of someone who had refused to be interviewed, probably because he had had something to hide, and had quickly pulled up roots and left Canada, where he had been living with his family, in order to avoid further investigation. The Project did not attach a caveat to this information.

Earlier in this chapter, I discuss the importance of providing accurate and precise information. The provision of this inaccurate information, particularly without a caveat, at what turned out to be a critically important time in Mr. Arar's ordeal was unfortunate, to put it mildly, and totally unacceptable.

On October 3, 2002, [***] sought the assistance of the RCMP's CID in a fax containing seven specific questions about Mr. Arar and his activities and associations. The fax indicated two potential purposes for the information: Mr. Arar's removal from the United States pursuant to the INS process, and law enforcement proceedings. CID forwarded the fax to Project A-O Canada, which responded the next day.

I am satisfied that it was appropriate for the RCMP to respond to the questions. Importantly, the response made it clear that the Project had yet to complete a detailed investigation of Mr. Arar and was unable to indicate links to al-Qaeda. Moreover, the information in the response was accurate, the way it was provided complied with RCMP screening policies, and a caveat was attached. It is also worth noting that, at the time, the RCMP still did not know that the United States was contemplating sending Mr. Arar to Syria.

Unfortunately, the RCMP did not take the opportunity presented by this exchange to point out that all previous disclosures of information made without written caveats were subject to the same caveat as the October 4 response. Further, while the Project pointed out that it was unable to indicate links between Mr. Arar and al-Qaeda, it did not go further and correct the inaccurate information already provided to the American agencies about Mr. Arar, including the label of Islamic extremist.

Finally, I note that, in its response, the RCMP provided information received from CSIS that was subject to caveats without obtaining the consent of CSIS to do so. This was a breach of both the CSIS caveats and RCMP policy.

The RCMP's third communication of note with American authorities during Mr. Arar's detention in New York actually involved two phone calls between Corporal Rick Flewelling of CID and an FBI agent, the first on October 4 and the second on October 5. During the second call, the FBI agent said that the United States did not have enough information to charge Mr. Arar and was looking to remove him. He indicated that Mr. Arar had asked to be sent to Canada, and Washington wanted to know whether the RCMP could charge him or refuse him entry to Canada. The corporal responded that there was not enough evidence to charge Mr. Arar in Canada and that it was likely that he could not be refused entry to Canada.

I accept Corporal Flewelling's evidence that it did not occur to him that the American authorities were considering Syria as an option. He believed that Mr. Arar would either be returned to Zurich or be sent to Canada. I am satisfied that the RCMP was not informed of the possibility of Syria as a destination until at least October 7.

On October 7, 2002, the U.S. INS ordered that Mr. Arar be removed from the United States because he had been found to be a member of al-Qaeda. Much of the information relied upon to make the order was contained in an appendix that has not been disclosed publicly.

I reach the following conclusions in regard to the two American decisions of interest to my mandate, that is, the decision to detain Mr. Arar in New York and the decision to remove him to Syria:

- Canadian officials did not participate or acquiesce in the American decisions to detain Mr. Arar and remove him to Syria. I have thoroughly reviewed all of the evidence relating to events both before and during Mr. Arar's detention in New York, and there is no evidence that any Canadian authorities—the RCMP, CSIS or others—were complicit in those decisions.
- It is very likely that, in making the decisions to detain and remove Mr. Arar to Syria, the U.S. authorities relied on information about Mr. Arar provided by the RCMP. Although I cannot be certain without the evidence of the American authorities, the evidence strongly supports this conclusion. Over time, a good deal of information about Mr. Arar that would undoubtedly have raised suspicions about him was supplied without caveats to the American agencies by the RCMP. Indeed, although the appendix containing the confidential information in the removal order has not been disclosed, the publicly available portion of the order refers to information that originated in Canada. Moreover, on many occasions after the event, several American officials, including then Secretary of State Colin Powell, said that the American authorities had relied on information provided by Canada in making the decision to send Mr. Arar to Syria. Tellingly, the Americans have never provided the Canadian authorities with any information of their own about Mr. Arar that would have supported the removal order. Given the close co-operation between the RCMP and the American agencies, it seems likely that, if they had such information, they would have supplied it to the Canadians.
- Finally, without the evidence of the American authorities, I am unable to conclude what role, if any, the TECS lookout for Mr. Arar requested by the RCMP in late October 2002 played in the American decisions to detain Mr. Arar and remove him to Syria.

5.2.2 Consular Officials

DFAIT first became aware of the possibility that Mr. Arar was being detained in New York on September 29 and was actually informed that he was being detained on October 1.

I conclude that, during Mr. Arar's detention in New York, DFAIT officials took reasonable steps to provide Mr. Arar with consular services, including addressing the possibility that he might be sent to Syria.

A number of signs alerted consular officials to the possibility that the United States was considering sending Mr. Arar to Syria. On October 1, Mr. Arar's brother informed DFAIT that Mr. Arar had told him that he would be sent to Syria. On the same day, a senior U.S. INS officer advised that the case was of such seriousness that it should be taken to the highest level, and on October 3, Mr. Arar told the Canadian consul that investigating officers had informed him that they were going to send him to Syria.

The DFAIT officials considered these warning signs, but based on their past experience with individuals in "terrorism-related" cases and the information they had received, they did not believe that there was an imminent risk that Mr. Arar would be sent to Syria. Individuals in these types of cases had always been held for months. Moreover, the officials had never known the Americans to remove a Canadian citizen to a country other than Canada when the individual had requested to be sent to Canada and was travelling with Canadian documents, as was the case with Mr. Arar.

At no time did the American authorities give consular officials any indication of their intention to send Mr. Arar to Syria. They were not open and forthcoming about what was happening with respect to the detainee. Canadian officials were caught completely off guard when they learned of Mr. Arar's fate.

A point of note is that, five days before Mr. Arar's removal, consular officials assisted Mr. Arar and his family in retaining counsel to represent his legal interest in any American proceeding. It was reasonable for consular officials to expect that the American lawyer who would represent Mr. Arar would take appropriate steps to protect his interests and would notify them if there was anything that they could do to assist with the case. The lawyer, who visited Mr. Arar on October 5 and also spoke with INS officials, did not raise the possibility of removal to Syria with Canadian consular officials or suggest any further action by Canadian officials to assist Mr. Arar. That lawyer declined an invitation to testify at the Inquiry. However, it appears that she, like the consular officials, was unaware that the American authorities were intending to remove Mr. Arar to Syria in the very sudden way that they did.

5.2.3 Interagency Communication

As discussed above, during the period of Mr. Arar's detention in New York, DFAIT and the RCMP were each dealing directly with American authorities in regard to Mr. Arar's situation without knowledge of what the other was doing and without benefit of the information in the other's possession.

The RCMP has no policy requiring it to communicate with DFAIT when it learns that someone connected with one of its investigations has been detained abroad. Canadians detained outside Canada are entitled to consular services on request, and the RCMP's general approach is based on the notion that detainees will be able to contact a consular officer if they wish. In Mr. Arar's case, it had no reason to believe that any request made by Mr. Arar for consular assistance in the United States would not be granted. There was consequently no reason for the RCMP to contact DFAIT about Mr. Arar's situation. Further, I am satisfied that there was no requirement for the RCMP to notify DFAIT that it was providing information about Mr. Arar to the U.S. authorities.

DFAIT, for its part, undertook a reasonable course of action in trying to sort out what was actually occurring and in involving legal counsel to act for Mr. Arar. I do not think that, in the circumstances, DFAIT should be faulted for not having informed the RCMP about the threat of Syria as it was assessed at that time.

Nevertheless, given the international environment in which they must operate when someone is detained in connection with a terrorism investigation, Canadian agencies in any way involved in such cases should consult with one another and develop a coherent and consistent approach to the situation for all Canadian agencies. The reality of terrorism investigations calls for extraordinary care by Canadian officials in relation to Canadians detained abroad for suspected links to terrorism.[8]

5.3 Imprisonment and Mistreatment in Syria

5.3.1 Initial Period

Mr. Arar arrived in Syria on October 9, 2002. He was held incommunicado by the Syrian Military Intelligence (SMI) at its Palestine Branch until October 21, when the Canadian ambassador, Franco Pillarella, was informed that Mr. Arar was in Syria. Prior to that time, Canadian officials had made a number of inquiries of Syrian officials about Mr. Arar's whereabouts and had been told that he was not in Syria. This was false.

---

[8] See Chapter IX.

In view of what followed, I conclude that Syrian officials would not say that Mr. Arar was in Syria during the initial period of his imprisonment because the SMI wanted to interrogate and torture him in order to obtain a statement. Clearly, the SMI did not want any interference from Canadian officials while it was conducting "the interrogation."

The actions of the SMI with respect to Mr. Arar were entirely consistent with Syria's widespread reputation for abusing prisoners being held in connection with terrorism-related investigations. The U.S. State Department and Amnesty International have publicly reported on Syria's poor human rights record in relation to prisoners. In particular, these reports state that Syrian intelligence agencies such as the SMI are known to hold prisoners incommunicado at the beginning of their imprisonment for purposes of interrogation using torture.

I am satisfied that, during the period Mr. Arar was held incommunicado, Canadian officials did everything they reasonably could to locate him. The fact is that the Syrian officials lied to them and there was little more they could do.

On October 21, the Syrian deputy foreign minister contacted Ambassador Pillarella and advised him that Mr. Arar was in fact in Syria, having just arrived from Jordan earlier that day. The next day, General Hassan Khalil, the head of the SMI, also told Ambassador Pillarella that Mr. Arar had just arrived in Syria, and that he had already admitted having connections with terrorist organizations. The general agreed to allow Canadian consular officials to visit Mr. Arar and the first visit was arranged for the following day, October 23.

Léo Martel, the Canadian consul in Damascus, visited Mr. Arar the next day in an office at the Palestine Branch. He did not observe any physical signs of torture on Mr. Arar and indicated in his report of the meeting that Mr. Arar had appeared healthy, but added, "of course, it is difficult to assess."

There were actually many indications that all was not well. The visit was very controlled and Mr. Arar's demeanour was submissive. Syrian officials were present throughout and insisted that Mr. Arar speak in Arabic, with one of them serving as interpreter. Mr. Arar sent eye signals communicating that he could not speak freely. He was made to say that he was "happy to have come back to Syria" and "my Syrian brothers have not exercised pressure on me," statements that were transparently artificial and contrived. He did manage to say that he had spent only "a few hours" in Jordan, which meant that he had been in Syria for about 12 days.

5.3.2 Torture

I am satisfied that the October 23 consular visit should have alerted Canadian officials to the likelihood that Mr. Arar had been tortured when interrogated while held incommunicado by the SMI. As I said earlier, what happened to Mr. Arar fit squarely within the publicly reported Syrian practices of torturing prisoners. The fact that Syrian officials misled the Canadians about when Mr. Arar had arrived in Syria suggests they had something to hide. And if there was any doubt, the controlled nature of the first consular visit and Mr. Arar's submissive demeanour and prompted statements during that visit were further indications that he had been abused.

Some Canadian officials did operate under the "working assumption" that Mr. Arar had been tortured. Others, including the Ambassador, were not prepared to go that far based on the information available. In my view, after the first consular visit, all Canadian officials dealing with Mr. Arar in any way should have proceeded on the assumption that he had been tortured during the initial stages of his imprisonment and, equally of importance, that the "statement" he had made to the SMI had been the product of that torture.

5.3.3 Continuing Investigations

5.3.3.1 *Bout de Papier*

On November 3, 2002, the SMI provided Ambassador Pillarella with a *bout de papier*, or informal written communication, setting out certain information that the SMI had obtained from Mr. Arar, including the fact that he had taken *mujahedeen* training in Afghanistan in 1993.

The Ambassador passed the *bout de papier* on to DFAIT Headquarters, which distributed it to the RCMP and CSIS. By this point, DFAIT should have been aware that Mr. Arar's statements to the SMI were likely the product of torture.

Given the circumstances, I do not think that it was improper or inappropriate for the Ambassador to receive the *bout de papier* from the SMI. By this point, the SMI was permitting Canada access to Mr. Arar and it would have seemed unlikely that he would be subjected to any physical abuse in the future. Moreover, it was General Khalil who raised the subject of information obtained from Mr. Arar and made the information available to the Ambassador. Furthermore, there was potentially a benefit to Canadian officials' knowing what Syrian authorities considered to be "the case" against Mr. Arar. As stated by Gar Pardy, Director General of Consular Affairs at DFAIT, they might have been better able to assist him armed with that information.

That said, when they received the information, DFAIT officials should have conducted a proper assessment of its reliability. Had they done so, they would have concluded that it was likely the product of torture and therefore of doubtful reliability. That assessment should then have accompanied the *bout de papier* when DFAIT distributed it to the RCMP and CSIS. As it turned out, some RCMP officers did not consider the likelihood of torture when assessing Mr. Arar's possible involvement in terrorism-related activities. This was unfortunate and unfair to Mr. Arar. In Chapter IX, I recommend that, when Canadian officials receive information from a country with a questionable human rights record, such as Syria, they conduct a reliability assessment and ensure that their conclusions accompany the information if they disseminate it.

5.3.3.2 CSIS Trip

On November 19, 2002, CSIS officials travelled to Syria for the purpose of meeting with the Syrian Military Intelligence (SMI). One of the purposes of the trip was to obtain information on Mr. Arar's case.

When they met with the SMI, the CSIS officials received some information regarding Mr. Arar's case, but did not provide the Syrians with any information about him. They did not visit Mr. Arar, nor did they provide the Syrians with any questions for him. However, I am not satisfied that CSIS did an adequate reliability assessment of the information received from the SMI, in particular with respect to whether the information could be a product of torture. Indeed, its assessment was that it was probably not the product of torture, which I find was not the case. As a result, any reliance on this information by CSIS or others was misguided or misplaced.

I am satisfied that it was appropriate for CSIS officials to meet with the SMI in the circumstances that existed in November 2002. There was a legitimate investigative reason for the trip, and DFAIT was consulted and approved of the trip, even though it had reservations about the timing. The Minister of Foreign Affairs was informed. The CSIS officials involved did nothing more than receive information in regard to Mr. Arar's case. They testified that they had been careful not to say anything that could negatively affect Mr. Arar's circumstances or his release.

That said, there are significant risks whenever Canadian investigators interact with a country with a questionable human rights record, particularly when a Canadian is being detained in that country. Although decisions to interact must be made on a case-by-case basis, they should be made in a way that is politically accountable, and interactions should be strictly controlled to guard against Canadian complicity in human rights abuses or a perception that Canada condones such abuses. In Chapter IX, I recommend a process for making such decisions.

5.3.3.3 RCMP Investigation

Project A-O Canada continued its investigation from October 2002 until after Mr. Arar's return to Canada and took steps to gather as much information about Mr. Arar as it could. The investigation was comprehensive and thorough, and involved co-operation with American agencies. In the end, this extensive investigation of Mr. Arar did not turn up any evidence that he had committed any criminal offence. Further, there is no evidence indicating that Mr. Arar constitutes a threat to the security of Canada.

5.3.4 Efforts to Obtain Release

5.3.4.1 Mr. Edelson's Letter

On October 31, 2002, Michael Edelson, a lawyer who had previously acted for Mr. Arar, wrote Project A-O Canada a letter requesting confirmation of information it was hoped could be used to try to obtain Mr. Arar's release. Mr. Edelson sought confirmation that 1) the RCMP had not requested that Mr. Arar be deported to Syria; 2) Mr. Arar did not have a criminal record; 3) Mr. Arar was not wanted in Canada for any offence; and 4) Mr. Arar was not a suspect with respect to a terrorism-related offence.

There was considerable discussion within the RCMP about how to respond. On November 16, 2002, Inspector Michel Cabana, the officer in charge of Project A-O Canada, sent a reply confirming only the first two points, adding that it would be improper for the RCMP to comment on Mr. Arar's position in relation to the RCMP investigation and referring Mr. Edelson back to DFAIT. Not surprisingly, the response was of no use to those seeking Mr. Arar's release and return to Canada.

I have two observations to make about this issue. First, the response to Mr. Edelson's request reveals a lack of a coordinated and cohesive approach by Canadian officials with respect to obtaining Mr. Arar's release. The Director General of Consular Affairs at DFAIT was supportive of Mr. Edelson's efforts to obtain a letter. However, the RCMP was of the view that the matter was entirely DFAIT's responsibility and that the RCMP had no role to play. In fact, the RCMP officers were quite upset about even being asked to write a letter. DFAIT and the RCMP had potentially different interests in relation to what should be done. There were no policies or guidelines addressing the need to reconcile differing positions regarding cases of Canadians detained abroad. A process is needed to ensure that Canadian officials proceed in a coherent and co-operative way. In Chapter IX, I recommend such a process.

My second observation about Mr. Edelson's request is that at least one RCMP officer was disinclined to indicate that Mr. Arar was not a suspect because the *bout de papier* received from Syria stated that Mr. Arar had admitted attending a training camp in Afghanistan in 1993. However, in attaching significance to this admission, the officer gave no weight to the fact that the so-called admission was likely the product of torture.

When the *bout de papier* was distributed within the Canadian government, a cautionary note about the likelihood of torture should have been attached.

5.3.4.2 Ambassador and Minister

During the months that Mr. Arar was imprisoned in Syria, Ambassador Pillarella met with General Khalil and other Syrian officials on many occasions. The Ambassador testified that he had stated repeatedly that Canada's position was that Mr. Arar should be released and returned to Canada. According to the Ambassador, there could not have been any doubt in the minds of the Syrians that he, as Canada's representative in Syria, had held that position. However, the Ambassador also testified that dealing with Syrian officials could be difficult. They were not always forthcoming and their practice in regard to prisoners detained in terrorism-related cases was to do what suited their best interests as they saw them.

Ambassador Pillarella testified that the fact that the SMI had permitted Canadian consular access to Mr. Arar was unprecedented. He also described the cordial relationship that he had developed with General Khalil, the head of the SMI. In the end, however, despite the Ambassador's efforts, the Syrian authorities were not responsive to the many requests that Mr. Arar be released.

While no one can say for sure why Mr. Arar was finally released in early October 2003, it does not appear that the Ambassador's entreaties played a role. I do not make this comment as a criticism, but rather to underline the Ambassador's point that making requests of the Syrian authorities was often an exercise in futility.

Canada's Foreign Affairs Minister Bill Graham also became involved in attempting to secure Mr. Arar's release. Beginning in November, plans were made for him to speak directly to Syria's Foreign Minister about Mr. Arar's case. However, a phone call scheduled for November 19, 2002 was delayed to allow the Minister to be briefed on the results of the CSIS trip to Syria, planned for about the same time. It made sense for him to have as much information as possible about Syria's view of Mr. Arar's case before discussing the matter with the Syrian minister. In December, the phone call was further delayed because of scheduling problems. Minister Graham eventually spoke to his Syrian counterpart on January 16, 2003. By then, Syrian officials were alleging that CSIS had said it did not want Mr. Arar returned to Canada. In his phone call, Minister Graham spelled out clearly and forcefully that Canada wanted Mr. Arar returned. I will come back to the alleged statement by CSIS below.

I am satisfied that Minister Graham's message to Syria's Foreign Minister was entirely appropriate and that his decision to become involved in the case was the correct step. Although the Syrian authorities did not respond positively to Minister Graham's entreaty, it was important nonetheless that a senior government minister clearly and firmly state Canada's position to the Syrians. Minister Graham did that.

5.3.4.3 Mixed Signals

5.3.4.3.1 Questions for Mr. Almalki

On January 15, 2003, the Canadian consul, on the instructions of the Ambassador, delivered a letter from the RCMP to General Khalil enclosing a series of questions to be posed to Abdullah Almalki, who, like Mr. Arar, was imprisoned at the Palestine Branch at the time. In the letter, the RCMP offered to share with the SMI "large volumes of highly sensitive documents and information, seized during investigative efforts or obtained from confidential informants associated to terrorist cells operating in Canada."[9]

Among the questions for Mr. Almalki were some about his relationships with a number of individuals, most of whom the SMI would have considered to be very heavily involved in terrorist activities. Mr. Arar, although only a person of interest and not a terrorist suspect, was included with these individuals.

There was conflicting evidence about whether DFAIT had given its approval to the RCMP to send the questions for Mr. Almalki.

In the latter part of 2002, the RCMP and DFAIT's Foreign Intelligence Division, referred to as "ISI," had a number of discussions about sending questions for Mr. Almalki to Syria. ISI witnesses testified that they had believed that a "credible risk" existed that the SMI would use torture in seeking answers to any questions sent and had advised the RCMP against sending questions.

In contrast, RCMP witnesses testified that DFAIT had never advised against sending questions; indeed, Ambassador Pillarella had obviously approved, as he had arranged for delivery of the questions to the SMI.

Ambassador Pillarella stated that he had understood from the RCMP liaison officer (LO) from whom he had received the questions that Ottawa had given its approval. The LO could not recall the conversation. There is virtually no written record of what was discussed among the parties.

What emerges is a complete failure of communication among Canadian officials with regard to whether or not the questions should have been sent. I am satisfied that DFAIT ISI properly assessed the situation. Sending questions raised a "credible risk" that the SMI would torture Mr. Almalki

[9] Exhibit C-359, Tab 10.

to obtain answers. In those circumstances, questions should not have been sent.

In any event, what is relevant for the Inquiry is that the questions were delivered to the SMI on January 15, 2003, the day before Minister Graham telephoned Syria's Foreign Minister to ask for Mr. Arar's release. The problem is that providing the questions to the SMI created a risk that the SMI would conclude that the RCMP considered Mr. Arar a serious terrorist threat (which it did not) and that, despite Minister Graham's entreaty, it would decide to hold Mr. Arar until it had completed all of its investigations that might involve Mr. Arar, including the one relating to Mr. Almalki. Ambassador Pillarella testified that, in the Syrian officials' minds, the cases of Mr. Arar and Mr. Almalki had been linked. I have no way of knowing whether the SMI in fact interpreted the letter and questions in this fashion. The fact remains, however, that sending the questions created a risk that they would be interpreted as a "mixed signal" from Canada.

5.3.4.3.2 Alleged CSIS Statement

In early 2003, Syrian officials informed Ambassador Pillarella on three separate occasions that the SMI had been told by CSIS that it did not want Mr. Arar returned to Canada. If true, this would have undermined Canadian efforts to obtain Mr. Arar's release. They did not indicate exactly who at CSIS had made the statement or under what circumstances it had been made. CSIS denied that any of its personnel had made the statement.

Each time Ambassador Pillarella was told about the CSIS statement, he assured the Syrian officials that Canada did want Mr. Arar back. In addition, when Minister Graham spoke with Syria's Foreign Minister by telephone on January 16, Minister Graham specifically raised the matter of the suggestion that Canada did not want Mr. Arar returned and emphasized that the Government of Canada's official and complete position was that Canada wanted him back and that there was no impediment to his return.

It seems to me that, in the circumstances, the Minister's telephone call was a reasonable way to address the concern about the CSIS statement. The Minister made Canada's position very clear and one could reasonably expect that a minister-to-minister conversation would be sufficient to deal with the issue. There was nothing in the responses of the Syrian foreign minister at the time or in the responses of other Syrian officials on hearing of the phone call that signalled that more needed to be done.

The issue remained dormant for about two months, until March 2003, when the Syrian ambassador to Canada, Ahmad Arnous, raised it again. He mentioned it to the two Canadian members of Parliament who were planning to visit Mr. Arar in Syria. The MPs reiterated the official Canadian position that Canada wanted Mr. Arar returned and reported the matter to DFAIT.

DFAIT did nothing further to try to clarify the matter at that time. The fact that the issue surfaced again two months after Minister Graham's phone call is troubling. Without the evidence of Syrian authorities, I cannot know what their thinking might have been about the "CSIS statement." However, it seems to me that, when the issue was raised again in March, more should have been done to address the matter.

It would have been helpful and sensible at that time for DFAIT to have asked that CSIS clarify directly with the SMI that it was not opposed to Mr. Arar's return and that it agreed with the official Canadian position. CSIS should have been asked to dispel any misperception on the part of the Syrians that Canada was sending mixed messages. Unfortunately that did not happen.

5.3.4.4 Visit by Members of Parliament

In the period from late October 2002 to February 2003, the SMI permitted the Canadian consul to meet with Mr. Arar on seven occasions.

Moreover, on April 22, 2003, two Canadian members of Parliament, Marlene Catterall and Sarkis Assadourian, visited Mr. Arar while he was in custody in Syria. They also delivered a letter from Minister Graham to the Syrian foreign minister seeking Mr. Arar's release. In that letter, Minister Graham indicated that there was no impediment to Mr. Arar's return to Canada. The MPs were informed that Mr. Arar was soon to be sent to trial on charges of belonging to al-Qaeda.

The MPs, together with Ambassador Pillarella, met with Mr. Arar for approximately twenty minutes. The meeting was very controlled. The MPs were confined to discussing Mr. Arar's health and family. Mr. Arar was required to answer in Arabic and his responses were then translated for the visitors. Mr. Arar appeared somewhat disoriented and thin. During the meeting, Ms. Catterall assured Mr. Arar that the Canadian government was doing everything it could to have him returned to Canada.

Prior to the meeting with Mr. Arar, Ambassador Pillarella had met with the MPs and told them that the Syrian authorities had serious concerns that Mr. Arar might be involved with al-Qaeda and might have attended a training camp in Afghanistan. Although the source of this latter information was probably the Syrian interrogation of Mr. Arar, the Ambassador did not caution the MPs that the information was likely the result of torture.

In his report to Ottawa concerning that meeting, Ambassador Pillarella noted that, had the MPs been more fully briefed in Ottawa, they would have reconsidered going to Damascus. Ms. Catterall denied that the Ambassador had been told this and indicated that she did not know where the Ambassador had gained that impression. DFAIT distributed the report of the consular visit to the RCMP and CSIS. I discuss the issue of the distribution of consular reports below.

5.3.4.5 "One Voice" Letter

During the months of May and June 2003, the concern that Syrian officials believed or said that they believed that CSIS did not want Mr. Arar returned to Canada lingered on. DFAIT made a number of proposals for a letter from Canada to Syria seeking Mr. Arar's release. The thrust of the proposals was to send a message that Canada—including the RCMP and CSIS—spoke with one voice in seeking Mr. Arar's release and that there was no reason Mr. Arar could not be returned to Canada. There were a number of meetings or discussions between officials from DFAIT, the RCMP and CSIS to discuss the "one voice" letter. However, in my view, the RCMP and CSIS were not supportive of DFAIT's efforts.

The first proposal was for a letter to be signed by both the Minister of Foreign Affairs and the Solicitor General, the minister responsible for the RCMP and CSIS. Initially, DFAIT suggested that the letter state that there was "no evidence" that Mr. Arar was a member of al-Qaeda or was involved in terrorist activity. In point of fact, the RCMP, the lead Canadian investigator, had no evidence to lead it to suspect that Mr. Arar had committed any offence. He was merely a person of interest, whom the RCMP wished to interview as a witness because of certain associations with others suspected of terrorism-related activity.

The RCMP and CSIS objected, understandably I think, to the unequivocal nature of the proposed "no evidence" language, taking the position that there was information that made Mr. Arar a person of interest to the Canadian investigators. However, the result of that objection was that CSIS advised the Solicitor General "very strongly" against signing any letter. Moreover, when the proposal evolved into the idea of a letter from the Minister of Foreign Affairs alone, the RCMP, with CSIS approval, suggested language that was unhelpful and indeed overstated Mr. Arar's status. It indicated that "Mr. Arar was a subject of a national security investigation," when he was not. This language would have had a prejudicial effect on DFAIT's efforts to have Mr. Arar released.

In the end, the Minister of Foreign Affairs did not send a letter and the Prime Minister did. I will come back to the Prime Minister's letter.

I conclude that the RCMP and CSIS should have supported DFAIT's efforts to obtain a "one voice" letter, because of a number of factors. First, it was clear, or should have been clear, to everyone that Mr. Arar's human rights had been and likely continued to be seriously abused. Syria's reputation for mistreating prisoners was well known and the likelihood of Mr. Arar receiving a fair trial in Syria was remote. By this time, it was also clear that the U.S. authorities had relied on information from Canada in removing Mr. Arar to Syria using their questionable practice of extraordinary rendition. In addition, the official Canadian position was that Canada should seek Mr. Arar's release. Next to the Prime Minister, the Minister of Foreign Affairs was the most senior Canadian official politically accountable for handling Mr. Arar's case. Minister Graham wanted Mr. Arar released. Moreover, it was likely that the support of CSIS and possibly the RCMP would be very important to the Syrian government. It was well known that the SMI, which was holding Mr. Arar, would be more influenced by the views of a security intelligence agency (CSIS) than those of a politician (Minister Graham). Finally, Mr. Arar, a Canadian husband and father, had been separated from his young family for over half a year.

Had the RCMP and CSIS put their minds to the task and approached it with a view to offering real support, they could have done so. In the end, proposing a letter that inaccurately said that Mr. Arar was a subject of a national security investigation was not helpful.

In Chapter IX, I recommend a protocol for addressing situations such as Mr. Arar's in the future. When Canadians are detained abroad in connection with a terrorism-related matter, there should be a consultative and coherent process for developing a Canadian course of action. Decisions should be made in a politically accountable way and, once a course of action is adopted, all agencies should be supportive.

5.3.4.6 Prime Minister's Letter

When DFAIT's initiatives to obtain a "one voice" letter that would be helpful in obtaining Mr. Arar's release stalled, DFAIT struck on the idea of obtaining a letter from the Prime Minister.

As a result, the Prime Minister sent a letter seeking Mr. Arar's release to Syria's President through an envoy, Senator Pierre De Bané. The letter, delivered on July 22, 2003, stated that there was no Canadian impediment to Mr. Arar's return. It did not contain the "no evidence" language about which

the RCMP and CSIS had expressed concern. In the end, the letter coming from Canada's Prime Minister likely went a long way towards sending the message that all Canadian agencies, including the RCMP and CSIS, wanted Mr. Arar returned. I note that the letter was sent about three and a half months after DFAIT first attempted to obtain a "one voice" letter.

5.3.5 Consular Services

5.3.5.1 Consular Visits

In the period of approximately one year during which he was imprisoned in Syria, Mr. Arar had nine consular visits. Mr. Martel, the Canadian consul, was the only person permitted to visit him, except once, on April 22, 2003, when the two Canadian members of Parliament, Marlene Catterall and Sarkis Assadourian, and Ambassador Pillarella were allowed to see him.

I am satisfied that Mr. Martel and Ambassador Pillarella did everything reasonably possible to obtain access to Mr. Arar. Mr. Arar is a dual citizen of Canada and Syria. The Syrian government, however, does not recognize any other citizenship if a person was born in Syria, as is the case with Mr. Arar. It consequently does not accept that a dual citizen is entitled to consular services from another country. Given this position, the ability of Canadian officials to obtain access to Mr. Arar depended entirely on the willingness of the SMI to grant what it considered favourable treatment. Over time, the SMI became much less responsive to requests to visit Mr. Arar. I believe Ambassador Pillarella and Mr. Martel exercised good judgment in seeking as much access as possible without unduly provoking Syrian officials.

Dealing with a country such as Syria, which may act arbitrarily and unpre-dictably, can at times require difficult decisions about how hard to press requests. While some might have adopted a more aggressive approach with Syrian officials, I see no reason to question the judgments the Ambassador and Mr. Martel made at the time.

5.3.5.2 Consular Reports

I am satisfied that, with the exception of the report on the August 14, 2003 visit, the reports of the consular visits were satisfactory.

Admittedly, the reports did not describe the terrible conditions in which Mr. Arar was being held. However, the controlled nature of the visits made it impossible for Mr. Martel to explore this issue with him. The one exception in this respect occurred during the August 14 visit, when Mr. Arar told Mr. Martel that he was being held in a cell that measured three by six by seven feet. This was important information, yet Mr. Martel failed to include it in his report. During that visit, Mr. Arar also told Mr. Martel that the press would know the truth when he returned home, suggesting that he did not consider it wise to provide details about his treatment while still in Syrian custody.

During the August 14 visit, Mr. Arar also said that he had not been beaten, tortured or paralyzed. Mr. Martel was understandably sceptical of this last comment, yet his report made no reference to his scepticism. As I indicate below, the report was distributed to other agencies and Mr. Arar's statement about not being tortured was accepted by some as fact.

After the August 14, 2003 consular visit, Minister Graham made a public statement to the effect that Mr. Arar had had an independent consular visit—which he had not—and had said he had not been tortured. While Mr. Arar had made such a statement, its accuracy was highly doubtful. It appears that the Minister had not been fully or properly briefed. His statement that Mr. Arar had said he had not been tortured was particularly unfortunate, as that piece of misinformation became the accepted fact for many and worked most unfairly against Mr. Arar.

DFAIT distributed a number of the consular reports on visits with Mr. Arar, including the report of the August 14 visit, to the RCMP and/or CSIS. Consular visits are intended to assist detainees, not to help collect information for investigative agencies. Reports of consular visits should accordingly be kept confidential except in certain specified situations. The purpose behind distributing the reports about Mr. Arar to the RCMP was ostensibly to assist Mr. Arar by dissuading RCMP officers from travelling to Syria in connection with his case. However, that purpose was never communicated to either the RCMP or CSIS, and the reports were used as part of the investigative file. Moreover, the Consular Affairs Bureau distributed the report of the August 14 visit, which stated that Mr. Arar had said he had not been tortured, to others without attaching an explanatory note indicating that this statement should be viewed with serious scepticism. In the recommendations in Chapter IX, I address issues relating to consular visits and the preparation and distribution of consular reports.

5.3.5.3 Legal Assistance

Prior to August 14, 2003, consular officials did not take any steps to obtain a lawyer in Syria for Mr. Arar. In my view, this was understandable. Clearly, it would have been possible for consular officials to put Mr. Arar's family in touch with a lawyer, or to at least suggest they contact one. However, Mr. Martel considered that retaining a lawyer at that time would be pointless, as the SMI was still investigating, there were no charges, and there were no legal proceedings underway. As a matter of practice, Syria did not permit lawyers to have access to detainees.

On August 14, the SMI indicated that Mr. Arar would be going to trial shortly. A search for the best lawyer began. Consular officials were strongly of the view that Mr. Arar and his family should retain a particular lawyer and conveyed that preference to the family. I am satisfied that their preference was motivated solely by Mr. Arar's best interests. In any event, in relatively short order, before any legal steps were necessary, the family retained counsel of its own choice. Consular officials could have acted more quickly in providing that lawyer with assistance; however, it is important to note that, throughout this period, the Syrians did not inform anyone of the charges against Mr. Arar and the case remained rather amorphous. I have no doubt that, if the case had crystallized, consular officials would have been as supportive as they could of Mr. Arar and his counsel.

5.3.5.4 Mr. Arar's Release

On October 5, 2003, Mr. Arar was released to Mr. Martel. Mr. Arar had lived through a nightmare. While the physical beatings had ended after the first few weeks, the conditions of his imprisonment in the Palestine Branch had been abysmal. He had been confined in a tiny cell with no natural light. He had slept on the floor and endured disgusting sanitary conditions. Mr. Arar had suffered enormously. He continues to experience the after-effects to this day.

Mr. Martel accompanied Mr. Arar back to Canada, where Mr. Arar was reunited with his family at the Montréal-Dorval International Airport on October 6, 2003.

5.4 Post-Return

5.4.1 Mr. Arar's Statement

On the plane trip home to Canada, Mr. Arar related to Mr. Martel some of what had happened to him in Syrian detention. Among other things, he told him that he had had a "difficult time" during the first two weeks of detention and that he had been hit from time to time, but nothing really serious. He also described the degrading conditions of imprisonment.

On October 7, 2003, at a meeting with DFAIT officials, Mr. Martel repeated what Mr. Arar had told him on the trip home—that he had been "beaten" occasionally during the first two weeks of detention.

On November 4, 2003, Mr. Arar spoke about his ordeal publicly for the first time. In his public statement, he described how he had been beaten while being interrogated by his Syrian jailers during the first two weeks of his detention. I note that the description of the abuse Mr. Arar gave during his press conference was essentially the same, albeit more detailed, as that he had given Mr. Martel on the plane trip home.

In November 2003, Mr. Martel prepared a memorandum and other written communications in which he stated that Mr. Arar had not told him during the trip home that he had been beaten while in Syrian custody.

In his testimony, Mr. Martel acknowledged that these were incorrect. He explained that he had prepared them from memory and had forgotten that Mr. Arar had told him that he had been beaten.

The reason I raise these written communications is to point out the potential harm that can flow from recording information inaccurately. After Mr. Arar's return, some officials in the Canadian government did not believe Mr. Arar's public statements that he had been beaten or tortured. As it turns out, their conclusions were wrong. Mr. Arar had indeed been beaten and physically tortured during the first two weeks of his imprisonment in Syria. Inaccurate memoranda and other written communications such as those I refer to above can contribute to and support false conclusions. The need for accurate and fair reporting is obvious.

5.4.2 Leaks

When Mr. Arar returned to Canada, his torment did not end, as some government officials took it upon themselves to leak information to the media, much of which was unfair to Mr. Arar and damaging to his reputation.

Over a period of time, Government of Canada officials intentionally released selected classified information about Mr. Arar or his case to the media. The first leak occurred in July 2003, even before Mr. Arar's return to Canada, and the leaks intensified in the period immediately following his return in October 2003.

There were at least eight media stories containing leaked information about Mr. Arar and/or the investigation that involved him. Typically, the leaked information was attributed to an unnamed government official, an official closely involved in the case, or some similar source. Some of the leaks sought to portray Mr. Arar as someone who had been involved in terrorist activities, mentioning, for example, that he had trained in Afghanistan. In one, he was described as a "very bad guy;"[10] in another, the source was reported to have said that the guy was "not a virgin,"[11] adding that there was more there than met the eye.

Several of the leaks were inaccurate, unsupported by the information available from the investigations, and grossly unfair to Mr. Arar. At least one leak sought to downplay the mistreatment and torture Mr. Arar had suffered in Syria.

---

[10] Exhibit P-80, pp. 1–2. Robert Fife, "Terror threats in Ottawa: Two kinds of fear: Report says Syrian intelligence helped U.S. to foil al-Qaeda plot on target in Ottawa," *Ottawa Citizen* (July 24, 2003), A1.

[11] Ibid., pp. 7–8, Robert Fife, "U.S., Canada '100% sure' Arar trained with al-Qaeda: Family spokeswoman accuses intelligence officers of anonymous smear campaign," *Ottawa Citizen* (December 30, 2003), A1.

The most notorious of the leaks occurred on November 8, 2003, when information from classified documents was published in the *Ottawa Citizen*, in a lengthy article by Juliet O'Neill that contained a large amount of previously confidential information.

The O'Neill article reported that security officials had leaked allegations against Mr. Arar in the weeks leading to his return to Canada "in defence of their investigative work—against suggestions that the RCMP and the Canadian Security Intelligence Service had either bungled Mr. Arar's case or, worse, purposefully sent an innocent man to be tortured in Syria."[12] This rationale implies that officials believe leaking confidential information is justified if it suits the interests of investigators. According to this thinking, leakors get to be selective—picking and choosing what to leak to paint the picture that suits their interests.

There have been several investigations into the sources of the Arar leaks. To date, none of the sources have been identified. All witnesses at the Inquiry who were asked about them denied any knowledge. The sources of the leaks appear to be a complete mystery to everyone and the prospects of identifying those responsible seem uncertain at best. The only remaining investigation is the criminal investigation into the O'Neill leak, which is now two years old.

Leaking confidential information is a serious breach of trust. Obviously, it is important that all available steps be taken to prevent it.

Quite predictably, the leaks had a devastating effect on Mr. Arar's reputation and on him personally. The impact on an individual's reputation of being called a terrorist in the national media is severe. As I have stated elsewhere, labels, even unfair and inaccurate ones, have a tendency to stick.

Professor Toope, the fact-finder I appointed to report on the circumstances of Mr. Arar's detention in Syria, has indicated that the leaks have had severe psychological and emotional impacts on Mr. Arar. Moreover, Mr. Arar, an educated, hard-working engineer, has had great difficulty finding employment. It seems likely that the smear of his reputation by the leakors has taken its toll.

5.4.3 Incomplete Briefing

When briefing the Privy Council Office and senior government officials about the investigation relating to Mr. Arar, the RCMP omitted certain key facts that could have reflected adversely on its investigation.

[12] Ibid., pp. 5–6, Juliet O'Neill, "Canada's dossier on Maher Arar: The existence of a group of Ottawa men with alleged ties to al-Qaeda is at the root of why the government opposes an inquiry into the case," *Ottawa Citizen* (November 8, 2003), A1.

After Mr. Arar's press conference on November 4, 2003, the RCMP was asked to prepare a detailed timeline relating to the Arar investigation to assist the government in deciding how to proceed, including in particular whether to call a public inquiry.

On November 14, the RCMP produced a timeline that omitted several significant facts. It did not disclose that, throughout its investigation, the RCMP had provided information to American agencies without attaching written caveats, as required by RCMP policy. It also failed to reveal that, in April 2002, the RCMP had taken the unprecedented step of supplying its entire Supertext database containing the relevant investigation file to the U.S. agencies, and that it had done so without screening the information for relevance or accuracy and without attaching caveats, as required by policy. The timeline also did not disclose that the RCMP had contacted U.S. Customs to request border lookouts for Mr. Arar and his wife and, in doing so, had described them as Islamic extremists suspected of having links to al-Qaeda. Moreover, the timeline omitted to mention the two phone calls that Corporal Flewelling of RCMP CID had had with an American agent on October 4 and 5, 2002, during the critically important time Mr. Arar was being detained in New York.

These omissions were serious and the effect of the timeline was to downplay the potential problems with the RCMP investigation. In the circumstances that existed in November 2003, it was very important that the RCMP accurately brief the government on what had occurred, to enable the government to make an informed decision on how to proceed. Since the RCMP had in effect been asked to report on itself, there was a heightened obligation for it to be complete and forthcoming. I would expect that, in future, briefings such as that provided through the timeline would be accurate and balanced.

DOCUMENT NO. 9

JUDICIAL SESSION FOR A PRELIMINARY INVESTIGATION OF CUSTODIAL MATTERS FOR ADLER *ET AL*

Tribunal of Milan

April 24, 2004

n. 10838/05 R.G.N.R.

n. 1966/05 R.G.GIP

The Judge Presiding Over Preliminary Investigations

Having examined the Prosecutor's request, in which custodial measures are sought for:

1) ADLER Monica Courtney, born in Seattle (Washington—USA) on 02/02/1973, US citizen with US passport n. 017017139 (issued on 07.25.01), international driver's licence (copy acquired) n. 66605387, issued by US Authority in Heatrow (Florida) on 04.03.2002, Diners Club credit card n. 38541798540000 (expiry date May/2004), residient at *2001 N.Adams, Arlington—VIRGINIA—22201;*

2) ASHERLEIGH Gregory, born in Hyattsville—Maryland (USA) on 12/23/1955, *Coachmen Enterprises Washington, DC P.O. Box 91228 Washington DC (USA)* or *STS Inc. P.O. Box 1606 Hyattsville (Maryland) 20788 (USA),* telephone number 3015953823; US citizen with US passport n. 015135635, issued on 06.04.96; US driver's licence n. 66605685; Visa Card credit card n. 4118160311575248 (expiry date June/2005)

3) CARRERA Lorenzo Gabriel, born in Texas (USA) il 01.29.71, US citizen with US passport n. 016422583, issued on 02.12.95, or n. 016422583, issued on 01.28.00; Visa Card credit card n. 4118160306976955 (expiry date October/2005) and Diners Club credit card n. 38502203140000 (expiry date October/2004)

4) CASTALDO Eliana, born in Florida (USA) on 11/14/1969, *P.O. Box 1041 Norristown 19404 PA (USA),* telephone number 6102786893.

US citizen with US passport n. 026138038 issued on 11.02.98; Visa Card credit card n. 4118165006438370 (expiry date February/2005);

5) CASTELLANO Victor, born in Texas (USA) on 05/01/1968, *P.O. Box 41471 Arlington VA 22204,* US citizen with US passport n. 015914097 (issued on 07.14.97), Diners Club credit card n. 38184636950006 (expiry date December/2004) and Visa Card credit card n. 4118160152726694 (expiry date March/2005);

6) CHANNING Drew Carlyle, born in New York (USA) on 04/26/1965, US citizen with US passport n. 017121103, issued on 06.10.02 (copy acquired); Diners Club credit card n. 385030097360001 (expiry date April/2005)

7) **DUFFIN John Kevin,** born in Illinois (USA) on 05/03/1952, *P.O. Box 60031 19406 King of Prussia PA (USA) or 649 South Henderson Rd, King of Prussia—19406 PA* or at *Krauss Nannette 329 Prince Frederick St—King of Prussia, PA 19406 (tel. 6102650563);* US citizen with US passport n. 016434535 issued on 09.15.99 (copy acquired), Diners Club credit card n. 38650098880006 (expiry date April/2005), Visa Card credit card n. 4118165007626908 (expiry date March/2005);

8) GURLEY John Thomas, born in Los Angeles (USA) on 07/10/1969, *2783 Lb Mcloud Rd 32805 Orlando (USA),* US citizen with US passport n. 045029843, issued on 12.10.99; Visa Card credit card n. 4118160151941278 (expiry date December/2004)

9) HARBAUGH Raymond, born in Alaska (USA) on 06.09.39, *Box 73 Newington 22122 VA (USA),* US citizen with US passport n. 016136600, issued on 03.17.99; Visa Card credit cards n. 4486025001058371 (expiry date June/2005), n. 4316440000154988 (expiry date March/2003);

10) HARTY Ben Amar, born in Iowa (USA) on 10.20.44, *Box 73 Newington 22122 VA (USA),* US citizen with US passport n. 017120164, issued on 11.09.2001 and valid until 11.09.07; Visa Card credit cards n. 4486029500095512 (expiry date giugno 2003) e 4316440000221555 (expiry date March/2003), SPG card (Special Preferred Guest Westin Palace), type "A", n. 50426336577

11) KIRKLAND James Robert, born in Tennessee (USA) on 07.13.42, US citizen with US passport n. 045032045, issued on 10.01.1998 by the *Passport Agency* in Miami, expiry date 30.9.2008; Diners Club credit card n. 38541799470009 (expiry date gennaio/2004)

12) JENKINS Anne Lidia, born in Florida on 09/24/1946, US citizen with US passport n. 016698784 (copy acquired), issued on 06.28.01 by the *Passport Agency* in Washington, and valid until 06.27.2011;

13) IBANEZ Brenda Liliana, born in New York (USA) on 01.07.60, *Coachmen Enterprises Washington, DC P.O. Box 91228 Washington*

DC (USA). Telephone number in Washington DC. 2026823098; US citizen with US passport n. 017018953; Visa Card credit card n. 4118165007635784 (expiry date aprile/2003) and Delta Airlines *Frequent flyer* card n. 2349251336;

14) LADY Robert Seldon, born in Tegucigalpa (Honduras) on 21.05.54, US citizen, domiciled or residente in via Don Bosco n. 40, in Penango (AT), Italy;

15) LOGAN Cyntia Dame, born in Maryland (USA) on 05/01/1960; *Coachmen Enterprises Washington, DC P.O. Box 91228 Washington DC (USA).* US citizen with US passport n. 016430730 (copy acqured), issued on 01.03.2000 by the *Passport Agency* in Washington, Visa Card credit card n. 4118165007635768 (expiry date April/2003), SPG card (Special Preferred Guest Westin Hotel), type "A", n. 50556297010, United Airlines *Frequent flyer* card n. 01394828870;

16) PURVIS L. George, born in China on 05.29.59, 21008 Matchlock Ct 20147 Ashburn—Virginia (USA), US citizen with US passport n. 015645726, issued on 05.20.97; Master Card credit card n. 5466160067501849 (expiry date March/2003); e-mail address "loiep53@aol.com"; United Airlines *Frequent flyer* card n. 01208942316; Hilton Honors card n. 441369809

17) RUEDA Pilar, born in California (USA) on 05.08.61, *P.O.Box 80027 Washington D.C. 20618 (USA);* US citizen with US passport n. 016518173, issued on 02.27.01; Visa Card credit card n. 4118165007854492 (expiry date September/2003); SPG card (Special Preferred Guest Westin Hotel), type "A", n. 50426336887,

18) SOFIN Joseph, born in Moldova on 02/13/1953, P.O. 4173 Arlington 22203 VA (USA), telephone number 7032185346, or Blake Lane Fairfay Virginia; US citizen with US passport n. 016138217 issued on 11.18.99; Diners Club credit card n. 38643304300000; SPG card (Special Preferred Guest Westin Hotel), type "A", n. 716587012;

19) VASILIOU Michalis born in Greece on 11.05.62, US citizen with US passport n. 015456173, issued on 10.11.1995.

Are Under Investigation For The Following Offences:

Felony ex Arts. 110, 112 n° 1, 605 criminal code, whereby among themselves and together with others (also Egyptian nationals), including ROMANO Joseph L. III—with the consequent aggravating circumstance of the offence being committed by over five persons -for having kidnapped, depriving him of personal freedom, Nasr Osama Mustafa Hassan alias Abu Omar, apprehending him by force and forcibly

making him enter a van, thereafter taking him first to the US military airbase at Aviano, where the United States of America Air Force 31st FW (Fighter Wing) is stationed, and thence to Egypt; parties to the crime being Jenkins Anne Lidia, Kirkland James Robert, Castaldo Eliana Isabella, Ibanez Brenda Liliana, Castellano Victor and **Gurley John Thomas in participating to the preparatory stages of the abduction (preliminary scouting and assessment of the location where it would take place, scrutiny of Abu Omar's habits, research into neighboring areas to that of the planned abduction, as well evaluation of the most suitable route for a safe and hasty access to the freeway bound for Aviano); parties to the crime being Asherleigh Gregory, Purvis George, Carrera Lorenzo, Harty Benamar, Harbaugh Raymond, Rueda Pilar, Sofin Joseph, Adler Monica Courtney, Logan Cynthia Dame, Duffin John Kevin, Channing Drew Carlyle,** and **Vasiliou Michalis in participating to the abovementioned preparatory stages, and to the actual execution of the kidnapping together with the victim's transfer to Aviano; party to the crime being Romano Joseph, US head officer in charge of security at Aviano base, for receiving the abductors and the victim at the said base, ensuring the formers benefited from a safe access to the base, and were able to put the victim on a plane taking him outside Italy; party to the crime being Lady Robert Seldon, for coordinating the action, as well as for guaranteeing connections and assistance to other parties to the crime, also as a consequence of his earlier presence and working activity in Milan.**

Abduction carried out in Milan, on 02\17\2003

THE FACTS OUTLINED BELOW ARE DRAWN ON CLASSIFIED RECORDS SUBMITTED BY THE PROSECUTION

1. Notification of Criminal Conduct

In the month of February 2003, the Egyptian citizen Nasr Osama Muostafa Hassan a.k.a. Abu Omar was reported missing in Milan, Italy. He had no longer been seen or heard since the morning of February 17th 2003.

Abu Omar is an Egyptian citizen who had been granted political asylum by the Italian authorities in 2001 and was under investigation in a separate inquiry for crimes connected with international terrorism (on this first point see the DIGOS note of 6.21.2005 and attachments, stating that Abu Omar had been granted political asylum with the legislative measure of 2.22.2001; on the second point see the informative note issued by DIGOS in Milan on 2.11.2002, submitted in the scope of proceedings n. 5236/02 R.G.N.R.).

It later emerged that Abu Omar had not departed of his own free will, but had been forcibly loaded into a van by strangers.

Indeed, subsequent to a public plea made by the Imam of the Mosque located in Milan's Viale Jenner, whom the missing person's wife had appealed for help, it emerged that an Egyptian woman had confided to a number of women from the same mosque that, on the very morning of 2.17.2003, she had witnessed the following event: a dark-bearded man of Arab origin, dressed in a tunic, had been stopped in Via Guerzoni by two men in Western clothing who, after checking his papers, forced him to get into a white van and drove off immediately at great speed.

The Egyptian woman was identified as Rezk Merfat. She was later interviewed for the first time on 2.26.2003, and confirmed in substance the version given to her friends, except the part relating to having witnessed the Arab man's forcible entry in the white van, while struggling and crying for help. The event had taken place in Via Guerzoni in Milan, between 11.30 and 12.00 pm on 2.17.03.

It has never been possible to interview the eyewitness regarding the partial conflict between the above reconstruction of events and the version acquired from subsequent phone tappings and from statements made by Abu Omar's wife.

In fact the witness moved back to Egypt straight after the abovementioned deposition before the Public Prosecutor.

This circumstance was recounted by her husband who, at first, confirmed his wife's account and added: "It is also true that she left Italy to return to Egypt the day after she was heard by the magistrate from the District Attorney's office in Milan. She did so out of fear, and also because my income as a laborer (in the construction business) does not allow me to support my whole family in Milan. She currently lives in Kaloubia (Egypt) and I go and see her from time to time. . . ."

Rezk Merfat's initial statement, though, were later questioned by the same person whom she had disclosed the information.

HASSANEIN Hayam Abdelmoneim Mohamed, declared on 3.15.2005:

> ". . . I recall fully well what my friend told me. In the late morning of February 17th 2003, Merfat was walking home, along via Guerzoni. As she was going, she had noticed a white van with no windows in the back, and two men of Western appearance standing nearby. As she carried on walking, she crossed a full-bearded Arab-looking man dressed in a white Jalabia, who was heading towards Viale Jenner. Moments later she heard a loud noise and the man cry out in Arabic, asking for help. She turned round quickly, shocked by the commotion, and saw the van drive off at full speed with no trace of the Arab-looking man; she therefore presumed he had been abducted. ADR. I do not recall other details on the matter; just that Merfat admitted to me she had already spoken with her husband of what she had witnessed. (. . .) I then went to Merfat's home to pick up my child, and told her of the Imam's

> announcement at the mosque about Abu Omar's disappearance. Concerned, Merfat asked me if I had disclosed her story to anyone, but I denied doing so, to spare her further worry. About a week later I received a call from Merfat who had been summoned by the police. She was weeping and asked me why I had betrayed her trust; indeed, she was terrified of her husband's reaction. At that point she confessed she hadn't told the police the whole story, because her husband forbade her to. I answered that I had done so, because I believed it could help save a man's life and—in an attempt to reassure her—I passed the phone to my husband who tried to explain to her that it was a religious duty to provide information that could reveal who had captured Abu Omar, and that she had nothing to fear. That same evening Merfat's husband came to our house in Vermezzo, and asked my husband and myself not to disclose to the police all the details his wife had told me; he added that Merfat had been unforthcoming with the police. (. . .) Merfat confessed to me that she had decided to return to Egypt lest anything should happen to her or her children after what she had witnessed."

Summoned again by the Public Prosecutor, SALEM SHAWKI BAKRY, Rezk Merfat's husband, was challenged with the statements made by HASSANEIN Hayam Abdelmoneim Mohamed, and gave the following account on 3.18.05, finally revealing the truth and admitting to both his and his wife's reticent behavior:

> "I must indeed make changes to my statement given only a few days ago, but I wish to stress that it was not my intention to hinder Italian justice, as I was solely concerned for the fear that gripped my wife as a result of what she had seen.
>
> Well, although I confirm to not having paid great attention to my wife's words on 2.17.03, I admit to having omitted parts of her account. She truly feared that a similar fate could befall me. It is especially true that she saw two Western-dressed men attack a bearded Arab, dressed in a white jalabia, who struggled and cried for help while being violently grabbed and forcibly made to enter a van. I confirm she was unaware of the Arab's identity, as I did ask her the question. Regarding the van color, I believe she said it was white or gray, anyhow it was light-colored. I don not recall if she told me the van windows in the back or not: it may well be she told her friend more details than what she told me.
>
> Anyhow, she had seen the man being loaded, despite his opposition, into the van that took off with two men on board. I do not know if the driver was a third man, as my wife did not specify this. (. . .)"

Gaps in the eyewitness account had already emerged subsequent to several phone tappings.

No significant progress was made in the investigation for over one year after the abduction. Indeed, investigators had almost disregarded the matter after a communication forwarded in March 2003 by "American authorities" to the Direzione Centrale della Polizia di Prevenzione in Rome, stating that

Abu Omar had relocated to an unknown Balkan location. Addressed by the above Direzione Centrale, the US authorities stressed the presumptive nature of the news, to which no further detail was provided. The statement made to the Italian authorities would later be proven to be utterly groundless.

In fact, within the framework of investigations relating to Islamic terrorist activities, a number of conversations were tapped in April 2004 between Abu Omar, his wife Ghali Nabila and Elbadry Mohamed Reda, wherein the former stated that he was in Egypt (he had been deprived of his papers and was forced to live there), and that he had been abducted, taken to a US base, and from there flown to Egypt, where he had been detained until then, and subjected to serious torture.

Conversation of 4.20.2004 at 18.28 between Abu Omar (int) and his wife (ut)
(. . .)
Ut: Osama, from the day they took you I have written to everyone, and thank God it's all over.
Int: it is not a problem. Listen, they warned me that reporters from all Europe will come looking for you. You must meet nobody, I must stress this, no journalists. That is what they said.
Ut: rest assured, I'll meet no-one.
Int: neither press nor TV!
Ut: sure, sure
Int: do not speak with any channel (TV, translator's note)
Ut: nobody, nobody
Int: tell the brothers I am back
(. . .)

Conversation of 5.8.2004 between Elbadry Mohammed Reda (U) and Abu Omar (I).
(. . .)
I = they tormented me with questions on may things . . . I was freed for health reasons, I have a kind of paralysis. To this day I cannot walk for more than 200 meters. I'm always sitting down. I was incontinent, suffered from liver trouble, with high blood pressure . . . so they let me out on health grounds (. . .).
U = God is great
(. . .)
U = (. . .) you disappeared on Monday 17th . . .
I = no, on 16th
U = you can't know more than us: it was 17th, a Monday
I – no, Monday 16th
U = the reports were made on the 17th, a Monday
I = I don't know if Monday was the 16th or 17th

U = it was February 17th . . .
I = they took me straight to a military base and there they put me on board a military plane . . . and then . . .
(. . .)
U = the people here . . . every time we went to report things, they didn't believe it, and they said they know nothing about you, and that they started an investigation, and that an eyewitness saw you . . .
I =I saw her . . . she lives in the next street
U = this woman . . . they put pressure on her husband and he changed his statement after ten days (. . .)

The existence of such conversations in the records of the wire tappings constitute an important corroboration to the statements made by the abducted man's wife and by Elbadry Mohamed Reda, as below

It must be stressed at this stage that wire tapping in this proceedings may only be used as a notitia criminis (therefore amounting to a formal complaint).

Furthermore, the contents of such tappings (lawfully permitted and protracted by the competent magistrate, through a formal filing of the relevant warrant and extension, for the purposes of the present proceedings) will be analytically reported below. In this instance it is merely necessary to emphasize that, though allowed in the context of separate actions, they may certainly be used in this instance, if anything as the starting point for further investigations.

On this subject, case law is utterly consistent in maintaining that "for the purposes of Art.270 Code of Criminal Procedure, on the legal use of data arising from wire-tapping in instances other than the one for which it was sanctioned, the use must be understood as evaluation of the said data as sources of evidence. To this effect, therefore, such tappings can lawfully provide information relating to additional offences, and may be used as a starting point for the ensuing inquiries and probative acquirements, unconstrained from the limits laid down in Art. 270 of the above code" (Cass., Sez. V, n. 23894 del 2.5.2003, Luciani; nello stesso senso vedi anche Supreme Court., Sez. VI, n. 31 del 26.11.2002, Chiarenza; Sez. VI, n. 3129 del 10.10.1992, Donzelli).

2. Witness Statements (De Relato) Re The Kidnapping—First Description of the Offence—Account of the Abductors' Escape on a White Van and Statements as to Their Subsequent Aircraft Boarding.

Abu Omar's wife, Ghali Nabila, was later heard again, and she declared the following:

> ". . . my husband disappeared from Milan last February 17th and I had no news for about one year. . . . Suddenly on April 20th this year, I received

a phone call from my husband to my Milan home . . . (. . .) . . . he told me he had been kidnapped in Milan, in a street I can't recall now—but I mentioned the name in my previous statement—and that some people had captured him with violence and taken him away in a white van . . . a woman, according to my husband, had witnessed the event.

My husband . . . told me he hadn't been kidnapped by Egyptians, although he didn't know who had . . . moreover, he neither told me how many people took part in the action, nor what nationality he thought they were.

After a few hours, maybe after one night, he was put on a plane and flown straight to Egypt, where he remained continuously detained until April 20th 2004 . . . he had always been kept blindfolded during the kidnapping and hadn't even been able to make out the abductors' language, as they had always remained silent . . . I have learnt some news also in conversations with my husband's sister . . . he was certainly flown to Egypt with a military aircraft, surely not a civilian plane.

(. . .) . . . he told me he had always been detained, and subject to awful torture . . . all kinds of torture . . . because the Egyptians wanted information from him that he was unable to give . . . he added that he was made to sign a statement after the torture where he declared he had turned himself in to the Egyptian authorities of his own free will . . .

According to my husband, at first the Egyptians were astounded at having him there with them; this fueled my husband's belief that he had not been kidnapped by Egyptians . . . once freed, the Egyptian authorities told him he could go back to his work in Egypt, open up a store or even take up studying again, but he had to stay away from spreading any kind of Islamic propaganda. Some of the details I am recounting have also been learnt by my sister-in-law . . . I cannot provide precise information as to the traumas he endured . . . I heard about the torture from his kin . . . at any rate, he said he had lost about 20 kilos as a result of the detention . . . I do not believe my husband was able to provide any of the information they were after . . . they merely ordered him to quit his propaganda activities . . .

(. . .) On April 19th 2004, an Egyptian official whose name I do not know called my husband's home in Alexandria and, speaking with his brother Hisham, told him he could fetch my husband from a certain police station in the city . . . on 20th my brother-in-law fetched him and took him home immediately . . . in fact, the first call I got from my husband was made on April 20th a few minutes after getting home . . .

(. . .)

Since he was freed and then disappeared again . . . around may 13/15th . . . my husband had always stayed in Alexandria . . . he told me the Egyptian authorities called him from time to time . . . after asking a few questions and never keeping him more than a couple of hours, they let him go home . . . I have no news of my husband since may 12th."

The same circumstances were described to operators by Elbadry Mohamed Reda, who provided further details, recorded in the statement on June 15th 2004:

> "(. . .) I obtained the first news on Abu Omar's actual fate from his wife . . . I learnt that on April 20th Abu Omar had called his wife from Egypt, telling her he had been detained and then freed after over a year . . . his wife spread the news throughout the community, and contacted me a short time later, saying that her husband wanted to talk to me and that I should call him . . . she gave me the number of the Abu Omar's family house in Alexandria, Egypt, where I called him. During that conversation . . . it took place 3/4 days after his release . . . we merely exchanged greetings . . . it was quite a call . . . Abu Omar said that he would tell me about important matters in a subsequent call . . . he feared his family's telephone was tapped . . . he said he would give me a mobile phone number where I could reach him . . . Some days went by . . . Abu Omar's wife gave me his Egyptian mobile number and I called him on May 7th 2004 . . . from a call center in Viale Jenner . . . during the conversation . . . Abu Omar told me what had happened . . . On February 17th 2003 he had left home around midday to go and pray in the V.le Jenner mosque . . . he had noticed a white van with two people close to his doorway . . . he didn't suspect anything . . . he made his way on foot to the mosque and as he got closer he noticed again the parked, white van; it had clearly driven round the block the other way as it could not have followed him due to the one way system . . .
>
> The same two people he had noticed before approached him, and one asked him his papers in Italian . . . he presented his passport, which testifies to his asylum holder status . . . the two men were sure of his identity . . . At that point one of them sprayed something on his nose and mouth . . . and they pushed him into the van . . . Abu Omar just about noticed that an Arab women with two children was witnessing the scene . . . Inside the vehicle the two men sealed his mouth with tape . . . Abu Omar did not lose consciousness and came to immediately.
>
> Speaking perfect Italian the two men told Abu Omar to keep quiet and remain still, otherwise he would be dead . . . the windows had tinted glass in the back so Abu Omar was unable to see where the vehicle was going and the itinerary followed. Thanks to his watch, he was able to ascertain that he had traveled by car with the two men for about 5 hours . . .
>
> He told me that he had kept the sticky tape on his mouth for the whole time, and the men had removed it only once their destination had been reached . . . The two abductors handed Abu Omar to other people inside a military base that he believed to be American, judging from the US military aircraft . . . with the US flag on them . . . He gave me no other clue as to what base it was . . . he didn't say whether the captors were Italian . . . just that they spoke Italian.
>
> The two men departed and left him with a group of English- and Italian-speaking people . . . who availed themselves of an Arab interpreter.

The Italian and English speakers . . . whom Abu Omar believed to be Americans . . . asked him questions repeatedly, accompanied with outbursts of violence, on three specific issues . . . on his dealings with Al Quaeda . . . on his activities related with the war in Iraq, asking him if he was sending volunteers to fight the US in those areas . . . and on his relationship with Albanian Islamic groups . . . He told me he had been beaten . . . tortured . . . questioned . . . At dawn he was loaded onto a US military aircraft and traveled for just under one hour . . . he told me that, due to the short trip and to the size of the city, which he had seen from the window . . . he thought he had been taken to a Rome airport . . . The aircraft had stationed in a restricted area inside this huge airport, probably military . . . Abu Omar was taken off the plane . . . got on to another US military plane . . . and took off again immediately . . . They were US aircraft . . . the second plane landed at a US base in the Red Sea in Egypt . . . Abu Omar saw other planes with US flags . . . From this base . . . he was flown to a Cairo airport, this time Egyptian and military . . . he was blindfolded and taken by car, with Egyptians on board, to a secret service building in Cairo . . . an office inside a well-known government building in Cairo, I also happen to know its location, in a neighborhood known as LADOGHLJ . . . He had to meet an important personality . . . the Egyptian Home Secretary HABIB AL ADLY . . . In fact the minister . . . basically told him that if he agreed to work as an infiltrator for the Egyptian secret service, he would be home in 48 hours . . . otherwise he would have to bear full responsibility for his refusal . . . Abu Omar refused . . . he was forthwith taken to other Cairo premises, also managed by the secret service, where he stayed continually until his release on April 20th 2004 . . . He was subjected to serious torture . . . the first measure was to leave him in a room where incredibly loud and unbearable noise was made . . . he has experienced damage to his hearing . . . The second kind of torture was to place him in a sauna at tremendous temperature and straight after to put him in a cold storeroom . . . occasioning terrible pain to his bones . . . as if they were cracking . . . The third was to hang him upside down . . . and apply live wires to the sensitive parts of the body including his genitals . . . and producing electric shocks . . . he has suffered damage to his motory and urinary systems . . . he became incontinent . . . They tortured him accusing him of being an Al Quaeda terrorist and a militant against the Egyptian regime . . . they wanted to wrest information from him that he was unable to give . . . they told him to consider himself, along with myself, Abu Imad (i.e. the imam of V.le Jenner) and Abu Saleh as terrorists . . . and that sooner or later the same fate would befall the three of us . . . they would catch us as soon as possible . . . they said they had agreements with the Italian authorities . . . that could easily ensure our capture . . . If we didn't turn ourselves in voluntarily . . . they would kidnap us . . .

He told me the torture had been particularly ferocious for the first seven months in detention . . . it had then diminished . . . except whenever questions were asked about his role and his alleged involvement . . . in the final stage of detention . . . he underwent medical treatment . . . also after his release . . . He told me that he had been summoned one day by one of the

> superintendents of the secret service, who said that if he wanted to get out alive from that jail, he would have to declare he had left Italy for Egypt voluntarily, in order to clear his position . . . he would have to keep quiet on everything else . . . from the abduction to the torture . . . they told him they would find out about any violation of the rules since everything was "under surveillance" also with the backing of the Egyptian judiciary . . . if he rejected this proposal . . . he would not leave the prison alive . . . Before making a decision Abu Omar consulted other inmates . . . who told him nobody gets out alive from that jail . . . so they told him to accept . . . So he did . . . he was taken to an office in Alexandria . . . he brother was told to fetch him there . . . upon release Abu Omar was deprived of his papers . . . and he was ordered not to disclose anything to anyone neither in Italy, nor Egypt, and certainly not to the press . . . Abu Omar "breached" the agreement . . . and for fear of being arrested again, he asked me not to divulge the information I had given him . . . I had no other direct communication with Abu Omar aside from that first time and on May 7th . . . for all other matters, I just got news from his wife . . ."

We later shall dwell upon the extent to which Elbadry Mohamed Reda and his account are trustworthy.

Thanks to Ghali Nabila, who had meanwhile gone to her husband's family in Egypt, it was ascertained that Omar had been detained in a Cairo prison since May 12th 2004, thence transferred to an Alexandria jail, and then back to Cairo around 2.20.2005, where the mistreatment seems to have resumed.

Ghali Nabila states to have last seen her husband on 02.21.2005 at the prison near Alexandria, and on such occasion he had told her that, due to the widespread and detailed news of his abduction in the press (first in the Italian daily "La Repubblica", with the contents of the article taken up and circulating widely in the Egyptian press), he was once more being subjected to physical harm, to the extent that he went on a hunger strike. Upon reaching Alexandria jail on 2.24.2005 to visit her husband, Ghali was informed of his transfer to Cairo. Nobody has heard of Abu Omar since then.

Though de relato, yet fully exploitable for the purposes of Art. 195 of the above code, the circumstances revealed by Ghali Nabila and Elbadry Mohamed Reda especially, in addition to the account given by the eyewitness Rezk Merfat, are of fundamental importance, allowing us to confirm without doubt that, sometime between 11.30 and noon on February 17th 2003 in Via Guerzoni, Milan, Abu Omar was approached by two Caucasian, Italian-speaking men, who apprehended him and forcibly dragged him into a white van (Abu Omar struggled and cried for help throughout).

3. The Absence of Either National or International Documentation Certifying Custodial Measures

The question arose as to whether the withholding of personal freedom, as described above, might in fact have flowed from a lawful warrant for the man's arrest.

The competent DIGOS Bureaus ascertained the utter inexistence, also at an international level, of any warrants providing for Abu Omar's tracking or arrest.

Investigations have been directed towards establishing Abu Omar's presence in Egypt, in order to ascertain, by means of a formal request of judicial assistance forwarded on 08.30.2004, if the man:

- Was present on Egyptian soil and, if so, was he free or detained;
- Had been detained in Egypt in the time ranging from 02.17.2003 and 08.30.2004;
- Had entered Egyptian territory in any way and at any time.

Also, a request was made to Egyptian authorities to interrogate (the questioning could even be carried out by Egyptian authorities and Italian officials) ABU OMAR (allegedly detained in Egypt, going by his wife's statement) as well as his close family, and to learn the names of the owners and holders of the landline number 002034963879, along with the mobile numbers. 0020127619802 and. 0020123347735, most likely used by NASR Osama Moustafa Hassan (alias ABU OMAR).

Despite the full and effective collaboration of the Italian Justice Ministry, the above request for judicial assistance has yielded no reply as of yet from the competent foreign authority.

Anyhow, it remains a proven fact that Abu Omar did not leave Via Guerzoni voluntarily as a result of lawfully issued constraint measures but, instead, he was deprived of his personal freedom and abducted by force: consequently, the material element for the offence of kidnapping is existent.

4. The Relevance of the Lack of any Documentation Certifying Custodial Measures, as of the Absence of any Communication to Italian Authorities

It must be stressed that the incident is made much more serious due to a range of factors that transcend the mere crime of kidnapping.

Firstly, the fact that the subject enjoyed refugee status in Italy, and that such status had been granted by the same Italian authorities, has entailed that a refugee's willful abduction from the protection and shelter afforded by the host State—in absence of any provisions issued by the latter and clearly against the will of the former—amounts to a most serious assault against the authority of the Italian State and of international treaties on such matters.

Secondly, we are confronted with the fact that the operation was conducted by foreign citizens—as we shall examine later—for the purpose of securing a detention abroad in such a manner that no Italian authority was made privy to the fact, and in the absence of any document certifying custodial measures, or in any way sanctioning a limitation of personal freedom.

Thirdly, the fact that the person involved was under investigation by Italian authorities, and his consequent disappearance constituted an objective hindrance to the Judicial Authority's ability to effectively ascertain the facts.

5. Corroboration of the Account of the Abduction, and the Specific Technical Investigation That Lead to the Identification of those Involved in the Abduction

As mentioned before, based on the accounts given by Abu Omar to his wife and to Elbadry Mohamed Reda, and reported by the two, Abu Omar was later transferred—after a journey of ***several hours, perhaps one night*** according to the wife, and of ***about five hours*** according to Reda—to a military airbase—allegedly American—whence he was placed onto an aircraft.

Following the inquiries made by DIGOS, it ensues that the only base fitting the description is the USAF airbase at Aviano.

In an effort to further their investigation, operators sought to establish whether there had been transfers from the abduction scene to Aviano airbase, starting from the fact, as recounted by the eyewitness, that one of the persons who approached Abu Omar had been talking on the phone.

It was possible to establish this point by examining the communication exchange between mobile phones that took place within the radio cells covering the abduction scene and its immediate vicinity, thereafter ascertaining whether any of them had subsequently headed for Aviano airbase.

This activity—later analytically reported below—enabled the identification of a set of SIM cards that were operating on the crime scene, and mutually interactive, amounting to a total of 62 calls of very short length, and reaching their highpoint at the moment of Abu Omar's disappearance.

As a result of this verification, it has been possible to distinguish two sets of telephone subscribers: the first was present on the scene of the abduction; it headed towards Cormano, and there met up with the members of the second one. Straight after the abduction, nine people belonging to the second group (four of whom have been identified: Carrera Lorenzo, Logan Cynthia Dame, Channing Drew Carlyle e Vasiliou Michailis) left the area and picked up the radio cells situated along the stretch of motorway Milan—Aviano. During the journey some subscribers made calls to mobiles used by officers stationed at the said airbase. After about five hours all the subscribers picked up the radio cells surrounding the USAF airbase in Aviano.

As stated above, one of the nine subscribers (334/176579), whose identity was impossible to establish but will be henceforth referred to as ALFA, after having picked up the cell located in Via Gramsci in Cormano at 12.35 pm, took the eastbound A4 motorway. Along the way, he made contact for three times (between 14.44 and 16.42 on 02.17.2003) with a mobile phone, which turned out to be registered with the 31 Contracting Squadron (USAF Base—Aviano), and its user was proven to be Colonel Joseph L. III Romano, then head of security at Aviano airbase.

Another of these nine subscribers (334/3101143), whose identity was impossible to establish but will be henceforth referred to as BETA, picked up on the day of the abduction all the cells in the area around Via Guerzoni and the Cormano motorway entrance, in a time spanning 11.15am and 12.41, at which time he picked up the cell in Via Gramsci, Cormano, accessing the A4 motorway, and was "followed" all the way to Aviano.

Notably, the user of the 334/3101143 subscription (BETA), was located around Cormano about two hours before the abduction and there met a member of the said second group; he then approached the Viale Jenner area (where the kidnapping occurred), made contact with the "first group", then headed back to Cormano together with the "first group", and joined the "second group"; from there he headed toward Aviano with the "second group" users.

The utterly amazing aspect stemming from the technical data gathered, is that the factual description made by the victim and passed on to Elbadry Mohamed Reda faithfully matches BETA's movements. This individual indeed approached the area where the victim was living and picked up the TIM mobile phone signal repeater in Via Litta Modignani at 11:21:16. As he moved closer, he picked up the repeater in Via Butti 9 at 11:39:51.

The latter TIM signal repeater caters for the area facing both the victim's house and the mosque.

In order to pick up the above signal without picking up the TIM repeater in Via Imbriani 40 first, BETA's vehicle must necessarily have followed the road adjacent to the victim's house.

By so doing, the one-way system obliged him to take Via Cesare Brivio (otherwise he would have picked up the repeater in Via Imbriani 40, being sent off track by the one-way system).

The actual transit along Via Cesare Brivio constitutes the first surprising corroboration of the account given by Elbadry Mohamed Reda: this street is an unavoidable section of the route taken by the victim on his way to the mosque, and also by BETA's vehicle as it approached the signal repeater.

Time is another surprisingly matching element in the story recounted by Elbadry Mohamed Reda and BETA's route. BETA stayed hooked to the repeater in Via Butti 9 from 11.39.51 to 11.46.32. The place of the abduction is about 500 meters away from the junction between Via Conte Verde and Via Guerzoni. It takes about 6 minutes to walk, whereas it only takes about one and a half minutes to drive.

Also, according to the story recounted by Elbadry Mohamed Reda, the abductors' van crossed the victim outside his home, and later on the crime scene, where the vehicle had arrived by taking a different route from the victim on foot. This is corroborated by the examining a map of the area. After the sighting, whereas the victim could have headed straight for Via Guerzoni, the van would have had to drive round the block since Via Guerzoni is a one-way street from Viale Jenner to Via Davanzati. Even this detail matches BETA's movements in full, as "witnessed" by the mobile phone.

The time of all these movements is perfectly compatible with the time of the abduction. This occurred between 11.30 and 12.00 on 02.17.2003. BETA was present in those location at the exact same time.

Furthermore, the story recounted by Elbadry Mohamed Reda—with reference to the circumstances surrounding the movements—was corroborated by the eyewitness statement.

She maintains, in fact, that the incident took place near the Purple Cross (in Via Guerzoni 34).

Such detail is not only compatible with BETA's established position, but it also matches the forced route taken by the van so as to catch up with the victim.

Indeed, when going round the block to get back to Via Guerzoni from Via Conte Verde, the abductors' van would have necessarily had to drive down Via Carlo Cafiero, actually leading up to the Purple Cross, which the van would have to drive past as Via Guerzoni is a one-way street.

It must be inferred that the "suspicious" movements recorded match Elbadry Mohamed Reda's story too greatly to be coincidental.

After all, Elbadry was not and could not be aware of the results yielded by screening the cell communication exchange.

According to further verifications made possible by the albeit partial testimony of the woman who witnessed the crime, it ensues that Elbadry

Mohamed Reda statement is completely truthful, even though it pertains to reported events.

As mentioned before, others telephone subscription users—established as being on the scenes—traveled contextually with BETA.

The subsequent moves take BETA back to Cormano, where along with the other telephone subscription users he heads towards Aviano.

During the journey towards the US military base in Aviano, those users of "suspect" telephones whose identity has been established contacted a number of individuals inside actual airbase.

The evident examination of registration holders, movements, and telephone communication exchange of all the above subscribers has yielded surprising results.

It become apparent that a great deal of subscribed numbers were registered to names that did not match those of the actual users; many numbers in fact were never matched to a user name. The remaining ones have been established as being used by US citizens.

Practically all the "suspicious" subscribed numbers share a further range of common features. In particular:

- As said before, the users of the relevant subscribed numbers, located within the same cell therefore at a short distance from one another, exchanged numerous calls on 02.17.2003; almost all of them were very brief, and adding up to a total of 62.
- The frequency of the calls intensified around the time coinciding with Abu Omar's disappearance.
- All the SIM cards operated by TIM had been activated/sold between November 2002 and January 2003.
- Virtually all the subscribed numbers stopped functioning in Italy immediately after the abduction, mostly between February 18th and 20th 2003.
- The vast majority of these SIM cards were registered to subscribers, in whose name at least other ten subscribed numbers had been registered; most of them had been assigned to "fronts" (the names were often identical: 6 numbers were in the name of a Timofte Mihai, a Rumanian citizen unconnected with the incident, and 3 to a company known as "Riva Beniamino snc"); at any rate, for virtually all the subscribed numbers it had not been possible to identify the actual user from the outset . . .
- As explained below, the sole exception to the above rule is the Vodafone number registered in the name of a US citizen, Adler

Monica Courtney, whose identity has actually been confirmed as authentic.

- One of the two mobile numbers present in via Guerzoni at the time of the kidnapping **(3397946739),** after having arrived in Aviano went straight back to Milan;
- BETA **(3343101143),** instead, arrived in Aviano and returned to Milan in the early hours of the following morning;
- As a result of the close scrutiny to which the communication exchange among the examined subscribed numbers (over 40 in total) were subject, some of which registered to US citizens, it has emerged that, even days before the incident, virtually all the users of the numbers had been present on the route that **Abu Omar** habitually followed from his house to the Viale Jenner mosque; this technical point provides added confirmation to their direct involvement in planning the crime, since to all intents and purposes the preparatory activities entailed on the spot investigation and careful observation of the victim's movements.

The tables below demonstrates how frequently the users of suspect numbers were present in the days prior to the abduction (the numbers that were then traced as subsequently traveling to Aviano are highlighted).

Subscribed Numbers Active in the Cells in Via Butti

Number	*Number of connections*	*First connection Date—Time*	*Last connection Date—Time*
3388952825 TIMOFTE MIHAI n. 4 of Table 2	*95*	*23/01/2003 12.00.02*	*16/02/2003 12.51.56*
3354369 70 DE L UCCI DA VIDE, n. 7 of Table 2	*86*	*16/01/2003 11.59.48*	*16/02/2003 12.57.36*
3387079723 TIMOFTE MIHAI, n. 3 of Table 2	*78*	*23/01/2003 12.36.37*	*16/02/2003 12.48.06*
3389383879 AGOSTINICARLA, n. 9 of Table 2	*59*	*26/01/2003 10.59.33*	*16/02/2003 12.50.09*
3338577471KOLAZE & GHELONSRL, n. 6 of Table 2	*48*	*11/01/2003 11.38.41*	*16/02/2003 12.51.56*
3386567958JA UREGUICRIBILLERO, n.8ofTable2	*47*	*31/01/2003 11.10.02*	*16/02/2003 12.58.26*
3336364075 RIVA BENIAMINO, n. 1 of Table 2	*27*	*31/01/2003 11.12.11*	*16/02/2003 12.48.53*

Number	*Number of connections*	*First connection Date—Time*	*Last connection Date—Time*
3343170 79 7 TIMOFTE MIHAI, n. 54 of Table 2	*24*	*29/01/2003 11.21.25*	*09/02/2003 12.30.54*
3409849532 ADLER MONICA C., n. 17 of Table 2	*23*	*14/01/2003 12.25.27*	*16/02/2003 12.38.33*
3343101143, registered to unknown, n. 11 of Table 2	*22*	*31/01/2003 11.45.51*	*16/02/2003 12.26.39*
3397946739 TIMOFTE MIHAI, n. 15 of Table 2	*20*	*18/01/2003 10.01.50*	*12/02/2003 12.17.43*
3387849290, registered to unknown, n. 49 of Table 2	*18*	*12/12/2002 12.52.11*	*16/12/2002 12.54.16*
3387570943 DUFFIN JOHN KEVIN, n. 25 of Table 2	*18*	*18/01/2003 12.45.38*	*07/02/2003 12.31.50*
3333504739 CASTALDO E., n. 26 of Table 2	*18*	*18/01/2003 11.18.14*	*31/01/2003 11.49.12*
3333026990 JENKINS ANNE LIDIA, n. 28 of Table 2	*17*	*22/01/2003 12.41.40*	*08/02/2003 12.48.47*
3386410348 SOFIN JOSEPH, n. 29 of Table 2	*15*	*11/12/2002 12.14.12*	*16/12/2002 12.54.16*
3498928671HARBA UGH R., n. 39 of Table 2	*12*	*14/12/2002 11.26.54*	*17/12/2002 12.42.10*
3386432346 RUSSO Domenico, n. 44 of Table 2	*11*	*13/12/2002 12.21.33*	*16/12/2002 11.44.07*
3406958386 KIRKLAND JAMES R., n. 32 of Table 2	*11*	*16/01/2003 10.48.20*	*09/02/2003 10.59.34*
3387905706 LOGAN CYNTIA D., n. 27 of Table 2	*10*	*24/01/2003 12.24.43*	*16/02/2003 12.57.36*
3201166281 DUMMY CUSTOMER, n. 36 of Table 2	*7*	*09/01/2003 12.51.56*	*19/01/2003 12.43.05*
3397672462 KOLAZE & GHELON, n. 52 of Table 2	*7*	*24/01/2003 12.10.39*	*11/02/2003 12.33.18*
3387570941 CASTELLANO VICTOR, n. 24 of Table 2	*7*	*25/01/2003 11.07.09*	*07/02/2003 12.31.50*
3337642102 TIMOFTE MIHAI, n.2 of Table 2	*6*	*15/02/2003 11.29.49*	*16/02/2003 12.48.06*
3201166255 DUMMY CUSTOMER, n. 37 of Table 2	*5*	*09/01/2003 12.51.56*	*18/01/2003 12.19.27*
3398675142 LODI DONATELLA, n. 10 of Table 2	*4*	*15/02/2003 11.46.03*	*16/02/2003 11.44.44*

Number	*Number of connections*	*First connection Date—Time*	*Last connection Date—Time*
3338579242 TIMOFTE MIHAI, n. 5 of Table 2	*3*	*08/02/2003 11.47.29*	*08/02/2003 12.16.53*
3383 79089 7 IBANEZ BRENDA L., n. 40 of Table 2	*2*	*13/12/2002 12.24.30*	*15/12/2002 10.24.37*
3397942963 TIMOFTE MIHAI, n. 53 of Table 2	*1*	*15/02/2003 11.43.11*	*15/02/2003 11.43.11*

Subscribed Numbers Active in the Cells North of V. Guerzoni

Numbers	*Number of Connections*	*First Connection Date—Time*	*Last Connection Date—Time*
3343101143 registered to unknown, n. 11 of Table 2	*25*	*31/01/2003 12.45.17*	*16/02/2003 12.54.44*
3343211730 RIVA BENIAMINO, n. 14 of Table 2	*18*	*05/02/2003 10.08.00*	*16/02/2003 12.52.26*
3397946739 TIMOFTEMIHAI, n. 15 of Table 2	*10*	*22/01/2003 12.31.30*	*16/02/2003 12.54.29*
3343176579 DISCOVERY SRL, n. 13 of Table 2	*7*	*26/01/2003 10.58.35*	*08/02/2003 12.57.57*
3337934123 registered to unknown, n. 35 of Tabella 2	*7*	*29/01/2003 10.18.53*	*16/02/2003 12.56.46*
3470502758 CHANNING DREW, n. 30 of Table 2	*1*	*16/02/2003 12.38.33*	*16/02/2003 12.38.33*
3389383879 AGOSTINI CARLA, n. 9 of Table 2	*1*	*27/01/2003 11.46.27*	*27/01/2003 11.46.27*
338 7905 706 LOGAN CYNTIA D., n. 27 of Table 2	*1*	*15/02/2003 11.17.53*	*15/02/2003 11.17.53*
3387570941 CASTELLANO V., n. 24 of Table 2	*1*	*05/02/2003 12.15.36*	*05/02/2003 12.15.36*
3338577471 KOLAZE & GHELON, n. 6 of Table 2	*1*	*17/01/2003 12.59.34*	*17/01/2003 12.59.34*
3337693263 registered to unknown, n. 34 of Table 2	*1*	*27/01/2003 10.36.31*	*27/01/2003 10.36.31*

It is patently clear from this table that a number of people had been present in that street almost one hundred times during the month prior to the incident.

Bearing in mind that they had never appeared to have visited that place neither before nor after, one can safely state that the whole body of circumstances—unitarily considered—does lead to the conclusion that the numbers examined belong to individuals who first plotted, then executed the abduction.

As stated above, one of the four subscribed numbers that reached Aviano (3343176579) made three calls to a mobile **3356121879** registered with the "31st Contracting Squadron (Base USAF-Aviano)"—as for its user some has been said and more will follow—between 14.44 and 16.32 on February 17th 2003; one can easily infer that, each time, the purpose of this was to inform that the vehicles were approaching Aviano base: indeed, **at the time of the said events the number was proven to be assigned to, owned and used by Lt. Col. Joseph L. III Romano, Commander of the 31st SFS (Security Forces Squadron) USAF, i.e. American head of security at Aviano Airport, responsible for the access areas to the airbase itself.** Lt. Col. Romano was transferred after the events to "Pentagon 3 1P" in Washington DC (USA), where he is currently employed.

The nature of the contacts made during the journey by the group explain the reason why at Aviano airbase there is no trace of their passage.

With the informative report dated 02.23.2005, the Commander of the Compagnia CC. Aeronautica in Vicenza had elaborated on the following point: *"it is decided that admission to the base through gates reserved to USAF staff will require no registration, but the mere display of the pass. Indeed, intelligence personnel (e.g. O.S.I. or C.I.A.) will be merely required to present customary ID badges, while army security staff is not entitled to carry out any inspection, even though other people may be on board the vehicle".*

Furthermore, at Aviano airbase, it has been possible to establish the departure of an aircraft at a time that is compatible with Abu Omar's (recounted) story; the final destination of the aircraft was Egypt (where the victim claims to have been detained) and an intermediate stop was made compatibly with the victim's (recounted) story. In actual fact the stopover did not take place in Rome but in a US airbase, although the flight time coincides clearly with the victim's account to Elbadry Mohamed Reda.

As if to substantiate the whole story further, one of the individuals in closer contact with the abovementioned "groups" traveled to Egypt straight after the abduction. The individual is the user of a subscribed number, which one of the group members called minutes after the abduction, and subsequently at regular intervals; the individual has been named as Lady Robert Seldon, a then attaché to the US Consulate and CIA superintendent.

Yet another surprising element bringing together the individuals who own the subscribed numbers is their credit card numbers.

Most of them have credit card numbers starting with the same figures.

By examining the people in the group sharing this feature, it can be pointed out that two people share the first 14 numbers (out of 16); highlighted below are the identical numbers and the names of those who traveled to Aviano).

LOGAN Cyntia Dame	Visa	n.4118165007635768
IBANEZ Brenda Liliana "	Visa	n.4118165007635784

Another man shares the first 11 figures (out of 16) with the two abovementioned individuals.

DUFFIN John Kevin	Visa	n.4118165007626908

As a curious note, Duffin and Logan also share the first five figures of their passport numbers.

Examining now less astounding correlations, though statistically noteworthy all the same, it can be noted that other two people share the first 9 figures with the abovementioned.

CASTALDO Eliana	Visa	n. 4118165006438370
RUEDA Pilar	Visa	n.4118165007854492

There are then two groups of two people each sharing the first 8 figures

ADLER Monica Courtney	Diners Club	n. 38541798540000
KIRKLAND James Robert	Diners Club	n. 38541799470009

ASHERLEIGH Gregory	Visa	n.4118160311575248
CARRERA Lorenzo Gabriel	Visa	n.4118160306976955

On the basis of such "coincidences" and following a meticulous process of authentication, it was possible to establish that the two "groups" had not met for the first time on the crime scene, nor in Cormano.

They had all stayed in Italy before; they had all stayed at the same hotels in Milan, La Spezia, and Florence, at times together and other times at closely successive intervals.

Different members of such "groups" often gave the same address at hotel receptions, claiming it was their own.

The above circumstances will be clearly dealt with later, however, one can safely claim that on 02.17.2003, two groups of US citizens operating in steady, coordinated and constant contact, were accessory to the kidnapping of Abu Omar.

Investigations made have allowed the identities of such groups to be known.

The first group is present in the abduction area (in fact the following cells were picked up: Via Imbriani, Via Butti, Via Bernina, Via B. Crespi, Via Imbonati, Via Pellegrino Rossi and Via Pedroni), and is constituted by the individuals below, along with the user of the BETA subscribed number (334/3101143) who, though unknown, is a key proof of the two groups' connection:

RUEDA PILAR

HARTY BENAMAR

HARBAUGH RAYMOND

ASHERLEIGH GREGORY

PURVIS GEORGE

SOFIN JOSEPH

ADLER MONICA COURTNEY

LOGAN CYNTHIA DAME, who will quickly move towards the second group.

The second group is located in an area north of the abduction scene, i.e. the border between Milan and Cormano (in fact the following cells were picked up Via Modignani, Via G. Sand, Via Martinazzoli, Via Senigallia e Via Gramsci), and is constituted by the individuals below, along with the users of the BETA (334/3101143) and ALFA (334/3176579) subscribed numbers, as well as others, whose users remain unidentified:

CARRERA LORENZO

LOGAN CYNTHIA DAME

CHANNING DREW CARLYLE

VASILIOU MICHAILIS.

It is important to stress that all the second group numbers moved along the Milan—Aviano route straight after the kidnapping.

The "Aviano group" was surely joined later by DUFFIN JOHN KEVIN in the Verona area, as outlined below.

Examinations made with the motorway company proved that two vans and a car traveled at the following times: accessed motorway at Milano Est at 12.46—12.47 and 12.54 respectively; exitedat Venezia Mestre at 15.18.02—15.18.22—15.26.27; accessed at Venezia Est and exited at Portogruaro at 16.00 and at 16.07. One of the vans was found to have returned to Milan on the very same day, while the other drove to Padua.

Screenings of the telephone communications showed that the user of the BETA subscribed number was most likely on board one of the vans, as the number hooked up with cells steadily covering the movements made, as confirmed by the entry and exit times

Finally, a number of significant elements have been acquired, allowing the identification of the plane that departed from the USAF airbase in Aviano and carried Abu Omar to Egypt.

****

The position of said Robert Lady Seldon remains to be examined

In order to assess the value of the probative elements that were found against Lady Robert Seldon, user of the Vodafone **3480614737** subscribed number, it is necessary to examine closely the communication exchange effected by the said SIM card.

The screening will be made in relation to the communication exchange dating from the first three months of 2003, as it is the relevant period for the purposes of this investigation, showing that the said number has made calls since its activation in October 2000 until last October, proving it was operational throughout.

This first table shows the contacts made by the telephone user from January 12th 2003 until February 19th 2003, two days after the crime was committed.

In this timeframe the user had always stayed in Milan and established contacts (see chart 27 attached to the DIGOS informative report dated 02.24.05) with the following SIM cards: **3388952825—3338579242—3386567958** (detailed at point 4, 5, 8 of table nr.1). Such mobile numbers had all been present on the scene of the crime during the abduction, as stated in detail above.

The following table clearly shows that contact with one of the numbers below **3386567958 (sub n. 8 table)** was also made on February 17th 2003, straight after the abduction (highlighted in yellow).

Call made	Call received	Date, Time	Duration	Cell
3480614737	3386567958	12/01/2003 13.47	0.00.37	MILANO—Via de Alessandri, 11, Sector 1
3386567958	**3480614737**	15/01/2003 11.39	0.00.51	MILANO—Via Crispi, 5—Milano, Sector 9
3386567958	**3480614737**	15/01/2003 13.28	0.00.11	MILANO—C.so di P. taNuova, 7/V. Cernaia, 10, Sector 2

Call made	Call received	Date, Time	Duration	Cell
3386567958	**3480614737**	17/01/2003 10.05	0.00.15	MILANO—C.so Garibaldi 68 (Hotel Ritter), Sector 2
3386567958	**3480614737**	17/01/2003 13.10	0.00.11	MILANO—Via Napo Torriani, 31, Sector 1
3386567958	**3480614737**	17/01/2003 17.46	0.01.00	MILANO—C.so di P.ta Nuova, 7/V. Cernaia, 10, Sector 2
3480614737	3386567958	21/01/2003 9.49	0.00.18	MILANO—C.so di P.ta Nuova, 7/V. Cernaia, 10, Sector. 2
3386567958	**3480614737**	21/01/2003 17.17	0.01.09	MILANO—C.so di P.ta Nuova, 7/V. Cernaia, 10, Sector 2
3386567958	**3480614737**	22/01/2003 13.32	0.00.27	MILANO—Via Crispi, 5—Milano, Sector. 2
3480614737	3386567958	22/01/2003 13.56	0.00.18	MILANO—C.so di P.ta Nuova, 7/V. Cernaia, 10, Sector 2
3386567958	**3480614737**	22/01/2003 14.00	0.01.01	MILANO—C.so di P.ta Nuova, 7/V. Cernaia, 10, Sector 2
3480614737	3386567958	23/01/2003 8.47	0.00.32	TREZZO SULU ADDA—Via del Cimitero, c/o Cimitero Comunale, Sector 1
3386567958	**3480614737**	23/01/2003 14.42	0.00.33	PN—SAN QUIRINO—Via Roiata, 43, Sector 3
3480614737	3386567958	24/01/2003 9.56	0.00.23	MILANO—Via Crispi, 5—Milano, Sector 2
3386567958	**3480614737**	24/01/2003 12.50	0.01.16	MILANO—C.so di P.ta Nuova, 7/V. Cernaia, 10, Sector 2
3386567958	**3480614737**	24/01/2003 13.15	0.00.23	MILANO—Via Galileo Galilei, 2 Milano, Sector 8
3480614737	3386567958	24/01/2003 14.50	0.00.28	MILANO—C.so di P.ta Nuova, 7/V. Cernaia, 10, Sector 2
3480614737	3386567958	24/01/2003 14.51	0.00.50	MILANO—C.so di P.ta Nuova, 7/V. Cernaia, 10, Sector 2

Call made	Call received	Date, Time	Duration	Cell
3386567958	**3480614737**	25/01/2003 12.25	0.00.38	MILANO—Building owned by RAS Via Canonica, 54—Milan, Sector 7
3386567958	**3480614737**	25/01/2003 17.28	0.01.01	MILANO—Via de Alessandri, 11, Sector 1
3480614737	3386567958	25/01/2003 19.01	0.00.22	MILANO—Via Napo Torriani, 31, Sector 3
3480614737	3386567958	25/01/2003 19.09	0.01.04	MILANO—Via Galileo Galilei, 2 Milano, Sector 2
3480614737	3386567958	26/01/2003 9.56	0.00.27	MILANO—C.so Garibaldi 68 (Hotel Ritter), Sector 2
3480614737	3386567958	27/01/2003 8.17	0.00.13	MILANO—Via Manzoni, 31, Sector 3
3480614737	3386567958	27/01/2003 11.31	0.00.16	MILANO—C.so di P.ta Nuova, 7/V. Cernaia, 10, Sector 2
3480614737	3386567958	27/01/2003 12.03	0.00.12	MILANO—Via Galileo Galilei, 2 Milano, Sector 8
3480614737	3386567958	28/01/2003 8.57	0.00.25	MILANO—Via Crispi, 5—Milano, Sector. 2
3386567958	**3480614737**	31/01/2003 14.44	0.01.20	MILANO—C.so di P.ta Nuova, 7/V. Cernaia, 10, Sector 2
3480614737	3386567958	31/01/2003 16.14	0.01.53	MILANO—Viale Jenner, n 4, Sector 3
3338579242	**3480614737**	04/02/2003 10.09	0.00.46	MILANO—C.so di P.ta Nuova, 7/V. Cernaia, 10, Sector 2
3338579242	**3480614737**	04/02/2003 10.22	0.00.10	MILANO—C.so di P.ta Nuova, 7/V. Cernaia, 10, Sector. 2
3338579242	**3480614737**	04/02/2003 13.44	0.00.08	MILANO—C.so di P.ta Nuova, 7/V. Cernaia, 10, Sector 8
3386567958	**3480614737**	07/02/2003 13.45	0.00.24	MILANO—C.so di P.ta Nuova, 7/V. Cernaia, 10, Sector 7
3480614737	3386567958	08/02/2003 20.37	0.00.20	MILANO—Via Ripamonti, 66, Sector 7
3386567958	**3480614737**	10/02/2003 9.26	0.00.15	MILANO—Via Crispi, 5—Milano, Sector 2

Call made	Call received	Date, Time	Duration	Cell
3480614737	3386567958	11/02/2003 15.40	0.01.05	MILANO—ATM car-park. Subway station Famagosta 75, Sector. 7
3386567958	**3480614737**	11/02/2003 17.06	0.00.21	MILANO—Via de Alessandri, 11, Sector 1
3480614737	3386567958	12/02/2003 8.50	0.00.31	MILANO—C.so di P.ta Nuova, 7/V. Cernaia, 10, Sector 2
3386567958	**3480614737**	12/02/2003 13.52	0.00.12	MILANO—Via Crispi, 5—Milano, Sector 2
3480614737	3386567958	13/02/2003 8.12	0.01.18	MILANO—Via F.lli Bettinelli, 3—Centrale Telecom Italia, Sector 7
3386567958	**3480614737**	13/02/2003 11.23	0.00.35	MILANO—Parcheggio ATM Cascina Gobba, Sector 2
3480614737	3386567958	13/02/2003 14.43	0.00.19	MILANO—L.go Cordusio, 4, Sector 1
3386567958	**3480614737**	14/02/2003 10.40	0.00.12	MILANO—C.so di P.ta Nuova, 7/V. Cernaia, 10, Sector 2
3480614737	3386567958	14/02/2003 15.45	0.00.34	MILANO—C.so di P.ta Nuova, 7/V. Cernaia, 10, Sector 8
3386567958	**3480614737**	14/02/2003 16.13	0.00.06	MILANO—C.so di P.ta Nuova, 7/V. Cernaia, 10, Sector 2
3386567958	**3480614737**	14/02/2003 16.58	0.00.21	MILANO—C.so di P.ta Nuova, 7/V. Cernaia, 10, Sector 2
3386567958	**3480614737**	14/02/2003 17.37	0.00.24	MILANO—C.so di P.ta Nuova, 7/V. Cernaia, 10, Sector 8
3386567958	**3480614737**	14/02/2003 19.41	0.00.30	MILANO—C.so di P.ta Nuova, 7/V. Cernaia, 10, Sector 1
3386567958	**3480614737**	16/02/2003 14.01	0.00.10	MILANO—Via Pancaldo, 11, Sector 3
3386567958	**3480614737**	17/02/2003 12.56	0.00.29	MILANO—Via Crispi, 5—Milano, Sector 2
3386567958	**3480614737**	17/02/2003 14.20	0.00.21	MILANO—Via Crispi, 5—Milano, Sector 2

Call made	Call received	Date, Time	Duration	Cell
3386567958	**3480614737**	17/02/2003 14.28	0.00.06	MILANO—C.so di P.ta Nuova, 7/V. Cernaia, 10, Sector 8
3386567958	**3480614737**	17/02/2003 16.25	0.00.08	MILANO—Viale Majno 10, Sector 1
3386567958	**3480614737**	18/02/2003 10.43	0.01.03	MILANO—C.so di P.ta Nuova, 7/V. Cernaia, 10, Sector 8
3386567958	**3480614737**	18/02/2003 11.50	0.00.08	MILANO—C.so di P.ta Nuova, 7/V. Cernaia, 10, Sector 2
3386567958	**3480614737**	18/02/2003 15.29	0.00.08	MILANO—C.so di P.ta Nuova, 7/V. Cernaia, 10, Sector 1
3388952825	**3480614737**	18/02/2003 20.23	0.01.20	MILANO—Via Duilio n 6, Sector 2
3388952825	**3480614737**	19/02/2003 11.53	0.00.28	MILANO—C.so di P.ta Nuova, 7/V. Cernaia, 10, Sector 1

Since 02/19/2003 to 02/22/2003 the number 3480614737 was in contact with other numbers currently unrelated to the issues dealt with in the present proceedings, and maintained its location in the city of Milan.

On February 23rd 2003 the user of the appliance moves to the province of Gorizia, and from that day no calls are made/received by the said number until 03/03/2003 when it receives two calls from an unidentified number, *while occupying a radio "cell" in Egypt.*

Days later, on 03/15/2003, the number picks up Italian cells again, confirming it has entered Italian territory.

One can comfortably assume that the user of the said Vodafone card stayed in Egypt from February 22nd to March 15th 2003, i.e. during the first days of Abu Omar's unlawful detention in Egypt, and when he was most likely being subject to the first spate of "treatment".

These circumstances have been confirmed by the witness account made by **Elbadry Mohamed Reda,** according to whom *Abu Omar* (who had informed him) had already been transferred to Egypt in those days.

Call Made	Call Received	Date, Time	Duration	Cell
3477619320	**3480614737**	19/02/2003 12:19:06	72	MILANO—C.so di P.ta Nuova, 7/V. Cernaia, 10, Sett. 2

Call Made	Call Received	Date, Time	Duration	Cell
3473204821	**3480614737**	19/02/2003 16:42:39	46	MILANO—C.so di P.ta Nuova, 7/V. Cernaia, 10, Sett. 1
3480614737	0276024801	19/02/2003 18:29:05	25	MILANO—Via Galileo Galilei, 2 Milano, Sett. 2
3480614737	3281508898	20/02/2003 09:26:37	9	MILANO—C.so di P.ta Nuova, 7/V. Cernaia, 10, Sett. 2
3478344302	**3480614737**	20/02/2003 10:55:19	59	MILANO—C.so di P.ta Nuova, 7/V. Cernaia, 10, Sett. 2
3480614737	0262265138	20/02/2003 11:23:54	1	MILANO—C.so di P.ta Nuova, 7/V. Cernaia, 10, Sett. 7
3480614737	3478344302	20/02/2003 12:48:26	0	MILANO—C.so di P.ta Nuova, 7/V. Cernaia, 10, Sett. 2
3478344302	**3480614737**	20/02/2003 12:48:43	39	MILANO—C.so di P.ta Nuova, 7/V. Cernaia, 10, Sett. 2
3477619320	**3480614737**	20/02/2003 14:15:24	141	MILANO—Via Crispi, 5—Milano, Sett. 2
3480614737	3477619320	20/02/2003 14:18:06	361	MILANO—C.so di P.ta Nuova, 7/V. Cernaia, 10, Sett. 2
3480614737	3406712600	20/02/2003 14:28:24	90	MILANO—Via Crispi, 5—Milano, Sett. 2
3473204821	**3480614737**	20/02/2003 15:06:17	83	MILANO—Via Crispi, 5—Milano, Sett. 2
3480614737	3406712600	20/02/2003 16:00:48	25	MILANO—C.so di P.ta Nuova, 7/V. Cernaia, 10, Sett. 2
3473204821	**3480614737**	20/02/2003 20:43:34	38	MILANO—Via Marco Aurelio 26—Centrale Telecom Italia Mil, Sett. 9
3477619320	**3480614737**	20/02/2003 22:16:29	28	MILANO—Via Marco Aurelio 26—Centrale Telecom Italia Mil, Sett. 3
3477619320	**3480614737**	21/02/2003 08:44:04	113	MILANO—C.so di P.ta Nuova, 7/V. Cernaia, 10, Sett. 8
3478344302	**3480614737**	21/02/2003 08:57:26	67	MILANO—C.so Garibaldi 68 (Hotel Ritter), Sett. 8

Call Made	Call Received	Date, Time	Duration	Cell
3478344302	**3480614737**	21/02/2003 09:05:02	11	MILANO—C.so di P.ta Nuova, 7/V. Cernaia, 10, Sett. 2
3480614737	043426764	21/02/2003 17:34:41	43	VI—MONTECCHIO MAGGIORE—Via Madonnetta, Sett. 1
3480614737	3331729183	22/02/2003 09:52:44	22	VI—GRUMOLO DELLE ABBADESSE—A4 - km 121,3, Sett. 7
3478344302	**3480614737**	22/02/2003 10:13:42	23	VE—VENEZIA—Via dei Salici 32, Sett. 7
3480614737	3331729183	22/02/2003 11:01:14	105	VE—PORTOGRUARO—Viale Trieste, 3, Sett. 9
3480614737	3331729183	22/02/2003 11:27:34	22	GO—MONFALCONE—Terreno in loc. Cima di Pietrarossa, Sett. 1
3480614737	3331729183	22/02/2003 11:31:17	15	GO—MONFALCONE—Via Terza Armata, 21, Sett. 3
3480614737	335204587	03/03/2003 09:35:51	10	
	3480614737	03/03/2003 11:34:23	30	**Egypt**
	3480614737	03/03/2003 11:35:13	165	**Egypt**
3480614737	3477619320	15/03/2003 10:29:58	42	CO—CARIMATE—Via Stazione, Sett. 3
3480614737	3477619320	15/03/2003 10:31:28	43	MI—MEDA—Via S. Maria c/o Torre acqua comunale, Sett. 3
3480614737	3483948952	15/03/2003 10:34:28	38	MI—SEREGNO—Via S.Stefano da Seregno, 39 c/o centrale Telecom, Sett. 3
3478344302	**3480614737**	15/03/2003 10:46:23	9	MI—MILANO—Viale Monza 139, Sett. 3
3478344302	**3480614737**	15/03/2003 11:56:18	63	MI—MILANO—Via de Alessandri, 11, Sett. 1

Lady Robert Seldon has long since retired from diplomatic service, and taken up residence it Italy. Indeed, he purchased a farmhouse in the hamlet of Penango (Asti), and lives together with his family in via Don Bosco nr. 40.

A substantial body of serious circumstantial evidence weighs upon him, mainly due to the fact that exchanges have been picked up between Lady and telephone subscriptions belonging to other suspects believed to have been involved in the abduction (especially those operated by Purvis George and Harbaugh Raymond); furthermore, on 02.17.2003, four contacts were made with the number operated by Harbaugh Raymond (n. 8), at 12:56, 14:20, 14:28 and 16:25.

Another noteworthy circumstance is that the said Lady was certainly present in Egypt on 3.3.2003 (two calls to the number in his use were recorded on this day), and he had most likely been there since 02.22.03.

An additional element is that one of the telephone subscriptions implicated most in the operations, transfers, and communication exchanges related to the kidnapping was officially assigned to a person (De Sousa Sabrina), a CIA agent appointed to the American Consulate in Milan: for his part, as pointed out before, Lady Robert Seldon, was an intelligence attaché to the American Consulate in Milan, operating as CIA superintendent.

Besides, access to Aviano without registering formally would have only been possible for CIA agents.

In addition to all this, one must point out the substantial similarity among passport and credit card numbers belonging to the "task force", as well as its members' significant financial means, since they lodged for long periods of time, and at a very considerable expense in some of the most exclusive hotels in Milan and other locations.

Such a great deal of correspondence, which cannot amount to mere coincidence is only feasible among persons belonging to an organization with practically unlimited resources.

****

Also with a view on providing further details on the investigative activities, **it is necessary at this stage to go back to examining analytically the developments and the findings of the investigation itself, based on the reconstruction contained in the Prosecutor's request.:**

"A) The incident, the first witness statements, the first investigations

On February 20th 2003 Antonio Nebuloni, a Milan-based attorney, contacted the D.I.G.O.S. office at the Police headquarters in Milan with the intent to obtain information on the alleged detention of ***Nasr Osama Moustafa Hassan,*** *an Egyptian citizen also known as* ***Abu Omar,*** *who had been missing from his Milan abode since February 17th of the same year; on that same day* ***Ghali Nabila,*** *wife of the missing man, went to the local police station "Cenisio" where she formally reported the disappearance of the said* ***Abu Omar,*** *and declared to have last seen her husband on February 17th at noon.*

It must be forthrightly said that ***Abu Omar*** *is notoriously a member of Al Jama 'a Al Islamiya, a radical Egyptian group, and for this reason believed by local authorities* *to be an opponent of ts of political refugee in Rome. He later moved to Milan and renewed his residence permit on political asylum grounds until June 7th 2003.* ***He was formally under investigation within the ambit of proceedings n. 5236/02.21 pending at this Office, for breach of Art.270 bis cp*** *(connection with an organization for the purposes of international terrorism): for this reason the telephone installed in his Milan house in via Conte Verde was subject to wire-tapping, as warranted by the judge for preliminary investigation in Milan.*

On matters relating to his disappearance, the D.I.G.O.S. in Milan learnt from trustworthy sources that on February 17th Abu Omar had been forcibly loaded onto a white van by at least two men while walking down via Guerzoni, on his way to the nearby Center for Islamic Culture, where he usually went at that time *(see report by Insp. Piredda dated 02.21.03 and attached to the informative report of 02.25.03).*

The confidential information was rapidly confirmed by records later admitted and filed: Ghali Nabila, *wife of the missing man, was summoned on February 24th for the purposes of providing additional elements to the initial statement, and she confirmed that before leaving the house her husband told her he was first going to the mosque in v.le Jenner, then to pay the rent, and after that he would come home. Having established that he was unreachable, and before making an official report, the woman contacted the community leaders at the Viale Jenner mosque, a frequent haunt of her husband's. At the end of the collective prayer of Friday, February 21st the ICI imam* ***Arman Ahmed El Hissini Helmy,*** *known as* ***Abu Imad,*** *who then recounted everything to her, had asked if anyone had news of* ***Abu Omar,*** *and described the man's appearance and clothing. After the imam's appeal an Egyptian woman confided to two of her sisters that on Monday (February 21st) a friend of hers had witnessed a man being stopped via Guerzoni, on the corner with via Cafiero, by two men in Western dress who had asked to see his papers first.* ***(Ghali Nabila*** *added that every time her husband left the house he took all his papers with him, especially the residence permit, the travel document he was given confirming his refugee status, and his ID card) He was then forcibly loaded onto a white van, despite his efforts to put up resistance. Not an habitual frequenter of the mosque, the woman at that moment was walking with her children down via Guerzoni on her way home after calling at the nearby butcher's; she confided to her friend that she had distinctly heard the men issue their demands to see the papers in Italian. So shaken was the eye-witness by the whole scene, that she told her husband it was her intention to return to Egypt. According to his wife, during the week prior to his disappearance* ***Abu Omar*** *had only left home to visit the v.le Jenner mosque for the noon prayer, had presided over the Friday collective prayer at the Gallarate mosque, had visited the Varese mosque on Saturday evening, and had held religious lessons at the one in Como on Sunday afternoon. On all these occasions his brethren had picked him up and taken him home.*

On February 25th 2003 ***Ahmed El Hissini alias Abu Imad,*** *suitably examined by police for a summary account, substantially confirmed Ghali's deposition, adding however that although he was unacquainted with the woman in question (i.e. the eyewitness), she had to be Egyptian. For the purposes of identifying her, he had arranged extensive searches throughout the Islamic community.*

The foreign woman who had witnessed the scene was named by police shortly after as being the Egyptian national ***Rezk Merfat,*** *born in Kalubia (Egypt) on 02.13.1980, residing with her husband in via Guerzoni nr. 33 Milan; the latter was heard as a person informed of events on February 26th 2003 by Digos, and on 03.04.03 by the Prosecutor in charge of proceedings. During the two hearings, the visibly fearful woman declared she lived in via Guerzoni at number 33, first floor. Between 11.30 and noon on Monday February 17th she was walking back from a medical appointment with her two daughters after having left her husband in viale Jenner, as he had other errands to run. After buying some bread, she accessed via Guerzoni and kept to the left-hand sidewalk on her way home. Having come level with the access to a ramp leading to underground parking lots, she noticed a light-colored van parked crosswise on the sidewalk, its front facing the wall and obstructing the way for pedestrians. Consequently, she crossed the road, reaching the opposite side, and continued her course, meanwhile noticing, somewhat ahead of the parked van, a bearded Arab-looking man wearing a traditional tunic walking down the left-hand side of the street, and another man, Western-looking and wearing sunglasses, who was talking into a mobile phone resting between his head and shoulder. The Egyptian woman was unable to provide any further details on the people present, also because by now she claimed she had distanced them by about 20 meters. Having reached the opposite side of the street, at a level with the entrance to the Purple Cross, she stopped a few seconds to let her younger daughter play with some young volunteers standing outside, then proceeded to resume her walk and cross via Guerzoni again. In that moment she heard a loud noise and, assuming an accident had occurred, she noticed the previously parked van back out quickly into the road and head off in the opposite direction to v.le Jenner, driving past her at great speed while she was about to cross the road on the pedestrian crossing at a level with the junction with via Cafiero. The load noise she heard was like a thud (plausibly the sound of the heavy van door slamming hard—ed.), and as the vehicle disappeared none of the people she had previously seen standing on the sidewalk were in sight. The modus operandi (load noise, high speed van) led her to believe that something had happened, and that the Arab man had been abducted. Specifically, during the account given to the Prosecutor on 03.04.03, the woman confirmed that the man standing before the bearded Arab man wearing a tunic had Western features and clothing, and was reading a document while talking over the phone. Consequently, the eyewitness had believed this to be a typical procedure of law enforcement officers when examining papers. She added also that, after walking past the van, she heard a loud noise like a falling object or a collision between two vehicles. The van had then sped past her and the people were no longer standing in the street. She maintained that the light-colored van was parked in the vicinity of the Purple Cross premises in via Guerzoni.*

During the same occasion on 03.04.03, ***Arman Ahmed El Hissini alias Abu Imad,*** *who was present at the eyewitness' examination, told investigators that a phone call was made to the Institute for Islamic Culture switchboard at 16.00 on February 26th 2003, in the course of which the anonymous caller, most likely an Egyptian, was quoted as saying that "Abu Omar was in Cairo and had been abducted by the Egyptian secret service with the help of Italian intelligence."*

On the basis of the above facts, criminal proceedings were initiated at this District Attorney's office with the charge of kidnapping (Art. 605 criminal code), and the Digos from the Milan Police headquarters was assigned the task of carrying out factual verifications: wire-tappings were ordered to be maintained on the telephones used by the missing man's relatives, and especially by his wife ***Ghali Nabila;*** *the authorities also ordered the acquisition of telecommunication logs showing all conversations on the mobile telephone cells in and around Via Guerzoni at the relevant time. As the exceptional results of the probe conducted with the abovementioned means will be expanded on later, it must be pointed out here that, due to a blatant mistake in the original warrant re the actual date of the abduction, the data on* ***cell communication exchange*** *at the time and place of the kidnapping that was first obtained and examined did not refer to 02.17.03 (correct date of the incident) but to 03.17.03 (see Digos informative report of 10.08.03).* ***Once the mistake had been corrected, the pertinent data was acquired forthwith, and as stated before immediately produced information of exceptional importance.***

Meanwhile, many witnesses were heard including the ***staff at the Purple Cross*** *who were present in via Guerzoni at the time of the incident, and had been named by the witness Rezk Merfat in her deposition: Davide Vignati, Fabio Fusi, Alessandro Tetta, Giusepe Tripicchio, Emiliano Bocci, Ermelinda Maria Teresa Beretta, Luigi Claudio Papa, Aniello Fariello, Giovanni Grisoli, Cosimo Tripaldi, Mirko Malavoglia and Fabio Paolo Viganò, all being employees and volunteers of the Purple Cross in via Guerzoni (the location where the witness* ***REZK Merfat*** *had said the relevant facts had taken place) on duty on that morning of February 17th 2003, and unanimously declaring that they had witnessed nothing out of place at the time and place in question.*

The examination of further foreigners belonging to the local Islamic community in Milan or in neighboring towns, and who had habitual dealings with the missing man proved equally unproductive, even though some witnesses had implicitly admitted they feared ***Abu Omar*** *had fallen victim to an abduction, as had befallen other member of the same radical Egyptian organization in the past.*[1]

Specifically:

— ***Arman Ahmed El Hissiny Helmy,*** *imam of the Milan-Viale Jenner mosque, declared on 08.04.03 to have learnt from Shaw ki Mohammed, head of the Mosque of Vienna, that some days after Omar's disappearance,*

[1] In September 1995 the Egyptian extremist **Talaat Fouad Kassem,** alias ***Abu Talal*** disappeared in mysterious circumstances from Zagreb (Croatia); he was spokesman for the Egyptian ***Al Jama'a Al Islamica*** group and was a political refugee living in Europe. A week later, on October 20th 1995, *Jama 'a Al Islamiya* carried out a bomb attack against a local police force building in Rijeka (Croatia) killing one person and wounding other 29. The action was believed to have been carried out in retaliation for the notorious leader's alleged kidnapping. The news was reported by the Milan Digos in the informative note dated 02.24.05.

Shawki had been contacted by a man known to him as belonging to the Austrian secret service, who had asked him information on Abu Omar;

— ***El Ashmawi Sherif Hafez,*** *administrative consultant at the House of Islamic Culture in Italy -based in Via Quaranta 54 in Milan—stated on 08.11.03 to have learnt from Ghali Nabila, Abu Omar's wife, that her husband had told her how he had noticed that every time he came back from the Gallarate or Varese mosques he was followed by a car or a white Fiat Fiorino van. The witness also stated, as told him by Abu Omar's wife, that during a lesson at the Como mosque the latter had criticized some Arab countries, such as Libya and Tunisia, whose governments trample on human rights;*

— ***Shaari Abdelhanid,*** *president of the Milan Institute for Islamic Culture, based at Viale Jenner 50, merely stated on 08.06.03 that he had never been on goods terms with the missing man since a pre-existing divergence arising from the handling of public relations with a number of Tunisian inmates presently in jail;*

— ***Abd El Aly Aly Aly,*** *administrative supervisor at the House of Islamic Culture in Italy—based in Via Quaranta 54 in Milan—believed the abduction to have been carried out by American or Egyptian security forces for the purposes of questioning Abu Omar on the September 11th terrorist attacks directed at the USA. This statement was based on Egyptian dailies reports that, while on his way from Denmark to Yugoslavia, Abu Talal had been forcibly taken to Egypt with American assistance;*

— ***Elbadry Mohamed Reda,*** *teacher at the House of Islamic Culture in Italy—based in Via Quaranta 54 in Milan—who, after admitting on 08.14.03 that at times Abu Omar was more involved in political than religious activity, in which he expressed his dissent against the Egyptian government, did recount impressions gathered in Islamic quarters in Milan, whereby Abu Omar's disappearance was ascribable to an abduction masterminded by Italian intelligence, the CIA or by the Egyptian secret service, backing this up with similar precedents that had befallen Egyptian nationals, also confirmed by the Egyptian president Mubarak;* ***Rezk Mohamed Ali,*** *principal of the school inside the mosque in Via Quaranta 54, Milan, after stating on 08.21.03 that he had learnt from Omar himself of his previous arrest in Albania, back from Afghanistan, and of his subsequent escape to Germany, did maintain that Omar may have been kidnapped by the Americans for reasons connected with Albania (i.e. Afghanistan);* ***Bouhaddou Mohamed,*** *head of the Varese mosque until 1998, provided on 09.10.03 no useful evaluation on Omar's disappearance;*

— ***Snoussi Hassine,*** *head of the Como mosque provided on 08.20.03 no useful evaluation on Omar's disappearance;*

— ***Zergout Abdelmajid,*** *imam of the mosque in Varese, stated on 09.10.03 that Omar's position with regard to the well-known current political events and international affairs was certainly not among the most moderate; also, he felt that Omar's disappearance surely could not be ascribed to a voluntary departure, but, based on elements gathered in Islamic circles he frequented, it was most likely the result of an abduction either operated by the Italian secret service in conjunction with US intelligence, or by Italian intelligence with the intent to hand him over to Egyptian authorities, or-lastly—by Egyptian secret services with the assistance of common Italian criminals.*

On the dynamics surrounding Abu Omar's kidnapping, other important information was acquired between February and March 2005.

Specifically, on 02.26.05 a statement by Elbadry Mohamed Reda was taken, *in his position as a person informed of the facts, and whose telephone had long been under surveillance by the Carabinieri of the R.O.S. in Milan (since the man is under investigation for belonging to an organization with terrorist aims ex art. 270 bis cp). Other important conversations recorded on this number will later be elaborated on; suffice it here to say that during the 02.26.05 questioning the Prosecutor asked for details of a conversation between the witness and a friend on the subject of Omar's disappearance, wherein the witness had mentioned that the eyewitness's husband had been subject to some pressure, to persuade her to change her account. The reference seemed clearly made at the eyewitness* ***Rezk Merfat, who had actually been heard by both the police and the Prosecutor, and had submitted an account that differed from the one known to the heads of the V.le Jenner mosque*** *(according to whom the woman had been a witness throughout the abduction, including Omar's failed attempt to break free from his abductors).* ***Elbadry Mohamed Reda*** *declared to this effect:*

> *". . . I'm talking about news that I was told by two Egyptian men, friends or family of the eyewitness' husband. They certainly all come from the same Egyptian village but I don not know if the two are related to the man or just friends. I learnt from the two that the woman had changed her version of the incident as witnessed by her, after unspecified characters had pressurized her to do so, saying that if she had confirmed the first version, her husband's residence permit would have been revoked and he would have been whisked off to Egypt. Indeed, I can confirm that this eyewitness has been named thanks to a fellow-Egyptian friend of hers (whose name I do not know) whom the woman had confided in. Her husband had spoken with Abu Imad and Abu Imad had gone to speak to the eyewitness. The change in the account revolves around this: the woman had told Abu Imad that she had seen the complete crime scene, with Abu Omar being apprehended by other people and forcibly loaded into a van, which she had described as white. I must also point out that the woman did not know Abu Omar personally, and had only give a physical description of the abducted man. When she was later called by the police, and by the Italian magistrate, the woman amended her version, saying that she neither recalled the color of the van, and that she had not witnessed the man's actual kidnapping. As far as*

I know, the frightened eyewitness to the abduction left Italy after her deposition before the Prosecutor, and is now in Egypt, while the husband is still in Milan. "

Consequently, on ***03.15.05, the Prosecutor recorded the statement made by Salem Shawki Bakry,*** *a person informed of the facts, and husband of the Egyptian national* ***Rezk Merfat,*** *eyewitness to the event:*

"On the day the incident occurred we (i.e. the whole family) had gone to a medical center in via Ragosa where my firstborn had been visited for a hearing ailment. After the visit, around noon, we were heading home. I was driving the car and, almost home, I dropped my wife at the top of via Guerzoni and drove off as I also had a medical appointment to get to. My wife and the girls (the youngest was in her arms) had about 200/300 meters to walk.

When I got home that late afternoon I recall finding my wife still very shaken, and she told me she had seen a fight in via Guerzoni between two men, one she believed was a policeman, and the other was an Arab. Regarding the details of what she had seen, I cannot but confirm the version she gave to the magistrate from the D.A. in Milan when she was heard. I was also present in that occasion. I also recall that Abu Imad, the imam from the viale Jenner mosque was also present. (The Prosecutor acknowledges it is stated in the statement of March 4th 2003).

Going back to that day, my told me she was also worried for me, as I could also be clearly subject to police inspection. But I conforted her saying that not only police was seldom seen in that area (it indeed was a very quiet area) but also because I had nothing to fear. Indeed, I had little to do with the mosque scene. After calming my wife down, that was the end of the matter so I did not know the details of what she had seen, nor did I consider asking her further questins on the matter. A few days later, Abu Imad (I do not recall whether directly or through someone else) told me that my wife had witnessed Abu Omar's abduction, and that she therefore had to inform the Italian police. I was flummoxed because I knew nothing of this, and at that time did not even make the connection with the "fight" she had told me about on February 17th 2003. Speaking with my wife and with Abu Imad I established how Abu Imad himself had come to know about this. Basically, my wife had confided herself with a friend of hers who had come to our house (I only know her name, Hayam, and that at the time she lived in Vermezzo, Milan), and this woman had recounted the tale with people from the viale Jenner mosque. For this reason, then, my wife was first called by the police, and then by the magistrate, and told what she saw.

I acknowledge that, it is claimed in certain statements you have collected (collected by the Prosecutor—ed.) *that my wife gave the authorities a different version of the facts she had witnessed because someone had pressurized her to keep quiet or not give a complete account, under threat that her or my residence permit would be revoked.*

I am unaware as to who may have made such statements, but I assure you they are false. No-one has ever threatened us directly or indirectly and, anyway, I am familiar enough with Italian legislation to know that a residence permit cannot be revoked from an honest hardworking citizen for no reason.

> *Yet, it is true that my wife was certainly shocked and shaken, all the more so when she learnt the identity of that person, whose abduction was being investigated by the Italian authorities.*
>
> *It is also true that she left Italy to go back to Egypt the day after she was heard by the magistrate from the Milan D.A. office. She did so because she was afraid and because I could not afford to support the whole family in Milan with my income as manual laborer in the construction business. She currently lives in Kaloubia (Egypt) and I go and see her from time to time. . . . I can confirm that my wife told me she had seen two people near the van, not three, and that one of them was surely an Arab."*

However, speaking on the very same day of 03.15.05 with ***Arman Ahmed El Hissini alias Abu Imad,*** *the latter stated:*

> *"I heard from no-one, and neither from those directly involved, of any kind of threats issued against Mrs.Rezk Merfat or against her husband. I only know, though, that she changed her version when she was heard by the police and by the magistrate. The change consisted in the following: I had known beforehand that she had beheld the crime scene, not only because she had seen several people around Abu Omar, but also that she had witnessed the eventa that occurred outside the Purple Cross, i.e. the moment when those men grabbed Abu Omar violently and forced him into a van. And she also heard the noises coming from the van, probably made by Omar as he was trying to break free. When she was later questioned by police and the magistrate, she changed her account, saying that she had merely seen a man, who looked like a policeman, speak with Abu Omar next to the van, and that she saw the van drive off and no-one was left in the street.*
>
> *As a result of this change I harbored the belief that someone may have induced the woman to change the description of the facts.*
>
> *I first found out of the existence of an eyewitness to the incident from a regular of the mosque called Sayed Shaban. I had spurred all community members to strive to gather information, and Sayed told me he learnt from another man, whose identity I do not know, that an eyewitness had seen the abduction, describing it as I recounted it earlier (being the violent account of the abduction in all its phases). I do not know the man who told Sayed of the eyewitness' existence but, anyway, Sayed knew who she was: he did not name her to me, but he acted as a go-between between myself and her husband, inviting him, upon my request, to come to see me at the mosque. The man, whom I had never seen before, undoubtedly came before his wife had been summoned by the police. I told him we knew that his wife had witnessed the abduction, and that he should report everything to the authorities. We did not specifically speak about how events occurred, as Sayed had recounted to me, but only generally about Abu Omar's kidnapping. For his part, he did not tell me what he had learnt from his wife, but he confessed that she had seen an extremely serious and dangerous incident, so much that he too seemed absolutely terrified. He kept saying that he did not want to get involved, and even said he would send his wife back to Egypt for this reason. At that point I told him that if Abu Omar were killed, he would also be*

to blame. He understood my plea as strongly based on religious grounds, and accepted that I pass on to the authorities his wife's name as eyewitness.

ADR: I therefore confirm that the woman's husband told me he wanted to send her back to Egypt, and I figured it was due to her fear of being involved in the grave matter she had witnessed. He uttered a typical expression reflecting our culture, that "he did not want to fling open the doors of Hell", by involving his wife and himself in such serious circumstances. He never mentioned financial grounds as a reason for his wife's return to Egypt."

Also on 03.15.05, a direct comparison was immediately arranged between ***Shawki Bakry*** *and* ***Arman Ahmed El Hissini alias Abu Imad;*** *both men confirmed their own accounts, although the former did admit to being terrified, along with his wife, at the prospect that she would be called upon to give evidence:*

"I can first of all confirm that I was approached by Sayed Shaban who told me that Abu Imad, here present, wished to speak with me in relation to what my wife had seen. It is also true, after what Sayed had told me (whom I had known for a long time as being a friend of acquaintances of mine), that I grew afraid and was also scared as I went to speak with Abu Imad. Yet the fear was not because my wife had witnessed the whole scene, but because I understood that the incident was politically motivated, and I was not interested in its reasons.

It is also true that I told Abu Imad it was my intention to have my wife return to Egypt. Yet, I also confirm that everything I learnt from my wife relating to what she had seen amounts to what my wife declared to the police and the magistrate. As I said before, I did not even pay much attention to what she told me on February 17th 2003.

So, I have no idea what source produced a different account of the facts as witnessed by my wife and recorded in her statements made to the authorities.

Sayed also told me that rumours were spreading around the mosque, saying that I did not want her to testify, but I denied all that."

He admitted though that only at the imam Abu Imad's insistence did he accept that his wife 's name was made to the police as eyewitness . . .

SALEM SHAWKI BAKRY's *reticence grew increasingly more apparent when, on the same day of 03.15.05,* ***HASSANEIN Hayam Abdelmoneim Mohamed,*** *the Egyptian woman friend of the eyewitness was summoned and heard as a person informed on the facts. She stated, in fact:*

". . . I remember perfectly well what my friend had told me. In the late morning of February 17th 2003 Merfat was walking home along via Guerzoni. On the way she had spotted a white van and two Western-looking man standing next to it; also, the back of the van had no windows. As she walked on, she passed an Arab-looking man dressed in a white Jalabia and sporting a big black beard who was directed towards viale Jenner. She heard a loud noise straight afterwards and realized the man was crying for help in Arabic. She turned round suddenly, scared by the commotion,

and noticed the van drive off at high speed with no trace of the Arab-looking man. For this reason she believed he had been taken away.

ADR. I do not remember other details on this event, just that Merfat admitted to having already spoken with her husband of what she had witnessed.

. . . The conversation with my friend Merfat took place on Friday. That morning I had taken my little girl to her house, so she could look after her for the time my husband and I were at the mosque for the collective prayer. During our conversation my husband was waiting in the car outside, but when I got in and we drove to the mosque I recounted to him Merfat's tale. When we got to the mosque I went to pray in the women's section. That day the imam made an appeal to the worshippers, asking anyone who had news on Abu Omar to come forward. I confided the story I learnt from Merfat to a fellow-worshipper, whose name escapes me. The woman urged me to approach the imam with this information. I protested that I could not go into the men's section, so the woman went up to the imam's wife, since she was also present at the prayer, and told her everything. She committed herself to pass this news on to her husband without delay. I met up with my husband outside the mosque and told him that I had spoken with other women about the event, and asked him if I had done the right thing. He reassured me, adding that he too had mentioned the affair to two young men who worked at the viale Jenner mosque. I then went back to Merfat's house to pick my child up, and told her of the imam's appeal concerning Abu Omar's disappearance. Merfat worriedly asked me if I had spoken with anyone about her story, and I said no because I did not want her to scare her further. One week later my friend merfat called me saying she had been summoned by the police. She asked me in tears why I had betrayed her trust, indeed she was terrified by her husband's reactions. She added that she had not told the complete story to the police, because her husband had forbidden her to. I told her I had talked because it could help to save a man's life, and to reassure her further I passed the phone to my husband, who tried to explain to her it was a religious duty to provide useful information that could shed light on who had kidnapped Abu Omar, and that she had nothing to fear. That same evening merfat's husband came to our house in Vermezzo, and asked my husband and myself not to report to the police those details that his wife had told me; he also told us that, when speaking with the police, she had kept quiet about something . . . Merfat revealed to me that she had decided tnce of what she had seen."

Summoned again by the Prosecutor, ***SALEM SHAWKI BAKRY was confronted with the statements made by HASSANEIN Hayam Abdelmoneim Mohamed,*** *and on 03.18.05 declared the following, finally revealing the truth and owing up to his and his wife's earlier reticence:*

"I must indeed make changes to my statement given only a few days ago, but I wish to stress that it was not my intention to hinder Italian justice, as I was solely concerned for the fear that gripped my wife as a result of what she had seen.

Well, although I confirm to not having paid great attention to my wife's words on 2.17.03, I admit to having omitted parts of her account. She truly feared that a similar fate could befall me. It is especially true that she saw two Western-dressed men attack a bearded Arab, dressed in a white jalabia, who struggled and cried for help while being violently grabbed and forcibly made to enter a van. I confirm she was unaware of the Arab's identity, as I did ask her the question. Regarding the van color, I believe she said it was white or gray, anyhow it was light-colored. I don not recall if she told me the van windows in the back or not: it may well be she told her friend more details than what she told me.

Anyhow, she had seen the man being loaded, despite his opposition, into the van that took off with two men on board. I do not know if the driver was a third man, as my wife did not specify this.

I also confirm that I did not link this event with the Abu Omar's abduction (which I had known nothing about) until Sayed, friend of mine and Abu Imad's, told me he knew what my wife had seen because she had spoken with a friend, who had informed others within the mosqu.

First I went to Abu Imad, who told me what he had learnt (and this matched exactly my wife's account to me, and presumably to her friend), adding that my wife had better inform the authorities of the whole thing.

I went home and asked my wife if she had told others what she had witnessed. I was angry but my wife denied doing so, and I did not wish to insist because our second baby had been born only a few weeks back.

All the same, when we appeared before the police and then the magistrate, I did not tell my wife to hide the truth: she was so scared that she decided to give only a partial account of what she had seen.

It is also true that I went to Mrs.Hassanein's house, and spoke with both her husband and her, but chiefly to say that they would soon be called by the police (whom I had given their address); I made no plea to them to conceal the truth. Foe sure, I told them my wife was terrified, and for this reason I imagine Mrs.Hassanein decided not to tell the police everything."

At this stage, ***it is quite clear that events unfolded in the following manner: two people (most likely three, considering the driver of the van) had assaulted and apprehended Abu Omar by force. Despite his cries for help and his efforts to break free, the man had been loaded onto the white or light-colored van, which drove off immediately.***

The garnered information, moreover, went a long way to confirm the Milanese and provincial Islamic community's widely-held belief. Either due to firsthand knowledge of Omar's past or present lifestyle, or based on rumours picked up within the Islamic community, none of its members, in fact, had ever believed that **Abu Omar** *could have possibly departed from Milan of his own free will. Indeed, everyone was convinced that he had been abducted by Italian, US, or Egyptian government agencies, not necessarily in mutual collaboration, but harboring the common intent of handing him over to Egyptian authorities, who thought (along with the Americans) he was not altogether unrelated to the recent upsurge of international terrorist activity.*

This belief is supported by Abu Omar's wife's conversations with third parties (the family phone was being tapped from long before the abduction): since 02.18.03 and the following days, in fact, Ghabi Nabila had been visibly concerned for her husband's safety and had endeavored to gather news, and spread the word around that he was missing.

This is the transcript of three recorded telephone conversations proving the woman's genuine concern, and Omar's friends and family's attempt to verify whether Omar had been arrested; this possibilty having been ruled out by the missing man's lawyer:

Interception of the telephone number 02.45479222, located at 18, via Conte Verde, Milan and used by Ghali Nabila (wife of Abu Omar), *carried out in the course of crimnal proceedings number n. 5236/02 by D.I.G.O.S. at Milan police headquarters.*

> ***1) 02.18.03, 21.50 hrs, conversation between Ghali Nabila and an Egyptian woman***
> *Ut: Ghali Nabila*
> *Int: Egyptian woman*
>
> *The unknown woman calls Ghali asking her if she has any news of Abu Omar. Ghali says she went to the police (Central office) and reported the mysterious disappearance.*
>
> ***2) 02.20.03,14.27hrs, conversation between a woman called Asma (who answers the phone belonging to Ghali Nabila) and Ummu Alai (Egyptian woman)***
> *Ut: Asma*
> *Int: Ummu Alai, Egyptian woman*
>
> *The woman asks for Nabila who is not in. A friendly conversation ensues wholly dedicated to Nabila's husband's disappearance. The woman insists that a thorough search of all hospitals should be made, as he may have been admitted due to an accident . . .*
> *Ut: even if he is in hospital . . . they must inform the relatives . . . because he carries his personal papers with him . . . anyway, Nabila has already reported the matter to the police, and they told her to come back and make a new report . . . if he were not to come home . . . anyway, he left to go to the mosque ans never arrived . . .*
> *Int: tell me, Fowad knows nothing yet!*
> *Ut: no, Fowad knows nothing . . .*
> *Int: I think he's in hospital . . .*
> *Ut: many people are looking for him, they checked in many hospitals and didn't find him . . .*
> *Int: listen, a similar thing happened some time ago to a brother named Salah . . . he was found at the San Carlo hospital nine days later . . .*
> *Ut: he has been missing since Monday afternoon . . . today is the fourth day . . . he never even made it to the mosque . . . may God give Nabila the strength and the patience . . . poor soul, she is suffering greatly.*
> *The conversation shifts to Nabila's suffering and her condition.*

3) 02.20.03, 14.37 hrs, conversation between an Egyptian man and woman
Ut: Egyptian woman,
int: Egyptian man.

The conversation starts in a familiar tone, and then
Ut: listen . . . the lawyer told her there is no-one . . . he told her there is no-one with that name . . . he is certainly not there . . . now she went and reported the matter . . .
Int: yes, to whom ?
Ut: with Iman . . . the Italian sister . . .
Int: . . . at the main police station, then ?
Ut: yes, at the main police station . . .
Int: all right, all right . . . let's hope for the best . . . by the way, Fowad has got a passport . . .
Ut: thank God . . . when did he get it?
Int: . . . he told me yesterday at 12.30 . . .
Ut: that means he claimed it last Monday . . . anyway, praise God . . . listen, this kind of thing makes you think . . . since he is not in that place (does not specify) . . . at first we hoped he was in that place . . . but now
Int: is he sure?
Ut. what?
Int: is the lawyer sure . . . ?
Ut: the lawyer has someone working there . . . she called Nabila and told her there is nobody there by that name . . . maybe he's somewhere else . . . but today she told her there is nobody there either . . . Nabila told her he may be with someone outside Milan . . . that is, three days outside Milan . . . anyway if he were outside Milan . . . but he lives here . . .
Int: what does 'outside Milan' mean . . . what are they doing with him outside Milan . . . ?
Ut: because he holds lessons outside Milan . . . also in Como . . . but since he lives here . . . they must take him away from here . . . and then they must advise that they have taken him away . . . if at all, they should have taken him from here . . . I mean from Milan . . . let us hope God protects us
Int: I think you should speak with her . . . maybe thereis trouble between him and his wife?
Ut: no, because when we asked her this, she said . . . no, it's nothing like that . . . He wants to divorce her, but she doesn't want to be rejected there . . . he kept saying 'I'll reject you and I'll give you the money you need' . . . but she doesn't want the divorce, she wants to continue being married to him . . .
Int: let's hope for the best . . . say, has she left already?
Ut: yes, she left a quarter of an hour ago . . .
Int: did she take a photo with her ?
Ut: yes, she took a copy of the permit . . . and a photocopy of the passport . . . that is, the Italian passport . . .
Int: alright, let's hope for the best . . .
Ut: say, are you going back to worj as soon as you 're done?
Int: no, I've got to finish a job alone . . .
Ut: alright.
They say good-bye.

Abu Omar's abduction has therefore taken place for sure: this certainty amounts to a starting point, which gives rise to the factual description and evaluations that follow.

For over one year after the abduction no significant progress was made in the investigation *on the disappearance of the* ***Abu Omar,*** *the Egyptian extremist.*

Moreover, on April 24th 2004, D.I.G.O.S. in Milan formally notified to this District Attorney office the contents of ***a March 2003 communique', and forwarded by "American authorities" to the Direzione Centrale della Polizia di Prevenzione in Rome stating that Abu Omar had relocated to an unknown Balkan location.*** *Addressed by the above Direzione Centrale, the US authorities stressed the presumptive nature of the news, to which no further detail was provided.* ***The statement made to the Italian authorities would later be proven to be utterly groundless.***

****

DOCUMENT NO. 10

NINETEENTH REPORT, SECTION 8: EXTRAORDINARY RENDITIONS

UK Parliament Joint Committee On Human Rights

May 18, 2006

8 Extraordinary Renditions [Part of the larger report]

148. Growing concerns about the phenomenon of extraordinary rendition, and in particular, allegations that British airports are being used for stopovers by CIA chartered aircraft operating renditions of suspects to jurisdictions where they will be interrogated under torture, led us to extend our inquiry to consider the obligations of the UK under UNCAT in respect of these allegations.[204] We heard oral evidence on the issue and sought and received additional written evidence on extraordinary renditions from a number of NGOs.

149. The existence of a practice of rendition to face torture is disputed. In a recent statement, the US Secretary of State, Condoleezza Rice, denied that the US transported detainees to other jurisdictions "for the purpose of interrogation using torture" or that it sent suspects to jurisdictions where it "believed" they would be tortured.[205] She nevertheless acknowledged and justified the extra-legal "renditions" process, and left open the possibility that suspects were being rendered to countries where torture is routinely practised, or where they may be subjected to inhuman or degrading treatment, or to other practices which fall short of the US Government's definition of torture, but which may nevertheless be prescribed by UNCAT.

[204] The Guardian, 12/9/20005, Destination Cairo: Human Rights fears over CIA flights, 12 September 2005; The Herald, Britain to be Hub for CIA Terror prisoner flights, 16 November 2005. Amnesty International, Rendition and "Disappearances" in the "War on Terror", http://web.amnesty.org/pages/stoptorture-renditions-eng Back.

[205] Ev 92 Back.

150. At a European level, investigations into allegations of extraordinary rendition and of the complicity of European governments in such renditions are still ongoing. Some preliminary findings have emerged, however: the Interim Memorandum by Senator Dick Marty of Switzerland, Rapporteur to the Council of Europe Parliamentary Assembly on Allegations of Secret detentions in Europe, found clear evidence to establish that individuals were being abducted, detained and transported within Europe, and handed over to countries where they faced torture.[206] A European Parliament Temporary Committee of Inquiry into the alleged use of European countries by the CIA for the transportation and illegal detention of prisoners began work in February and expects to produce its first interim report in May 2006. A number of European states including Germany, Italy and Spain are now undertaking official investigations into the possible use of their airports in extraordinary renditions.[207]

151. In the UK, Government Ministers have repeatedly stated their belief that renditions to torture are not taking place through UK airports or airspace.[208] These assertions are based on the assurances given by the US authorities, and by the absence of any formal requests from the US authorities to render suspects through the UK. The Foreign Secretary has stated that there have been no requests from the US government to effect renditions through UK airspace since 1998. In that year, two requests relating to renditions of suspects to face trial in the US were granted.[209] Also in 1998, one request to refuel an aircraft carrying two detainees to the US was denied.[210] In a letter to us, Mr Straw stated:

I have no reason to believe that suspected terrorists have been rendited through UK territory or airspace during the Bush Administration. None of the information published recently has demonstrated otherwise . . . we see no value and have no intention of checking every flight transiting the UK which may have some connections with the US Government.[211]

206 Parliamentary Assembly of the Council of Europe, Committee on Legal Affairs and Human Rights, *Alleged Secret Detentions in Council of Europe Member States*, Information Memorandum II AS/Jur (2006) 03 rev, 22 January 2006.See also *Alleged existence of secret detention centres in Council of Europe member states*, statement by Dick Marty, Rapporteur of the Committee on Legal Affairs and Human Rights, Strasbourg, 13.12.2005 Back.

207 Ev 181 Back.

208 The Rt Hon Jack Straw MP, Oral evidence taken before the Foreign Affairs Committee on 13 December 2005, HC (2005-06) HC 768i, Q23; Baroness Ashton of Upholland, Qq 137-180; Rt Hon Adam Ingram MP, Qq 236-270 Back.

209 HC Deb., 12 December 2005, cols 1652-3W Back.

210 10 HC Deb., 10 January 2006, Col 5WS Back.

211 Ev 91 Back.

152. Evidence has emerged, however, that aircraft believed to have been involved in previous renditions have passed through the UK, stopping for refuelling purposes en route, to countries known to practise torture.[212]

153. Evidence to us questioned the sufficiency of the inquiries undertaken by the Government. Liberty and JUSTICE considered it unrealistic to expect that the United States Government would have sought specific permission to use the UK for extraordinary rendition and argued that a proactive investigation was needed to establish whether UK airspace or airports are being used in the practice of extraordinary rendition.[213]

154. We note the conclusions of the House of Commons Foreign Affairs Committee, which on 15 February published its views on extraordinary renditions in its Human Rights Annual Report. It regretted the Government's unwillingness to request information from the US Government concerning rendition flights,[214] and concluded that:

> the Government has a duty to inquire into allegations of extraordinary rendition and black sites under the Convention Against Torture, and to make clear to the USA that any extraordinary rendition to states where suspects may be tortured is completely unacceptable.[215]

155. There has been pressure to take action to investigate renditions at operational as well as diplomatic levels. We note that the Chief Constable of Greater Manchester Police opened an inquiry into extraordinary rendition flights on behalf of the Association of Chief Police Officers (ACPO),[216] and we understand that this inquiry is still open.

Human Rights Compliance

156. In regard to extraordinary renditions, as elsewhere, compliance with the Convention against Torture and other human rights standards requires more than passive non-cooperation in torture; it requires active investigative and law enforcement action to prevent torture or inhuman and degrading treatment. Credible allegations that UK airports or airspace is being used to render suspects to face torture engage the UK's positive obligations to prevent and investigate acts of torture under UNCAT, as well as under Article 3 of the European Convention on Human Rights, given force in

---

[212] In a letter of 6 March 2006 to Sir Menzies Campbell, Mr Ingram disclosed that aircraft known to have been chartered by the CIA landed on 14 occasions at two RAF bases, RAF Brize Norton and RAF Northholt: The Guardian, *Minister Admits Rendition flights used RAF bases*, 7 March 2006 Back.

[213] Ev 159-169 Back.

[214] Foreign Affairs Committee, First Report of Session 2005-06, *Human Rights Annual Report 2005*, HC 574, para 51 Back.

[215] Ibid., para 52 Back.

[216] Ev 160, para 6 Back.

domestic law by the Human Rights Act,[217]and under the customary international law prohibition on torture.

157. Under Article 3 of UNCAT, there is an obligation not to return anyone to a country where there are substantial grounds to consider that they will face a real risk of torture; this is reflected by similar obligations under Article 3 ECHR[218] and Article 7 ICCPR.[219] This obligation is also likely to apply where an individual is "rendered" through the UK by foreign intelligence agents, to face such a risk of torture outside the UK.[220]

158. Liberty and JUSTICE further suggest that extraordinary renditions may in themselves amount to torture, since "detaining someone where the detainee is aware that the purpose of the detention is to bring him to a place where he will be subjected to physical torture might in itself amount to torture as it will undoubtedly inflict severe mental suffering on the detainee".[221] This argument relies on an analogy with the case of *Soering v UK*, where it was held that the prolonged wait for the death penalty known as the "death row phenomenon", amounted to inhuman and degrading treatment in breach of Article 3 ECHR.

159. The Convention places a number of specific duties on states to investigate allegations of torture, both within the jurisdiction, and elsewhere. Under Article 12, there is a duty to investigate wherever there are reasonable grounds to suspect that an act of torture has been committed in the jurisdiction. Under Article 6, where persons alleged to have committed offences of torture or complicity in torture are present in the territory of the State, there is an obligation to take the suspect into custody or otherwise secure his presence in the territory, and make a preliminary inquiry into the facts, with a view to either prosecution or extradition in accordance with Article 7.[222] Therefore, the effect of UNCAT is that where there are credible allegations that an aircraft present at a UK airport is involved in the transport of a suspect to torture, or that persons present on the aircraft are involved in the transfer of suspects to torture, there is an obligation to conduct a preliminary investigation into its involvement in any possible offences of torture. Where this preliminary investigation unearths

[217] *Soering v UK* (1989) 11 EHRR 439; *Chahal v UK* (1997) 23 EHRR 413; Back.

[218] *Chahal v UK, op. cit.* Back.

[219] Liberty, JUSTICE and REDRESS argue in their evidence that this obligation will be breached where the UK permits a transfer to torture by foreign agents through the UK. Back.

[220] See the comments of the Venice Commission (The Council of Europe Commission on Democracy through Law, Opinion on the International Legal Obligations of Council of Europe Member States in Respect of Secret Detention Facilities and Inter-State Transport of Prisoners, 17 March 2006, CDL-AD (2006) 009 Back.

[221] Ev 159-169 Back.

[222] Article 5.2 UNCAT provides for universal jurisdiction over crimes of torture, stipulating that states must establish jurisdiction over offences of torture, including complicity and participation in torture, and attempted torture, where the alleged offender is present within the jurisdiction, irrespective of where the offence has occurred. Back.

sufficient information to justify arrests, there is an obligation to prevent the aircraft from leaving UK territory, and to arrest any suspects present on the aircraft. Where there is sufficient evidence, the suspects must be either prosecuted, or extradited.

The Chicago Convention

160. The principal international treaty which regulates civil aviation is the Chicago Convention on International Civil Aviation 1944 (The Chicago Convention). Under the Convention, if extraordinary rendition aircraft are identified as state aircraft, then in order to fly through UK airspace, or land at UK airports, they require prior authorisation, and must abide by the terms of such authorisation (Article 3(d)). If extraordinary rendition aircraft are identified as civil aircraft, then under Article 5 of the Chicago Convention, they must be permitted to fly through UK airspace and to stop for refuelling or other similar ("non-traffic") purposes at UK airports, without obtaining prior permission. However, the Chicago Convention expressly permits State authorities to search the aircraft on landing or departure, and to inspect relevant certificates and other documents relating to the aircraft (Article 16). Under Article 23, these include the journey log book of the aircraft, a list of passengers, their names and places of embarkation and destination, and a detailed description of any cargo. There is therefore nothing in the Convention which would prevent a police search of a civil aircraft stopped for refuelling at a UK airport, or the arrest of persons aboard the aircraft who were suspected of crimes of torture.

161. Furthermore, Article 4 of the Chicago Convention stipulates that states must not use civil aviation for any purpose inconsistent with the overall aims of the Convention.[223] Civil flights established to be transporting suspects to torture would be likely to be considered inconsistent with the aims of the Convention, and therefore outside its protection, in particular given the need to interpret and apply the Convention in light of the UK's obligations under UNCAT and under customary international law. Given the status of the prohibition on torture as a norm of higher international law or *jus cogens*, an interpretation of the Chicago Convention which permitted free passage to aircraft known to be involved in renditions to torture would be likely to render the relevant provisions of the Chicago Convention inapplicable, since under the Vienna Convention on the Law of Treaties, a treaty which conflicts with a norm of *jus cogens* is void.[224]

[223] The Preamble to the Convention notes that development of international civil aviation can "create and preserve friendship and understanding among the nations and peoples of the world" whilst its abuse can "become a threat to the general security" and states the Convention's aim to develop international civil aviation in a "safe and orderly manner." Back.

[224] Vienna Convention on the Law of Treaties, Article 53 and Article 64 Back.

Status of Aircraft

162. The status of aircraft alleged to be used in extraordinary renditions, as either State or civil aircraft, is unclear. The question is significant, since a State aircraft, though it will require permission to land in the UK, will not be subject to search by UK authorities, except by agreement. Whether an aircraft is classified as State or civil may depend on the nature of the aircraft. Where it is a military aircraft or lands at a military base for example, its status as a civil aircraft may be open to question. The Venice Commission on Democracy through Law, in its recent legal opinion on renditions, considered that where an aircraft, chartered by agents of a foreign State, represents itself as a civil aircraft, then it forfeits the right to claim State aircraft status under the Chicago Convention as well as the right to state immunity.[225] It nevertheless considered that aircraft presenting themselves as State aircraft would enjoy immunity and could not be searched.[226] The Secretary General of the Council of Europe, in a recent Report on these matters, recommended clarification of the law on human rights exceptions to State immunity, and co-operation between the Governments of Council of Europe states to achieve this.[227]

The Government View

163. Although there has been some confusion as to the effect of international civil aviation law on the Government and police powers to investigate allegations of extraordinary rendition, it now appears to be accepted that the current law creates no barrier to investigation. Initial Government suggestions that the Chicago Convention prevented investigation of the matter[228] were later withdrawn. At report stage debates on the Civil Aviation Bill in the House of Lords, in response to amendments tabled by Baroness D'Souza which would have provided for express powers to require aircraft to land, and to board and search aircraft where they were suspected of involvement in extraordinary rendition, Lord Davies of Oldham argued that the amendments were unnecessary since such powers already existed under international civil aviation law. He stated:

> The Chicago Convention is clear on this. We certainly have the right to investigate an aircraft, but, of course, we have to have good grounds for doing so. If credible intelligence of serious illegal activity comes to light regarding an aircraft in flight, the Government can certainly require the aircraft to land. Article 3 of the Chicago Convention allows states to require aircraft to land if there are reasonable grounds to conclude that the aircraft

[225] Venice Commission legal opinion, *op. cit.*, para 103 and para 148 Back.
[226] *Ibid.*, para 149 Back.
[227] Secretary General's report under Article 52 ECHR on the question of secret detention and transport of detainees suspected of terrorist acts, 28 February 2006, SG/Inf (2006) 5, para 71 Back.
[228] HL Deb., 12 October 2005, col 376 Back.

> is being used for any purpose that is inconsistent with the aims of the Convention.
>
> If the aircraft is on the ground the control authorities—police, Customs and immigration—have a variety of powers to enter, take evidence and make arrests.[229]

164. In evidence to us, Ms Harman accepted there was an obligation to investigate allegations of flights transporting individuals to torture. She further accepted that the Chicago Convention should not "be a shield behind which acts preparatory to torture should take place".[230] She considered that the primary duty of investigation lay with the police, rather than with central government.[231] **We welcome the Government's acceptance that international civil aviation law permits thorough investigation of civil flights alleged to be involved in extraordinary rendition.**

165. The Government's position has been that whilst in principle it would be willing to investigate where there is evidence of extraordinary renditions passing through the UK, at present there is no such evidence.[232] It does not consider information that aircraft landing in the UK can be demonstrated to have been previously involved in extraordinary renditions, to be sufficient in itself to warrant further investigation. Mr Ingram stated, in respect of the aircraft disclosed to have landed at RAF bases: "there is no evidence to show that any of those aircraft were carrying any passengers of the type [alleged to be transported in renditions]".[233] Baroness Ashton of Upholland confirmed the Government's view that there was "no basis for further action".[234]

Conclusions

166. One obstacle to obtaining clear evidence that a particular flight is transporting a detainee as part of a rendition is the current lack of a requirement for chartered civil aircraft passing through the UK to provide lists of passengers on board. Ms Harman confirmed that such information was not required or recorded.[235] We note, however, that there is nothing in the Chicago Convention which would prevent the UK from requiring transiting civil aircraft to provide such information. Given the potential for abuse of free passage for civil aircraft under the Chicago Convention, by aircraft involved in extraordinary renditions, **we recommend that the**

[229] HL Deb, 8 March 2006, col 844 Back.
[230] Q 165 Back.
[231] Q 168 Back.
[232] Lord Davies of Oldham, report stage debate on Civil Aviation Bill, *op. cit;* Rt Hon Adam Ingram MP, Qq 236-270; DCA Qq 137-180 Back.
[233] Q 251 Back.
[234] Ev 85-88 Back.
[235] Q 180 Back.

Government should take steps to require staff and passenger lists to be provided to the UK authorities when chartered civil aircraft land at UK airports, or transit UK airspace. In the long term, if effective unilateral Government action is not taken, there would be a case for amendment of the Chicago Convention, to require the provision of passenger lists.

167. In relation to the question of whether there have been extraordinary renditions in the past few years using UK airspace or airports, and the extent to which the Government should initiate an investigation, we note that the Government has recently rejected the view of the House of Commons Foreign Affairs Committee that it is under a duty to enquire into the allegations of extraordinary rendition and black sites under the Convention against Torture. In its response to the Foreign Affairs Committee's Annual Report on Human Rights for 2005, the Government states that a "search of all relevant records" has not found any evidence of detainees being rendered through UK airspace since 11 September 2001, and that in the absence of such evidence it does not consider that there is a requirement under Article 12 UNCAT for it to carry out a further investigation.[236] This accords with the Government's view expressed in evidence to us, as described above.

168. We consider that there is now a reasonable suspicion that certain aircraft passing through the UK may have been carrying suspects to countries where they may have faced torture, or to have been returning from rendering suspects to such countries. This reasonable suspicion is in our view sufficient to trigger the duty to investigate, and to look behind the assurances received from foreign Governments. **It follows that we do not accept the Government's view that, by the means described in its response to the Foreign Affairs Committee, it has adequately demonstrated that it has satisfied the obligation under domestic and international human rights law to investigate credible allegations of renditions of suspects through the UK to face torture abroad. In order to satisfy the obligation to investigate in relation to possible renditions to face torture which may already have taken place, we believe the Government should now take active steps to ascertain more details about the flights which it is now known used UK airports, including, in relation to each flight, who was on them, and their precise itinerary and the purpose of their journey. If evidence of extraordinary renditions come to light from such investigations, the Government should report such evidence promptly to Parliament.**

169. **We recognise that there are growing calls for an independent public inquiry into alleged use of UK airports in extraordinary renditions, and**

[236] Response of the Secretary of State for Foreign and Commonwealth Affairs to the First Report from the Foreign Affairs Committee, Session 2005-06, *Annual Report on Human Rights 2005*, Cm 6774, paras 27 and 28 Back.

that the piecemeal way in which information has so far reached the public domain does not inspire confidence in the Government's willingness to investigate, but nevertheless we consider that such an inquiry would be premature. Whether a public inquiry is necessary should be determined in light of the extent to which inquiries by the Government leads to the publication of the detailed information required.

170. For the future, in addition to the steps which the Government has taken to make its position on extraordinary renditions clear to the United States authorities,[237] we believe the Government should establish a clear policy as to the action to be taken in cases where aircraft alleged to have been previously involved in renditions transit the UK. Where there are credible allegations arising from previous records that a particular civil aircraft transiting UK airspace has been involved in renditions, and where the aircraft is travelling to or from a country known to practise torture or inhuman or degrading treatment, it should be required to land. Where such an aircraft lands at a UK airport for refuelling or similar purposes, it should be required to provide a full list of all those on board, both staff and passengers. On landing, it should be boarded and searched by the police, and the identity of all those on board verified. Wherever appropriate, a criminal investigation should be initiated. Where an aircraft suspected of involvement in extraordinary renditions identifies itself as a state aircraft, it should not be permitted to transit UK airspace, in the absence of permission for UK authorities to search the aircraft. We consider that these steps are not only permitted by the current law, but required to ensure full compliance with the Convention Against Torture.

[237] *Ibid.*, para 29 Back.

DOCUMENT NO. 11

EXTRAORDINARY RENDITION: CLOSING THE GAP—A PROPOSAL TO CRIMINALIZE UK INVOLVEMENT (EXCERPTS)

UK Parliamentary Group on Extraordinary Rendition

November 5, 2009

2. Introduction

The All Party Parliamentary Group on Extraordinary Rendition

2.1 This consultation document has been prepared by the All Party Parliamentary Group on Extraordinary Rendition (the ***APPG***) following consultation with Freshfields Bruckhaus Deringer. The APPG is a cross-party grouping of over 60 MPs and Peers from the British Parliament who have come together to examine extraordinary rendition and related issues. It was established by Andrew Tyrie MP in December 2005, in response to allegations that the United Kingdom had been involved in the United States rendition programme. The Chairman of the APPG is Andrew Tyrie MP, the Vice-Chairmen are Chris Mullin MP and Norman Lamb MP, and the Treasurer is Lord Hodgson.

2.2 All Party Parliamentary Groups are informal, cross-party groupings of Parliamentarians. They have no official status within Parliament. The APPG does not receive any money from any government. The APPG's entry in the Register of All-Party Groups can be viewed at http://www.publications.parliament.uk/pa/cm/cmallparty/memi01.htm.

2.3 The APPG aims to collect, examine, and publicly disseminate information about rendition, the involvement of the UK in such practices, and related issues. It publishes almost all of the information that it obtains on its website, www.extraordinaryrendition.org.

2.4 Some of the aspects of extraordinary rendition of most concern to the APPG are summarised below. However, it considers generally that the process is illegal, immoral, a stark breach of the rule of law and ineffective as a counterterrorism tool.

2.5 In particular, the APPG seeks to determine whether:

(a) UK territory has been used to facilitate rendition programmes, in particular the US programme, in any way, including by allowing the facilitation, over-flight or refuelling of rendition flights through or on UK territory or airspace;

(b) the UK has assisted in renditions of British nationals or residents;

(c) UK officials or Armed Forces have conducted or facilitated renditions; and

(d) the UK has in place adequate procedures that can give the public confidence that the UK will not be involved in extraordinary renditions in the future.

2.6 The Obama Administration in the US initially signalled positive steps to curtail practices on the part of US military and intelligence personnel in connection with extraordinary rendition. The APPG welcomes this development, for which it has been campaigning (although it remains very concerned as to whether these steps are being sufficiently implemented so as to bring about a substantive change). However, the APPG does not believe that it is appropriate for the UK to allow the regulation of rendition conduct on UK territory to occur through changes in the policies of whichever Administration happens to be in power in Washington D.C. US executive decisions do not absolve the UK of its obligations under its own domestic law and under international law.

2.7 Extraordinary rendition has allowed authorities to circumvent the proper procedures imposed under international and domestic law for the protection of suspected terrorists; has led to a denial of justice and has exposed those individuals to physical mistreatment and torture, and to the risk of such treatment. The APPG considers it right that there be effective legislation to ensure that the UK does not facilitate or support such a practice now or in the future. Existing domestic criminal law does not sufficiently address the issue. It is not focussed on the necessary acts for extraordinary rendition and its requirements make prosecution extremely difficult. There have been no prosecutions to date.

2.8 Positive and identifiable steps by the UK Government to prevent UK involvement in extraordinary rendition, conducted by any country, are, and remain, critical. They enable the UK to underline its commitment to meeting its international legal obligations, to set a standard in the international community and to make a clear statement about the way in which governments should conduct themselves, even in the face of the threat of global terrorism.

Objective

2.9 The purposes of this Consultation Paper (CP) are:

(a) to examine the current weaknesses in the legal framework in the UK for dealing with the phenomenon of extraordinary rendition;

(b) to examine those weaknesses in the international context; and

(c) to propose a practical legislative route to ensure both that the UK is not used for the purposes of extraordinary rendition, and that organisations or individuals in the UK do not facilitate this practice in any way.

This CP does not attempt to deal with all the purposes, consequences, or results of extraordinary rendition, some of which are fully addressed by other legal provisions, Rather it proposes a route to stamp out the phenomenon itself, at least so far as the infrastructure of the UK and its Overseas Territories are concerned.

2.10 The APPG believes that its proposals will be effective in preventing the use of UK facilities for the purpose of extraordinary rendition. It would, however, welcome the comments of consultees as to how these proposals can be improved.

Consultation Process

2.11 This CP reviews the elements of domestic and international law applicable to conduct constituting extraordinary rendition. It considers the issues arising from trying to apply the UK's domestic law to extraordinary rendition. It then considers possible amendments to existing statutory offences to strengthen the law in this respect, before setting out, in detail, the new offences the APPG considers to be necessary. The recommendations are intended to:

(a) provide coherent and clear new offences which protect individuals and society and provide clarity for investigators and prosecutors by focusing on identifiable and provable acts necessary for extraordinary rendition involving the UK;

(b) enable relevant conduct to be appropriately sanctioned;

(c) be, and be apt to be, applied in a manner which is fair and non-discriminatory, in accordance with the UK's obligations under the European Convention for the Protection of Human Rights and Fundamental Freedoms, the Treaty on European Union and the Treaty establishing the European Community, the UK's other international obligations, and the obligations of UK public authorities under the Human Rights Act 1998; and

(d) continue to ensure consistency with the UK's international obligations in the field of international transport.

2.12 This CP is part of a process that is open, inclusive and evidence-based. It involves:

(a) a review structure that will look to include those affected (for example, key players in the UK transport infrastructure are being contacted directly and asked for their views on the proposals, in addition to this wider consultation);

(b) consultation with criminal justice practitioners, academics, parliamentarians, non-governmental organisations, victims of rendition and the wider public.

Next Steps and Contact Details

2.13 This CP is circulated for comment and criticism. It does not necessarily represent the final views of the APPG. Following its review of the responses to this consultation it will, where appropriate, amend its recommendations. The APPG's present intention is to submit its proposal for consideration by Parliament.

2.14 Recipients of this CP are invited to submit their responses in writing to Andrew Tyrie MP by **31 December 2009.** Comments may be sent either—

By post to:
Andrew Tyrie MP
Chairman, APPG on Extraordinary Rendition
House of Commons
London
SW1A 0AA
United Kingdom

By email (with subject heading 'Response to Consultation') to:
mailto:mccrackens@parliament.uk

2.15 It would be helpful if, where possible, responses sent by post could also be sent to the APPG in electronic format: either on disk, or by email to the above address.

2.16 The APPG will treat all responses as public documents in accordance with the Freedom of Information Act and it may attribute comments and include a list of all respondents' names in any final report it publishes. Those who wish to submit a confidential response should contact the APPG before sending the response.

2.17 This consultation paper is available on the APPG's website at: http://www.extraordinaryrendition.org

2.18 The APPG thanks you for your attention to this CP, and for any response you may choose to submit.

3. Executive Summary

3.1 There is cogent and broad-based evidence that extraordinary rendition has been taking place for a considerable period of time. However, the APPG is particularly concerned that extraordinary rendition has become more frequent in the context of the US-led 'War on Terror' and current related geo-political concerns.

3.2 Extraordinary rendition, broadly the secret transfer of people from one country to another, against their will and without due process of law, is linked with torture, with cruel, inhuman and degrading treatment, with protracted detention without trial and without access to legal or medical help, and with related human rights abuses. It operates in breach of criminal and international law. That the Obama Administration has commenced a review of the legality of certain of its detention policies is recognition of this.

3.3 In May 2009 the APPG visited Washington DC for meetings with the new Administration and on Capitol Hill. There is a real determination to clear this up but the Administration has been left with a difficult legacy. It is currently wrestling with the dilemmas of reconciling the requirements of justice with the need to protect itself and other western democracies.

3.4 The APPG considers that involvement in extraordinary rendition has significant adverse implications for a country's reputation and international standing. It is concerned that, to the extent that the UK may be condoning, or turning a blind eye to, or be implicated in such practices, it increases the terrorist risk that the UK faces. Moreover, as extraordinary rendition is, by definition, taking place outside any legal structure, it is fundamentally inconsistent with the rule of law, a fact that has been consistently recognised by our courts, and has been affirmed most recently in the case of Binyam Mohamed (discussed at paragraph 4.18 below). Indeed, it is the opinion of the Eminent Jurists Panel of the International Commission of Jurists (the **EJP**) that by eroding international humanitarian law and human rights law standards, aspects of the 'War on Terror', including rendition, States *"have put the possibility of short term gains from illegal actions over the more enduring long term harm that they cause"*.[1] This has been the APPG's view from its inception.

[1] EJP Report on Terrorism, Counter-Terrorism and Human Rights, *Assessing Damage, Urging Action* (the ***EJP Report***), 16 February 2009, at Chapter 7, page 160.

3.5 It is quite possible that UK citizens have been directly involved in the apprehension, detention and/or physical mistreatment of those subjected to extraordinary rendition. Moreover, there is clear evidence that aspects of the process of extraordinary rendition have involved the UK's transport infrastructure and there is a strong likelihood that people acting within the UK (or its Overseas Territories) have directly, or indirectly, facilitated or supported this process. There is no specific offence in English law that criminalises the extraordinary rendition process.

3.6 The APPG recognises that criminal offences exist in English law which do criminalise certain elements of extraordinary rendition (in particular, kidnap, false imprisonment, certain statutory offences against the person and involvement in torture). However, those offences only apply effectively to those who have directly committed particular acts which may form part of the process of extraordinary rendition. Those people are, in practice, very difficult to apprehend and the legal requirements for a conviction are not well suited to the facts of extraordinary rendition. No prosecutions have taken place to date. It is clear that English criminal law, as it stands, is not well adapted to the task of prohibiting the practice effectively. Further, to the extent that the principal actors in an extraordinary rendition case are members of foreign (or even UK) military, paramilitary, intelligence or police forces operating clandestinely, it is difficult for UK authorities to identify, arrest and prosecute them. English criminal law is constrained in pursuing secondary participants in the extraordinary rendition process who are within the UK (i.e. those who aid, abet or assist extraordinary rendition).

3.7 Consequently, the APPG considers that the UK should take appropriate steps to reform its criminal law to criminalise extraordinary rendition involving the UK (and its Overseas Territories). Doing so would penalise conduct which is identifiable, reprehensible and contrary to the public interest.

3.8 Moreover, the UK's international obligations under both treaty and general international law both prohibit it from participating in extraordinary rendition and require it to take appropriate steps to detect and deter extraordinary rendition. Enhancing the criminal law to target such behaviour, and then applying it, will hold the UK to compliance with its international obligations. It also distinguishes the UK in the international community by making a clear statement in this respect as to its credentials in connection with the rule of law and the protection of human rights. In so doing, it offers the prospect of creating higher standards globally.

3.9 The APPG therefore proposes reforms to the criminal law that seek to prohibit:

(a) specifically the use of transport facilities in the UK or any of its Overseas Territories for the purpose of extraordinary rendition;

(b) the use of such transport facilities for the purposes of facilitating extraordinary rendition;

(c) appropriate failures by controllers of transport facilities to prevent the use of those facilities for the purpose of extraordinary rendition (subject to an effective system of safe harbours to protect those undertaking their usual activities in the transport sector); and

(d) 'circuit flights' (where the UK is used as part of an itinerary for extraordinary rendition purposes but without a detainee being transported through the UK) by extending the proposed criminal liability in certain circumstances where the actual transfer of the individual is not through the UK but the overall process is, itself, enabled by the use of UK transport infrastructure.

3.10 It is proposed that extraordinary rendition is defined by reference to the transport of an individual without his consent where the transfer is without lawful excuse (i.e. in effect, not subject to a recognised legal process capable of being controlled by the courts). This clearly imports a rule of law approach to deterring the process itself, rather than simply the mistreatment at the destination.

3.11 This approach does not include any concept of risk of torture or inhuman or degrading treatment. Although these issues are commonly associated with extraordinary rendition, introducing such a requirement complicates the proposed offence and raises very considerable problems of evidence and achieving a successful conviction. It risks creating legislation which satisfies the emotional response to rendition, and its context, but which may not be sufficient effectively to change behaviour.

3.12 For related reasons, the proposal does not change the law relating to the conduct of British armed forces or security services in the field. To the extent that they might (say) seize an individual in country A and then transfer him to the custody of another country or to be held in country B, without involving the territory of the UK, it would not be caught by the proposed legislation. This is a very important topic and raises very serious issues of international and national law and their impact on the UK's operations overseas which involve such conduct. The APPG would welcome comments in the consultation as to whether these issues should also be encompassed in this proposal or addressed through other means.

3.13 The APPG wishes to ensure that liability should not be imposed on those going about their normal jobs. It is proposed that the necessary mental element for the offence is, therefore, set high so that only those who are sufficiently involved and culpable are exposed to liability.

3.14 The exception to this is the 'failure to prevent' offence. This is intended to ensure that those in the management or control of the critical transport infrastructure which is used in extraordinary rendition do take the necessary steps to ensure that their facilities could not be used for this purpose. However, to protect them from inappropriate risk, there would be an extensive 'safe harbour' requiring the existence of adequate procedures to identify individuals being transferred against their consent and, if so, whether that any such transfer is without lawful excuse. The APPG recognises that this is a more difficult area but believes that it is important that, if the UK's performance in the area of extraordinary rendition is to be materially improved, those who control the essential facilities should not be permitted to turn a blind eye but must take reasonable steps to avoid abuse of their facilities.

3.15 This CP focuses on the law of England and Wales. It does not specifically cover Scotland and Northern Ireland, which have their own separate legal systems. Parliament has the power to legislate for Scotland and Northern Ireland (although under the Sewel Convention, the consent of the Scottish Parliament is sought if the legislation relates to a devolved matter).[2] However, the general principles set out in this CP are of broad application and similar policy considerations would apply to extending the proposed legislation to Scotland and Northern Ireland. Indeed, the APPG seeks such an extension, regarding it as particularly important given the reputed role of Prestwick Airport in Scotland in rendition activity.

4. Factual and Political Background

Defining 'Extraordinary Rendition'

4.1 Our research indicates that no formal or legal definition of extraordinary rendition has been adopted in the UK, or elsewhere. However, consistent themes can be discerned from the views of legislative,[3] quasi-legislative[4] and academic and non-governmental sources,[5] that extraordinary rendition should be defined as an extra-judicial practice involving the apprehension and transfer of persons from one jurisdiction to another outside the parameters of lawful processes. Extraordinary rendition also frequently connotes that persons so transferred face the risk of torture or other cruel, inhuman or degrading treatment. It is a process that by its inherent nature

[2] Schedule 5 of the Scotland Act 1998 provides that matters relating to international relations (Part I, paragraph 7) and matters relating to the regulation, security and safety of air and other forms of transport (Part II, Head E) are reserved to the UK Parliament.

[3] Congressional Research Service Report for U.S. Congress, Renditions: *Constraints Imposed by Laws on Torture*, 12 October 2007.

[4] Council of Europe, Secretary General's report under Article 52 ECHR on the question of secret detention and transport of detainees suspected of terrorist acts, 28 February 2006, at paragraph 22.

[5] *UK Involvement in Extraordinary Rendition*, Joint Supplementary Submission to the Joint Committee on Human Rights, Liberty/Justice, December 2005.

operates outside the law; and the English courts have consistently asserted that involvement in rendition operations is an affront to the rule of law.[6]

4.2 The following working definition captures the popular, inclusive sense:

> *Extraordinary rendition is the apprehension and forced transfer of persons from one State to another, outside the due process of law, where there is a risk that such persons will be exposed to torture or inhuman or degrading treatment.*

'Due process of law' is to include extradition pursuant to treaty or ad hoc arrangements, deportation or prisoner transfers. The definition is also in line with the Council of Europe's working definition reflecting the European Convention on Human Rights (the *ECHR)*.

4.3 However, the proposal discussed in the CP is focussed on certain aspects of this definition. Because of the fundamental difficulties in defining whether an individual has been exposed to torture or inhuman or degrading treatment (or that people involved in any act of rendition were sufficiently aware at the relevant time that this would be the case), the proposal concentrates on prohibiting the specific elements of the practice which can be subject to simple and effective criminal control in the UK and for which it is realistic that a credible prosecution can be brought. In this way, it is intended to ensure that the use of UK infrastructure to assist in rendition is prohibited.

The Recent Context—the US Detention Programme and The Risk of Torture

4.4 The 21st Century practice of extraordinary rendition is closely linked to the conduct of the US government as it pursues its policies in combating what it has defined as the global 'War on Terror'. The US has a longstanding policy of using rendition as a counter-terrorism tool. Under

President Reagan, rendition was used to bring people to justice in the US, and under President Clinton the use of rendition included transferring detainees to third countries in which they were wanted for terrorism offences.[7] Both former US Secretary of State Condoleezza Rice and former President Bush acknowledged that the US carries out rendition as a matter of policy, and vigorously defended the programme as a vital component in US counterterrorism strategy. Secretary Rice set out the policy in the following terms:

> *For decades, the United States and other countries have used 'renditions' to transport terrorist suspects from the country where they were captured to their*

[6] See R (Binyam Mohamed) v Secretary of State for the Foreign and Commonwealth Office [2008] EWHC 2048 (Admin) at paragraph 9(iii), citing R v Mullen [2000] QB 520.

[7] Stephen Grey, *Ghost Plane*, (Hurst & Co, London, 2006), 119; Michael Scheuer, 'Testimony to the House Foreign Affairs Committee', 17 April 2007, available online at http://foreignaffairs.house.gov/110/34712.pdf.

home country or to other countries where they can be questioned, held, or brought to justice.[8]

4.5 However, as the EJP has stated, there is a difference in nature between rendition operations as historically understood, and those carried out presently, in that *"the main objective now is intelligence gathering, with its focus on interrogation and detention"* as opposed to transferring persons for criminal prosecution.[9]

4.6 The places to which people have been transferred include States known to practice torture, and cruel, inhuman or degrading treatment on people in their custody, including Uzbekistan, Pakistan, Morocco and Syria.[10] Destinations also include US detention facilities, such as Guantánamo Bay and military facilities in Iraq and Afghanistan.

4.7 The Council of Europe has commented on the likely existence of secret CIA detention facilities in Eastern Europe.[11] It has also endorsed the findings of the report of the Council of Europe's rapporteur on extraordinary rendition, Senator Dick Marty (the ***Marty Report),*** as to the alleged conduct of extraordinary rendition operations.[12] On the basis of concurring testimony from persons alleged to have been subject to rendition, Senator Marty suggests that such operations carried out by intelligence personnel demonstrate a great deal of consistency, reflecting the highly trained nature of the operatives allegedly involved. In most cases, terrorist suspects are asked to step aside for a 'security check'. This is the start of the extraordinary rendition process, colloquially referred to as 'black-bagging'. Those taken aside are then normally taken to a small room at the relevant transport facility where they are blindfolded, and stripped by teams of up to six intelligence officers. Senator Marty suggests that detainees are then shackled, subject to intimate searches, a hood is placed over their head and headphones or earmuffs are used to deprive them of visual and

[8] Secretary Condoleezza Rice, 'Remarks Upon her Departure for Europe', 5 December 2005, emphasis added, available at http://www.state.gov/secretary/rm/2005/57602.htm (retrieved on 26 November 2008).

[9] EJP Report at Chapter 4, Section 3.1, page 80.

[10] The Explanatory Memorandum to the 2006 draft report of Senator Dick Marty to the Committee on Legal Affairs and Human Rights of the Parliamentary Assembly of the Council of Europe, *Alleged secret detentions and unlawful inter-state transfers involving Council of Europe member states* (the *Marty Report),* names Tashkent and Rabat as 'Category D' detainee transfer or drop-off points. A Canadian Commission of Inquiry has accepted in the case of Maher Arar (discussed at paragraph 4.9 of this CP) that renditions have occurred to Syria. The US State Department, in its 2007 Country Reports on Human Rights Practices published on 11 March 2008, documented instances and allegations of torture in Morocco, Syria and Uzbekistan. See http://www.state.gov/g/drl/rls/hrrpt/2007/.

[11] Marty Report, Section Two and Resolution 1507 (2006) of the Parliamentary Assembly of the Council of Europe, and Recommendation 1754 (2006) of the Parliamentary Assembly recommending the Committee of Ministers introduce a minimum standard of human rights protection in respect of extraordinary rendition.

[12] Marty Report, Section Two, at paragraphs 84-86, and Resolution 1507 (2006) and Recommendation 1754 (2006), cited above.

auditory sensation. They are then transferred, directly or indirectly, to detention sites, normally by aircraft.

4.8 President Bush publicly elaborated on the detention programme in September 2006:

> *In addition to the terrorists held at Guantánamo, a small number of suspected terrorist leaders and operatives captured during the war have been held and questioned outside the United States, in a separate program operated by the Central Intelligence Agency . . . Many specifics of this program, including where these detainees have been held and the details of their confinement, cannot be divulged . . . But as more high-ranking terrorists are captured, the need to obtain intelligence from them will remain critical—and having a CIA program for questioning terrorists will continue to be crucial to getting life-saving information.*[13]

4.9 There is no doubt that those subject to extraordinary rendition may face torture. As one example, a Canadian Commission of Inquiry has determined that a rendered individual, Maher Arar, a Canadian citizen, was subjected to torture in Syria having been rendered to that country following his arrest by US officials at New York's JFK airport in September 2002, partly on the basis of inaccurate and over-stated intelligence furnished to the US by the relevant Canadian services. He received an apology from the Canadian Government and was awarded $10.5m in compensation.[14] The EJP views the Arar case as emblematic of the risks to human rights that extraordinary rendition operations (carried out with the cooperation of different intelligence services) present.[15] In addition, the British High Court has accepted in the case of Binyam Mohamed, a British resident rendered to Guantánamo Bay (discussed in detail at paragraph 4.18 below), that there is, at a minimum, an *"arguable case . . . that cruel, inhuman or degrading treatment had been inflicted."*[16]

4.10 Moreover, the Convening Authority for the Department of Defense Office of Military Commissions has accepted[17] that the US Joint Task Force

---

[13] President George W Bush, 'President Discusses Creation of Military Commissions to Try Suspected Terrorists', 6 September 2006, http://www.whitehouse.gov/news/releases/ 2006/09/20060906-3.html.

[14] Office of the Prime Minister,'Prime Minister Releases Letter of Apology to Maher Arar and his Family and Announces Completion of Mediation Process', 26 January 2007, http://news.gc.ca/web/view/en/index.jsp?articleid=270739&keyword=maher+arar& (retrieved on 26 November 2008); 'Canada offers rendition victim compensation', The Guardian, 26 January 2007, http://www.guardian.co.uk/world/2007/jan/26/ usa.ciarendition.

[15] EJP Report at Chapter 4, Section 3.2, pages 83-84.

[16] R (Binyam Mohamed) v Secretary of State for the Foreign and Commonwealth Office [2009] EWHC 152 (Admin) at paragraph 20.

[17] Her Honor Judge Susan J. Crawford made this admission in an interview with the Washington Post on 14 January 2009 (Washington Post, 14 January 2009 at A01, available at http://www.washingtonpost.com/wp-dyn/content/article/2009/01/13/ AR2009011303372.html). Judge Crawford refused to refer the case of suspected 9/11 conspirator Mohammed al-Qhatani to a military commission on the basis of ill-treatment amounting to torture. The Department of Defense has confirmed that the treatment of al-Qhatani was contrary to the Army Field Manual (see Department of Defense

at Guantánamo Bay, which the Marty Report also identifies as a rendition drop-off point[18] has engaged in coercive interrogation techniques, the totality of which amount to torture as understood in domestic and international law. This represents quasi-judicial acceptance that US personnel have committed acts of torture. President Bush also acknowledged that "an *alternative set of [interrogation] procedures*" were being practiced by the CIA, and had been used on Abu Zubaydah, an alleged Al Qaeda senior strategist captured in Spring 2002 at the inception of the secret detention programme. Several US Government memoranda and legal opinions are now in the public domain, and document the US Administration's restrictive view of its anti-torture obligations. [19]This includes the Bybee Memorandum (known colloquially as the 'Torture Memo') of August 2002. This adopted what has been widely accepted as an overly narrow view of what amounted to torture in US law implementing State obligations under the Geneva Conventions and the UN Convention Against Torture.[20] Many interrogation techniques implemented by the US are illegal under English law.[21]

The Extent of Extraordinary Rendition and the US Detention Programme

4.11 CIA Director Michael Hayden has publicly clarified certain aspects of the US rendition programme. He has elaborated on the number of people rendered to third countries, and to CIA secret detention, since the programme's inception in spring 2002 with the capture of Abu Zubaydah:

> *in the life of this [CIA secret detention] program it's fewer than a hundred, with regard to [enhanced] interrogation techniques it's fewer than a third, and the number of renditions [to third countries] is actually smaller than that, mid-range, two figures.*[22]

press release of 14 January 2009, available at http://www.defenselink.mil/ news/newsarticle.aspx?id=52680).

[18] See Marty Report at paragraph 43.

[19] See a Joint Task Force Memorandum of 11 October 2002, setting out three categories of 'lawful' interrogation techniques, and requesting that they be authorised, including: "(1) The use of scenarios designed to convince the detainee that death or severely painful consequences are imminent for him and/or his family . . . (3) Use of a wet towel and dripping water to induce the misperception of suffocation", available at http://www.npr.org/documents/2004/dod_prisoners/20040622doc3.pdf (retrieved on 26 November 2008).

[20] Memorandum from Jay Bybee, Assistant Attorney General for the Office of Legal Counsel, to Alberto Gonzales, Counsel to the President, of 1 August 2002 on the interpretation of torture for the purposes of 18 U.S.C. 2340 (available at http://fl1.findlaw.com/news.findlaw.com/nytimes/docs/doj/bybee80102mem.pdf). This Memorandum suggested that an act would only constitute torture "[w]here the pain is physical, it must be of an intensity akin to that which accompanies serious physical injury such as death or organ failure". This Memorandum has now been rescinded by the Office of Legal Counsel and was repudiated by Attorney General Michael Mukasey at his 2007 Senate confirmation hearings (reported in The Boston Globe, 17 October 2007).

[21] Professor James Crawford, Whewell Professor of International Law at Cambridge University, and Kylie Evans, Research Fellow at the Lauterpacht Centre for International Law, *Opinion: Extraordinary Rendition of Terrorist Suspects through the United Kingdom,* 9 December 2005, paragraphs 10-13. The Foreign Secretary has stated publicly that waterboarding is torture.

[22] CIA, 'Transcript of Director Hayden's Interview with Charlie Rose', 24 October 2007, available at https://www.cia.gov/news-information/press-releases-statements/press-release-archive-2007/

Of these *"fewer than a third"*, three were subjected to the technique known as waterboarding: Khalid Sheikh Mohamed, Abu Zubaydah, and Abd al-Rahim al-Nashiri.[23] Other organisations believe that the number of extraordinary renditions carried out by the US Administration is much higher.[24]

4.12 On 14 February 2008, Steven Bradbury, Assistant Attorney General for the Office of Legal Counsel, testified that the CIA programme was being run in accordance with a new executive order from the President, which was issued on 20 July 2007.[25] In March 2008, US intelligence officials admitted holding Muhammad Rahim, currently detained at Guantánamo Bay, in secret CIA custody for at least six months previously. He was the first detainee in almost a year that US intelligence officials admitted to holding in CIA secret detention.[26]

4.13 President Obama, by Executive Order on 22 January 2009, ordered the closure of the US detention facility at Guantánamo Bay within one year.[27] He has also ordered the closure of CIA detention facilities across the globe[28] and instituted a high-level review of lawful options for the apprehension, detention, interrogation and prosecution of suspects.[29] These steps, if they were effectively implemented, would undoubtedly have an impact on extraordinary rendition and its associated practices. However, it is currently unclear what impact these steps, however welcome at the time they were announced, will in fact have.

4.14 We note, however, that there has been no specific executive or legislative prohibition on extraordinary rendition; indeed it is apparent that US Governments of both stripes have engaged in forms of rendition since the late 1990s. Nor is the President's Order protected from future amendment or repeal. Moreover, on its face the relevant Order merely provides that the Administration shall *"identify such [detention] options as*

interview-with-charlie-rose.html. Director Hayden has stated that the capture of Abu Zubaydah in spring 2002 marked the start of the CIA's programme of secret detention and interrogation. See Council on Foreign Relations, 'A Conversation with Michael Hayden', 7 September 2007, http://www.cfr.org/publication/14162/conversation_with_michael_hayden_rush_transcript_federal_news_service.html.

[23] BBC, 'CIA Admits Waterboarding Inmates', 5 February 2008, http://news.bbc.co.uk/1/hi/world/americas/7229169.stm.

[24] Amnesty International USA stated in April 2007 that "[t]he number of renditions cases currently appears to be in the hundreds". Amnesty International USA, 'Statement submitted for the record by Amnesty International USA', Extraordinary Rendition in US Counterterrorism Policy: The Impact on Transatlantic Relations, Joint Hearing of the US House of Representatives Committee on Foreign Affairs, 17 April 2007, http://foreignaffairs.house.gov/110/34712.pdf.

[25] Steven G. Bradbury, 'Prepared Statement of Steven G. Bradbury before the House Committee on the Judiciary, Subcommittee on the Constitution, Civil Rights, and Civil Liberties', 14 February 2008, 4, http://judiciary.house.gov/hearings/pdf/Bradbury080214.pdf.

[26] Mark Mazzetti, 'C.I.A. Secretly Held Qaeda Suspect, Officials Say', 15 March 2008, http://www.nytimes.com/2008/03/15/washington/15detain.html?ref=asia.

[27] Executive Order 13492 of January 22, 2009.

[28] Ibid.

[29] Executive Order 13493 of January 22, 2009.

are consistent with the national security and foreign policy interests of the United States and the interests of justice" and *"there shall be established a Special Task Force on Interrogation and Transfer Policies (Special Task Force) to review interrogation and transfer policies"*.[30] This does not preclude a form of rendition continuing. In addition, the closure of Guantánamo Bay and CIA detention facilities does not address the transfer of detainees to third States where they may be subject to ill-treatment, as in the Arar case described in paragraph 4.9 of this CP. Therefore the opportunities for a continuation of past practice still exist. Indeed, CIA Director Leon Panetta has affirmed before the US Senate that the use of third States would remain an option for the US.[31] In addition, we cannot state with any certainty that the new Administration will acknowledge past misdeeds and move forward in a transparent manner -we note that Director Panetta and Attorney General Holder have suggested that Department of Defense officials that relied on the dubious legal authority of opinions such as the Bybee Memorandum are unlikely to face investigation or prosecution.[32] In addition, the Department of Justice has affirmed the Bush Administration's position of an arguably overbroad state secrets privilege in respect of a US civil action against those allegedly involved in extraordinary rendition. This claim of privilege has been rejected by the US Ninth Circuit Court of Appeals.[33]

The United Kingdom's Role

Confirmed Involvement

4.15 There is no doubt that the UK has been involved in the US rendition programme. In February 2008, the Foreign Secretary disclosed to the House of Commons that, on two occasions in 2002, a rendition flight with a detainee onboard had refuelled at the British island of Diego Garcia. This was despite regular and explicit US assurances to the contrary.[34] To date, the Government has failed to disclose the identities of the two individuals concerned and the locations to and from which they were rendered (although it was disclosed at the time of the Foreign Secretary's Statement that one of the individuals had been released and one was being held at

---

[30] Ibid, at Section 1(e).

[31] Testimony of CIA Director-designate, the Honorable Leon E. Panetta to the Senate Intelligence Committee, 6 February 2009.

[32] Testimony of Director-designate Panetta to the Senate Intelligence Committee, 6 February 2009; written response 3C of Attorney General Eric H. Holder Jr. to Senator John Kyl (R-AZ), 28 January 2009.

[33] *Mohamed et al. v Jeppesen DataPlan, Inc.* 563 F.3d 992 (9th Cir. 2009), Opinion of Circuit Judge Hawkins, rejecting the oral submissions of the Department of Justice of 9 February 2009.

[34] Rt Hon David Miliband MP, 'Terrorist Suspects (Renditions) Statement', 21 February 2008, available at http://www.publications.parliament.uk/pa/cm200708/cmhansrd/cm080221/debtext/80221-0007.htm#08022198000007. The full list of assurances on this issue was released to the APPG on Extraordinary Rendition by the Foreign Office on 2 September 2008, and is available at www.extraordinaryrendition.org. The information shows that on seven separate occasions the US provided inaccurate assurances on Diego Garcia. It also shows that the first such assurance was in June 2003, just nine months after the second rendition flight had refuelled on Diego Garcia.

Guantánamo Bay). Subsequent Parliamentary Answers have confirmed that both have now been returned to their country of nationality.[35]

4.16 There have been five further acknowledged occasions since 1997 when the US has sought permission from the UK to render someone through UK territory or airspace: on two occasions in 1998, permission was granted for the rendition of suspects to trial in the US; on a further two occasions in 1998, permission was refused;[36] in 2004, an approach was made by the US for permission to conduct a rendition, but the UK indicated that permission would be refused if they were asked to give it.[37]

4.17 In February 2009, the Defence Secretary disclosed to the House of Commons that, in 2004, two individuals captured by UK Forces in Iraq, and transferred to US detention, had subsequently been rendered to Afghanistan.[38] Parliamentary Answers subsequently confirmed that both individuals were rendered to Bagram Air Base.[39]

Binyam Mohamed

4.18 In August 2008, the High Court held in the case of Binyam Mohamed that information passed from the UK Security Service had *"facilitated"* the interrogation of Binyam Mohamed by US authorities at times when they knew he was being held incommunicado and without access to a lawyer by providing information and questions to their US counterparts.[40] Mr Mohamed is a British resident who was detained in Pakistan in April 2002 and detained incommunicado at various undisclosed locations until May 2004. He was subsequently rendered to Morocco, where he alleges he was severely tortured; then to Afghanistan; and finally to Guantánamo Bay where he was held until his release on 23 February 2009. He alleges that he was subjected to serious torture whilst in US military custody. The Court has ruled that *"the relationship between the United Kingdom Government and the United States authorities in connection with BM was far beyond that of a bystander or witness to the alleged wrongdoing"*.[41] The Foreign

---

[35] Bill Rammell MP, 'Written Answer to Andrew Tyrie MP', 11 February 2009, available at http://www.publications.parliament.uk/pa/cm200809/cmhansrd/cm090211 /text/90211 w0007.htm.

[36] Rt Hon Jack Straw MP, 'Rendition Allegations (Inquiries) Statement', 20 January 2006, available at http://www.publications.parliament.uk/pa/cm200506/cmhansrd/vo060120/wmstext/60120m01.htm. The two rendered detainees were Mohammed Rashid and Mohamed Rashed Daoud Al-Owhali. See letter from Kim Howells MP to Andrew Tyrie MP, available at www.extraordinaryrendition.org.

[37] Rt Hon Jack Straw MP, 'Letter to Rt Hon William Hague MP', 6 February 2006.

[38] Rt Hon John Hutton MP, 'Records of Detention (Review Conclusions) Statement', 26 February 2009, available at http://www.publications.parliament.uk/pa/cm200809/cmhansrd/cm090226/debtext/90226-0008.htm#09022651000004.

[39] Rt Hon Bob Ainsworth MP, 'Written Answer to Andrew Tyrie MP', 6 July 2009, available at http://www.publications.parliament.uk/pa/cm200809/cmhansrd/cm090706/text/90706w0010.htm#09070625001975.

[40] R (on the application of Binyam Mohamed) v Secretary of State for the Foreign and Commonwealth Office [2008] EWHC 2048 (Admin) at paragraph 88(i).

[41] Ibid. at paragraph 88(v).

Secretary has accepted that there is an arguable case that Mr Mohamed had been subject to torture and cruel, inhuman and degrading treatment by or on behalf of the United States authorities during the his two year period of incommunicado incarceration.[42]

4.19 UK intelligence services have conceded that they have used information obtained from detainees who had been rendered and/or held in CIA secret custody.[43] Indeed, in the case of Binyam Mohamed, the Security Service was found to have provided questions for Mr Mohamed's interrogation, and UK officials have been alleged to have been present at such interrogations.[44] The Attorney General, in consultation with the Director of Public Prosecutions, has referred the alleged complicity of an MI5 officer in Binyam Mohamed's case to the police for investigation.[45] In July 2009, the Metropolitan Police confirmed that they would investigate these allegations.[46] Notwithstanding whether there is any eventual finding of liability for the direct involvement of MI5 officers in such conduct, to the extent that UK intelligence services actively sought and used such information where there was a real risk that detainees were subject to torture, the APPG notes the strong criticism of the use of torture evidence by the House of Lords in the *A* case[47] and the view of the EJP that the systematic use of such intelligence renders a State *"complicit, wittingly or unwittingly, in the serious human rights violations committed by their partners in counterterrorism"*.[48] The Joint Committee on Human Rights recently considered the concept of complicity in its Report on Allegations of UK

[42] R (on the application of Binyam Mohamed) v Secretary of State for the Foreign and Commonwealth Office [2009] EWHC 152 (Admin) at paragraph 2.

[43] See, for example, ISC, 'Report into Rendition', 28 June 2007, at paragraph 28, quoting the Director General of the Security Service: *"When [Khalid Sheikh Mohammed] was in detention in 2003, place unknown, he provided [the pseudonyms of] six individuals . . . who were involved in [Al Qaeda] activities in or against the UK. The Americans gave us this information . . . These included high-profile terrorists—an illustration of the huge amount of significant information that came from one man in detention in an unknown place"*; and the speech of President George W. Bush, 'President Discusses Creation of Military Commissions to Try Suspected Terrorists', 6 September 2006, stating that information obtained by the CIA's secret detention programme *"helped stop a plot to hijack passenger planes and fly them into Heathrow or the Canary Wharf in London . . . It's helped our allies protect their people from deadly enemies."*

[44] The High Court has ordered that closed portions of its initial judgment in Mr. Mohamed's case, which may cast light on whether domestic security services were involved in the mistreatment of Mr. Mohamed, should now be made public, there being no compelling interest in maintaining secrecy over the closed portion, when balanced against considerations of the rule of law and the need to ensure democratic accountability over the British Security Services. See *R (on the application of Binyam Mohamed) v Secretary of State for Foreign and Commonwealth Affairs* [2009] EWHC 2549, in particular at paragraphs 101-109. At the time of publication, this information had not yet been released, pending appeal.

[45] Written ministerial statement of the Attorney General, Baroness Scotland QC, on Binyam Mohamed, dated 26 March 2009, available at http://www.attorneygeneral. gov.uk/NewsCentre/Pages/AttorneyGeneralDecisionOnBinyamMohamedInvestigation. aspx.

[46] James Sturcke, 'Police launch investigation into Binyam Mohamed torture allegations', The Guardian, 10 July 2009, http://www.guardian.co.uk/world/2009/jul/10/binyam-mohamed-torture-investigation-police.

[47] A v *Secretary of State for the Home Department* [2005] UKHL 71. In particular, see the judgment of Lord Bingham of Cornhill at [10]–[45].

[48] EJP Report at Chapter 4, Section 3.2, page 85.

Complicity in Torture. The Committee concluded that the systematic receipt of information known or thought likely to have been obtained from detainees subjected to torture would amount to complicity in torture.[49]

Further Allegations—Facilitating Rendition

4.20 The foregoing demonstrates that UK territory has been used for the purpose of rendition; the UK Government has, historically, actively consented to a form of rendition; that the UK Government was involved in the rendition of a British resident; and that the UK Government was involved in the rendition of two individuals captured by UK Forces in Iraq and rendered to Afghanistan. There are, however, allegations that the extent of UK involvement may run deeper.

4.21 Documents disclosed by the Foreign Office in respect of the claim for judicial review of Bisher al-Rawi and Jamil el-Banna, two British residents who travelled to the Gambia in November 2002 and were subsequently detained, transferred to US authorities and rendered to Afghanistan and Guantánamo Bay, indicate the Security Service had passed information to the US authorities that may have facilitated their detention.[50] While there is no indication that this was the intention of the UK Security Service, nonetheless the Intelligence and Security Committee (the ***ISC***) found that "*greater care*" could have been exercised by the Service, and noted "a *lack of regard, on the part of the US, for UK concerns*".[51]

4.22 On 25 February 2008, former SAS soldier Ben Griffin alleged that UK Forces in Iraq had been capturing people who were handed over to US forces, and subsequently rendered or mistreated.[52]

4.23 On 11 September 2009 MI6 referred one of its own officers to the Attorney General over allegations of complicity in torture.[53]

Further Allegations—Use of UK territory

4.24 The APPG was also concerned by the conclusion of the Marty Report, that Prestwick Airport is a 'Category A' stopover facility for rendition

---

[49] Joint Committee on Human Rights, 'Allegations of UK Complicity in Torture', 4 August 2009, Conclusion 5, available at http://www.publications.parliament.uk/pa/ jt200809/jtselect/jtrights/152/15202.htm.

[50] Several telegrams sent by the Security Service to US authorities in relation to al-Rawi and el-Banna were released to the APPG. These telegrams set out intelligence in relation to al-Rawi and el-Banna, and their travel plans. They are available at http://www.extraordinaryrendition.org/index.php/information-sessions/bisher-al-rawi-a-jamil-el-banna.

[51] ISC, 'Report on Rendition', July 2007, conclusions U and V, available at http://www.cabinetoffice.gov.uk/intelligence/special_reports.aspx. See also paragraphs 111-147.

[52] Statement of Mr Ben Griffin, 25 February 2008, available at http://www.stopwar.org.uk/ index.php?option=com_content&task=view&id=533.

[53] Richard Norton-Taylor and Ian Cobain, 'MI6 officer investigated over torture allegation', The Guardian, 11 September 2009, http://www.guardian.co.uk/world/2009/ sep/11/mi6-investigated-over-torture-allegation.

flights, providing refuelling and support services.[54] This conclusion was based on evidence in the form of detainee testimonies, exhibits placed before judicial and parliamentary enquiries, information obtained under Freedom of Information legislation, interviews with legal representatives and insider sources, the accounts of investigative journalists and research conducted by non-governmental organisations.[55] Senator Marty has also reported *"concurring confirmations"* that Diego Garcia had been used in the 'processing' of detainees.[56]

4.25 These findings have been endorsed by the Parliamentary Assembly of the Council of Europe.[57] Moreover, questions have been raised by the European Parliament in respect of over 100 flights made by planes linked to renditions that have transited the UK or its Overseas Territories.[58] We also note that Manfred Nowak, the UN Special Rapporteur on Torture, has claimed to have received *"credible evidence from well-placed sources familiar with the situation on the island that detainees were held on Diego Garcia between 2002 and 2003"*.[59] Similar allegations have been made by NGOs and the mainstream media.[60]

4.26 The APPG notes that, as highlighted by the ISC, inadequate record-keeping means that it will be difficult to discern the full extent of any such involvement.[61]

---

[54] Marty Report, at paragraph 43.

[55] Marty Report, at paragraph 43, footnote 38.

[56] Committee on Legal Affairs and Human Rights of the Parliamentary Assembly of the Council of Europe, 'Secret detentions and illegal transfers of detainees involving Council of Europe member states: second report', 11 June 2007, page 16, http://assembly.coe.int/Documents/WorkingDocs/Doc07/edoc11302.pdf.

[57] Resolutions 1507 (2006) and 1562 (2007) of the Parliamentary Assembly of the Council of Europe.

[58] European Parliament Temporary Committee on the alleged use of European countries by the CIA for the transportation and illegal detention of prisoners, 'Report on the alleged use of European countries by the CIA for the transportation and illegal detention of prisoners', 30 January 2007, The European Parliament referred to *"170 stopovers made by CIA-operated aircraft at UK airports, which on many occasions came from or were bound for countries linked with extraordinary rendition circuits and the transfer of detainees"*. See http://www.europarl.europa.eu/comparl/tempcom/tdip/ default_en.htm. See also the list of flights sent by the Foreign Secretary to the US Administration for specific assurances that they were not involved in renditions, available at www.extraordinaryrendition.org.

[59] Jamie Doward, 'British island "used by US for rendition", The Guardian, 2 March 2008, http://www.guardian.co.uk/world/2008/mar/02/ciarendition.unitednations.

[60] See Reprieve, 'Enforced Disappearance, Illegal Interstate Transfer, and Other Human Rights Abuses Involving the UK Overseas Territories', http://www.reprieve.org.uk/ documents/FinalRepreiveSubmissionFASC.pdf (retrieved on 26 November 2008); Adam Zagorin, 'Source: British Territory Used for US Terror Interrogation', Time Magazine, 31 July 2008, http://www.time.com/time/world/article/0,8599, 1828469,00.html; BBC 2, 'Newsnight', 31 July 2008, http://news.bbc.co.uk/1/hi/ programmes/newsnight/7536477.stm.

[61] ISC, 'Report into Rendition', conclusion B. The then Foreign Secretary Jack Straw confirmed in a Written Answer to Sir Menzies Campbell that much of the information on rendition flights through UK airspace was based on the recollections of officials. Sir Menzies Campbell WPQ 12 December 2005 [36414].

The UK Government'S Position

4.27 The Foreign Secretary has stated that *"[t]he Government never uses torture for any purpose, nor would we instigate or encourage others to do so. Our allies are fully aware of our rejection of torture"*.[62] The Government has maintained this position in the light of allegations relating to Binyam Mohamed discussed above, but has accepted that the current allegations merit police investigation.[63] The Prime Minister has undertaken to make public guidelines on interrogation procedures to be followed by UK intelligence services, with compliance to be monitored by the Intelligence Service Commissioner, but has stopped short of establishing an independent judicial inquiry into such allegations.[64] In relation to extraordinary rendition specifically, the Government has described the existing measures applicable to the granting of permission to rendition flights in the following terms:

> *We would expect the US authorities to seek permission to render detainees via UK territory and airspace, including overseas territories, and we will grant permission only if we are satisfied that the rendition would accord with UK law and our international obligations.*[65]

4.28 It is apparent from the allegations and reports discussed above that this system has failed. The two Diego Garcia rendition flights discussed at paragraph 4.15 of this CP demonstrate that rendition flights are able to use UK territory and airspace apparently without seeking authorisation. Clearly, expecting the US to seek permission for rendition flights does not provide adequate protection against UK involvement.

4.29 In order to legitimise its practice of rendition, the US Government has provided repeated assurances that those rendered are not subject to torture. It has also provided assurances that rendition flights have not used UK territory. The Diego Garcia admissions suggest that the UK cannot rely on such assurances. Nonetheless, the Government has indicated it will continue to accept US assurances in good faith.[66] The Foreign Secretary compiled a list of almost 400 flights, which was submitted to the US State Department on 15 May 2008 for specific assurances that they had not been involved in renditions. No such assurances were given. Furthermore,

[62] Rt Hon David Miliband MP, 'Letter to Andrew Tyrie MP', 5 June 2008, available at www.extraordinaryrendition.org.

[63] Remarks of the Prime Minister, the Rt Hon Gordon Brown MP, to the press on 26 March 2009, available at http://www.independent.co.uk/news/uk/home-news/statement-due-in-torture-row-1654668.html

[64] Rt Hon Gordon Brown MP, 'Detainees Statement', 18 March 2009 at Col 55WS.

[65] Andrew Tyrie WPQ 20 March 2006 [59974]. The government has confirmed that this is a legal requirement and that it derives from *"an aspect of the principle of State sovereignty over territory"*, Andrew Tyrie WPQ 18 April 2006 [61538].

[66] Rt Hon David Miliband MP, 'Terrorist Suspects (Renditions) Statement', 21 February 2008 at Col 553.

the Foreign Secretary has refused to seek assurances in respect of 'circuit flights'[67] notwithstanding the recommendation of the Foreign Affairs Committee (the ***FAC***) that he should do so, based on its finding that there is a legal obligation to prevent flights to or from a rendition using UK airspace.[68] It reiterated this conclusion in its Human Rights Annual Report 2008.[69]

Criticism of the UK Government's Position

4.30 The FAC has criticised reliance on assurances in respect of torture given the conflicting standards adopted by the US and the UK in this area. It has also strongly condemned the inaccurate assurances given to the UK Government in respect of rendition flights using UK territory. It has criticised the Government's lack of transparency on rendition, and called for the publication of further information on the Diego Garcia renditions, the renditions from Iraq to Afghanistan and the historical guidance given to intelligence officers.[70] The ISC has noted that *"[a]lthough the US may take note of UK protests and concerns; this does not appear materially to affect its strategy on rendition."*[71] The Joint Committee on Human Rights has concluded that *"[i]n view of the large number of unanswered questions, we conclude that there is now no other way to restore public confidence in the intelligence services than by setting up an independent inquiry into the numerous allegations about the UK's complicity in torture"*.[72]

4.31 Moreover, a Legal Opinion prepared by Michael Fordham QC and Tom Hickman, and published by the APPG in September 2008[73], suggests, in line with the view of the European Court of Human Rights, that it is improper for the UK Government to rely on US assurances on this issue.

4.32 The UK Government's refusal to address the issue of extraordinary rendition, openly and transparently, has been widely criticised. The European Parliament *"deplore[d] the manner in which the UK Government, as represented by its Minister for Europe, cooperated with the Temporary Committee"*. The Council of Europe cited the UK's acceptance of assurances on Diego

[67] The US provided renewed assurances that referred only to rendition flights that had landed at the UK, and not those that had transited the UK. In an earlier letter to the Foreign Affairs Committee the Foreign Secretary had stated that the Government's purpose in sending the list of flights was: *"to identify whether rendition (i.e. of an individual) through UK territory or airspace in fact occurred"*.

[68] FAC, 'Human Rights Annual Report 2007', paragraph 47.

[69] Foreign Affairs Committee, 'Human Rights Annual Report 2008', 9 August 2009, available at http://www.publications.parliament.uk/pa/cm200809/cmselect/cmfaff/557/ 55702.htm.

[70] FAC, 'Human Rights Annual Report 2008', Conclusions and recommendations.

[71] ISC, 'Report into Rendition', conclusion Y.

[72] JCHR, 'Allegations of UK Complicity in Torture', paragraph 99.

[73] FAC, 'Human Rights Annual Report 2007', 20 July 2008, paragraph 53, available at http://www.publications.parliament.uk/pa/cm200708/cmselect/cmfaff/533/ 53306.htm#a8; Michael Fordham QC et al, 'Joint Legal Opinion in the Matter of the Human Rights Responsibility Arising from Military Detainee Handovers in Iraq', available at www.extraordinaryrendition.org.

Garcia *"without independently or transparently inquiring into the allegations itself, or accounting to the public in a sufficiently thorough manner"*. The Foreign Affairs Committee has criticised the Government's *"policy of obfuscation"* on rendition.[74]

Prosecutions in the United Kingdom

4.33 We examine in more detail at Section 5 the limitations of domestic law as it currently stands. However, we note here that, despite the known instances of UK involvement in rendition and further credible allegations, to date, no UK prosecutions have been brought against any UK or US officials. In response to a request from Liberty, the human rights NGO, the Association of Chief Police Officers asked Chief Constable Michael Todd to examine whether there was a basis under English law for a police inquiry.[75] His response in June 2007 indicated that there was not.

4.34 This UK assessment is in clear contrast to that of other European countries, including Italy and Germany, both of which have initiated prosecutions against officials involved in renditions using their territory. These prosecutions and the applicable law in other key jurisdictions are examined in more detail in Section 7 below.

5. A Summary of the Current Domestic Law

Introduction

5.1 In this part, we provide a summary of the domestic law relating to extraordinary rendition, as it currently stands.

5.2 Certain constituent elements of extraordinary rendition are already substantively criminalised at common law and by statute. These offences apply in the first instance to those directly involved in extraordinary rendition. We discuss the limitations of this at paragraph 5.26 of this CP, before turning to the scope of accessory liability for secondary participants

[74] European Parliament, 'Report on the alleged use of European countries by the CIA for the transportation and illegal detention of prisoners'; Council of Europe, 'Secret detentions and illegal transfers of detainees involving Council of Europe member states: second report', page 16; Foreign Affairs Committee, 'Foreign Policy Aspects of the War against Terrorism', 5 April 2005, paragraph 98, http://www.publications.parliament.uk/ pa/cm200405/cmselect/cmfaff/36/3607.htm#a14.

[75] Letter from Chief Constable Michael Todd to Shami Chakrabarti, available at http://www.liberty-human-rights.org.uk/news-and-events/pdfs/er-acpo-response-june-07.pdf, stating: *"none of the information available contributes to the evidential base to support allegations that offences have been committed on UK territory. The material is put together and draws conclusions on a wholly different basis to that needed for the criminal process here in the UK. Much of the information is circumstantial and without any means of testing or corroborating the claims made. Original sources are either outside UK jurisdiction, anonymous or otherwise unavailable for interview to a standard that would support a case brought in this Country . . . None of the accounts given by those involved include allegations that such operations transited UK soil . . . there are considerable practical difficulties dealing with these matters, in particular, in bringing the facts together with the law/procedure in this area."*

in offences related to extraordinary rendition. We then examine briefly the limited deterrence of rendition offered by the Human Rights Act 1998 and the writ of habeas corpus. We conclude by assessing the weaknesses of the current legal position and the problems of bringing a prosecution, and by briefly outlining how the proposal set out in Section 8 addresses those weaknesses.

5.3 In essence, our domestic law fails to provide for the effective criminalisation, and hence deterrence, of extraordinary rendition activity. This is primarily because those parties that have committed primary offences (being frequently intelligence or military personnel) cannot, in the event, be apprehended. The law on secondary liability (i.e. aiding and abetting) is too uncertain and too rarely applied, even in more obvious cases, to act as an effective (as opposed to theoretical) sanction. Further, English criminal law does not, currently, address corporate liability. Finally, English criminal law does not effectively address the 'turning of a blind eye' to rendition activity when, by its very covert nature, it is an activity in relation to which it is not, in practice, realistic to establish either the necessary acts or the necessary mental state in the absence of a new targeted, specific offence.

Common Law Offences of General Application

5.4 At common law, the offences of kidnapping and false imprisonment will, in the absence of legal authority for such practices, prohibit the extra-judicial apprehension of those subjected to extraordinary rendition and their subsequent detention on board aircraft or other forms of transport that may pass through the UK or an Overseas Territory.

Kidnapping

5.5 Kidnapping is a common law offence which consists of the taking or carrying away of one person by another by force (or fraud[76]) without the consent of the person so taken or carried away and without lawful excuse.[77] For the purposes of this offence, 'taking or carrying away' merely means a deprivation of liberty, coupled with the physical removal of the victim from a place he wishes to be.[78] 'Force' is also broadly construed, relating not merely to physical force, but any conduct which, together with the carrying away of the victim, is such as to override the consent of the victim.[79]

[76] *R v Cort* [2004] 1 Cr App Rep 199.

[77] *R v D* [1984] AC 778.

[78] *R v Wellard* [1978] 3 All ER 161. It is, thus, unnecessary to prove that the kidnapper had carried the victim to the place he intended.

[79] The exercise of a mental or moral power or influence to compel or force another to do something against his will would suffice if it is sufficiently compelling to overcome that person's will: *R v Singh, R v Southward* [1995] 8 Archbold News 3, CA.

Such conduct will, however, be 'lawfully excused' where it is pursuant to a valid power of arrest or court order.[80]

5.6 Consequently, the initial detention of persons then subjected to extraordinary rendition (so-called 'black-bagging')[81] will amount to kidnapping under English law, and where such operations are carried out in the UK, the military, intelligence or other personnel directly involved may be subject to prosecution as principal offenders. We are unaware of any provision of domestic law that would give any such conduct the cloak of lawful excuse.

5.7 The offence of kidnapping is punishable by a fine or imprisonment at the discretion of the court. The sentencing guideline indicates that, in cases involving violence or prolonged detention, a sentence of more than eight years' imprisonment will be appropriate.[82] Consequently, it is likely that kidnapping as part of the process of extraordinary rendition would attract a significant custodial sentence.

False Imprisonment

5.8 A person is guilty of the offence of false imprisonment at common law where he or she unlawfully restrains the victim's freedom of movement from a particular place.[83] 'Restraint' for these purposes is broadly construed, and encompasses the physical restraint of an individual, as well as circumstances in which the victim submits to intimidation or commands.[84] An 'unlawful' restraint simply means restraint without lawful authority.[85]

5.9 The accused must have intended to restrain the victim, or to have been subjectively reckless[86] as to the risk that the victim would be so restrained (i.e. the accused knew there was such a risk, but nonetheless ran that risk).

5.10 Consequently, in the absence of legal authority for their detention, rendered persons that are detained on planes that transit through UK territory are falsely imprisoned on such planes. We are unaware of any provision of English or Welsh law that accords UK or US personnel any law enforcement status that would entitle them to detain persons in this manner. Those military, intelligence or other personnel that are directly involved in such a rendition and secure detainees held on a rendition transport will clearly

[80] *Greaves v Keene* (1879) 4 Cox D 73, *Mee v Cruickshank* (1902) 20 Ex CC 210.
[81] As discussed at paragraph 4.7 of this CP.
[82] *R v Spence and Thomas* (1983) 5 Cr.App.R. (S) 413.
[83] *R v Rahman* (1985) 81 Cr App Rep 349, CA.
[84] *R v Linsberg and Leies* (1905) 69 JP 107, CCC) and *R v James* (1997) Times, 2 October, CA. Indeed, a restraint may consist simply of being prevented from proceeding in a particular direction (2 Co Inst 482 at 589).
[85] As discussed in relation to kidnapping, at paragraph 5.5 of this CP.
[86] *R v James* (1997) Times, 2 October, CA.

have sufficient intent or knowledge to satisfy the mens rea requirement for this offence.

5.11 False imprisonment is punishable by a fine or imprisonment at the discretion of the court, on its determination of the seriousness of the offence. In so determining, the court will have regard to the purpose for which the imprisonment was carried out. It is likely, on this basis, that persons found guilty of false imprisonment in relation to extraordinary rendition would also face a substantial sentence of imprisonment.

Statutory Offences of General Application

5.12 Statutory offences will apply in respect of any violent conduct towards persons subject to extraordinary rendition while in the UK. Thus, persons involved in the renditions process are susceptible to prosecution for assault and battery, actual bodily harm and grievous bodily harm. The principal statutory offences are set out in the Offences Against the Persons Act 1861 (the ***OAPA***).

Battery or Assault Occasioning Actual Bodily Harm

5.13 Battery is a summary offence under Section 39 of the Criminal Justice Act 1988 (the ***CJA 1988***), committed where any person touches or applies unlawful force to another. The level of force required is relatively superficial—minor bruising will suffice.[87] However, where more significant harm is caused, for example extensive bruising, the accused may be charged with assault occasioning actual bodily harm under Section 47 of the OAPA.[88]

5.14 For both offences, a person is guilty of the offence where he intends to inflict unlawful force or is subjectively reckless as to the infliction of unlawful force. It is unnecessary that a person charged with the more serious offence of assault occasioning actual bodily harm intended or foresaw the more serious harm that occurred.

5.15 Consequently, the appropriate UK authorities may prosecute those (including military, intelligence or related personnel) that inflict minor or moderate ill-treatment on any person subjected to extraordinary rendition whilst being held in the United Kingdom or an Overseas Territory (for example to subdue a detainee). Assault occasioning actual bodily harm is punishable by up to five years' imprisonment.

[87] The Charging Standards for the offence state "grazes, scratches, abrasions, minor bruising, swellings, reddening of the skin, superficial cuts, black eye" are sufficient to engage liability.

[88] In Boyea [1992] Crim. LR 574, the Court held that "any hurt or injury calculated to interfere with the health or comfort . . . [provided it is more than] trifling or transient" was sufficient.

Wounding and Grievous Bodily Harm

5.16 Where military, intelligence or other personnel inflict more serious injury to any person subject to extraordinary rendition, they may face prosecution under Sections 20 and 18 of the OAPA that relate to wounding or grievous bodily harm. For the purposes of these offences, 'wounding' merely requires all layers of the skin to be pierced. 'Grievous bodily harm' has been broadly defined in case law as encompassing serious harm, with regard to the totality of injuries inflicted.[89] A person will be guilty of the Section 20 offence where he is merely subjectively reckless as to the risk of inflicting some minor bodily harm. Where a person intends to wound or inflict grievous bodily harm, he will be guilty of the offence under Section 18, which carries a maximum penalty of life imprisonment.

Military Law

5.17 Under English law, members of the Armed Forces do not obtain immunity from the ordinary law applicable to citizens by virtue of their uniformed status.[90] Consequently, UK service personnel that have committed any offences in support of renditions are liable to be prosecuted under any applicable domestic law. In addition they may be guilty of offences under the uniformed services' Disciplinary Codes, as set out in the Naval Discipline Act 1957, Part II of the Army Act 1955 and the Air Force Act 1955.[91] In particular, each Code makes it an offence to act in a manner amounting to *"disgraceful conduct of a cruel, indecent or unnatural kind"*, punishable by up to two years' imprisonment following trial by court-martial.[92] It is also an offence to aid, abet, encourage or assist in the commission of any offence contrary to a service Disciplinary Code.[93]

Aviation Law

5.18 Pursuant to Article 148 of the Air Navigation Order 2005 (as modified)[94] (the ***ANO***), it is a criminal offence, punishable by fine or imprisonment, to contravene certain of the provisions regulating air transport. Article 149 of the ANO makes clear that the terms of the ANO extend to non-UK registered planes when transiting the UK. Whilst the majority of these provisions relate to the observance of proper technical and safety standards,

---

[89] *R* v *Grundy* [1977] Crim. LR 543.

[90] *Burdett v Abbot* (1812) 4 Taunt 401 at 449-450. In addition the Human Rights Act 1998 applies to a member of the armed forces as it applies to a civilian.

[91] As set out in the Naval Discipline Act 1957, Part II of the Army Act 1955 and the Air Force Act 1955.

[92] Section 37 Naval Discipline Act 1957; Section 66 Army Act 1955; and Section 66 Air Force Act 1955.

[93] Section 41 Naval Discipline Act 1957; Section 68A Army Act 1955; and Section 68A Air Force Act 1955.

[94] SI 2005/1970.

particular actions by those operating rendition flights (to the extent that such flights use civil aircraft)[95] could be caught on specific occasions.

5.19 Specifically, pursuant to Article 94 of the ANO, it is an offence for any person with intent to deceive to file or use any certificate, licence, approval, permission, exemption or other document issued or required by the ANO which has been forged, altered, revoked or suspended, or to which that person is not entitled. A person found to violate this provision is liable on indictment to a term of imprisonment of two years, or an unlimited fine, or both.

5.20 In addition, Article 148(5) and Schedule 14, Part A, of the ANO makes it an offence, punishable on summary conviction by a Level 4 fine, to breach the Civil Aviation (Rules of the Air) Regulations 2007 (the ***Rules of the Air***).[96] The Rules of the Air govern, inter alia, the proper filing of flight plans. Consequently it is an offence under the ANO to file false flight plan information.

5.21 To the extent that those persons operating rendition flights provide false information to mask their activities, they will fall foul of the air transport regulatory framework, and face enforcement action by the Civil Aviation Authority (the ***CAA***). However, it is apparent that the sanctions available are weak, and the CAA would face significant difficulties in collecting satisfactory evidence of infringing conduct on the part of persons operating rendition flights through UK territory and then prosecuting such persons. Moreover, it is not clear that a rendition flight would necessarily violate these provions. The deterrent value and effect of these regulatory offences, has not been, and is not, sufficient to deter rendition.

Torture

5.22 Individual criminal liability for the offence of torture is provided for under the CJA 1988, which gives effect to the prohibition on torture set out in the United Nations Convention Against Torture and Other Cruel, Inhuman or Degrading Treatment or Punishment (the *Torture Convention).*

[95] The Marty Report observes that rendition flights operated by the CIA have used civilian aircraft (see the individual case studies contained in Section 3 of the Explanatory Memorandum to the 2006 draft report, which refer, in particular, to "rendition planes" designated N313P and N379P, which were privately owned). It has also been alleged that certain rendition planes were chartered from the US company Jeppesen International Trip Planning (see Jane Mayer, 'The CIA's Travel Agent', The New Yorker, 30 October 2006 (http://www.newyorker.com/archive/2006/10/30/061030ta_talk mayer) and Jeppesen DataPlan Inc. case noted at footnote 33, above). Pursuant to the Chicago Convention (see paragraph 6.18 below), "State" as opposed to "civil" aircraft require prior authorisation to overfly a State party to the Convention and must abide by the terms of such authorisation. While the Convention makes clear that it is the nature of the flight that is determinative of whether it enjoys State or civil status it has been argued that the use of privately chartered plans is part of a strategy to ensure that such flights are deemed "civil" and as such benefit from fewer overflight restrictions. The corollary of this is that such flights should be considered civil for the purposes of the ANO.

[96] SI 2007/734.

The substantive obligations imposed on the UK by the Torture Convention are discussed in paragraphs 6.4 to 6.6 of this CP.

5.23 Section 134 of the CJA 1988 provides that it is an offence for a public official intentionally to inflict severe pain or suffering on another in the performance or purported performance of his official duties or for any other person to inflict such pain with the consent or acquiescence of a public official. The act of torture must, therefore, be intentional and covers treatment inflicted for the purpose of obtaining information or a confession. For these purposes, the term 'public official' is construed relatively broadly, and will include persons acting in a non-private capacity, e.g. as a de facto organ of a State or any other authority-wielding entity.[97] The offence under the CJA 1988 is of universal jurisdiction, thus any act amounting to torture committed anywhere may be prosecuted by UK authorities. The offence is punishable by a maximum of life imprisonment.

5.24 The focus of the Section 134 offence is, thus, the substantive act of torture. Consequently, any prosecution under the CJA 1988 would most likely be directed at any ill-treatment that a rendered person is subjected when interrogated at the end of the rendition process.[98]

5.25 We note, however, that the process of extraordinary rendition in and of itself arguably amounts to conduct theoretically contrary to the Torture Convention, as recognised by the Eminent Jurists Panel,[99] and as such could conceivably be prosecuted directly under the CJA 1988, although no such prosecution has yet been attempted.[100] It is also possible that persons who provide support or clearance to rendition flights or other rendition transports may be liable as accessories to the Section 134 offence. The possibility of a successful prosecution on this basis is discussed in more detail below.

Analysis of the Principal Offences

5.26 The foregoing survey of applicable offences under English law demonstrates that specific aspects of the process of extraordinary rendition,

[97] *Prosecutor v Furund'ija* (ICTY) (10 December 1998/IT-95-17/1-T).

[98] We note that the only prosecution as yet undertaken for the Section 134 offence targeted the most direct and egregious form of the systematic and physical mistreatment of individuals (see *R* v *Zardad* (2005) (unreported)).

[99] EJP Report at Chapter 4, Section 3.1, page 81.

[100] This point is discussed in more detail at paragraphs 6.4-6.6 of this CP. The Attorney General, Baroness Scotland QC, in concert with the Director of Public Prosecutions, Keir Starmer QC, has invited the Commissioner of the Metropolitan Police to investigate the allegations made in the case of Binyam Mohamed (as discussed at paragraph 4.18 above). Baroness Scotland had previously indicated that the role of British officials in facilitating conduct linked to torture would form part of any investigation she may subsequently invite the police to initiate (see letter of Baroness Scotland to the Rt. Hon. Andrew Dismore MP, Chairman of the Joint Committee on Human Rights relating to the Binyam Mohamed case, dated 12 February 2009, and available at http://www.attorneygeneral.gov.uk/attachments/Attorney%20General%20letter%20re%20Binyam%20Mohamed%20case.pdf(retrieved on 1 June 2009).

from initial detention through to the alleged mistreatment of interrogated persons, are, arguably, substantively criminalised. However, the offences discussed in paragraphs 5.4 to 5.25 apply only to those who are directly involved as principals in the elements of extraordinary rendition identified. The involvement of UK citizens (whether members of the Armed Forces, Security Services or otherwise) and UK territory is thought to have largely been, to the extent that information is available, a less direct involvement in the apprehension, detention and physical mistreatment of those subjected to extraordinary rendition. However, as discussed in Section 4 of this CP, UK territory has been used for the transit of persons to detention and for rendition 'circuit flights'. Consequently, conduct on UK territory, and possibly the conduct of UK nationals, has supported the passage of rendition transports through the United Kingdom or an Overseas Territory. The provision of assistance to such flights will be governed by principles of accessory liability but it is ill-adapted to prosecutions for extraordinary rendition.

Complicity in the Offence

5.27 It is unlawful to aid, abet, counsel or procure the commission of a criminal offence.[101] These terms are given their ordinary meaning and so will cover circumstances in which a person (the ***accessory***) assists in or encourages the commission of a crime by the offender (the ***principal***).[102] An accessory that is proven to have aided or abetted an offence may be tried as a principal offender, and faces the same penalties as the principal offender. Thus, as described above, an accessory to a rendition transport may face penalties up to and including life imprisonment.

Accessory Liability—the Conduct Element

5.28 A non-technical approach should be taken in determining what conduct engages accessory liability. Thus 'assistance' as it is generally understood will be sufficient to engage accessory liability. Although the commission of the principal offence must be proved, it is not necessary to demonstrate that the principal would not have committed the offence but for the assistance given by the accessory.[103] It is not necessary, thus, that the assistance given is significant, nor does the principal have to be aware of the assistance.

5.29 Consequently, it is theoretically conceivable that the provision of technical support, refuelling and any necessary clearances for rendition

[101] Section 8 Accessories and Abettors Act 1861 in relation to indictable offences, and Section 44 Magistrates' Courts Act 1980 in relation to summary offences.
[102] A-G's Reference (No 1 of 1975) [1975] QB 773.
[103] *A-G v Able* [1984] 1 QB 795 per Woolf J.

flights or other transports that transit the UK would amount to assistance for the substantive offences committed by the principal perpetrators of a rendition (i.e. the military or intelligence personnel that participate in kidnap, false imprisonment or physical mistreatment as discussed above). It is not necessary that the principal offenders on board the plane know that they have received such assistance, or from whom that assistance emanates. However, the use of accessory liability in such circumstances is problematic and there has been no tradition of seeking to apply it in cases analogous to extraordinary rendition.

Accessory Liability—the Mental Element

5.30 For an accessory to be convicted it must be proved that his assistance was done:

(a) intentionally, in the sense that he did it deliberately (and not accidentally), knowing that his act was capable of encouraging the commission of the principal offence; and

(b) with intent to assist the principal offender (and not to obstruct or hinder him).[104]

5.31 In addition, an accessory cannot be convicted unless he was aware of all the essential circumstances which make the principal offence a crime, which is to be assessed on the evidence in the case.[105] Where the defendant is wilfully blind to the circumstances, he will be judged as having knowledge.[106] Lastly, a secondary party must be proved to have foreseen as a real possibility that the principal is acting, or may act, with the mental element required for the principal offence.[107]

5.32 It is not necessary, then, that the principal offender and the accessory have a shared intention or criminal plan as to rendition.[108] It is technically possible that any person providing, say, airside services to a plane, knowing that rendered persons are held on that plane and that those persons have been ill-treated or face ill-treatment, could be guilty as an accessory.

Circuit Flights—Accessory Liability and Universal Jurisdiction Under Section 134 CJA 1988

5.33 While domestic judicial interpretation of the Section 134 offence is limited, Article 4 and 5 of the Torture Convention clearly establish that

[104] *R v Bryce* [2004] 2 Cr App Rep 592, CA.
[105] *Johnson* v *Youden* [1950] 1 KB 544. It is however not necessary that the accessory knows as a matter of law that the principal offence is a crime.
[106] *R v Griffiths* (1974) 60 Cr App Rep 14 at 18.
[107] R v Powell, R v English [1999] 1 AC 1.
[108] A-G's Reference (No 1 of 1975) [1975] QB 773.

universal jurisdiction for complicity in torture was intended at the international level.[109]

5.34 Consequently, providing any assistance to extraordinary rendition that involves transit through the UK of persons who may be subject to mistreatment at the hands of foreign nationals outside of the UK could be prosecutable here. It is also theoretically conceivable that providing such assistance to an empty plane, which is used to subsequently transport a rendered person to a site where that person is tortured, may similarly engage such accessory liability on an identical basis to that described in paragraphs 5.27 to 5.32 above (i.e. where that assistance enabled the torture to occur and where the defendant intends to assist torture).

Analysis of the Scope of Accessory Liability

5.35 Accessory liability is essentially parasitic. It requires the facts amounting to the principal offence to be demonstrated (though it does not actually require someone to be prosecuted for that offence). Thus, to be convicted as an accessory, it must be demonstrated that the elements of rendition amounting to kidnap, false imprisonment, offences against the person or torture existed, and that the accessory had knowledge of those circumstances.

5.36 This clearly presents a significant evidential hurdle to a successful prosecution. By their very nature, rendition flights operate clandestinely. It is unlikely that persons operating UK transport facilities know of the purpose of such flights. Moreover, it will likely only be in the most egregious of cases (for example where a detainee tries to escape a flight) that airside personnel providing simple refuelling, maintenance and hangaring to the exterior of a plane would become sufficiently aware of the circumstances surrounding the principal offence to warrant the imposition of accessory liability.

5.37 These difficulties are manifest in respect of circuit flights. In order for accessory liability to be established, it would be necessary to establish that, subsequent to the overflight of an empty plane, a rendered individual was then detained and transferred for torture. This will be very difficult given the lack of specific evidence, even in respect of planes carrying persons. In addition, the requirement that the person giving the assistance intended that someone be subjected to ill-treatment is a high threshold and would effectively capture only those persons who were intimately involved in the rendition process with sufficient knowledge that the purpose of the flight in question was to torture. This would not, then, cover assistance in the form of refuelling, maintenance and hangaring that is given by employees

[109] As to which, see paragraphs 6.4-6.6 of this CP.

at aerodromes in the absence of knowledge of the true purpose of such flights, including the treatment that any captive would receive.[110]

5.38 At common law, a legal person may incur secondary liability where he, she or it has a legal duty to act or is entitled to exercise control over or prevent the actions of the principal offender, but fails to do so.[111] The latter has applied to the owner of a motor vehicle whose car may have been driven dangerously by a fellow traveller,[112] a licensee that allowed customers to drink outside of licensed hours[113] and, most recently, to a company manager that failed to prevent employees being racially harassed.[114]

5.39 These extensions of accessory liability could theoretically inculpate those in positions of responsibility or seniority at airports, aerodromes and logistics suppliers, rather than mere employees. Liability for omissions, though generally treated negatively in English law, is justified in respect of those with special responsibilities that are in a position to prevent extraordinary rendition.

5.40 However, the scope of any extensions is extremely uncertain and there is no established line of precedent for such extension. The examples that have been established to date are based on particular and clear facts.[115] Given the substantial practical problems involved in the rendition area, there is no credible basis for suggesting that accessory liability provides a control on extraordinary rendition processes generally or that it is capable of deterring behaviour by those in a position of control over transport facilities.

Corporate Liability

5.41 It is possible to extend criminal liability to companies for acts committed by employees acting in the course of their employment. However corporate liability cannot arise where imprisonment is the only sanction. Consequently, corporate liability is not available for the most serious offences discussed above (wounding or grievous bodily harm with intent and torture). Moreover, as a company can only act through its employees, a criminal prosecution against a company will only proceed successfully,

[110] Note that the proposal in this CP does not criminalise innocent behaviour by people involved in such activities.

[111] *Russell v Russell* (1987) 85 Cr App R 388 at 397 per Lord Lane CJ, referring to the responsibility of parents in relation to children. Academic authorities suggest that the principle may extend to employment cases, where, for example, a security guard has deliberately omitted to lock a door, enabling burglars to enter, and where a store detective has deliberately ignored thefts by customers (Simester and Sullivan, *Criminal Law Theory and Doctrine* (2nd ed. 2003) at page 204).

[112] *Du Cros v Lambourne* [1907] 1 KB 40.

[113] *Tuck v Robson* [1970] 1 WLR 741.

[114] *R v Gaunt* [2004] 2 Cr App R 37.

[115] The Law Commission has stated "the ambit of the exception is unclear and it is questionable whether it represents a general principle." (Law Commission, Participation in Crime, Law Com No. 305, at paragraph 2.29).

in practice, where the requisite conduct was carried out by an employee of sufficient seniority to be identified as a directing mind of the company.[116] While there have been strong judicial statements supporting a widening of this position, so that a company may be liable for the acts of more junior employees, it is nonetheless likely that the involvement of senior management is required.[117] This may capture UK companies in the unlikely case that they have entered into very specific agreements to provide material support to rendition flights, where those agreements were concluded by those of sufficient authority to represent the company.[118] However, it is unlikely that such senior management would be involved in more general support roles in relation to rendition flights. Consequently, the impact of corporate liability under existing law appears limited.

Prospects for Prosecution

5.42 While individuals committing acts forming part of the process of extraordinary rendition could theoretically be prosecuted as principal offenders or accessories for a range of offences, it is highly unlikely that such prosecutions will be pursued. The Code for Crown Prosecutors stipulates that a prosecution should only be brought where the evidence is such that there is a real likelihood of securing a conviction.[119] Given that the principal offenders are likely to be foreign military, paramilitary or intelligence personnel,[120] the prospects of identifying such persons and securing their presence for investigation and subsequent arrest and trial must be viewed as slender.[121] In the absence of specific information on particular rendition transports, it is unlikely that the CPS will initiate such a prosecution. The position is particularly stark in respect of accessory liability for circuit flights. The strict requirements of knowledge and intention would require convincing evidence to be presented before personnel could be prosecuted. As the Association of Chief Police Officers has made clear, the direct and specific evidence currently available in respect

---

[116] Tesco Supermarkets Ltd v Nattrass [1971] 2 All ER 127.

[117] Meridian Global Funds Management Asia Ltd v Securities Commission [1995] 3 All ER 918.

[118] We are, however, unaware of any such agreements, which are most likely to have been concluded in secret.

[119] Paragraph 5.2 of the CPS Code.

[120] The Marty Report makes clear that rendition flights are likely to have been operated by CIA personnel. In the case of Abu Omar, the Milanese court issued arrest warrants for 26 US nationals (including a number of alleged CIA agents) for his alleged rendition on 17 February 2003.

[121] The APPG notes, in this regard, the fact that of the above-mentioned 26 US nationals whose arrest was ordered in the Abu Omar case, none have been brought before the Italian authorities. It should also be noted that in limited circumstances a member of the Intelligence Services may be immune from prosecution for criminal or civil offences under Section 7 of the Intelligence Services Act 1994 (the ***ISA** 1994)*. In particular, he will not be liable for an act done outside the British Islands if his act was authorised by the Secretary of State. Authorisations will only apply to acts that are *"necessary for the proper discharge of a function of the Intelligence Service or GCHQ"* (section 7(3) ISA 1994). An authorisation may then cover enhanced interrogation techniques that could amount to cruel, inhuman or degrading treatment, as long as it is carried out outside the British Islands.

of prosecution under the existing offences in cases of rendition involving the UK falls far below the required standard.[122]

5.43 It is the view of the APPG that English criminal law, as it currently stands, is ineffective to penalise the practice of extraordinary rendition involving the UK or any Overseas Territory. The common law extension of accessory liability to omissions where persons have a legal duty to act or are entitled to exercise control over other persons does not create sufficient pressure on those controlling transport facilities to ensure that they are not used to facilitate extraordinary rendition. The uncertain scope of this doctrine provides neither sufficient clarity for the conduct of business, nor sufficiently rigorous protection for those who may be subjected to processes in flagrant violation of domestic and international laws. In the absence of any realistic prospect of prosecution, let alone conviction, the criminal law fails to operate as an adequate deterrent for involvement in extraordinary rendition. The APPG considers that, to be effective, the legal framework should require those operating transport facilities to act proactively with greater diligence to ensure their facilities are not used to provide logistical or other support to rendition transports.

Other Domestic Avenues of Redress—Human Rights Act 1998 and Habeas Corpus

5.44 Section 6 of the Human Rights Act 1998 (the ***HRA***) prohibits public authorities from acting in a manner that is incompatible with those rights under the ECHR that are scheduled to the HRA.[123] A 'public authority' is defined as an entity whose functions are *"of a public nature"*,[124] and as such encompasses military and government personnel. In addition, the HRA requires domestic courts to have regard to the principles and case law of the European Court of Human Rights in determining cases that involve a Convention right.

5.45 We discuss at Sections 6.3-6.11 of this CP certain of the Convention rights that are affected by extraordinary rendition. In particular, Articles 2 (the right to life), 3 (freedom from torture and other cruel, inhuman or degrading treatment) and 5 (freedom from unlawful deprivation of liberty) are likely to be engaged. Under the HRA framework, such rights are directly applicable in domestic law. Consequently, if military or other governmental personnel act in a manner that infringes any such rights through participation in extraordinary rendition, a domestic court may provide relief (in the form of a court order to restrain such conduct, or, in certain cases,

[122] As discussed at paragraph 4.33 of this CP.
[123] Articles 2-12 and 14-18 of the ECHR, Articles 1-3 of the First Protocol to the ECHR, and the Sixth Protocol to the ECHR.
[124] Section 6(3)(b) HRA.

an award of damages). Moreover, consistent with the jurisprudence of the European Court on the ambit of the Convention, the HRA will apply to the conduct of UK military or other governmental personnel abroad, where the territory in question is within the jurisdiction of the UK. Consequently the activities of military or governmental personnel at, for example, UK military bases abroad, are susceptible to challenge on HRA grounds.[125]

5.46 However, the HRA does not impose criminal liability on those that may act inconsistently with Convention rights: it only gives rise to civil compensation or restraint. Moreover, given the extra-legal nature of extraordinary rendition, it is very unlikely that persons with sufficient standing will have the opportunity to challenge the process on HRA grounds through judicial review. In addition, the APPG views the availability of damages as providing only limited ex post censure of actions that can be readily established. Accordingly, its deterrent value must be viewed as limited.

5.47 The common law writ of habeas corpus ad subjiciendum is an ancient remedy available in all cases of wrongful deprivation of personal liberty to secure the release of any such person unlawfully detained. The protection of the writ extends not only to subjects of the Crown, but to all persons within the United Kingdom under the protection of the Crown and entitled to resort to the courts to secure their rights, even where they are alien enemies. As such the writ would be available to persons temporarily resident in the United Kingdom that have been subject to extraordinary rendition, or persons that are held in private detention in the United Kingdom or its territory. Consequently persons that are alleged to be detained in UK territory at Diego Garcia may be entitled to the protection of the writ. However, it does not apply to protect people who were subject to extraordinary rendition within the UK but are then held outside the jurisdiction of the UK courts.

5.48 Section 11 of the Habeas Corpus Act 1679, provides that UK subjects that are transferred outside of the United Kingdom to be illegally imprisoned will nonetheless be able to bring a claim of false imprisonment before the UK courts against all or any person or persons that authorised such transfer or advised, aided or abetted any such transportation. Moreover, the persons that knowingly unlawfully detain, imprison or transport such persons, or authorise, advise, aid or assist such conduct, shall be subject to a maximum of life imprisonment.[126] This is an anti-avoidance provision

[125] R (Al-Skeini) v Secretary of State for Defence [2008] 1 AC 153 and R (Al-Jedda) v Secretary of State for Defence [2008] 1 AC 332 relating to UK military bases in Iraq, and most recently R (on the application of Al-Saadoon and another) v Secretary of State for Defence [2008] EWHC 3098 (Admin) where it was held that the claimants in an HRA claim were within the jurisdiction of the United Kingdom for the purposes of the HRA, though on the facts no breach was found.

[126] Criminal Law Act 1967, Sections 10(2), 13(2) and Schedule 3 Part III and Schedule 4, Part III.

aimed against conduct that may take persons outside the protection of the writ of habeas corpus.[127]

5.49 The APPG does not consider that this (albeit ancient and noble) provision is appropriate to control extraordinary rendition in the modern world. In particular:

(a) the Section 11 offence appears limited to UK 'subjects' that *"now or hereafter shall be an inhabitant or resident"* of England and Wales. Whilst Section 11 could apply to UK nationals or residents, it is unlikely that it would extend to persons with no connection to the UK that are merely transited through UK territory or to people who were in the UK on a more temporary basis but 'kidnapped' and rendered from the UK;

(b) more importantly, the parts of the section 11 offence which are more relevant to the issues arising in extraordinary rendition are essentially secondary 'aiding or abetting' offences, albeit statutorily defined. Thus, it is subject to the same deficiencies as outlined above in relation to secondary offences and, arguably, at least, requires proof of the underlying primary offence;

(c) the Section 11 offence does not deal with either circuit flights, or the wider 'failure prevent' issues which are addressed in the proposal and which the APPG considers are necessary to create a comprehensive and effective UK criminalisation of the practice;

(d) the mental element is the relatively strict one of 'knowing' which would be too limiting to give rise to an effective prohibition;

(e) so far as can be identified, the provision has never been used (and certainly not in modern times) and there is room for a more defined and focussed provision that takes account of the developments in the law over the past 330 years;

(f) the extra-legal and secret nature of detention under the process of extraordinary rendition would inhibit in practice successful recourse to the court under this provision.

The Draft Legislative Proposal

5.50 The APPG considers that its legislative proposal, set forth in Section 8, remedies the key weaknesses in English criminal law outlined above.

(a) By establishing a specific primary offence that criminalises the use of transport facilities for the transfer of persons without lawful

[127] It seems that Section 11 was originally designed to prevent Charles II from sending political opponents to Scotland to be tortured (see P.R. Chandler, *Praemunire and the Habeas Corpus Act,* (1923) Columbia LR 273 at 276).

excuse (and which thus focuses on extraordinary rendition itself), the proposal clearly addresses the conduct that forms the core of extraordinary rendition, insofar as that process involves the UK or its Overseas Territories. As such, the APPG's view is that this proposal provides for the first time a proper deterrent to extraordinary rendition.

(b) By clearly prohibiting the facilitation of extraordinary rendition, the proposal avoids the difficulties of relying on the theoretical and unclear possible extension of accessory liability to prosecute those that have provided support to extraordinary rendition. It provides clear definitions of criminal behaviour and avoids the current unsatisfactory position of a low but uncertain risk of being prosecuted as an accessory when the necessary acts and mental state are difficult to establish and where there will, almost certainly, be no prosecution for the primary offence. In addition, the creation of a specific offence relating to circuit flights avoids reliance on the limited scope of accessory liability in relation to the statutory offence of torture under the CJA 1988.

(c) The imposition of liability on those who manage or control transport facilities, subject to various defences, places the common law extension of accessory liability for certain omissions on a clear statutory basis. This strengthens the regulation of persons and organisations that may find themselves in a position to support extraordinary rendition. As such it will provide a more practical bar to extraordinary rendition than the current domestic legal framework.

8. The Proposal

Introduction

8.1 The preceding sections have shown that:

(a) UK transport facilities have been used by rendition flights;

(b) although certain acts, including holding captives in planes on UK soil, are criminal offences under English law, the existing criminal law is inadequate in relation to the range of activities associated with extraordinary rendition in the 21st century;

(c) in any event, there have been no prosecutions in the UK (although there are ongoing criminal prosecutions related to extraordinary rendition in Italy, Germany and Spain), in part because the evidential requirements for the current criminal offences are difficult to meet in the circumstances of extraordinary rendition;

(d) the position under our domestic law is consistent with the position taken across European and common law States: there is no express prohibition on extraordinary rendition; criminal law prohibitions attach to elements of the extraordinary rendition process; there is overreliance on narrow accessory liability to deter the facilitation of this process;

(e) reliance on international standards, subject to idiosyncratic and restrictive interpretations in key States, have had little effect in curtailing extraordinary rendition;

(f) UK government policy is stated to be against extraordinary rendition flights;

(g) there is both:

(i) a gap in the UK criminal structure in that there has been a failure to prosecute, or to provide the tools to prosecute, behaviour that has occurred, which is abhorrent and which needs to be remedied; and also

(ii) the possibility for the UK to lead countries in taking a clear public stand against extraordinary rendition by the adoption of focussed criminal legislation which would seek properly to criminalise such behaviour.

8.2 Accordingly, we propose an extension to the current criminal law to criminalise certain actions forming an essential part of extraordinary rendition activities, insofar as they take place within the UK or its Overseas Territories. This would be achieved, as set out in more detail below, by four sets of measures which we propose:

(a) a primary offence of using transport facilities in the UK or any of its Overseas Territories, for the purpose of transferring an individual, without his or her consent, to or from the UK (or any Overseas Territory) from or to another State, without lawful excuse.

(b) it would also be an offence for a person to facilitate another person in carrying out the primary offence. Specifically, this offence would target the facilitation of the transfer of an individual, without his or her consent, to or from the UK (or any Overseas Territory) from or to another State, without lawful excuse. The formulation of a facilitation offence, by way of primary legislation, would help obviate some of the evidential difficulties that exist in relation to accessory liability.

(c) since, for the control of extraordinary rendition to be effective, criminal liability should also be extended to persons controlling transport facilities that are used for the purpose of extraordinary rendition, we propose that any legislation in this field should create a new offence of failing to prevent the transfer of an individual, without his consent, to or from the UK (or any Overseas Territory) from or to another State without lawful excuse. We propose that liability for such an offence should attach to any person, whether an individual or a body corporate, which has the 'management or control of transport facilities'.

(d) Finally, there should be a specific extension of this liability to so-called 'circuit flights' where UK facilities are used in a secondary way to support extraordinary rendition between third countries.

A preliminary draft of the legislation proposed to establish these offences is contained in Annex 1 to this CP. This draft is indicative only and the APPG welcomes comments on its terms.

8.3 This proposal does not address all the acts or events associated with extraordinary rendition, as discussed in Section 3 of this CP. In particular, the following aspects of extraordinary rendition are not captured by the proposal:

- the conduct of extraordinary rendition operations globally that do not involve the use of transport facilities in the UK or any Overseas Territory (as with the transfer of detainees from UK to US custody in Iraq, those detainees then being subject to later rendition, of the type recently admitted to by the Defence Secretary);
- the facilitation of extraordinary rendition by the provision of intelligence to third States (as in the Binyam Mohamed case); or
- the participation of UK intelligence or other personnel in the interrogation of detainees previously subject to extraordinary rendition and thus detained unlawfully.

8.4 The APPG also regards these practices as abhorrent. However, some of these acts (particularly the facilitation of rendition and participation in interrogations) are likely already substantively addressed by the UK's obligations under the Torture Convention (discussed at paragraphs 6.4-6.6 above) and the domestic offence of torture under Section 134 of the CJA 1988 (as discussed at paragraphs 5.22-5.25 above)—depending on their facts. In some cases, for example in connection with the case of Binyam Mohamed, they are currently the subject of criminal investigation by the authorities. The APPG is wary of creating new offences that serve to duplicate existing prohibitions where it is better enforcement, rather than new legislation, that is required. Accordingly, the proposal, as currently cast in the CP, represents a focussed step to deter extraordinary rendition, insofar as that process is likely to involve the UK or its Overseas Territories, in a way that English law can effectively control. It is our intention to create a criminal framework that targets the essence of rendition activity, itself, involving the UK that is not otherwise effectively addressed. Our proposal does so in a fashion that will provide clarity to those potentially involved; that will effectively deter future involvement and which is readily prosecutable. It may, however, be necessary to give further consideration to behaviour not caught by the proposal, as discussed above, in the light of further experience.

8.5 **We would welcome consultees' views on whether the criminal law should, nevertheless, be extended to criminalise certain actions usually connected with extraordinary rendition activities, either insofar as they take place within the UK or the Overseas Territories or, potentially overseas, provided that there is a sufficient connection with the UK, or, indeed, on a universal jurisdiction basis. If so, should such an extension be part of this proposal or a separate exercise?**

8.6 We would also welcome consultees' views on whether the scope of the proposal, in directly targeting conduct related to extraordinary rendition through the UK and Overseas Territories, is appropriate, or whether it should be extended to cover other geographical areas.

8.7 We would also welcome consultees' views on whether administrative changes, such as the introduction of a Code of Conduct, could achieve an equally effective framework.

The Alternative Approach

8.8 We considered, but rejected, an alternative approach. This was to use a discrete amendment to Sections 4 and 5 of the Asylum and Immigration (Treatment of Claims, etc.) Act 2004 (the ***2004 Act)*** to address the issues arising from extraordinary rendition

8.9 Section 4(1) of the 2004 Act provides that a person commits the offence of trafficking people for exploitation where he arranges or facilitates the arrival into the UK of an individual, whom he intends to exploit within the UK or elsewhere (Section 4(1)(a)), or where he believes that another person is likely to exploit the individual in the UK or elsewhere (Section 4(1)(b)). Sections 4(2) and 4(3) of the 2004 Act replicate this offence in relation to assisting or facilitating transit to another part of the UK, or exit from the UK.

8.10 As of 31 January 2008, the Act has been widened to include entry, in addition to arrival, into the UK to capture conduct where there is an argument that those being trafficked have not formally arrived in the UK for immigration purposes. Section 4(4) provides that a person is *"exploited"* for the purposes of this offence if, among other criteria, he is the victim of behaviour that contravenes Article 4 of the ECHR concerning slavery and forced labour.

8.11 The alternative considered was to extend the definition of exploitation in Section 4(4) to cover conduct that is contrary to Articles 2 and 3 of the ECHR (the right to life and the right to freedom from torture, respectively).

8.12 Although this was attractive in terms of requiring very limited amendments, it was felt unsatisfactory in that:

(a) it would be a considerable extension of the scope of the 2004 Act and might be said to be inappropriate in that respect;

(b) critically, substantively, it would require the prosecution to prove that the defendant intended that an individual would be subject to treatment contrary to the right to life and the right to freedom from torture. This was thought likely to present real problems of evidence and definition for a criminal offence; and

(c) we felt that the scope of the offence was too narrow, in that it would not criminalise behaviour that was directly supportive of rendition flights (or not do so in a way that was likely to be capable of being effectively used by the criminal authorities, given the problems of prosecuting people for accessory liability). It was also felt that it did not make a sufficiently strong public statement, or create a sufficiently powerful prohibition to constitute a firm statement by the UK that it was against, and criminalising, extraordinary rendition activity.

8.13 **We invite the views of consultees as to whether the use of a discrete amendment to Sections 4 and 5 of the Asylum and Immigration (Treatment of Claims, etc.) Act 2004 would be an appropriate way to criminalise extraordinary rendition.**

The Proposal

8.14 Accordingly, the proposal on which we seek consultation is that outlined at paragraph 8.2 of this CP. The reasoning is summarised below to assist in the consultation process.

8.15 The primary offence would be:

> *using transport facilities in the United Kingdom or any of its Overseas Territories, for the purpose of transferring an individual, without his or her consent, to or from the United Kingdom (or any Overseas Territory) from or to another State, without lawful excuse.*

8.16 Any person, whether an individual or a body corporate, using transport facilities in this way would be exposed to liability.

The Actus Reus of the Use of Transport Facilities Offence

8.17 *Use of transport facilities*—'Transport facilities' would be defined in the legislation in a very broad manner, encompassing all vehicles, vessels and craft, all transport installations, airports, ports, ground transport terminals and all ancillary facilities, including all facilities for refuelling, maintenance, and storage. 'Use' would be left undefined, on the basis that it is not needed and could be applied widely so that any substantive use whatsoever should be covered.

8.18 *In the UK or any Overseas Territory*—The intention here would not be that the UK should legislate for its Overseas Territories, but that it should extend criminal jurisdiction in the UK over acts of extraordinary rendition carried out in Overseas Territories. This would mean that the use of facilities in, for example, Diego Garcia for the purposes of extraordinary rendition could be charged as an offence in any jurisdiction within the UK. Although there does not appear to be a specific precedent for this in English criminal law, a number of criminal statutes assert the criminal jurisdiction of the UK on an extraterritorial basis and there seems to be no theoretical reason why criminal liability should not be extended in this way.

8.19 *For the purposes of transferring an individual*—The primary focus of the offence would be to criminalise the specific acts whereby an individual is transferred. However, the offence would be broad enough to encompass acts preparatory or ancillary to the rendition itself.

8.20 *Without consent*—While the law in relation to the absence or presence of consent is extensive, the question of consent is capable of erecting a substantial obstacle to prosecution. Consequently, we propose that a provision be included to the effect that the absence of consent will be presumed in certain circumstances. These would include the omission of a passenger from the vessel's official manifest or the non-presentation of an individual's documentation in connection with a particular journey.

8.21 *To or from the UK or any Overseas Territory*—It will be necessary for the purposes of this offence that the individual is transited through the UK.

8.22 *From or to another State*—It will not be necessary for the purpose of establishing this element of the actus reus to show that the individual has been transferred from or to any particular jurisdiction. It will be sufficient to show that he or she has been brought from, or taken outside of, the UK or the relevant Overseas Territory.

8.23 *Without lawful excuse*—This requirement is critical. The essence of the proposal is that all forced transit that is not conducted under recognised legal procedures that are capable of review and independent decision (such as extradition) should be illegal. The purpose of this criterion is to establish that any 'extraordinary' rendition other than by way of lawful extradition, deportation, prisoner transfer or removal direction (each of these forms of transfer being appropriately defined in the legislation) is covered by this offence, but that the offence does not extend to what might be termed 'judicially-authorised rendition'. We have consciously adopted the term *"without lawful excuse"* so that the proposed offence is linked to the judicially developed concept that conduct be without lawful excuse as required in the common law offences of kidnap and false imprisonment, discussed at paragraphs 5.5-5.7 above. In this way, the APPG considers that the offence will capture conduct that falls outside of due process of law, but will benefit from developed case law for kidnap and false imprisonment, and so obviate difficulties relating to whether the transfer or conduct in question has a legitimate aim (for example the emergency transfer of sedated persons for medical treatment, or the exercise of reasonable parental discipline in transferring a difficult child). By importing this standard from the law relating to kidnap and false imprisonment, it is the APPG's hope that the Court will be able to adopt a reasoned approach in assessing individual cases before it with regard to established authority.[128] Moreover, the APPG notes that this requirement mirrors in tone the defence of "lawful authority, justification or excuse" that exists in respect of the domestic offence of torture.[129] The APPG is aware that this standard leaves open the possibility of overbroad claims of "lawful excuse" on the part of persons that may claim they are acting under the colour of explicit or tacit governmental acquiescence or instruction. The APPG considers that this can be judicially controlled by placing the onus on defendants to establish the basis for a claim of lawful excuse,[130] with regard to the approach taken to kidnapping and false imprisonment. However, the APPG would welcome consultees' views on this point.

8.24 We have also considered, in this regard, whether it is necessary to include, as a constituent element in the offence, that the individual is being transferred for the purposes of or in connection with his interrogation, detention or trial in another jurisdiction (or that of any other person). However, it is thought that it is unnecessary to add to the complexity of the offence in this way. Such an additional hurdle would present a considerable obstacle to prosecution, and would, in any event, operate as a distraction from the principal intent of the proposed offence i.e. that any extraordinary rendition of an individual which involves the UK should give rise to criminal liability. Such an additional requirement would take the offence back into the territory of the alternative discussed above.

---

[128] See in this regard *R v D* [1984] AC 778, setting out the criteria for the common-law offence of kidnap (discussed at paragraph 5.5 *et seq.* above), *R* v *Rahman* (1985) 81 Cr. App. R. 349 and *R* v *Faraj* [2007] 2 Cr. App. R. 25. It would appear from discussion in these cases that conduct that is "lawfully excused" includes lawful arrest, the use of reasonable parental force, and the reasonable defence of property.

[129] Section 133(4) CJA 1988.

[130] It would be a matter for the Court to interpret whether this provision would place an evidential or persuasive burden on the defendant in determining its consistency with Article 6(2) ECHR (see *R* v *DPP, ex p Kebilene* [1999] 4 All ER 801 at 842, per Lord Hope of Craighead; *R v Lambert* [2001] 1 All ER 1014 at 1022, per Lord Woolf CJ).

8.25 In addition, the APPG has concluded that the offence should not require the establishment of a risk of torture. While this risk is undoubtedly part of the backdrop of extraordinary rendition in its modern sense, it is our opinion that a requirement that a defendant intended or was reckless to the risk that an individual would be tortured would likely result in liability for the criminal offence of torture under Section 134 of the CJA 1988. The APPG's purpose in establishing a new offence is to strengthen, not repeat, existing criminal law. Moreover, as concluded at paragraph 7.39(d) above, the experience of some States has demonstrated that linking a domestic criminal prohibition to the international standards relating to torture in practice is difficult and raises significant evidence issues. Consequently, we consider it appropriate to focus on the more objective element that the individual's transfer is other than under due process of law. This conduct is at the core of extraordinary rendition as it might be facilitated in the United Kingdom. Moreover, it is the absence of legal process, and the erosion of the standards of the rule of law,[131] that give rise to the possibility of ill-treatment. As such, addressing this aspect of extraordinary rendition and promoting a renewed respect for the rule of law will effectively curtail the mistreatment of persons in any event. Our approach is consistent with the key recommendation of the Eminent Jurists Panel that it is incumbent on States, at the national level, to review their legal frameworks and *"make such changes as are necessary to ensure that they are fully consistent with the rule of law and the respect for human rights, and to avoid all over-broad definitions which might facilitate misuse"*.[132]

The Mens Rea of the Use of Transport Facilities Offence

8.26 It is proposed that a person be guilty of this offence where he knows that an individual is being transferred to another State, and:

(a) either knows that the individual is being transferred without his or her consent, or is reckless as to whether the transfer is consensual; and

(b) either knows that, or is reckless as to whether, the transfer is being made without lawful excuse.

In each of limbs (a) and (b) above 'recklessness' is the taking of an unreasonable risk of which the risk-taker is aware. Consequently, a person would

[131] The APPG notes that the British courts have strongly criticised earlier instances of rendition on the basis that it is an affront to the rule of law, irrespective of whether there was in those cases a risk of torture. See, in particular, *R v Horseferry Road Magistrates' Court ex p Bennett* [1994] 1 AC 42 per Lord Griffiths at 61-62: *". . . the judiciary accept a responsibility for the maintenance of the rule of law that embraces a willingness to oversee executive action and to refuse to countenance behaviour that threatens either basic human rights or the rule of law"*. That case concerned the unlawful transfer of an alleged criminal where there was no suggestion he faced torture.

[132] EJP Report, key recommendation 1(c) at Chapter 7, page 164.

be guilty of an offence where he is aware that there is a risk that an individual being transferred out of the UK is being transferred without his consent and without lawful excuse, and nonetheless proceeds with his involvement in the transfer of the individual.

8.27 **We would welcome consultees' views on the following:**

- **(a) whether they agree with the proposed elements of the actus reus of the primary offence;**
- **(b) whether they agree with the proposed mens rea of the primary offence;**
- **(c) whether they are aware of any appropriate circumstances in which there should be a presumption of absence of consent;**
- **(d) whether they agree with the proposed definitions and, in particular, whether they are aware of any procedures which should be included in the definition of 'lawful excuse'.**

The 'Facilitation' Offence

8.28 It is also proposed that it be made an offence for any person to facilitate another person in carrying out the primary offence referred to at paragraphs 8.2(a) and 8.15 above. Specifically, the offence would target the facilitation of the transfer of an individual, without his consent, to or from the UK (or any Overseas Territory) from or to another State, without lawful excuse.

8.29 It is thought that the formulation of a facilitation offence by way of primary legislation would reduce some of the evidential difficulties that exist in relation to accessory liability. The facilitation offence would be intended to sanction, and therefore prevent, the support of extraordinary rendition by those who, whilst not actually carrying out the extraordinary rendition process, make it possible and so are complicit in the process.

The Actus Reus of the Facilitation Offence

8.30 We propose to define 'facilitation' in the legislation. The definition would include the provision of any material assistance (including material, technical, financial and logistical assistance) by any person (whether an individual or a body corporate) to any person, in connection with an extra-judicial transfer of a person. This would include simply permitting the use of any facilities for such purposes.

The Mens Rea of the Facilitation Offence

8.31 The mental element for the facilitation offence would adopt the same knowledge or recklessness standard as the primary offence. Consequently, a person would be guilty of an offence where he is aware that there is a risk that an individual being transferred in to, or out of, the UK (or the relevant Overseas Territory) is being transferred without his consent and without lawful excuse, and nonetheless proceeds to facilitate the transfer of the individual. An advantage of this approach is that an individual, being 'put on notice' of the risk, would come under an obligation to make due and proper enquiry if he or she were not to be reckless in permitting the use of transport facilities. This approach would also ensure that a person unknowingly or non-recklessly providing services to a rendition flight would not be criminalised.

8.32 **We invite consultees' views on the following:**

(a) **whether they consider it appropriate to create a secondary offence of facilitating the primary 'use of transport facilities' offence;**

(b) **whether they agree with the actus reus of the 'facilitation' offence;**

(c) **whether they agree with the mens rea of the 'facilitation' offence.**

The 'Failure to Prevent' Offence

8.33 To achieve the purpose of effectively banning extraordinary rendition in the UK, we propose to extend criminal liability to persons controlling any transport facilities used for the purpose of extraordinary rendition, where those persons have not taken sufficient steps to prevent their use for this purpose. Consequently, we propose a new offence of failing to prevent the transfer of an individual, without his consent, from or to the UK (or any Overseas Territory) to or from another State without lawful excuse. Liability for such an offence will attach to any person, whether an individual or a body corporate, which has the 'management or control of transport facilities'.

8.34 It is critical, however, that the proper administration of the transport infrastructure is not criminalised, and unreasonable costs are not imposed on the parties undertaking that administration. We therefore propose a general offence but with clearly defined 'safe harbours' for transport operators administering transport facilities to the required standard to prevent extraordinary rendition.

The Actus Reus of the Failure to Prevent Offence

8.35 This offence would, subject to the safe harbours detailed below, be committed by any person managing or controlling any transport facilities used in the transfer of a person without his consent to or from the UK (or any Overseas Territory) from or to another State without lawful excuse (i.e. the primary offence must have occurred). The expressions 'managing' and 'controlling' would be defined broadly in the legislation. Liability would extend not only to those people with day-to-day oversight of the operation of facilities, but also to those individuals and companies with overall responsibility for ensuring that adequate regulatory and legal compliance safeguards are observed.

The Mens Rea of the Failure to Prevent Offence

8.36 Liability for this offence will be strict, subject to the safe harbour defence set out at paragraph 8.37 below. Consequently, any person controlling transport facilities which are used in any act of extraordinary rendition will be liable for this offence unless they can show that they fall within the safe harbour.

'Safe harbour' Defence in Respect of the Failure to Prevent Offence

8.37 The 'failure to prevent' offence would criminalise a controller of a facility for failing to put in place adequate procedures by way of safeguards against the facility being exploited for the purposes of extraordinary rendition, and/or failing to observe those procedures. It would be a complete defence to a charge of failing to prevent the primary offence for the defendant to show the following:

(a) there were in place, at the date on which the act of extraordinary rendition occurred, effective procedures requiring persons controlling vehicles, vessels or aircraft using the facilities for the purpose of transit from the UK to another State to identify any individuals being transferred outside of the UK against their will, and to confirm that those individuals are being transferred with lawful excuse (including by way of extradition, deportation, prisoner transfer or removal direction); and

(b) the procedures required that any reasonable suspicion that such a transfer might be occurring was to be notified to individuals controlling the facilities and to the appropriate UK authorities. The notification was to be made sufficiently promptly to prevent the facilities being used for the purpose of a further transfer. In the meantime, steps were to be taken to prevent further transfer pending obtaining reasonable satisfaction that any such reasonable suspicion was unfounded.

The procedures would have to have been properly operated and carried out in good faith.

8.38 In substance, this is akin to a due diligence defence. We consider that it would promote a culture of compliance across the transport sector.

The requirement for due diligence and on-site verification on the part of persons with responsibility in this sector, rather than reliance on government certification or diplomatic assurance, is consistent with the view expressed by the Foreign Affairs Committee that greater active scrutiny was required on the part of the UK to avoid participation in the extraordinary rendition process.

8.39 **We invite consultees' views on the following:**

- (a) **whether they consider it appropriate to criminalise persons managing or controlling UK transport facilities who fail to prevent the further transfer of an individual, without his consent, from or to the UK (or any Overseas Territory) to or from another State without lawful excuse;**
- (b) **whether they agree with the proposed actus reus of the 'failure to prevent' offence;**
- (c) **whether they agree with the proposed strict liability element of the 'failure to prevent' offence;**
- (d) **whether they consider the proposed safe harbour defence to be adequate and sufficient.**

The 'Circuit Flights' Offence

8.40 The APPG has been particularly concerned by so-called 'circuit flights', whereby a plane containing no captives uses UK transport facilities as part of a broader itinerary that involves picking up individuals in other jurisdictions and transporting them to third countries. We would like to see the conscious giving of assistance to extraordinary rendition activities in this way also criminalised.

8.41 However, we are acutely aware of the difficulties of drafting such a proposal in a way that avoids criminalising innocent conduct. We therefore propose a separate, specific extension of the facilitation offence.

8.42 We propose that it would be also an offence in the UK to undertake the facilitation offence where the primary offence does not involve the transport facilities of the UK or its overseas territories but those of another country. The elements of that offence would be the same as for the UK-based facilitation offence.

8.43 However, the mens rea element would be different. A person would not be guilty of the offence unless he or she intended that the use of the facilities in the UK was to facilitate the conduct of the primary offence in relation to those overseas countries. Whilst setting the mens rea element at the level of intent imposes real hurdles for any prosecution, this seems appropriate given the genuine difficulties faced by those in control of transport facilities in the UK and the Overseas Territories in determining the purpose of a particular flight (or other journey). The unknowing provision of services to a circuit flight would not be criminalised by this proposal.

8.44 **We invite consultees' views on the following:**

- (a) **whether they consider it appropriate to create an offence criminalising the use of UK transport facilities as part of a 'circuit flight' involving extraordinary rendition activities in other jurisdictions;**
- (b) **whether they agree with the proposed actus reus of the offence;**
- (c) **whether they agree with the proposed mens rea of the offence.**

Penalties

8.45 We provisionally propose that persons guilty of the primary and facilitation offences outlined above would be liable on indictment to imprisonment for a term of 8 years and/or an unlimited fine. This is consistent with the penalty recommended under current sentencing guidelines for aggravated forms of kidnap[133] and is thus, in our preliminary view, appropriate for the commission of an offence of recklessly or intentionally facilitating extraordinary rendition. In respect of the 'failure to prevent' offence, we recommend a penalty of five years' imprisonment and/or an unlimited fine. We note that this latter penalty is equivalent to that imposed for failures to disclose in respect of money laundering,[134] and may, thus, be thought appropriate for an offence related to the failure of responsible persons to respond adequately to reasonable suspicions.

8.46 **We invite consultees' views on appropriate penalties for the proposed offences.**

Crown Application

8.47 Under the principle of Crown immunity, it is presumed that the Crown will not be bound by onerous legislation unless Parliament expresses a contrary intention. This presumption particularly applies to criminal legislation, and extends to all bodies and persons acting as servants or agents of the Crown, whether in its private or public capacity, including all elements of the Government, from Ministers of the Crown downwards. Government departments, civil servants, members of the armed forces and other public bodies or persons are, therefore, included within the scope of the immunity. Given the nature of extraordinary rendition operations as discussed in

[133] See paragraph 5.7, above.
[134] See Sections 330-334 of the Proceeds of Crime Act 2002.

this CP, the APPG is of the view that those likely to be in a position to facilitate such operations include Crown servants, particularly military or intelligence personnel. It is therefore appropriate expressly to extend the scope of the legislation to the Crown.

8.48 **We welcome consultees' views on whether it is appropriate to extend the scope of the legislation to the Crown.**

Extent

8.49 As discussed in paragraph 3.15 of this CP, this analysis does not cover Scotland and Northern Ireland. However, it is recommended that it would also be extended, on analogous reasoning, to Scotland and Northern Ireland.

8.50 **We welcome consultees' views on whether it is appropriate to extend the scope of the legislation to Scotland and Northern Ireland.**

Annex 1—Draft Legislation

Rendition Flight Offences

1. The offences

(1) A person (A) is guilty of an offence if –

(a) A uses transport facilities located in the United Kingdom or any of its Overseas Territories for the purpose of transferring an individual (B) to or from the United Kingdom or any of its Overseas Territories from or to another State,

(b) B does not consent to the transfer,

(c) the transfer is without lawful excuse,

(d) A knows the transfer is without B's consent or is reckless as to whether the transfer is without B's consent, and

(e) A knows the transfer is without lawful excuse or is reckless as to whether the transfer is without lawful excuse.

(2) A person (C) is guilty of an offence if –

(a) C facilitates a transfer in the circumstances of subsection (1) above,

(b) C knows the transfer is without B's consent or is reckless as to whether the transfer is without B's consent, and

(c) C knows the transfer is without lawful excuse or is reckless as to whether the transfer is without lawful excuse,

provided that C shall not be guilty of an offence if the actions which would constitute the offence are necessary for the safety and proper administration of the transport facilities.

(3) Subject to section 7, a person is guilty of an offence if he manages or controls the transport facilities that are used in an offence under subsection (1) above and fails to prevent the transfer.

(4) For the purposes of this part –

(a) "transport facilities" means facilities for transport services (whether for passenger transport services or otherwise), including all vehicles, vessels, trains, aeroplanes, airports, ports, air traffic control systems, ground or air transport terminals, refuelling facilities, storage facilities and maintenance facilities;

(b) "consent" has the meaning given by sections 2 and 3;

(c) "facilitating" has the meaning given by section 5;

(d) "managing and controlling" has the meaning given by section 6.

(5) To prove that an individual has been transferred 'from or to another State' it is sufficient to show that he or she has transferred from or to the United Kingdom or the relevant Overseas Territory and it is not necessary to prove that he or she has been transferred to or from any specific or identified State.

2. "Consent"

(1) For the purposes of this part a person consents if he agrees freely to the transfer, having the freedom and capacity to do so.

3. Evidence of Consent

(1) If, in proceedings for an offence specified in this part, it is proved –

(a) that the defendant did the act specified in section 1(1), and

(b) that any of the circumstances specified in section 3(2) existed,

the individual will be deemed not to have consented to the transfer in the absence of positive evidence to the contrary.

(2) The circumstances are that –

(a) the individual was physically constrained or concealed during the transfer;

(b) the individual's name was omitted from the papers relating to the transfer;

(c) the individual's identification or travel documentation was not presented during the transfer on any occasion when the documentation of passengers would usually be presented.

4. "Without lawful excuse"

(1) Without limitation to section 1(1)(c) for the purposes of this part if an individual is transferred by way of the procedures specified in subsection (2) below, the transfer will not be without lawful excuse.

(2) The procedures are any process prescribed in legislation in the United Kingdom for –

(a) extradition;

(b) deportation and removal direction; and

(c) prisoner transfer.

(3) In any prosecution brought for an offence under section 1 it will be for the defendant to establish the basis on which he considers his conduct to be lawfully excused.

5. "Facilitates"

(1) A person facilitates a transfer if he either makes it possible or makes it materially easier (irrespective of whether another person might

otherwise have facilitated should the facilitation in question not have occurred) whether by the physical or administrative or legal acts that he takes.

6. "Managing and Controlling"

(1) A person manages transport facilities if he takes operational decisions in relation to those transport facilities which could, directly or indirectly, affect whether they can be used for the purpose of the offence in section 1(1).

(2) A person controls transport facilities if he can exercise a dominant influence over the management or strategic decisions taken in connection with those transport facilities.

7. Defences

(1) In proceedings for an offence under section 1(3), it will be a defence if, at the time at which the offence under section 1(1) occurred–

(a) there were adequate procedures in place–

(i) to identify any individuals potentially being transferred to or from the United Kingdom or any of its Overseas Territories from or to another State without their consent, and

(ii) to confirm that any individuals being transferred without their consent were not being transferred without lawful excuse; and

(b) those procedures required –

(i) any reasonable suspicion that the acts specified in section 1(1) might be occurring to be notified to individuals controlling the facilities and to the appropriate UK authorities sufficiently promptly to prevent the facilities being used for the purpose of a further transfer,

(ii) steps to be taken to prevent further transfers pending obtaining reasonable satisfaction that any such reasonable suspicion was unfounded, and

(iii) the necessary administrative and operational powers to enable the prevention of further transfers to be granted;

(c) those procedures were being properly operated.

(2) The defence under subsection (1) only applies if the procedures were implemented and operated in good faith.

8. Circuit Flight Offence

(1) A person (D) is guilty of an offence if he knowingly uses transport facilities located in the United Kingdom or any of its Overseas Territories

to facilitate the subsequent or prior transfer of any person (E) from a State other than the United Kingdom or any of its Overseas Territories to another State other than the United Kingdom or any of its Overseas Territories knowing that E:

(a) does not consent to the transfer; and

(b) the transfer is without lawful excuse.

9. Penalties

(1) Where a person is guilty of an offence under sections 1(1), 1(2) and 8 of this part, he shall be liable on conviction on indictment to imprisonment for a term not exceeding 8 years and/or an unlimited fine.

(2) Where a person is guilty of an offence under section 1(3) of this part, he shall be liable on conviction on indictment to imprisonment for a term not exceeding 5 years and/or an unlimited fine.

10. Crown application

(1) This Act binds the Crown.

11. Extent

(1) This Act extends to [. . . . .] only.

12. Interpretation

In this Act –

"consent" has the meaning given by sections 2 and 3; "facilitating" has the meaning given by section 5;

"managing and controlling" has the meaning given by section 6;

"Overseas Territories" has the same meaning that "British Overseas Territories" has in the British Nationality Act 1981;

"transport facilities" has the meaning given by section 1(4)(a).

DOCUMENT NO. 12

A REVIEW OF THE ENFORCEMENT BY THE SECURITY POLICE OF A GOVERNMENT DECISION TO EXPEL TWO EGYPTIAN CITIZENS

Parliamentary Ombudsman of Sweden

March 22, 2005

Registration Number: 2169-2004

In an adjudication of March 22, 2005, the Chief Parliamentary Ombudsman, *MatsMelin*, made the following observations.

1. Summary of the Ombudsman's Criticism

My review of the enforcement by the Security Police of the Government's decision to expel two Egyptian citizens, A. and E.Z., on December 18, 2001, reveals serious shortcomings in the way in which this case was handled by the Security Police. I have therefore found reason to express extremely grave criticism of the Security Police. This criticism can be summarised as follows.

–Relinquishment of official authority

At Bromma airport the security police already failed to maintain control of the enforcement, thereby allowing American officials free hands to exercise public authority on Swedish territory. Relinquishing Swedish public authority in this way to foreign officials is not compatible with Swedish law.

–Degrading treatment

The enforcement was carried out in an inhuman and therefore unacceptable manner. The way in which A. and E.Z. were treated is alien to Swedish police procedures and cannot be tolerated. The treatment to which the two men were subjected was in some respects unlawful and must be characterised overall as degrading. Questions may also be raised as to whether the way in which the enforcement was carried out constituted a breach of Article 3 of the European Convention. The Security Police should have intervened to prevent this inhuman treatment.

–Passivity

The way in which the Security Police dealt with this case was characterised throughout by passivity—from the acceptance of the offer of the use of an American aircraft until completion of the enforcement. One example that can be mentioned is the failure of the Security Police to ask for information about what the security check demanded by the Americans would involve.

–Inadequate organisation

None of the officers present at Bromma airport had been assigned command of the operation. The officers from the Security Police who were there had relatively subordinate ranks. None of them considered that they bore the ultimate responsibility for the enforcement. They also acted with remarkable deference to the American officials.

2. Background and Inquiry

2.1 Introduction

During the spring of 2001, the Swedish Security Police (SÄPO) launched a case involving two Egyptian citizens, A. and E.Z. The Security Police then investigated and maintained surveillance of the two men for about six months. At the same time the Migration Board were dealing with applications for asylum from A. and E.Z. However, the Migration Board came to the opinion that in view of the nature of the case the final decision rested with the Government. The case was therefore referred to the Government offices during the autumn of 2001 for continued consideration.

On December 18, 2001, the Government decided to reject the applications submitted by A. and E.Z. for residence and labour permits and that the two men were to be expelled. In addition, it was decided that the expulsion order should be enforced without delay by the Security Police and that their destination was to be Egypt. In the decision it was stated that A. and E.Z. had occupied leading positions in an organisation that was guilty of terrorist acts and that they could be held responsible for the actions of the organisation in question. On the same day, A. and E.Z. were detained and taken to Bromma airport to await transport to Cairo in an American aircraft. Apart from Swedish and Egyptian officials, the plane was also carrying American security personnel. Before the plane took off, the American officials undertook a security check of A. and E.Z. inside the police station at the airport. This inspection involved various forms of force and coercive measures.

After the expulsion had been described in a programme called *KallaFakta* on the Swedish television channel TV4, I decided on May 25, 2004, to launch an inquiry on my own initiative.

2.2 The Parliamentary Ombudsman's Inquiry and the Public Prosecutor's Appraisal of the Case etc.

2.2.1 The Extent of the Parliamentary Ombudsman's Inquiry

The Act with Instructions for the Parliamentary Ombudsmen (1986:765) contains provisions on the extent and the limits of the supervisory powers exercised by the Parliamentary Ombudsmen. These state, for instance, that public agencies, their officials and others employed by these agencies are subject to the supervision of the Parliamentary Ombudsmen, while this does not apply to the Government or Ministers. It can also be added that the Parliamentary Ombudsmen's supervisory powers only apply to Swedish public authorities.

In this case I have examined how the Security Police enforced the expulsion order made by the Government. My inquiry has therefore focused on establishing what occurred at Bromma airport and the manner in which the expulsion of the two Egyptians was carried out. Central issues in my inquiry concerned the actions of the Security Police in connection with the use of public authority by foreign officials on Swedish territory and the use of force and coercive measures. The surveillance and investigation carried out by the Security Police in the months prior to the expulsion will not, however, be dealt with in any further detail.

In view of the restrictions that apply to the Parliamentary Ombudsmen's supervisory powers, my review does not therefore include the Government's expulsion order, nor on what its decision was based. Consequently, no opinion is expressed on the suspicions about A. and E.Z. On the same grounds, it does not concern the question of whether enforcement of the expulsion was possible in view of the provisions of Section 1 of Chapter 8 of the Aliens Act (1989:529) and Sweden's commitments according to international conventions, nor, therefore, does it include the issue of the value of any "assurances" made by Egypt. Furthermore, my review does not include the measures adopted by the Government to monitor the commitments made in the assurances, nor statements made by the Government to international inspection bodies.

The way in which the Government dealt with the expulsion of A. and E.Z. is subject to a review by the Parliamentary Committee on the Constitution.

2.2.2 The Public Prosecutor's Appraisal of the Case

The events in question were reported by an individual to the police and the prosecution agency for consideration of whether any crime had been committed in connection with the enforcement by the Security Police of the Government's expulsion order. On June 18, 2004, K.E., Assistant Chief District Prosecutor, decided not to institute a preliminary inquiry as there were no grounds for suspecting that any offence subject to criminal prosecution had been committed by a representative of the Swedish police force (reg. no. C00-7-565-04). In this decision a note was made that the question of whether any case arose from the actions of foreign citizens during the enforcement on board the aircraft had been referred to the Director of the Public Prosecution Agency in Stockholm.

In the exercise of her supervisory powers, A.B., at that time Acting Director of the Public Prosecution Agency, then conducted a review of the decision made by K.E. In her decision of November 3, 2004, she found that in view of the stringent safety and security requirements—in particular during the period in question—the measures invoked could not be considered to constitute a breach of the general principles applying to the actions of the police. She noted specifically in her decision that it concerned the measures adopted by foreign personnel as they were not operating independently at the time. In addition, A.B. made the assessment that there were no grounds for assuming that any offence subject to public prosecution had been committed by the captain of the foreign aircraft (reg. no.100 2004/0653).

2.3 Conduct of the Inquiry

To begin with, documentation relating to the case was requested from the Security Police and the Government offices (the Ministry for Foreign Affairs and the Ministry of Justice). Then information was acquired verbally from Deputy Police Commissioner M.L., Chief Superintendent A.A., five other senior officers at the Security Police, Inspector P.F. of the Stockholm County Police Authority's Border Control Unit at Bromma Airport and from K.J., E.Z.'s legal counsel. In addition P.F. showed the Parliamentary Ombudsman the premises used by the police at Bromma airport. The Security Police were then asked to submit written answers to certain specific questions. The response of the Security Police was supplemented by a written statement from M.L. and A.A. and two other officers. Finally a number of additional documents were requested from the Security Police.

2.4 The result of the Inquiry

In the course of the Parliamentary Ombudsman's review relatively extensive information has come to light. In what follows a chronological account will be given of the way in which the case was dealt with and the main circumstances considered significant for the issues pertinent to my adjudication.

2.4.1 Initial Measures

In May 2001, the Security Police initiated surveillance and investigation procedures concerning A. and E.Z. A. was then living in Karlstad and E.Z. in Stockholm. A.A. had overall responsibility for the handling of the case.

At this time, applications for asylum from A. and E.Z. were being considered by the Migration Board. In June 2001, the Security Police presented certain aspects of their case to representatives of the Migration Board and at the end of October 2001 the Security Police lodged objections to A. and E.Z.'s applications for asylum. At the beginning of November 2001, as laid down by Section 11 of Chapter 7 of the Aliens Act, the Migration Board referred the case to the Government. In the same month, the Security Police reported on the case to officials at the Department for Migration and Asylum at the Ministry for Foreign Affairs.

In November 2001, the Security Police came to the conclusion that expulsion could be required in this case. Planning began for the enforcement of an expulsion order, for instance of how arrests could be made in Karlstad and Stockholm and how the subsequent transport to Egypt could be arranged. Initially it was stated that no Government decision could be expected before January 2002. According to information on file at the Security Police, it was then intended that the Government would reach its decision on December 13, 2001, so that the journey was therefore planned to take place on December 15. On December 5, the Ministry for Foreign Affairs then announced that no decision could be expected before December 20.

The Ministry for Foreign Affairs and the Security Police seem, therefore, to have continued to discuss when, for instance, the Government could reach a decision in this case. On December 14, 2001, there is a journal entry in the Security Police's case file: "Inf. Foreign Ministry—decision Tuesday!" (i.e. December 18) and "Plane booked Wed. 8.15 a.m." (i.e. December 19) and also "place booked Kronoberg [Detention Centre] Tues-Wed". The Security Police had contacted the transport service of the National Prison and Probation Administration to request assistance in arranging air transport for A. and E.Z. to Egypt. Transport was chartered and departure scheduled for the morning of December 19, 2001. According to the Security Police it was difficult to arrange slots to fly over Europe before that time. A.A. has stated that at some stage before December 17, 2001, he was informed that the Government intended to deal with the case on December 18, 2001, which meant that the expulsion could not take place immediately after the decision had been made. Some time before the expulsion decision was made, however, the Security Police received an offer from the American Central Intelligence Agency (CIA) of the use of a plane that was said to have what was referred to as direct access so that it could fly over Europe without having to touch down. Enforcement could then take place immediately after the Government made its decision on December 18, 2001. A.A. has said that the Americans attached no conditions to the use of this aircraft by the Security Police. He did in fact assume—as the aircraft was American—that some American personnel would be on board but also that officers from the Security Police would be able to accompany the flight. According to A.A., however, it was "purely a transport service" that the Americans were offering and no mention was made of any specific category of American personnel being on the plane.

2.4.2 Security Police Presentation of the Case to the Foreign Minister on December 17, 2001

On Monday December 17, 2001, the Security Police presented the case to A.L., then Foreign Minister. The Security Police officers present were A.A. and X, the case officer. A number of officials from the Ministry for Foreign Affairs were present, among them G.-B.A., State Secretary, S.-O.P., Director General, and staff from the Department for Migration and Asylum.

After a presentation by the staff from Department for Migration and Asylum, X presented the case from the perspective of the Security Police. He has stated that the Foreign Minister seemed satisfied with the presentation and with the grounds offered by the Security Police for rejection of the applications for asylum. Representatives of the Security Police have provided the Parliamentary Ombudsman with the following information on discussions about enforcement. A.A. presented the two alternative transport possibilities available: the aircraft booked for December 19, 2001 and the American offer. As there were security reasons for arranging the expulsion immediately after the Government had made its decision, the alternative of using the plane booked for December 19th was not considered satisfactory: there were demands that enforcement should take place without delay. According to A.A., great weight was probably given to the security considerations by both the Government offices and the Security Police during the presentation. He felt that there was some concern in the Government offices about this case. During the presentation, A.A. reported that if the American offer were accepted, enforcement could already take place during the evening of December 18, 2001. According to A.A. the Foreign Minister then withdrew with her most senior officials to discuss the issue, before assenting to acceptance of the American offer by saying "we'll do it that way". Even though A.A. was aware that neither the Government nor a Minister could make decisions concerning the exercise of the powers of a public agency, he construed the statement as a "direct signal". Officer X has also testified that the Foreign Minister was positive to the American offer. According to officer X, the Foreign Minister asked whether any members of her staff had a different opinion and, this not being the case, then said "That's what we'll do, we take the American offer" or something similar. M.L. has stated that she was informed that both transport alternatives had been mentioned during the presentation. K.J. has stated that the officials at the Ministry for Foreign Affairs told him that during the presentation there was some concern that either the UN Committee against Torture or the European Court of Human Rights would have time to issue a staying order before enforcement could take place. There is also information in this case that there were fears that an attempt would be made to free A. and E.Z.

In the Security Police file one of the journal entries for December 17, 2001 reads "Presentation Ministry for Foreign Affairs/A.L.—Foreign Min. wants enforcement Tuesday evening—Yes to ordering plane through USA". A memorandum drawn up by the Security Police on February 7, 2002 contains the note: "After some consultation with the staff of the Ministry for Foreign Affairs the Foreign Minister then gave approval of the acceptance by SÄPO/RPS of the help offered by the USA for the transport of A. and E.Z.". In a memorandum dated February 12, 2002, J.D., then Head of the Security Police writes: "Representatives of the Ministry for Foreign Affairs were aware of who was to undertake the transport".

In May/June 2004 the Ministry for Foreign Affairs carried out its own internal analysis of what was said about this issue during the presentation. This involved asking a number of officials at the ministry to account for their memory of the meeting and some of the findings were as follows. One individual was extremely uncertain about whether enforcement was discussed but was of the opinion that if so, the aircraft was more probably Egyptian. His recollection was furthermore that he was surprised when he found out that an American plane was involved. Some had no recollection whatsoever of discussion of enforcement apart from that it was to be undertaken rapidly and by the Security Police. Some individuals remembered that there had been discussion of logistical problems in the airspace between Stockholm and Cairo. According to one official, the Americans were to provide assistance in this respect, while another stated that the Security Police needed help, probably from "our colleagues in the West". One individual had a clear memory of talking to A.A. on some occasion before the meeting, who then mentioned that the Security Police could not arrange Swedish transport at such short notice and therefore had to try to get hold of a foreign plane. It is likely that the Foreign Minister had been informed to this effect prior to the meeting so that she would be ready for the question. The Foreign Minister had, to the best of his recollection, no opinion about who should undertake the transport. He does not remember whether they discussed an aircraft of any particular nationality but was fairly convinced that the Foreign Minister would at least "have raised her eyebrows considerably if SÄPO had reported that it was to be an American plane".

The same official also made a note that after the enforcement A.A. had rung to report that all had gone well but that the plane had turned out to be American and not Egyptian. Overall assessment of the information provided gave, according to the Ministry for Foreign Affairs, no support for the claim that during the presentation the Security Police had stated that the enforcement would take place using an American aircraft or with American participation. On the other hand, the information could suggest that American help would be provided in arranging slots for the flight. In addition, it was also pointed out that different "information cultures" were involved.

After this presentation the Security Police contacted the American intelligence service.

2.4.3 December 18, 2001, the Day of Enforcement

At lunchtime on Tuesday December 18, 2001, Y—the security police officer who had planned the enforcement—met American officials at Bromma airport. During the meeting he was informed that American security personnel would be on the plane, which was expected to land at Bromma at about 9 p.m. The Americans also stated that there was no room on the aircraft for Swedish police officers. Officer Y has stated that he emphasised that this was "our enforcement so we have to go along as well". The Americans then arranged for Security Police officers to travel on the flight.

During the meeting it was also said that the security personnel on the plane might be wearing hoods and that they wished to conduct a security check of A. and E.Z. before they boarded the plane. Without this examination the men could not be transported on the plane. According to Y this involved a body-search; no other procedures were discussed. As the Americans preferably wanted access to a room in which to perform the security check, the police unit responsible for passport control at Bromma airport was approached and it was agreed that the checks could be carried out there.

Officer Y contacted A.A. to inform him that the American officials wanted to conduct their own security check at Bromma. According to Y, A.A. had no objection to this. A.A. has stated that he probably was contacted on this matter but that he has no memory of it happening. He has also said that "purely hypothetically" he probably considered it was "relatively OK" to conduct a security check before permitting the Egyptians to board the aircraft "but obviously under the direction of or with the participation, as it were, of Swedish officers".

Later that day the Government decided, pursuant to the Aliens Act, to reject the applications of A. and E.Z. for residence and labour permits and that the two men were to be expelled. In addition it was decided that the

Security Police were to enforce the expulsions without delay and that the destination was to be Egypt. According to the Security Police journal in the case file, notification of the Government's decision was received at 3.10 p.m.

As the officer with overall responsibility for the case, A.A. remained at Security Police headquarters in Stockholm for the entire day. At 4.43 p.m. he decided that A. and E.Z. were to be apprehended. At the request of the Security Police, the Migration Board decided that E.Z., who was in Stockholm, could be placed in a detention centre or a police cell until enforcement could take place. The grounds cited for this request involved both reasons of security and logistical considerations. At about the same time the units were alerted that were to apprehend the deportees, who were both, as has previously been pointed out, under surveillance.

The Security Police apprehended A. relatively quickly at a bus stop in Karlstad. A body search was carried out but no weapons or other dangerous objects were discovered. A. was informed of the decision in his own language, placed in a vehicle and driven to Bromma airport. According to the journal entry, A. was "apprehended and informed" at 4.55 p.m. No coercion was required during the apprehension nor was A. handcuffed during the journey to Bromma. The medication needed by A. for his stomach problems was also procured from Karlstad.

The National Counter-terrorist Unit apprehended E.Z. at about 5 p.m. at his workplace in Stockholm. He was then taken to the Kronoberg Detention Centre, where he was detained until transport to Bromma airport could be arranged. A body search was also made of E.Z. and he was informed of the Government's decision in his own language. After a few hours E.Z. was taken to Bromma by the National Counter-terrorist Unit. At this time he was in handcuffs. However, no other coercive measures seem to have been invoked during his apprehension.

According to a log entry by officer Y dated December 21, 2001, about the transport of A. and E.Z., the two vehicles arrived at Bromma airport at 8.20 p.m. and 8.30 p.m. After they had been guided into the restricted area of the airport by authorised staff, the vehicles were parked outside the airport police station, where they then waited for some time. According to one Security Police officer, E.Z. became indignant when he understood that he had been taken to an airport and one of his remarks in his own language was that there would be bloodshed.

At this time there were five Security Police officers at the airport, among them officers X and Y. None of these five held senior rank, nor had any of them been assigned command of the operation. The American officials that Y had previously met during the day also arrived at the airport. Their task was to ensure that everything took place as agreed and they remained in the background all the time. In addition, Paul Forell, an officer of the Border Police, and some members of the National Counter-terrorist Unit and police officers from Karlstad were also present.

Just before 9 p.m. the American plane touched down. Officer Y went to speak to the occupants of the plane. These included, in addition to its crew, a security team of seven or eight, among them a doctor and two Egyptian officials. Officer Y informed the American officials that A. and E.Z. were waiting in the vehicles parked in front of the police station and the Americans were taken to them.

The security team, all of whom were disguised by hoods around their heads, then went up to the vehicles in which A. and E.Z. were sitting. One of the men was taken first to the police station by the team. Inside the station, in a small changing room, the American officials conducted what they had referred to as a security check. According to reports, a doctor was present in the changing room. When the check had been completed, the second man was sent for and the same procedure repeated.

The inquiry has revealed that this security check comprised at least the following. A. and E.Z. were subjected to a body search, their clothes were cut to pieces and placed in bags, their hair was thoroughly examined, as were their oral cavities and ears. In addition they were handcuffed and their ankles fettered, each was then dressed in an overall and photographed. Finally loose hoods without holes for their eyes were placed over their heads. A. and E.Z. were then taken out of the police station in bare feet and led to the aircraft.

In addition, K.J. has reported that E.Z. said that the security team had forced him to lean forwards in the changing room and he had then felt some object being inserted into his anal cavity. Afterwards he was equipped with a diaper. According to K.J., E.Z. then felt calmer, as if "all the muscles in his body were slack". E.Z. was, however, fully conscious for the entire journey. K.J. has added that E.Z. was blindfolded and placed in a hood and also forced to lie in an uncomfortable position on board the aircraft.

Officer Y has stated that "he has the impression" that he asked two of his fellow-officers to keep an eye on the two security cheks so that they had "some grasp as it were" of what was going on. There was only room for a very few people in the changing room. While the security cheks were taking place, Y himself was standing some distance away and could not see what was happening. The two Security Police employees, a police officer and a civilian interpreter, who were with the security team in the changing room have stated that they did not see suppositories being administered to A. and E.Z. or diapers being used. Their information reveals, however, that the changing room was very crowded and so they had difficulty in observing what was going on for the entire time. The Security Police officer says that because it was so crowded he left the changing room after only a short time. He did not, therefore, even see the garments being cut to pieces. The interpreter says that he was present for the entire time but that when E.Z. had been undressed he turned away for about 20 seconds. When he looked back, E.Z. was in principle fully clothed. According to both witnesses, the security team conducted the security inspection rapidly, efficiently and professionally. The members of the team did not speak to each other but communicated using hand signals. Nor did any of the other Security Police officials in attendance at Bromma state that they had noticed or been informed that A. and E.Z. had been administered suppositories or equipped with diapers.

The two men were then taken to the aircraft. Just before 10 p.m. the plane took off from Bromma for the flight to Egypt. Two representatives of the Security Police were on board the plane: officer Y and the civilian interpreter. The original intention had been for three people to accompany the plane to Egypt but late in the day they were informed by the captain of the plane that there was only room for two from the Swedish Security Police. A. and E.Z. were placed at the rear of the plane, each lying on a mattress to which they were strapped. Their handcuffs, ankle fetters and hoods were not removed during the flight to Egypt.

The transport log drawn up by officer Y contains the following entry: "They were kept under observation for the entire time and the guards were changed every other hour. The doctor in the escort inspected them all the time (A. and E.Z. were probably given a tranquilliser by the doctor before take-off)". According to officer Y these notes in the log should be regarded as his speculations, as this is what "one could gather as a doctor was with them". He did not, however, see this taking place.

Officer Y also wrote a memorandum dated December 18, 2001, about the measures adopted in connection with the expulsion. It contained the information that the body-search at the airport and the use of handcuffs and fetters was at the express order of the captain of the aircraft. In addition, it was noted that the explanation for requiring A. and E.Z. to wear hoods was that this was a policy that had been laid down on the basis of the events of September 11, 2001, about the transport of deportees with terrorist links.

At about 3 a.m. the plane landed at Cairo. A. and E.Z. disembarked and were received by Egyptian officials. They were then driven off in a transit bus. At this point the Security Police officers considered that the enforcement had been completed.

2.4.4 Subsequent Measures

On their return to Sweden, a meeting was held at Security Police headquarters about the enforcement. Those present at this meeting included officer

Y, A.A. and M.L. The meeting was informed, for instance, that the Egyptians had been required to wear hoods. According to M.L. there may also have been discussion of the use of diapers and that one of the Egyptians was suffering from stomach problems, which was why this was needed. She has, however, pointed out that she is not certain on this point. A.A. has also said that he is uncertain about what was discussed at the meeting but believes that the diapers and the medication were raised in view of the entry on tranquillisers in officer Y's log of the journey.

Officer Y then reported the case to J.D. As has previously been noted, in February 2002 Jan Danielsson drew up a memorandum on the expulsion. In it he states, inter alia, that he can find no grounds for criticising those involved in the expulsion. This memorandum was submitted to the Ministry of Justice, which, on April 12, 2002, conducted a judicial appraisal of the way in which the Security Police had dealt with the enforcement. The Ministry of Justice accepted the Security Police's procedures, in principle, and noted that the Ministry's assessment concurred with the judgement expressed by J.D.

2.5 The Parliamentary Ombudsman's Referral of the Case to the Security Police

The case was referred to the Security Police with the request for a response on the following issues.

1. What legal grounds are there for allowing foreign officials to assist Swedish police officers in connection with the enforcement of a deportation or expulsion order and for permitting them to use coercive measures on Swedish territory?—What appraisal was made of these issues by the Security Police in this case?
2. What legal grounds are there for the use of force or coercion in the enforcement of a deportation or expulsion order ("repatriation")?—Were the coercive measures invoked in the case in question necessary and acceptable?
3. What assessment has been made by the Security Police of the conduct of its officers on this occasion?
4. Had command of the enforcement been assigned to any of the Swedish police officers present at Bromma airport, i.e. could any officer be considered to have operational command?—If not, for what reason had command not been assigned?
5. What judgement has been made by the Security Police on the question of who was in fact in control of the enforcement from the arrival of the two Egyptians at Bromma airport?

2.6 The Response of the Security Police

The Security Police submitted a response to which were attached written statements by M.L. and A.A. and also officers X and Y (whose statements have been omitted). After beginning with an account of the legal provisions, K.B. went on to state the following.

The events at Bromma

The Security Police officers who carried out the enforcement have been questioned by the Parliamentary Ombudsman in this case and provided information that deals with the issues raised from different perspectives. In this response from the Security Police I have enabled these officers to submit additional information on which assessment of the questions raised by the Parliamentary Ombudsman may be based. The statements they have submitted are attached to this response. Two officers have informed me that they have nothing to add to what they have previously said. The Director General at the time, Jan Danielsson, has not submitted any further statement. This, of course, makes it difficult for me now, three years later, to undertake renewed review of the appraisals made of the issues raised by the Parliamentary Ombudsman by senior Security Police officers at the time of the enforcement.

The Security Police has, in the memorandum submitted by J.D. to the Ministry of Justice on the circumstances of the enforcement, undertaken an appraisal of the case in question in accordance with the issues raised by the Parliamentary Ombudsman. The memorandum was drawn up on the basis of the actual circumstances that were then known about the enforcement and have not changed in substance since then. I must therefore refer to this memorandum. The Ministry of Justice has, on the basis of this account, taken a standpoint in a memorandum dated April 12, 2002 on the measures that were justified in connection with the enforcement. The Ministry of Justice then found that the measures adopted were not obviously incompatible with Swedish law but that at the same time they were not totally in accord with Swedish police procedures. The conclusions reached by the Ministry were presented to the Minister of Justice on March 26, 2002. The Ministry of Justice took no measures as a result of the account presented in the Security Police's memorandum.

The issue of command is not touched upon in J.D.'s memorandum. From the information I have gathered it is clear that no specific officer had been assigned command at Bromma airport. As far as can be seen, the Security Police came to the conclusion that this was not the kind of operation that made it necessary to assign operational command at Bromma airport.

With regard to the actions of the Security Police officers, I can merely point out that the enforcement has been reviewed by the public prosecutor and that the Director of the Public Prosecution Agency in Stockholm as part of a review process—have found no grounds for initiating a preliminary enquiry as a result of the measures adopted in connection with the enforcement. I assume that this review also comprised any use of coercion that took place during the enforcement.

Experiences and measures

One result of the appraisal made by the Ministry of Justice and other conclusions that can be drawn about the enforcement is, in my opinion, that the Security Police must develop in some respects and further improve both its decision-making procedures and the operational conduct of enforcement cases.

Effective counter-terrorism obviously requires active Swedish participation in international endeavours in this area. This must never, however, result in foreign officials being permitted to exercise their authority in Sweden. There is in my opinion, an essential difference between the enforcement of a Swedish deportation or expulsion order and international cooperation. For my part, I would find it alien to use a foreign aircraft with foreign security staff, as in this instance. The Security Police must have total control over the enforcement, although due consideration must be taken of the role of the captain of the aircraft.

The National Police Board is currently formulating regulations and general guidelines on the responsibilities of police officers and the management of cases involving enforcement of deportation and expulsion orders. One section will deal with repatriations by air. Pending the issue of these regulations, the National Police Board published a circular on October 14, 2002, with guidance for repatriation by air. The Security Police will, of course, comply with these instructions.

In my judgement, it is clear that some of the measures adopted after the two Egyptians had arrived at Bromma airport were excessive in relation to the actual risks that existed, in particular as Security Police officers had already made body-searches of the two men. There were also other shortcomings in the case, for instance in allowing foreign officials to take measures without adequate participation by Swedish police officers and the lack of any designated operational commander at Bromma airport.

We cannot, of course, exclude the possibility that, within the framework of international cooperation in counter terrorism, foreign officials may be present during some measures in Sweden, at interrogations for instance. In view of previous experience, including this case, the Security Police will, however, carefully consider in advance to what extent and in what way these officials will participate and inform them of the conditions that apply.

In this context, I would also like to mention some organisational and procedural changes that will, overall, help to raise the quality and reliability of Security Police operational measures, including enforcement cases.

The governance of the Security Police is being reorganised and augmented at the moment to enable strategic planning and substantially enhanced direction and monitoring of its operational activities. The new structure will provide greater scope for more intensive analysis of various possible alternative courses of action, and also improved risk analysis for complex operations.

The allocation of authority and accountability in the Security Police will be made more explicit so that responsibility for the conduct of operational measures will more explicitly rest with the head of the unit concerned in certain operational areas. New and more stringent requirements will be introduced for documentary records and reports on operations. This will facilitate retrospective review and appraisal of sensitive and difficult operations.

The Director General will have at his disposal a special unit for internal review, which will provide support for senior officers on issues relating to the focus of and risks involved in major, sensitive operations, and also enable their quality, security and effectiveness to be monitored and evaluated. This unit will consist of senior commanders with considerable operational experience. The unit will also have access to legal expertise from the legal unit. At the moment the Security Police possesses good general competence in the area of international law and human rights on the issues relating to its operations, but additional specialist expertise at an advanced level will be made available in this area.

During 2005 an extensive training programme for newly recruited personnel will begin, which is intended to provide both enhanced basic training and training at specialist levels. In-service training for all personnel will be linked to this programme. Important elements in this training will involve international criminal and procedural law, international law and human rights. Special seminars will also be arranged to deal with the new regulations relating to the conduct of counter-terrorist measures.

3. The Parliamentary Ombudsman's Appraisal

3.1 The Security Police actions in Connection with the Exercise of Public Authority by American Personnel on Swedish Territory etc.

3.1.1 The Legal Framework

The Instrument of Government (IG) is posited on the assumption that judicial and administrative measures are the concern of Swedish authorities.

The constitution is based therefore on the principle that only Swedish police officers are empowered to use force or coercive measures, for instance, against individuals or exercise their authority in any other form (cf. SOU 2003:25 p. 194). However, the Riksdag can decide on exceptions to this principle (IG Chapter 10, Section 5, fourth paragraph).

One exception of this kind has been made in the Act on International Police Cooperation (2000:343), enacted as a result of Sweden's accession to the Schengen Convention. This act contains provisions that give foreign officials legal rights in specific circumstances to invoke measures on Swedish territory in the case of what is specified as cross border pursuit and surveillance.

However, there is no exception to the principle referred to in the case of police enforcement of deportation and expulsion orders. In situations like this, the fundamental rule that only Swedish police officers may exercise public authority on Swedish territory applies. This issue has recently been considered in a Government inquiry. On April 4, 2002, a special commissioner was appointed to review certain issues concerning the enforcement of deportation and expulsion orders. The inquiry, which was called the Inquiry into review of the regulations and praxis in connection with the enforcement of deportation and expulsion orders (Enforcement Inquiry) submitted its report *Enforcement when identity is unclear etc.* (SOU 2003:25) in March 2003. The report contained the following evaluation of this issue (p. 199).

The conclusion reached in the Enforcement Inquiry is that the fundamental principle on which the current regulations are based, i.e. that public authority can only be exercised by the officials of the country whose territory it is, is apposite. The opinion of the inquiry is therefore that there is no reason at the moment to consider any legislative amendments to enable foreign officials to invoke coercive measures on Swedish territory over and above the possibilities afforded by the existing statutes.

The legal situation that applies today has been subject to the appraisal of the Parliamentary Ombudsmen in a number of previous adjudications. In a case concerning the regular police (JO 1974 p. 93) the Parliamentary Ombudsman, Wigelius, expressed the following opinion.

The participation [of foreign personnel] has been raised in a number of different cases. It is more than likely that there are grounds for adopting a liberal approach to foreign participation, but when it comes to the closer forms of participation there is good reason to advocate a more restrictive stance. One general endeavour should, of course, be to preclude as far as possible the kind of participation in which the foreign police officer, either because of lack of knowledge of the regulations that apply to police procedures in Sweden or for some other reason, may commit actions that would be regarded as the abuse of authority if committed by a Swedish police officer. It is of course of the utmost importance that all forms of participation are monitored continually on the part of Sweden, which in principle probably requires all such participation to take place in the presence of a Swedish officer.

A corresponding argument was presented in an adjudication by the Parliamentary Ombudsmen in 1984 (JO 1984/85 p. 131). In a case involving contacts between the Swedish Security Police and foreign security services, the Chief Parliamentary Ombudsman, Eklundh, endorsed the opinion cited above. He stressed in particular that the legal regulations in this area do not permit foreign police officers to conduct police activities in Sweden other than while assisting Swedish police officers, and that the participation of these police officers in Swedish police operations must always take place in the presence of Swedish officers.

It should be pointed out that these previous adjudications by the Parliamentary Ombudsmen have mainly involved the participation of foreign police officers in interrogations that have taken place in Sweden.

A memorandum recently drawn up by the Ministry of Justice on international legal assistance in criminal cases (Ds 2004:50) contains the statement that a fundamental requirement for both the participation of foreign police officers in Sweden and of Swedish officers abroad is that this may not involve measures that according to Swedish law would be considered to be the exercise of public authority. In addition, it is pointed out, with reference to the Parliamentary Ombudsmen's adjudications cited above, that this general principle should be considered to apply if there are no regulations permitting more extensive measures, as is the case, for instance, with the Act on International Police Cooperation (p. 116 f.)

The Security Police's own internal procedural directives lay down, for instance, that cooperation with foreign services or other authorities may not include exercise of their powers in Sweden.

As pointed out above, the Enforcement Inquiry found no reason to propose any legislative amendments in this respect. On the other hand, the agencies responsible were recommended to issue regulations on how their officials must act when involved in repatriation transport. In view of this, in February 2005 the National Police Board issued regulations and general guidelines for the enforcement of deportation and expulsion orders involving travel by air (FAP 638-1). These lay down that the police authority is the enforcement agency even when assisted by a foreign agency (§15). Another stipulation is that security controls that involve body-searches or other methods that require statutory endorsement must be carried out on Swedish territory by Swedish police officers (§17). The general guidelines under this last regulation state that there may be reasons for foreign police officers or other officials representing foreign agencies to assist Swedish police officers in enforcement situations on Swedish territory, for instance in cases pursuant to the Act concerning Special Controls in Respect of Aliens (1991:572). This can occur in cases when another state assists by providing transport. The general guidelines under §17 also point out that a foreign police officer or other official may, on the orders of the captain or in some other emergency, use coercive measures on board an aircraft.

In its report the Enforcement Inquiry also raised another aspect that may be of some significance in this context, which is the position and powers of the captain on board an aircraft.

Section 1 of Chapter 5 of the Aviation Act (1957:297) lays down that the captain of an aircraft is the supreme authority on board. The captain may take the measures required to avoid danger, if the behaviour of any individual constitutes an immediate risk to the safety of the aircraft or safety on board. In carrying out these measures the captain may not adopt greater force than the circumstances require and force may only be used when other methods are of no avail. If force is resorted to, only the mildest form likely to achieve the desired result may be used and only for as long as is absolutely necessary. Members of the crew are to provide the captain with any assistance he may require. Passengers may also provide such assistance, if requested by the captain. If, because of imminent danger, measures must be taken immediately, members of the crew or passengers may themselves act without the captain's order (Chapter 5.4). A captain may also refuse to allow members of the crew, passengers or cargo on board the aircraft when the circumstances so demand (Chapter 5.3). The captain of a foreign aircraft has the same powers even in Swedish areas (Chapter 5.6).

In view of these regulations, the Enforcement Inquiry contained the following statement (p. 199).

In the case of a foreign aircraft, certain security controls may be demanded before the individual in question is at all permitted to board the aircraft for transport from Sweden. In cases where security controls of this kind include body-searches or other coercive physical measures that require some basis in law, it is reasonable to assume that these measures may not be carried out on Swedish territory by foreign officials without such a legal basis. In view of the captain's responsibility for safety on board the aircraft and the regulations entitling him in certain cases to invoke violent measures, it cannot, however, be excluded that foreign officials may have the right, on his orders or in an emergency, to resort to some degree of coercion.

It can be pointed out that the Ministry of Justice's memorandum of April 2002 about this particular enforcement concluded with a reference to the appointment a few days earlier of a special commissioner to review regulations and praxis in connection with the enforcement of deportation and expulsion orders, i.e. the Enforcement Inquiry. In addition, it was pointed out that experience of the Egypt case had been taken into account when drafting the directives for this inquiry.

Finally, it may added that there are no regulations governing the possibilities open to the police of using foreign aircraft in enforcing deportation and expulsion orders.

3.1.2 Adjudication

For a long time the police in Sweden have had extensive international cooperation with the police in other countries and with international police organisations. This occurs, for instance, through participation in Interpol, Europol and Schengen, commitments in international conventions, bilateral agreements or simply through the exchange of valuable police information. It also seems as if international police cooperation is becoming more intensive, both within the scope of the European Union and at a more general international level. There may be good reasons for cooperation of this kind in itself and it may be necessary to prevent and oppose terrorism and other forms of cross-border criminality.

This international cooperation naturally involves the work of the Security Police to a great extent. It was pointed out, for example, in 1989 in a report on the working methods of the Security Police that international cooperation plays a very important role in enabling the security service to operate effectively, for instance in the field of counter-terrorism (SOU 1989:18 p. 61). Sweden has also ratified various conventions on combating international terrorism, such as the UN International Convention for the Suppression of the Financing of Terrorism.

It is therefore hardly remarkable that during its surveillance and investigation of A. and E.Z. the Security Police had contacts with the security services of other countries. However, a completely different state of affairs arises when this kind of cooperation evolves from merely exchanging information to permitting foreign police officers or security agents to take an active part in police operations and to exercise public authority in Sweden. There is, as K.B. remarks, an essential difference between the enforcement of a Swedish deportation or expulsion order and other forms of international cooperation.

To begin with, I wish to point out that the mere fact that a foreign police officer or official is present when Swedish police officers exercise their authority is not in conflict with current legislation. I can, therefore, envisage a situation in which a foreign security agent assists a Swedish police officer in a terrorist case by, for instance, being present and asking additional questions during an interrogation (cf. the opinions expressed in JO 1974 p. 93 and JO 1993/94 p. 88). Another conceivable situation could involve the presence of a foreign police officer while Swedish police officers are searching premises. Nor do I have any objections to the presence of a foreign official during the enforcement of a deportation and expulsion order. It is, however, important to point out that in these cases the public authority must be explicitly exercised by Swedish police officers and that the foreign officials have to remain in the background and adopt what is basically a passive role.

The inquiry into this case reveals, however, that during the brief period of time, about one hour, during which the American and Egyptian officials were on Swedish territory, the opposite circumstances applied. The Swedish Security Police officers remained in the background while the American officials exercised public authority on their own by, for instance, adopting coercive measures such as body- searches, physical examination and some degree of force in the use of fetters and handcuffs. In section 3.2 below I will present my opinion of the force and coercive measures that were invoked during the enforcement in more detail.

Before dealing with the question of whether or not the exercise of public authority by American officials on Swedish territory was legal, there are grounds for touching to some extent on the reason for accepting the American offer.

The inquiry reveals, as has already been described, that from November 2001 and onwards, continuous discussions were taking place between the Ministry for Foreign Affairs and the Security Police concerning, among other things, when a Government decision could be expected. It transpires that it was said initially that no decision could be expected before January 2002. Information on file at the Security Police shows that subsequently it was intended that the Government should reach its decision on December 13, 2001, and the enforcement was therefore arranged for December 15. On December 5, the Ministry for Foreign Affairs then announced that no decision could be expected before December 20. This information must have been revised, however, as on December 14, the Ministry announced that the Government intended to make a decision in the case only four days later.

In other words, there seems to have been far from adequate planning. This lack of foresightedness appears to have contributed to the fact that the American offer came under discussion.

Indeed, the inquiry reveals that when the Security Police were attempting to charter a plan in the customary way via the National Prisons and Probation Administration's transport service, it was difficult at short notice to arrange slots for flights through Europe on the day when the decision would be made, December 18 2001. As the plane chartered could not leave until the morning of December 19 places were requisitioned for A. and E.Z.

at the Kronoberg Detention Centre for the night of December 18. The difficulty of arranging the desired transport in immediate connection with the anticipated Government decision must be considered to be the reason why it was only shortly before the expulsion order was issued that the Security Police received the CIA offer of the use of a plane with a direct flight path through Europe on the day of the decision itself.

One question is whether this offer was discussed during the presentation of the case to the Ministry for Foreign Affairs on December 17, 2001. As the inquiry shows, the Security Police and the Ministry for Foreign Affairs have different opinions on this issue. A.A. and officer X have both stated that the two transport alternatives were presented at the meeting and that the Foreign Minister gave the "go-ahead" to acceptance of the American offer. The Ministry for Foreign Affairs claims, on its part, that there is no support for the assertion that the Security Police mentioned the American alternative during the presentation. I may conclude that the inquiry (by the Ministry for Foreign Affairs) into this issue was made in May/June 2004, i.e. about 2,5 years after the event, that the recollections of those interviewed seem to be vague and extremely disparate and that the information provided by the Security Police is corroborated by a journal entry and other written documents drawn up shortly after the meeting. Appraisal on the basis of the information available to me strongly suggests, therefore, that at this meeting the Foreign Minister was informed about the alternative involving the use of an American aircraft for enforcement and the Security Police received the impression that this procedure had been accepted.

It should be emphasised that full responsibility for how the enforcement was implemented rests of course with the Security Police. In my opinion, it is nevertheless understandable that in the choice of transport the Security Police also took into account what it had come to believe was the Foreign Minister's attitude in this respect.

Here I would already like to point out that scarcely any objection on principle can be raised to the use of a foreign aircraft for the enforcement of a deportation or expulsion order, even though, of course, there may be situations when such a course of action may appear to be less than suitable.

It is also clear that during the presentation on December 17, 2001, nothing was said about the participation of foreign security personnel in the enforcement. As far as I have been able to determine, this information was not given to the Security Police until lunchtime on December 18, 2001.

Against this background, I have found no reason to go any further in my inquiry into what was discussed at the presentation to the Foreign Minister. In addition, as pointed out initially, Ministers are not subject to the supervision of the Parliamentary Ombudsmen.

With respect to the acceptance by the Security Police of the American offer, it is worth pointing out that, after the terrorist attack on September 11, 2001, the USA began what was termed a war against terrorism. There are therefore good reasons for asserting that the offer of the use of an American aircraft for transport by the American intelligence service only three months after the terrorist attack should have given rise to explicit questions from the Security Police about whether this offer was conditional on the requirement of any particular arrangements with regard to security. If such questions had been asked when the offer was received, it is likely that the required participation of American security personnel and security checks could have been taken into consideration when deciding whether to accept it or not. Questions like this would probably have been answered, not least in view of the fact that there seems to have been an American policy, developed on the basis of the events of September 11, 2001, that applied to the transport of deportees with terrorist links.

A.A., who handled contacts with the CIA, has said that no conditions were attached by the Americans to the use of the American plane by the Security Police. However, during my inquiry, no information has been submitted to suggest that this was ever discussed at all. Instead, the Security Police seems to have accepted the offer almost passively without investigating what it would mean in practice, merely assuming that they were talking about a "pure transport service". The circumstance that, according M.L., this was probably the first time the Security Police had used a foreign aircraft in a case like this, should have given rise to appraisal of the problems, for instance from a legal point of view, that acceptance of the American offer might entail. In this respect the Security Police displayed remarkable inadvertence.

After this, there is reason to turn to what occurred during officer Y's meeting at Bromma at lunchtime on December 18, 2001. As far as I have been able to determine, this is when the Security Police received information that security personnel would be accompanying the aircraft, that the personnel would be hooded, that they wanted to conduct their own security checks of A. and E.Z. and that there would not be room on the plane for any Swedish police officers. This information should have given rise to considerable apprehension about the ability of the Security Police to retain control over the enforcement. It was therefore not sufficient for the Security Police to assert that Swedish police officers were responsible for the enforcement by merely demanding that a pair of its representatives should be enabled to accompany the plane to Egypt. Information about the extent of the American involvement should at any rate have prompted those responsible at the Security Police to assign immediate operational command to an officer of sufficiently high rank to ensure on the spot that the Swedish police officers would retain control of events at Bromma in every respect and also during the flight to Egypt. In addition, the Security Police at this stage should have asked for information about what the security checks would comprise. If this had been provided, the Security Police would have had time to undertake a judicial appraisal of whether—and if so to what extent—checks of this kind were acceptable.

The inquiry suggests that officer Y informed A.A. and that the latter, without any further probing or consideration, approved that security checks could be made. Once again the Security Police acted passively. Officer Y has admittedly stated that a security check was all that had been mentioned, but the turn that the events took shows that these inspections went further than this and the measures taken by the American officials followed what appeared to be a well-drilled pattern. The fact that the Americans wanted access to a room should have raised doubts about whether it was merely a question of frisking the two men in the usual way.

The closer implications of the American demand to be allowed to make security checks do not therefore appear to have been clear to the Security Police before the inspections were being carried out at Bromma airport—if even then.

I will now turn to a discussion of the question of whether the behaviour of the Security Police in connection with the conduct of the American security personnel on Swedish territory is compatible with Swedish law.

As has been made clear by the account of the legal regulations, the legal situation in this area is relatively clear. Insofar as Swedish law does not otherwise provide, the Swedish legal system is based on the premise that police activities in Sweden are dealt with by Swedish police officers. At the moment, in other words, the Swedish legal system does not permit foreign officials to undertake police operations in Sweden unless they are assisting the Swedish police force and the participation of such officials in police operations in Sweden must always take place in the presence of a Swedish police officer.

One cogent reason for adhering to this principle is that criminal liability for misuse of office applies only to the exercise of Swedish authority (Criminal Code 20.1). In the cases where provision has been made for a foreign police officer to exercise certain public authority in Sweden—as a result of agreement with other states—this liability has been extended to include officers in this position. Section 12 of the Act on International Police Cooperation (Schengen cooperation) stipulates that liability for misuse of office as laid down in 20.1 of the Criminal Code applies to foreign officials exercising their authority in Sweden on the same terms as if they were exercising Swedish authority. The foreign officials are therefore placed on the same footing in this respect as Swedish police officers. In my opinion it would be unacceptable to have a system which enabled foreign officials to exercise public authority in Sweden without being subject to the liability laid down in the Criminal Code for misuse of office. In addition, it may be worth pointing out that problems may arise in civil suits for indemnity for injuries or damage caused by foreign officials in Sweden (cf. Section 13 of the Act on International Police Cooperation).

In his statement A.A. has raised the issue of whether, in view of the international developments that have taken place in recent years both in and outside the EU, any change has taken place in attitudes to the extent to which foreign officials from other security or intelligence services can participate in operations in Sweden. As has already been shown, the answer must be in the negative. The previous opinions of the Parliamentary Ombudsman cited here still apply and also seem to have gained general support. Nor can I, for my part, see any reason for excluding the Security Police from the current system. On the contrary, there may be grounds for particular restrictiveness in allowing foreign security and intelligence services to operate on Swedish territory. In addition, it is my opinion that the growth in the extent and intensity of international police cooperation augments the need for firm and clear regulations.

Another question that has been raised in this case is whether the provisions of Chapter 5 of the Aviation Act can be invoked in support of the actions of the American officials on Swedish territory. Such support could be derived from the observations of the Enforcement Inquiry that in view of the captain's responsibility for security on board an aircraft and the regulations that entitle him in certain cases to use force, the possibility cannot be excluded that at his request or in an emergency foreign officials have the right to use some coercion.

However, the Aviation Act only grants the captain, and, in principle, if he so decides, members of the crew and passengers, power to resort to the use of force to maintain order and safety on board the aircraft. Recourse to force may only take place when other means are ineffectual and it may be invoked for no longer than is absolutely necessary. On the other hand, the captain does not have the right to order the use of force towards someone who is not on board his plane. Here his power is restricted to the right to refuse to allow passengers to board when the circumstances so require. If a captain, by virtue of this entitlement, demands at a Swedish airport that a passenger undergo some coercive measure before being allowed on board, it is obvious that this measure may not be implemented by anyone other than a Swedish police officer (cf. Section 17 in FAP 638-1).

Here too, therefore, I agree with the opinion that generally prevails that, to the extent that Swedish legislation does not provide otherwise, according to the current law foreign officials are not allowed to undertake police operations in Sweden except when assisting Swedish police officers and that the participation of such officials in Swedish police operations must always take place in the presence of a Swedish officer. In my opinion there are particularly cogent reasons for upholding this principle when the police operation concerned may involve subjecting individuals to force or coercive measures.

The inquiry in this case shows that the American security officials did not merely assist the Security Police in their enforcement but that in reality they took over and were in control from the moment of their arrival at Bromma airport. Admittedly Swedish Security Police officers were present, but they remained passively in the background while the American officials were allowed to conduct the security checks on their own. This kind of complete transfer of the exercise of public authority to foreign officials on Swedish territory is not compatible with Swedish law.

Nor can the Security Police be considered to have been in control of the enforcement on board the aircraft. The enforcement of an expulsion is not complete until the deportee has been received in the destination country. The Swedish police therefore have full responsibility for the enforcement until that time. In this case it has even been shown that initially there was no room for Security Police officers on board the aircraft but that after objections had been raised by Swedish representatives two Swedish officials were allowed to accompany the flight. Of the two selected to do so, one had been assigned no explicit command and the other was a civilian interpreter who could not exercise police authority.

To sum up, it can be concluded that at Bromma airport the Security Police had already lost control of the enforcement. In reality, the Security Police officers at the airport relinquished the enforcement to American officials and gave them free hands to exercise public authority. There is no basis in law for conduct of this kind.

3.2 The Use of Force and Coercive Measures etc.

3.2.1 The Legal Framework

The European convention on the Protection of Human Rights and Fundamental Freedoms (European Convention) has had the force of domestic law in Sweden since 1994. Article 3 lays down that no one shall be subjected to torture or to inhuman or degrading treatment or punishment. A definition of the concept of torture may be found in the United Nations Convention against Torture or Other Cruel, Inhuman or Degrading Treatment or Punishment, which is known as the Torture Convention (see also Danelius, *Mänskligarättigheterieuropeiskpraxis (Human rights in European Praxis)*, 2002, p. 71 f.).

In addition Chapter 2 of the Instrument of Government contains provisions about the fundamental freedoms and rights of citizens. All citizens shall be protected in their relations with the public administration against any physical violation and physical search (Section 6). The expression physical violation refers principally to the use of force against the human body but also includes medical examination, minor operations such as vaccination or taking blood samples and also similar actions of the kind often referred to as physical examination (Govt. Bill 1975/76:209 p. 147). Physical examination is defined in its turn as an inspection of the surface and interior of the human body and examination of samples taken from the human body (Procedural Code 28.12, second paragraph). Body-search refers to the examination of garments and other items worn and also of bags, packages and other objects that someone is carrying (Procedural Code 28.12, third paragraph).

Foreigners in Sweden are, unless some other provision is made by legal statute, on the same footing as Swedish citizens in these respects (IG 22.2, second paragraph).

The use by the police of force and coercive measures implies a restriction of the protection against coercive physical violation and physical search cited above. This protection may only be restricted by law (IG 2:12, first paragraph).

The Aliens Act lacks provisions on the use of force and coercive measures in the enforcement of an expulsion order. Instead, when police assistance is required in the course of enforcement the provisions that regulate the actions of the police in general apply.

It should first be pointed out that in all forms of police operation, the principle of necessity and proportionality referred to in the first paragraph of Section 8 of the Police Act (1984:387) must be taken into account. According to this statute, a police officer may, in the execution of his official duties, only act in ways that can be justified in terms of the objective of his actions and other circumstances. If coercion has to be used, this may only be in the form and to the extent needed to attain the intended result.

The legal basis for the powers of the police to use force can be found in Section 10 of the Police Act. This lays down that a police officer, insofar as other methods are ineffectual and it can be justified in view of the circumstances, may use force to discharge his duties, for instance, if he is offered violence or the threat of violence (point 1), if someone who is to be detained, apprehended or in some other way lawfully deprived of liberty attempts to escape or the officer encounters some other form of resistance when enforcing such a deprivation of liberty (point 2), to prevent a criminal act or danger to life, health or valuable property or extensive damage to the environment (point 3), or if the action is needful in other respects for the sake of public order and security and that it is obvious that it cannot be carried out without violence (point 7).

The powers of the police to restrain individuals are regulated in Section 10a of the Police Act, together with the first paragraph of Section 15 of the Act on the Treatment of those Detained and Arrested, etc. (1976:371). These provisions permit a detainee to be restrained during transport and on other occasions outside the place of detention whenever this is required for the sake of safety or in order to prevent violent behaviour by the detainee, if other remedies are seen to be ineffectual and when required to safeguard the life and health of the detainee or other individuals. According to Section 10a of the Police Act, a police officer has the same rights to use restraints when he apprehends or restricts the liberty of an individual in some other way. Restraint is normally used to refer to a device that binds the hands or feet together (Berggren and Munck, *Polislagen (The Police Act)*, 4. ed., p. 80). The manual issued by the Prison and Probation Administration states that the following types of restraints may be used: handcuffs, ankle fetters, waist chains, plastic restraints, stretchers and straitjackets.

Apart from the areas laid down in these statutes, there are no others, except for the special situations referred to in Chapter 24 of the Criminal Code on the general grounds for exemption from criminal responsibility, in which the police may resort to the use of force.

The provisions in the Police Act entitling police officers to use force do not apply to foreign police officers. It is quite another matter that a foreign police officer, like any other individual, is exempt from criminal responsibility if he comes to the assistance of a Swedish police officer (see 24.5 of the Criminal Code, cf. as well SOU 1987:14 p. 185).

The Police Act also contains a provision on body-searches. A police officer who makes a legal arrest or otherwise apprehends someone or removes them may, in connection with this measure, also conduct a body-search to the extent that this is required for the sake of safety, for instance, so that weapons and other dangerous objects can be impounded (Section 19). The kind of search required for the sake of order or safety when someone has been detained by the police is normally referred to in everyday terms as "frisking" (see Berggren and Munck, p. 120 f.). There are, however, no provisions in the Police Act that provide a legal basis for physical examinations.

Chapter 6 of the Aliens Act includes regulations on detention. If an alien is detained and placed in a Criminal Correction facility, detention centre or police cell, the rules laid down in Sections 2 and 2a-2c in the Act on the Treatment of those Detained and Arrested, etc. apply to physical searches and physical examinations. (Aliens Act 6.2, second paragraph).

There are no provisions that deal with the rights of police officers to wear masks in the course of their operations. Conduct of this kind, with the possible exceptions that may arise in the course of operations by the National Counter-terrorist Unit, are alien to the spirit of regular police activities. It has however been considered that in view of the duties of the Security Police, its officers are often required to use methods that are rarely adopted by the regular police. One example that may be cited is that Security Police officers sometimes have to assume another identity in order to safeguard both themselves and their families from being exposed to threat and other forms of reprisal (see for instance JO 1993/94 p. 88 and SOU 1990:51 p. 153).

There are also what are known as the protective regulations for civil aviation (see, for instance, the Act on the Protection of Civil Aviation (2004:1100) which came into force on January 1, 2005. This Act enables body-searches to be made in the course of a security check at an airport. Similar regulations were previously contained in the Act on Special Controls at Airports (1970:926).

In the regulations and general guidelines on the enforcement of deportation and expulsion orders by air (FAP 638-1) recently issued by the National Police Board, it is stipulated that if during the enforcement procedure an alien is treated by foreign officials in a way that is obviously incompatible with what is regarded as acceptable in terms of Swedish law, the Swedish police officer responsible for the enforcement must intervene without delay. The police authorities shall in such cases promptly consider whether the enforcement is to be cancelled (Section 3, cf. also Section 16). One of the general guidelines under Section 3 states that if the treatment of the alien referred to in the regulation is of extremely brief duration and no repetition may be anticipated, the enforcement should not be cancelled.

3.2.2 Adjudication

To begin with, I should like to point out that for me it is self-evident that in a democratic state, subject to the rule of law, police officers must treat all those who become the object of police actions in a humane and dignified manner. This means that nobody may be subjected to degrading or humiliating treatment in the course of a police operation. Among its other provisions, the European Convention also lays down, as has been pointed out, as an unconditional rule that nobody may be subjected to inhuman or degrading treatment (Article 3). The following adjudication is therefore based on this fundamental acknowledgement of and respect for the freedoms and rights of every individual.

As can be seen from the presentation of the legal regulations, there are grounds in law for the use by the police of force and to some extent coercive measures in the enforcement of a deportation or expulsion order. Actions of this kind, such as the use of restraints, may not, however, become a matter of routine and in every individual case an appraisal must be made of whether the situation requires recourse to such means. There are, therefore, grounds for studying more closely whether the measures adopted in the case of A. and E.Z. were compatible with Swedish legislation and, if so, whether they were necessary.

In this case, it has been revealed that Swedish police officers made body-searches of A. and E.Z. when they were apprehended. They were then subjected to a security check at Bromma airport conducted by American officials. As has already been made clear, these checks comprised at least the following elements. A. and E.Z. were subjected to body-searches, their clothes were cut to pieces and placed in bags, their hair was thoroughly examined, as were their oral cavities and ears. In addition they were handcuffed and their ankles fettered, dressed in overalls and photographed. Finally loose hoods without holes for their eyes were placed over their heads. A. and E.Z. were then taken out of the police station in bare feet and conveyed to the aircraft where they were laid on mattresses to which they were strapped. The hoods, handcuffs and fetters were not removed during the flight to Egypt.

Where the body-searches are concerned, it can be observed that for the sake of safety, for instance, it is of course a matter of police routine to conduct a body-search of individuals when they are apprehended. I therefore have no objection to the body searches made by the Security Police officers of A. and E.Z. and can also, in view of the regulations and safety requirements that apply to air transport, accept that a second-body search was made immediately before boarding the aircraft.

I can also understand that for the sake of safety on board an aircraft, there may be grounds for handcuffing someone during a repatriation. I therefore have no objections to the decision to handcuff A. and E.Z. during the flight to Egypt. However, there seems to have been no obvious need for ankle fetters as well. At no stage during the enforcement had A. and E.Z. attempted to resist, either actively or passively, or shown any tendency to want to escape. In addition they were surrounded all the time by a large number of American, Swedish and Egyptian officials. The only incident that took place consisted of the remark E.Z. made at the airport.

The inspection of A. and E.Z.'s hair and the scrutiny of their oral cavities and ears must be considered to constitute a physical examination. There is no legal support for the use of this kind of coercive measure in this particular case.

A. and E.Z. were also made to wear hoods. Actions of this kind are alien to the conduct of the Swedish police although, in one or two cases, similar measures have unfortunately been adopted in Sweden recently. The response of the Security Police asserts, as does the memorandum drawn up by the Ministry of Justice in April 2002, that it is most appropriate to consider the use of hoods on the basis of Section 10 of the Police Act. In my opinion, there is a great deal to suggest that a measure of this kind cannot be evaluated by reference to this provision but that, instead, there are no regulations that apply. Even if the measure were to be appraised on the basis of Section 10 of the Police Act, in this case it was manifestly not a necessary element in the performance of official duties (cf. Berggren and Munck, p. 71). Moreover, in my judgement, it is patently obvious that the requirements for the use of force laid down in point 7, which the Security Police refer to in particular, were not fulfilled. In other words, there were no legal grounds for this measure. In this context it may also be pointed out that the UN's general principles for the protection of individuals deprived of their liberty emphasise, inter alia, that detainees may not be deprived of the ability to use their senses, vision or hearing, nor their sense of orientation in time and space.

I have no reason to comment on the fact that the American officials were wearing masks other than to point out that, as can be seen from the account of the legal regulations, in principle such conduct cannot be accepted in Sweden.

It has also been claimed that in the changing room tranquillisers were administered to A. and E.Z. rectally and that they were even made to wear diapers before being dressed in overalls. The Security Police officers who have been heard, including the two who were present in the changing room, have however stated that they did not at that time observe and were not subsequently informed that this was the case. Their accounts leave, however, some scope for the possibility that these actions may have taken place without their notice. Some support for the belief that drugs were administered coercively can be found in the information given by E.Z. to K.J. and the entry made by officer Y in the enforcement log, "A. and E.Z. were probably given a tranquilliser by the doctor before take-off". Officer Y has asserted that the entry was mere speculation on his behalf but has not, in my opinion, been able to provide any reasonable explanation as to what, in this case, his speculation was based on. I am therefore obliged to conclude that the inquiry cannot show with certainty whether a coercive measure such as the forcible administration of drugs did take place or not. The same applies to whether the two men were made to wear diapers.

The lack of certainty that therefore prevails on this point is, as far as I can see, one outcome of the shortcomings in the way in which the Security Police organised the operation. As no Swedish police officers even diligently supervised the measures adopted by the foreign officials, it has been impossible subsequently to establish or repudiate the allegations of forcible medication.

Even though the inquiry has not, therefore, been able shed light on the circumstances in this respect, I would like to point out that coercive medication is one of the kinds of coercive physical measures referred to in 2.6 of the Instrument of Government and which therefore requires the support of law to be permitted. There is no such support in the Police Act. In the *travauxpréparatoires*to the legislation, it is specifically pointed out that in a society like Sweden, it can never be permissible for the police to use psychopharmaceuticals or other drugs in the course of an official enforcement. No support for methods of this kind may be derived from the Police Act but they should be considered unlawful. In addition, it is stated that this does not exclude the possibility that a court of law, by virtue of the general rule about emergencies in the Criminal Code, may consider it justifiable, in exceptional cases, for a police officer to have administered medicine to someone against their will in a situation of extreme emergency. (Govt. Bill. 1983/84:111 p. 92 f.).

Coercive medication in the current case would therefore have been unlawful.

I also have reason to consider whether the treatment of A. and E.Z. during the enforcement was compatible with the prohibition against torture and inhuman and degrading treatment enshrined in the European Convention and elsewhere. On this issue I would first like to point out that in both from the Torture Convention and from application by the European Court of Human Rights of the distinction made in Article 3 of the European Convention between torture and other forms of unlawful treatment, it is clear that torture is a concept reserved for cases involving the intentional infliction of severe pain or grave suffering intended, for instance, to obtain information or to punish or intimidate (see for example the judgment of the European Court of Human Rights of June 27, 2000 in the case of Salman v. Turkey). I, for my part, do not consider that the treatment to which A. and E.Z. were subjected in Sweden and during the flight to Egypt can be regarded as torture.

For some action to be considered to be in breach of article 3 in the European Convention in some other respect, the European Court of Human Rights has taken the view that the treatment, when all the circumstances have been taken into account, such as how long it lasted, its effect on the physical or mental health of the victim, as well as the victim's age and health, must attain a certain level of severity (see for instance the judgment issued on January 18, 1978, in the case of Ireland v. the United Kingdom). In particular, when the issue concerns whether or not some form of treatment is to be considered degrading, the court has taken into account whether the object has been to humiliate the individual concerned and also its effect on the individual's personality. When such treatment has occurred in connection with the deprivation of liberty, it must involve a violation that exceeds the humiliation inherent in arrest or detention (see for instance the judgment of March 12, 2003, in the case of Öcalan v. Turkey). It should be noted in particular that in the case mentioned the court considered that the circumstance that Öcalan for security reasons was blindfolded and handcuffed during a flight from Kenya to Turkey did not constitute a violation of Article 3 of the European Convention.

Nevertheless, I consider that the treatment to which A. and E.Z. were subjected, from the moment when their clothes were cut up and removed and they were hooded at Bromma airport until they arrived in Cairo, still wearing hoods, fettered and strapped to mattresses, must in its entirety be characterised as degrading. The possibility cannot be excluded that this treatment, even if it may have been prompted mainly for reasons of security, could also have been intended to humiliate. In my opinion therefore, questions could be raised as to whether the enforcement was implemented in a manner that constituted a breach of article 3 of the European Convention. Irrespective of whether or not this was the case, it is nevertheless clear that in the end the enforcement was carried out in an inhuman and therefore unacceptable manner.

I have previously observed that there was no basis in law for allowing the American officials to exercise public authority on Swedish territory. The Security Police should have reacted, therefore, as I have already pointed out, when a demand was made on December 18, 2001, to be allowed to conduct a security check. As has been made clear, the representatives of the Security Police remained passive on this issue. The officers present at Bromma airport were therefore surprised by the extent of the examinations. For this reason—and in view of the rapidity with which the examinations were made—I can understand that the Security Police officers made no analysis of the legality of the measures adopted. They should, however, even without such an analysis, have realised that there were grounds for intervening to prevent the inhuman treatment that A. and E.Z. were being subjected to.

Certain other circumstances may be assumed to have played a role when the Security Police allowed these events to occur. To begin with, no officer had been assigned operational command at Bromma airport. As a result none of the Swedish officers present—all of whom were of relatively junior rank—considered that they were ultimately responsible for the enforcement. K.B. has also referred to this shortcoming. It cannot be excluded that an operational commander with a relatively senior rank could have influenced the course of events. Instead, the Swedish Security Police officers were remarkably submissive to the American officials. The unclear organisation of the Swedish team may also have contributed to give the Americans the impression that there was no need to give the Security Police more detailed information about what was about to happen. Secondly, it cannot be excluded, either, that the Security Police officers present may have been burdened by their knowledge that the Government had decided on enforcement without delay and that the Ministry for Foreign Affairs, for instance, considered it important for enforcement to take place on the day the decision had been made.

It is mainly against this background that I have decided, albeit with some hesitation, to take no further action than to express my criticism in this adjudication.

3.3 Concluding Comments

In the public debate, information has been offered to suggest that what occurred was the first American transport of prisoners in the hunt for presumed terrorists after September 11, 2001, and that the American officials were part of a special commando that undertook what have been called "extraordinary renditions". This term is used to refer to a process in which individuals suspected of being terrorists are secretly and with no basis in law taken to certain states that cooperate with the USA so that they can be interrogated there in a brutal manner. For instance, in *Chain of Command—the Road from 9/11 to AbuGhraib*, London 2004, Seymour M. Hersh alleges of the events at Bromma airport that "American operatives participated in what amounted to the kidnapping of two Egyptians" (p. 53).

My impression is that the enforcement involving A. and E.Z. cannot be regarded as a rendition of this kind. It is important to remember that the Security Police were conducting certain investigations and surveillance, that the Migration Board studied the applications for asylum submitted by the two men and that, above all, the Government rejected, by virtue of the Aliens Act, A. and E.Z.'s applications for residence and labour permits and decided that the two men were to be expelled to their native country. This was not therefore a case in which "American agents" alone removed the two men.

In international police cooperation it is important to consider the legal aspects and restrictions that apply. It is obvious that the Security Police did not pay sufficient consideration to the difficulties that could be linked to acceptance of the American offer. In this adjudication I have accounted for considerable shortcomings in the way in which the Security Police dealt with the enforcement. In my opinion, the most striking deficiency is the passivity shown by the Security Police throughout. This failing, combined with the lack of any designated operational commander at Bromma airport, resulted, in my view, in the Security Police losing control of the way in which events developed.

I have also pointed out that A. and E.Z. were subjected to inhuman treatment. I would like to emphasise that treatment of this kind is alien to Swedish police procedures and cannot be tolerated.

Foreign officials who assist Swedish police officers in Sweden are not, in principle, entitled to use force and may not resort to other forms of coercion. If, nevertheless, foreign officials take such measures or, as in this case, go so far as to act in a way that is not acceptable according to Swedish legal standards, Swedish police officers must intervene to put a stop to this without delay. I consider that in this case the Security Police officers should have aborted the enforcement. Had they done so, it could then have taken place with the aircraft that was ready to depart on the morning of the following day.

Finally, I find reason to comment on the contents of the statements submitted by officers X and Y to the Parliamentary Ombudsman. In important respects they fail to express self-critical reflection. In their opinion, for instance, the Security Police had control of the enforcement. In addition, Security Police officer Y states that the enforcement of A. and E.Z. "did not go so far that the two concerned were subject to any more discomfort that can be considered necessary given the order that was being enforced". I am disturbed by the lack of self-criticism in this attitude, particularly in an operational area that is characterised by secrecy and closed to public control. At the same time, I note with satisfaction K.B.'s assertion that it would be alien for him to use a foreign aircraft with foreign security personnel in the way this occurred in this case.

I take it for granted that the Security Police will adopt cogent measures to avoid any repetition of what occurred. As can be seen from its official response, work has already started on reorganising its operations, enhancing its internal controls and training. In addition, the National Police Board recently issued regulations and general guidelines in this area.

With the extremely grave criticism of the Security Police that I have found reason to express, I conclude this case.

DOCUMENT NO. 13

RESPONSE TO A LETTER ENTITLED "EVIDENCE OF EXTRAORDINARY RENDITION"

Office of the Minister of Foreign Affairs, Ireland

July 25, 2006

Dear Dr Manning,

Thank you again for your further thoughts on the subject of extraordinary rendition, contained in your letter of 24 May. As my Private Secretary stated in his initial reply to you of 6 June, I greatly value our dialogue on the fundamentally important issues with which your correspondence has been concerned.

I must, however, strongly disagree with the suggestion made in Part (1) of your letter—*Evidence of extraordinary rendition*—that I consider the matter of so-called extraordinary rendition to be largely an "academic matter". On the contrary, it is a matter which exercises the Government greatly. We have gone to great lengths not only to voice our complete opposition to the practice, but also to raise our concerns at the very highest levels of the US government. In this respect, I have been active at the General Affairs and External Relations Council of EU Foreign Ministers, and also in my bilateral dealings with the US authorities. As a result, Ireland is in the unique position in Europe, to the best of my knowledge, of having explicit, categorical, bilateral assurances in this matter, confirmed at the level of the US Secretary of State, Condoleezza Rice.

I would reiterate the fact that there is no evidence, nor even any concrete and specific allegation, that prisoners have been brought through Ireland as part of an extraordinary rendition operation. Let me be clear: I am not denying that the practice exists elsewhere. That much is clear from public statements by US officials. However, the Government have received explicit assurances from the US authorities that Irish territory is not, and has not been, used for this purpose.

I look forward, in the coming months, to the publication of the recommendations of the Secretary General of the Council of Europe, Mr Terry Davis. I would reiterate the Government's intention to consider carefully with partners any specific and workable recommendations that may be made by the Council of Europe in this area. I would anticipate that when such recommendations emerge they will require coordinated action at a European level if they are to be implemented in an effective manner.

I am attaching a note responding in some detail to the legal issues raised in your letter. Let me say that I have found our exchanges to be most valuable. They have helped to clarify the underlying concerns that exist in Ireland on this matter—concerns I have then been able to raise in my bilateral dealings with the US Government, and among EU partners. They have also, I hope, enabled me to clarify for you the Government's position on this complex matter.

I would suggest that if there are any further points you might wish to raise these could be considered between officials.

Yours sincerely,

Dermot Ahern, T.D.
Minister for Foreign Affairs

Comments on the Document Enclosed with the Letter Dated 24 May 2006 to the Minister for Foreign Affairs From the President of the Irish Human Rights Commission

Positive Obligations

In Part (2) of the document, ("Article 3 of the European Convention on Human Rights: The Positive obligation to Prevent Torture"), the Commission takes issue with the Minister's reference, in describing the scope of a State's positive obligation to prevent torture under Article 3 of the Convention, to the judgment of the European Court of Human Rights in the case of *Osman v UK*.[1] The Commission points out that this case dealt with Article 2 of the Convention (on the right to life) and not Article 3, and state that the Minister's reference to it 'could be quite misleading in this context'. The Minister wishes to make clear that he never intended to suggest that the *Osman* case concerned Article 3 of the Convention. The Minister's letter of 4 April, written as it was to a Commission of human rights experts, simply referred to that case as generally indicative of the scope of a State's positive obligation under Article 3, having regard to the well established link

[1] Osman v The United Kingdom, Judgment of the European court of Human Rights, 28 October 1998.

between the two Articles in the Court's jurisprudence. In fact, the relevance of the *Osman* standard to a State's positive obligation to prevent torture is confirmed by the Court's judgment in *E. and Others* v *UK*.[2]

With regard to the Commission's comments on a State's obligation under Article 3 to conduct an effective, official investigation where an arguable claim is raised that ill-treatment is being committed by third parties within Irish jurisdiction, the Minister would point out that all credible complaints of illegal activity connected to so-called extraordinary rendition have been investigated by An Garda Siochana. To date, owing to a lack of evidence that any unlawful activity had occurred, no further action has been found to have been warranted. In this context, the Minister wishes to remind the Commission that the Government have consistently made clear that any person with specific evidence of illegal activity should present this to An Garda Siochana.

Diplomatic Assurances

Turning to the Commission's comments in Part (2) of its letter dealing with diplomatic assurances, the assertion is repeated that the State is not permitted to rely upon these in order to fulfil its positive obligation to prevent use of Irish airports to facilitate so-called extraordinary rendition. In stating this, the Commission refers to comments on diplomatic assurances in the decisions of the European Court of Human Rights in the cases of *Soering v UK*[3] and *Chahal v UK*[4] and the decision of the UN Committee Against Torture in the case of *Ahmed Agiza v Sweden*.[5]

The Minister wishes to points out that the three cases cited did not deal, as the Commission suggests, with the general duty of States to prevent torture, but with the specific obligation of States with regard to non-refoulement. In these cases, both the nature of the diplomatic assurance given and, more particularly, the legal obligation of the relevant States in deciding whether to rely on these assurances differed significantly from those which apply in the current situation.

As the Commission will be aware, a State's obligation of non-refoulement is an explicit requirement of Article 3 of the Convention Against Torture in respect of torture and such a requirement may be implied in respect of other forms of ill-treatment falling within the scope of that Convention. It is also an inherent requirement under Article 3 of the ECHR. The essential

[2] E. and Others v The United Kingdom, Judgment of the European Court of Human Rights, 26 November 2002.
[3] Soering v the United Kingdom, Judgment of the European Court of Human Rights, 7 July 1989.
[4] Chahal v the United Kingdom, Judgment of the European Court of Human Rights, 15 November 1996.
[5] *Agiza v. Sweden*, UN Committee Against Torture, Communication No. 233/2003 (Decision of 20 May 2005).

elements for the obligation to arise, present in all three cases cited by the Commission, is that a State is contemplating the return, through its own action (by mechanisms such as extradition, deportation or expulsion), of a specific individual to another State where there is a substantial risk that he or she might be tortured or ill-treated[6]. The diplomatic assurances considered by States in such situations (again, including all three cases cited) are concerned with how the individual will be treated by or in the potential receiving State. In these situations, international tribunals have considered the weight to be attached by potential sending States to such diplomatic assurances, having regard to their clear legal obligation to determine, on the basis of *all* relevant considerations, whether there are grounds for believing that the individual would be in danger of being subjected to torture or other prohibited ill-treatment.

In the current situation, the above elements are not present. The Government are not contemplating whether to return a particular individual to another State, and are not therefore engaged in an assessment of the risk that that person may be subjected to torture if returned to another State. The matter on which the Government need to satisfy themselves is simply whether a category of persons, alleged without evidence by some commentators to be present on Irish territory, are actually so present. The diplomatic assurances received from the US and accepted by the Government in this context are specific, factual and relate to the very existence of such persons.

It is perhaps worth illustrating this point by a detailed reference to the facts of the *Ahmed Agiza* case. This case was not referred to in the Minister's letter of 4 April precisely because the facts on which it is based are simply absent in the current situation. In the *Agiza* case, the complainant was undoubtedly present in Sweden, and had applied to the Swedish authorities for asylum there. The authorities decided to reject his application, ordered his deportation and subsequently handed him over to foreign agents. In arriving at their decision to deport the applicant, the authorities sought to satisfy themselves that he would not face torture in Egypt, and in this regard appear to have relied upon the assurances of the Egyptian authorities that he would be treated in accordance with international law upon his return to Egypt.[7] The question faced by the Committee Against Torture was whether Sweden's act of handing the complainant over to foreign authorities violated Article 3 of the UN Convention Against Torture. It was in this context that Sweden's reliance on diplomatic assurances was considered by the Committee. No analogous facts are present in the current situation.

---

[6] These specific requirements for such an obligation to arise are evident in your own general point made on page 6 of your letter: '***prisoners*** must not be ***deported*** or ***handed over*** in circumstances where there is a substantial risk that they might be tortured or ill-treated' (emphasis added).

[7] see paragraph 4.12 of the decision.

The fact that a State's obligation in respect of non-refoulement does not arise in the abstract, but requires the existence of an actual person is evident in the *Agiza* decision itself. In paragraph 13.3 of the decision, the Committee states the need to consider whether the complainant was '*personally* at risk of being subjected to torture in the country to which he was returned' (emphasis added). In the same paragraph it considers that the assessment of the *personal* risk to a complainant is a separate matter to the existence of a consistent pattern of gross, flagrant or mass violations of human rights in the relevant country. This is further indication of the fact that States' very specific obligations in respect of non-refoulement cannot be applied to the present situation.

In this context, it is worth nothing that in their joint statement on extraordinary rendition of 27 June 2006, Amnesty International, Human Rights Watch, the International Commission of Jurists and the Association for the Prevention of Torture all confine their criticism to "diplomatic assurances **against torture or inhuman or degrading treatment**." There is no suggestion that diplomatic assurances, as a class, cannot be relied upon.

To complete the Minister's response to the Commission on this matter, the content of the diplomatic assurances received from the US will be briefly addressed. Diplomatic assurances, by their nature, can often involve uncertainties as to the meaning of the language used, or the practical ability of States to guarantee the treatment promised. The assurances obtained from the US in the context of extraordinary rendition are that prisoners have not been and will not be transported through Irish territory without the Government's consent.

As such they are simple, factual and categoric. They state unambiguously a factual situation, over which (contrary to the Commission's suggestion) the Minister is confident the US Government have complete control.

CONCLUSION

The policy of extraordinary rendition is closely associated with the Administration of George W. Bush. That linkage, however, does not mean that the policy has ended or will end with a new Administration of a manifestly more internationalist bent. In January 2009, immediately after taking the oath of office, President Barack Obama announced his intention to close the detention facility at the Guantánamo Bay Naval Based in Cuba and to bar categorically the use of "enhanced" interrogation measures that violate domestic federal and international law. Obama thus renounced what were the two most contentious and, in the case of Guantánamo, visible parts of the Bush-era approach to counter-terrorism.

But the Obama's Administration's approach to the lower salience issue of extraordinary rendition has been rather different. Instead of renouncing transfers to countries that do not respect anti-torture norms, the Obama Administration has indicated that it intends to keep the practice available as an option. According to news reports, the Administration "is now relying heavily on foreign intelligence services to capture, interrogate and detain all but the highest-level terrorist suspects seized outside the battlefields of Iraq and Afghanistan." [1] Among the countries named in news reports are Libya—where at least one rendered prisoner is reported to have died in custody—and Pakistan. In the domestic arena too, the Obama Administration has persisted with, rather than abandoning Bush-era policies that touch on extraordinary rendition. The most telling evidence of this fundamental continuity in policy emerges in the context of federal court tort litigation in which subjects of extraordinary rendition challenge the practice in pursuit of money damages. At the beginning of the Obama Administration, there were two law suits pending in federal court concerning extraordinary rendition. In both, the Bush Administration had vigorously argued that federal judges had no authority to hear the cases. In both, the Obama Administration took the same line. In the law suit filed by Maher Arar, the Holder Justice Department persuaded a federal court of appeals to dismiss Arar's damages suit notwithstanding the absence of any other form of remediation, legal or political, available in the United

[1] Eric Schmitt and Mark Mazzetti, US Relies More on Aid of Allies in Terrorism Cases, *New York Times*, May 23, 2009.

States.[2] In the second suit, the Holder Justice Department has at the time of this writing successfully secured en banc review—i.e., review by the whole appellate bench—of a court of appeals judgment in favor of tort plaintiffs.[3] In sum, not only has the Obama Administration signaled a willingness to continue the use of extraordinary rendition, it has also indicated its willingness to stymie any effort at remediation on behalf of those inadvertently or erroneously swept up in the practice.

The documents in this volume squarely present the question whether the United States' international partners and international organizations will continue to resist the practice of extraordinary rendition. From the perspective of human rights advocates who oppose extraordinary rendition, the prospects for policy amelioration appear dim. By renouncing torture and Guantanamo, Obama signaled an apparent willingness to play by the shared rules of international law. With considerable strategic acumen, he drew the sting from international criticism of the United States without renouncing or stepping away from the more operationally significant parts of counter-terrorism policy—the reliance on cooperating countries with looser approaches to torture and human rights. No longer is the United States, moreover, a manifest outlier. President's Obama's receipt of the Nobel Peace Prize "for his extraordinary efforts to strengthen international diplomacy and cooperation between peoples" is a sign of this sea change.

The documents in this volume, therefore, may well be monuments to an era whose time has expired. Although the practice of extraordinary rendition may continue without significant variance in frequency from the Bush years, it is unlikely that there will be many more Dick Martys or Armando Spataros in coming years. What is collected here, therefore, is the rare moment whether the enforcement of human rights norms by international actors against the United States has force and effect due to the momentary marginalization of America.

---

[2] *Arar v Ashcroft*, 532 F3d 157, 164 (2d Cir 2008)., vacated and superseded – F3d – (2d Cir Nov 2 2009) (No. 06-4216-CV).

[3] *Mohamed v Jeppeson Dataplan, Inc.*, 563 F3d 992, 997 (9th Cir 2009), rehearing en banc granted – F3d – (9th Cir Oct. 27, 2009) (No. 08-15693).

SUBJECT INDEX

Child Detainees

Consular Visits

Corporate Liability

Credit Cards

Criminal Prosecution

Cyprus

Czech Republic

Denmark

Diapers, Use of

Diplomatic Assurances against Torture

Dogs, Use of

Drugs, Administration of

Egypt

Enforced Disappearances

Estonia

Europe

Habeas Corpus

Hoods

Hungary

Iraq

Ireland

Italy

Kidnapping

Kosovo

Latvia

Switzerland

Syria

TDIP (Temporary Committee on Alleged Use of European Countries by CIA for Transport and Illegal Detention of Prisoners)

Telephone Communications

Territories under U.S. Jurisdiction

Torture

Turkey

Ukraine

United Kingdom

United States

Venice Commission Opinion

War

Waterboarding

Women

Wounding

www.ingramcontent.com/pod-product-compliance
Ingram Content Group UK Ltd.
Pitfield, Milton Keynes, MK11 3LW, UK
UKHW051048150926
475595UK00005B/170